THE CONQUEST OF NATURE

Water, Landscape and the
Making of Modern Germany

THE CONQUEST
OF NATURE

Water, Landscape and the
Making of Modern Germany

DAVID BLACKBOURN

JONATHAN CAPE
LONDON

Published by Jonathan Cape 2006

2 4 6 8 10 9 7 5 3 1

Copyright © David Blackbourn 2006

David Blackbourn has asserted his right under the Copyright, Designs
and Patents Act 1988 to be identified as the author of this work

First published in Great Britain in 2006 by
Jonathan Cape
Random House, 20 Vauxhall Bridge Road,
London SW1V 2SA

Random House Australia (Pty) Limited
20 Alfred Street, Milsons Point, Sydney,
New South Wales 2061, Australia

Random House New Zealand Limited
18 Poland Road, Glenfield,
Auckland 10, New Zealand

Random House South Africa (Pty) Limited
Isle of Houghton, Corner of Boundary Road & Carse O'Gowrie,
Houghton 2198, South Africa

The Random House Group Limited Reg. No. 954009
www.randomhouse.co.uk

A CIP catalogue record for this book
is available from the British Library

ISBN 0-224-06071-6

Papers used by The Random House Group Limited are natural,
recyclable products made from wood grown in sustainable forests;
the manufacturing processes conform to the environmental
regulations of the country of origin

Typeset by Palimpsest Book Production Limited,
Polmont, Stirlingshire

Printed and bound in Great Britain by
William Clowes Ltd, Beccles, Suffolk

To my grandparents
In loving memory

CONTENTS

LIST OF MAPS

ACKNOWLEDGEMENTS

I am very grateful to the following for permission to use illustrations: Bärenreiter Verlag, Kassel and Basel (1); Geheimes Staatsarchiv, Preussischer Kulturbesitz (2); Oderlandsmuseum, Bad Freienwalde (4); Jürgens Photo, Berlin (5); Kunstmuseum, Basel (6); Generallandesarchiv, Karlsruhe (7, 9); Reiss-Engelhorn Museum, Mannheim, photo by Jean Christen (8); Stadtmuseum, Oldenburg (10); Stadtarchiv, Wilhelmshaven (11); Staatstheater, Oldenburg (12); Niedersächsisches Freilichtmuseum (13); Landschaftsbibliothek, Ostfriesische Landschaft, Aurich (14); Verlag Haus am Weyerberg, Worpswede (15); Archiv der Stadt Remscheid (17); Hochschularchiv, TH Aachen, Fotosammlung (18); Deutsches Museum, Munich (21); Ruhrtal Museum, Schwerte (23); Deutsches Historisches Museum, Berlin, Bildarchiv (24); Ullstein Bild (25, 26); Bundesarchiv, Koblenz (27); Agnes-Miegel-Gesellschaft (30); Barbara Klemm, Frankfurt am Main (31).

PREFACE

The idea of writing this book goes back a long way, to California in the spring of 1990, when I was a visiting professor at Stanford University and began to read the work of American 'New Western' historians. That was when I drafted the first outline of the present work, which was to be the book after the book after the one I was then writing. Two years later I moved permanently to the USA. Research on the project was begun during a trip to Germany in 1995 and completed over the following years. The book was written between the end of 1999 and the beginning of 2005. I like to think it has benefited from this long period of gestation, but – to paraphrase the famous words of Mandy Rice-Davies – I would, wouldn't I?

It is a pleasure to thank the many people and institutions who have made the book possible. My research was supported by the John Simon Guggenheim Memorial Foundation, the Alexander von Humboldt Foundation and the Clark Fund of Harvard University. I am grateful to Harvard University for periods of leave that allowed me to work on the book, and for providing an atmosphere of intellectual stimulation that I have come to treasure. I want to offer special thanks to friends and colleagues at the Center for European Studies and to my graduate students, past and present, whose commitment to the common enterprise of history has done more to sustain my sense of optimism than they probably realize. In Germany I have benefited from the continued support and hospitality of the Institute for European History in Mainz, where Andreas Kunz and Martin Vogt were especially helpful in the early stages of research. I am also very grateful to the friendly staff of the Generallandesarchiv Karlsruhe and the Staatsbibliothek Berlin, as well as to the libraries across Germany that made many hundreds of obscure printed materials available to me through inter-library loan. Closer to home, I owe a huge debt to the staff of the Houghton and Widener libraries at Harvard. I should also like to express my gratitude to a series of research assistants – Ben Hett, Kevin Ostoyich, Katharina Plück and Luise Tremel – who were efficient and good-humoured in helping with bibliographical research and the ordering of books and inter-library loan materials. Thanks also to Katja Zelljadt, who brought her remarkable energy to bear on the task of tracking down illustrations and permissions.

I have had the good fortune to be asked to talk about the material in this book to many different gatherings of historians and others. It would be hard to overstate how much I gained from these opportunities to formulate and discuss my ideas. The research was first presented at a conference on water held in 1998 at the Kunst- und Ausstellungshalle der Bundesrepublik in Bonn, the first of four meetings devoted – an inspired notion – to the elements. In the following years, while the book was being written, I was able to try out my ideas in front of audiences in Oslo, Berlin and Vancouver, and at conferences, seminars and lectures across the USA from California, Oregon and Arizona to Florida, New Jersey and Washington DC. Many of those who encouraged me or helped me to work out what I really wanted to say were not German historians, or historians at all. Thanks go to them all. An even larger debt of gratitude is owed to those writers and scholars in a variety of different fields whose work I have read with profit. The notes at the end of the book indicate the size of that debt. I am, of course, solely responsible for any factual errors or wayward interpretations the book may contain.

It is a pleasure, finally, to thank those who have been closest to this book. I am grateful as always to my agents, Maggie Hanbury and Robin Straus, and to Will Sulkin and Jörg Hensgen at Jonathan Cape, for their support and confidence. My family, and a changing cast of quadrupeds, have lived with this book for a long time. I thank my wife, Debbie, and our children, Ellen and Matthew, for their patience and above all for their love. I also want to thank my parents for their loving support over so many years. Books are fed from many sources. This one was conceived and written in the country I now call home and it deals with a country where I have spent enough years to feel that its landscape is a part of my life. But, from the time I first set out to write it, this book has felt personal in ways that may go back even further. My wife says that the sight and smell of fenland or saltmarsh induce in me a kind of reverie. If she is right (and she usually is), then perhaps this book owes something to my earliest years in Lincolnshire. That is one of many reasons why the book is dedicated to the memory of my grandparents.

David Blackbourn
Lexington, Massachusetts
May 2005

INTRODUCTION:
NATURE AND LANDSCAPE
IN GERMAN HISTORY

When German soldiers went off to war in August 1914, Kaiser Wilhelm II promised that they would be home, victorious, before the autumn leaves fell. By 1915, soldiers and civilians alike were forced to recognize that Germany would not be able to impose its will on the enemy so easily. That year the writer Wilhelm Bölsche published a book on *The German Landscape Past and Present*. Bölsche was a prominent social reformer in early twentieth-century Germany, a popularizer of Charles Darwin and a founding member of the Garden City movement that promoted more green space in Germany's expanding cities. The book was his contribution to the war effort, just one of many attempts to mobilize nature behind the national cause. A preface to the volume drove the message home. It was written by Franz Goerke, a fellow social reformer who combined an interest in popular scientific education with a passion for 'green' causes like nature conservation. 'In this time of struggle and battle', wrote Goerke, the German landscape was 'the greatest thing we have to defend'.[1] Here was a call to sacrifice familiar to millions of Germans who fought in the wars of the twentieth century. The landscape they were asked to defend was the 'great green garden of Germany', a homeland or *Heimat* whose meadows, woodlands and meandering streams were the cradle of German character and spirit.[2] Whatever cataclysmic changes the war might bring about, the natural landscape – like the people it nurtured – was reassuringly there, unchanging.

Except, of course, that it wasn't. A German of 1915 or 1940, transported back to 1750, would have been astounded at how different the 'natural' landscape looked – much less of it was cultivated, much more of it dominated by sand or scrub and especially by water. The visitor from the twentieth century would not have needed to journey far before stumbling upon pools, ponds and lakes long drained and forgotten. A complete loss of bearings would threaten the modern traveller in the low-lying marsh and fenland that still occupied so much of the North German plain in the eighteenth century. There was a reason why educated contemporaries likened them to the wetlands of the New World, even to Amazonia. Dark and waterlogged, filled with snaking channels half-hidden by overhanging lianas and navigable only in a flat-bottomed boat, these dwelling places of mosquitoes, frogs, fish, wild boar and wolves would not only have looked but smelled and sounded quite different from the open landscape of windmills and mani-cured fields familiar to twentieth-century Germans. The modern trav-eller in any German river valley would surely register the same feeling of being transported into a lost world. The river itself looked quite different in 1750. It did not even flow in the same places. Unlike the familiar modern artery, engineered to flow swiftly in a single channel between embankments, the eighteenth-century river meandered over its floodplain or made its way through hundreds of separate channels divided by sandbars, gravel banks and islands. It ran fast or slow according to the season, not at a pace adapted to the needs of year-round navigation. And along the river for miles on either side lay wetland forests, which had not yet given way to farmland and indus-trial installations. That was what the eighteenth-century Rhine looked like, the river in which Goethe fished for salmon and hundreds of people still sifted through the gravel for gold. The Rhine became the supreme symbol of German identity over the 150 years that followed, but it was a new and different river where the salmon and the Rhine gold had no place.

That was lowland Germany around 1750, much of it barely recog-nizable to twentieth-century eyes. Upland Germany had changed less, but still enough to shock our hypothetical traveller. Consider, for example, someone brought up in the twentieth century on the East Friesland peninsula, or in one of the many parts of Bavaria once covered by moorland. Great expanses of high peat moor that had formed over centuries remained largely untouched in 1750, not yet traversed by roads or canals and given over to arable farming. Only in a few places had peat-cutting started to change the appearance of regions that were still regarded with fear; for it was not until the moors began to disappear that Germans – some Germans – would learn to view them as 'romantic'. Climbing higher still, into the uplands of the Eifel or Sauerland, the Harz or Erzgebirge, the traveller might encounter an even more poignant example of something that had since disappeared: one of the hundreds of valleys later drowned by dams. Their fields and villages had not yet been covered by water, just as the waterlogged high moors had not yet been covered by fields and villages. The German landscape was many things: unchanging was not one of them.

This book tells the story of how Germans transformed their landscape over the last 250 years by reclaiming marsh and fen, draining moors, straightening rivers and building dams in the high valleys. None of these human undertakings was entirely new. Cistercian monks had drained marshes in the Middle Ages and the first successful 'cut' to remove a bend in the Rhine was made in 1391. There were even dams of a kind hundreds of years earlier in the central mountains of Germany, built to provide a source of energy for draining mine-shafts – using water to raise water. What was novel after 1750 was the scale and impact of hydrological projects. They changed the face of the land as much as familiar and obvious symbols of the modern age like the factory chimney, the railway and the burgeoning city. Why were these measures taken, who decided on them, what were the consequences? Those are the questions that concern me. I have called this book *The Conquest of Nature* because that is how contemporaries described what they were doing. The tone shifted over the years, from the sunny Enlightenment optimism of the eighteenth century, to the earnest nineteenth-century belief in science and progress, to the technocratic certainties that marked so much of the twentieth century. (Read the utopian claims in 1900 about hydro-electric power, a clean and modern source of energy created by men in white coats, and it sounds just like the enthusiasm for nuclear power sixty years later.) What did not change is the basic idea that nature was an adversary to be manacled, tamed, subjugated, conquered, and so on through a dozen variations.

'Let us learn to wage war with the elements, not with our own kind'.[3] That was the Scot, James Dunbar, writing in 1780. His view that there was a just war to be fought against nature became a familiar refrain through more than two hundred years of German history. Dunbar's contemporary, Frederick the Great of Prussia, who drained more marshland and fen than any other ruler of the time, looked down on the newly reclaimed Oder marshes and proclaimed: 'Here I have conquered a province peacefully'.[4] In the nineteenth century, moorland colonies and steamship navigation were the causes of progressive men. In the golden age of natural science, mastery over nature was supposed to mark the moral advance of humankind; it was the antithesis of war. This attitude persisted even into the catastrophe of the First World War, which many commentators saw as a break in the natural trajectory of human progress. When Sigmund Freud wrote his *Thoughts for the Times on War and Death* in 1915, he counted it among the 'disillusionments' of war that 'our technical advances towards the control of nature' had encouraged a belief in the peaceful settlement of human conflicts; for the civilized values of orderliness and law were 'among the qualities which have made mankind the lords of the earth'.[5] After the war the Marxist cultural critic Walter Benjamin offered a variation on the same theme, lamenting that 'instead of draining rivers, society directs a human stream into a bed of trenches'.[6] When it came to water projects, this swords-into-ploughshares optimism remained common ground among liberals and socialists well beyond the middle of the twentieth century.

The historical reality was rather different. More often than we like to think, draining a marsh or redirecting the course of a river was not so much the 'moral equivalent of war' (to use William James's term) as the by-product, even the handmaiden, of war. Take the reclamation projects pursued by Frederick the Great. Draining marshes removed the dark haunts that harboured deserters and impeded Frederick's clockwork army on its line of march. The canals and ditches were dug by soldiers, the settlement of colonists was overseen by former army suppliers. And the conquest of nature was undertaken, often enough, on territory that had been won by conquest of the literal kind. Or consider the unprecedentedly ambitious project to 'rectify' the Rhine in the nineteenth century, which would not have come about when and how it did if Napoleon had not helpfully simplified the political map of Germany by destroying the Holy Roman Empire, opening the way for the transformation of the river. Similar examples abound. Why did Prussian engineers and thousands of workers struggle for ten years against the North Sea and the malarial mudflats of the Jade Bay? To build a deepwater harbour for the Prussian, later the German, battle fleet. Why did the pace of moorland drainage and colonization accelerate after the First World War? Because Germans came to see themselves after the Treaty of Versailles as a 'people without space', a *Volk ohne Raum,* so that every cultivated acre counted. In their preparations for the next war the National Socialists carried this battle for food, which was simultaneously a battle against nature, even further. And after 1939 they developed hydrological plans for eastern Europe that combined technocratic hubris with racial contempt for the peoples whose 'disorderly' land they had subjugated. Race, reclamation and genocide were intertwined.

What generations of Germans called the conquest of nature could be described equally well with another military metaphor, as a series of water wars. And that was true at home as well as abroad. Water serves a very large number of human purposes. Rivers alone are a source of drinking water, and of water for washing and bathing. They irrigate crops and provide calorific energy directly in the form of fish. They flush away waste and serve as a means of transportation (a river is a road that moves, said Blaise Pascal). They provide water for cooling and other industrial processes. And they drive both simple water-wheels and complex turbines, this being an instance in human history where the wheel really was reinvented. Some of these many ways of harnessing the river are mutually compatible; but others are not. Every rearrangement of German hydrology described in this book, whether redirecting and diking a river, draining a marsh, digging a canal or building a dam, set rival users against each other. These were rupture points, when rivers and wetlands were remade to serve new interests. In the early years the conflict was typically between fishing or hunting and agriculture, later it was between agriculture and industry, later still between one powerful modern interest group (like inland shipping) and another (like hydro-electric power). Almost always there was a clash of some kind between local or small-scale claims and larger interests; and almost always it was the big battalions who came out on top. As one of Germany's leading dam experts remarked: 'With mastery of the water comes the opportunity for conflict over it'.[7]

Achieving that mastery depended on modern forms of knowledge: maps, charts, inventories, scientific theory, the expertise of hydraulic engineers. It was also a measure of political power. These transformations of the German landscape were coercive. Germany's water wars were sometimes overtly violent. Fenland fishing communities resisted their displacement; so did small boatmen driven off the river by steamships. They were met with military force. Open violence waned after the middle of the nineteenth century (except when Germans were rearranging other people's waterways), and the domestic water wars moved into the law courts, parliaments and ministerial offices. But what the French call 'soft coercion', or *violence douce*, was always there in the background. Look at how German waterways were remade, and you see where the lines of power ran. The human domination of nature has a lot to tell us about the nature of human domination.

But this book also tells a story of consent as well as coercion. For all the fierceness of debate about a given canal or dam, over who would pay and who would benefit, there was a remarkably long-standing consensus among politicians, lobbyists, officials and opinion-makers on the underlying principle that German waters could be reshaped at will. Could be – and should be. The elite was not alone in taking this view. Mastering nature came to be widely seen as natural – or 'second nature', as we say. There was popular enthusiasm for the great civil engineering projects that changed the shape of the land. It was evident in the speeches that accompanied every festive inauguration of a newly completed river correction or dam, the lionizing of celebrated engineers like Johann Tulla and Otto Intze, and the tremulous tone adopted by mass-circulation family magazines when reporting on these triumphs of human ingenuity. When Dr Jakob Zinssmeister, an advocate of harnessing hydro-electric power, wrote in 1909 that 'mankind is after all there to dominate nature not to serve it', he was only stating what most people believed.[8] It is often said that modern Germans were less amenable to 'modernity' than the British or French, less worldly and materialist, more hostile to mechanical civilization. This has been presented as one explanation for the appeal of National Socialism. If you believe that, I hope this book will make you think again.

Not that the right of humans to assert their mastery over nature went unchallenged. If Jakob Zinssmeister's comments seem rather insistent, even impatient, that is because they were made in response to conservationists who questioned the impact of dam-building on the local landscape, flora and fauna. The dam was a new cause of concern; the underlying disquiet was not. Poets and naturalists had worried about human arrogance even in the eighteenth century. Doubting voices multiplied in the noisy 'age of progress' that followed. The sceptics had different reasons for questioning the dominant, instrumental view of humankind's relationship with the natural world. For more than two centuries the most persistent basis for concern was (and perhaps still is) aesthetic. From the lamentations of Romantic poets to the pressure-groups of the twentieth century that tried to block hydro-electric projects, the threat to the natural beauty of the landscape took centre-stage. Another concern was already being expressed when the first proposals to remake the Rhine were unveiled in the early 1800s. What if the remedy proved worse than the disease? What if – terrible thought – it was human actions themselves that led to 'natural' disasters? Both concerns, the aesthetic and the practical, had human interests at their core, even if it was a view of human interests different from Jakob Zinssmeister's. Other Germans had religious grounds for questioning the human right to 'improve on creation'. The decline in bird species that followed the loss of wetland habitats animated much of this concern, for ornithology was a popular pursuit in Germany. Bird protection societies were formed earlier than in most other countries and enjoyed huge support. Then there was a final contrarian strand of doubt, one that would become increasingly important in the future. In 1866, German physiologist Ernst Haeckel coined the term 'ecology'. This marked the emergence of a body of thought that forced humans to confront their complex interrelationship with other species. Germans made a pioneering contribution to modern ecological ideas; and it was the study of aquatic species and habitats that propelled much of the new thinking.

These Cassandras were diverse; they are hard to pigeon-hole intellectually or politically. A German nature conservation movement emerged at the beginning of the twentieth century, but it was not a direct forerunner of the environmental activism that recast German politics eighty years later. The earlier movement shared some of the ecological concerns that drove the Greens, but it was more preoccupied with landscape aesthetics and more conservative. After 1933 the movement entered into a passionate but mostly unrequited love affair with National Socialism, and some of the same attitudes (often espoused by the same people) persisted into the post-war years. Where the later Greens were committed to 'think globally, act locally', earlier nature conservationists tended to their local 'homeland' regions but within a strongly nationalist, often racialist framework. Even the adjective 'green' is an unreliable indicator if it leads us to imagine a straightforward continuity of environmentalist beliefs. In the first half of the twentieth century, as in the nineteenth, 'green' was often a code-word for German superiority: 'German and verdant', as opposed to the Slav 'desert' or 'wilderness'. 'The German village can only ever be a green village' wrote one Nazi landscape planner.[9] His view, which combined landscape aesthetics, ecological concern and racial pride, was shared by most conservationists. The modern Green movement has constructed for itself (as movements do) a pre-history of prophets before their time, and there are certainly connecting threads; but the line connecting past and present was more broken than continuous.

To write about the shaping of the modern German landscape is to write about how modern Germany itself was shaped. Anyone trying to do it is faced today with two very different ways of framing the story. Call them the optimistic and pessimistic approaches, one an account cast in the heroic mode, the other a modern morality tale of just deserts. The first tells a straightforward story of progress. Growing human control over the natural world meant new land for colonization and more food to support a growing population; it removed the scourge of malaria and checked the age-old threat of floods; it provided safe drinking water and a new source of energy through the retention of the waters of upland streams; and it brought freedom from the confines of closed-off local worlds by removing obstacles to communication, speeding the flow of people and goods along previously twisting rivers as surely as steamships drove through ocean sea lanes. This is a story of emancipation from constraints, bringing short-term losses for a few but long-term gains for the many. Until about a generation ago, when 'modernization' and the gospel of progress began to lose their lustre, this was the upbeat register in which the story was usually told. *It's getting better all the time* sang the Beatles in 1967, and most historians would have sung along.

That is the optimistic version.

Few historians still write this way. Attention has shifted to the darker side of progress. The 'conquest' of water led to a decline in biodiversity, and (the other side of the same coin) brought damaging invasive species, the algaes, molluscs and more 'adaptable' fish that established themselves in already damaged eco-systems. Hydrological projects also wiped out human communities, and with them valuable forms of local knowledge: carefully calibrated ways of living with and from the water. Every benefit of progress had its price: the water-borne pollution from industry and chemical fertilizer that caused fish-kills and human health hazards, the vulnerable monocultures introduced on newly cultivated land, the lowering of water tables caused by wholesale drainage. Old constraints and insecurities were removed, but new ones took their place. The city fathers who built reservoirs a century ago boasted that they had increased water use, but they had also established a pattern of unchecked consumption that is simply unsustainable. Dams, for whatever purpose they were built, often failed to deliver the goods, but they did present later generations with unforeseen problems. The habit of treating river basins as a series of gutters and drainpipes to speed the water on its way was perhaps the most obvious instance of how technocratic water management had unintended consequences. Increase the velocity of a river and its tributaries, confine that river within a narrow channel and encourage human settlement on the former flood-plain, and what you have done is exchange regular local flooding for less frequent but far more extensive and damaging inundations – although, as we have seen in the many 'once in a century' floods on the Rhine, Oder and Elbe since the 1980s, these have become quite frequent enough.

That is the pessimistic version.

Neither way of framing this history is really satisfactory. Both tell a one-eyed tale. Even in our age of sound-bites and simple story lines, with its inbuilt bias against complexity, it is surely still possible to hold two contradictory ideas in our heads. These German passages to modernity were, like Dickens's French Revolution, the best of times and the worst of times. The conquest of nature was a kind of Faustian bargain. Faust laboured to tame the threatening waters, to create new land by 'bringing the earth back to itself', and he succeeded – but at a price.[10] (In Goethe's play it is the elderly couple, Philomen and Baucis, who pay the price: early 'victims of modernization'.) Both gains and losses were real; it depends which groups you look at and the time-scale you adopt. That is not an argument for splitting the difference, simply the starting point for an honest reckoning. The evidence in this book suggests that it was usually the poorest and most powerless who made the greatest sacrifices in the cause of material betterment. The immigrant labourers and convicts who dug canals before 1914, the foreign prisoners of war who drained moorland in the First World War, and the slave workers who did both of those things and more under grotesquely inhumane conditions in the Second World War represent an extreme version of that generalization. But it is also true that in Germany, as in other European countries, the costs of large hydrological projects were not shunted on to the poor as they so often have been in the modern Third World. The transformation described in this book brought great material benefits to most Germans: new land, a regular supply of clean water in the household, water transformed into energy or used in industrial processes that made mass consumption a reality. The Faustian bargain is still in place, but now it takes a different form. Over the last two hundred years, and at an accelerating pace in the twentieth century when war did not intervene, Germany made the transition from a world where most people lived very short lives that were constantly exposed to insecurity and material constraints, to an ageing society that enjoys an ease unprecedented in human history – a society with the luxury of examining its own prodigal ways, although many (myself included) would argue that doing so is actually a necessity rather than a luxury. That is surely the real question now about the long-term consequences of manipulating and mechanizing German water resources. It is the question of sustainability. When do 'needs' become 'wants', and who will decide which wants deserve to be satisfied? And those who reject the thinking behind that question have to answer another one: Can things go on the way they have been without a hard reckoning in the future? As the last two chapters of this book suggest, Germans have been more willing than most to face that question.

This concern is at the root of present-day pessimism, which has taken on a different quality since historians began to pay attention to species other than humans, when they placed human history more squarely within the history of the world that people inhabit: the lithosphere, the atmosphere and – not least – the hydrosphere.[11] The 'pessimists' in the debate that once raged over the social consequences of the Industrial Revolution were not pessimistic about the future of humankind. They wanted to expose the inequities of past human societies, but looked forward to a fairer distribution of material resources in the future. Doubts about the wisdom of subjugating the natural world to human uses did not enter the argument. That has changed. The very projects that once symbolized a future of human emancipation – like the huge Soviet hydrological projects on the rivers that fed the Aral Sea – can now be seen as human and environmental catastrophes. It is impossible for any book dealing with long-term changes in human relations with the natural world not to be overshadowed in some way by the serious global crises we face today – climate change, growing rates of species extinction, 'desertification', and the gloomy long-term future of the world's fresh water supply. Readers of this book will find many examples of the negative environmental effects brought about by the hydrological revolution in Germany – drainage projects and river 'corrections' that created mini-dust bowls by drying out the land (and caused the coining of a new word, *Versteppung*), widespread loss of wetlands and species, habitat fragmentation on an ever larger scale, irreversible changes of the kind ecologists call 'Humpty-Dumpty effects'.[12]

So why do I nonetheless find a 'pessimistic' account inadequate? Partly because we can point to other changes that were reversible and have in fact been reversed over the last thirty years, notably water-borne pollution and the whole German approach to flood control in river basins. There are, moreover, instances where the outcome of human interventions has been paradoxical, like the reservoirs that became links in the flyways of migratory birds and are now managed as valuable eco-systems in their own right. This is a modest German variant on a global story, most dramatically illustrated by the Salton Sea in the American south-west, a disaster of human hydrological engineering gone wrong that now attracts more bird species than anywhere else in the continental United States. A history that takes the environment seriously is bound to turn up warnings from the past, but it is likely to be bad history (and probably unhelpful for grasping our present-day problems) if it is nothing but a jeremiad. The history of humans and the natural world is bound to be morally charged, which makes it all the more important to retain a feeling for historical irony. Not everything is or was a downward glide to perdition.

The almost religious sense of a 'fall' in some writing about human relations with the natural world is palpable. Humankind has transgressed, has lost its innocence and been expelled from Eden. It has even – a figure of speech drawn from later in the Book of Genesis – been branded with 'the permanent mark of Cain' for its murderous attack on nature.[13] In most history books the sense of a fall from grace is, of course, much less insistent than this. Still, the habit of mind is familiar enough that thoughtful environmental historians have found it worth reflecting on.[14] It is not a stance I find very helpful, and the call to embrace an 'unblemished' nature that so often goes with it is even more problematic. No one has stated the issue more trenchantly than the American environmental historian Richard White:[15]

To call for a return to nature is posturing. It is a religious ritual in which the recantation of our sins and a pledge to sin no more promises to restore purity. Some people believe sins go away. History does not go away.

Can that history be told other than through human eyes? Many non-human species find a place in the following pages, from the humble caddisfly to the salmon, from the wolf which Germans largely succeeded in exterminating in the eighteenth century to the *Bacillus thuringiensis* which ate its way through so many fields of German maize in the twentieth century. But I have not tried to tell the story that follows from the perspective of any of these species – and if I had, it would be no more than a form of ventriloquism. The perspective of this book is resolutely human and anthropocentric. I have not (as Arnold Toynbee once did) given speaking roles to plants, although I have drawn on a wonderful book by Ernst Candèze that relates the building of a dam through the eyes of an enterprising group of beetles, ants and grasshoppers who felt the consequences.[16] I do not believe that we could (as one American environmental historian has suggested) 'think like a river', even if we wanted to.[17] I write as an all too human observer, a chastened progressive old enough to remember when things were getting better all the time but now more often tempted by the thought, equally unhistorical, that they are getting worse all the time. A desire to show readers the contradictions of Germany's passage to modernity gives this book its underlying rhythm, its point and counterpoint.

The book is built on a series of dramatic episodes that allow us to recover what contemporaries thought they were doing (or trying to prevent someone else from doing). That is a way to counter the pervasive sense of inevitability that coats the past as soon as it becomes the past. Those I have called optimists and pessimists both have a tendency, from their opposite perspectives, to make the process of change seem too straightforward, too smooth and self-evident. I have tried to restore a sense of the options that confronted people at the time, to show the grit and friction that was evident in every one of these episodes. But the longer perspective is necessary as well. All history is the history of unintended consequences, but that is especially true when we are trying to untangle humanity's relationship with the natural environment. Flash-forwards allow us to see how often contemporary expectations were confounded. Whether the effects in a given instance were for better or worse (or both), remaking German rivers and wetlands was not only arduous and ambiguous but unpredictable. This book is full of examples. We regularly encounter engineers trying to fix problems that were problems only because the previous fix had not worked. And every time their mantra was the same: *This* time things would be different! Score one for the pessimists. But the same point also cuts the other way. What nature conservationists wanted to conserve at any given time was the status quo at a particular point between one set of human interventions and another – the residue of yesterday's 'progress', after it had acquired a patina of 'naturalness'. If the apostles of progress were too often dazzled by the once-and-for-all solutions of the present, environmentalist critics have too often painted an unrealistic picture of the past, attributing pristine qualities to habitats that had long carried the traces of human use.[18] That argument, and the many ironies that flow from it, is one that runs like a red thread (or perhaps it is a green thread) through the book. The point was unwittingly made by the moorland painter Otto Modersohn, who confided to his diary that 'nature should be our teacher', then noted that this not very original thought occurred to him 'on the bridge that leads over the canal'.[19]

This book is full of people looking down, like Modersohn, on German waterlands, although usually from a greater height than the bridge over the canal. These observers provide us with a series of 'before' and 'after' snapshots of the German landscape. We know what the labyrinth of the old Oder marshes looked like thanks to a seventeenth-century engraving that frames the view from the surrounding heights; then, a hundred years later, Frederick the Great looked out proudly over the reclaimed land that stretched before him, the 'beautiful garden' of later cliché. Hundreds of miles to the west, unaware that he was recording a world that would soon disappear, Peter Birmann painted an Upper Rhine we no longer recognize; he was followed in the nineteenth century by a host of observers who looked down over the plain and saw (as August Becker did) a land 'so fruitful and luxuriantly green . . . that it seems like one great garden'.[20] In just the same way, clergymen and conservationists gazed down and wrote elegies to river valleys that would soon be drowned by dams, then yielded their place to the technocrats and travel writers who celebrated a different panorama and a new kind of beauty – the 'reservoir romanticism' that is still alive in aerial photographs of shimmering man-made lakes in the Eifel and Sauerland.

Like the privilege of hindsight, these elevated perspectives are valuable, but they do not tell the whole story. They do not tell us what it meant on the ground when the 'before' turned into the 'after'. You can see a lot of things when you look down at them from above, but you miss a lot as well. So I have also made a point of going down to ground and water level: to the fisher people whose lives are so easy to sentimentalize when they are seen from a great height, the construction workers who paid with their health (and sometimes their lives) to accomplish the feats that others rhapsodized about from a distance, the farmers on reclaimed fens who took generations to establish themselves and were never free from the fear of flooding, the moorland colonists whose lives were no less precarious. Writers like to think they are in charge, but there are things in the writing of any book that creep up behind the author's back and insinuate themselves. In this case it was the mud that took me by surprise: in chapter after chapter there were people up to their waists in mud. I have not tried to clean them off: the idea was always to offer multiple perspectives, and this one is important. Readers can expect a book that takes them up to the heights, but also down to where the earth meets the water.

These are more than just differences in perspective, more even than a shorthand for different social experiences. They are two different ways of saying that history occurs in space as well as time. Real space and imagined space. The landscapes that feature in the title of this book come in two kinds. There is the cultural construct framed by the observer; and there is the physical reality of rock, soil, vegetation and water. Germans distinguish between 'nature' (a cultural projection of human ideas and emotions) and 'nature in itself' (the complex of life-forms on earth, which includes humans).[21] When I write about the making of the modern German landscape, it is in this double sense. The two meanings complement each other. They represent two halves of a single history.

Human beings are metaphorical creatures. We think of time, and we represent it as a river. 'Time is a violent torrent', said Marcus Aurelius. Machiavelli used the same idea when he wrote in *The Prince* that history, or *fortuna*, was like 'one of those violent rivers which, when they become enraged, flood the plain, ruin the trees and buildings, lift earth from this part, drop it in another'.[22] It was already a cliché when the eminent German historian Leopold von Ranke claimed in the nineteenth century that history 'flowed' like a river, adding that historians

were caught up in the 'irresistible current' but tried to 'master' it. The
metaphorical instinct works the other way round as well. We see a river
and we turn it into a source of myth and legend. That is as old as the
river valley civilizations of the Euphrates, Nile and Ganges. Modern
Germans also fashioned their waterlands into repositories of cultural
and political meaning. Artists, writers, historians, travellers, politicians,
planners – all invested the German landscape with symbolic values, and
I have tried to show the variety of ways in which they did so. The
Rhine, at once Romantic, fruitful and 'German', is only the best-known
case.[23] Everywhere we look, German rivers, moors and fens became
markers for larger, more abstract things: conquest and loss, of course,
the twin themes of the book, but many other qualities besides, both
positive and negative – beauty and ugliness, abundance and scarcity,
harmony and disharmony. During the nineteenth century it is particularly striking how often Germans came to map their own imagined
virtues onto the landscape. Many historians have devoted themselves
in recent years to these mental topographies, and with good reason.
What we call landscapes are neither natural nor innocent; they are
human constructs. How and why they were constructed (many would
say 'imagined', even 'invented') belongs to the stuff of history.

But when I read yet another book or article about an 'imagined landscape', it is sometimes tempting to complain, like Gertrude Stein, that
'there's no *there* there'. And I want to ask: Are all topographies in the
mind, is every river nothing more than a flowing symbol? There was
a time when a sharply physical sense of place was an essential ingredient of history. Peter Heylyn, a seventeenth-century English writer on
religion and history, made the point with commendable vigour in 1652:
'Historie without Geographie like a dead carkasse hath neither life nor
motion at all'.[24] Some of the most celebrated historians of the nineteenth century would have agreed. Think of Thomas Babbington
Macaulay in England; or of Jules Michelet, who wrote in his *History
of France* that 'without a geographical basis, the people, the makers of
history, seem to be walking on air, as in those Chinese pictures where
the ground is wanting.'[25] In Germany, home to the great pioneers of
geography as a discipline, historians took the same line. Heinrich von
Treitschke is most often associated with stirring political narratives
about the rise of Prussia. But his pages contain much more interest in
the contours of the land than those who have not read him (or read
him only for the plot) imagine.

By the 1920s, it is true, professional history had come to define itself increasingly by the practice of document-based research, leaving vulgar geography to local antiquarians and popularizers. Nowhere was that more true than in Germany. But the revolutionary challenge mounted by historians associated with the French journal *Annales* (founded in 1929) changed all that. They insisted that the physical environment was more than just an empty stage on which humankind performed. The greatest of them, Marc Bloch, taught that human history was to be found not only in the archives but 'behind the features of landscape'.[26] This new departure (or return to an older wisdom) was not just a Gallic affair. It had its counterparts in Britain, the United States and Germany. A belief that the historian should possess a pair of stout walking shoes transcended national borders, then and for some years to come.

Now it sounds faintly old-fashioned. Electronic media have supposedly left us with 'no sense of place'.[27] We associate those stout walking shoes with people of a certain age, like the venerable French historian Georges Duby, looking back wistfully to the days when he walked the countryside and examined 'a document . . . open to sunlight and to life itself, namely the landscape'.[28] But things were changing even as Duby wrote these words in 1991. Historians and the general public have both shown a renewed interest in places and landscapes. The growing popularity of books on environmental history and the natural world suggests that a shift is taking place. Restoring the connection between the broad sweep of history and the physical environment opens up new perspectives. While researching this book, I walked many of the landscapes it describes and this only enhanced my appreciation for the sheer scale of the transformation that humans imposed. I also became convinced that the book should make use of what geographers, botanists and ecologists had to say. Making inferences from pollen analysis or mapping changes in species are, of course, also ways in which humans impose meaning on the natural world. The taxonomies are ours. Rivers flow and do their work whether or not people are present. That is to say, they do what we call 'flow' and 'work': the river has no name for these things, which are human constructs every bit as much as saying that the river has been 'conquered'. But looking closely at what happened when that flow and work were radically altered by human actions is still a very different enterprise from showing how Germans came to view a landscape as harmonious, or ordered, or quintessentially German.

That brings me to the really difficult question. There is a special reason why efforts to connect history to the physical environment disappeared off the map in Germany. The reason is National Socialism, which sullied this as it did so much else. There were historians in 1920s Germany who pioneered a new kind of regional history that looked closely at human interactions with the landscape. But they also held racist views and were seriously compromised under National Socialism.[29] A whole historical approach was discredited, its vocabulary tainted. Two American environmentalist authors can write a book called *Rooted in the Land* without causing offence; but put that into German and you have something all too close to the Nazi adjective *schollengebunden*, or 'rooted in the soil'.[30] French regional histories routinely have a chapter called *La Terre et les Hommes*, and nobody thinks twice about it. Try that in German and you have *Land und Leute* (land and people), which immediately summons up dark associations because it was the title of a book by Wilhelm Heinrich Riehl, the nineteenth-century writer often seen as an intellectual precursor of National Socialism.[31]

Is it playing with fire to suggest that we pay more attention to the land as well as the people? I am tempted to reply: We're adults, we're allowed to handle fire (and, as we shall see below, fire is also an eminently historical subject).[32] But the issue of the Nazi taint deserves a more direct answer. It really is time that we stopped letting National Socialism dictate who we read and how we read them. Take Wilhelm Heinrich Riehl. He was admired by his contemporary, George Eliot, that formidable freethinker and model of the emancipated woman; Greens as well as Nazis have claimed him (with equal plausibility, or implausibility) as a forerunner. His book on land and people remains a striking, original piece of work. Why should we shun him because what he wrote resonated with some National Socialists seventy years after he wrote it? Intellectual lineages are ambiguous and unpredictable; they cannot be policed or quarantined. There is no reason, anyway, to fear that we shall burn our fingers by restoring the historical importance of the physical environment. It has in fact slowly been making its way back into German history through studies of regions, rivers, ecosystems, villages. None of this writing bears the slightest trace of the nationalist or *völkisch* baggage of the past.[33] Nor does it open the door to geography-is-destiny conclusions – the kind often associated with Nazism. The real irony here is that National Socialists were actually anything but geographical determinists. They spoke all the time about landscape, but were deeply suspicious of anything – including the physical environment – that might be seen as trumping the primacy of human will, especially the 'blood inheritance' of race. We shall see that demonstrated repeatedly in chapter five of this book. When the Nazi 'landcape planner' Heinrich Wiepking-Jürgensmann wrote that 'landscape is history and history is landscape', it was the plasticity of landscape he wanted to assert – the capacity of 'superior' races to shape it according to their will.[34]

Landscapes are both real and imagined. Germans transformed their river valleys, lakes, moors and fenlands in the modern era. They drained, diverted and dammed, changing the hydrological cycle, the balance of species and the relationship of people to their environment. Yet contemporaries also invested this process of transformation with a variety of metaphorical meanings. They called it the conquest of nature, celebrated it as progress or mourned it as loss, praised the new landscape as ordered or deplored it as geometrical. German waterlands were a screen on to which a changing society projected its hopes and fears. From the Rhine to the Vistula, they also became symbols of German national identity. One German moorland expert has referred to 'the wet book of history'.[35] That is one of the histories I have tried to write, but interwoven with the history of perceptions and meanings, politics and race. History is as various as life; its sub-divisions are cross-sections through the same reality. The generous vision of 'total history' can never be achieved, but it is still worth reaching for.

This is a book about transformation on an epic scale. In the eighteenth century, German-speaking Europe looked so different from the way it looks today that many parts of it would seem entirely alien if we could travel back in time. The physical world pressed up hard against contemporaries, and enlightened opinion supported the view held by most German territorial rulers that nature was there to be mastered or conquered. As for 'Germany', it existed only in the mind. When this book opens, the French Revolution had not yet occurred and unified Germany was still a century away. *The Conquest of Nature* describes a series of dramatic changes in the physical environment over the last 250 years. I try to show how they were linked to absolutism in the eighteenth century, to revolution and nationalism in the nineteenth century, to Nazism, communism and democracy in the twentieth century, and to war in almost every period. And I want to suggest, finally, that attitudes towards nature went through as many changes over those 250 years as the natural world. This is a book about the reshaping of the German landscape that also tries to show how modern Germany itself was shaped in the process.

I

CONQUESTS FROM BARBARISM

A Wilderness of Water and Marsh

German-speaking Europe in the 1770s was a study in contrasts. Life for many of its twenty-two million inhabitants resembled something lifted straight out of one of those fairy tales the Grimm brothers collected just forty years later. It was a world shaped by bereavement, peopled with orphans and widows. Half of all children died before the age of ten and only one person in ten reached the age of sixty. Epidemic disease threatened, and so did harvest failure that was still capable of producing widespread starvation, as it did in Saxony, Prussia and parts of southern Germany in the early 1770s. Wolves roamed the forests and swamplands, especially in the east, while filthy and noxious towns killed so many of their inhabitants that they needed a constant influx from rural areas to maintain their populations. In town and country alike this was in many ways a rigidly stratified society. Rural lords enjoyed seigneurial rights that were harsher the further east you went. Most town-dwellers were not citizens of the places where they lived; urban guilds and church foundations enjoyed special prerogatives and privileges. Across the hundreds of principalities, large and small, that made up the loosely-knit Holy Roman Empire of the German Nation, restrictions were imposed by princes, lords, town patricians, churches and guild masters on where you could live, what you could wear, the occupations you could practise and who you could marry.

Yet this was also a society in flux. At the most basic material level, the threat posed by famine and disease was less severe than it had been even forty years earlier. Agricultural yields were higher, while modest changes in diet and hygiene brought an improvement in mortality rates.

The population was climbing steadily. Some of the improvement was down to the actions of princely rulers. Won over by contemporary arguments that their populations were a valuable human resource, they encouraged new crops and began to take measures against some of the most obvious sources of household disaster in an insecure world – fire and flood as well as epidemic disease. As we shall see, the attempt to eradicate 'predatory' animals like wolves was a part of this larger ambition.

These actions were also a sign that the rulers of some German territorial states were flexing their muscles. Whether we look at the Kingdom of Prussia in northern and eastern Germany (large, and getting larger by conquest), or the more modest Margraviate of Baden-Durlach in the south-western corner of German-speaking Europe, we find rulers asserting themselves. They were doing this not only against the 'disorderly' natural world, but against the rival claims of institutions that stood between them and their subjects: church foundations, guilds, urban patriciates, even seigneurialism. The growing power and reach of the absolutist state was one of the dynamic elements that was changing German-speaking Europe in these years. But it was not the only one. Population growth drove the search for new land to cultivate. It also created a reserve army of labour in the countryside that engaged in the so-called putting-out system: merchants provided raw materials (like textiles) to rural families, who worked them up into the finished product. This was a direct challenge to the guilds. Merchants and businessmen were growing in wealth in the 1770s. So was an educated class of nobles, officials, clergy and professional men who gathered in the burgeoning bookshops, coffee houses and masonic lodges of the era. They formed the reading public that sustained the German Enlightenment as it came into full flower after the 1760s, men (and they were almost all men) who devoured the printed word and debated the virtues of improvement, utility, harmony and reason, the key ideas of an enlightened age.

In all of these ways, the German lands were changing in the 1770s; they were on the move. That was literally true. Travel did much to widen the horizons of Germans in these years. The most spectacular example was the father-and-son team of Johann Reinhold and Georg Forster, who sailed around the world with Captain Cook in 1772–5. The son's account of the journey, *Voyage around the World*, made him famous when the German edition appeared in 1778. The book fed what was already a mania for travel and travel writing among the enlight-ened German public. Frederick the Great of Prussia mocked the 'modish' belief in travel.[1] At the University of Göttingen, where Forster made a triumphant visit, leading professors even taught courses on the subject.[2] Despite poor roads and a threat from bandits serious enough that the Berlin intellectual Friedrich Nicolai packed a stick along with his pen and measuring instruments, educated Germans of the 1770s were trav-elling as never before. They went to view buildings, to examine collec-tions of every imaginable kind or to seek out minerals and botanical specimens for themselves, to look at the results of the model husbandry that was bringing new crops and animal breeds to German fields. And, of course, they went to meet and talk with each other – at spas like Carlsbad, in the learned societies and reading clubs springing up across Germany, and in country houses, if the owners were like-minded and hospitable.

One such traveller, in the year 1777, was Johann Bernoulli. An astronomer, mathematician and physicist, Bernoulli came from a distinguished Swiss-Dutch family of scholars and was a member of the Royal Academy of Science in Berlin. It was from the Prussian capital, a city whose population had grown rapidly to over 100,000, that he set off in the middle of May, heading east, his ultimate desti-nation St Petersburg. The journey there and back would take him eighteen months to complete and six volumes to describe.[3] Bernoulli was prompted to undertake his journey by an invitation to visit the Pomeranian estates of his friend, the Prussian diplomat Count Otto Christoph von Podewils, across the River Oder to the east. But he stopped off first, just nine leisurely days after leaving Berlin, at the main Podewils estate in Gusow, which lay on the south-western edge of the area known as the Oderbruch.

Bernoulli was a man of austere tastes, and his description of Gusow wastes little time on the manor house, recently rebuilt in Baroque style, and no time at all on rooms or furnishings. Even the paintings are noted impatiently, although he concedes that some (a Cranach, 'a few Rembrandts') might interest a lover of the fine arts. But not Bernoulli. His attention is fixed on serious things – things in glass cases. He admires the count's 'very systematically ordered' library of history, liter-ature and botany, then a collection of mathematical instruments and mechanical devices like the odometer that can be attached to a cart wheel. Bernoulli also inspects the countess's natural history specimens.

MAP 1 *Prussia in the age of Frederick the Great.*

In cabinets assembled with 'care, order and meticulousness' are rocks, minerals, seeds, dried fruit, pickled animals, and the two stars of her collection: a set of shells and conches, including South Sea conches just acquired in London, and one of the largest collections of butterflies to be found under glass anywhere in Germany.[4]

Bernoulli was, if anything, even more impressed by the Gusow estates,

BALTIC SEA

Memel
Tauroggen
Memel
Tilsit
PRUSSIAN
Königsberg
Insterburg
Pregel
Gumbinnen
Lauenburg
Danzig
ERMLAND
Bartenstein
Angerburg
Kolberg
Köslin
Bütow
LOWER
POMERANIA
Elbing
EAST
PRUSSIA
LITHUANIA
Marienwerder
WEST PRUSSIA
Mockrau
Neidenburg
‧RANIA
Draheim
Graudenz
‧tettin
Kulm
KULMERLD
NETZE - Fordon
Bromberg
DISTRICT
Thorn
Vistula
‧berg
Netze
Küstrin
‧rankfurt
Warthe
Schwiebus
‧bus
Glogau
Wohlau
Liegnitz
Breslau
S I L E S I A
Brieg
Oppeln
Hirschberg
Schweidnitz
Neisse
Neisse
Oder
Beuthen
Glatz
Cosel
Vistula
Jägerndorf
Troppau

AUSTRIA

which showed the effects of the same enlightened taste, botanical bent and impulse to order. The reader's first introduction to Gusow is a long and rapturous account of the fertile cabbage fields, wrested from soil that once bore only reeds and coarse grass. Bernoulli notes with satisfaction that modern husbandry allows the land to support a larger population. Everywhere he looks – at the ditched and manicured fields, the willow plantings, the trees and shrubs in the 'American garden' – he sees evidence of agricultural improvement. And all this had happened in a generation, since the Countess Podewils inherited the property from her uncle in the 1740s.[5] Over the next eighteen months Bernoulli would often find himself referring to the dramatic changes in the land that occurred between the 1740s and the 1770s. So it amounts almost to the appearance of a main theme when, before leaving Gusow to cross the 'rich soil' of the Oderbruch en route to the Oder ferry at Zellin, he notes: 'Thirty years ago this place was a marshy waste'.[6]

Thirty years before, most of the area that lay north and east of Gusow was a marshy waste, at least in the eyes of educated contemporaries. This was the Oderbruch, or Oder Marshes, which extended along the west bank of the River Oder, some ten to twelve miles wide, from Oderberg in the north to Lebus in the south, a distance of around thirty-five miles. Before the middle of the eighteenth century, this was 'barren, valueless swamp land', 'a wilderness of water and marsh'.[7] Areas of this kind could be found everywhere in Prussia. To the west, on the doorstep of Berlin, were the Wustrau marshes. Across the Oder to the east, beyond the fortress of Küstrin, lay the Warthe and Netze river valleys, another 'marshy and watery waste'.[8] And north of that, where Count Podewils' Pomeranian estates lay, were similar tracts of land like the Madüe and the marshes of the River Plöne. In fact, as Johann Bernoulli pushed on east, through West Prussia and East Prussia into the Courland, he was seldom far from areas that, thirty years before, had been thinly inhabited except by frogs, storks and wild pigs. The waterlogged valley of the Vistula, the German Weichsel, was among the most notorious.

These marsh regions had a common geological origin. During the last ice age a huge ice cap pushed south across Scandinavia, the Baltic and the North Sea, and continued on across what is now the North European Plain until it reached the central highlands of present-day Germany and Poland. Then, around 10,000 years ago, the ice sheet retreated. Trapped between the retreating ice-face and the high ground, the huge volume of meltwater was unable to flow directly away from the ice so instead moved laterally along it. This created a number of great east–west depressions, known in German as *Urstromtäler*, in Polish as *pradoliny*, and in English as ancient river valleys. They stretched from the Pripet and Bug in the east to the Elbe in the west. Eventually this water mass was captured by rivers flowing from south to north and emptying into the Baltic or North Sea, the drainage system familiar to us. But the marshy floors of the ancient river valleys remained.[9]

The retreating ice sheet shaped the future hydrological system of the area in two other ways. It deposited debris through which the sluggish rivers of the North European plain flowed, making numerous side-arms as they did so and creating swampy regions in between them. And it gouged out so-called tongue basins, small depressions caused by the lobes of the ice sheet, which gradually filled up with silt. That was what happened in the marshy lower reaches of the Vistula and Oder. Through the middle of the eighteenth century, much of the sandy plain continued to be punctuated by areas of swamp and marsh. Unlike the Paris or London basins, these lowlands were decidedly not 'rich, fertile, smiling areas'.[10]

We have a fairly good idea of what the Oderbruch must have looked like in 1744, when the Podewils arrived in Gusow. Just a year later three artists made an excursion into the Bruch to paint the landscape. What they captured in oils still resembled quite closely the scene in an engraving made a century earlier by Matthäus Merian, in which the observer gazes down from the heights on a labyrinthine network of waterways that wind their way across the flats, creating countless islands in the process (Fig. 1).[11] These are stylized landscapes, of course; and the view from above probably makes the undergrowth of brush seem more dense than it actually was. But if these depictions tend to romanticize in one way, they undercut romantic legend in another. Contrary to the image of the pre-reclamation Oderbruch that the German writer Theodor Fontane fostered in his *Rambles through the March Brandenburg*, published in 1861, which has been endlessly recycled ever since, this was no primeval forest with trailing creepers. As the cartographic evidence confirms, areas of solid woodland were few.[12] Open patches of marsh and pools, where the main vegetation was grass or reeds, alternated with areas of thick, waterlogged brush and alder trees. Twice a year the Oderbruch was under water to a depth of ten to twelve feet, once in spring after the snow melt, and again in summer when local storms and run-off from the distant highlands combined to swell the river. And twice a year, after the waters retreated, old passages had closed and new side-arms of the river appeared. It was an area over which mists swirled, home to many species of birds, fish and animals, where the columns of insects were so thick that they made a sound 'like a distant drumbeat'.[13]

Efforts to tame these inhospitable waterlands went back centuries, to the medieval Teutonic Knights and the Cistercian order. They were continued by the Hohenzollern dynasty as it established itself in the region after 1500 and cautiously began to expand its territories through marriage and purchase. Joachim I of Brandenburg built summer dikes along the river on the upper, southern part of the Oderbruch between Lebus and Küstrin; his sons Joachim and Hans tried to cut off some side-arms of the river. In the 1590s Johann Georg ordered the height of the dikes to be raised; then at the beginning of the seventeenth century regular dike inspections were instituted. The focus of all these efforts, which consisted mostly of trying to do better what the previous generation had not done well enough, was the southern Oderbruch. There the land was slightly higher and the river less intractable. The south also received priority because diking helped to safeguard the fortress of Küstrin and prevent the unruly waters from closing the commercially and strategically important road that ran west, past Selow and Gusow, to Berlin. But during the Thirty Years War (1618–48) that caused such devastation in Germany, invading Swedish armies not only seized Küstrin but destroyed many of the dikes.[14]

When the war was over, Frederick William, the Great Elector, did what everyone else in Europe did: he called in the Dutch. By the middle of the seventeenth century the inhabitants of the Low Countries were securely established as the hydraulic masters of the Continent. This reputation was based partly on the deeds of its celebrated engineers. Jan Leeghwater had drained Lake Beemster and scores of other inland lakes in North Holland; Cornelis Vermuyden had done the same in the English Fens. Their countrymen were working as hired experts from Italy to Muscovy. More anonymously, Dutch colonists draining and settling land were familiar across the deltas and estuaries of northern Europe, as far east as the Nogat and Vistula.[15] Frederick William, who had lived in the Low Countries as a young man and married a Dutch princess, encouraged colonists to settle the marshlands of Brandenburg. More than one 'New Holland' bore witness to their efforts.[16] These settlements were mostly established close to Berlin, on the fringes of the Dosse and Havel marshes that had once been 'a paradise of frogs'.[17] In 1653, the same year that Vermuyden finished draining the English Fens, the Great Elector brought in Dutch colonists to plant themselves further east, in the Oderbruch. But they lacked the resources to establish successful settlements, and their piecemeal efforts to construct dikes were, like those of so many predecessors, washed away.[18]

The Dutch connection was to play an important part in bringing about more lasting change in the eighteenth century. It began with King Frederick William I. The 'Soldier King', who doubled the standing army to 80,000 men, had in mind the needs of the cavalry, for new land could grow feedstuff in winter and provide grazing in summer. His response to the degradation and repeated collapse of the Oderbruch dikes was a rebuilding programme. The new dikes would be higher and thicker; new regulations were crafted to enforce their maintenance. (It was characteristic of the king and the state he ruled that Friedrich von Derfflinger, the head of the new Dike Commission, was an officer and the son of a seventeenth-century Prussian military hero. He also happened to be the owner of the Gusow estate until his death in 1724.) In the 1730s six main drains were constructed to reclaim the land behind the new protective wall, some 70,000 acres in all. The problem was that, once again, these measures dealt only with the southern part of the Bruch. Water was drained away, using the natural lie of the land, to the northern, lower-lying part of the Oder Marsh. Squeezed out of one place, the water only made its presence more powerfully felt elsewhere. Worse: when the river ran unusually high in the northern marshes, water backed up and inundated the newly won land to the south, as the catastrophic floods of 1736 were to show. It was the ninth major flooding in the area in forty years, the fourth in just eight years.[19]

That is where Simon Leonhard Haerlem, hydraulic engineer, entered the picture. As the name suggests, his family's origins were Dutch (some authors give the name as Haarlem, or Häarlem), although its members had long settled in Hanover, where Simon Leonhard's father and grandfather had both been dike masters. Born in 1701, Haerlem entered Prussian service in the 1730s, working on reclamation projects on the lower Elbe and later drawing up a plan to drain the Warthe and Netze marshes.[20] In 1736, Frederick William summoned him to the Oderbruch, where his immediate task was to supervise repairs to the main Oder dike that had been breached at Neuendorf. But his presence set off a more far-reaching proposal. That same year, Frederick William went heron hunting in the still unimproved Lower Bruch and noticed that the Ranft estates of his host, Minister of State Samuel von Marschall, had been spared the general flooding thanks to the local construction of polders. Was the same thing possible throughout the Lower Bruch, he asked Haerlem? Yes, came the reply, but it would be complex – and costly. The Soldier King, parsimonious even by

Hohenzollern standards and mindful of his advancing years, made a note that this task would be left 'for my son Friedrich'.[21]

That son, Frederick II ('the Great'), knew the Oderbruch at first hand from a harsh youthful experience. Every life of Frederick has something to say about the incident that occurred when he was just eighteen. It was a classic political confrontation between a ruling monarch and an independent-minded crown prince, a conflict of wills sharpened by the tension between an unyielding, disciplinarian father and a son who wrote poetry, played the flute and passed his time with philosophers: a 'French windbag', in the father's words. Frederick, tired of the paternal bawling and blows that were supposed to make a good Prussian out of him, tried to flee the state with his closest friend, an officer called Hans-Hermann von Katte. They were caught and tried as deserters. Katte was sentenced to life imprisonment, but on Frederick William's insistence he was executed and the crown prince forced to watch.[22] It is the less dramatic sequel that principally concerns us. After two and a half months under guard in the fortress of Küstrin, Frederick asked his father for forgiveness and was instructed to work in the local provincial administration, where he would learn 'economics from the ground up'. This became his 'Küstrin galley'. He became familiar with royal agricultural domains like Carzig and Wollup, enclaves in the partly tamed Upper Oderbruch. As the nineteenth-century historian Leopold von Ranke put it: 'He inspected buildings, animals, fields, everything, and found that further improvements were still possible, especially if one drained the marshes that had no human use'.[23]

It was a brutal way to learn about the virtues of land reclamation, and Frederick later complained that his youth had been stolen. But rational husbandry also appealed to the philosophical, enlightened side of Frederick that his father had tried to suppress. Three years before coming to the throne he wrote: 'Making domain lands cultivable interests me more than murdering people'.[24] He was to end up doing a good deal of both. But the point is that Frederick's experience of riding around the royal domains and mastering the details of husbandry reinforced his enlightened reading to make him a strong supporter of contemporary ideas about improving the land. 'Agriculture', he wrote in one of the many letters he exchanged with the French philosopher Voltaire, 'is the first of all the arts, without which there would be no merchants, kings, poets, philosophers'.[25] This conviction had a playful side. Earlier Hohenzollerns had drained marshes to establish dairies; Frederick once gave a large Emmenthaler as a wedding present, accompanied by a poem in praise of cheese.[26] But his belief in the primacy of the fruits of the earth was no pose, and it went together with the anti-water prejudice of an extreme, incorrigible landman. Frederick once complained that even taking the waters at a spa made him feel *deplaciert*: water was best left to the eels, flounders, pike and ducks.[27]

He became king in 1740, exchanging the pleasures of reading, music and good conversation at his Rheinsberg estate for the isolation of power in Berlin. Frederick's harsh youthful experiences had made him more self-confident but harder, leaving behind an icy self-command and a dark, cynical side that became increasingly prominent during the forty-six years of his reign. He was close to very few people: not the officers in his immediate entourage, not the foreign philosophers he collected in Berlin, and certainly not his wife, the former Elisabeth Christina of Brunswick, with whom he spent as little time as possible and rarely appeared in public. A distant and self-contained figure, he 'spread awe and coldness' all around him. Even before assuming the throne Frederick had become much more interested in military affairs, although he never took to his father's soldierly pursuits like hunting. But he still read and wrote extensively as king, and maintained a serious interest in enlightened ideas. He remained strongly drawn to the tasks of agricultural improvement and internal colonization.

Frederick issued a flurry of rescripts on these subjects as soon as he was king. In 1746, ten years after his father's conversation with Haerlem, he requested answers from officials to a series of questions about the Lower Oderbruch: where should dikes be built, what would they cost, what return could be expected from the reclaimed land? It was Haerlem who drafted the response, outlining plans for 'a large-scale drainage of the Oderbruch'. In a formulation nicely gauged to appeal to the monarch's prejudices, he expressed confidence that 'in spots that now feed a few fish, it will be possible in the future to maintain a cow'.[28] Haerlem's report was written in early January 1747, and passed on to Frederick by a senior official called von Beggerow. On 21 January the king instructed Minister of State Samuel von Marschall – the same man whose local efforts had impressed his father ten years earlier – to chair an Oderbruch Commission that would include Haerlem, Beggerow and a senior member of the provincial administration. Three days later they had their man, seconded to the commission by royal decree: Heinrich

Wilhelm von Schmettau, scion of an extended family clan of Prussian officials and officers, who was deputy director of the War and Domains Office in Brandenburg.[29] Less than three weeks after that a contract was signed with the engineer Mahistre, who had worked on the construction of the Plauen Canal a few years earlier.[30]

Many popular accounts of the Lower Oderbruch reclamation assume that the eventual, radical project was on the agenda from the start. Haerlem's original proposal did indeed contain a bold proposal, but it was not the one that was actually carried out. His report in January 1747 had suggested that, in addition to further diking of the Oder and cutting off side-arms where possible, a new channel be cut for the river at the northern end of the Oderbruch, between the Neuenhagen mill and Oderberg. At some point in the early months of 1747 this plan was modified. It was now proposed to construct a new channel for the Oder, twelve miles in length, between Güstebiese and Hohen-Saaten. This would shorten the river by fifteen miles, speed the flow of water, and make it easier to drain the land over which the Oder meandered so unpredictably. The commission suggested three great advantages for the new plan: it would improve navigability, it would lower costs by shortening the length of the dikes, above all it would permit a more comprehensive reclamation. But there was one large obstacle: at its northern end, the new channel would have to be dug through a tongue of high land. This would be a major undertaking. Frederick II therefore ordered an on-site inspection.[31]

Three men were deputed to conduct it. Haerlem and Schmettau were accompanied by one of the most celebrated mathematicians of the eighteenth century, the Swiss-born Leonhard Euler, a man who (in the words of a later French eulogist) reached a 'pitch of glory' that neither Descartes nor Newton had enjoyed.[32] Just turned forty, Euler had moved to Berlin from St Petersburg in 1741, a star acquisition in Frederick's attempt to restore the reputation of the Academy of Sciences. Euler's reputation rested on his work in geometry, algebra, probability theory and optics. But he also had a practical bent, displayed in a 1736 *Treatise on Mechanics*.[33] Frederick had already used his expertise in hydrological questions. Euler helped to design the aquaduct at the new royal castle of Sans-Souci, and – like Mahistre – he had worked on the Plauen Canal. Given this background, and his good connections at court, he was the obvious person to send into the Oderbruch.[34]

Haerlem, Schmettau and Euler, the engineer, the bureaucrat and the scientist, left Berlin on 7 July, travelling – as Bernoulli was to do almost exactly thirty years later – to the Zellin ferry. (The parallel is no idle detail: Euler had studied with Bernoulli's grandfather and was a life-long friend of Bernoulli's uncle, Daniel, the man who established Bernoulli's Principle in 1738: that the velocity of water forced into a narrower channel will increase.[35]) Over the next two days the three men went downriver and back, maps and surveying instruments to hand. Euler saw for himself the great bend in the Oder at Güstebiese and measured the drop in the proposed new channel that would replace it; for, as he was to write a few years later in his *Letters to a Princess*, 'before digging a canal, you must be well assured that one of the extrem-ities is more elevated than the other'.[36] Which was true enough, even if it was hardly an insight that called for Newtonian brilliance. At one point the three travellers encountered Mahistre's men, already gath-ering to begin excavations; everywhere they encountered the side-arms of the existing river, dozens of them, and shook their heads. It is tempting to call them three men in a boat, but that is not quite accurate, because from time to time they were forced overland. The most striking aspect of their journey, in retrospect, is that they were travelling on water that would soon become land, and on land that would soon become water. Their report to the king concluded that the radical plan to create a new course for the river should go ahead.[37] Little more than a week later, on 17 July, it did.

It would take seven years to carry out the Haerlem plan, not counting the much longer period required to people the land that emerged out of the water. It was an epic undertaking. There is no other word for it, although it is a word that has to be handled with care. Frederick the Great was a hero to generations of Prussian historians for taming the Oderbruch and planting colonists on reclaimed land. Popular writers followed suit. A century later in 1848, year of revolutions, the dike inspector Carl Heuer described in verse how a 'mighty vassal . . . stormed through hearth and home' until a royal hero 'drove him from the field'.[38]

The vanquished power is our River Oder
And its terrain the Oder Marshes
The hero who cast him in chains
Has risen to the vault of heaven

The tourist brochures that now summon Germans to the Brandenburg Oderland offer a toned-down version of the same story. They are
careful to avoid any suggestion that Old Prussia is being venerated, but
'Old Fritz' remains at the centre of the story. Indeed his role has been
cast in stone, the memorial stone that celebrates Frederick's achievement in draining the Oderbruch.[39]

There is plenty to object to in an account that reduces what was
accomplished to the work of one man. As Bertolt Brecht's poem sardon-
ically asked of the kings who built the seven gates of Thebes: And did
they carry all the stones themselves?[40] But necessary though it is to
scratch away at legend, it is just as important not to fall into another
trap that lies in wait for historians as well as tourist offices. That is
the temptation to assume that the draining of the Oderbruch, like the
many similar undertakings that followed, was somehow natural, the
way things were bound to be. For if there is one thing that Carl Heuer's
doggerel and the books of the old Prussian historians had right, it is
their insistence that this was indeed a struggle: against the elements and
against human resistance.

The project was star-crossed from the outset.[41] The construction
engineer Mahistre died just three months after work was underway, his
place taken by the Brothers Rottengatter. Samuel von Marschall,
chairman of the Oderbruch Commission, died in 1749, Haerlem
assuming his responsibilities. A more serious threat to the tempo of
construction were the outbreaks of fever that occurred every year, taking
lives and causing serious illness among many more. Frederick, who
followed the progress of work with vast impatience and demanded
weekly progress reports, ordered doctors sent in from Berlin. But in
autumn 1752 the outbreaks of fever were worse than ever. This was
marshy, malarial terrain, and the physically punishing work made the
labourers susceptible to illness. While the science of hydrological engineering and the quality of measuring instruments were advancing rapidly,
the mechanical arts of construction still rested on the ancient principles of wedge, lever and pulley. Carts carried work materials to the site
from as far away as Berlin and Stettin, but it was human muscle power
that did the rest, men standing waist-deep in water, wielding buckets,
shovels and long-handled spades.

Illness made already serious labour shortages worse. Experienced
dike-builders and canal-diggers were hard to come by and expensive.
Military service and harvests took labourers away from the project.[42]

Some would-be colonists who arrived early in the area were engaged in construction; but work still languished through much of 1750 and 1751, when there were no more than 700 men instead of the expected 1500–1600 on site. The slow rate of progress exposed the project to the elements: ice build-ups in winter and high water that breached half-completed dikes and led to floods. Alt-Wriezen was inundated twice in these years. An often unreliable labour force working in dreadful conditions and discontented about their pay also faced non-cooperation from local people. When their petitions were brushed aside, some reacted by refusing to provide the wood that made up the fascines needed for dike construction, or withheld use of their boats to transport materials. There were acts of sabotage. Local fears and resentments over the larger goal of the project were hardly smoothed by the reported thefts of food, hay and wood by canal workers. In July 1751, a weary official reported on 'another major brawl' between carters and locals in Güstebiese.[43]

It was in 1751 that Frederick finally lost patience, and the under-taking was put on a military footing. Colonel von Retzow assumed overall command of the project in January, and informed his monarch from the Oderbruch that only with good weather and 1600 labourers – half of whom would have to be soldiers – was there any hope of completing the project that year. Neither condition was satisfied; Haerlem reported to Retzow in April that because of high water only 242 men were at work. But things changed that summer. Another soldier, Captain Petri, was dispatched to the Oderbruch to assist Haerlem, and in August 1200 men were on site, 950 of them soldiers. In earlier years the demands of military service had impeded work; now the situation was reversed. Here, in microcosm, was proof that the Prussian army was indeed – as one historian has put it – 'the flywheel of the economy'.[44] The entire project increasingly assumed the char-acter of a military operation. After Petri's arrival with special orders in 1751, followed by an aide-de-camp called Groschopp the following spring to keep him up to the mark, boats were requisitioned from reluc-tant villagers, resisters were threatened with severe punishment, and construction went ahead under military guard. Despite continuing prob-lems with illness and desertions, the pace of work picked up and the project was finally completed in 1753. On 2 July, water was allowed to flow into the new bed that had been dug for it. Three days later Haerlem and Petri took a party of dignitaries from Berlin down the

'New Oder' (or Petri Canal, for it was the soldier not the engineer whose name was commemorated), and found its waters smooth and 'tranquil'. From the Eichhorn mill that served as their base, they reported triumphantly to Retzow that 'there is now really no doubt that all the former enemies and detractors of this work, which transcends their own horizons, should be ashamed of themselves.'[45]

Frederick himself, looking down on the new Oderbruch from the surrounding heights, was no less triumphant: 'Here I have conquered a province in peace'.[46] Later writers would take his cue. Carl Heuer's 1848 verse was quite typical in using the language of conquest to describe the reclamation. Whether it was achieved peacefully is another matter. Contemporaries who referred to a 'silently conducted Seven Years War' were nearer the mark.[47] Violence was an essential part of the transformation: without the use of soldiers and military coercion the project would not have been completed when it was. Yet there is no reason to question the importance of what was achieved. True, there had been earlier, partial efforts to tame the Oder Marshes; and there was another precedent of sorts, in the draining of the Havel Marshes under Frederick William I, begun in 1718, a project that was also bedevilled by engineering problems and local resistance, and completed only when Dutch engineering was bolstered by Prussian military strength.[48] If the Seven Years War that broke out in 1756 had marked the end of Frederick II's ambitions to make 'peaceful' conquests from Prussia's marshes, perhaps we should view the draining of the Oderbruch differently. Like his father's efforts on the Havel, it would have remained a historical curiosity.

But that was not what happened. The war, fought by Prussia to retain the province of Silesia that had been seized from Austria at the beginning of Frederick's reign, was certainly costly and destructive. The devastation inflicted by Prussian power in the territories it overran, like neighbouring Saxony, was matched by the suffering of Prussians whose lives were affected by war and its indirect effects – disease and a disrupted food supply. Those living east of the River Oder were especially vulnerable: the population fell briefly in the province of Pomerania. But these effects of war only placed a greater premium on colonization as a task of post-war reconstruction. With the return of peace in 1763, further reclamation projects were pushed ahead with an almost manic intensity. With the benefit of hindsight, the Oderbruch was the place where it all began.

The Lords and Masters of Nature

It is hard to grasp the sheer scale of the new land that was won in 1740–86, the years when Frederick II was on the throne. The activity began in the first decade of the reign with the Oderbruch scheme and a number of more modest projects in the Priegnitz, the Stettin marshes and the valley of the Dölln; it continued until the year of the king's death, when he wrote to President von der Goltz in Königsberg instructing him 'to drain the large marsh close to Tilsit'.[49] Throughout the intervening period there were always projects underway, sometimes dozens of them at various stages of completion, so that the men in charge had to shuttle backwards and forwards from one to another. Military campaigns did not stop the work. In fact, officials could almost count on the fact that during his travels to and from hostilities Frederick would spot yet another patch of swamp and ask for a full report.

The one exception was the period of the Seven Years War, when no new projects were begun. But the existing ones went on, despite their cost in human and financial resources. The most important was a large-scale scheme to reclaim the marshes of the Warthe and Netze valleys, which rivalled the draining of the Oderbruch in complexity and ultimately took much longer to complete. Like the Oderbruch, this was an area that Frederick knew well from his time in Küstrin, when a liaison with Frau von Wreech often took him to Tamsel on the heights that looked down over the Warthe.[50] This project was entrusted, like many others right across the kingdom, to Franz Balthasar Schönberg von Brenckenhoff, a swashbuckling native of Anhalt-Dessau who began his controversial years of service to the Prussian state as an army supplier, and ended as Frederick's troubleshooter-in-chief in hydrological projects.[51] After 1763 the pace of reclamation became more frenetic, reaching its peak in the 1770s. No part of the kingdom escaped the parties of officials and labourers, whose requirements in the way of carts, provisioning and lodgings made them resemble small armies – here, Brenckenhoff's background stood him in good stead. In the 1770s alone there were projects underway in Brandenburg, Pomerania, East Prussia and Lithuania; in Silesia, seized from Austria in the early 1740s; in East Friesland, annexed in 1744; and in West Prussia, part of the booty from the first Polish partition of 1772. The fact that Prussia was growing (it doubled in size during Frederick's reign) drove the gathering pace of activity through the 1770s. External conquests created additional territory on which to make internal conquests, spaces on the map out of which new land could be made.

Work went on in the valleys or estuaries of major rivers like the Elbe, Oder, Warthe, Netze and Vistula. It also went on along waterways whose names, many of them now no longer German, will be familiar only to those who have looked at old Prussian maps or read Theodor Fontane's *Rambles through the March Brandenburg* with unusually close attention. Rivers like the Rhin, the Dosse and the Jäglitz, the Aland, the Briese and the Milde, the Notte, the Nuthe and the Nieplitz. We find the same story, the same attention to both large and small, when it comes to Prussia's disappearing marshes. Some were very extensive, such as the Drömling in the Old March, drained at the end of the 1770s. Twenty-six miles long and thirteen miles wide, it yielded over 220,000 acres of new land. The marshes around Lake Madüe and on the Plöne in Pomerania, some 75,000 acres all told, presented special difficulties. This was one of Brenckenhoff's major projects. At the other end of the scale, pocket-sized by comparison, was the Hopfenbruch, which lay between Berlin's botanical gardens and Charlottenburg until it was drained in 1774.

Even as work began or plans were drawn up to deal with the most obvious candidates for improvement, a restless, energetic Frederick would demand more maps and lists of the 'Brücher und Lücher', the marshes and bogs, in this or that province. A roll-call of these lost wetlands reads like a gazetteer of old Prussia: Altranft in the Oderbruch, the Bartschbruch, the Great Camminer Marsh, the Damscher Bruch, the Elbewische, the Fienerbruch, the Golm'scher Bruch, the Havelländisches Luch, the Ihna Bruch, the Jaemischwald Bruch, the Kremmensee marshes, the Lebasee, the Madüe, the Netzebruch, the Obrabruch, the Priegnitz, the Rhinluch, the Schmolsiner Marsh, the Thurbruch on the island of Usedom, the Vilmersee, the Warthebruch, the Zehden marshes. This was activity on a scale quite different from anything the Cistercians or the early Electors of Brandenburg could have imagined. Like similar undertakings elsewhere in Germany during these years – the draining of lakes on the Magdeburg Plain, the diking and ditching of fens in the Emsland, the reclamation work on the Danube Moor in Bavaria – these were more extensive, more comprehensive, than anything that had come before.[52]

One of the things that made these projects possible in the first place was information. Even half a century earlier no ruler in Germany could have laid his hands on the kind of detailed knowledge needed to carry out what Frederick demanded. This was the heroic age of the statistician, a new breed of men like Anton Friedrich Büsching and Johann Peter Süssmilch who counted not only births, deaths and marriages but land, people and raw materials. Statistics became an important part of the German 'science of government' known as cameralism, which emphasized the training of future officials in useful knowledge that would help rulers to develop the natural resources of the realm.[53] Frederick the Great was unusually thirsty for information, and cameralism was a German label, but there was nothing distinctively Prussian or German about what was happening. The growing use of statistics can be found across Europe, in the Britain of George III, the France of Louis XVI, the Russia of Catherine the Great, and in many smaller states. By the middle of the eighteenth century, the well-tempered state was one in which the prince had access to computations, tabulations, and classifications on everything under the sun, including those tracts of 'useless' land that might, one day, produce a field of corn or support a herd of Frisians.

Tabulating space – it sounds so obvious. But gathering all this information rested on major advances in surveying skills. The measuring instruments that Friedrich Nicolai carried on his travels to southern Germany and the odometer that Johann Bernoulli admired at Gusow were signs of the times. But putting the information to use required something that was perhaps even more important: new ways of representing information on the map. By the middle of the eighteenth century maps were changing. Instead of being crowded with visual symbols like towns or castles, with little sense of their connection to each other and no sense of topography, maps were showing something that we take for granted: a continuous physical terrain. This change was driven partly by military demands, for armies on the move needed accurate information about the ground they were crossing. Military maps remained secret; the new cartographic conventions became standard. (Their experience with mapping terrain was one reason why so many Prussian officers found themselves drafted to reclamation projects in the lulls between Frederick's wars.) The emerging discipline of geography also helped to establish this new kind of map. Philippe Buache was a French pioneer in classifying the 'natural boundaries' of the earth's surface in terms of watersheds. Johann Christoph Gatterer's

Outline of Geography went in a similar direction; so did the historical-geographical-topographical accounts written by the prominent cameralist Bernhard Ludwig Bekmann, with their detailed attention to mountains, rivers and plains.[54]

Tables, maps, topographical descriptions: these put power in the hands of a ruler like Frederick the Great. Information made the great reclamation projects possible. It was a 'how' – a prerequisite. But was it also a 'why' – a motive? Certainly it was one of them. The maps and statistical tables did not turn up by chance. Frederick encouraged the early work of Süssmilch; the descriptions compiled by Bekmann, a member of the Academy of Sciences, were written at royal command.[55] Officials were constantly being chased up for detailed reports, backed by the threat of a summons to Berlin to explain themselves if one was not forthcoming. Information was the fuel that fed the machine of the absolutist state, but the larger purpose has been summed up by Henning Eichberg: to 'order, measure, discipline'.[56]

Marshland offended egregiously against this sense of order. Unimproved, marshes resisted the cadastral surveys on which land taxes rested, impeded soldiers on the march, and provided a bolthole for 'disorderly' elements such as bandits and deserters. Like the new high roads or *Chausseen* of this period, the roads built on reclaimed land and the milestones strung along them were visible symbols that order had been established. Viewed from the perspective of organizing the interior space of the state, administrative lines on the map were now matched by lines on the ground. And the same was true of the boundary lines drawn around the state. These were the years when European state borders were starting to become more fixed. But how could a boundary be established when seasonal flooding or the wild meanders of a river altered the disposition of the land from year to year? When Bishop Maximilian Franz of Münster drained and settled moorland in the 1780s, one of his major aims was to secure the borders of his ecclesiastical territory.[57] Many of the great projects entrusted to Brenckenhoff were undertaken on the expanding eastern margins of the state.[58] This was an issue that faced every German prince, but it faced the ruler in Berlin with particular force. For Prussia, a state that was expanding through military conquest across the swampy North European Plain, borders and reclamation went together.

To adapt a famous remark of Clausewitz's, waging war on nature was the pursuit of politics by other means. But the relationship also ran the other way. The language of war infused contemporary thinking about the natural world. That was why the draining of the Oderbruch could be described as a 'conquest'. Or, as Frederick put the matter on another occasion: 'Whoever improves the soil, cultivates land lying waste and drains swamps, is making conquests from barbarism'.[59] This was the authentic voice of eighteenth-century enlightened absolutism. The desire to order, measure and discipline applied not only to soldiers and subjects, to land and raw materials, but to nature itself, where the Creator had left dark or 'barbarous' corners that served no useful purpose. The perspective of the prince was in harmony with educated opinion among academicians and cameralist officials, who echoed the view that humankind, 'the lords and masters of nature' (in Descartes' words), the 'master of the domain of earth' (in Buffon's), had a right and duty to 'repair' or 'improve' a *natura lapsa*.[60]

Human mastery was not asserted only against disorderly waters. Another element – fire – received plenty of attention in these years. Fires regularly burned towns to the ground, helped by the use of wood and straw as building materials.[61] They caused both loss of life and (from a cameralist perspective) the destruction of resources, human and material. Prussia was an eighteenth-century pioneer in fireplace inspections, edicts on roofing materials and directives about fire pumps.[62] Perhaps more important, certainly more widely influential, was the campaign conducted in German states against rural wildfires and the peasant practice of fire farming, or *Brandwirtschaft*, what used to be known in England as swiddening. As Stephen Pyne has argued, to absolutist rulers and officials 'fire was dangerous, irrational, unpredictable, wasteful in its consumption, mischievous in its migratory habits, an inducement to sloth and violence. Fire was power. It was something to be controlled.'[63] And controlled it was. Rationally-minded forestry officials led the efforts to wipe out this affront to enlightened management of timber resources, through edicts on burning, the construction of firebreaks and more orderly planting of trees. Nowhere else in Europe did scientific forestry make such advances in the second half of the eighteenth century as it did in Germany. What the Swedish botanist Linnaeus did for plants, Wilhelm Gottfried Moser and J. F. Stahl did for the arboreal world in their *Principles of Forest Economy* (1757). And, just as the Dutch provided Europe with its hydraulic engineers, Germany ('the fatherland of forestry') exported its forestry officials to the rest of Europe and the European empires overseas.[64]

Planting trees was also one of the solutions seized upon by contemporaries who worked to master nature in a different way. Not fire, but
sand, was the irritant across many parts of the north German plain.
Giant shifting dunes filled the air with fine particles that obscured roads
and drifted on to the fields, ruining standing crops. 'With the exception of Libya, few states can boast of being our equal when it comes
to sand', wrote Frederick the Great to Voltaire, with rather heavy
irony.[65] It was a vexation to which he repeatedly returned. One measure
urged on officials was the planting of pine trees to anchor the shifting
sands; another was drilling down experimentally to see what lay beneath
the sand, so that any layers of marl under the surface could be turned
over and brought to the top.[66] Frederick expressed some scepticism
about the chances of winning this particular battle, as things stood in
the 1770s, and he was right. Prussia would not so easily throw off its
reputation as a sandbox. Another Frederick – Engels – was still referring in 1840, with similar irony but rather more affection, to the 'north
German Sahara'.[67]

Meanwhile, the war against untamed nature was being waged more
successfully on another front, and with weapons more lethal than spades
or drills. This was the culling or eradication of creatures that directly
challenged humans for resources. Unamenable to domestication and
ranked low on the Great Chain of Being, these species were considered
verminous or predatory. The list was long. It included, of course, rats,
mice and foxes, but also moles, weasels, polecats and beavers, and a
wide variety of birds and insects that represented a threat to livestock,
orchards or crops. There was a regular running battle against many of
these, symbolized by the figures of the mole-catcher and rat-catcher
(whose lowly status as members of 'dishonourable occupations' said
something about a society that considered their work essential, yet also
tainted by their contact with vermin).[68] Campaigns were also mounted
against this or that species as the season or local needs dictated. In
Brandenburg plagues of locusts prompted both Frederick William I and
Frederick the Great to issue edicts. Around Magdeburg and Halberstadt
it was hamsters devastating the cornfields who were subject to 'extermination measures'. (When it became apparent that local catchers were
deliberately releasing females to maintain the hamster population, partly
because of their profits from the pelts, Frederick responded with a 1764
decree threatening offenders with corporal punishment.) Wild boar were
hunted down from Lithuania to the gates of Berlin. In terms of sheer

numbers, however, nothing matched the pursuit of the sparrow. Between 1734 and 1767, within the borders of the Old March Brandenburg alone, somewhere between eleven and twelve million were killed and their heads turned over for payment.[69]

Sparrows were not eradicated. Other species were, in Prussia and throughout German-speaking central Europe. The most dramatic aspect of this story is the hunting to extinction of the bear, lynx and wolf. All had increased in numbers during the devastation of the Thirty Years War. In the period of recovery that followed, as humans reoccupied abandoned tracts of land, different populations found themselves trying to live at high densities in the same area. Wild species came into direct conflict with humans and their stocks of domesticated animals. There was little doubt about the outcome. When the war ended the battle against predatory animals began. George II of Saxony and his hunting companions killed no fewer than 2195 wolves and 239 bears between 1656 and 1680; in Prussia, 4300 wolves, 229 lynx and 147 bears were killed in the year 1700 alone.[70] When Frederick William visited East Prussia in the early years of the eighteenth century, he was still complaining that there were 'more wolves than sheep'. Generous bounties were offered, then increased; hunters were instructed 'to seek out, pursue, shoot and eradicate' the scourge. In 1734, officials in the March and Pomerania received special instructions to report all sightings. Professional hunters were employed and as many as 130 men took part in some large-scale wolf hunts. Similar measures were taken against the smaller numbers of bears. Frederick the Great, like his German contemporaries, continued these campaigns. When it came to wolves, attention was focused on the eastern margins of the kingdom where the largest numbers remained.[71] Less than two months before his death, in June 1786, Frederick exhorted his senior official in Königsberg not to relax the hunts, 'so that these predatory animals do not once more gain the upper hand, but rather, so far as possible, are eradicated'.[72]

Both anxiety and determination are evident in this letter from the dying king. These were not hunts for pleasure: they were strictly a matter of utility. On this subject, at least, Frederick took the same view as his father. When an official was unwise enough to point out that the wild boar of the Warthebruch offered opportunities for hunting, Frederick William replied laconically: 'Sooner people than pigs'.[73] Nor was hunting down these creatures incompatible with a changing sensibility regarding animals. Frederick the Great disliked bear-baiting as a degrading spectacle; it did not make him less certain of the need to hunt down bears in the wild. The practical justification for doing so – predations on human resources – was underwritten by complicated cross-currents in contemporary thinking. These species were still commonly regarded as cruel and rapacious. Human projections of this kind were especially numerous in the case of the wolf, to which greed, cunning and depravity were readily attributed.[74] The new systems of classifying the natural world associated with Buffon and Linnaeus were starting to challenge these established anthropomorphic stereotypes found in folk tales and earlier bestiaries. They even raised potential questions about a human-centred view of the world. But the main lesson drawn from these new taxonomies by amateur naturalists and the rest of the educated public, including officials, was that they reinforced claims for human mastery of the world. Any more subversive implications came too late to prevent many species from being hunted to extinction. The wolf, the bear and the lynx largely disappeared from the German states between 1750 and 1790. From then, until the final eradication in the nineteenth century, it became common to see stones commemorating 'the last wolf killed here' on such and such a date.[75]

Wild fire, shifting sands, predatory animals: all belonged, in contemporaries' eyes, to the dangerous, disorderly side of nature. But none was thought so dangerous an enemy as untamed water. The element presented its most destructive face in the floods that periodically devastated coastal and inland areas. North Sea floods were the most catastrophic, like the Christmas storm flood of 1717 that claimed 8,000 lives in East Friesland, the Jeverland, Oldenburg, Schleswig and Holstein. In some areas half the population perished.[76] Inland floods were never so deadly, but they were frequent and destructive. One calculation based on local chronicles suggests that a 'major flood' occurred in the Warthe valley roughly every ten years after 1500.[77] The evidence points to something similar in the lower Oder valley, occasions when waters higher than those that brought the normal twice-yearly floods spilled out to inundate neighbouring towns. That happened sixteen times between 1595 and 1737. It usually occurred in spring, although it was in July that the devastating flood of 1736 took place, when the river rose for nine days before it breached the dikes on 17 July and flooded the towns of Küstrin, Wriezen, Oderberg and Schwedt. Crops and animals were destroyed. People saved themselves by clambering on to roofs; but they lacked food or fresh water, so that 1500 sickened and 170 died of dysentery and other infections contracted from eating putrid fish or drinking contaminated water.[78] Like major fires, like the outbreaks of disease to which they sometimes led, floods of this magnitude were disasters to which the eighteenth-century state responded with growing attention. German states were especially active. Canalization and dike building were to the threat of water what new urban regulations and changing forestry practices were to fire, or quarantines and inoculation to epidemics: a form of disaster management before the event.[79] The alleviation of human misery and the safeguarding of valuable resources (including people) were the inseparable ends. Controlling the flood waters unleashed by unruly nature – Carl Heuer's 'dangerous vassal' – was the means.

The damage done by floods was obvious; but contemporaries saw a greater problem. Wetlands, they believed, harboured dangers that were particularly insidious and always present. On no other aspect of the natural world was there such agreement within enlightened opinion as there was on the need to drain marsh and swamp. Whether we look at Buffon and Montesquieu in France, William Falconer and William Robertson in Britain, Georg Forster and Johann Gottfried Herder in Germany, the argument is the same. Marshes are dark, foetid places, where decaying vegetation and the decomposing animal matter emit noxious effluvia. If their odours offended the nose (for Europeans in the second half of the eighteenth century were becoming much more sensitive to the smell of decay), their dank disorder also offended the eye and their noisy animal cries the ear, an unwelcome reminder of nature's pandaemonium.[80]

Every association of marshland and swamp was negative. Their inhabitants were considered taciturn, clannish and superstitious, people who saw marsh gases and believed them to be will o' the wisps. Just as the seventeenth-century English traveller John Camden called the old Fenlanders 'barbarians', eighteenth-century Germans – officials, writers, those who lived on the surrounding heights – were suspicious of these semi-amphibious marsh-dwellers.[81] The stereotypes tended, if anything, to be reinforced by a growing interest in the relationship between climate and society that was being fostered by travel. No less firmly established in contemporary minds was the link between the 'pestilent marsh' and disease, a perfectly reasonable association, in fact, although one expressed in the prevailing language of 'miasmas'. Not least, marshlands were seen as the haunts of wild animals, again with good reason.

Frederick the Great, frustrated by the failure to eradicate wolves in West Prussia, knew where to place the blame and where to find the solution: 'In order better to achieve the final objective, one must devise means of gradually draining the impenetrable marshes and bogs where the wolves stay, and making them accessible'.[82] August Gottlob Meissner made the same connection in 1782 when he wrote about the Warthebruch before it was drained: 'No plough had ever been here, no human industry had ever sought its fortune . . . one encountered nothing but swamp and dense undergrowth, the habitation of snakes and wolves'.[83] As another contemporary noted of the same area, 'the whole region remained for a long time a dwelling place for wild animals, wolves, not infrequently bears, otters and other vermin of every kind'.[84] Marshes, swamp and fen were dark corners that harboured decay, disease and deadly vermin. The solution to all these problems was repeated by writer after writer: it was to drain the water and clear the vegetation, to let in air and sunlight so that the recovered land could be put to use.

Colonists

The huge scale of the reclamation projects in these years was matched by the huge scale of the migrations that filled the new land. This was a movement of people comparable to the German expansion into eastern Europe in the Middle Ages, and it was happening at the same time as the peopling of North America. Like those other great migrations it was an experience that generated both hardships and pioneer myths. And, as we shall see later in this book, all three episodes of colonization would be taken up and used by National Socialism in the twentieth century. 300,000 immigrants entered Prussia during the reign of Frederick the Great, enough to fill the Berlin of Frederick's youth four times over. Like the French Huguenots before them, some of the immigrants did in fact establish themselves in the capital, or in towns like Landsberg and Driesen that had been devastated in the Seven Years War and were now being rebuilt. But the majority settled in rural areas. There, territorial expansion and reclamation together produced the empty spaces on the map that Frederician population policy, or *Peuplierungspolitik*, was designed to fill. All told, some twelve hundred new villages or rural settlements were established in Prussia between 1740 and 1786. They housed the colonists so dear to Frederick's heart. It was colonists who were expected to make new-won land productive, colonists who would grow the feed that fattened the herds, tend the meadows that grazed the cavalry horses, and raise the corn that was needed in the growing capital.

In an age when the resources available to the state, including human beings, were viewed as part of a zero-sum game, population policy meant that colonists were solicited throughout Germany and beyond. Permanent recruitment stations were set up in key cities like Frankfurt am Main and Hamburg. Edicts were regularly posted and inserted in the press, advertising Prussia as a promised land for hard-working immigrants.[85] This aggressive policy antagonized other rulers, and some responded by trying to ban emigration. The need to calm ruffled feathers for diplomatic reasons sometimes led to a temporary suspension of recruitment here or there. But, as the numbers show, these efforts to sell a new future in Prussia proved successful. Both 'push' and 'pull' were involved. Religiously persecuted Protestants in almost every part of the Holy Roman Empire and beyond, peasants and craftsmen from south-western areas of Germany where rural over-population was becoming a problem, victims of the famines that affected Saxony and Bohemia in the early 1770s, all felt the push. The inducements – the pull – included the payment of travel costs, freedom from customs charges on personal possessions brought into Prussia, exemption from military service, billeting and other imposts, and special privileges like free wood. There was also land on a long lease, plus a house, farm equipment and stock for peasant settlers, a house, workshop and tools in the case of craftsmen.[86]

Some arrived with nothing to their name, urgently in need of the travel money that was paid when they reached the Prussian border at Halle or Treuenbrietzen, and even more desperate when the rules changed and the cash became available only on arrival at the final destination. But many brought substantial assets with them. The fourteen families who established themselves in Berkenwerder in the Warthebruch carried 280 Taler each in cash.[87] That was probably on the high side. The 2712 families who settled the Netzebruch, Warthebruch and Friedeberg-Bruch a few years later brought just over 100 Taler each.[88] We see a very similar figure if we look at the six different 'transports' of immigrants from the Palatinate who arrived in Pomerania in 1747. They numbered 1120 people in 250 families. Each family possessed on average 114 Taler, 80 Taler of which they carried with them.[89] To put this in perspective, 80 Taler in the middle of the eighteenth century was enough to stock a smallholding. It would buy you three horses, two cows, four pigs, four sheep, four geese, four chickens, a bed, household utensils, a cart, plough, harrow, scythe, axe and other farm equipment.[90] Most new arrivals were not starting from scratch, anyway. They brought household possessions, equipment and four-legged assets as well as cash to the Prussian El Dorado. The 688 families who arrived to settle the reclaimed Netzebruch were accompanied by 434 horses, 130 oxen, nearly 800 head of cattle and more than 500 head of young stock.[91]

We have to imagine the sight they presented, streaming into Prussia from every point of the compass: Swabians moving north, Mecklenburgers moving south, Saxons moving east, Germans from Poland moving west. And all moving slowly, for the wagons on which the young and the old travelled were forced to move at the pace set by pushcarts and livestock. Like the wagon trains heading west in nineteenth-century America, these columns of hopefuls sometimes lost people along the way. But it could also happen that their numbers grew. One party from the German parish of Seiberdorf in Poland set off for Silesia in 1770 300 strong. By the time they arrived another twenty families – 100 people – had joined them.[92] The journey out of Poland in these politically tense years was the most likely to meet with attempts at physical resistance from the local power holders. The Seiberdorf party received an escort of Prussians hussars. But it was, at least, a short journey, a reminder that not all of these mass migrations were long-distance affairs. The logic of geographical proximity was at work when Germans from across the Polish border settled mainly in the eastern provinces of Prussia closest to them, Mecklenburgers established themselves most often in Brandenburg or Pomerania, and Saxons in Brandenburg or Magdeburg.[93]

But what about those who came from much further afield, from Austria, Switzerland, or the German south-west? There was no obvious geographical logic here to act as a guide, although patterns eventually became established that acquired a lasting momentum. Later migrants went where family or friends had gone, while officials became familiar with particular travel routes, dialects and regional characteristics. In this way, many Swabian settlements were established in West Prussia, while Pomerania became a favoured destination of immigrants from the Palatinate. In these cases the distances *were* great and the journeys long.

It was over 800 miles from the Württemberg homeland of the Swabians, in the Neckar valley 'near Stuckert', to West Prussian Marien-werder on the Vistula. It was a shorter distance, but still almost 700 miles, for the French-speaking Swiss emigrants who travelled from Neuchâtel to the Oderbruch. All who made the journey began by taking a boat from Neuchâtel to Solothurn, travelled overland to Basel, and then down the Rhine as far as Mainz. There, some groups would continue on down the Rhine to Rotterdam, travel by sea to Hamburg, and then by boat via the Elbe, Havel and Spree to Berlin, completing the last stage on foot. But most of these families chose to leave the Rhine at Mainz, travel the short stretch along the Main by boat to Frankfurt, then complete their journey overland, through Kassel, Halberstadt and Magdeburg to Berlin.[94] The roads made for slow going. When the poet Klopstock travelled between Halberstadt and Magde-burg in 1750, progress at the rate of six Prussian miles (about thirty-five English miles) in six hours struck him as so remarkable that he compared it to the races of the ancient Olympics – and he was riding in a light carriage with four horses.[95] The journey from Switzerland could not be completed in less than four weeks, and usually took closer to six.

For one group of Austrians bound for the Oderbruch in the same years, the journey took longer than that. Like the 22,000 of their fellow religionists who had emigrated to Prussia a generation earlier, they were Protestants from Catholic Salzburg.[96] We first encounter the group in Regensburg, seat of the Holy Roman Empire's parliament, where the Prussian embassy served as a conduit that funnelled immigrants into the state. At the beginning of April 1754, correspondence between Councillor von Viereck and Frederick the Great indicates arrangements being made for the Austrians' journey on. This must have taken some time (probably because of serious doubts in the Oderbruch about when the project would be completed), for it was not until the following month, on 12 May, that Viereck wrote to tell the Prussian representa-tive in neighbouring Hof that a group of twenty peasants and weavers had just set off, with sixty or seventy more due to follow. Some of the second party probably caught up with the first, for a group of forty Salzburgers reached Hof on 20 May. There, thanks to the generosity of a Protestant nobleman, they were given carts and sent on to Prussian

Halle the same day. On 29 May the General Directory in Berlin advised Colonel Retzow, who was in overall charge of work in the Oderbruch, about the pending arrival of this group, which was still somewhere between Hof and Halle. The party duly arrived in Halle, received 77 Taler and 14 Groschen in travel costs, and set off for Potsdam and Berlin 'full of humility and patience', singing a song of exile ('*I bin ein armer Exulant*'). Perhaps their singing was too lusty, because after the first groups of Salzburgers had passed through the capital Frederick ordered that 'the Austrians coming from Regensburg now and in the future, should the case arise, are to be directed not via Berlin but on side roads in order to avoid all unnecessary *eclat* and *bruit*'.[97] Eventually the two groups, numbering 65 people in all, reached Wriezen, the main centre of activity for placing newly arrived colonists, just one day apart, on 7 and 8 June. It had been over nine weeks since they waited in Regensburg for their fate to be settled, longer than that since they left their native valleys.[98]

Should we be surprised about these hundreds of thousands of people on the move? Not really. German-speaking Europe in the last decades of the Old Regime, the years before the French Revolution, was not the static society that is sometimes depicted. In many ways it was bursting out of its corsets, as the existing social order came under strain from a newly growing population, new ways of organizing business that bypassed the guilds, new rural settlements on new land, new kinds of commercialized agriculture, new ideas. People on the move were the embodiment of the change, for the Old Regime was in fact highly mobile, although in ways that are different from the ones we take for granted. It was not only enlightened men, the Bernoullis and the Nicolais, or young noblemen making the grand tour, who went on the road in these years. At any given time, as many as one German in ten was on the move. Some were permanent itinerants, pedlars, hawkers, gypsies, knife-grinders, prostitutes, troupes of players and musicians, a segment of society that had grown in numbers as the population rose and was sometimes difficult to distinguish, in the minds of the many who feared them, from beggars and thieves.[99] They shared the road with pilgrims journeying to shrines and other devotional sites, despite the best efforts of the Catholic Enlightenment to discourage their deplorable 'superstition'. Others travelled seasonally, like the shepherds from the German south-west who took their flocks down from the high meadows to winter over in the Danube and Rhine valleys, making the return journey to the Swabian or Franconian Alps in March. These routes could be hundreds of miles long: some Franconian flocks were driven as far north as Thuringia, even to the Dutch border.[100] Yet others hit the road at a particular stage in their lives, like the journeymen who went 'on the tramp' in search of work, typically for two years, after serving their apprenticeships.

The columns of colonists had something in common with each of these groups, although they resembled none of them exactly. Perhaps we should label them hybrid types – like the new crops and breeds that were often introduced into reclaimed areas at the same time they were. Like the Catholic pilgrims heading to their devotional sites, Protestant immigrants often sang hymns as they went and were fired by a sense of religious purpose, even deliverance. Like the shepherds, they travelled long distances with their animals in tow. Like the true itinerants they carried their possessions with them, whether these were stored in a cart or carried over the shoulder in a knotted bundle. Like the troupes of travelling players, their arrival in a town often caused a commotion because of the unfamiliar way they dressed and spoke – or sang. And yet, like the tramping journeymen, their time on the road was an interlude, a movement between one settled life and another. The journeyman aspired to become a master. The colonists, when they unharnessed their wagons and wiped off the dirt of the road, wanted to plant themselves on the land.

They met with a sour reception. Although, like their new neighbours, they were peasants and craftsmen, and mostly fellow Protestants as well, they were distrusted because they were different. But they were disliked and resented most of all because of the land and special privileges that had attracted them in the first place. For the whole point of the exercise was to settle new land with new colonists: to increase the population of the state, not just shift the existing population around. The locals were not the only people hostile to the newcomers. State officials were less than enraptured by the settlers streaming in. Everyone knew, of course, that colonists were one of Frederick's driving passions, and individuals responsible for the settlements – Brenckenhoff, for one – became genuine enthusiasts for this or that group, especially Swabians and Palatines. In theory, cameralist theory, all officials should have welcomed these new additions to the inventory of Prussia's two-legged resources. In practice, they complained: the parties of colonists harboured 'undesirable' elements, they met with mishaps on the way, then haggled over travel costs, they arrived later than expected, or (much worse) they turned up too early, before their new land was ready. In short, from the unsympathetic bureaucratic perspective, colonists caused extra work and disrupted familiar routines.[101] Hence the many cases of abusive treatment meted out to the new arrivals, if brusqueness from officials needs any special explanation in eighteenth-century Prussia.

Frederick the Great's idolaters have always pointed to the great man's fits of rage upon hearing about instances like these.[102] And it is true that royal displeasure over the mistreatment of colonists and the related problem of official foot-dragging produced strings of edicts – a sure sign that the message was not being heeded. No one doubts that Frederick followed the everyday problems of settlement with intense personal interest. Whether it was a dike in Pomerania that was behind schedule, or a disputed bill run up by Oderbruch colonists at the Black Bear in Potsdam, the king wanted to know the facts. This desire to micromanage everything that went on had two aspects to it, one might almost say that it was fed by two contradictory impulses, and these pulled in opposite directions. The plans to settle reclaimed land amounted almost to a parody of the desire to order a disorderly world, to impose a machine-like regularity. But the chosen methods had a frenzied, volcanic quality that threatened to undercut the original aim. The tension between the two left its imprint on the land and its inhabitants.

The ordered aspect leaps to the eye. It is what yielded the exquisitely detailed 'colonist tables' and accounts, so that – to take an example – the sum of 36,231 Taler expended in the Madüe led to 7795 Morgen of new land on royal domains and 6543 Morgen of new noble-owned land, enough to settle a total of 150 families, or 712 people.[103] (One Morgen was a quarter of a hectare, or rather more than half an acre.) These settlements had nothing about them that was left to chance, in the Madüe or anywhere else. Everything was prescribed. The empty spaces on the map were filled up with villages placed at regular intervals, and in each village specifications were laid down for the sizes of houses, gardens, fields, meadows and stock, down to the last goose and goat. Even the layout was uniform and rectilinear. Straight lines, squares and crosses were preferred, curves nowhere to be seen.[104] Few things testified more eloquently to the enlightened-absolutist search for order than the shape of the new settlements. Here was a textbook case of what Johannes Kunisch has called 'geometrical thinking'.[105] Geometrical – and machine-like. Contemporaries liked the metaphor of a mechanical universe, the earth as 'a vast machine'. La Mettrie, one of the fashionable intellectuals Frederick brought to Berlin, even looked ahead to the production of a mechanical man, *L'homme Machine*.[106] The machine metaphor was often applied to the absolutist state, with its automaton-like subjects. Perhaps it was this background buzz of language in his sources that led the nineteenth-century historian, Max Beheim-Schwarzbach, to describe Frederician colonization in mechanical terms. As he puts it, looking back on the whole process, when the king died 'the whole work fell still, the machine rested'.[107] The metaphor seems very reasonable when we think of all those tables and inventories.

So what are we to make of it when Beheim-Schwarzbach describes Frederick's colonization policy as a 'violent, abrupt, even dangerous experiment'?[108] This sounds like an altogether different, more convulsive enterprise. And so, in its methods, it was. Frederick was always anxious not to be trapped in the bureaucratic net. He played officials off against each other, especially in the later years of his reign, and liked to assign special tasks on an ad hoc basis.[109] A notorious example is his habit of appointing officers to conduct judicial investigations when the legal mills ground slow, or their findings proved inconvenient. But in no other aspect of domestic policy was Frederick's 'impetuous creativity' so prominent as it was when it came to implementing the great reclamation and colonization projects.[110] Whenever possible he bypassed the machine, the General Directory in Berlin and officials in the local administration, believing them inadequate to 'Les plus Grands eforts' that were needed.[111] Instead he appointed and granted special powers to men who received their instructions from and reported direct to him. Brenckenhoff, the semi-literate but energetic former war supplier from Anhalt-Dessau, was the archetype, the impatient problem-solver who cut a swathe though the marshlands of the New March and Pomerania.[112] Johann Friedrich Domhardt enjoyed a similar loose rein in the eastern provinces. Like Brenckenhoff, he was born outside Prussia (in Brunswick), and like Brenckenhoff he was an improving landowner and horse-breeder, an intensely practical as well as ambitious 'self-made man'. Frederick raised Domhardt to the nobility to bolster his authority against suspicious local officials, but his real power always derived from the personal support of the monarch. If Brenckenhoff was a king on the Netze, Domhardt was a king on the Vistula and Haerlem in the Oderbruch.[113]

These troubleshooters found the task of colonization no easier than reclaiming the land had been. They may have had wide powers, but they faced a wide range of problems. One of them was money. The projects had special budgets siphoned off by Frederick from the general accounts and other sources, including the surpluses that came out of Silesia and West Prussia.[114] But these funds flowed unevenly, and Frederick was always reluctant to release extra money, however urgent the need. His marginal comments on documents ('non habeo pecuniam', 'I haven't a Groschen to spare') were notorious.[115] Given the wide discretion they enjoyed and the pace at which they worked, it is not surprising that the king's men sometimes stumbled into financial trouble. The General Directory pursued Haerlem for four years over a missing statement of accounts, finally forcing him to explain himself in Berlin.[116] But it was Brenckenhoff, further away from Berlin and very casual about bookkeeping, who contrived to land himself in the hottest water. After his death in 1780 the family property was seized by an ungrateful Frederick when it proved impossible to account for 100,000 Taler of the money that had passed through his hands.

No one has ever claimed that Brenckenhoff was strong on balance sheets; one admiring historian even called him 'a brazen speculator with a careless contempt for orderly accounts'.[117] Was he actively dishonest, or was it his habit of mixing up private and public monies that led to 'devilish confusion' in the accounts? Probably the latter, as Brenckenhoff dipped into his own wealth to finance urgent work and reimbursed himself later. But the real question is why Frederick not only gave such latitude to a man he already suspected of 'intrigues and deceptions', but even held him up as a model to more sluggish officials.[118] The answer is that the king was willing to tolerate rough and ready frontier methods if it got the job done. Brenckenhoff eventually paid the price for this. For their part, local officials in the New March and Pomerania had to work out how it was possible to 'keep a close eye' on Brenckenhoff while they were simultaneously under warning 'not to place the slightest obstacle in his path'.[119] They were doubtless as confused as Brenckenhoff's accounts. But then, confusion was the signature of the reclamation and colonization projects, as Frederick's passion for quick results clashed with regular bureaucratic procedures. When it was not money, it was some other problem – although most led back to money in the end. Millers complained about the effect of diverted waterways and had to be compensated; in some cases mills were dismantled and rebuilt on new sites. Guilds complained that newly arrived craftsmen would cause unfair competition. There were lengthy negotiations to be conducted with those who shared rights in the reclaimed land with the crown: towns, religious orders, above all the nobility. Then the same parties had to be persuaded to build colonies on their new land as fast as Frederick wanted to do on the royal domains. The difficult relationship between the king's plenipotentiaries and ruffled local officials did not make any of these tasks easier. Many wondered at the time if the results could justify 'the heavy toil, the general vexations, the complications and misunderstandings'.[120]

All of this provided the discordant background music to the main task: settling the colonists. For those time-consuming schemes on the Oder, Warthe, Plöne and the rest did no more than create the preconditions. The cuts in the rivers had been made, the major dikes and embankments built (although not always completed). The task of filling in the squares on Frederick's grids remained. That meant ditching and diking the future fields, constructing sluices, uprooting the old vegetation and planting willows by the new drainage canals, preparing the still heavy, intractable soil, building paths and bridges, houses, farms and schools, all the while maintaining the new defences against the water. Wood and other construction materials had to be found, then rafted and carted on site; and even though newly arrived colonists did much of the heavy work themselves, carpenters and woodcutters and labourers had to be 'sent for from far and wide', as Haerlem complained.[121] The demands of war interrupted this work, especially in the Oderbruch, where the Seven Years War came at a critical moment. Retzow and Petri rejoined their regiments in 1756, placing direction of the project in the hands of a bean-counting bureaucrat and leaving Haerlem to face a multitude of everyday problems on his own. Materials became even more difficult to find, the labour force was temporarily depleted.

The war on the elements was hard enough even when it was not made harder by war between the European powers. The time that had to be spent on the road was one of the strains. There were supplies to be checked, hundreds of workers to be found and supervised, buildings to be inspected and progress reports to be written. Brenckenhoff once said that his entire salary was insufficient to meet the cost of carriages and tips to grooms. This was doubtless an exaggerated claim, and a self-serving one at that, but it gives a true indication of

Brenckenhoff's peripatetic life, which impressed Johann Bernoulli, who sought him out in Pomerania and marvelled that the 'great colonizer' was a man 'of exceedingly corpulent figure'.[122] This was also Petri's life, then Haerlem's, on the Oder; Domhardt lived 'a veritable nomad's existence' out in the great spaces of the eastern provinces.[123] Getting things done meant staying on the move. A financial expert who was seconded from Berlin to assist both Domhardt and Brenckenhoff at different times, received instructions from Frederick 'to ride around like a good fellow' and return to the capital thin and healthy, a remark that the king may have wanted him to pass on to the portly Brenckenhoff.[124]

What complicated this work was the fact that the colonists were arriving even as their new land was being prepared for occupation – or, if they were unlucky, before the preparations had even begun. Some groups had to be housed in temporary accommodation, like refugees in our own time. Others arrived confused or truculent after being handed around from one unhelpful minor official to another. Still others arrived too lightly clad for the raw northern climate, or without the boots that were necessary to negotiate the ever-present mud. Given the many problems they presented, it is possible that being on the move actually provided Brenckenhoff, Haerlem and Domhardt with some relief, for on every return to base from an on-site inspection they were swarmed by settlers. According to the loyal and protective Petri, Haerlem was exhausted by colonists who 'hung around the neck . . . from morning to night'.[125]

Through the problems caused by money or men, warfare or the elements, the great colonization projects moved forward irregularly, convulsively. They put one in mind of the frenzied energy that drives the land reclamation schemes at the climax of *Faust*: 'Daily they would vainly storm,/Pick and shovel, stroke for stroke.'[126] In Goethe's great drama, Faust eventually achieves his desire of 'bringing the earth back to itself'. Human mastery is asserted over the anarchic water, and the new land becomes a 'veritable paradise' for settlers from the old Germany. It is not too fanciful to see Frederick's reclamation and colonization schemes as a real-life anticipation of this epic of development:[127]

> Green are the meadows, fertile; and in mirth,
> Both men and herds live on this newest earth.

Fields of Joy and Abundance

In *Faust* a price is paid for the triumph of progress. There are victims. The same was certainly true of Frederick's 'conquests'. Reclamation and colonization created a new world but destroyed an old one. What was lost must be measured in human and environmental terms. The changes brought a new physical security to men and women who settled once inhospitable land, yet they exposed much larger numbers of people to potential insecurity. They also destroyed ecologically valuable wetland habitats. How do we strike a balance? With difficulty, for short-term and long-term consequences are hard to weigh in the scales, and the many unintended consequences make it even harder. We can choose to celebrate a triumph of modernity, or lament a world that was lost, but neither really does justice to what the transformation meant.

The brave new world of dikes, ditches, windmills, fields and meadows, a landscape of 'wealth and almost Dutch cleanliness', delivered many undeniable benefits.[128] New land was created for colonists, the food supply was increased. When Pastor Rehfeldt delivered the memorial oration at Brenckenhoff's funeral, he painted a picture of barren land transformed into 'fields of joy and abundance'.[129] And it is true that reclaimed land often proved exceptionally rich and productive, nowhere more so than in the Oderbruch. As the soil dried out, livestock raising and dairying were joined by very diverse arable farming – rye, wheat, oats, barley, clover, rape, caraway and specialized cash crops.[130] Just as, to the east, Brenckenhoff planted vines on the hills between Küstrin and Bromberg, experimented with different varieties of peas and lentils, and filled the new land with Danish cattle, English sheep, Turkish goats, Don Cossack buffalo, even camels, so the Oderbruch provided almost laboratory conditions for scientific husbandry.[131] Here, in a newly organized landscape, the contemporary obsession with improved crops and rotations (especially from England) could be put into practice. It is wonderfully appropriate that the German pioneer of scientific agriculture, Daniel Albrecht Thaer, should have settled in the area – at Möglin – in 1804, where he published the four volumes of his *Principles of Rational Agriculture*.[132] Later commentators, who so often looked down on the Bruch (as Frederick had always done) from the surrounding heights, invariably painted the same picture. This was a 'blooming province' (Walter Christiani), a 'green land in the sandy marches', 'a large and beautiful garden' (Ernst Breitkreutz).[133] Theodor Fontane, describing the Oderbruch of the early nineteenth century in his novel *Before the Storm*, was moved to Biblical comparison:[134]

> To wander through this region at Whitsuntide, when the fields of rape were in bloom and scattering their gold and odour far and wide, was to fancy yourself transported from the March away to some distant, more opulent land. The fruitfulness of this virgin soil moved the heart to a feeling of joyful gratitude, such as the Patriarchs may have felt when, in regions empty of men, they numbered the God-given yield of their house and their herds.

The Oderbruch also did well by its inhabitants – those who farmed and later owned the new land, at any rate. By the third decade of the nineteenth century, the Oderbruch peasant had gained a reputation for acquisitiveness that was striking even by prevailing standards of criticism among officials, clergymen and other middle-class observers who found such wealth unseemly. The red-tiled and green-shuttered farmhouses, the carriages and finery, the consumption of tobacco and wines, the cards and skittles: these were the conventional symbols of vulgar prosperity. Few were more sardonic than Fontane, in the *Rambles through the March Brandenburg* and in novels like *Under the Pear Tree*. Yet Fontane had no doubt that a 'barren and worthless marshland' had been transformed into 'the granary of our land'.[135] The promised opportunities held out by Frederician colonist-recruiters had apparently been redeemed.

Nor was that all. Contemporaries may have had the wrong explanation when they associated malarial fevers with 'miasmas', but they were not wrong to link the disease with marsh and fen. With reclamation, malaria was no longer endemic across the north German plain, disappearing as it had in the English Fens a century earlier. Not only was standing water removed as a breeding ground; where the new husbandry of livestock and dairy farming was practised it provided the malaria-carrying anopheles mosquito with a preferred source of blood.[136] The disappearance of malaria had far-reaching consequences. It meant the end of a disease that weakened the human immune system, so that people were now less vulnerable to chronic diseases like anaemia and to killers such as pneumonia and gastro-intestinal infections in children. Like other by-products of reclamation, this one signalled the 'end of the biological old regime', or at least the beginning of the end.[137]

It was benefits such as these that Paul Wagret, a modern Dutch expert on reclamation, had in mind when he wrote in 1959 about 'the conquest of marshlands by civilization'.[138] It is harder today to summon up such unqualified enthusiasm, which passes over the costs of that conquest. Like Philomen and Baucis, the elderly couple who stood in the way of Faust's great land reclamation project, there were people who impeded Frederician colonization schemes. The old Oderbruch provides a perfect example. It contained a thin scatter of villages built on higher sandy mounds. Their inhabitants, no more than 170 families in the Bruch proper, were amphibious. They lived primarily as fishermen, from the rich stocks of carp, perch, pike, bream, barbel, ide, tench, lamprey, burbot, eel and crabs. But they also produced hay and pastured animals when water-levels were lower, using animal dung mixed with mud and bundles of twigs, or fascines, to construct protective walls against floods; and on those walls they grew marrows and other vegetables. For much of the year, except during low water and winter ice, their only means of communication through the labyrinthine waterways was by flat-bottomed boat.[139]

This way of life was destroyed, although not without a struggle. The resistance echoed the stubbornness heard in the English Fens more than a century earlier:[140]

> For they do mean all fens to drain
> And water overmaster,
> All will be dry and we must die,
> 'cause Essex calves want pasture . . .
> We must give place (oh grievous case)
> To horned beast and cattle,
> Except that we can all agree
> To drive them out by battle.

The Fens had witnessed riots and disorders; on the Oder there were attempts to sabotage the work of reclamation, not only – as we have seen – during the initial phase of construction, but beyond. After the spring floods of 1754, Haerlem reported that breaches in the dikes had been caused not only by the force of water, 'but malicious inhabitants of the marsh, perhaps because of their fishing interest, had clandestinely pierced the dikes in three places and thereby caused major damage to the defences'.[141] The inhabitants of Old Mädewitz, according to Hans Künkel, 'offered resistance from their fortresses of marrows' – not, perhaps, the best of strategic positions. The authorities, once again, used soldiers and now threatened capital punishment against offenders.[142] Philomen and Baucis, having declined money and resettlement, were killed by Mephisto and his men when Faust ran out of patience. The former marsh-dwellers were offered and mostly accepted new land as compensation, land that was equal in size to the largest of the new colonist settlements (about 55 acres) although smaller than the expanses of marsh and water they had been used to. Physical resistance ended; instead, fisher families used petitions and lawsuits to ensure that they received at least the compensation due to them, especially from the noble and municipal landowners.[143] But there were plenty who clung defiantly, painfully, to a world that was disappearing, who found it impossible to exchange a fish-hook for a plough, although their children and grandchildren of course adapted (as we say) to the new regime of *terra firma*.

It is true that before the change these marsh-dwellers had hardly lived free from constraints. They owed a variety of seigneurial dues to their lords – money in lieu of labour service, three geese per year, 'fish money', and so on. They also faced the monopoly power of the fish-processors' guild (literally, the *Hechtreisser*, or 'pike-rippers' guild'), whose members took their catches in Wriezen, then salted, prepared and sold the fish. The fisher people of the Bruch may have lived in misty isolation, but they were part of a developing market economy as well as a surviving feudal system.[144] The harshness of their environment and a diet of 'fish and crabs and crabs and fish' should also discourage any idealization of their former existence, notwithstanding golden-age myths about extraordinary longevity.[145] On the other hand, their way of life was neither so irrational nor so abjectly vulnerable to the elements as officials and later writers often assumed. Their economy was carefully geared to the normal cycle of floods that occurred, before the reclamation, each spring and summer. Like the inhabitants of the Havelland and east Münsterland recently examined by Rita Gudermann, and numerous others across the marshes and fens of the north German plain, they had evolved small-scale local solutions that permitted them to survive and fashion a livelihood from the waters until large-scale state 'improvement' came along.[146] We should not overlook this evidence of resourcefulness and ingenuity, wiped out by technological hubris married to state power.[147] Something was lost, and that is one of the registers in which we should tell the history of reclamation.

It was not only the immediate inhabitants of the marshes whose former lives came slowly but inexorably to an end. The waters had supported fishing families from many surrounding towns and villages. At the time of the reclamation, they accounted for 350 of the 430 families living on royal domains in the Lower Oderbruch. With the disappearance of ponds, lakes and eel-weirs on the river they, too, had to seek a future elsewhere. Even the physical appearance of a town like Wriezen was transformed. As the pike-rippers' guild complained: 'In places where the fishermen once cast their great nets one now sees meadows, even wheat and other kinds of corn'.[148] The guild, once such a powerful force, declined from forty-two members in 1740 to twenty-eight in 1766; by 1827 it was down to thirteen. By then the guild house had been sold to the state, which converted it into a synagogue. As brewing and distilling flourished and Wriezen acquired a cattle show, the fishing business died, the old fish containers rotted and abandoned boats became wracks.[149]

It was the colonists who represented the future. But the first two generations of incomers also paid a high price as they built the basis for later prosperity. Disease and heavy labour culled their ranks; many widows showed up in the tables of colonists compiled for Frederick's scrutiny. In many new colonies the original houses and outbuildings, thrown up too quickly with skimpy foundations, collapsed or subsided. Animals died from infections after grazing on still water-logged meadows.[150] As the colonist saying went: 'The first generation meets with death, the second with privation, only the third with prosperity'.[151] (In his own brutal variation on this, Frederick the Great once remarked: 'The first generation of colonists usually does not amount to much'.[152]) Some moved on, or returned home, like the luckless Herr Paulsen. In 1759, his first year at Neu-Rüdnitz in the Oderbruch, he and his wife were robbed and assaulted by a band of Cossacks. In the second year he lost fourteen head of cattle to disease and had three horses stolen. In the third year his fields were flooded, weeds ruined half his crop and a plague of mice ate the rest. In the fourth year he was flooded out again, losing all of his pigs and poultry. Then he sold up and went home.[153]

Of course, all settler or frontier societies have a stock of stories about the epic struggle of starting over. Whether it is the Oderbruch, the Western Frontier, or the Great Trek, there is a common shape to these narratives of endurance: the hopeful journey, setbacks that test resolve, eventual success in the face of the elements. Tales like these, worn smooth by the tellers, acquire a timeless quality. But they seldom lose their sense of place, for that is what gives them meaning, and in the hardships that befell German colonists we find important evidence about the costs of reclamation. Take those diseases and infections of humans and livestock, or the infestations of mice and weeds. These were not just bad luck, the vagaries of a cruel nature. Environmental historians have made us familiar with the problems that arise when humans migrate from one ecosystem to another; for people carry their biota and pathogens with them, in this case from every part of Germany and much of Europe beyond: France, Denmark, Sweden, the Low Countries, Switzerland, Piedmont, Savoy. To which we must, of course, add the breeds and species deliberately introduced to the new land with promiscuous zeal and mixed success by a Brenckenhoff. That some failed and others brought infections, or that some 'servant species' got above themselves, is not really a surprise.[154]

Some of the familiar disasters of development were largely avoided on these reclaimed lands. The rich alluvial soil (although not everywhere as rich as in the Oderbruch) did not suffer the soil exhaustion found in some other marginal, especially upland, areas brought into cultivation or used more intensively. Mixed farming helped here, in sharp contrast to the crisis that eventually overtook the monocropped German pine forests. And a combination of climate and topography meant that soil erosion was not the problem that it was in other parts of Germany, or in the great plains of America, even though (as we shall see) there were to be major arguments in the future about the danger of *Versteppung*, the creation of a dried-out, steppe landscape in Central Europe.[155] There was, though, one obvious cause of soil erosion: the flooding that continued to overrun reclaimed marshes and low-lying valleys. It is hardly an exaggeration to say that floods occurred everywhere some of the time and somewhere all of the time along the rivers of the plain. For writers reluctant to give up metaphors of a vanquished enemy that had been confined, periodic inundations were evidence of a powerful foe that still 'rattled its chains mightily'.[156] Major post-reclamation floods swept through the Oderbruch in 1754, 1770, three times in the 1780s (including the catastrophic year 1785), again in 1805, 1813, 1827, 1829, in 1830, with severe consequences, and twice more in the 1830s, in 1843, 1854, 1868, 1871, 1876, three more times from 1888 to 1893, and so on into the twentieth century – most recently in 1997, the 250th anniversary of Frederick's handiwork.[157] In the worst cases, more soldiers and labourers were drafted in to make repairs than had been been engaged in the original reclamation, with costs in the same proportion.

In the Oderbruch and other lowlands floods had a variety of causes. They were usually a result of downpours or abnormal snow run-off in the distant highlands where the river had its origins. The shortcomings of hydrological engineering, or short-sightedness, made the impact of the floodwaters more severe. Dikes were inadequate to the volumes of water they were supposed to handle. Or the work of reclamation was simply left incomplete, as it was at the western end of the Warthebruch, where even contemporaries like Captain Petri were sceptical of Brenckenhoff's hasty improvisations and corner-cutting.[158] Or older patterns asserted themselves in ways that had not been anticipated, such as the 'New Oder' silting up its bed just as the river had always done. Or the improvement schemes had other unforeseen consequences, as water squeezed out of one place returned in another, which happened almost everywhere to some degree.[159]

How people reacted to these reverses has changed over the last 250 years. But for most of that time it was the specific remedies that changed, not the underlying assumptions. Each major setback led to a rethinking; and to study these well-intended responses one after the other is to be reminded very forcibly of something that historians know well about their work, but hydrological engineers found it harder to accept about theirs: that the state of the art is always provisional. Read the series of confident prescriptions for the Oderbruch, and you find that each set of proposed new measures promises to turn the trick and *finally* overcome the ignorance, or engineering mistakes, or political constraints of earlier generations, right down to Werner Michalsky's claim in 1983 that under East German planning 'the centuries-old dream of humanity to control the forces of nature has been realized under socialist conditions'.[160] The reality was that none of these supposedly definitive solutions – not raising the height of dikes after the inundations of the 1770s, not blocking off the 'Old Oder' following the 1830 flood, not the major corrective scheme in the 1850s, not the advent of steam pumps and dredgers, not the new plan in the 1920s that used electrically powered pumps, not the repeated reorganizations of Dike Associations, not even socialist conditions – none of these was able to prevent floods that were now a threat to the work-cycle rather than a part of it.[161] Over a period of more than two centuries, no definitive security against the water could be established in these reclaimed lands. Instead, in a pattern that has become familiar elsewhere, floods eventually became less frequent but more catastrophic when they did occur, right down to the disaster of 1997, the second 'once-in-a-century' flood in fifty years.[162]

Paradise Lost?

'Let us learn to wage war with the elements, not with our own kind; to recover, if one may say so, our patrimony from Chaos, and not to add to his empire'. That was the call to arms of Scottish philosopher James Dunbar in 1780.[163] On the north German plain, waging war on 'chaotic' waters also led to heavy casualties among the indigenous flora and fauna. The environmental impact of reclamation could be dramatic. A contemporary described what happened in the Oderbruch after the rooting up of the former tangled and waterlogged undergrowth. Left for months in huge piles to dry out, it became a refuge for wildlife of every kind. When the wood was finally lit, birds and animals fled the fire and smoke, an easy prey for the hunters. Wild cats, hares, deer, weasels, martens, foxes and wolves raced for cover that was now gone, together with fen chickens and wild ducks and magpies, owls and hawks that screeched and cawed as they left their temporary habitats. Theodor Fontane, who later retold the story in his *Rambles*, called it a 'war of extermination'.[164]

But the true extent of the change went far beyond violent episodes like this; it was felt cumulatively in the serious loss of biodiversity. These had been rich wetlands, a complex ecosystem that supported a now almost unimaginable range of insect, fish, bird and animal life. The damage done by blazing guns was much less significant over time than the loss of a habitat that supported the bounteous volumes and varieties of fish once found in the Oderbruch, which in turn made the area a home for cranes, storks, lapwings, geese and wild ducks.[165] In 1741 Jacques de Vaucanson had exhibited his famous mechanical duck, a model that could waddle, flap its wings, wag its head and even pick up pieces of corn that it 'digested' and excreted. This marvel was admired by advanced contemporaries across Europe and described in the French *Encyclopédie*. Frederick the Great tried to attract Vaucanson to Prussia. But even as the mechanical duck enthralled educated audiences, the real duck was disappearing from the reclaimed Oderbruch and other former wetlands.[166]

That something important was being lost in this process was a note sounded more and more often in the second half of the eighteenth century. In Britain, where Dunbar saw a war to be waged, others counted the cost. 'I grieve, when on the darker side of this great change I look', wrote Wordsworth; 'nature has her proper interest', reminded Coleridge.[167] The same reminder was being issued in Germany. Novalis complained in 1799 that human dominance had 'made the eternal creative music of the universe into the monotonous clapping of a monstrous mill'.[168] This was the lament of full-voiced Romanticism, bellows working to pump out the message. But a quieter shift of sensibility can be traced back over the previous decades. The 'Anacreontic' poets of Halle celebrated the beauties of nature in elegiac verse; so did Salomon Gessner in his *Idylls*.[169] It is true that Daphnis and Chloe, nymphs and dryads still wander through these pastoral works, coating the sense of loss with a stylized sweetness. Not so in the case of Friedrich Klopstock, who spoke more directly to nature's 'proper interest':[170]

Fair is the majesty of all thy works
On the green earth, O Mother Nature fair!

Klopstock was an important figure for a number of reasons. Not only was he a literary celebrity with an influence well beyond the 'Sylvan League' of nature poets who came within his orbit. As a lion of the learned societies and reading clubs, a traveller, collector and botanizer, he was also the archetype of the educated contemporary who had learnt from Buffon and from his own observations to respect the natural world for its intrinsic qualities. In his emphasis on beauty, not utility, and his sense of wonder at the richness of nature's economy (both qualities he shared with the young Goethe of the 1770s) Klopstock was an intellectual bell-wether of the times.

He was also a conduit through which Rousseau's arguments about a 'return to nature' entered Germany, but not the only one. German writers seized on Rousseau's cult of the natural with the same intensity that marked their (belated) enthusiasm for the 'natural' English landscape garden, the antithesis of the formal, geometrical French or Dutch garden. (Although he admired the cabbage fields at Gusow, Johann Bernoulli noted that the symmetrical lay-out of the gardens was already a little old-fashioned.[171]) Johann Georg Sulzer's *Conversations on the Beauty of Nature* (1770) argued that only children 'educated in the school of nature' would achieve that 'delightful innocence and simplicity' that was the source of true wisdom. The pedagogical reformer Johann Bernhard Baselow went one better by opening a series of model schools to preach this gospel of nature, the first of them – in 1774 – established in Brenckenhoff's old stamping ground of Anhalt-Dessau.[172]

When we think about the new appreciation for untamed nature so typical of these years, it is the mountains and the seashore that come to mind. These provided the starkest contrast with a natural world that was supposedly being levelled and confined, and they were the places where the new cult of 'natural movement' could be exercised in the form of mountain-climbing and swimming. The Germans discovered the Alps in the 1770s, and the seashore not long after. It was not until well into the next century that marshland and moor would acquire comparable celebrity. But these habitats were not entirely neglected, nor was their fate. Rousseau had established the theme. His first *Discourse* on the sciences and arts, like *Emile*, criticized the draining of marshes as one of the destructive interventions in nature that threatened to obliterate physical distinctions in the face of the land.[173] The 'barren marsh' also joined the 'wild forest' and other favoured sites in German poetry, as a place where the writer could shed artifice and find solitude.[174]

A more complex example is Goethe's *The Sorrows of Young Werther*, a work about a young man's obsessive love that leads him to suicide. The book that made the author's name when it appeared in 1774 is suffused with the lovesick protagonist's concern with every aspect of the 'inner, glowing sacred life of Nature', including the solitary worlds of mists and reeds.[175] The reader is also struck by the use of the flood-metaphor to signify, not danger, but freedom. An example occurs early in the book. Why is it, asks Werther rhetorically, that 'the stream of genius so seldom breaks out as a torrent'? The answer: Because there are cool and composed men 'whose garden houses, tulip beds and cabbage fields would be devastated if they had not in good time known how to meet the threatening danger by building ditches and dikes'.[176] Have cabbage fields and ditches ever been cast in such a villainous role? And when Werther seeks a term of contempt for the straitjacketed world of bureaucracy, the opposite of wild nature (and genius), he chooses an example that might have been drawn straight from the new model husbandry of the Oderbruch, the drudgery of 'count[ing] peas or lentils'.[177]

One of the ideas that runs through the book and places *Young Werther* in its time is the description of unspoiled nature as a 'paradise'. It reminds us that the travellers of the later eighteenth century and those who read their books were encountering new worlds that expanded their sense of nature's diversity. We can hardly miss this theme in contemporary reactions to reclaimed marshes and swamps. It served as a touchstone. Sometimes, of course, the analogy served to confirm the rightness of what was being done. The old Havelland marsh, we are told, had been 'a savage, primitive land, as the hand of nature had created it, a counterpart to the primeval forests of South America'. As for the old Warthebruch, 'anyone who had dared to enter it would have felt himself transposed to one of the most unknown parts of the world'. A Danish traveller to the same area in the 1780s shuddered when he compared the 'Canadian wilderness' that was still undrained with those parts of the marsh that had already been improved. It was the ordered and manicured areas whose 'beauty' he found 'paradisal'.[178]

But the identification of paradise in the opposite sense, as something natural and unspoiled, was becoming a more familiar idea. It gained strength when the Forsters returned from their journey on the *Resolution* with evidence about the pristine beauty of Tahiti. The son, Georg Forster, popularized the idea in his *Voyage around the World*, which inspired an 'island paradise' genre of books set in places where no animals were killed or eaten and the fruits fell unbidden from the trees.[179] The father, Johann Reinhold Forster, was a sort of German Gilbert White, a naturalist with a sense of delight in diverse forms of life and a gift for description. What he saw on the Cook voyage led him to voice some of the same environmental concerns that troubled French naturalists like Commerson and Poivre who had spent time on Mauritius. A mounting sense of foreboding can be found in his journals, as he came to see the darker side of human 'improvements'.[180] The Americas taught their own lessons about the impact of deforestation and land reclamation. Some were already pointing to the New World to warn about the possible consequences of human arrogance. In *Travels into North America*, the Swedish naturalist Peter Kalm noted the changing climate and reduced numbers of fish and birds where swamps had been cleared in North America, urging his own countrymen not to be 'blind to the future'. It was a work that influenced the elder Forster, who translated it into English. Herder drew on similar evidence when he insisted that living things were interrelated and humans 'should act prudently in altering this interdependence'. Nature was 'a living whole'; it should not be 'mastered by force'.[181]

The poets, naturalists and travellers were responding, with doubts, sometimes even dismay, to a visibly changing world. Their reactions formed the first 'green wave' in German culture. At a moment when discovery and destruction were delicately poised, it is hardly surprising that some contemporaries came to see pristine nature as a 'green utopia', or 'paradise'.[182] It is an idea that has retained its evocative power. Writing almost two hundred years later about the Oderbruch and Warthebruch from which his ancestors came, Hans Künkel tells us that before reclamation these areas were 'a paradise of creatures great and small'.[183] Even so hard-headed a historian as Fernand Braudel suggests that 'at the end of the eighteenth century, vast areas of the earth were still a garden of Eden for animal life. Man's intrusion upon these paradises was a tragic innovation'.[184]

A paradise lost, then? There is certainly no denying the magnitude of the destructive human impact on the natural world in the later eighteenth century. This occurred before the fossil fuel-based era of industrialization, and in the wetlands of the north German plain it led to a devastating loss of biodiversity. It is no more misleading to couch this great transformation in terms of a 'paradise lost' than it is to speak of a 'conquest of marshlands by civilization', as Paul Wagret did. But it is no less misleading either. A lost paradise rests on the idea of a fall, a distinct before-and-after. The natural world was stable, harmonious and self-equilibriating, until disturbed by a human impact that brought instability, disharmony and disequilibrium. When environmental historians and others argue for a break of this kind, they are following the impulse of the Romantics, whose holistic categories did much to tinge modern ecological thinking. But the argument is as problematic in its own way as the wishful thinking of the heedless modernizers. If the great illusion of the 'improvers' was the belief that they had found a once-and-for-all technical solution, the opposite snare for the green-minded has been the belief in a once-and-for-all state of nature. Yet that flies in the face of modern ecologists' well-founded evidence on the unstable dynamism of natural systems. Some environmental historians clearly suspect these findings and the application of chaos theory on which they rest, as if questioning the organic harmony of nature somehow prevents us from identifying destructive human actions.[185] It does not. But when we write about human impact on the natural world, we should recognize that we are dealing with the interaction of two dynamic systems.

There is something else. When we consider these apparently pristine wetland habitats, the question arises: How pristine were they? Going back to that eighteenth-century commentator, was this in fact a 'land created by the hand of nature'? Not really, is the answer. For within both distant and fairly recent history it had been shaped and reshaped, although less dramatically than it was to be in the reign of Frederick the Great, by local systems of human exchange with the natural environment. The reclamation projects themselves often turned up the remains of early human settlements. But we do not even have to go back that far. There is evidence that just five hundred years earlier there had been settlements in what became the impenetrable marshlands of the north German plain, until a combination of climatic change and human actions, especially deforestation, caused catastrophic floods that drove people to higher ground.[186] It was only in the following centuries that fisher people and hunter-gatherers developed their own micro-economies in areas like the Oderbruch and Warthebruch, adapting themselves to conditions that were then new.

This chequered and discontinuous history of human activity does not make Frederician 'conquest' less novel or far-reaching, any more than long centuries of Native American activity undercut the impact of European conquest and settlement in the New World. But it does undermine arguments about an undisturbed natural world. Settlements were only one part of the story. There were many other ways in which human use had shaped this supposedly pristine natural world. Hunting is a good example. There is probably no better depiction of the ecological old regime than Jan Brueghel the Elder's *Interior of the Woods with Huntsman*; but as our eyes are drawn into the scene we can hardly miss the point that without the huntsman there would be no picture of this wooded waterland in the first place.[187] And the same goes for much of the wildlife within it. The 3000-strong herd of red deer reported from the seventeenth-century Warthebruch owed as much to the hand of man as the hand of nature.[188] Almost all of the reclaimed wetlands were in fact hunting preserves before they became pastures or fields of corn, which is why so many Prussian nobles protested against the process of reclamation. Examine these apparently natural habitats closely, and it becomes apparent just how much they owed, directly or indirectly, to human interventions. Those high water levels were sometimes high because they had been raised by the operation of nearby mills.[189] The hydrology of lowland marshes was affected by the adaptation of upland streams for wood rafting or to power hammer mills. Alluvial deposits continued to occur in flood-prone river valleys because of topsoil erosion caused by deforestation in distant uplands.[190] There is, in the end, no obvious baseline for measuring the world that was 'lost' during reclamation. To put it in the sharp terms used by Elizabeth Ann Bird, it is possible to 'argue against environmentally destructive technologies, but not on the grounds that they are anti-natural'.[191]

The wetlands of the north German plain were physically transformed in the second half of the eighteenth century. What happened in places like the Oderbruch is best understood as a history in which three major strands were intertwined. This was, in the first place, a dramatic chapter in the history of human intervention in the natural world, with damaging effects for the ecology of the region as well as complex implications, both benign and less benign, on the growing human population. The transformation also shows us how power operated: who drained the land, who resisted it, what forms of knowledge came out on top. The alchemy that turned water into land in Frederician Prussia revealed where the lines of power ran in the late absolutist state. Finally, the disappearing marshlands represented a nature on to which human emotions were projected, as if on to a screen. These episodes were perceived as conquest, the taming of a dangerous foe, but they were also starting to be seen as the sundering of a harmonious natural world, as loss.

THE MAN WHO TAMED
THE WILD RHINE

The Bells of Pfotz

One Sunday morning fishermen set off from a village near Leimersheim on the Rhine to haul in their nets from one of the old arms of the river. Pleased by their catch of tench, roach and eels, they pulled up their oars and let the flat-bottomed boat drift. Then they heard the sound of distant bells, more solemn than any bells they had ever heard and growing louder as they approached the middle of the river. The men looked at each other: the sound was coming from below the surface. The boldest, Hansadam, bent over the side of the boat, and after gazing into the water called his friends over to look. The bells were tolling from the tower of a church that was visible beneath them, surrounded by a few simple huts. The boat moved slowly overhead. Fearful that they would capsize, the men grabbed their oars and pulled as hard as they could for the bank. Stowing the catch quickly, they hurried to the village and told their story. It was met with disbelief and mockery, until other fishermen reported having the same experience on another quiet Sunday morning. From then on fishermen avoided the spot. But the sound of the bells was still heard in the village when the river rose and floods threatened.[1]

This seventeenth-century legend belongs to a familiar type. Bells are often associated in Christian culture with driving away supernatural beings, warding off the devil, or warning about an impending natural disaster.[2] The Rhineland, like other regions in Germany, boasts many stories of ghostly bells that ring to admonish or warn.[3] Often they are based on the fate of real villages, as this one is. The fishermen in the story came from New Pfotz; the bells belonged to the former village of Pfotz where their ancestors had lived. Like many left bank settlements along this stretch of the Rhine, Pfotz had been founded in the late thirteenth century as a fishing village. It disappeared less than three hundred years later. The site on a broad bend of the meandering Rhine was steadily eaten away by the river. Finally, in 1535, the village was moved to higher ground a few hundred yards to the west and renamed New Pfotz. Old Pfotz, abandoned, eventually slid entirely under the water.[4]

It was not the only village to disappear in this way. Winden, which lay between Leimersheim and New Pfotz, was also swallowed by the river. A century later and just to the south the same happened to Wörth, when flood waters broke through in the 1620s and villagers fled to higher ground, where they resettled in the deserted village of Forlach. Two more substantial settlements also went under along the same short stretch of the Upper Rhine. Knaudenheim was a farming and fishing village with 400 inhabitants when the floods of 1740 drowned two people and fifty head of cattle. Not for the first time the village moved its protective dikes further back. But in 1758 Knaudenheim was even more disastrously flooded. The water stood eight feet high, covering the crops, damaging foundations, and driving the inhabitants on to their roofs. Given the damage to the dikes and the hopelessness of their long-term future, villagers petitioned their bishop for permission to resettle on the high bank of the river three quarters of an hour away by foot. Even this 'sandy, unfruitful and quite barren spot' was preferable to constant insecurity. Bishop Hutten gave his approval, provided the settlement was laid out along the geometrical lines so beloved of the period, and the new village of Huttenheim bore his name. Only a commemorative stone marked the spot where Knaudenheim had stood. Then there was Dettenheim, a pure fishing village established in 788 and one of the oldest settlements along this part of the Rhine. By the middle of the eighteenth century it too was being repeatedly threatened by the river. Permission to move to a safer site was first requested in 1766. The case was tied up in jurisdictional squabbles and then by war, so that it was not until 1813 that the village finally moved, leaving 'former Dettenheim' behind it as an empty space on the map.[5]

All of these villages, like others that barely escaped the same fate, lay within a few dozen bends of the river between Karlsruhe and Speyer. Further upstream it was the same story, as settlements along another stretch of the Upper Rhine were either destroyed, or abandoned and rebuilt on another site. The once important trading town of Neuenburg was swept into the river, complete with the nave of its cathedral, at the end of the fifteenth century, the town of Rheinau destroyed in the sixteenth. Dunhausen, Geiling, Goldscheuer, Grauelsbaun, Grefferen, Hundsfeld, Ihrigheim, Muffelnheim, Plittersdorf, Söllingen, Wittenweiler, all were villages that disappeared completely, leaving nothing more than a field name behind.[6]

There are many reasons for deserted or abandoned villages, among them the twin scourges of plague and war. Those who lived on the banks of the Upper Rhine were familiar with war, and the plague it so often brought, from the Thirty Years War in the seventeenth century through the campaigns of Louis XIV to the conflicts of the eighteenth century. In this cockpit of early modern European warfare, some villages were repeatedly laid to waste. But, like the fortresses that dotted the area, they were rebuilt, and rebuilt where they stood. Not so the settlements that found themselves in the wrong place when the river changed its course. These were deserted villages that drowned, with their fields, huts, houses, church and bells.

There is no great mystery why these human settlements should have proved so fragile. It comes down to geomorphology and hydrology: the way in which, until modern times, the river pursued its unpredictable course across the lowlands of the Upper Rhine.[7] Before it reaches Basel the Rhine flows west. There it turns to the north, until it reaches the great massif of the Taunus mountains at Mainz. This is the Upper Rhine plain, 185 miles long and about twenty miles wide, a great rift valley dating from the Tertiary period. It is flanked on both sides by mountains, the Black Forest and Odenwald to the east, the Vosges and the Palatine Forest to the west. Once, before it dropped like a fallen capstone, the plain formed the central arch of these highlands. Now it is dominated by the river, which did not create it, but uses it as a corridor to the sea. The Rhine at this point has left the falls and torrents of its highland youth behind; it flows with a shallower drop through the sand and gravel on the valley floor, adding its own deposits of rocky debris and sediment.

Until the nineteenth century, the Rhine did not flow through one defined bed. In the southern part of the Upper Rhine Plain, the actions of the river created countless channels divided by gravel banks and sandbars. These were built up by the river when it was swollen with

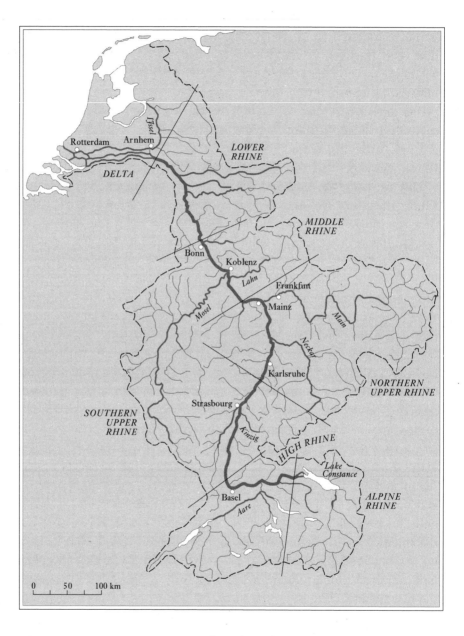

MAP 2 *The Rhine basin.*

floodwaters and its force was greatest, becoming obstacles when the current slackened. Over the centuries, season by season, this cycle created a labyrinth of waterways and islands – as many as 1600 islands in the 70-mile stretch of the river below Strasbourg. This was the Rhine that Peter Birmann saw and painted from the cliffs above Istein at the beginning of the nineteenth century (Fig.6).[8] It looks more like a series of lagoons, a broad, confusing waterworld that fills the canvas. The eye is drawn first one way then the other as the viewer tries unsuccessfully to identify the main course of the river, as it winds through a tangle of channels and wooded islands. This section of the Upper Rhine was called the furcation zone.

Downstream, beyond the point where it receives the waters of the Murg, the Rhine flowed more as a single stream. But it still did not flow in a single channel, instead winding in great curls and loops across its floodplain. This was the meander zone. Figure 7 shows what this had led to by the early nineteenth century: a main channel that was itself lazy and serpentine, flanked on both sides by the snaking curves of former channels, like a Medusa's Head. The oldest of these channels went back as far as 8000 BC, according to pollen analysis of the sediment that gradually filled the channels in. In later centuries the river never stopped redirecting itself. The basic dynamics were simple.[9] Even when its flow was sluggish, the water on the outside of the bends in the river would speed up (to compensate for the greater distance it needed to travel), eroding the far bank and depositing sediment on the near one. Over time, the loops became so pronounced and the neck of the loop so narrow that the river almost doubled back on itself. Come high water, and the river would flow across the neck of the loop, turning the former main channel into a side-arm, and eventually into an oxbow lake, until the time, perhaps hundreds of years later, when the force and direction of the floodwater made the side-arm or oxbow lake into the main channel once again. When the river ran high it might carve itself a new bed anywhere on the floodplain that lay between the high banks, where the natural terrace of the valley began. In some places the floodplain stretched for miles, and at some point in its long history the Rhine would use all of it. The river in full spate also scoured away at the high banks, as the many irregular bays and spurs along it clearly showed.

Many of the human settlements along the Upper Rhine were sited on the edge of the high bank, overlooking the floodplain, a position from which it was possible to take advantage of what the river had to offer, whether animal, vegetable or mineral, with less risk from inundation. Others ventured down closer to the river to build, closer to the fish, the fowl and the rich alluvial soil. That is where most of the drowned villages had been. Like the more meagre scattering of villages in the old Oderbruch, they were usually built on slightly elevated land with a gravel or sand bank beneath it. From about the twelfth century a series of terms evolved sufficiently differentiated to suggest close familiarity with the workings of the river. For the various kinds of side-arms, narrow channels, oxbows and pools there was one vocabulary: *Altrhein, Giessen, Kehlen, Schlute, Lachen*. For the more or less dry land beyond and within the meanders there was another: *Aue, Wörth, Grund, Bruch*. But as the fate of Pfotz showed, no amount of local knowledge was proof against the river.[10]

We should not imagine that the villagers of the riverbank threw up their hands. For centuries they looked for ways to protect themselves from the threatening waters. Dikes and ditches were constructed from the Middle Ages onwards. The first artificial cut in the river to divert water from a threatened site dated back to 1391. By the seventeenth century human agency was responsible for as many cuts in the meander zone as the river itself. Dikes to protect fields and meadows could be found on both banks, some of them major undertakings. The new Linkenheimer dike, completed in the 1660s, was over 600 yards long. And the constructions of the busy seventeenth century took place despite the shortages of men, money and materials caused by war ('there used to be eight or ten people where now there is one, and 300 carts where now there are just forty').[11] As the population grew in the eighteenth century, so did the efforts to hold the river at bay. Up and down the meander zone dikes were built and rebuilt at a frantic tempo. Between 1770 and 1783 Leimersheim alone used almost 400,000 fascines to augment its protective wall.[12] The mounting activity was necessary, because the Rhine posed a growing threat. One reason was the rise in the river bed, as debris and sediment was gradually deposited further downriver. By the end of the eighteenth century, the southern part of the meander zone was starting to resemble the wild Rhine further upstream. The rising level of the river increased erosion of the high bank and meant that villages in the flood-plain had to keep raising the height of their dikes. But despite these efforts, it was obvious that the threat of destruction (or the need for relocation) was working its way downstream.

Climatic fluctuations made the situation worse. For these were years in which Europe went through a 'Little Ice Age'. Whatever the cause or causes, whether it was the result of sunspots or volcanic activity, or simply part of a long series of climatic fluctuations, there is no doubt that the period from the late sixteenth century into the nineteenth was climatically distinct from what came before and after. On this, the evidence of tree rings, glacier movements, harvests and chronicles agrees. Central Europe experienced snowier winters, springs that were colder and later, and wetter summers. Virtually every summer from 1760 to 1790 had unusually high rainfall. The same climate that caused the glaciers to advance and the growing season to retreat also brought about a rise in river levels.[13] On the Rhine, as on the Oder, greater volumes of snow-melt and heavy rains brought decade after decade of exceptionally high waters after the 1730s. They arrived around once every three years between the 'great winter' of 1740 and the floods of 1786, then virtually every year from 1799 to 1808.[14]

Piecemeal efforts to shore up the defences had no chance of holding back the river over 800 square miles of floodplain, on which woodland was increasingly giving way to vulnerable pasture and arable land. In many ways this losing struggle only made things worse. Attempts to confine the river within a narrower channel only added to its destructive power when high waters came. Once the water had made a breach, the dikes meant that it flowed more slowly out of flooded areas. The fields at Schröck lay under water for eighteen weeks in 1661.[15] An equally persistent problem was that efforts to achieve protection from the river at one point almost always increased the threat somewhere else. In the seventeenth century, an artificial cut through the loop in the Rhine at New Pfotz (which came too late to save Old Pfotz) simply redirected the main channel of the river from the left bank towards Schröck and Linkenheim on the right bank; and a further cut that relieved this pressure increased the threat of flooding in Leimersheim and Hördt on the left bank. Hördt responded in 1756–63 with a cut that redirected the river through the fields of Dettenheim, which effectively doomed the village.[16] These games of hydrological leapfrog were power struggles between the Palatine left bank and the Badenese right bank communities, and they were occurring more frequently in the eighteenth century. Nothing illustrates better the ineffectiveness of piecemeal local efforts to tame the increasingly threatening river.

By the beginning of the nineteenth century the situation was clearly worsening. Dettenheim and Knaudenheim had to be moved. Even Philippsburg, which lay on higher ground, considered the same step in 1801; so did Liedolsheim a few years later. There was hardly a village within the meander zone that was not seriously threatened at least once, and usually more than once, in the decades after 1740. The possibility of a comprehensive solution was first raised by local rulers in the final years of the Holy Roman Empire. But there were too many rulers, and their conflicting interests created a stalemate. Political sovereignty was exceptionally fragmented on the south-western margins of the old German Empire. A large-scale plan to 'tame' the Rhine would be enacted only after the cataclysm of the French Revolution had destroyed the Holy Roman Empire and redrawn the political map of Germany.

Tulla's Plan

In the Paris cemetery of Montmartre stands a gravestone commissioned by the Grand Duke of Baden. It depicts a relief map of the Rhine, flanked by a book of mathematics open at Pythagoras' theorem and an arched bridge surmounted by a globe. The map of the Rhine shows the former winding course of the river, and the new 'corrected' course established in the nineteenth century.[17] This stone marks the grave of a German engineer from the south-western state of Baden, Johann Gottfried Tulla. It was Tulla who conceived and drove through the first stages of the project that remade the river. A modern French writer has called him 'the true father of the modern Rhine'.[18] A commemorative stone in his birthplace of Karlsruhe has an inscription that summarizes his life's work in more dramatic terms: 'To Johann Gottfried Tulla: The Man Who Tamed the Wild Rhine'.[19]

The Tulla family was of Dutch origin, from a small town near Maastricht. In the seventeenth century, Cornelius Tulla served with the Swedish army during the Thirty Years War. His son remained in Germany with foster parents when Cornelius followed his paymasters, and started a dynasty of Lutheran pastors in the small margraviate of Baden-Durlach. Johann Gottfried, born in 1770, was also intended for the clergy, but at the Karlsruhe Lyzeum he showed a talent for mathematics and physics. The local margrave, Karl Friedrich, keen to encourage the 'useful sciences', had hired a number of outstanding pure and applied scientists to teach at the Lyzeum. There Tulla not only studied mathematical theory, trigonometry and geometry, but received a practical grounding in mechanics, surveying and drawing up blueprints. Spotted as a precocious talent by his teachers, Tulla was encouraged to further his education. Thanks to a series of state stipends he was able to spend a further eight years in a programme of extended study.[20]

They would turn out to be some of the most tumultuous years in modern German history. Tulla's first request for financial support was considered by the Karlsruhe treasury in March 1789, just six weeks before the French Estates General was scheduled to meet in Paris. His apprentice years were spent against the background of the French Revolutionary events that followed. The fall of the Bastille in July 1789 initially touched off enthusiasm in the German lands. French political writings were quickly translated and discussed. Writers like Christoph Wieland and Ludwig Tieck expressed their support; so did the young Georg Wilhelm Friedrich Hegel, then a student in Tübingen. Intellectual 'pilgrims of revolution' set off for Paris to bear witness, and the pride of the Hamburg reading clubs, Friedrich Klopstock, put aside his poems to 'Mother Nature fair' and began to write 'odes to liberty'. Even some of Germany's rulers sympathized with the early stages of the revolution, seeing in its hostility to aristocratic, guild and clerical privilege no more than a variation on their own enlightened programmes of the previous decades – a kind of catching-up with what they themselves had been doing. The Duke of Gotha and the Duke of Brunswick were among those who took this view; so, more prominently, was the enlightened Joseph II of Austria. Joseph, who died in 1790, believed to the end that the French were merely borrowing his own ideas.

Even before the French Revolution took a radical turn in 1792, however, there were German rulers alarmed by the repercussions that events in France were having in their own lands. In the years from 1789 to 1792, while Tulla sat quietly in Karlsruhe mastering the arts of surveying and drawing blueprints, riots were taking place further down the Rhine in Mainz, Boppard, Koblenz and Cologne. There were further disturbances just across the river in the Rhenish Palatinate. In 1792–3 there was even a short-lived 'Jacobin Republic' in Mainz, its most famous participant the same Georg Forster who had made his name sailing round the world with Captain Cook. None of these episodes, not even the Mainz Republic, came close to bringing down the social and political order in Germany. Rural insurrections further east, in Silesia and Saxony, were more of a threat; but they were crushed by armed force. It was not home-grown revolutionaries, whether self-styled Jacobin intellectuals or pitchfork-wielding peasants in Saxony, who would transform the Holy Roman Empire. It was French armies that would do that, and in the process create a new world for men like Johann Tulla in Baden.

By 1792, when it was decided to send Tulla outside Baden to complete his training, the state found itself at war with France. The new French constitution of 1791 had renounced conquests and the use of force against 'the liberty of any people', but the following year France declared war against the 'despotic powers' of Prussia and Austria. The smaller German states were sucked in, Baden among them. From the French capture of left-bank towns like Speyer and Worms in autumn 1792, the Rhineland became – as it had been so often in the past – one of the major fronts. The victories won by the French Revolutionary Army eventually led Prussia to seek a separate peace in 1795. Baden did the same a year later.

During these dangerous years, Tulla was studying with Professor Karl Christian von Langsdorf at Gerabronn, a mathematician and engineer who was director of the salt works for the principality of Ansbach. Tulla lodged with the family of his mentor. Langsdorf's careful accounts suggest a comfortable but modest middle-class regimen: coffee in the mornings and afternoons, a glass of beer to accompany lunch, local wine with the evening meal, otherwise 'as much bread as he wishes to eat, but without butter, for I do not keep a cow'. The receipts for doctors' visits and miscellaneous medicines, tonics and powders also point to the poor health from which Tulla would always suffer, and increasingly so as he spent more of his time in damp, watery environments. At Gerabronn he received further instruction in mathematics; he also began to develop his knowledge of hydraulic engineering, in which he already showed a strong interest. It helped that he had access to Langsdorf's own still unpublished work on the subject, for – as Tulla reported proudly to Karlsruhe – this contained 'everything new' that had been written in the field in German or French.[21]

After two years Langsdorf proposed that the ambitious, serious-minded Tulla undertake a journey to broaden his understanding of the hydraulic sciences, so that he could see 'how in general art is able to influence nature, and the circumstances in which it is able to do so'.[22] A more than usually nervous treasury in Karlsruhe, counting the costs of the war that was still going on, agreed to this. Tulla left Gerabronn in April 1794 on a journey that would last over two years. His itinerary included the Lower Rhine, the Netherlands, Hamburg, Scandinavia, Saxony and Bohemia, areas that were in many cases feeling the effects of war and further, war-related social unrest. There were renewed peasant disturbances in Saxony, for example, in 1794. For Tulla, these years were partly devoted to formal study, notably at Germany's leading engineering school, the Mining Academy at Freiberg in unsettled Saxony. He also visited Göttingen to speak with professors and visit the observatory. Most of all, though, he spent time on site at hydraulic projects, getting to know the men in charge and the machinery they were using. This was what the Badenese state expected, and it was what the intensely practical Tulla most enjoyed.[23]

On the Rhine at Düsseldorf he viewed projects initiated by Director of Hydraulic Engineering Wiebeking, studied the dynamics of the river closely and saw the results of efforts that had been made to cut off side-arms. In a diary entry made by the twenty-four-year-old we can already hear the confident tone that would be the hallmark of the later expert: 'Most hydro-technicians have studied the effects of engineering work on a river only on the surface'.[24] He moved on, strongly encouraged by Karlsruhe, which saw the practical applications, to the Prussian district of Cleve, where the problems posed by the Rhine were similar to those on the Upper Rhine. Next stop was the Mecca of all would-be water engineers, the Netherlands, where he made excerpts from the latest Dutch specialist literature, feasted his mind on windmills and bucket-wheels, and was nearly arrested for espionage when he sketched an ice-breaker. And so the trip went on, a grand tour of locks and embankments, groyne dams and pumping equipment. Small wonder that, by July 1794, he was already requesting money 'in order that I may replace my coat and other necessary articles of clothing, which I have ruined unbelievably.'[25]

Delayed somewhat by a bout of fever, he returned to Gerabronn in June 1796. There he was required to pass an examination set in Karlsruhe and administered by Professor Langsdorf. Part of this was theoretical, part consisted of writing reports on eminently practical hydraulic questions, for example how the Rhine at Daxlanden could be 'brought to order'. This series of tests having been passed (Langsdorf enthused that the money invested in the young engineer had 'borne fruit a hundred-fold'), Tulla finally presented himself back in Karlsruhe for an oral examination by the leading scientists of the principality, which included answering questions on the notes, sketches and calculations in the travel journal he had been required to keep during his two-year trip. That took place in November 1796, and ended with similar plaudits from the examiners. The following year Tulla was appointed as a state engineer with primary responsibility for Rhine construction works in the Rastatt district. His salary was 400 gulden a year, plus 2 *malter* of rye, 8 *malter* of spelt (a kind of wheat), and 8 awms of wine, second class.[26]

The long years of apprenticeship over, Tulla's career advanced quickly. As a further sign of the confidence it placed in the rising star, Karlsruhe sent him on a tour of France in 1801–3, so that he was there during the years when Napoleon, who had seized power in 1799, was busy promoting himself from First Consul to Consul for Life (he would proclaim himself Emperor in 1804). That Tulla should journey to Paris at this time was also a sign of the way the political wind was blowing in his home state. As we shall see, Baden was to be one of the major beneficiaries when the Holy Roman Empire was destroyed by Napoleon in 1803, and after 1805 the state was a loyal French ally. While in Paris, Tulla examined hydraulic projects and exchanged ideas with French specialists. Promoted to senior engineer with the military rank of captain on his return in 1803 (his remuneration in kind was now upgraded to 'wine, first class'), Tulla assumed responsibility for river construction works throughout Baden the following year. In 1805 he was offered two posts and declined them both. He turned down a chair in mathematics at Heidelberg in order to pursue his practical ambitions, and a senior engineering position in Munich in order to pursue those ambitions on the Rhine. He seems to have been everywhere in these years, busy with maps and measurements, examining the latest construction of fascines, travelling from site to site in his chaise with the energy of a Brenckenhoff.

Tulla worked on various stretches of the Rhine, and initiated a project to regulate one of its tributaries, the Wiese. He drew up and supervised the scheme, which began in 1806 and was not completed until 1823. The year after work started on the Wiese he received an offer from Switzerland that would allow him to tackle a major hydrological undertaking without giving up his long-term ambitions in Baden. He was asked to devise a solution to the flooded and swampy lower valley of the Linthe at the point where it entered the Walensee. War and

French exactions had emptied the coffers of his native state, slowing the pace of work – Tulla was still sharing complaints with a fellow engineer several years later about the 'continual lack of resources' that 'daily' eroded the efficiency of the Waterways and Roads department.[27] The Badenese state was happy to grant Tulla leave for an undertaking that promised to provide him with valuable experience at someone else's expense. His work on the Linthe and Walensee, which lasted five years and eventually cost one million Swiss Francs, reinforced Tulla's already strong inclination to think on a large scale. It was during this Swiss interlude, in 1809, that Tulla for the first time put down on paper his proposal for a wholesale 'rectification' of the troublesome Rhine.[28]

By the early nineteenth century German hydraulic engineers showed a confidence born of growing experience and technical expertise. For two generations the basic principles established by scientists like Daniel Bernoulli and Leonhard Euler had been practised on rivers that found themselves straightened, redirected and fitted out with locks. That was true above all across the North German Plain, from the Oder and Warthe in the east to the Lower Rhine and tributaries like the Ruhr and Niers in the west.[29] Trial and error honed the judgement of the specialists and led to a growing body of written work. David Gilly, a leading Prussian hydraulic engineer who worked on many projects with Brenckenhoff, wrote and lectured extensively in the 1790s. In 1805 Gilly and his Prussian colleague Johann Eytelwein, who at the time was drawing up plans to improve on the earlier Frederician regulation of the Oder, produced the first volume of *Practical Directions on Hydraulic Engineering*.[30] Gilly and Eytelwein were just two of many contemporary writers on what was starting to be called technology – the word was first used in the title of a German book in 1777.[31] The turn of the eighteenth and nineteenth centuries saw a burst of new engineering handbooks, syntheses, dictionaries and bibliographies.[32]

Tulla devoured this literature, including the work of his own mentor, Langsdorf, whose *Handbook of Hydraulics* appeared in 1796. Tulla's practical bent meant that he also stored away for future use what he had seen for himself, not only in the Netherlands and France but in Germany. By the early years of the nineteenth century, German states were no longer dependent on imported Dutch expertise to remake their rivers; a cohort of native practitioners had formed. Gilly and Eytelwein were active in Prussia. Reinhard Woltmann was at work on regulating the Elbe. Tulla met him during his visit to Hamburg, and was sufficiently impressed by an instrument designed to measure the river current that he had a replica made by a Karlsruhe mechanic. Tulla would become the first person to use the Woltmann water gauge to measure the velocity of the Rhine. Then there was the immodest and much-travelled Karl Friedrich Ritter von Wiebeking, whose career eventually took him to Vienna and Munich. Tulla first met him on the Lower Rhine in 1794. In 1796, Wiebeking moved to Darmstadt, a carefully laid-out residential city of a local ruler not dissimilar to Karlsruhe, where for six years he had overall responsibility for the stretches of the Rhine that flowed through Hesse-Darmstadt. Tulla found him unbearably pompous. More congenial was another Hessian engineer, Claus Kröncke, who became a close friend and later an important ally on the Rhine project. These were men who still got their clothes muddy and complained about their expenses, but in other ways they were very different from the Haerlem and Brenckenhoff generation. The growth of professional knowledge and collective expertise were evident even in their rivalries.

Northern Germany may have defined the state of the art, but the technical means available to tame unruly rivers had long been perfectly familiar in Baden. The Rhine was of central importance to the riparian state, and the first rudimentary cuts to re-channel the river had after all been made over 400 years earlier. In the course of a 1787 lecture to celebrate the 200th anniversary of the Karlsruhe Lyzeum, the mathematician Johann Lorenz Böckmann – one of Tulla's teachers – asked rhetorically: 'What progress have mathematics and the natural sciences made in the Badenese lands?' In answering this question, he praised the works recently undertaken by his colleagues 'against incursions and against the frequent flooding of the Rhine, the Murg and other, smaller but dangerous rivers'.[33] He was right. As we have seen, the later years of the eighteenth century had witnessed intense activity: dikes, embankments, cuts. The large investment in Tulla by the state signalled the belief that further improvements would be needed. That was true right down to particular sites. Many of the cuts in Tulla's eventual Rhine-rectification had been proposed earlier as individual measures. One of the first, at Daxlanden, had even been presented to him as an examination question.

It was their scale, not this or that specific innovation, which made Tulla's proposals distinctive, even startling. As he observed a few years later, 'for state water and road construction projects a general plan should always be established to guide all the undertakings – an ideal of how everything should be'.[34] His ideas, first put forward in 1809, were reiterated in a memorandum three years later: *The Principles According to Which Future Work on the Rhine Should Be Conducted.*[35] The title was matter-of-fact, the content radical. Tulla envisaged work along the whole of the Upper Rhine from the Swiss border at Basel to the Hessian border at Worms, a distance of 354 kilometres. The river should be 'directed into a single bed with gentle curves adapted to nature or . . . where it is practicable, a straight line'.[36] This artificial bed would significantly shorten the length of the Rhine and speed the flow of water, causing the river to cut a deeper bed, thereby protecting riverside communities from flooding and allowing former marshland to be cultivated as the water table fell. A uniform width of between 200 and 250 metres was to be established along the 'corrected' river. This amounted to a remaking of the Rhine.

Tulla was three weeks short of his forty-second birthday when he wrote the 1812 memorandum, just a few years younger than Daniel Albrecht Thaer when he wrote his first major book, *Introduction to the Knowledge of English Agriculture and its Recent Practical and Theoretical Advances, with Respect to the Improvement of German Agriculture,* another work whose radical content could hardly be guessed from the title.[37] There are some illuminating parallels between the man who symbolized the new relationship with nature in the reclaimed Oderbruch and the man who wanted to tame the wild Rhine. Both believed in fusing theory and practice, rejected conventional academic positions, and instead created new educational institutions. Thaer's practical-based pedagogy at Möglin, and his decision to leave the University of Berlin after initially accepting a chair, established the principle that the university was not the best place to study agriculture. Tulla turned down the Heidelberg chair partly because of his commitment to practical training for engineers, and was later instrumental in creating the Karlsruhe Polytechnic in 1825.[38] When it came to their hallmark achievements, both men were synthesizers with a distaste for the piecemeal. And both distilled their message about the practical application of theory into a dictum. 'Agriculture is a trade whose purpose is to earn a profit through the production of vegetables and livestock'. Those were Thaer's words, not universally accepted two hundred years ago. 'No river or stream, including the Rhine, needs more than one bed'.[39] That was Tulla, setting out an axiom that was still a provocation at the begining of the nineteenth century.

Tulla and Thaer had something else in common. Their advanced thinking was not restricted to technical concerns. Both saw the German Old Regime, the Holy Roman Empire they had grown up in, as an obstacle to technological and economic progress, which made them symbols as well as beneficiaries of the changes that came to Germany when the French Revolution transformed the existing political structure. It was Prussian reformers reacting to the French challenge who invited Thaer to establish himself in Möglin, and Thaer reciprocated by helping to draft the decree that emancipated the Prussian peasantry from serfdom – something that Frederick the Great had achieved in royal domains, including the new-won land, but not on noble property. Tulla, too, was an opponent of feudal ties in the countryside, having seen peasants drafted in to perform compulsory labour service on dike and embankment projects. In his view, the system was both inequitable and inefficient. Tulla's enthusiasm for the 'modern' and 'rational' went beyond his commitment to the latest measuring devices. Conversely, as far as the Rhine was concerned, the changing institutional and political background of the early nineteenth century was decisive for the realization of his great project. For if technological advances and cumulative expertise made the Rhine rectification thinkable, it was the political convulsions sparked by French armies that made it possible.

Remaking the Upper Rhine

'A force appeared that beggared all imagination': that was how the military theorist Carl von Clausewitz described the French Revolutionary, later the Napoleonic, armies.[40] This was a new kind of army, the nation in arms, that rolled over opponents. In Germany the campaigns of 1792–1806 led to a series of imposed peace treaties and in their wake came a seismic shift in the German political landscape. The Holy Roman Empire of the German Nation disappeared, along with the hundreds of tiny principalities that had sheltered within it. Borders were redrawn, populations changed rulers, old forms of sovereignty ended, new states emerged.[41]

Baden was one of the winners. Like other German states it signed a peace treaty with France that sanctioned French annexations, in this case on the left bank of the Rhine, but it received generous territorial

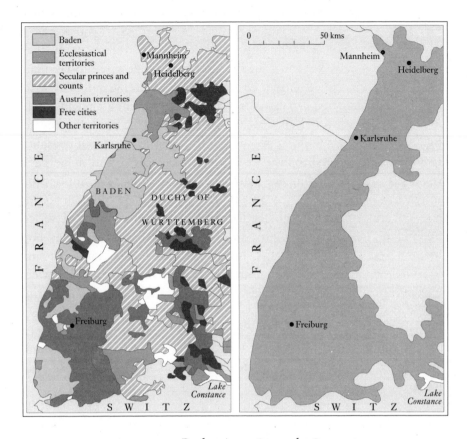

MAP 3 *Baden in 1789 and 1815.*

compensation. At the beginning of the nineteenth century, in the years when Tulla was honing his skills and becoming convinced that whole-sale rectification of the Rhine was necessary, Baden fattened up by swal-lowing the tiny right-bank territories that were expunged from the map, most of them in 1803, the rest in 1806: imperial cities, the lands held by imperial knights, ecclesiastical principalities. The state increased its population six-fold, its territory four-fold. And if the Margrave of Baden did not become a fully-fledged king, like the Elector of Bavaria and the Duke of Württemberg, at least he became a Grand Duke. There was a price to be paid for this good fortune, in the shape of French finan-cial demands, but the fact remains that Baden emerged from the wreckage of the Holy Roman Empire no longer a regional principality but an important middle-sized German state, one of the three dozen or so that were to make up the new Germany after the eventual defeat of France.

In 1806 Napoleon set up an organization of German states, a combination of military alliance and French-sponsored counterweight to Prussia and Austria. He called it the Confederation of the Rhine, although some of its members (like Mecklenburg) were a very long way from the river in question.[42] But what of the Rhine itself? From the standpoint of those who wanted to remake the river, to rationalize it as Napoleon had rationalized the map of Germany, the dramatic changes brought by French dominance provided both a motive and an opportunity. The opportunity was presented by the disappearance of the dozens of small territorial jurisdictions that had always frustrated earlier attempts at comprehensive work on the Rhine. The motive arose from the same shift of fortunes. The previously disjointed collection of Badenese lands now had the look of a modern territorial state; but, like other beneficiaries of Napoleon, Karlsruhe needed to find ways of creating a common identity among its new lands and subjects.

The following years saw a wave of bureaucratic centralization, efforts to gather information about the new acquisitions, new maps, revised legal codes, revamped tax systems, newly standardized weights and measures.[43] Rhine rectification held up a mirror to these changes. Dive into the sprawling archival record, look at any one stage of the project, and it is like drawing a cross-section through the life of the state. River regulation threw up issues of every imaginable kind. Who would provide the labour? Where would the fascines, the sand and the gravel come from? Were new arrangements necessary to guard the forests that provided the all-important fascines? How would the whole thing be paid for and what contributions could be levied on local communities? What about the compensation urgently requested by villages that lost land when the river was channelled into a new bed? Conversely, what about the new land created by rectification: should it all revert to local villagers, and what about the land that fell on the 'wrong' side of the new river and was no longer Badenese at all?[44] Tulla's project meant, in effect, that the whole apparatus of state was mobilized. The departments that were called on for opinions and action included Foreign Affairs, Finance, Interior, Forestry and Mines, Domains, Waterways and Roads.[45] But if the Rhine project reflected a larger pattern of state-building, it also contributed to that process. It was an undertaking that advocates hoped would integrate the new state along its major artery.[46]

French military success had another important consequence. It eased the diplomatic agreements necessary for large-scale rectification of the Rhine. While the Holy Roman Empire still existed, any proposed improvement by Baden on the right bank had to be negotiated with one or more of the motley group of territorial rulers on the left bank: the Elector Palatine, the Prince-Bishop of Speyer, the Duke of Pfalz-Zweibrücken, the Counts of Leiningen (all three of them). French annexation of the left bank put a brutal end to that inconvenience. Now negotiators from Baden and France could sit down one on one. There had, in fact, been earlier discussions between the two states after the floods of 1778, over possible joint measures along the stretch of the river around Strasbourg. Agreements were even struck in 1782 and 1791, but were overtaken by war. The separate peace that Baden signed with France in 1796 contained two clauses that left the way open for future measures.[47]

Rhine rectification was linked at every stage with diplomacy, and Karlsruhe was well aware of the connection.[48] Tulla himself was sent on his lengthy trip to France in 1801 so that he could establish useful contacts with local specialists and improve his French with an eye to future negotiations. Then, and in the years that followed, Baden tried to sell Rhine rectification to France as a solution to the border question. This suited Karlsruhe, which would be able to consolidate an expanded right bank. It was reasonable to think that the French would feel the same way. The idea took hold in eighteenth-century France that the best national boundaries were 'natural', defined not by custom or history but geographically. 'It is good to take streams, rivers, watersheds . . . as the boundaries of territories', as a French Foreign Office memorandum put it in 1772.[49] That was the basis on which France signed a number of 'treaties of limits' with its territorial neighbours in the 1770s and 1780s, the River Doubs serving as the frontier marker with the Duchy of Württemberg, the Saar as the boundary with the Elector of Trier. The French revolutionaries took over the idea and applied it to the Rhine, but with a new twist. Since they were unwilling to present annexations as 'conquests', and occupation of the left bank of the Rhine could hardly be presented as something that enjoyed popular support, the idea of the 'Rhine barrier' as a defensive 'natural frontier' became an article of patriotic faith.

The problem, of course, was that rivers in their natural state make very uncertain boundaries. France found this out on all of its frontiers, before the revolution and after. Nowhere was the problem more evident than it was on the Rhine. As a Strasbourg engineer noted gloomily:

> Everybody agrees that all boundaries should be as fixed and invariable as possible; yet what is more variable than the middle of the Rhine, that is to say, the navigable part of the river? The Rhine changes its course every year, sometimes two or three times. With the floods, an island or a commune, which in the spring was French, is German the following winter, then becomes French again in two or three years . . .

Patchwork human intervention only made things worse, because

> by means of dams or dikes, the riverfront inhabitants and sometimes the contiguous states bring back an island to their respective banks. These islands, without stable and recognized masters, facilitate disorders of every kind.[50]

Tulla's proposals offered a solution that would fix the border by taming these 'disorders'. It was the border issue that caused Tulla to write his 1812 memorandum, presented on behalf of Baden to the Magistracy of the Rhine. Established by Napoleon in 1809, this body was responsible for dealing with both territorial and hydrological issues along the whole stretch of the river between the Swiss and Dutch borders. Tulla's plan was accepted by the Magistracy, despite some French scepticism. In 1812 Baden and France agreed to make six cuts in the Rhine between Knielingen and Schröck, but the agreement was overtaken by the collapse of the Napoleonic Empire in 1814. The Magistracy of the Rhine ended with it, and so for the moment did the prospect of realizing Tulla's ideas.[51]

The European peace settlements of 1814 and 1815 pushed France back from the Rhine everywhere except in Alsace. As a result, Baden now began negotiations with Bavaria. Another south German state that had done well out of the dismantling of the Holy Roman Empire, Bavaria had acquired the Palatinate on the left bank, the stretch of the Rhine that was the most obvious candidate for the first phase of Tulla's proposals. Discussions were stalled until the major floods of 1816–17, which concentrated the minds of the negotiators. Under the terms of a treaty signed in 1817, the two states agreed to cooperate in making five cuts; a further agreement followed in 1825 to make fifteen more.[52]

There would be many more rounds of diplomacy. Some led to further agreements between the Upper Rhine states of Baden, Bavaria and Hesse. Others involved allaying the fears of downstream states like Prussia and the Netherlands that the new hydrology of the river could prove damaging. Finally, closing the circle opened by talks that went back to the 1770s, the Rhine Boundary Treaty of 1840 finally made possible the correction of the river where it flowed between Baden and French Alsace.

Hydrology and diplomacy were inseparable elements of Rhine rectification. It was the French revolutionary and Napoleonic armies that radically simplified the map of Germany and created the political space for Tulla's ideas to receive their first hearing. 'In the beginning was Napoleon' runs the celebrated opening line of one modern German history.[53] It might stand as a verdict on the remaking of the Rhine. But the Napoleonic era was only the beginning, for the time-scale of the project was much longer than anything we associate with political generations. Tulla's dream was not realized until the 1870s. By then the map of Germany and Europe had been transformed once again by Otto von Bismarck, a man born six years after Tulla first proposed to tame the Rhine.

This was the largest civil engineering project that had ever been undertaken in Germany. The Rhine between Basel and Worms was shortened from 354 to 273 kilometres, almost a quarter of its length. Dozens of cuts were made, more than 2200 islands removed. Along the stretch between Basel and Strasbourg alone, well over a thousand million square metres of island or peninsula were excavated and 240 kilometres of main dikes constructed containing five million cubic metres of material.[54] During the 1860s the number of fascines being used was running at up to 800,000 a year.[55] Consider Rhine rectification as the single giant project of Tulla's imagination, and all of the numbers are dauntingly large. Turn the magnification up, however, look at how the goal was realized one stretch at a time, and the sheer arduousness of the project becomes easier to grasp. It took seven years to make the cut in the river at Mechtersheim, begun in 1837 and completed when the river finally flowed within its new bed in 1844. That was fairly typical of progress in the meander zone. A channel would be dug along the predetermined new course of the Rhine, usually 18–24 metres in width, sometimes narrower. When the channel had been excavated the ends were knocked out, allowing the river to follow the line of least resistance and rush through the shorter route, eventually widening the artificial channel through the power of its current. Fascines then secured the new banks and cut off the old arms of the river, so that water reached them only when the river was running very high.[56]

That was the theory, anyway, the same one that had guided the digging of the New Oder between Güstebiese and Hohen-Saaten almost a century earlier. The looser the soil, the greater the drop in the river and the shorter the cut in relation to the meander, the quicker the river did the work assigned to it. But local geological vagaries often delayed the desired effect. Stubborn seams of clay along the new bed caused the biggest problem. Then it was necessary to excavate some more, to build up an extra head of water artificially as a way of scouring the channel, or simply to wait. Of the twenty cuts made between Lauterburg and Worms over the years 1817 to 1878, the average length of time between making the cut and watching the river establish its new bed was almost nine years. In two extreme cases, the Anglhofer and Friesenheimer cuts, the interval was thirty-four years and fifty years. Even leaving those two aside, the average interval was still five years.[57] The scale of the task was even greater along the severely braided Rhine in the furcation zone between Baden and Alsace. That was where the islands were most numerous and the largest amounts of debris had to be moved. Although, once again, the erosive force of the river was harnessed, work on a single stage of the rectification could still take a generation to complete. At Freistett, where consolidating a single river bed meant making cuts and removing large islands (including a local landmark, the *Rauher Kopf*), work began in 1820 and went on until 1864.[58]

The nature of contemporary construction work did as much as anything to determine the pace of the project. Maps, measuring instruments and the science of hydraulic engineering had all advanced since the eighteenth century; the technology of digging ditches had not. At least through the 1850s it was human muscles wielding picks, shovels, spades and buckets that did most of the work. The other main source of energy was horses. In that respect Rhine rectification resembled the draining of the Oderbruch. In fact, it bore more than a passing resemblance to Charlemagne's fruitless attempts more than a thousand years earlier to build a canal connecting the Main and the Danube. Up to 10,000 workers were digging the Fossa Carolina in 793. As many as

3000 men laboured on each stage of Rhine rectification – reinforced (as in the Oderbruch) by soldiers, around 800 of whom helped to dig the Eggenstein cut.[59] Tulla's dream was largely realized before the mechanization of construction, at a time when the population was booming. The result was that, like the great road and railway building projects of the era, remaking the Rhine was carried through by swarms of manual labourers.

Sometimes, another parallel with the great Frederician project on the Oder, they worked with military detachments to guard them from attacks. The backlash against Tulla's scheme came mostly from villagers who feared that the new course of the Rhine would make them more vulnerable to flooding or cost them valuable arable and woodland. Protests came from communities on both banks of the river, and they had a precedent in the opposition mounted in Auenheim and Rheinsheim against cuts proposed by the French in 1801–2. The most sustained rearguard action against Tulla's proposal came from Knielingen, a right-bank village that today forms part of Karlsruhe. Protests began earlier, in 1812, when a proposed cut in the river would have moved the course of the Rhine eastwards and left village-owned lands stranded on the far bank, potentially lost to France. But resistance continued after the war. It became most intense in 1816–17, when attempts by the Badenese state to embark on Tulla's project coincided with bad harvests and heightened rural anxiety. Now villagers did more than send letters of protest or seek audiences. They disrupted the work of surveyors, refused to provide fascines or labour for the correction work and threatened those from neighbouring villages who did. After thirty men from Eggenstein trying to work on the correction were driven off at the beginning of September 1817 ('beaten off by the Knielinger so that several of them were injured'), a detachment of infantry was billeted on the village and the right of assembly suspended.[60]

Tulla was inclined to see every form of opposition as an expression of ignorance and petty-mindedness. As he wrote to his sympathetic colleague, the Hessian engineer Kröncke, in 1825:[61]

The difficulties and obstacles that stand in the way of rectification of the Rhine do not lie in the task itself, in the river and the areas that surround it, or in excessive costs, or inadequate returns, or in the need to make exceptional sacrifices, but make themselves felt for the most part according to the degree to which individual interests or the interests of whole communities come into play, and whether the active agents are more or less enlightened and moral.

Tulla often expressed scepticism about the power of reason to dispel the fog of prejudice, as he saw it, concluding that only further flood disasters could teach the hard lessons that needed to be learnt. His tone was typically confident and dismissive of those who refused to recognize the obvious. It was the voice of the German state official, impatient with social conflicts, and the voice of the zealous technocrat. 'Many things could have been done much better', he snapped, 'had ignorant and sometimes malicious people not interfered, and had I been able to act entirely in accordance with my own convictions'. Comprehensive rectification was 'the only means of rescue for the inhabitants of the riverbank', and Tulla had little time for those – like politicians – who did not take his word for it.[62] 'People who are not specialists' (this was a reference to members of the Hessian parliament) 'can only have opinions, and it is very wrong when people with opinions can dismiss the arguments that experts have put forward with complete conviction'.[63]

Alas, there were even experts who failed to see the light. Some of Tulla's sharpest barbs were reserved for his fellow engineers. Of Herr Arnold, a sceptical colleague in the downstream Rhine city of Mainz, he wrote:

> I believe that he will not allow himself to change his mind, because he has too little knowledge of river works and perhaps it tickles his vanity to hold a different point of view . . . As a rule I consider it to be largely wasted effort to try to educate people on things that lie beyond their area of competence.

Then there were the Bavarians, partners in the first stages of the project. Herr Spatz had 'limited views' and was too strongly attached to earlier piecemeal efforts of his own; he cherished his 'little dikes' like 'immortal children'. He had, complained Tulla in February 1825, won over the senior Bavarian hydraulic engineer Wiebeking, with the result that they 'have almost entirely abandoned the rectification of the Rhine'. These two influential Bavarian specialists had been joined by a third, Herr von Rechmann, 'who understands nothing of river works'. If both banks of the river had belonged to Baden, 'we should long ago have been further on'.[64]

But there were also sceptics in Baden who questioned Tulla's grand design. Treasury officials, parliamentarians and local communities voiced their concerns; so did influential senior engineers. Tulla's *bête noire* was Friedrich Weinbrenner, Baden's Director of Construction Work and the brother-in-law of the incorrigible Herr Arnold in Mainz (the nascent profession of engineering officials was as dynastic in Germany as the department of *Ponts et Chaussées* in France). 'Our Herr Weinbrenner is the most conceited man in the world, he regards himself as the greatest genius and believes that there is nothing in the universe about which he cannot write and instruct people'.[65] This was Tulla's uncharitable judgement on Weinbrenner in 1825, the crucial year in determining whether Rhine rectification would move forward or not.

By the end of 1825 the second agreement had been signed with Bavaria and the project acquired new momentum. There were a number of reasons why Tulla's plan eventually carried the day. Older critics retired or died off while Tulla himself rose through the engineering bureaucracy. The floods of 1824, initially a weapon in the hands of the doubters, came to be seen as a vindication of Tulla's proposals, not a reason to reject them. Tulla himself worked hard to persuade those who mattered. He conducted Badenese parliamentarians through the earliest cuts. Above all, he wrote. The *Memorandum* of 1822 and *On the Rectification of the Rhine* (1825) were not timeless contributions to hydraulic wisdom. They were occasional works, even polemics, written to sway opinion.[66] The bulk of the rectification still lay ahead in 1825, dependent on agreement from the Grand Duchy of Hesse, France and the downstream states of Prussia and the Netherlands. But there were to be no more memoranda from Tulla. Troubled by colic and rheumatic pains, Tulla grew increasingly irritable as his health declined and went to Paris to have an operation. He was still fretting about the Rhine as he lay in the French capital preparing to undergo a medical procedure he failed to survive. The young engineer August Sprenger, a trusted protégé, was sent from Baden to Paris at the end of March 1828 to attend to his ailing mentor, but Tulla died before Sprenger arrived.[67] The fame of the man who tamed the wild Rhine was to be largely posthumous.

Winners and Losers

Some plaudits came while Tulla could still enjoy them. One of the earliest cuts in the river was made between Knielingen and Eggenstein, and while Knielingen protested, the inhabitants of Eggenstein welcomed a measure that removed the threatening river to a safe distance. The cut was opened on the afternoon of 20 January 1818, watched by thousands. Six days later Tulla travelled through the cut with a party of engineers and soldiers. It was an occasion for toasts from the Eggensteiners and many assembled dignitaries from beyond. A local official, Bernhard Dillmann, read Tulla a poem:

> Praise and thanks are due to this man,
> Who through the wisdom of his plan
> Which he has now seen through to its end
> Has liberated us from the Rhine.

Tulla had 'rescued us from our plight for a hundred years to come', ran one line of Dillmann's verse. He closed with two verses of Luke: Lord, now lettest thou thy servant depart in peace, according to thy word: For mine eyes have seen thy salvation. The mayor and citizens of the commune voiced similar sentiments in a formal vote of thanks to their 'father', as they styled Tulla, who 'by means of the canal constructed through the Neupforzer woods has created a defence against the Rhine, so that it will not continue – as it has done for so long – to carry away our land and the hard-earned property of our citizens'.[68]

Protecting land and property from the flood waters: that had always been the main objective in Tulla's mind. As early as 1805 he referred to Baden as a state 'where cultural improvements and the securing of property depend heavily on hydraulic and hydro-technical undertakings'. This conviction drove him to an especially bitter condemnation of his local adversary, Weinbrenner, for indifference to 'the well-being . . . of many hundreds of thousands of people'.[69] The Faustian theme of bringing the land back home, of human mastery, runs through his writings. It was for humans to shape the river in their own interests: 'in cultivated lands, brooks, rivers and streams should as a rule be – canals, and where the water flows should be in the power of the inhabitants'.[70]

That objective was largely achieved. A comprehensive system of Rhine dikes was not part of the Tulla plan; that came later. But the re-engineered course of the river through the Upper Rhine plain by itself removed the threat of inundation from dozens of towns and villages. One by-product, as Tulla had foreseen, was psychological: a 'gain for the riverbank inhabitants that cannot be expressed numerically, that they will become less fearful'.[71] Confidence and security meant that land was reclaimed from the former floodplain and intensely cultivated. That was important in a corner of Germany where rising population and land hunger, especially in the Palatinate, had already created a significant stream of eighteenth-century emigration to America, Hungary – and to Frederick the Great's Prussia. It was also fertile land. As one modern observer describes it, 'we feel the easy fruitfulness of this land as an inner blessing and take pleasure in the colours in the foreground'. For August Becker, writing in the nineteenth century after Tulla had worked his magic, the plain was 'so fruitful and luxuriantly green, so thoroughly planted and cultivated, that it seems like one great garden'.[72] The idea that rectification 'turned the Rhine plain into a blooming garden', an image familiar from the Oderbruch, will make sense to anyone who travels today on one of the trains that traverse both banks of the river, and sees mile after mile of crops that make the land resemble a colourful and symmetrical quilt.[73] Arable farming and cash crops were not directly created by river rectification, as they were in the Oderbruch by drainage. But the realization of Tulla's scheme brought new security as well as new land, and both led to more inten-sive settlement. Even today the inhabitants of Maximiliansau celebrate harvest festival in the Tulla Hall.[74]

'The attitude and productivity of the riverbank inhabitants will improve in proportion to the amount of protection their houses, posses-sions and harvests receive', Tulla had written. 'The climate along the Rhine will become more pleasant and the air cleaner, and there will be less mist, because the water table will be lowered by nearly a third and swamps will disappear'.[75] His optimism proved well-founded on this score as well. Prior to rectification, the Upper Rhine plain had been a breeding-ground of malaria, typhus and dysentery.[76] Malaria claimed the life of the Elector Palatine Karl in 1685, who died after conducting military exercises on marshy ground near the confluence of the Rhine and Neckar.[77] Parish records show that in 1720 more than a hundred people died of malaria in Burkheim. The disease was equally endemic in neighbouring communities like Philippsburg and Mechtersheim.[78] Malarial sickness was a greater killer than war in the eighteenth century. Altering the course of the river hastened the end of the biological old regime: after 1885 there were only isolated cases of the disease. Some, it is true, have argued about whether it was the recast river itself, or the increase in cattle grazing that followed it, or broader medical and nutritional advances that was most responsible for the disappearance of malaria. The case has even been made that in the bifurcation zone the severing of former side-arms from the flow of the main river created more favourable breeding grounds locally. But most writers emphasize the overall improvement in health of those living on the banks of the Upper Rhine, another boon – like greater security and productivity – that they enjoyed thanks to the comprehensive plan of rectification.[79]

Were there, then, no losers? With the benefit of hindsight it is clear that Tulla set in train changes more dramatic than even he could envisage. He was the first to remake the Upper Rhine. It was to be remade more than once, mainly with the needs of navigation in mind, until the river came to resemble the fully canalized, modern commercial waterway of today, its banks dotted with large ports and industrial plants. What came later, for better and worse, makes it hard to draw up the balance sheet of Tulla's achievement. Hard, but worth attempting. Against the greater wellbeing of those now freed from local flooding, we have to set a variety of worlds that were lost. Even for river engineers of Tulla's generation, the logic of reconfiguring the stream meant that some familiar landmarks of the Rhine like ferries and floating mills were sacrificed to the larger long-term good. They were obstructions; the future lay with bridges and with the great commercial mills of Mannheim.[80] More dramatic, certainly more symbolically charged, was another loss: the disappearance of the Rhine gold that had been extracted from the river for two millennia, together with the 'gold-washers' whose livelihoods the precious metal had sustained.[81]

Flecks of gold were washed down the Rhine from the Aar region of Switzerland. They were deposited along with quartz, mica and feldspar as sediment in the gravel banks of the river, the largest and richest seams forming as a result of moderate high water that flowed away slowly.[82] Sifting the sand and gravel for gold was one of the oldest occupations on the Rhine. The Celts had done it in the third century BC. Strabo reported on the river's riches around the time of Christ's birth, and the Romans supposedly shipped so much Rhine gold back to Italy that they depressed the price. Early medieval records document the continued existence of gold beds. The Emperor Frederick II decreed in 1232 that these belonged to the local lords, but the prospecting rights were usually parcelled out.[83] The physical extraction of the gold was an uncomfortable, time-consuming business of shovelling and sifting with sieves and wooden boards. About 700 tons of sand and gravel had to be processed to yield 100 grams of gold. The vagaries of the river meant that gold-bearing gravel banks regularly shifted and sometimes disappeared completely, just like the drowned villages. A report in 1721 about one rich but shifting gold bed recorded that it had been hotly disputed between claimants from Germersheim, Speyer and Leimersheim, but ended with the lapidary note: 'Since then frequented by no one; now under water'.[84]

Yet on the eve of the great changes brought by Tulla, Rhine gold remained important. It enriched the lords sufficiently for them to be concerned about sticky fingers and smuggling; it mattered enough to those who actually extracted the gold that all kinds of chicanery were practised over contested seams.[85] Thanks to the disturbances caused by construction work the old Rhine produced tantalizingly higher yields of gold in its last years, before the negative long-term effects of the correction were felt. On the left bank, around two kilos a year were sent from the Palatinate to the royal mint in Munich during the 1830s and 1840s. This dropped off to less than one kilo in the 1850s, and when just 278 grams were delivered in 1862 the Bavarian state relinquished its rights to Palatine Rhine gold.[86] On the Baden side almost 150 kilos of gold went to the Karlsruhe mint in the thirty years from 1804 to 1834, as much as thirteen kilos a year around 1830. The figure stayed close to historic levels until mid-century, then fell steeply, to just 500 grams a year in the 1860s, less than 100 grams by the early 1870s. The amount was insignificant when the state stopped keeping records in 1874.[87]

The new hydrological conditions created by river rectification made it impossible to continue extracting gold from the gravel: the high waters came and went too quickly to leave anything other than tiny and irregular deposits. And so, at some point between the California gold rush of 1849 and the South African gold rush of the late nineteenth century, gold effectively disappeared from the Rhine after more than two thousand years. To most people today, 'Rhine Gold' means only an opera by Wagner, first produced in 1869 just as the stuff itself vanished. What did it leave behind? Local names (*Goldgrund, Goldgrube*), and a dwindling number of people who had once made a living as gold washers in Wörth, Neuburg, Hördt, Leimersheim, Germersheim, Sondernheim, Neupotz, Philippsburg, Oberhausen, Rheinhausen and Speyer. The Baden census of 1838 listed 400 gold washers on the right bank of the river alone.[88] A generation later there were almost none to be found on either bank. The last full-time gold washers gave up in the 1860s or 1870s, ruefully accepting (like Georg Michael Kuhn, the last of the breed in Leimersheim) that the river was simply not the same. The last gold washer in Speyer died in 1896, survived by his equipment, which found its way into the Historical Museum of the Palatinate. Only a few solitary ancients still went through the motions in side channels of the Rhine, photographed by contemporaries at the moment that marked the end of their craft.[89]

The new Rhine brought changes to every aspect of life on the riverbank. As river marshes gave way to meadows and meadows to arable, as orchards and fields of potatoes or sugar beet moved down to occupy the rich alluvial soil, older uses were displaced. Reed cutters disappeared. So did the fowlers who had worked the *Vogelgründe*, the birding grounds once to be found thickly dotted around the broad bends in the river. A kind of cascade effect can be observed. Fowlers were driven ahead of the corrections from one part of the river to the next as their leases became valueless.[90] Like the seams of gold, the birding grounds survived only as historic place names, such as the busy tram interchange called *Entenfang* now to be found half-way between the centre of Karlsruhe and the river, marking what had once been an area alive with ducks and hunters.

Nothing symbolizes the changes better than the decline in Rhine fishing, the stuff of legends – legends that were being zealously collected by Romantic intellectuals in the very years when Tulla was beginning his work. From Strasbourg downriver to Speyer, all the larger urban settlements had important fish markets and sections of town that took their name from the trade. They were served by fishing communities on both banks of the river. The medieval fishing guilds may have been declining, but the business was not. For many towns and villages it was far and away the most important source of income, on the Upper Rhine probably more than on any other stretch of the river. In Burkheim, fishermen, boatmen and their families made up half of the population before the corrections. The fishermen's guild had ninety members. Further north, villages like Wörth, Pfortz and Neuburg lived almost entirely from fish.[91] These were often the poorer villages, from which fish-wives sold the catch house to house. But fishing also had an important ancillary role in wealthier, more diversified settlements along the river. Eighteenth-century Leimersheim had seventeen recorded fishermen; a further five of the twenty-four peasant families practised the occupation part-time.[92] Depending on the season and water conditions, they found their catch in a variety of places. They fished the main river and its side-arms, shallows and backwaters, unregulated tributaries and inland lakes or pools left by the floodwaters. They also fished from the countless islands in the Rhine, where the characteristic wood-and-reed fisher huts were as common as they were along the banks of the river. Goethe described visiting a number of them during his trip to Alsace of 1770–71, when 'we brought the cool inhabitants of the Rhine mercilessly into the pot, to fry in the sizzling fat'.[93]

At the time when Goethe was in Alsace there were forty-five species of fish in the Upper Rhine and its tributaries.[94] Some were freshwater fish that lived year-round and bred in the river, like perch, tench, roach, bream, barbel and gudgeon. Others were anadromous species, which lived in the sea but ran up the river to breed. They included the lamprey, sea trout and lavaret, allice shad and thwaite shad (shad are fat members of the herring family with the unherring-like habit of spawning in rivers), the sturgeon, and – of course – the salmon. If the shad was sometimes called the king of the herrings, the salmon was the king of all fish. Upper Rhine fishing distinguished historically between 'major fishing' (salmon) and 'minor fishing' (everything else). Salmon was not only king; it was plentiful. The best catches came in the period when the fish ran up the river from the sea, beginning in January and peaking in July. They were caught in a rich variety of drift nets and casting nets, and in a major fish market like Strasbourg a hundred or more would be sold in a single day.[95] That servants on the Upper Rhine complained about being forced to eat salmon three days a week is almost certainly a legend, but it still gives some measure of abundance in the pre-Tulla era.[96]

Correcting the river ended this plenty. Georg Friedrich Kolb was still reporting good catches of both migratory and stationary fish in 1831, but even then there were signs of decline. Concern grew in the following decades. Fishermen from Speyer, Frankenthal and Germersheim were complaining in the early 1840s about the absence of salmon and sturgeon.[97] The main river could no longer be fished as it had been; the islands familiar to Goethe were gone. Some of the former side-arms of the Rhine, quiet refuges from Tulla's colder and speedier river, enjoyed an initial boost in stocks. What this meant to fishermen can be measured in the price of fishing leases, some of which remained robust through the late nineteenth century and even into the twentieth.[98] But many promising side-arms eventually turned into land. Other once rich sources of fish like shallow pools and unregulated tributary streams (such as the Herrenbach near Russheim) were hit as hard as anywhere, the value of their fishing leases collapsing to less than a tenth of their former value in the space of two decades.[99] Fisher families hung on as long as they could, to the 1860s, even the 1880s or beyond.[100] Then they, too, turned to the land, becoming small peasants or labourers. Others emigrated or found employment in the work of river correction itself, in occupations that were linked to it, like quarrying, or in industries like sugar refining that grew out of the new uses to which the Rhine floodplain was being put.

There were many long-term reasons for the decline in Rhine fishing, not all of which can be laid at Tulla's door. Pollution of the river by industrial effluents was one, a problem already attracting some attention in the 1840s. The growth of steamship traffic and the later dredging of a deep channel had a major impact on fish populations. And it was the twentieth-century building of dams connected with hydro-electric plants like Kembs that – fish-ladders notwithstanding – finally stopped migratory fish from swimming upstream. These were all stages in the cumulative degradation of an increasingly canalized river, which continued until the full extent of the damage was registered in the 1970s.[101] These changes were, at most, only indirectly linked to Tulla's original scheme. Yet his correction, the 'first and for fishing most consequential' of all the changes to the natural character of the river, certainly had a direct impact on fish stocks.[102] The effects began with the disturbances produced by the construction work itself. Then the faster flow and reduced water-surface of the river destroyed resting places and shelters, especially the shallows and gravel banks that made the best breeding grounds.[103] These changes had an especially damaging effect on migratory fish. As the Rhine was remade, salmon, sturgeon, shad and lamprey declined, then disappeared. The riparian states signed a series of treaties to protect the salmon, in 1840, 1869 and 1885. These agreements were a touchstone of contemporary concern, but they proved unable to reverse the trend. The resort to fish hatcheries followed a similar time-line and was no more successful when it came to migratory breeds. The first salmon farm on the Upper Rhine began operating in Alsace in 1850; others followed in Baden twenty years later. At best they delayed the impact of change. From the end of the nineteenth century the salmon catch on the Upper Rhine, and on other parts of the river and its major tributaries, collapsed sharply and inexorably. The river became the domain of a small number of tough, highly adaptable species – 'universalists'. Three members of the carp family (the roach, bleak and bream) came to make up three-quarters of all the fish in the Rhine; the zander (or pikeperch) and the eel also prospered in the changed conditions.[104]

The zander and the eel: both tell us something about what was happening to the river. The zander, like the North American rainbow trout, was introduced into the Rhine as a substitute for the disappearing migratory fish. Unlike the millions of salmon eggs that produced such a slim return, this was an experiment that worked; but its success marked the limits of what the newly engineered stream would bear.[105] The eel was significant in two ways. In part it thrived, like the zander, because it was tolerant of adverse new conditions. It was also successful because its life-cycle was exactly the reverse of the salmon's or sturgeon's. Eels breed in salt water, in the Atlantic Sargasso Sea between Bermuda and the West Indies, then the elvers drift with the Gulf Stream to the coast of Europe and run up rivers like the Rhine, where they live for eight to ten years before returning to the Atlantic to breed and die.[106] Their breeding grounds were not, therefore, disturbed by the Tulla correction and the measures that followed. As salmon fishing collapsed, the river eel became the new, high-value catch of Rhine fishermen in the twentieth century. Eel fishing spread from the Rhine delta and established itself on the Upper Rhine in the 1920s, first on the Baden side, then on the left bank, where an enterprising fisherman in Leimersheim started a fleet that had grown by 1938 to a dozen vessels.[107]

We happen to have a fictional account of this, Willi Gutting's *The Eel Fishermen*.[108] Gutting was a schoolteacher and regional writer who lived on the Upper Rhine, first in Hördt, then in Leimersheim itself, and the characters in the book are closely modelled on his neighbours. Gutting describes the annual cycle of the eel fishermen, working between

May and October to catch the adult eels running back to the sea and mending their nets during the winter. There are no longer any salmon, except for the young ones occasionally caught up in the nets of the eel-boats in spring. Wendelin Bäck still 'navigated the backwaters and ditches in his skiff, the master of the tench and pike, of the carp, barbel and whitefish', but he owes his living to Barbara, the commercial matri-arch of the village and widow of Rud Losche, founder of the eel-fishing fleet.[109] Gutting's book begins before the First World War and ends in 1940. What he describes (and his memoirs suggest that the account was largely accurate) is a riverbank community that has had to find a new way to live with, and from, a new Rhine.[110]

The Eel Fishermen includes a still more momentous episode of change, one that forces us to think about the long sweep of historical change on the Upper Rhine. Gutting's Leimersheim is a village divided between water and land, between the wetland margin along the river and the agricultural land behind it. We are told right at the beginning of the book about the marsh and woods, where the animals 'lived secretly behind the network of lianas and the yellow wall of rushes', and 'the great water fowl were lost in the solitariness of the reed-bound ponds and the softly drifting waterways'.[111] This waterland is the home of the duck hunter Hanns Bitterfuchs, in many ways the moral centre of the book, and the author returns again and again to describe the 'thick confusion of reeds and rushes', the waterlogged willows and alders, the 'jumble of roots, the miniature primeval forest'.[112] It sounds like the Oderbruch before it was drained. And this haunt of cranes and herons suffers the same fate, sacrificed to the needs of cultivation. The agent of change is Rud Losche, creator of the eel-fishing fleet, a man whose family has lived from the Rhine for generations, who, nonetheless, now throws his energy (and ultimately his life) into a plan to tame the river through a system of drainage ditches and pumps. The lowland near the river would become proper agricultural land and in place of the marsh 'the fruits of the earth would ripen happily'. Rud, looking at his handi-work, reflects: 'It was good to feel a ship under one's feet, to sail off with a fleet into the fresh summer. It was better to reclaim land, far-sightedly and with superior plans to snatch fruitful earth away from the great enemy'. And this becomes village lore, so that Rud's son Heiner hears how his father was a magician or sorcerer who 'banished water from all the land and directed it back to its place behind the dike, and now the peasants all around had dry fields and sweet meadows'.[113]

Rud Losche's reclamation project is precisely dated in the novel: 1931. So what did it have to do with Tulla, whose own project was completed more than half a century earlier? The answer is that Tulla was the first to put the river 'in its place', creating an expectation of security among those who lived and raised crops behind the dike.[114] 'Everybody must be in favour of progress', thinks Adam Hauck, Barbara Losche's father, writing about the drainage project in his journal.[115] By 1931 Tulla's legacy meant that progress had long been defined in one way only, as maximum safety from the river. It was not only a peasant like Adam Hauck who saw things this way; so did the duck hunter Bitterfuchs, who 'applauded like a madman' a scheme that would threaten his way of life.[116]

It remains the case, however, that water fowl still flew over Bitterfuchs's marshy haunts in 1931. Similar idylls were depicted in the same period by other Upper Rhine writers, like the poet-painter Carl Philipp Spitzer from Speyer, and by the landscape artists who turned the village of Wörth near Leimersheim into a fashionable bucolic retreat, the Worpswede of the south-west. No doubt there was a political dimension here. Celebrating an 'authentic' German Rhine landscape during a period of French post-war occupation that lasted until 1930 was likely to prompt idealization. But that is certainly not the whole story. There remains a question about when exactly the pre-Tulla Rhine became the abject canal, the symbol of 'outdoor geometry' deplored by ecologists and conservationists in recent decades.[117] Pursuing this subject is like chasing a view that is always just over the horizon. When a group of conservationists and other Rhine experts gathered in Speyer in 1977, some of the older ones looked back fondly to the river of their youth in the 1930s and 1940s.[118] When the playwright Carl Zuckmayer wrote his memoirs in 1966, he remembered the Old Rhine of his childhood, in the early years of the twentieth century. The main channel had been dredged, 'but the winding old bed of the river [wa]s still there, creeping through a jungle of willows and alders, rotting poplar trunks and vigorously sprouting second growth. Here was an unexplored, almost impenetrable web of brooks, branches, stagnant inlets, swampy patches, standing pools and stony tributaries'.[119] Go back to the years around 1900, however, and you find the great Upper Rhine naturalist Robert Lauterborn deploring the losses of flora and fauna on his beloved river. And Lauterborn's nineteenth-century predecessors were already telling a story about a world that had been lost.[120] It sounds like a classic

Golden Age myth: the river was always more pristine and diverse, less geometrical and denatured, in the previous generation. Yet this is one of those cases where everyone was right. From the time of Tulla's first cuts at least through the 1970s, when the alarm bells became too loud to ignore, the taming of the Rhine was accompanied by a cumulative ecological degradation. Like the changing fish population of the river, this larger loss of biodiversity began with Tulla and became progressively more severe.

The big picture is clear enough. Over a period of a century and a half, some 85 per cent of the Upper Rhine floodplain was lost. The Tulla project alone turned over more than 25,000 acres to new human uses. A broad wetland corridor was reduced to a narrow belt usually no more than 150 yards wide. With the lost natural floodplain went most of the extensive Auenwald, or riparian forest of oak, elm, alder, willow, along with the characteristic vegetation of wild fruit trees and dense bushes, marshes and water-meadows. Walk in what remains of this Auenwald today, by Leimersheim or Hördt, and it still has the power to enchant; but it is only a shadow of what it once was, a strip of wetland wedged between the agricultural activity of the plain and the constant traffic of the river. As seasonally flooded areas disappeared, as zones where the water flowed at different speeds became fewer, so the self-cleansing capacity of the river was damaged. What these changes also meant, of course, was a radical reduction and fragmentation of habitat, with consequent losses of species-diversity. Many species disappeared or were relegated to a precarious, marginal existence.[121]

The biologist Ragnar Kinzelbach has argued that the fauna of the Upper Rhine 'changed more fundamentally' in the 150 years after Tulla than in the previous 10,000 years.[122] The reduced number of species and the threats to many more can be registered all the way up the food chain from insects to amphibians to birds to mammals. So can the arrival of invasive species that moved into a damaged ecosystem, from the zebra mussels that have colonized the river-bottom to the muskrats that have taken over the niches once occupied by native mammals.[123] How much does all this have to do with Tulla? The original correction of the Rhine is only the first of eight reasons that Kinzelbach gives to explain the present dismal state of affairs. Some, like the warming of the river when its water was used for cooling by fossil fuel and nuclear power plants, are distinctly twentieth-century. (Tulla's changes had the opposite effect, making the water cooler and richer in oxygen, although this of course also constituted a disturbance to many species.) There are many examples where the loss or endangerment of species had other, usually later causes, whether the falling numbers of mayfly and caddisfly, which depended on clean water (the sharp drop came after 1900), or the final demise of the otter, which disappeared on the Upper Rhine in the interwar years as a combined result of habitat destruction, pollution and human predation. But it is often hard to make a clean separation between causes. Pollution included the run-off from agricultural fertilizer, a by-product of that 'blooming garden' Tulla made possible. Human predation and the loss of bird or animal habitat often went together, as human settlements steadily encroached on the former floodplain, and it is their combined effect that explains the threat to water fowl (like herons and duck) and the fact that after the middle of the nineteenth century the beaver could be found on the Upper Rhine only in museums. In the case of insects, frogs and many other bird species, the Tulla-related disappearance of riverbank wetlands was decisive.[124]

The changing flora of the Upper Rhine are better recorded, the evidence of botanists' notebooks supplemented by the information available from maps and herbaria. The broad story is once again one of loss and greater uniformity, although questions of timing and causation are just as hard to unscramble. Everyone agrees that there was a long-term decline in the old-growth forests and native vegetation characteristic of the former riparian wetlands and meadows: oak, alder, willow, many varieties of vine, bushes, flowers, herbs and mosses. In the case of some especially water-sensitive plants, it is clear that post-Tulla change – eutrophication, pollution – was primarily responsible for threatened species. But for those species that depended on riverside gravel banks, periodically flooded sites or one-time water-meadows now turned over to arable, the nineteenth-century correction was already a cause of major habitat disruption. Occasionally we catch sight of a species actually on the verge of disappearing. In his *Flora of the Palatinate* in 1846, F. W. Schulz noted that the marsh gladiolus was still ubiquitous; by 1863 it was 'once widely found', and he thought it wise to record specific locations.[125] By the middle of the century, Schulz was already deploring the larger loss of 'reedy areas', what we would today call wetlands.[126] Once again, though, if Tulla's impact was damaging, it was less devastating than the impact of his successors, even if they were merely following the logic of what he had begun. Georg Philippi, noting a variety of species like willows and bullrushes that declined because of the correction, is careful to point out that the decline was sharper after 1900, and progressively so. In Philippi's view, 'the Tulla correction reduced the Aue and in part reconfigured it, but it retained the Aue. The more recent Rhine development has severed the Rhine from its Aue and the surrounding areas, as a result of which the Aue has been largely destroyed'.[127] Later changes had been incomparably more damaging than Tulla's handiwork. Not only that: the slower pace and relatively less intensive human intrusion of the nineteenth-century correction meant that plants had time to find alternative habitats – and more alternative habitats to find. Both time and space would later be in much shorter supply.

The environmental effects of the Upper Rhine correction were different in the former meander zone to the north and the former furcation zone to the south. The basis of Tulla's approach had been to reduce flooding by speeding up the flow of the river and thereby lowering its surface. This is what happened; but it happened unevenly and with unanticipated consequences. In the southern zone between Basel and Karlsruhe the river scoured its bed more deeply, often quite soon after the correction work had been done, and to a degree that was as damaging as it was unexpected. The Rhine fell by over 16 feet (5 m.) at Neuenburg, by 23 feet (7 m.) at Rheinweiler, the height of a two-storey house.[128] Neuenburg had been repeatedly flooded in the eighteenth century. Now it faced the opposite problem: not too much water, but too little. As the water table fell, the roots of trees and plants were starved of moisture. In the Breisach, wetland was steadily degraded into dry grassland dominated by buckthorn, briar and bramble.[129] This contrasted starkly with the situation to the north. In the meander zone many former wetlands, backwaters cut off from the river, lost their white willows, alders and creeping vines but developed into habitats containing abundant reeds and aquatic plant life – an unintended consequence of Tulla's handiwork, the paradox is that they became botanically richer than the surviving patches of Auenwald still subject to flooding by a polluted main stream.[130] In the southern Upper Rhine the backwaters dried up and the water lilies disappeared. Here the correction produced something that in places resembles a steppe landscape. It was one of the most destructive effects of Tulla's 'time-bomb'.[131]

The dramatic lowering of the water table in the south was not fore-

seen. Another potential consequence of the Tulla correction was anticipated, indeed was forcibly presented by Tulla's opponents as a reason
not to proceed with his project. That was the danger of serious flooding
downstream, on the Middle and Lower Rhine, as a result of the
straighter, faster river. The high waters of the main river and of its
tributaries arrived naturally at staggered intervals, not all together.
Increasing the velocity of the Rhine threatened to disrupt that pattern,
making the risk of serious inundations downstream much greater. It
was a 'risky plan' that threatened to unleash 'catastrophes'. That, at
any rate, was what Tulla's contemporary critic Fritz André argued in
his 1828 pamphlet, *Observations on the Rectification of the Upper
Rhine and a Depiction of the Dreadful Consequences of this Undertaking for Inhabitants of the Middle and Lower Rhine.*[132] His views
were echoed in more temperate language by the Dutch hydraulic engineer Freiherr van der Wijck, who lived in Mannheim. The same fear
drove early opposition to Tulla's corrections from the Netherlands and
Prussia. It was informed in the case of the Prussian engineer Johann
Eytelwein by first-hand experience of the flood problems caused by
shortening the Oder.[133] There was even an apparent precedent, in microcosm, on the Upper Rhine. The correction of the Kinzig, a Rhine tributary, was begun by Tulla in 1814; its waters then reached the main
river more quickly, and flooding followed on the Rhine at Kehl in
1816.[134]

The critics did not win the argument at the time, but history seems
on the face of it to have vindicated them. Consider the devastating
floods of 1882–3, or those that followed a century later in 1983, 1988,
1993 and 1994. No one now doubts that the risk to downstream cities
like Koblenz, Bonn and Cologne has increased substantially. Those cities
are located right on the river bank because the Middle and Lower Rhine
were historically much less prone to flooding than the Upper Rhine.
Now that location makes them all the more vulnerable. But if the
long-term outcome is plain enough, the chain of causation is once again
complex. After the inundations of the early 1880s the engineers
exonerated Tulla from responsibility, blaming freak meteorological
conditions. This was the common sense of the time, an instinct to deny
any negative effects of earlier engineering measures that was heightened in the case of one leading defender – Max Honsell – by the fact
that he had himself worked on the later cuts of the Upper Rhine correction and saw himself as Tulla's heir.[135] While this insouciance is open

to criticism, the parliamentary enquiry of 1889 into the floods made a more interesting and valid point. It gave Tulla's corrections a clean bill of health because he had not completely cut off the old side-arms of the Rhine from the main river, and so had left areas in which Upper Rhine floodwaters could be retained. But precisely that was about to change. By the late twentieth century those side-arms had been completely closed off, and the modern engineering of the Rhine with navigation in mind had further increased its velocity. In the 1940s the high waters of the Rhine took 65 hours to pass from Basel to Maxau, near Karlsruhe, much faster than in the pre-Tulla era; but forty years later that interval had been more than halved, to just thirty hours. That hugely increased the likelihood that the high waters of the Rhine and its tributaries – Rench, Kinzig, Murg, Ill, Moder, Sauer, Neckar – would converge catastrophically on the Middle and Lower Rhine.[136]

Holding Tulla responsible for what was done a century and more after his death is like blaming Friedrich Nietzsche for what National Socialists later did in his name. But in the one case, as in the other, it is fair to identify responsibility at a certain level – in changing mental horizons, making certain things thinkable that had not been thinkable before. Two main issues stand out here. Tulla had always argued that the side-arms of the old Rhine should not be completely cut off. So why did his successors do so, and build the continuous system of dikes that definitively straitjacketed the river? Because Tulla had promised security for dwellers on the Upper Rhine floodplain; the measures taken in succeeding generations were designed to fulfil that promise still more comprehensively, attempting to purchase greater security, but at the cost of greater insecurity for downstream communities. We can see this happening, stage by stage, through the nineteenth century. The archival record reveals a kind of hydrological two-step being danced, decade by decade. One file will record 'flood damage in the year 1844', another 'the flood of 1851'. The result? Proposals for 'extending and strengthening the Rhine embankment'. Then comes another bulky folder on 'the floods and damage in the year 1876', prompting further plans to 'extend and strengthen' the river defences. The same cycle repeated itself in 1877, floods followed by proposals two years later for the 'extension and strengthening of the Rhine embankment in the districts of Daxlanden, Knielingen and Neuburgweier'. This time new floods arrived even as the work was being done. The response was exactly the same as it had been on each previous occasion. And so the cycle went on, the fruitless search for definitive security that was successful only to the extent that it pushed the problem downstream.[137] The most recent efforts to reopen some areas of the floodplain as water retention basins is, as Egon Kunz put it, 'a step into the past'.[138] These attempts to appease the 'river spirits awakened by Tulla's correction' (to quote Kunz again) mark a recognition that negative consequences were at least implicit in the original project.[139]

A similar logic, call it the logic of unintended consequences, was at work when it came to the post-Tulla projects that turned the Rhine into a shipping canal. That had not been Tulla's intention. It is true that he had himself drawn up plans as early as 1799 for a steam-powered ship (the plan has been lost, only a description survives), but navigation was never his main concern.[140] The first steamship reached the Upper Rhine only in 1831, three years after his death. The port installations and factories that soon dotted the banks of the river had no place at all in his visions. Yet the steamships, ports and factories came, and they came because of the shift that Tulla brought about in attitudes towards the once wild stream. But we can pull the chain of causation rather tighter than that. Some of the most serious side-effects of the original correction actually made the river less amenable to shipping. Where the Rhine unexpectedly scoured its bed in the former furcation zone, in some places like Istein right down to the rock, it became necessary to take further steps to neutralize this outcome. And the debris washed downstream by the scouring had different but equally undesirable effects on the main channel. The dredging and canalizing that took place years after Tulla's death was therefore undertaken to 'correct' the effects of his correction.[141] If Rud Losche in Leimersheim was regarded in village lore as a *Zauberer*, a sorcerer, Tulla was the original sorcerer along the whole length of the Upper Rhine.[142] Or perhaps, thinking of Goethe's ballad *Der Zauberlehrling*, we should regard him more as a sorcerer's apprentice.

GOLDEN AGE

The Jade Bay

In August 1852 two Prussian negotiators travelled to the Grand Duchy of Oldenburg in north-west Germany. They were an odd couple: Samuel Gottfried Kerst, 'energetic but crude', and the more diplomatically adroit Dr Ernst Gaebler.[1] A former Prussian artillery officer, Kerst had spent six years of his youth in Brazil as a captain of engineers, serving on a Brazilian battleship in the war against Argentina that broke out in 1825. Returning to Germany, he taught at a technical college in Danzig before being elected as a liberal to the Frankfurt National Assembly that came into being after the 1848 revolution. In contrast to Kerst, Gaebler was a more conventional Prussian bureaucrat, a senior official in the Berlin Police Prasidium under Chief of Police Carl von Hinckeldey, a powerful figure notorious for his spy-rings.[2] The only unexpected thing about Gaebler was his favoured position as a personal confidant of Otto von Manteuffel. Prussian Prime Minister from 1850–8, Manteuffel was a conservative realist. His political outlook partly foreshadowed the one espoused in the following decade by a much more famous conservative realist, Otto von Bismarck. Manteuffel was happy to expand police powers against liberal opponents; but he was also scornful of Prussian reactionaries who wanted to pretend that the 1848 revolution had never happened, and was prepared to use domestic political surveillance against right as well as left. He dominated Prussian politics in the uneasy years after the upheaval of 1848.

What Kerst and Gaebler had in common was a passion for German naval power. Kerst had been general secretary of the German naval ministry established by the Frankfurt parliament, which brought him into close contact with fellow enthusiasts who included Prince Adalbert of Prussia, first cousin of the king. The winding-up of the modest fleet after the revolution did not dampen his zeal. He entered Prussian service and continued to press the cause in memoranda and private conversations.[3] Gaebler was doing exactly the same, working directly on Manteuffel.[4] It was this shared commitment that made Kerst and Gaebler ideal for their mission in 1852. The ostensible reason for their journey was to buy ships for Prussia from the former German navy, then being auctioned off. Rumours were also spread that they were in Oldenburg to discuss emigration issues. Both were plausible cover stories. But their real objective was to negotiate Prussian purchase of a parcel of land to serve as a North Sea harbour for the new Prussian fleet.[5]

Prussia had become a great European power over the previous two hundred years through its military prowess on land. The trading companies established by the Great Elector in the seventeenth century did not alter that; nor did Prussia's brief possession of East Friesland, a North Sea foothold, during the reign of Frederick the Great. While Britain and France fought the Seven Years War in North America and India, Frederick the Great's Prussia fought a war on the European Continent. And the same had been true when Britain and Prussia fought together to topple the dominance of Napoleonic France. Prussia produced generals, not admirals. Earth remained the Hohenzollerns' element, not salt water. As Frederick himself said: 'Land animals like us are not accustomed to live among whales, dolphins, turbot and codfish'.[6]

Twice in the early decades of the nineteenth century there were tentative initiatives to establish a Prussian navy; twice they came to nothing. As one critic put it, Prussia was a 'giant on the Continent' but 'a dwarf on the sea'.[7] That began to change with the revolution of 1848–9. When conflict arose with Denmark over the disputed duchy of Schleswig it highlighted German naval impotence against even a minor European power. Germany was Neptune without a trident.[8] Liberal-nationalist enthusiasm for the German navy in 1848 suggested a way in which Prussia could win hearts and minds while furthering its own interests. This is what Wilhelm I, who ruled as regent in Prussia after 1858 and as king from 1861–88, would call 'making moral conquests', and the British ambassador in Berlin described more cynically as 'flatter[ing] popular passion'.[9] Buying ships from the defunct German fleet signalled a new Prussian naval ambition. But its own coastline lay exclusively along the Baltic, where it could be easily blockaded, not the North Sea.

The Jade Bay in Oldenburg offered a solution to that problem. Already proposed by Oldenburg in 1848 as an ideal site for the future German navy, a view strongly backed by Kerst and Prince Adalbert, the Jade Bay was a sheltered North Sea harbour that was largely ice-free and had a deepwater channel. The Jade Bay also had geographical advantages over other sites on the North Sea coast. It was further away from Denmark and the British island of Heligoland than the Elbe and Weser estuaries to the east, further away from the Netherlands than Emden to the west. A further point in favour, certainly in the eyes of Prince Adalbert, was that there were no towns nearby to threaten naval discipline, just the two small villages of Heppens and Neuende – although the potential isolation and lack of creature comforts seems to have prejudiced Admiral Brommy and other naval officers against the Jade Bay in 1848–9, a foretaste of things to come. Best of all from the Prussian point of view, Oldenburg had responded to discreet diplomatic soundings by making it known that it would welcome an agreement.[10]

Kerst arrived in Oldenburg on 10 August, Gaebler four days later. Negotiations were carried out in conditions of great secrecy to prevent word reaching the suspicious neighbouring power of Hanover. Manteuffel and Prince Adalbert were the only members of the Prussian cabinet who knew about the talks. The basis of an agreement was reached by Kerst, Gaebler and their negotiating partner in Oldenburg, Theodor Erdmann, by the beginning of September. Disagreement on the detailed terms and Manteuffel's nervousness about political opposition at home then delayed things, to the extreme frustration of Kerst and Gaebler. A final text was agreed in July 1853 ('this is the happiest day of my life' said Gaebler, when he signed on behalf of Prussia).[11] There were strong opponents in the Prussian cabinet – finance minister Bodelschwingh offered his resignation, nervous of the costs and piqued that he had been kept in the dark – but the agreement was approved by governments and parliaments in both states and made public in January 1854. Hanover protested this 'lightning bolt out of a clear blue sky', but found no support in Germany or abroad.[12] Under the terms of the treaty Prussia received sovereignty of a parcel of 380 acres on the west side of the Jade Bay, plus a tiny plot on the opposite side designated for a battery. Oldenburg received, among other considerations, 500,000 Taler.[13]

In late November 1854 Prince Adalbert went to Oldenburg, where he received the title deeds from the Grand Duke. He travelled on to the site of the future naval base to join senior Prussian and Oldenburg officials, completing the last leg of the journey by farmer's cart in a blinding snowstorm. A tent had been set up on the marshes and the formal transfer of sovereignty took place inside it. The Oldenburg flag was lowered, the Prussian flag raised, and a 21-gun salute was sounded by three Prussian ships anchored in the bay. The ceremonies completed, the party ate a 'simple luncheon' with champagne in the Eilers inn at Heppens.[14]

The peace-time buying and selling of territory among German states remained commonplace in the nineteenth century, as it had been in earlier eras. Add the vagaries of war and peacemaking and there were plenty of lands across the former Holy Roman Empire that had been bought, sold or exchanged half a dozen times. So it was with the small corner of the Oldenburg-East Friesland peninsula now acquired by Prussia. Since the late sixteenth century the domain of Jever had belonged to Oldenburg, Anhalt-Zerbst, Russia, the Netherlands, France, Russia again, then Oldenburg again.[15] If the territorial carousel was familiar enough, the unusual feature in this case was that just a few centuries earlier the bay itself, the whole point of the exercise, had not existed.

The Jade Bay. The name had nothing to do with the pale green mineral used in jewellery. It came from the Frisian (and English) word 'gat', meaning an opening between sandbanks, a channel or strait.[16] And that perfectly described the Jade Bay, an inlet joined to the sea by a narrow channel, resembling a bottle or vase with a long neck. When and how was it created? The southern coastline of the North Sea has never been fixed. Measured over the very long term, in millennia, it has seen a series of major advances and retreats by the sea, the most spectacular of which, the rising sea levels of the Atlantic Transgression between 6000 and 3000 BC, pushed the coastline much further to the south, eventually swallowing up the Dogger Bank and creating the English Channel.[17] In the very short term, from one tide to another, the coast is subject to constant small-scale shifts, as the sea erodes the land at one point, depositing sand and mud at another. In between those two scales, over the span of decades and centuries in which human history is usually measured, the sea has shaped and reshaped the contours of the coastline just as it made and unmade offshore islands. Change on this scale was typically the work of a major flood, or series of floods. That was what created the Jade Bay, as it did the similar indentations of the Dollart and the Zuider Zee further west (see Map 4).

Where the Jade Bay is now, was once land. Its earliest inhabitants resembled others all along the coast. They built knolls (*Wurten* or *Warfen*) as strongholds against the sea, and for perhaps a thousand years that provided their protection until systematic diking began in the eleventh century.[18] This part of East Friesland, known in the medieval period as Rüstringen, was not only land, but land that for centuries felt the imprint of European history: it was subjugated by the Carolingian empire, plundered by the Vikings, coveted by Henry the Lion, organized into parishes by the archbishops of Bremen.[19] Before it disappeared the floor of the later bay contained ploughed fields, pastures, market towns and villages whose parish churches showed every sign of wealth.[20] Then came the St Julian's flood of 1164, which cut a channel inland that was too deep to re-dike. The incursion was extended by the St Clement's flood in 1334, the St Marcellus flood in 1362 and finally by the St Anthony's flood in 1511.[21] Each time the sea scoured the interior of the new bay more settlements went under, or fields and villages were turned into islands that slowly disappeared. Where the drowned land lay in shallow water it might reappear at low tide. The Oberahneschen fields, a mudbank on which the fourteenth-century furrow marks were still visible, continued to provide reminders of themselves into the twentieth century.[22] In the Prussian years they were the scene of duck shoots when the tide was out.

The Oberahneschen fields were the remnants of a once large and important parish, Aldessen. Its fate over the centuries illustrated something else about the actions of the sea: that it both gave and took away. Aldessen benefited when the sea first cut its channel into the interior. In 1300 its market was flourishing. But further floods gnawed away at the land until nothing but a series of islands was left behind after the inundation of 1511.[23] What happened then was just one of many instances of how, after a certain point, people accepted what seemed to be inevitable and tried to salvage what they could, thereby hastening the disappearance of parishes like Aldessen. Where there was no hope of rebuilding the dikes around a town or village whose position had become hopeless, it was *ausgedeicht*, or 'diked out', left beyond the newly aligned protective wall. The remaining buildings were cannibalized

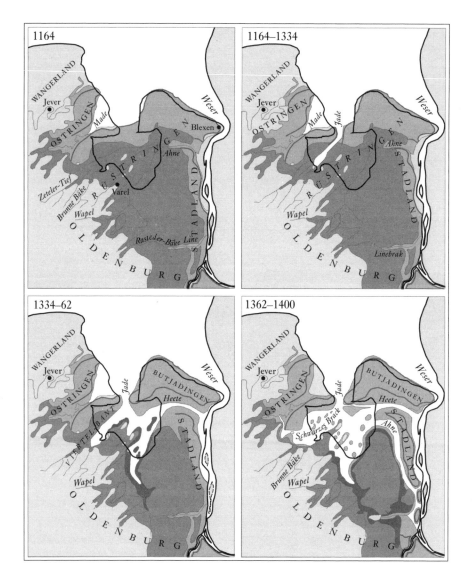

MAP 4 *The formation of the Jade Bay.*

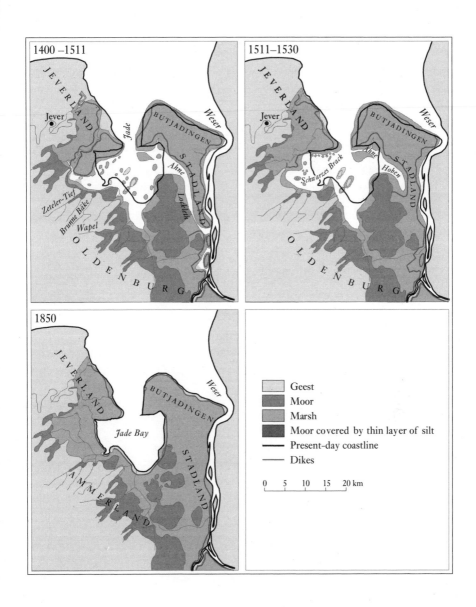

to provide materials for the new dike; church treasures were sold to defray the costs. There was something undeniably dramatic about this, although the drama was often painfully protracted. Villages sometimes disappeared during one terrible day or night; more often the process was slow and inexorable. A century ago, one of the earliest historians to write seriously about the hydrology of the Jade Bay and its lost settlements observed that the great signature floods that featured in the chronicles were 'rhetorically effective headings'.[24] Georg Sello was right. Even when decisive changes were set in motion by major floods they were likely to work themselves out afterwards, in the years when human energy had been so sapped by disaster that it was no longer equal to the task of repairing dikes and reclaiming what had been lost.

In one way or another, however, the late medieval centuries saw the formation of a Jade Bay roughly approximating to the one the Prussians looked out over in the 1850s. And beneath its surface, wherever they looked, lay lost villages like the drowned villages of the Upper Rhine. In the deepwater channel so attractive to the navy lay Humens. South-west of it, opposite what would become the entrance to the new harbour, lay Dauens. Across the bay, below the site chosen for the battery, were the remains of the villages that had made up the parish of Aldessen.[25] Like the drowned villages of the Rhine, and like the celebrated towns that disappeared under the North Sea at other points along the coast (Rungholt, Vineta), the communities lost to the Jade Bay left behind a rich stock of legends.[26] One of the bells from the parish church of Bant, destroyed in the 1511 flood, was believed to sound warnings when a new catastrophe threatened. It admonished villagers not to neglect the work of diking. That was the message of many legends: floods were a moral judgement, retribution upon communities that had become too wealthy or careless to maintain their guard against the sea. Another set of legends was associated with the deep holes, or *Kolke*, created by floods, which were believed to demand regular human sacrifices. In other stories the dike itself required an animal or human victim to appease the angry waters. One told of a deaf and dumb child sold by his mother and sacrificed to save the dike at Steinhausersiel. The child recovered his voice to cry out 'mother's heart is harder than stone'.[27] The archaeological evidence of human and canine skeletons recovered from old dikes might suggest that the legends had a basis in fact, but it is hard to be sure: the bloated bodies recovered after major floods had to be buried somewhere and the base of an unbreached dike was often the only dry land around.[28]

Common to all the legends was a powerful sense of unending human struggle against the dangerous, malicious sea. Like the German rivers that 'rattled their chains', the North Sea was anthropomorphized as the enemy: 'Rasmus', 'Shiny Hans'. Maintaining the dikes became the defining condition of life, a material necessity infused with moral urgency. '*Wer will nicht deichen, der muss weichen*', ran the stern injunction – whoever is unwilling to dike must step aside.[29] The permanent struggle against the sea provides the background to *Der Schimmelreiter* (The Rider on a White Horse), Theodor Storm's great novella of 1888, which relates the heroic efforts of Haike Hauen to preserve a dike in the face of selfishness and indifference, efforts which eventually cost him his life.[30] (There are echoes of Haike Hauen in Willi Gutting's Leimersheim hero, Rud Losche, who came to a similar end.) More than a trace of the heroic tone, mixed with pride in the latest technology, has found its way into the modern literature on coastal defences and the need for vigilance against the threat of natural disaster from the sea.[31]

That floods have been disastrous requires little argument. Whether they were natural is a more complicated question. In many ways coastal flooding could hardly have been more elemental, a product of winds, tides and changing sea levels. There were meteorological reasons why, in one century after another, the most devastating 'storm floods' occurred during the months from November to February. It was the greater tidal range between low and high water that made the southern coast of the North Sea more vulnerable to flooding than the Baltic coast or the eastern North Sea coast.[32] And records show that sea levels have fluctuated over the centuries, threatening coastal communities, for reasons unconnected with human activity. The active element was the rising sea, not – as used to be thought – the 'sinking coast'.[33] But humans also made an unwitting contribution to the problems that faced them. The earliest knoll settlers accepted that regular floods would occur and took advantage of the muddy nutrients washed up on the coastal marshes around them. Their settlements were not unlike those in the Oder Marshes before they were reclaimed. Eventually summer dikes were built to extend the area of protected land that could be used for agriculture, but these were still not designed to repel winter storm floods. It was the conversion of summer dikes to permanent, year-round structures that changed the equation. From then on any coastal area that had not been diked could expect to receive more flood water, a logic that led to the joining of one dike to another until, by the thirteenth century, a 'golden ring' had been drawn around the Frisian marshes. Now the flood waters, instead of spreading out a few inches deep over the marshland behind the tidal mudflats, built up against the dikes and battered at them, giving rise to the familiar image of the angry, growling sea. The earthen dikes were vulnerable, especially in periods when epidemic or war impeded regular maintenance – as occurred in the fourteenth century, when the Black Death coincided with internecine political conflict in Rüstringen.[34] If the dikes collapsed and the sea broke through, water poured into the painstakingly drained polders. These were all the more at risk because the land shrank as it dried out. In the absence of new deposits of mud it often settled below sea level. Flood water, cutting a powerful channel through a breached dike, also went where it had not been for many centuries, further inland, up to the sandy geest and moorland. Where peat had been dug, which also caused the land to sink, moors were vulnerable for the same reason as polders.[35] That was the reason for the 'swimming moors' recorded by so many startled observers, which became detached and floated disconcertingly on the water, complete with trees and bushes.[36]

Human ingenuity drew a sharp line between water and land in what had once been an amphibious zone. As a result, every flood became a problem and a major flood was devastating. The pent-up power of the water behind the dikes, in conjunction with the shrunken polders behind them, meant that if the sea did break through it could quickly carve its way inland. It is no coincidence that the Zuider Zee, the Dollart and the Jade Bay were all formed in the first centuries of comprehensive diking.

The Jade Bay was never larger than in the years after the St Anthony's flood of 1511. What followed was part of a process we find all along the coast, from the Low Countries to Schleswig. Over a period of centuries the sea was rolled back and land reclaimed. Dike design and materials improved. As the human toll of war and disease diminished, routine repairs and maintenance became more effective.[37] The political environment also changed. Rising territorial states were ambitious to claim new land, as the Hohenzollerns did on such a grand scale in the swamps of Brandenburg and points east. All of these elements were at work in the Jade Bay, which was slowly reduced in size and assumed the rounded, symmetrical contours it had by the nineteenth century. Dikes were built across the deep, jagged incursions made by earlier floods and the land was gradually drained, which is what happened to the Black Water on the western side of the bay close to the later site of Wilhelmshaven.[38] Reclamation had its ups and downs. If territorial ambitions prompted new projects, disputes between rulers disrupted them. The long lawsuit between the counts of Oldenburg and East Friesland over the diking of the Black Water is just one example.[39] Peasants, dike organizations and territorial princes argued over costs and responsibilities as the pace of reclamation quickened in the seventeenth century. ('There is always conflict over dikes among the marsh people', wrote Peter Saxby in 1637.[40]) Construction was even interrupted by a form of early industrial action unique to the northern coast, known as *Lawai*, wildcat strikes by the new breed of piece-rate workers drafted in for large or urgent projects.[41] The most urgent arose after new floods. These left their usual trail of broken dikes, dead bodies, drowned animals, ruined land and hopelessness; they also intensified every existing social conflict by adding mutual recrimination to material distress.[42]

Floods continued to add their counterpoint to the process of land reclamation from the sixteenth century into the nineteenth. Four major ones stand out. The All Saints' Day flood of 1570 was felt right along the coast from Calais to Scandinavia, taking thousands of lives. The parishes of Heppens and Neuende, where the Prussian naval base would be built, counted 147 dead.[43] Another large flood followed in 1634, although the coast around the Jade Bay was more directly affected by the St Peter's flood seventeen years later.[44] Both paled beside the Christmas flood of 1717, which remains one of the most destructive storm floods ever recorded on the North Sea coast. When the waters finally retreated fourteen days later the marshes were strewn with human and animal cadavers. Human bodies were found still tied together, where families had tried to prevent themselves from being separated in the floodwaters. Bodies had been washed into ditches or lay piled up wherever the water had deposited them, thirty at the foot of one bridge. Some had been gnawed by dogs or other animals. Iffe Diercks ensured that his wife avoided these indignities. The Dierckses escaped the flood by clambering into an apple tree, but Frau Diercks died of cold within a few hours. Her husband loosened her hair and used it to tie her body to the tree, so that she could later have a proper burial. Diercks himself, rescued after three days, survived with the loss of all his toes to frost-bite.[45] The Christmas flood took some 9000 lives in all, numbers that can be partly explained by the greater sense of security that had taken hold behind the higher dikes. There were parishes in the Jeverland and Butjadingen, on either side of the Jade Bay, where 80 per cent of the population perished. Over 400 died in Heppens and Neuende, 375 in neighbouring Kniphausen. The catastrophe had long-term effects on the demography of the entire region. The toll in domesticated animals was upward of 60,000.[46] The 'night of terror and dread' at Christmas 1717 became the yardstick for every modern flood.

Measured by high water levels, although not by casualties, it was exceeded by the February flood in 1825 that took the lives of nearly 800 people and 45,000 animals. Once again it caught the population by surprise. After a wet and blustery late autumn it had been an uneventful winter until a storm began to beat at the coast on 3 February. Just as in 1717 the flood trapped people in their beds, as it began around midnight. Church bells tolled through the night of 3 February as the sea rushed through holes in the dikes, sending people onto the highest roofs, as many as fifty huddled together on some. The retreating waters revealed what one eye-witness described as 'a complete desert in the fruitful green fields', a wasteland of sand and shingle as far as two hours' distance inland. Huge clumps of torn-off peat moor six feet high rose out of it like rocky outcrops in the desert.[47]

The ruinous losses and new costs caused by floods had an important social effect on the population of the coastal marshes. They culled the small, economically weaker peasantry, who lost their land and became agricultural labourers or emigrated. This led to the consolidation of a rich farming elite. The land on the western shore of the Jade Bay fell into the hands of wealthy family dynasties: the Irps, Harkens, Gerdes and Müller families in Heppens, the Andreae and Gummels families in Neuende. They were joined at the top of the social pyramid by merchants who had invested their profits in land, men from nearby towns like Mariensiel and Rüstersiel, which had grown up around the great sluice gates that drained the marshes and moors while denying access to the sea, then developed as ports and trading centres.[48]

These were the owners of the land that fell under Prussian sovereignty in 1853. A group photograph of the principal landowners taken in 1855 shows men in tailcoats who look very secure in their prosperity – who look, in fact, remarkably like the wealthy farmers of the

Oder marshes in the middle of the nineteenth century.[49] They had good reason to look satisfied in 1855, for they had just done very well out of the Prussian government. The Prussian admiralty used a local Olden-burg lawyer, Maximilian Heinrich Rüder (another liberal veteran of the Frankfurt parliament, like Kerst), to buy up the necessary land. The admiralty was prudent enough to have him begin his work in the winter of 1853–4, before the treaty was made public, in an effort to stifle speculation that would drive up the price. Rüder bought the first parcels of land as a straw man, in his own name. But it still cost as much to obtain title to the land as it did to purchase the sovereignty. Prussia committed a million Taler to the Jade Bay before a spade had been put into the ground.[50]

Neither the German parliamentarians of 1848, flushed with national enthusiasm, nor the Prussians in the 1850s were the first to think about using the Jade Bay as a harbour. Others had the same idea, going back to Count Mansfeld during the Thirty Years War. Christian V of Denmark, who was Duke of Oldenburg at the time, actually began to build a port in the south of the bay near Varel in 1681, but the tech-nical problems proved too great and Christiansburg was abandoned after twelve expensive years. Everything that had been built was torn down again. During the French and Napoleonic Wars the Jade Bay caught the eye of both sides in turn. The Russians surveyed the land around Heppens in 1795 but were intimidated by the construction costs. When France gained control of the area, some survey work was done at Eckwarden on the opposite side of the bay, while a reluctant work-force of 200 was mustered to begin building a battery at Heppens. Napoleon supposedly claimed that the Jade Bay had a 'great future', but nothing came of his plans either.[51] These episodes suggested a mixed message for the Prussian state in the 1850s. The good news was that they confirmed the Jade Bay as an ideal location; the bad news was that the technical and financial demands had scared everyone away. German naval enthusiasts liked to point to the enthusiasm shown by the great Napoleon, but even they accepted that harbour installations were 'abysses that swallow money', as the French had demonstrated by spending 56 years and twenty-eight million francs building one at Cherbourg.[52]

In September 1868, one year before the town of Wilhelmshaven was formally christened, a new local newspaper appeared. In its first edition the *Heppenser Nachrichten* published some verse. The poet, Franz

Poppe, began with a gloomy picture of the sea eating away at the land by the Jade Bay, but switched to a very different key:[53]

> And you, too, Heppens would have disappeared
> With your meadows and your pastureland,
> Demolished by the raging anger of the sea
> Had a hero not arisen, a saviour.
> A youthful giant burning with desire for deeds,
> Prussia stood tall within the German lands.
> One day our fleet will shelter here,
> So forward, and a harbour let us build.

This is very like Carl Heuer's tribute to the draining of the Oder Marshes, and there are parallels between the two projects undertaken a century apart. Wilhelmshaven was also an assertion of Hohenzollern will, a 'town on command'. And, like the 'conquest' of the Oderbruch, the making of the harbour and town beside the bay acquired a retrospective tinge of the heroic because it required such an arduous struggle against the elements. It was not so simple 'to conjure up a town out of moor and marsh'.[54]

The difficulties began even at the planning stage, when two celebrated harbour designers in Hamburg and London came up with proposals that the Prussian admiralty considered impractical (and, in Sir John Rendell's case, absurdly expensive as well). A home-grown plan was adopted instead. Chronic personnel problems then led to a false start. Within two years the first head of the local administration and two different directors of harbour construction had come and gone.[55] One reason why it was difficult to attract civil servants to the Jade Bay and keep them there was the utter isolation of the area and its well-deserved reputation for rain, wind and mud (it quickly acquired the nickname 'mudtown').[56] Even officers, who had no choice, regarded a posting there as a form of exile. Their wives were even less amused. Louise von Krohn, the wife of a naval officer, who arrived in 1859 to set up home in a damp and leaky farmhouse, later wrote her memoirs of the 'early hard times'.[57] She saw it as one of her tasks to console others who found themselves in the same position, like 'Grete', the young officer's wife informed by a white-faced spouse that she had to leave her elegant apartment on Berlin's Kurfürstendamm and move to the marshy, fever-ridden Jade Bay – a prospect 'so terrible that she could hardly grasp it'.[58] As far as its reputation was concerned, the Jade Bay might as well have been Hudson's Bay.

It was not just its reputation or the raw conditions that led directors of harbour construction Christiansen and Wallbaum to seek early transfers out. They faced problems they had never encountered before, problems that continued to bedevil their successor, Heinrich Göker. One was isolation. The future Wilhelmshaven was like 'an island cut off from the world'.[59] Letters took four or five days to reach Berlin. One of the first tasks was to build a road westwards and inland, to connect to the nearest main highway. Even then travelling times were painfully slow. Disagreements between Prussia and Oldenburg over the route and the sharing of costs delayed the building of a rail link. So, even more, did the deliberate obstructionism of Hanover. This was the kind of petty bickering between states – contemporaries called it *Kleinstaaterei* – so characteristic, still, of the years immediately before German unification. It was, in fact, precisely this kind of parochialism that strengthened liberal nationalism in these years – although it also eventually pulled many liberal nationalists towards Prussia, which was clearly the most dynamic German state and the one most likely to bring about some kind of German unification.

The rail link was established only in 1867. That was why, in the early days, most building materials and other provisions had to be shipped in. But that exposed the builders to problems on the seaward side. No sooner had the Prussians arrived than they encountered the New Year's storm of 1855, the second highest of the century after 1825, followed in short order by renewed flooding in February 1858 and January 1860. These seriously delayed the first stages of construction. Water swept away the pilings and weakened the new dike around the perimeter of the future harbour; it hampered construction of an unloading quay. Sometimes waves flooded the construction site, washing away materials. The most persistent and demoralizing difficulties involved the cofferdam that was supposed to protect the site of the future main harbour entrance. This was the perennial 'problem child' of local officials.[60] Constructed out of parallel pilings with earth in between them, it was eaten away by an infestation of ship's worm and collapsed in the 1860 storm. Work resumed behind a rebuilt protective barrier. Parts of this were also carried away by the current, forming a hazard to shipping. An admiralty official later referred grimly to the 'persistent struggle against the North Sea floods'.[61]

The deepwater channel, essential to the future harbour, caused even more concern. Other bays along the Dutch and Frisian coast had silted up naturally over time, as currents moved sand and mud from west to east. The flood of 1855 was especially untimely for the Prussian admiralty because it ravaged the offshore island of Wangerooge, sending islanders fleeing to the mainland and depositing the western end of the island into the North Sea, some of it landing in the Jade Bay. A second problem arose because the Grand Duchy of Oldenburg planned further land reclamation in the southern and eastern parts of the bay. This threatened to weaken the tidal current that flushed the bay and maintained the deepwater channel. As the difficulty of taking reliable soundings showed, the channel was far from stable.[62]

Early reverses, the slow pace of construction, a long-term threat of silting, steadily mounting costs: all ensured that the project had critics. This was different from the grumbling by some of Frederick the Great's officials about his colonization plans; it was more like the opposition that Johann Tulla had encountered in Baden's parliament, one of the most liberal and outspoken in all of Germany before 1848. In fact, Prussian criticism of the Jade Bay project as a 'bottomless' pit of expense was sharper than anything Tulla faced. For the period of construction coincided with a revival of liberal politics in Prussia that began in the late 1850s and culminated in the formation of the Progressive Party in 1861, the response to a major clash between king and parliament over a new military bill. This 'constitutional conflict', which led Wilhelm I to consider abdicating, was the event that brought Otto von Bismarck into power.

In this tense period the very future of the undertaking seemed to be at stake, as political and press critics were joined by sceptics in the administration.[63] Criticism persisted even through the years when the foundations of German unification were being laid by successful Prussian wars against Denmark and Austria. In 1864 a member of the Prussian parliament took up the question of silting. 'Nature', he argued, '[wa]s creating obstacles' in the Jade Bay that the local administration was powerless to deal with because it was hemmed in by the 1853 treaty. The treaty was in fact renegotiated the same year to expand the Prussian foothold, and the silting issue was addressed when Prussia took over responsibility for protecting Wangerooge and persuaded Oldenburg to stop reclamation work in the bay. The pace of work also picked up, especially after the 1864 war with Denmark. But opposition did not stop. In 1868 the temporary suspension of financial support led to huge lay-offs of construction workers.[64]

By then a great army of workers had been assembled. It passed the 1000 mark in 1861, reached 2000 in 1864 and stood at 2500 in August 1868 before the four-month lay-offs occurred. When work resumed the following year the figure grew to almost 5000, the highest it would ever reach. By 1869, when the final work was being done on the harbour facilities, half of the workers were skilled craftsmen.[65] But it was manual labourers who dominated before the last few years (craftsmen were not even counted until 1864), and it was they who gave the Jade Bay its reputation as a raw frontier settlement. It was likened again and again in the memoirs to a Californian gold-rush town, a 'little America' that attracted the hopeful and the desperate.[66] This in itself did not make the area unique in the 1850s and 60s. The pell-mell growth of the Saarland coalfield in the same years earned it the nickname 'black California' (black for coal); the even faster growing Ruhr was Germany's 'wild west'.[67] The difference between these areas and the Jade Bay is that the workforce responsible for building the harbour town was temporary. That, and the peculiar difficulty of the terrain, explains why its living conditions were even worse than those in the booming coal-fields.

The construction workers were casual labourers. Some were locals, seasonal agricultural workers and men who might previously have been employed in dike-building. Others came from the Prussian east, including Poles and Lithuanians. Many non-natives belonged to the nomadic army of workers who moved from one large construction site to the next, owners of a spade, a pair of thigh-boots and not much else. Yesterday they might have excavated earth for a railway or canal; today it was a harbour. Neither the back-breaking labour nor the long hours (from dawn to dusk in summer, with an hour off for lunch) would have been a novel experience for most.[68] But the physical environment of the Jade Bay was exceptionally punishing. The harbour entrance, the canal that led to the main installations, the docks themselves – all were excavated by hand. The material that had to be dug out could hardly have been more intractable. At the harbour entrance were mudflats. Inland, the site lay some two feet below the normal high water mark, and from the surface downwards it consisted of several feet of clay, just over a foot of peat, five feet of mud mixed with reeds, then sand.[69] All of this had to be shovelled into barrows, then wheeled across duckboards to tipping sites and used to raise the elevation of the later town. The men resembled a line of soldiers marching in single file as they pushed their loads across the boards, singing to keep in step, until a barrow slipped, stuck in the mud, and the whole column was delayed. Only at the very end was this labour replaced by mechanical tip-up trucks on rails, known as 'dogs' ('who feeds the dogs?', asked a bureaucrat in Berlin).[70]

Local topography also meant that the construction of every new dike, lock-gate, dry dock or jetty first required piles to be driven into the ground. Again, it was not until the middle of the 1860s, after much of the hardest work had been completed, that steam-driven mechanical piledrivers arrived on site. The original 'monarchs of the mud' hammered the piles in by hand. Wilhelmshaven was built by the same methods that built Venice and Amsterdam. It was created by the same methods that had also created St Petersburg 150 years earlier, another monument to political will that was built on a muddy river delta at huge human cost. To make the comparison is also to recognize the differences. Peter the Great's 'window on Europe' cost 10,000 lives. Prussian ambitions on the Jade Bay took a more modest toll. Official statistics recorded – although probably under-recorded – a total of 247 construction workers who died in the years 1857–72.[71] More than a tenth of the deaths were a result of accidents; almost another tenth were attributed to suicide or alcohol. The remainder were caused by illness, above all respiratory diseases like tuberculosis, pleurisy and pneumonia. These, together with influenza, were the great killers of German workers everywhere in this period, because their victims were already weakened by physical exhaustion and unhealthy living conditions. On the Jade Bay, where labourers worked in permanent damp, were crowded together in barracks, ate poorly and drank alcohol to fend off the cold, high sickness and mortality rates were hardly a surprise.[72]

Then there was malaria – 'marsh fever' or 'cold fever'. It was endemic in the surrounding marshlands, and the countless pools of standing water created by building works provided a perfect breeding ground for the anopheles mosquito.[73] Malaria, like mud, was simply a part of everyday life. A doctor still struggling to eradicate the disease in the early twentieth century was told by informants who remembered the 1860s that 'hardly anyone had avoided malaria'.[74] The mortality rate was low – more workers on the Jade Bay died of typhus than malaria

– but startlingly large numbers fell sick and the effects made sufferers more susceptible to other diseases. Close to 18,000 cases were recorded in all, the numbers always peaking in the summer months. In August 1868, thirty per cent of the workforce was sick; the following month it was thirty-six per cent, more than 1000 men.[75] The unavoidable presence of malaria lodged itself in the minds of later memoir writers.[76] It was one experience that upper-class residents shared with the army of workers. To Louise von Krohn malaria was one of life's 'calamities'. She, her maid and her husband all succumbed. Quinine interrupted but did not stop the fevers: Julius von Krohn would suffer recurrent bouts for years.[77]

Malaria was not the only hardship faced by the thin stratum of officers, officials and merchants in the early years.[78] Their privations did not, of course, compare with those of construction workers. They were spared the physical toil, had better food and lived in the first permanent houses (the Krohns moved from their leaky farmhouse to a home in the newly built Manteuffelstrasse in 1864). But conditions were still very raw. Prussian authorities received numerous complaints about flying sand from the construction site, which got into eyes and clothing, found its way through window frames and settled on the furniture. The short-term remedy was to strew mud on the sand, then throw straw on the mud.[79] But mud was more often the problem than the solution. It seemed to be everywhere, especially after the rain that fell on average every other day. High boots were worn on all occasions – by churchgoers, by officials greeting Prince Adalbert on one of his regular visits, by families making their way over the duckboards to a dance at the 'Zur Erholung' inn.[80] It was not just rain that caused the mud. The water table was high to begin with (sometimes the burial casket would bob in the grave) and construction disturbed local drainage ditches, causing streets and homes to flood. As the permanent population slowly grew through the 1860s, to 3000 by the end of the decade as against 4000 construction workers, a related problem arose as new buildings were built on former water-meadows and marshland. Subsidence was the predictable result.[81]

It is a paradox the Ancient Mariner would have appreciated that, for all the problems caused by excessive water, absence of water to drink was a major problem. This seems to have been a matter of unhelpful geology compounded by incompetence. Artesian wells were drilled in 1862 and 1864, with indifferent results. Dowsers were brought in to no avail. Until 1877, when the town was finally connected to a plentiful supply from the sandy geest more than six miles away, drinking water remained scarce. What came from the wells was quite inadequate. There were queues from 4 o'clock in the morning at the few stand-pipes, first the men, then the women. Residents also drew from a water hole near the first lock-up in the area, trying to ignore the occasional dead dog or cat, or from the ditches in which workers washed their muddy boots. During periods of drought, and they occurred even in this grey and rainy world, water had to be brought in by ship from Bremen and distributed to households by the bucket.[82] The provisioning of the new settlement was inadequate in other ways as well. Consumer goods were few and expensive. The original treaty allowed only for tradesmen to service the future naval base; a town on the Jade Bay site was expressly prohibited. But the port assumed more elaborate dimensions than originally envisaged, especially with the decision to add a shipyard to the docks, and the permanent population grew. Oldenburg lifted the restrictions in 1864 and shops began to establish themselves along the newly laid streets, their names lovingly intoned by Catharine Schwanhäuser in her later chronicle.[83] But until the 1870s anything other than basic needs required a trip to Jever, which meant two days and an overnight stay.

The sociability of reading circles, whist evenings and dances fortified early residents of the embryonic town. These civilizing touches are faithfully recorded in the memoirs that have come down to us. But their authors seem at least as pleased to recall the hard times: they had faced the wind and rain, the mud, the malaria, the shortages, yet somehow come through. The combined inn and store, covered with a tarpaper roof and known as the 'Grey Donkey' because of its gloomy appearance, is fondly recalled. Even the 'dissolute lives' of construction workers are sketched with a certain patronizing affection – the heavy alcohol consumption, gambling, fights, the raucous dancing at Andree's (although not the presence of prostitutes).[84] Recollected in tranquillity, the rough early days became a source of local pride, a creation myth of pioneer fortitude.

The modest ceremony in 1854 that saw the first raising of the Prussian flag by the Jade Bay was followed fifteen years later by a more festive inauguration. Much had changed in those years. Prussian victory over Austria (and most of the other German states) in 1866 marked the decisive stage in creating a unified 'Lesser Germany'. It laid the basis for the North German Confederation created in 1867, a stepping-stone to the German Empire established in 1871. On 17 June 1869 Wilhelm I of Prussia, soon to become German Kaiser, arrived by train from Oldenburg. He was accompanied by representatives of other German ruling houses, senior officials and ministers, Bismarck among them. Also present were members of the General Staff, led by Helmuth von Moltke. Chief of the General Staff since 1857, Moltke was the planner whose emphasis on strategic use of the railways had done so much to ensure Prussian victory over Austria and its German allies in 1866.

The party went through two specially constructed triumphal arches decked with green spruce to the harbour, where Minister of War and the Navy Albrecht von Roon read a short speech proclaiming the name chosen for the new town by Wilhelm I. Ernst Gaebler, by now retired, had written to the king reminding him of Prince Adalbert's wish that the town be called Zollern by the Sea, but the choice fell on Wilhelmshaven to honour Wilhelm's deceased brother and predecessor on the throne, Frederick William IV. The king then went aboard the British frigate *Minotaur*, sent by Queen Victoria and anchored in the bay as a mark of respect, which fired its guns in salute. The visit continued with a tour of the installation, before Wilhelm laid the foundation stone of a new garrison church.[85] But a king was not expected to face too much reality. The date of the visit was carefully chosen to coincide with a noon high tide, so that royal eyes would not have to gaze over the expanse of mudflats. Even so, a retired admiralty official wrote many years later that when Wilhelm christened the town 'he still looked out in every direction at a wasteland'. Crown Prince Frederick, who visited in July 1869, must have been thinking the same when he reportedly exclaimed in bewilderment: 'What has His Majesty inaugurated here?'[86]

It took another decade to turn the wasteland into a town. Wilhelmshaven became a normal Prussian administrative district in 1873, no longer subject to admiralty jurisdiction. But a greater transformation was taking place on the ground. The railway station had already become a proper station, not the imposter covered by canvas sailcloth stretched over wood, like a giant tent or a conceptual artwork ahead of its time.[87] In the 1870s, years of frenetic building everywhere in the new Germany, Wilhelmshaven acquired an infrastructure: gasworks, piped water, schools, government buildings. Roads were laid

down between the few main thoroughfares that already existed. The
topography familiar to early inhabitants disappeared in the process.
Water holes and streams were filled in; the Heikesche Cow Pasture
became the Bismarckplatz and the residential area around it. Tree plantings and a town park transformed the physical landscape just as choral
clubs transformed the social landscape. This 'civilizing' of a former
frontier settlement had its dark side. The poor natural drainage of the
area, made worse by construction, still caused problems. The housing
quickly built inside the town and in 'colonies' outside to accommodate
shipyard workers lacked modern sanitation. The stagnant, overgrown
ditches that ran alongside these areas became a repository for household and human waste and a serious health risk. Malaria remained
endemic into the early twentieth century, even as Louise von Krohn
insisted that it had 'disappeared'.[88] There was a renewed epidemic in
1907. Nearly 150 cases were reported, although all the local doctors
believed the true figure was higher. Some adults had been ill with the
disease in the past, but a detailed examination showed many new cases.
Mosquitoes were found inhabiting gardens, pig-sties, even houses, and
the repeated enlargement of the naval base – a second entrance was
built in 1876–86, a third in 1900–09 – kept recreating conditions in
which they could breed.

Early twentieth-century memoir writers were eager to draw a line
under the past, consigning the mud and malaria to an earlier time. Yet
it was neither fanciful nor simply local patriotism to believe that
Wilhelmshaven, forty years on, had become a symbol of a quite
different kind. No longer an isolated place of exile, it drew workers
from all over Germany to its shipyards. Wilhelmshaven as 'melting
pot' remains a cliché to this day, neatly closing the circle that began
with comparisons between the Jade Bay and American gold-rush towns.
Above all, the naval base made Wilhelmshaven into a symbol of
dynamism and modern times. The base dominated the town, and it
grew in step with the rising naval and imperial ambitions of unified
Germany. The festive arrival and departure of ships, the launching of
a new vessel, these gave rhythm to the life of the town. They linked
its inhabitants mentally to a larger world. In 1878 the celebrated
German explorer of Africa, Gerhard Rohlfs, spoke at the Viktoria
Hotel; in the 1880s, the decade when the first German overseas empire
was established, the town hosted a major exhibition of art, manufac-
tures and horticulture that included Chinese paintings, ivory carvings

and tropical birds. Most of the exhibits were provided by navy personnel.[89]

Nothing provides a better symbol of Wilhelmshaven's place in the new Germany than the attention bestowed on it by the wilful, narcissistic man who became Emperor Wilhelm II of Germany in 1888, just shy of his thirtieth birthday. He visited during naval manoeuvres in September 1888 just three months after coming to the throne, then again the following July. In later years only the sister naval base of Kiel was singled out so often for favour by the Kaiser. The 'feverish excitement' that Louise von Krohn recorded at the time of the July 1889 visit was, of course, a familiar enough affliction among middle-class Germans, not unique to Wilhelmshaven, but the town had a special stake in the Kaiser's pursuit of 'World Policy'.[90] The shipyards hummed in the years after 1898 when the new German battlefleet was under construction. Naval base and town both grew. The plan for the third harbour entrance (which had the incidental effect of destroying almost all the first buildings constructed in the 1850s) was drawn up in 1897, the same year that Admiral Tirpitz's first naval bill was unveiled. 'Our future lies on the water', the Kaiser had said, and the fortunes of Wilhelmshaven were closely linked to his boast.[91]

Set against the long history of human settlement along this part of the coast, the future imagined so eagerly by Kaiser, Navy League and 'navy professors' turned out to be a short one. Defeat in the First World War, when the battlefleet demonstrated its lack of strategic value, ended with a revolution sparked by a sailors' mutiny in Kiel and Wilhelmshaven at the beginning of November 1918. The engine fitter and Leading Seaman Bernhardt Kuhnt became president of the short-lived Socialist Republic of Oldenburg and East Friesland.[92] The town, all too dependent on the naval base, was badly hit in the 1920s by the loss of the German battlefleet, most of it handed over to the victorious powers and a good part of it scuttled at Scapa Flow. Despite efforts to attract other industries (including the ship-wrecking business, in which it led Europe in the early 1920s), Wilhelmshaven lost thousands of shipyard jobs even before the arrival of the depression that followed the 1929 Wall Street Crash. This made it very susceptible to National Socialism, which received strong support from small businesses and officials as much as unemployed shipyard workers. In the Reichstag elections of July 1932 the Nazis won almost half of all the votes cast in Wilhelmshaven (although less in the heavily proletarian areas just beyond the city limits), well above their average in Germany as a whole. The Third Reich brought rearmament and turned Wilhelmshaven back into a boomtown – the shipyards employed close to 30,000 workers on the eve of the Second World War. It also brought about the almost complete destruction of the town by Allied bombing raids in the last years of the war. Just ninety years after Prussia purchased its foothold on the Jade Bay the book was closed on the naval base.

Colonizing the Moors

A year before the National Socialists came to power in 1933, the Olden-burg regional writer August Hinrichs reminisced about a map on his schoolroom wall back in the 1880s. The map depicted his small, local universe and it was the colours that he remembered. At the top was the blue of the North Sea, with the Jade Bay on the right-hand side shaped 'like a plump side of ham'. Then came the three colours that denoted the different habitats and landscapes of the Oldenburg and East Friesland peninsula: green for the marshes, yellow for the sandy geest, brown for the moorland of the interior.[93] The colours remain the same on modern maps, but the advancing areas of cultivation and human settlement have altered their proportions. Hinrichs noted the changes in his own life-time. In fact they were occurring, sometimes dramatically, sometimes incrementally, even before that.

A traveller going due west from Wilhelmshaven in 1878, the year of Hinrichs's birth, would have seen the changes. That was also the year when work began on the Ems–Jade canal, which eventually linked Wilhelmshaven via Aurich with the port of Emden, so an enterprising traveller could simply have followed the line the engineers had laid down for the new waterway.[94] The first part of the journey would have crossed land shaded green on the map. These were the coastal marshes. Here the look of the land had changed least over the previous decades, for it had already been substantially reclaimed through coastal dikes and a grid of drainage ditches. Green was surely the right colour for this rich arable and pasture land which provided the marsh farmers with their wealth. After about ten miles the land rose slightly (the canal-builders dealt with this problem by building a series of locks). This was where the geest began. The word itself means 'infertile'; the soil is sandy and the vegetation heath-like. The ridge that crosses the Oldenburg-

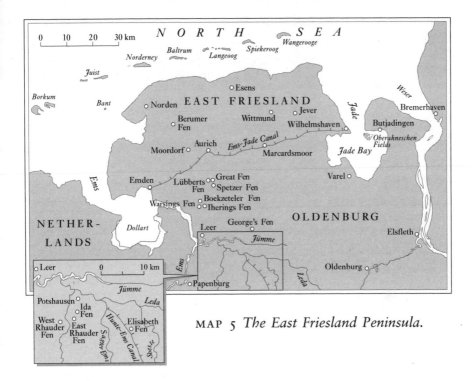

MAP 5 *The East Friesland Peninsula.*

East Friesland peninsula is first cousin to the better known and higher Lüneburg Heath that lies to the east. This was once heavily wooded land, cultivated – as we know from excavations and pollen analysis – as early as 3000 BC. But long years of settlement led to deforestation. Medieval agriculture was especially damaging. Overgrazing and the practice of stripping off the top layer of grass to provide nutrients for crops exposed the surface to winds that blew away the topsoil and uncovered the sand beneath. Through the years when the marsh farmers became rich, the geest provided grazing for sheep and an inhospitable soil on which small peasants eked out a living with their rye crops, supplemented by weaving and clog-making. But the landscape was changing again by the third quarter of the nineteenth century. Hedgerows were built as wind-breaks, manure was applied to the soil and fast-growing pines were planted to anchor the shifting sands. The characteristic appearance of the present-day geest farmland was starting to take shape.[95]

Just over six miles after the geest rose from the coastal plain the land changed once again. The terrain was now moorland. The route of the future canal ran straight through the 'completely desolate moors' that stretched across the peninsula from Aurich to Friedeburg, and south for another fifty miles.[96] Some of this great expanse, especially in the river valleys of the Leda and Jümme, was low moor, where water had turned gradually to land. Low moorland resembled the marshes drained by Frederick the Great. High moors, on the other hand, like those between Aurich and Friedeburg, lay well above the water table and grew independently of it. High moorland developed in areas with heavy rainfall, low evaporation and poor drainage. A sponge-like moss or sphagnum grew on the surface. When the bottom part died, water cut it off from oxygen so that it did not completely decompose and there were few bacteria to help it do so. Over time a dark, acidic, waterlogged peat-bog built up below ground. After several thousand years, the still growing moors of the peninsula often reached a depth of thirty feet.[97] The coastal climate and hydrology of north-west Germany created the perfect conditions for moors to grow. They covered a quarter of Oldenburg and East Friesland, more than in any other part of Germany.[98]

As the hundreds of mainly Polish labourers who dug the Ems–Jade canal could have testified, moorland was treacherous terrain. Crossing it was difficult until the modern era of drainage, and that era did not begin on the high moors until long after the first successful efforts to drain coastal marshes and other lowlands. True, there is evidence from prehistoric times of corduroy roads built across the moors, made up of logs laid together transversely, but these were eventually swallowed up.[99] As, sometimes, were people. It was not just 'eerie' to cross the moor, as the poet Annette Droste-Hülshoff wrote; it was also life-threatening. The Protestant Pastor Johann Wilhelm Hönert from Bremen warned in the late eighteenth century about moorlands that were either 'completely impassable or at least to be entered only with difficulty and danger'. Paths could be used year-round only if fascines were carefully laid down (Hönert likened it to building a dike) and covered with sand 'one shoe high'.[100] But even in the nineteenth century travellers disappeared when they left safe ground and were sucked down into the bog.[101] Until the nineteenth century, in fact, very few travellers would have chosen to do what Droste-Hülshoff did and cross the moor for pleasure or out of curiosity. Moorland was wasteland, barren and dangerous, its fickle surface marked by grassy tussocks, scrubby bracken, the occasional stunted birch and pools of black water that contained no fish, a place from which 'moor thunder' could be heard below ground.[102] Modern moor archaeology, a product of the late nine-teenth century, has uncovered the well-preserved traces of many earlier settlements, but these were situated either on the lakes that once lay beneath the low moors, or on the edges of the high moors.[103] For centuries, people on the Oldenburg and East Friesland peninsula approached the moorland cautiously, making forays from dry ground to cut peat for fuel.

Our traveller in 1878, after following the route of the future canal just a few miles into the moors, would have been in a good position to survey the different methods that had been used to bring this no man's land into use. A short distance to the south and west were a number of so-called fen colonies built along canals, the oldest going back to the seventeenth century, another very recent.[104] Then, dotted all around, were 'high moor colonies', mostly established in the second half of the eighteenth century. The largest (and most notorious) was Moordorf, which lay twenty miles further on, just beyond Aurich. Finally, on the very spot where the traveller stood, next to the line of the proposed canal, was the face of the future as contemporaries saw it. For this was where the colony of Marcards Moor would be built, an experiment in putting the 'German high moor culture' of the 1870s into practice. Some of these initiatives would leave more lines on the map than others; some would prove more successful than others. All brought fundamental change to a landscape that had been growing imperceptibly for millennia.

The first systematic efforts to tame the moors came in the seven-teenth century. These were the Fehn or fen colonies, a term used to describe both low and high moor settlements. They were founded because of the high price commanded by peat at a time when local supplies had been interrupted by the Thirty Years War. To build a fen colony a canal was first dug from the nearest waterway to the edge of the moor; then a trunk canal was cut through the moor itself, usually with main channels that branched off at right angles. Over time, a further series of side-arms, called *Inwieken*, were sometimes dug to give easier access to the peat. After the top layer of poorly combustible white peat had been removed and set aside, the dark peat was cut by hand with special spades, dried in large piles and shipped to market. The top layer was then mixed with sand into the subsoil to create an overlay of humus for raising crops. In theory, the colonists would extend the area of cultivated land as the peat was removed.

The fen colony was, like so much else that involved the manipulation of waterlands, borrowed from the Dutch. The first German example was Papenburg in the Emsland, founded in 1631. It was followed by a series of East Frisian fen colonies established by private companies. Many were formed by Emden merchants imitating their counterparts in Groningen, the true Dutch pioneers. Great Fen was set up in 1633, then Lübberts Fen, Hookser Fen, Boekzeteler Fen, and Iherings Fen. Another burst of activity in the eighteenth century saw the founding of Warsings Fen, New Fen and Spetzer Fen. These were all clustered close to earlier colonies. Not so two other, large fen colonies. Rhauder Fen was established in 1769, on a site first developed but then abandoned by Emden merchants twenty years earlier, and – a sign of the changing times – on land acquired from the moribund order of the Knights of St John of Jerusalem (the Knights of Malta, as they were often called). It became one of the most successful settlements of its kind. Berumer Fen, in the far north, was also successful, and unusual in that the company which developed it ran the colony on its own behalf, rather than bringing in leaseholders as 'colonists' to cut the peat and work the land.[105]

These were all private undertakings, designed to turn a profit. The states held back because of the heavy initial investment required by fen colonies (the Prussian state actually dug the canals at Spetzer Fen, then sold the enterprise to a private group to avoid further costs). But in the nineteenth century it was the states that made the running, looking to take the edge off the social question and create new land for a growing population that might otherwise have left for seasonal work in the Netherlands or a new start in America. Under Hanoverian rule, three new East Friesland fen colonies were established in the 1820s (North and South George's Fen and Holter Fen).[106] There was also a burst of activity by Prussia, closely linked to the process of German unification. Around 1860 there were proposals to extend the Great Fen eastwards towards the Jade Bay. Hanover obstructed this out of pique over the building of Wilhelmshaven – another example of small-state parochialism.[107] But what had been blocked by politics could also be unblocked by politics. One side-effect of Prussia's military triumph in 1866 was the crushing of Hanover and the reacquisition of East Friesland.

In the wake of this success, an enthusiastic official in the ministry of agriculture called Marcard drew up plans for a large-scale programme of canals and fen colonies. On the left bank of the Ems near the Prussian border a north–south canal was driven through the Bourtanger Moor, using prisoners captured in the Franco–Prussian War. An 1876 treaty with the Netherlands laid the basis for a series of lateral canals that would connect to the existing Dutch network. Further north, earlier proposals to extend the Great Fen towards the Jade Bay were reactivated, with a new twist: it was Spetzer Fen that was now extended east with the construction of the Auricher Wiesmoor Fen, completed in 1878. Two further colonies – Wilhelms Fen I and II – were added in the 1880s, the final fruits of Marcard's vision. But by then Prussian ideas for colonizing the moors had changed direction.[108]

It was Oldenburg that threw itself most vigorously into fen colonization. Further away than East Friesland from Dutch influence and perennially cash-strapped, the state had watched its neighbours practise the art for two centuries. In the middle of the nineteenth century Oldenburg joined in with the zeal of the convert. Starting in the 1840s, canals were driven through the moors and colonies established along them: August Fen in the 1850s, Elisabeth Fen in the 1860s, Mosles Fen in the 1870s. By 1881 they covered 2500 acres. Ida Fen was founded in 1865 as a private undertaking. Within a generation Oldenburg had successfully established the canal-based system of moor colonies long familiar further west.[109]

The canal was essential to the life of the fen colony. It drained the moor and provided the means of transporting peat and agricultural produce out and commodities like manure or building materials in. Papenburg was, in the words of its historian, 'the town on the canal', and the same was true of all its successors.[110] The fen colony had no town centre or market square; sandy roads usually ran along the water, but the canals formed the main arteries, crossed at intervals by swing-bridges, another import from the inventive Dutch. The importance of the canal went beyond the economic; it was a symbol of being connected to the larger world. A vivid, powerful contemporary account of this can be found in a series of four letters to a friend published by Ludwig Starklof in 1847. Its title, *Moor Canals and Moor Colonies between Hunte and Ems*, hardly hints at the author's passionate optimism about the future of canals and fen colonies.[111]

Starklof was an Oldenburger, a long-serving state official who was also a travel writer, historical novelist, amateur painter and the man responsible for founding the first public theatre in Oldenburg, which he managed for ten years in tandem with his official duties.[112] He was that classic type of the 1840s, the liberal-minded bureaucrat frustrated by the cramped, suffocating political atmosphere of the small state he served and concerned about the 'social question'. In 1846 Starklof wrote a novel, *Armin Galoor*, which criticized conditions in Oldenburg; he was peremptorily dismissed by the Grand Duke August after thirty-five years of service. It was in the following year that he travelled to view the terrain of the proposed Hunte–Ems canal. For Starklof, as for so many others of his kind, the canal (like the railway) was a symbol of progress. In the letters to a friend he is open about his convictions and refers self-mockingly to his 'canal enthusiasm'.[113] His early pages describe the anarchic hydrology of the area around the Sagter Ems and the Soeste, the two rivers that the canal would later bisect as it drove a straight line through the moors. He and his companions seek out the surveying team that was already at work, Surveyor Fimmen, his deputy Herr Kessel, and an unnamed man who carried the measuring chains, marvelling at the beauty and sensitivity of the instruments ('made by Breithaupt of Kassel').[114] Along the way Starklof finds people who invariably share his enthusiasm, like the old man who responds: 'A canal between the Hunte and Ems? Yes, sir, you're right about that! That's what we need to set our hands to! That is what East Friesland and Oldenburg lack! – I've been saying it for fifty years – that would be a great thing! And whoever accomplishes that will make a name for himself for all eternity'.[115]

But Starklof was also writing as an advocate of fen colonies, at a time when Oldenburg still had none. His account is framed as a contrast between backward Oldenburg and forward-looking East Friesland. When he and his companions rode across the border at the Potshausen bridge over the Leda, everything changed 'as if with the wave of a magic wand'. Gone were the dirt, the smoky huts and the poverty on the Oldenburg side; the East Frieslanders were living 'in the fresh, clear light of day, they are as neat and clean as a freshly shelled egg'.[116] Starklof was impressed (like most visitors) with Rhauder Fen. He describes its well-tended houses and small front gardens, the clean and orderly rooms with their well-filled larders, even the occasional Black Forest clock, and the fields of arable and meadow that stretched back behind the houses to the still unexcavated peat moor. These were scenes from a Dutch still life, 'a picture of progressing, advancing, growing'. As for the women, they not only had teeth, they had white teeth.[117]

And the reason for this orderliness and prosperity? Starklof had the answer: 'We are now in a region of canals, of trade, buying and selling, of large enterprises. These are forces that stretch their powerful arms out wide. The navigable, well-planned and canalized waterway washes these people, these houses with its invigorating influence, it washes them clean, prevents dirt from settling, will not permit going to seed'.[118] It is a point that Starklof hammers home. Trade, the traffic in goods, these are the key – 'here is the peat and there is the canal'. The waterway is the fen colonist's 'lifeline' to a wider world.[119] He was convinced that Oldenburg would reap the same rewards; the main thing was to make a start.

Starklof was hoping in 1847 that work on the Hunte–Ems canal would begin early the following year; but the spring of 1848 brought revolution instead. Crowds gathered in the town of Oldenburg, petitions rained in, craftsmen met to formulate their grievances, and liberal politicians called for representative government. The revolution was less radical than in Prussia or southern states like Baden – there were no revolts in the countryside and no barricades in the towns – but the issues were the same. There were demands for constitutional rule, an elected parliament, freedom of the press, reform of the legal system and measures to address the 'social question'. The Grand Duke acceded to the pressure and appointed a reforming 'March Ministry', similar to those being formed across Germany in the spring of 1848. Elections to an Oldenburg parliament and to the Frankfurt National Assembly followed. Starklof threw himself into the fray. He cultivated a popular following, convinced that the revolution would restore him to his former position. But his verbal radicalism antagonized many old liberal friends, and the Grand Duke refused to bring back a man he believed had personally insulted him.

Starklof stood but was not elected to the new Oldenburg assembly or the Frankfurt parliament. Frustrated, he went to Frankfurt to cover the dramatic events there for a Bremen newspaper. He reported the debates over the constitution and the national question, which took place against the onset of counter-revolution in Prussia and Austria after the autumn of 1848 and were punctuated by further insurrections. Starklof observed the final uprisings of the revolution in Baden in the summer of 1849, then travelled to Switzerland like so many political émigrés. He returned to Oldenburg that autumn, still intent on winning back his job. Friends in government interceded with the

Grand Duke. But the position Starklof really coveted, running a new organization to foster internal colonization in Oldenburg, was brusquely denied him. Despairing that his ambitions would ever be realized and concerned about his daughters, who were showing increasing signs of mental instability, Starklof disappeared on 11 October 1850. His body was found three weeks later, floating in the Hunte.[120]

Starklof had endured decades of political and social stultification by looking to the future. He took his own life just when that future began to take shape, as political life in Oldenburg opened out and the economic policies Starklof favoured were put into effect. A passionate advocate of wider economic connections and a pro-Prussian nationalist, he did not live to see Oldenburg join the German Customs Union in 1853 or the Jade Bay agreement (it was an old liberal friend, Maximilian Heinrich Rüder, who acted for the Prussian admiralty in buying up land in Heppens). Perhaps most poignantly of all, he threw himself in the Hunte just five years before work finally began on the Hunte–Ems canal that was so close to his heart. The project started in 1855 but proceeded slowly. A Hodges peat-ship was brought in after 1871 to excavate the moor mechanically, but progress remained slow because the white-peat surface still had to be removed by hand. There were bridges and locks to build, then feeder canals to open up further areas of moorland. The whole canal was not open until the 1890s.[121] But the section where Starklof had encountered the surveying team was finished much earlier. The first colonists moved into the Elisabeth Fen in the 1860s; a second wave followed in the 1870s. These fen colonies, a new settlement corridor right through the middle of the moors, were generally regarded as exemplary. They even attracted Dutch settlers, the ultimate accolade.

A case can be made that fen colonization in the middle decades of the nineteenth century justified the boundless belief in progress shown by liberals like Ludwig Starklof. Many existing colonies flourished in these years; some enjoyed their fastest growth. Great Fen was one. In 1833, a full two centuries after it was founded, this had grown to 1200 inhabitants. By the middle of the century the figure was over 2000, and by 1880 it had reached 3000.[122] A major improvement in the capital assets of the operating company made the difference here, allowing geographical expansion and technical improvements. Rhauder Fen, to no one's surprise, also thrived; so did Berumer Fen. But others barely grew at all (Iherings, Lübberts and Boekzeteler Fens), while some were evidently in crisis. Even the upbeat Ludwig Starklof could see in the 1840s that something was very wrong at South George's Fen, where the colonists' plight 'made my heart quake in my body'. The sullen, fearful tenants, with their mean huts and diet of rotten potatoes, made him think he had been 'transported into a miserable hovel in Ireland'.[123] Conditions remained 'wretched' in the years that followed. Many colonists fled to the new Oldenburg settlement of August Fen, others emigrated to the USA.[124] This was a vivid reminder (Ida Fen was another) that even when the moor had apparently been 'conquered' by the canal, success was not guaranteed.

How do we explain these differences? Why did South George's Fen fare so much worse than its sister colony to the north, or Ida Fen fail spectacularly to emulate neighboring Rhauder Fen? Later advocates of inner colonization spilled plenty of ink complaining about the quality of 'colonist material'. But even if we accept that some newcomers were ill-adapted to their new homes, this seems too global an explanation. In any case, as the same commentators frequently pointed out, so much depended on the terms and conditions that faced future colonists; and where these were unforgiving it was hardly surprising that older fen colonies failed to thrive, or that new ones attracted only those who (in the words of a Prussian official) had 'nothing more to lose'.[125] Those conditions included the size of the holding, the financial terms, the rent, the fees payable for services (such as 'lock money'), the schedule laid down for building a house or beginning agricultural cultivation. Quite small differences in these, given the way that each condition was likely to have an effect on the others, could produce major divergences over the long term – what would be called, many years later, sensitive dependence on initial conditions, or the 'Butterfly Effect'. But it was not just the legal and financial conditions that varied. The hydrology was not the same everywhere; nor was the accessibility or quality of the peat. It was problems of this kind – the difficulty of getting at good quality peat, a botched canal, frequent floods – that largely explain the decades of futility and frustration in South George's Fen.[126]

The waterways were so often the key. Hans Pflug, writing admiringly about Papenburg during the Nazi era, described 'canals cut straight as a die through the wilderness-like moorland'.[127] But this was highly idealized. Even Papenburg's canals did not measure up to the Dutch.[128] If eighteenth-century fen colonies generally did better than those founded in the seventeenth century, it was because the main canal did not hug the edge of the moor so timidly and the network of waterways was larger.[129] If privately developed fen colonies almost always fared better in East Friesland than those established by the state, whereas in Oldenburg it was the other way round, a major reason in each case was that good canals led to successful colonies. Conversely, when things went wrong, it could usually be traced back to flaws in the canal. It was built too narrow, or too shallow, or was poorly maintained, silting up and filling with weeds.[130] (A distinctly modern problem arose when an invasive species, the Canadian water weed, after escaping from the Berlin Botanical Gardens in 1857, began choking the waterways of north-west Germany after the 1870s.[131]) Summer low-water brought the worst problems, when even the shallow-keeled peat ships had to sail with lighter loads, reducing the economic return per trip. Locks caused special concern because of the water they used up: in summer a ship might wait hours for another one to arrive, so that they could be passed through together.

All systems of artificial waterways face problems in maintaining water levels. That was why the Oldenburg state built feeder canals – and why, at the end of the nineteenth century, the need to maintain water levels in canals helped to drive the construction of reservoirs.[132] Compounding the problem in East Friesland and Oldenburg was that fewer side-canals were dug than in Dutch fen colonies. For the larger the number of *Inwieken*, the greater the volume of black water that drained out of the moor to keep the waterway system topped up. Fewer side-canals also meant that peat had to be carried further overland to the nearest canal, raising the cost of production and doing nothing for the quality of the product. Even greater problems faced colonists in East Friesland settlements where the Hanoverian or Prussian state had built canals so quickly that the excavated peat and sand was simply piled up at the side, where it formed a wall between the colony and its lifeline to the world. As if to over-compensate, Prussia invested heavily in building an exemplary canal to cut through the Bourtanger Moor, but built it in the wrong place. Here the act of faith embodied in the principle 'build it and they will come' turned out to be misplaced – or, to take the charitable view, the canal was ahead of its time. The absence of nearby markets and the time-lag before connections were made with the Dutch canals made it hard to attract colonists. Alfred Hugenberg reported morosely in 1891 that 'for the most part one sees no ships on the canals, no life on the streets'.[133]

The fen colonist, or *Fehntjer*, was never likely to turn into a wealthy

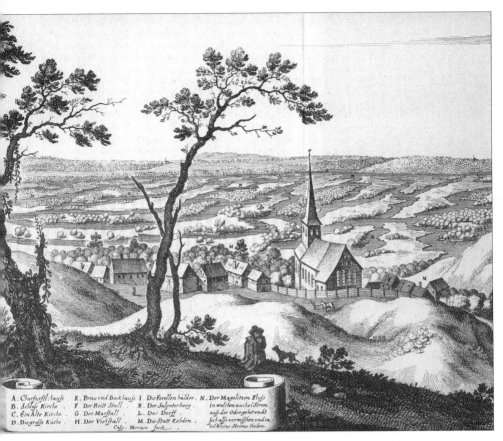

1. View of the Zehden Marshes, from a seventeenth-century engraving by Matthäus Merian.

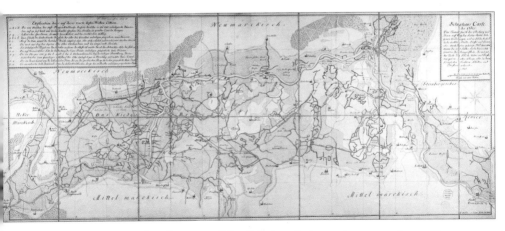

2. A contemporary planning map of the Oderbruch shows the proposal to redirect the course of the river.

3. The arduous work of hydrological improvement in eighteenth-century Prussia, depicted in David Gilly and Johann Albert Eytelwein, *Praktische Anweisung zur Wasserbaukunst* (Berlin, 1802).

4. Franz Balthasar Schönberg von Brenckenhoff, the former army supplier from Anhalt-Dessau who became one of Frederick the Great's main agents of land reclamation and colonization.

5. Frederick the Great Visits Newly Established Colonists in the Rhinluch,
oil painting by Johann Christoph Frisch (*c.* 1800)

6. Peter Birmann's *View of the Rhine from the Istein Cliffs,*
painted in the early nineteenth century.

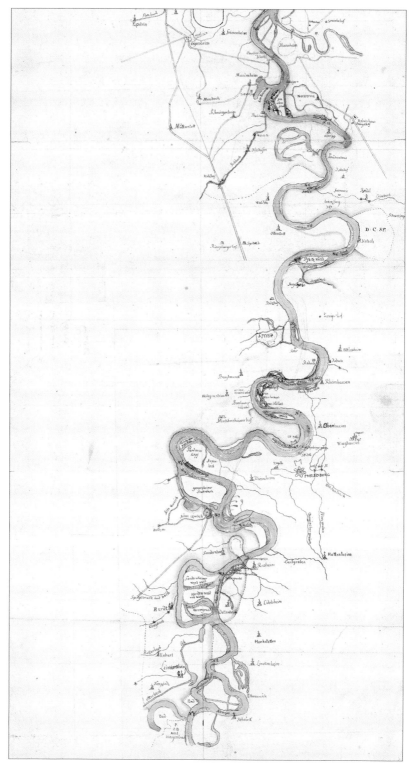

7. This 1789 map shows the serpentine course of the Rhine
prior to Johann Tulla's 'correction'.

8. Johann Gottfried Tulla, 'the man who tamed the wild Rhine'.

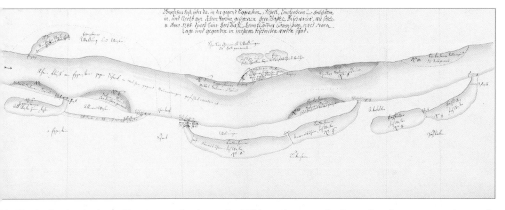

9. Typical salmon breeding grounds along the Rhine, destroyed when the river was engineered to run straighter and faster.

10. Julius Preller's drawing with sepia watercolour additions shows the isolated area that would later become Wilhelmshaven. The village of Heppens can be seen beyond the windmill, and beyond that the Oberahneschen fields are just visible above the waters of the Jade Bay.

11. Constructing the future Wilhelmshaven in the 1860s.

12. Ludwig Starklof, the Oldenburg liberal and passionate advocate
of fen colonies and the Hunte–Ems Canal.

13. Elisabeth Fen.

14. The moor colony of Moordorf.

15. Worpswede painter Fritz Mackensen's *Clog Maker in the Teufelsmoor* (1895) suggests the powerful effects of the moors on human emotions, but also the degree to which people have already drawn their straight lines through the landscape, in the form of the canal with its peat boat and the road that crosses the canal in the middle distance.

Oderbruch or marsh farmer. He and his family balanced three different occupations: peat-digger, agriculturalist and small boatman. Perhaps that is why the *Fehntjer* attracted so much sentimental regard, even from those (like Ludwig Starklof) who saw themselves as thoroughly modern men who relished the final conquest of the moors. The *Fehntjer*, even as he tamed the elements, had something of the craftsman about him, his three-in-one way of life a reproach to the modern division of labour.[134] The paradox is that, whether fen colonies failed or succeeded, the unity of the *Fehntjer* life was fragile. Failure meant that colonists incurred debts to merchants or peat-shippers, becoming in effect peat-diggers for the profit of others. Or they turned into day labourers on the peat-fired iron works established in some colonies, processing bog iron ore, or limonite. It was a sure sign that something like this was happening when a colony had few or no registered peat-ships of its own. But success also meant that the three different activities separated themselves out. The most spectacular sign of that was the emergence of shipping as the dynamic element. Despite suspect canals, there were fen colonies where nine out of ten families lived primarily from shipping by the mid-nineteenth century.[135] Papenburg had 150 sea-going ships in 1869, plus 70 peat-ships; East and West Rhauder Fen had 90 sea-going ships between them in 1882, plus 180 peat-ships.[136] To watch the larger, sea-going schooners sliding through the moorlands down to Emden must have been as strange as watching ships that seemed to cross the desert on the newly constructed Suez Canal. Shipping brought prosperity while it lasted, although it did not last for much longer: the number of sea-going ships harboured in the fen colonies declined sharply at the end of the century.[137] But even while it lasted, this was not exactly what the successful fen colony was supposed to be – an older part dominated by shipping, a newer part given over to peat-digging, and agricultural cultivation squeezed between.

The third quarter of the nineteenth century was the high water-mark of fen colonies. Older ones grew as never before, new ones were founded. Then the fen colony died out as an idea, after two and a half centuries: existing settlements survived, but inspired no further imitators. At first glance, the reason seems obvious. The original motive for the fen colonies, large-scale peat extraction, had surely had its day; King Coal was the fuel of the future, the all-purpose alternative. It was Ruhr coal that the naval administration in Wilhelmshaven wanted to import through the Ems–Jade canal, not peat.[138] All true. Yet peat remained in demand, mainly (but not exclusively) as a domestic fuel, and its price in the later nineteenth century was often high enough to bring a satisfactory return but low enough to make it competitive. As for demand, peat was – like coal, and the oil that later fired the cruisers in Wilhelmshaven – a non-renewable resource. Theodor Fontane, who had a well-informed fascination with peat-digging in the low moors of Brandenburg, was typically acute when he said that 'it is not its products that [the moor] brings to market, *but itself – the peat*'.[139] There were some fen colonies in East Friesland where peat stocks were nearly exhausted. But that was not true of most: the amount of peat dug in the Berumer Fen more than doubled between 1850 and 1880.[140] It was a measure of how robust peat stocks remained that, even while the number of sea-going ships declined, the number of peat-ships operating out of Papenburg and the East Friesland fen colonies in the 1880s (around 750) was larger than ever before. Meanwhile, the opening up of the Oldenburg moors brought new supplies on line. Elisabeth Fen alone harboured 120 peat-ships by the end of the century.[141] The founding of new fen colonies ended before the peat ran out or the demand for it turned down. Certainly the sense that coal represented the future played a part in this. Prussian officials were also disillusioned over their most recent efforts, especially the ghost canal in the Bourtanger Moor. What weighed most of all, perhaps, was the sheer slowness of fen colonies if the purpose was to produce agricultural settlements – especially when they ended up producing shipping communities.

By the 1870s there was a new model: one that arose, quite literally, out of the ashes of an older way of using the moors.

Moor burning was another Dutch import into Germany in the seventeenth century.[142] The surface of the moor was crudely hoed and left to dry, hoed over again, then burnt in May, after the last frosts. Buckwheat was sown in the ashes, and a crop appeared within ten to twelve weeks. Crops were generally good for three or four years, and this kind of fire farming required almost no capital. The first moor colony based on the practice was (like the first fen colony) established in the Emsland. It was called Piccardie after its founder, a doctor from the Netherlands.[143] Moor-burning colonies spread quickly, far more quickly than fen colonies because they were so much cheaper. They existed throughout Oldenburg; above all they were founded by the Prussian state in East Friesland after Frederick the Great's land reclamation edict of 1765, over eighty colonies in all.[144]

Moor burning had its supporters in the scientific community and among the advocates of agricultural improvement. One of them was the celebrated Arthur Young in England, where the practice was sufficiently widespread in the moorlands of the south-west that it was known as 'devonshiring'. Moor burning was also common and officially approved in other parts of England and Scotland ('it is scarcely possible to bring boggy, mossy, peat soils from a state of nature into cultivation without the assistance of fire').[145] The Danes and the Dutch also used it. But moor burning in isolation, without additional manuring beyond the nutrients provided by the ash, was not sustainable, and that was precisely the form of slash-and-burn cultivation practised in the Prussian moor colonies of East Friesland.[146] The colonies themselves were thrown together haphazardly with almost no preparatory work. Underlying their foundation was the familiar idea of planting a new population that could provide a return from the 'distant wilderness'.[147] Like those who were settled on reclaimed land in the 1770s and 80s, many of the colonists came from outside. But that was about all they had in common. The miserably unplanned moorland settlements were decidedly un-Frederician by comparison with the Oderbruch or Warthebruch. There are arguments about whether this was because of Prussia's 'stepmotherly' attitude to East Friesland, or because Frederick was insufficiently engaged to keep local bureaucrats up to the mark.[148] Whatever the cause, the result was an ecological and human disaster.

Taking the long view, it would be hard to deny that the fen colony also fell under the heading of what the Germans call *Raubbau* – a predatory, destructive exploitation of a natural resource. After all, it involved carving into the moor, stopping its growth, and shipping off its substance. But it did (usually) leave a sustainable agriculture behind. Moor burning and buckwheat-growing was more profligate. After seven years at most the nutrients had all been drained from the soil, which was then spent for thirty years. In the absence of additional fertilizer, the fire farmer had to move on, burning the next patch of moor until it too was exhausted. The long-term effects are visible in aerial photographs even today. Moor burning led to wild-fires; and it produced a blue-black smoke and haze that hovered over north-west Germany in the spring and, depending on the direction of the wind, carried as far as St Petersburg or Lisbon.[149] For the colonists, poor to begin with, it was a desperate existence. The buckwheat crop was vulnerable to the late frosts common on the high moors, where there were only two and a half frost-free months in an average year.[150] The failure of the crop meant penury. Then colonists found that the end of the 'free years' in which they owed no payment to the state coincided with the point at which the growing area no longer grew anything.[151] Small wonder that high moor colonies became associated with begging and criminality. The members of a newly-created underclass looked for support from the surrounding geest villages, which complained about this 'scourge'. Moordorf, the largest colony of all, became a by-word for indigence. These 'pioneers in the wilderness' lived poverty-stricken existences in tumbledown huts. Adults and children begged in the streets of Aurich where they were shunned as 'gypsies'.[152]

In the years of Hanoverian rule in East Friesland after 1815, new colonies were founded. Greater planning preceded their establishment, and they recruited the sons of local geest peasants as colonists; but the ground rents were pitched too high and the results were no better. In the 'hungry '40s' both old and new settlements were in crisis. Like the handloom weaving trade in Silesia, the buckwheat colonies of East Friesland (and Oldenburg) were incubators of poverty, a spur to the mass emigration from Germany in the 1840s and beyond, not a palliative against it.[153] Surveying the sorry history of high moor colonies in 1871, a Prussian official summed it up savagely: 'a more irresponsible colonization would be hard to imagine'.[154] After Prussia regained control over East Friesland in 1866 a commission of enquiry was set up to examine remedies. In 1876 a Central Moor Commission was created; it was followed a year later by a Moor Research Station in Bremen, jointly supported by Prussia and the city state of Bremen. Out of this bout of rethinking came a determination to pursue high moor colonies, but in a new, more 'scientific' way. German high moor culture had been invented.[155]

There were precedents already pointing in this direction. In the Oldenburg high moor settlements established around the middle of the century, colonists worked the surface of the moor but not through the discredited method of fire farming. They were allowed to burn the moor 'only as a prelude to rational practices' of husbandry, and never more than two years in a row. Loans were provided for manure and seeds.[156] This was a new departure, like Oldenburg's new investment in fen colonies. But it was not the self-consciously scientific path pursued by the

Research Station and the experts. They called for systematic draining, then stripping off the surface vegetation and enriching the subsoil with lime or alkaline fertilizer to counter its acidity. The Bourtanger Moor was chosen as the site of a major experimental colony: 400,000 Marks of public money were invested in Provinzial Moor, where the approved modern methods were employed and every aspect of the colonists' activities was minutely prescribed. A successful high moor settlement, divided between arable and animal raising, was launched.[157]

Was this the future of moorland colonization in the region? What happened along the new Ems–Jade canal suggested that it was. The canal had a primarily strategic purpose. It was supposed to carry Ruhr coal to the battlefleet in Wilhelmshaven, but that never happened because the waterway was too shallow. A 'violent interference in nature' – it cut more than thirty-five feet into the moor in some places – turned out to be a 'gigantic failed investment'.[158] But the canal did open up a large area of moorland: it could have formed an important outlet for new fen colonies – Ludwig Starklof's version of the future. Instead, the decision was taken to pursue the kind of high moor cultivation pioneered at Provinzial Moor. Marcard's Moor, named after the Prussian official who served for many years as chairman of the Central Moor Commission, was constructed along roads, not canals. Based on farming the chemically enriched surface of the moor, it produced potatoes, not peat. Roads, houses and future public buildings were also built before the colonists arrived, making use of a light railway that carried construction materials from the canal. The novelty of the new colony – starting a trend that was taken up in similar colonies across Germany – was the use of convict labour for construction. The houses they built were reportedly good ('too good!', sniffed one critic). The old moor-burning buckwheat colonies had a reputation for turning men into criminals; now convict labour was employed to construct new model colonies on the high moors.[159]

By the time Marcard's Moor was created, the landscape of the moors was changing at a faster pace. Beyond the colonies, large moor estates were being established, where gangs of seasonal labourers extracted peat. This was an extension of what had already occurred in some fen colonies. The large estates resembled the *Faktorei* in Brandenburg's Wustrau Moor that Theodor Fontane saw in 1859, where thousands of seasonal labourers worked at piece rates under the control of the 'peat-lord', watched over by the peat inspector (a figure who crops up repeatedly in his novels as well as the *Rambles*).[160] Large peat firms flourished, usually on the edge of the moors themselves: Rushmann of Varel, Lanwer and Company of Ramsloh, Dittmer-Kyritz of Oldenburg.[161] There was still cheap labour to be had for these large capitalist businesses. After the 1870s it even included Dutch peat-cutters, reversing the previous pattern that saw Germans labouring in the Netherlands.

But non-human energy was also making its appearance. Mechanized cutting machines, baling presses, the industrial processing of peat mould and peat litter, all were part of the same drive to industrialize the products of the moor. But arguably what made the most difference to the speed at which the moor disappeared was another machine, one that could cut deep under the surface and turn over the mineral riches underneath. The steam plough arrived later than those other symbols of the steam age, the railway engine and the steamship, but when it did the effects on the moor were comparably dramatic.

The Triumph of the Steamship

Ludwig Starklof's old man, the one who showed such remarkable enthusiasm for the Hunte–Ems canal, could remember the town of Oldenburg back in the late eighteenth century, when travellers were up to their knees in swamp as soon as they passed out of the gates. He would find things much changed, said Starklof; there were high roads now and the town had grown out beyond its old gates, doubling in size. Not least – and this was an obvious point of pride for the progress-minded Starklof – steamships plied the Hunte between Oldenburg and Elsfleth.[162] Such a thing would have been impossible even a decade earlier because of the shallows and meanders of the river. But a series of 'cuts' in the river, beginning in 1835 – a miniature version of those made in the Upper Rhine as a result of Johann Tulla's grand design – made the Hunte navigable. The steamships followed. Operated by the Weser-Hunte Steamship Company (Starklof was a member of the board of directors), they linked the growing capital with Oldenburg's small ports on the left bank of the Weser, Elsfleth and Brake, and in turn with Bremen and Bremerhaven. This marked the onset of something new. Through the 1850s and 60s, interrupted only by the brief economic downturn of 1857 that slowed trade, steamship traffic in Oldenburg rose steadily.[163]

What was happening in one backward corner of Germany was a sign of the times. River correction and regulation were going on everywhere. Sometimes flood prevention was the motive, or the search for new agricultural land; but increasingly it was shipping needs that drove the process. The Rhine provided the template. Work on Tulla's Upper Rhine went on through the third quarter of the nineteenth century. In 1851 a Rhine River Engineering Administration was established at Koblenz, capital of the Prussian Rhine Province, and set about taming the river as it passed through the rocky defile between Mainz and Koblenz – the Romantic Rhine that presented almost as many dangers to shipping as it did sights for tourists. Engineers addressed the whirlpool at St Goarshausen, the 'Wild Ride' at Bacharach, and the notorious Bingen Reef that caused so many shipwrecks at low water. Dynamite tripled the width of the Bingen Gap, the safe channel that ran between the rocks. Islands disappeared, as they had on the Upper Rhine. The mouths of tributaries were moved so that they entered the river at a sharper angle. The main bed was dredged to a uniform depth; wing dams of the latest design aimed to provide a uniform width.[164]

Where the Rhine led, other rivers followed. Building on a growing body of theory and experience, engineers set to work removing meanders and islands, rocky shoals and shallows. There were differences of timing and tempo. The Oder in the east and the Mosel in the west waited longer for comprehensive regulation. The Ruhr was regulated early because of its importance for carrying coal. The greatest efforts went on international waterways like the Rhine and Danube, then on rivers like the Elbe and Weser, but the attention paid to secondary streams like the Hunte and Aller showed how widespread river regulation had become.[165] Contemporaries hailed this wholesale canalization of German rivers as progress, that great keyword of the 1850s and 60s, and so did writers who looked back fondly on its fruits. Walter Tietze, from the perspective of the early twentieth century, contrasted the wild Oder that had 'conducted skirmishes against its banks' with the river that had been 'restrained and curbed by the improving hand of man'.[166]

Most educated Germans of the time believed that humans could and should 'improve' on nature. Enthusiasm for the technological by-products of human ingenuity was infused with a moral passion that it would be hard to exaggerate. Nothing better expressed this buoyant optimism than the almost magical properties attributed to steam power,

which meant the steamship as well as the railway. When the engineer
Ernst Mattern looked back on the years after mid-century, he turned
the steamship into a hero. His language is revealing. River regulation,
suggested Mattern, came 'only when the appearance of steamship traffic,
part of a larger rise in expectations associated with the new cultural
life, forced greater attention on the natural waterways in order to
harness the wealth that lay within them for the general well-being'.[167]
And it is true that the steamship was a key to the changing shape of
German rivers, just as it was a key symbol of the age.

Not that the steamer suddenly took over the river. Prussian statistics showed that there were more than 40,000 inland shipping businesses in 1849, the great majority consisting of one man and a boat;
twelve years later there were still nearly 36,000.[168] Look at almost any
of the numerous prints and engravings from the mid-nineteenth century
that depict a busy river crowded with boats. Whether the scene is the
Rhine or the Elbe the steamer is there, smoke issuing from its high,
brightly painted chimney; but so are sailing ships and flotillas of small
boats. All of them jostled together on Germany's straighter, deeper
rivers, which they also shared with steam tugs, horse-drawn barges and
the giant rafts (they weighed up to 3000 tons) that floated timber down
the Rhine, Elbe, Oder and Vistula.[169] Victor Hugo described this floating
miscellany on the Rhine in 1845:[170]

> Every moment some new object passes you, sometimes a barge so crowded
> with peasants that it is frightful to behold . . . Then the steam-boat, with
> its streamers, or one of the two-masted craft, with its cargo piled in the
> centre, descending the Rhine; the pilot with his vigilant eye, the active sailors,
> a woman chattering at the cabin-door . . . Or you see strings of horses on
> the bank, towing heavily-laden barges, or a single high-arched boat, bravely
> dragged by a single horse, just as an ant carries off a defunct beetle. Suddenly
> the river doubles upon itself, and you discover an immense raft from
> Namedy, majestically descending. Three hundred sailors man this monstrous
> craft; long oars, fore and aft, simultaneously strike the waters . . . a whole
> village floats upon this prodigious platform of wood.

These craft shared the river; but they did not share it on equal terms.
Small owners may have continued to dominate German waterways
numerically, especially where their craft (like the flat-keeled peat boats
of East Friesland) were well adapted to local conditions. But on larger,

regulated rivers the steamboat had obvious advantages of speed and freedom from the elements, especially moving upstream. When the propeller replaced the paddle wheel after the 1840s, making it easier for steamships to manoeuvre, it only reinforced their advantage. The steam tug was a major threat to the horse-drawn barge; and new deep-water inland ports with fixed quays allowed larger vessels to berth alongside the warehouse, cutting out the small lighters that carried cargoes from ship to shore. These economic and technological shifts were all taking place against a changing legal background. Navigation agreements over major rivers (Rhine, Elbe, Oder) abolished local shipping monopolies and tolls, removing commercial choke-points that had once granted shipping guilds a privileged position. This also worked to the advantage of steamship operators.[171] Displaced boatmen hired themselves out as pilots, or worked as ordinary sailors on larger vessels. Sometimes, most famously during the 1848 revolution in Mainz, they released their frustrations in physical attacks on the hated steamships.[172]

The rafting of timber, which went back to the fourteenth century, enjoyed a 'second flowering' during the second half of the eighteenth century and the first half of the nineteenth.[173] Rafts actually benefited at first from the removal of shoals and rapids, which made the business of rafting hugely risky as well as hugely profitable.[174] But these floating villages now faced dangers of a novel kind. Theodor Fontane described how steam tugs on the Oder took pleasure in swamping rafts, so that the cooking and sleeping quarters of the crew were deluged. It was like riders who spattered pedestrians with water and mud. The sight of Polish and Czech crew members leaping around to retrieve cooking pots or clothes seems to have added spice to the occasion for the German tug-boat captains. (Fontane, with his habitually sharp eye, noted that the same steam tugs sometimes assisted small boats that were in trouble, including vessels hemmed in by rafts – but the assistance was unappreciated, not just because it was expensive, but because of the gloating arrogance displayed by the steam-tug captain, who was both 'saviour and tyrant'.)[175] But rafts faced more fundamental problems than combative steam-tug captains. Timber moved on to the rails, then shipbuilders on the North Sea and Baltic moved to iron and steel-hulled ships. The swing-bridge at Mannheim still opened 405 times for rafts in 1860, 368 times in 1869, but the future held only decline. Just ten rafts passed Mannheim in 1890; ten years later it was none.[176]

Take a snapshot of the traffic on any large German river in the 1850s

or 60s, and it resembles a snapshot of a changing society: a mixture
of what is, what has been, and what is about to be. The craft on the
river were of every imaginable kind; but it was the steamship and steam
tug that would come out on top, and the diesel-powered vessels that
followed them. There were two aspects to this triumph. The unspec-
tacular part was the traffic in bulk goods: the coal that left the Ruhr
from the huge port of Duisburg-Ruhrort, the sugar carried to riverside
refineries. This aspect of inland shipping, linked to rapid industrialization as both cause and effect, was the one that interested the chambers of commerce and still dominates the economic history books. It
is what Victor Hugo had in mind when he wrote that the Rhine was
no longer a 'street of the priests' but a 'street of the merchants', or
when Eberhard Gothein enthused that 'Rhine shipping was a part of
every transformation of a nineteenth century that transformed everything'.[177] By the time Gothein was writing (1903) his words were undeniably true. A single statistic tells the story of how steam turned
navigation on Europe's busiest waterway upside down. In 1840, three
times more tonnage was carried downstream than upstream; by 1907
the proportions were reversed.[178] But this was a long-term process (even
more long-term on other rivers). Although the goods carried on German
rivers doubled in the years 1840–70, their share of all inland transportation fell because the railways grew faster. Only enormous invest-
ments in river regulation and canals after 1870 allowed inland shipping
to regain a larger share.[179]

But none of this mattered much to people in the middle decades of
the nineteenth century. What captured their imaginations was the
passenger steamer. It was usually coupled with the railway as a symbol
of progress and liberation, another instance of how the 'power and
reliability' of the steam engine had allowed men 'to triumph in the
struggle against the forces of Nature'. Those were the words of Max
Maria von Weber, eldest son of the composer, credited by his publisher
with inventing the 'technological novella'. The editor of Weber's
collected essays, Max Jähns, celebrated the steam engine in no less
extravagant terms: 'Mightier beyond compare than steed or chariot,
oar or sail, it is the new and powerful motor of our day'.[180] Similar
effusions, quite at odds with conventional notions about German
'inwardness' and dislike of mechanical civilization, could be found on
a regular basis in weekly magazines designed for family readership, like
Die Gartenlaube, *World Illustrated* or *Over Land and Sea*, all prod-

ucts of the 1850s. Large numbers of people were drawn by a new means of communication that made travel easier and brought more of the world within their grasp. Just as the railway became rapidly popular among journeymen and peasants, inspiring its own songs, so the twice-weekly Oder steamer between Frankfurt on Oder and Stettin carried not just businessmen and estate owners but day labourers and craftsmen bound for market.[181]

The first steamship sighting in a locality always attracted interest. It happened as early as 1816 in Cologne, when crowds gathered to admire a British ship travelling from London to Frankfurt. Astonishment was expressed that the journey from Rotterdam to Cologne, normally six weeks, had taken a mere four and a half days – a time that would soon seem unimaginably slow.[182] Oldenburgers saw their first steamship in 1844, when a Belgian vessel entered the harbour. It caused 'great excitement' and was recorded in an article by Ludwig Starklof, who wanted to charter the ship for a journey to Elsfleth and Brake.[183] The opening of a regularly scheduled service, like the first railway journey from a new station, was an occasion for speeches, bunting and hurrahs. More unexpectedly, perhaps, the regular arrival of the scheduled steamer continued to draw enthusiastic crowds in places where people depended on the service or simply welcomed news, visitors and excitement from the outside world. The historian of Trier notes how people made their way down to meet the Mosel steamers in the third quarter of the nineteenth century.[184] Theodor Fontane describes his Oder steamship rounding a bend in the river so that a landing stage became visible and an old wooden bridge filled with hundreds of people. When the steamer tied up there was 'a pressing forward, a greeting, accompanied by the ringing of a bell'. They had arrived in Schwedt.[185]

Things were different on the Rhine. Not that there was any shortage of 'bustle', the word used by English visitor Michael Quin to describe the quay at Koblenz one morning in 1842. As he noted: 'Steamers were smoking in all directions, some just arrived, some preparing to start either up or down the Rhine'.[186] The point is that this had become a matter of routine on the river. When the Prussian-Rhenish Steamship Company (later the Cologne-Düsseldorf line) began service between Cologne and Mainz in 1827 with the steamship *Concordia*, it carried 18,000 passengers. By the time of Michael Quin's visit the figure was almost 700,000; twenty years later it was more than a million. And there were other companies that competed over the same routes.[187]

Sheer numbers made the impact of Rhine steamships different. It was not the progress or arrival of a single vessel that made an impression, but the effect made by the sight of eight or ten of them on the same stretch of river. Michael Quin and Victor Hugo both remarked on this 'spectacle'.[188] But it was a later visitor who best captured this sense that the steamship itself was a part of the spectacle. Lucy Hill was a young American woman who spent an autumn in the mid-1870s as a guest at the Schiller Institute near Koblenz, an experience described in *Rhine Roamings*.[189] Lucy Hill and her companions made frequent trips, to Königswinter, Lahnstein, Mainz and many famous landmarks along the Middle Rhine. All involved steamers, which play a central role in her account – catching them, nearly missing them, eating on them, 'adventures' with fellow passengers aboard them. It is in keeping with the spirit of her book that each of its four illustrations depicting a celebrated Rhineland location also includes a steamship. Prolonged exposure led Lucy Hill to an insight that shines clearly through her sentimental prose:[190]

> [W]e feared the steamboat would be a few minutes early, and we should lose sight of it. But no; we had a few minutes to wait. When it made its appearance, it was greeted with an unanimous 'Oh! how beautiful! how fairy-like!' . . . The steamer was a double-decked American boat, the only one of its kind then on the Rhine; its decks were crowded with passengers, who, although seemingly enraptured with what they were witnessing, were wholly ignorant of the active part they were taking in the scene, – the body of the boat, its well-lighted saloons, its crowded decks, its flags and tall chimneys, and, lastly, the waving of handkerchiefs as the passengers descried us on the bank, were all truthfully reflected in the waters beneath.

The steamer had a starring role in the drama of winking lights and reflections that cast a 'magic spell'.

The opposite was, of course, the more conventional opinion: that the view *from* the steamship afforded 'panoramas'. The idea of the panorama, of nature arranging itself for the human eye to enjoy, belonged to the mental furniture of these years as much as the idea of progress.[191] Where eighteenth-century travellers collected mineral specimens or flowers, nineteenth-century travellers collected views or moods. When we think of modern communications opening up new panoramas to contemporaries, it is usually the railway that comes to mind.[192] But the steamship had the same effect – perhaps more so, because it allowed the traveller more time. Fontane found the steamer a perfect place from which to capture views that were 'scenic' (one of his favourite words). For travellers on the Middle Rhine, these sensations came one after the other, like an anthology of visual quotations. Victor Hugo thought that Bacharach resembled a 'gigantic curiosity shop' arranged for display. Michael Quin recommended travellers upstream to look at the scenery that had passed because '[t]he panorama always seemed to me more perfect in its outlines and accessories when contemplated that way'. Even those possessed of a more sceptical spirit found it hard to avoid the term. Karl Immermann, although declaring heretically that he found the Middle Rhine 'monotonous', conceded that he enjoyed 'the panorama of Mainz'.[193]

The Rhine was different because of the sheer number of travellers, their international composition (the English were especially prominent), and the unequalled mystique of the 'Romantic Rhine'.[194] The rocky gorge between Koblenz and Bingen was where, in Michael Quin's revealing phrase, 'the Rhine begins to look like itself', that is to say, where it began to resemble the guide-book accounts of what it was supposed to look like.[195]

Quin was one of the many who helped to establish this programmed response through his own writings. Friedrich Engels satirized the effect when he described John Bull, the Englishman who stayed in his steamship cabin from Rotterdam to Cologne 'and only then steps up on deck because that is where his Panorama of the Rhine from Cologne to Mainz or his Guide for travellers on the Rhine begins'.[196] This stretch of the river, with its dramatic striations of basalt and shale, its striking natural features that bore so many literary associations, like the Drachenfels and Lorelei, its vineyards and ruined castles, lived off a carefully cultivated reputation for the wild and Gothic, even as steamships, travel guides, Cooks Tours, hotels, guest houses and porters made the experience of travelling there increasingly comfortable.

But the Rhine was different only in scale. What was happening there also happened somewhat later and more modestly elsewhere. Faster and more reliable means of transportation were opening up the business of leisure everywhere. The first Baedeker guide was devoted to the Rhine (the firm was based in Koblenz), but the familiar red books, which included steamer schedules and railway connections, soon covered other regions of Germany.[197] And while the Rhine may have been unique in the combination of sights, legends and literary associations it offered (it certainly was in the eyes of its own promoters), other localities assiduously cultivated the virtues of their own landscapes and cultures. One irony of the decades that preceded unification is that, at the very moment when improved communications were stitching the future nation more closely together, there was a growing tendency to foster local identities.[198]

Take the case of spa towns, which were among the favoured destinations of these years.[199] Numbers of visitors rose substantially over the third quarter of the century. The Rhine certainly enjoyed a special position here: no other German river was so important as a conduit to the fashionable watering places that lay on or near it, such as Wiesbaden, Bad Ems and the spas in the Taunus mountains. That was one reason why the landing stages of Koblenz and Mainz were so busy during the 'season'. But other rivers served the same purpose on a more modest scale. Even Fontane's Oder steamer had a few travellers en route to Silesian spas.[200] There were over 300 places where people took the waters in Germany. The great majority were not glittering international meeting places, famous for their casinos, literary celebrities and royal visitors. They were more understated, geared to the middle class; they had no roulette, no real or pseudo-Englishmen, and they served *Frühstück*, not *Breakfast*.[201] These formed the backbone of the new culture of travel and leisure. And, like every town or region that looked to attract visitors, they combined the attraction of what was becoming familiar and routine (timetables, guide books) with the appeal of what was locally distinctive, whether the properties of its waters or the uniqueness of its views. The model of the Romantic Rhine, in short, was widely imitated.

Both railway and steamship played a large part in this new form of travel. Indeed, their timetables were coordinated. But there were two particular locations, other than the Middle Rhine, where the steamer really came into its own. One was on the lake. Through the eighteenth century the only kinds of recreational activity to be found on German lakes were the masques and mock battles that took place in the grounds of aristocratic estates.[202] But during the nineteenth century lakes came to be prized as places of leisure. Lake Constance, in the far south of Germany, is a perfect example. Resort towns like Nonnenhorn, Wasserburg, Überlingen, Meersburg and Bodman developed on the German side in the years after 1850, with the familiar infrastructure of promenades, hotels and guest houses – and landing stages. The first steamship appeared on the lake in 1827. As the area drew more visitors, steamers ferried passengers across to the Swiss side, on excursions to the 'island of flowers' and on moonlight trips. They were as central to the appeal of the area as firework displays or the view of the Alps on a clear day.[203] The steamship proved even more essential in attracting visitors to the North Sea islands. Norderney, established in 1797, remained for decades a fashionable playground of the elite because it was so hard to reach. Growth came in the middle years of the century, when rail links brought travellers to the coast and regular steamship service became available. Between 1830 and 1870 bathing resorts were established on the East Frisian islands of Langeoog, Juist, Borkum and Baltrum. Föhr and Sylt, which lay off the coast of Schleswig-Holstein, were opened up to leisure travellers in the same period.[204]

There were some echoes of the Rhineland in the popularity of the North Frisian islands. Both drew an international clientele: there were complaints that Sylt became 'a kind of new-America'.[205] Yet both were also attractive to some German visitors because of their symbolic importance to the national cause. Nationalist writers in the first half of the nineteenth century painted the Rhineland as a quintessentially 'German' landscape, responding heatedly to French claims on the left bank. This reached its height during the war scare of 1840.[206] The islands of Sylt and Föhr acquired a similarly 'German' pathos after 1848 because of their proximity to the disputed duchies of Schleswig and Holstein. This sentiment was apparent in accounts of the islands like Ernst Adolf Willkomm's *Journeys by the North Sea and the Baltic* (1850).[207]

Island and lakeside resorts, inland spa towns and the Rhineland all had something else in common. They represented the domestication of German waters. What travellers did on their trips amounted to another way in which water was 'conquered'. That was true whether they steamed through the water, boated on it, drank it from fountains and bottles, bathed in it, gazed at scenic panoramas of it, or took the opportunity (like Bismarck at Norderney) to shoot seals and dolphins that swam in it.[208] These more or less harmless recreational activities rested on an increasingly complex infrastructure that made travel less arduous and enjoyment of the natural landscape more convenient. Spa towns did their best to shield guests from floods and rockfalls, meanwhile constructing paths (even funicular railways) to suitable panoramas; the North Sea islands invested after 1850 not only in jetties, promenades and bathing machines, but in sea-walls and breakwaters against the wind-driven tides that threatened to eat away at the exposed western ends of the islands.[209]

It is a cliché that those who could afford to travel went to the seaside or lake as an escape from the hectic world of the growing city. But there was no need to leave home to reap the benefits of construction projects that put nature in its place. During the busy years of growth after the middle of the century, new wealth, civic pride and optimism reshaped German city centres. Like Ludwig Starklof's Oldenburg, but on a larger scale, they burst out beyond their old walls and gates, permanently altered by the arrival of the railway and hungry for more space. Homes, commercial buildings and symbols of cultural progress like museums and botanical gardens appeared along new gaslit boulevards.[210] Taming troublesome waters was often a prelude to these changes. Until the 1860s the area west of Leipzig's historic centre was marshland that flooded when the Elster and Pleisse overflowed their banks. There was even a popular song with the first line 'In the great seaside city of Leipzig, there was once a most terrible flood' (its most famous line ran: 'On the roof there sits an old man, who does not know what to do'). Then the Elster was canalized in the 1860s and the marshland drained, creating the handsome residential area that later housed the Supreme Court of unified Germany.[211] The Ohle in Breslau was filled in to create new streets in the same decade.[212] The area around the Alster in Hamburg was similarly rebuilt. Refashioning the Alster not only removed a potential peril; it added a public resource. In new city centres across Germany the seriousness of commerce and culture was leavened by riverside promenades and public parks, where artificial bodies of water were conjured up if none was already there to domesticate. Suburban sprawl, meanwhile, brought outlying lakes within the reach of city-dwellers. All this created new recreational opportunities by the water: orderly and respectable in public parks, more muscular or frankly hedonistic along the river and on outlying lakes. As small boats disappeared from the great commercial waterways, they found a niche on urban lakes. As professional fishermen struggled with the effects of river regulation, weekend anglers multiplied in the cities. These were the years in which the German mania for forming clubs led rowers and sailors to begin creating their own organizations. Bathing places proliferated. It was not until the end of the century that Heinrich Zille sketched the bathers and pipe-smoking clerks enjoying the waters of Berlin, but they were there before he recorded them.

The steamship naturally had its place in this waterborne playground, nowhere more than in Greater Berlin. The conditions for steamer services there were ideal. For one thing, new artificial waterways were being constantly built, following the line of natural but unnavigable streams. For another, the outlying areas into which the city was growing contained numerous lakes. These advantages unlocked entrepreneurial energies. At the end of the 1840s the proprietor of the Maass Swimming and Bathing Establishment for Gentleman By the Schlesisches Tor had started a modest steamship service for customers that left from the Island Bridge. When Louis Sachse took over the business in 1859 he extended service up the Spree to Treptow. Five years later he joined two investors from Stettin to found the Berlin and Cöpenick Steamship Company. From a floating landing stage by the Jannowitz Bridge, four 60-foot ships capable of holding 120 passengers each plied the waterways through the eastern and south-eastern suburbs. By 1866 the company, now called simply the Berlin Steamship Company, had a fleet of thirteen vessels. To the west of the city regular steamship service on the *Fortuna*, *Kladderadatsch* and *Trio* was offered by A. H. Berndt of Berlin, who competed on the same route with the shipbuilder August Gebhardt from Potsdam. After a battle of newspaper advertisements, Gebhardt eventually came out on top and bought up his rival's fleet. Routes radiated out in every direction from the centre of Berlin: east via Treptow and Köpenick to the Müggelsee, Erkner and on to Stietzensee, south-east through Köpenick up the Dahme to Scharmützelsee, west via Potsdam to Nedlitz and Paretz, north to the Heiligensee, Niederfinow and the Ruppiner See.[213]

'Nothing is more Berlinerisch than a steamer trip on the waters of the March', wrote the journalist Harry Schreck in 1929. Steamer trips like these, he thought, were among the few simple, traditional pleasures left in an age that had little time for tradition. The nostalgia was understandable enough, but it built in many ways on an illusion. Leisure activities themselves would become increasingly organized, commercialized and – under National Socialism – politicized in the twentieth century. For better and for worse, the innocent steamer trip on the waters of the March represented the real break with the past, the beginning of something new and modern.[214]

Further Victories over the Powers of Nature

In September 1844 the Association of German Natural Scientists and Physicians held its annual meeting in Bremen, where the chairman of the local branch greeted them with the ringing declaration that this was their 'golden age'.[215] Confidence was never in short supply at the Association's gatherings. A quarter of a century later the physicist and physiologist Hermann von Helmholtz told the audience in his opening address that what bound them together was the conviction that science would 'make the reasonless forces of nature subservient to the moral purposes of humanity'. Scientists, teachers, influential statesmen, members of the 'cultivated classes of the nation' – all 'look to us for further progress in civilization, further victories over the powers of nature'.[216]

There was no better place to announce the dawning of a golden age than Bremen, the city state perched on the German North Sea coast, facing the wider world. One reason for the boundless mid-century optimism was the girding of the globe with new technology. What the telegraph was doing within the nation, it was believed, the under-water cable would do internationally. And the same went for the power of steam. The steamship was a 'vehicle of universal communication', 'the mediator of the human omnipresence throughout the globe'.[217] If this was true, then Bremen was the word made flesh. Together with its new out-port of Bremerhaven, the Hanseatic city was a German window on a world that seemed to be getting smaller every year. In the 1860s it took forty-four days to sail across the Atlantic, but only two weeks under steam power; by the 1880s that was down to ten days. The arrival of the *Washington* in Bremerhaven on 19 June 1847 initiated regular steamship service between Europe and the United States. Over the following decades, as steam reduced the cost as well as duration of the crossing, Bremerhaven became one of the most important links between Germany and the Americas. The steamships brought cotton, tobacco, rice and coffee across the Atlantic. What they carried back was refined sugar, processed rice, beer – and people. Four million Germans left for the USA between the 1840s and the First World War. More emigrants departed from Bremerhaven than from any other port, 77,000 in 1854 alone. The Norddeutscher Lloyd, founded in Bremen in 1857, became one of the world's great shipping lines. After the end of the American Civil War eight of its steamers left for New York every week. Norddeutscher Lloyd vessels could be found across the world, in California, India, Hong Kong and Australia.[218]

None of this would have been possible without constant innovation close to home. Only twenty years after Bremerhaven first opened, a new port was built between 1847 and 1851 to handle larger ships. In 1858 it was rebuilt again. Bremerhaven went through a cycle of deepening its docks, like Wilhelmshaven, but it did so earlier and quicker. New light-ships, lighthouses, buoys and pilot stations safeguarded the main shipping channel and approaches to the Weser; the North German Marine Observatory was established at Hamburg in 1868.[219] The dimensions of docks and the positioning of navigation buoys: it sounds like something that only an antiquarian transport historian could love, on a par with collecting bus tickets – except that contemporaries showed a remarkable zeal for details of this sort, which were invariably used to demonstrate how everything was becoming bigger, stronger or faster. The message was also disseminated in books for the young, like Ernst Schick's *Detailed Description of Notable Buildings, Monuments, Bridges, Facilities, Hydraulic Constructions, Art Works, Machines, Instruments, Inventions and Undertakings of Modern and Recent Times, Adapted for the Instructive Entertainment of Mature Youth*. Schick did not stint on lighthouses or harbours.[220]

Beyond the buoys and pilot stations of the North Sea coast, the world's sea lanes were also becoming more secure in the third quarter of the century, and significantly shorter. Here we are perhaps more prepared for the interest displayed by contemporaries, although it is still possible to be taken aback by their zeal. In the one-volume version of his *Comparative General Geography*, published in 1868, Ernst Kapp hailed the navigation of the 'main roads' through the oceans as a 'triumph of the mind over [these] bodies of water'. Writing just one year before the Suez Canal opened, he had no doubt that 'with the completion of this correction, which is in the general interest of civilized humanity throughout the globe, the human mind will finally achieve mastery over even this disadvantage of nature it has suffered for thousands of years'. The word 'correction' was, of course, the same term used to describe what was being done to the Rhine and other German rivers. Kapp's use of it was no accident. He believed that, given the size of the oceans that were to be joined by the Suez Canal (and the Panama Canal of the future), blasting through an isthmus was comparable to removing the rocks that impeded the flow of a river – a mere trifle.[221]

How do we explain this habitual tone of confidence in human mastery? At least three currents of thought flowed into it. In the first place, belief in progress carried larger political and cultural hopes for the future. For a progressive like Ludwig Starklof, steamship and railway alike were symbols of a new, less cramped society, the view put most provocatively by Friedrich Harkort when he boasted that 'the locomotive is the hearse that will carry absolutism and feudalism to the graveyard'.[222] This was a familiar tone in the 1840s. We encounter it often in Heinrich Heine. The same utopian optimism rings clearly through Karl Mathy's 1846 article for that liberal bible, Rotteck and Welcker's *Staats-Lexikon*, on 'Railways and Canals, Steamships and Steam Transportation'. These powerful new forces would make the fields fruitful and bring new life to workshops, argued Mathy; they would 'also grant the lowest among us the power to educate themselves by visiting foreign lands, to seek work in faraway areas and to recover their health in distant watering places or seaside resorts'.[223] This optimism did not disappear with the end of the 1848 revolution. Ernst Kapp was himself a '48er who emigrated to America after the revolution, where he built himself a house in Texas, before returning to Germany in the 1860s as an unreconstructed apostle of progress.[224]

After the political semi-freeze of the 1850s, liberal optimism burst out again after 1859. The formation of the Progressive Party was one sign of it. Another was the combative rhetoric of the men who addressed the Association of German Natural Scientists and Physicians. None addressed them more often, or was more combative in the cause of progress, than Rudolf Virchow – physician, scientist, scientific popularizer, Progressive Party politician and ferocious anti-clerical.[225] This last is important. It was not only the lingering authoritarianism of German governments, but even more the resurgence of religious 'obscurantism' in the Catholic Church (the Syllabus of Errors in 1864, papal infallibility in 1870), that explains the shrill tone of progressive language in these years. The railway and the steamship were sticks with which to beat a Church that had hurled its anathemas at the modern world. Liberals and progressives saw themselves fighting a war on two fronts: against a nature that constrained humanity, and the 'backward-looking' humans who did the same.[226]

These views were infused with nationalism: united Germany would settle accounts with both Roman machinations and provincial narrow-mindedness. A distinctly German pride in modern scientific accomplishments was important in another way, and suggests a second reason for the peculiarly bombastic insistence on human mastery over nature. Germany had long seen itself and been viewed by others as the 'land of poets and thinkers' – dreamy, metaphysical, impractical. Brash celebration of science and technical invention was a reaction against this stereotype. The politicians, scientists and other members of the educated middle classes who thundered about the steamship and progress were disowning the dreamy image, and casting off another long-standing national symbol: the gentle, nightcap-wearing, unworldly figure of the 'German Michel'. Virchow, Helmholtz and Kapp had more energetic heroes. So did the editors of family weeklies like *Die Gartenlaube* and other publications that lauded modern technology. Otto Spamer's *Help Yourself!*, a series of portraits of 'men who have risen through their own initiative', paid special attention to scientific researchers, inventors and engineers. They deserved gratitude for their contributions to 'culture, intellectual development and human progress', because it was thanks to their 'path-breaking new ideas' that 'a fresh breeze blows through our present-day world'.[227]

There is a final reason for contemporary expressions of wonderment about human mastery over nature. The sense of wonder was, paradoxically, a tribute to the respect accorded to the natural, physical world as a force that shaped human affairs. Because this idea is now so unfamiliar, at least in the form it assumed in the nineteenth century, it requires a real effort of the imagination to enter the minds of men (and we are talking here about men) who believed that geography was destiny. But whether we read the works of the geographer Carl Ritter, the philosopher-geographer Ernst Kapp or the historian Heinrich von Treitschke, what runs through them all like a red thread is the belief that group and national destinies were shaped by geophysical features (and by climate) – in Ritter's shorthand phrase, 'the External Features of the Earth in their Influence on the Course of History'.[228] It was precisely because these prominent figures and the thousands who read them believed deeply in the determining effect of mountain ranges and coastlines on how human societies evolved that they were so impressed by the instruments of human ingenuity that exploded these constraints. Ritter was pleased to record that steam power had effectively reduced the length of rivers six- or sevenfold; even a canal through the isthmus of Suez appeared to be possible. He concluded: 'The whole physical conditions of earth are changed as the mind of man gains wider and firmer rule'.[229]

It was a cliché of these years that the world was getting smaller. You could travel around it in 100 days; soon it would be only 80. The power of steam navigation also brought hitherto unexplored areas within reach. Among the 'men of action' Otto Spamer so much admired were those Germans who travelled overseas to explore and map areas still unknown or little known (to Europeans). Neither the travel nor the celebrity it brought was new. A half-century or more earlier the same instinct had sent Carsten Niebuhr to Arabia, Alexander von Humboldt up the Orinoco and Georg Forster around the world. As recently as 1845 Ludwig Leichardt had set off to cross the Australian continent for the first time, dying in the desert three years later.[230] But journeys like this became more numerous in the third quarter of the nineteenth century, and the machinery for publicizing them became more energetic.

This was an imperialism of the imagination, an outburst of cultural confidence that was a prelude to the political and economic imperialism that would be such a central aspect of Germany after the 1880s. It also expressed a fascination with the 'exotic', which was the *alter ego* of the faith in progress that dominated the middle decades of the nineteenth century. The unfamiliar and different were taken as a challenge. Two destinations caught the contemporary imagination. One was Africa. Between 1849 and 1855 Heinrich Barth, a classicist-turned-geographer, travelled extensively in Africa north of the equator, becoming just the third European to enter Timbuktu. His *Travels and Discoveries in North and Central Africa*, initially published in five volumes, was later issued in an edition aimed at the general public, although it was mainly the 'men of science' who celebrated Barth on his return.[231] Better known to the public was Gerhard Rohlfs, who crossed the Sahara, then made a journey across Africa from Tripoli to the Gulf of Guinea in the 1860s. Rohlfs was a doctor, so his later journeys into Sudan make him the German Dr Livingstone – if Livingstone can be imagined serving, as Rohlfs had done, in the French Foreign Legion. German explorers were especially numerous in Africa during the 1860s and 70s. They included Georg Schweinfurth, Karl Mauch, Eduard Mohr and Oskar Lenz. Their travels embraced every part of the Continent, including the west coast and the interior, although most were drawn at some stage to the Sahara.[232]

If Africa in the German imagination stood for the hot and the 'dark', the cold, white Arctic was its opposite. Germans also devoted themselves to travel and research in Polar waters, beyond the point ever reached by German whaling ships that had once sailed out of the North Sea ports. The original stimulus came from the geographer August Petermann, whose talk at the national gathering of German geographers at Frankfurt in 1865 was enthusiastically received. Political uncertainties delayed things, but the first German North Pole Expedition was mounted in 1868. The 80-foot steamship *Germania*, captained by Karl Koldewey, spent four summer months in the Polar region before returning with scientific data but no major geographical findings. A second expedition was immediately planned for the following year. It used two vessels (the *Germania* joined by the sailing ship *Hansa*), and was led once again by Koldewey. The party included six scientists and a battery of scientific instruments. Departure from Bremerhaven on 15 June 1869 was graced by the presence of Wilhelm I and Bismarck, just two days before they travelled on to the formal inauguration of Wilhelmshaven. The expedition discovered and mapped the eastern coast of Greenland and wintered over in the pack ice. The crew of *Germania* returned to the Weser in September 1870, to discover that the Franco–Prussian War was underway. The *Hansa* had been lost, but its party survived the breaking ice in the spring and all were eventually brought home safely. They had spent a total of 237 days on an ice floe, basis enough for heroic accounts. At a meal to welcome back both crews, the chairman of the expedition committee offered a toast: 'We are now able to look with pride and joy on the achievements of the sailors and scientists, they have gloriously demonstrated German nautical proficiency, German persistence and German striving for the enrichment of science'.[233]

The emphasis on science was typical of the age. More natural history, natural science and geographical societies were founded in the decades from the 1840s through the 1870s than at any other time in the nineteenth century.[234] The Moor Research Station in Bremen and the North German Marine Observatory in Hamburg were also classic products of their time. But more than science was at stake in the voyages of exploration. Journeys up the Limpopo and expeditions to Polar waters tapped into a deeper contemporary belief that the constraints of the natural world could be overcome. The explorers added dramatic exclamation marks to a 'golden age' that saw a new naval base rise out of the mud, further conquest of the moors in the name of internal colonization, and wholesale domestication of German rivers through regulation and the steamship. In 1860, when Louis Thomas published his *Book of Miraculous Inventions* aimed at young people, he included an introduction with the title 'Man, the Master of the Earth'. After describing how humankind had overcome its inferiority to other creatures in strength, hearing or eyesight by superior ingenuity and technology, Thomas went on:[235]

> And so man is the crown of creation, and that he is the master of the whole earth is proved by the earth itself. He burrows through its very innards and sows its surface with plants of every kind; the plants that grow in the hot zones he is able to grow in more temperate climates; his canals, his railways plough through the earth, with his dynamite he can blow away and topple rocks; he builds roads over the highest mountains, he joins oceans by cutting through mighty isthmuses, and he transforms deserts into states rich in towns or into fruitful fields. Storm, rain or cold cannot stand in his way, distance can no longer keep him permanently from his goal, the oceans cannot divide him.

It was, of course, a partial view in more ways than one. The builders of Wilhelmshaven knew that it was not as easy as that. It took no time at all to write a rhapsody like Thomas's; taming the mud and keeping the North Sea at bay took years, and victory was never final. The engineers of the Hunte–Ems canal knew the same thing; so did the fen colonists of East Friesland and Oldenburg. These were the human costs of conquering unruly waters, paid by people with muddier boots and poorer health than the poets of progress. Sometimes the human cost took more dramatic form, like the boiler explosions that plagued the early steamships and the heavy losses of transatlantic vessels in the early years – 144 steamers went down in the North Atlantic between 1838 and 1878. The radical poet Ferdinand Freiligrath gave the point an extra twist, one designed to puncture the complacency of the well-off, when he noted that the safety of steamship passengers depended on the stokers and engineers who laboured below decks, away from the light and the scenery: one willed act by them, and the ship went up in the air.[236]

What went up in the air every time a steamer left its berth was smoke. The smoke from moor burning was diminishing, partly under the impact of societies formed to outlaw it, but the 'smoke scourge' produced by steamship funnels was already taking its place alongside other forms of pollution as one of the costs of progress.[237] Another was household and industrial waste that turned rivers into noxious threats to human health and aquatic life. A local newspaper described the Emscher in 1875 as 'dark black in colour and giving off a pestilential stink. Fish, crabs and frogs perish in the . . . river poisoned by ammonia and tar'.[238] The problem extended beyond the coal mining area of the Ruhr. In 1877 140 Saxon districts lodged complaints about polluted waterways. More than 90 per cent of them pointed to problems caused by industry.[239] The degradation of German rivers by industrialization (and 'industrialized' agriculture) was starting to arouse contemporaries. Societies were formed to combat it; scientists debated whether the self-cleansing capacities of German rivers could cope with an unprecedented burden. Wilhelm Raabe used a real-life court case as the basis of his 1884 novel, *Pfister's Mill*, which recounted the threat to a popular countryside inn by the pollution released from an upstream sugar refinery.[240]

These were among the human costs of progress; but what about the non-human costs? Friedrich Nietzsche, repelled by the pomposity of the progress-mongers and always ready to offer an untimely thought, had a word for what humans were doing to their environment: 'Our whole attitude towards nature, the way we violate nature with the help of machines and the heedless inventiveness of our technologists and engineers, is one of hubris'.[241] By the time he wrote that, in 1887, the darker side of progress was receiving plenty of attention. Botanists and zoologists lamented the disappearing habitats and threatened breeding grounds caused by river regulation and steamship traffic. The moors also had their anguished defenders. The Bavarian mineralogist Franz von Kobell complained that peat-digging and moorland drainage were destroying the local bird population. 'People behave as if the world was for their use only'; they wiped out the moorland birds 'as if they had the right to improve on creation'. 'In a few hundred years', so he worried in 1854, the moors would exist 'in name only'.[242] That turned out to be much too optimistic. Threatened bird species aroused very vocal concern. Franz von Kobell feared for the snipe that had once thrived on the Dachau moors; the botanist and pioneering moorland conservationist Carl Albert Weber was alarmed about the decline of blackcock and curlew. Others pointed to the retreat of the white stork as wetlands disappeared and with them the frogs on which the birds depended.[243] Similar trends were deplored across Germany. The teacher and ornithologist Karl Theodor Liebe, who spent forty years recording bird life in his native Thuringia, described in 1878 how many of the species observed in that time had disappeared. The same year he founded the German Association for Bird Protection, the first of five separate organizations with this aim established before the end of the century. Public pressure contributed to the passage of the Imperial Law on Bird Protection in 1888.[244]

The warning voices belonged to both amateurs and professionals. This was the great age of the amateur naturalist, as it was of the weekend archaeologist. Officials, clergymen and teachers combed the land with their nets and notebooks, recording, collecting and worrying. This was the other side of the culture of progress. The prestige of science, the reverence for detailed observation and hard facts, propelled members of natural history societies into the countryside, on the lookout for living species as well as fossils. What they found could be as disturbing in the one case as the other. For professional scientists the two things were connected, especially after publication of Darwin's *On the Origin of Species* in 1859, which had a major impact in Germany. The fate of species past led to fruitful thinking about species present and the relationship between them. In his evolution-inspired work on general morphology, published in 1866, physiologist Ernst Haeckel coined the term 'ecology', defined as the science of the relationship of an organism to its surrounding external environment – its 'conditions of existence'.[245]

German scientists played a vital role in the emergence of modern ecological thinking. This body of thought, in turn, owed a special debt to study of aquatic species and habitats. At the end of the 1850s, the zoologist and scientific popularizer Adolf Rossmässler, an expert on molluscs, energetically advanced the cause of the marine aquarium: an artificial environment, it is true, but one that demonstrated in microcosm the subtle interdependence of species, the pedagogical cause to which Rossmässler was passionately committed. Germany duly opened its first aquarium in 1864, in Hamburg. It was set up by August Möbius, a key figure in ecological thought. Möbius was a marine zoologist and another mollusc man. He worked on the fauna of the Kiel Bay, then wrote a pioneering account of oyster beds, noting the dangers of excessive harvesting. But he owes his subsequent fame to the fact that he coined the term 'biocoenosis', which would long remain the European term for what early American ecologists called a 'living community'. In the following decade Friedrich Junge, who had studied with Möbius, published his *Village Pond as a Living Community*. It was a forerunner of the holistic accounts that would soon be devoted to other habitats, like the moor (Carl Weber), the forest (Karl Gayer) and the lake (August Thienemann).[246] Common to all this work was the conclusion that disturbances to one species, or one part of an ecosystem, had ripple effects. And the lesson was that humans should not intervene heedlessly in complex webs of life.

Environmental disturbances were still most likely to cause alarm if one of the species that felt the negative impact was humans. Pollution was the prime example, but not the only one. One result of the greatly increased traffic across the world's oceans was what we would now call 'biological invasions'. It was not just people, cotton and tobacco that crossed the Atlantic; other species made these journeys as stowaways, in the cargo hold or attached to the hull of the ship. The invasive species that created most alarm in newly unified Germany were two arrivals from North America, the vine disease phylloxera and the Colorado beetle, which attacked potatoes. The government official charged with dealing with these threats to German agriculture later wrote a lightly ironic account in his memoirs about the 'war of extermination' waged against these and other harmful insects.[247] But humour was in short supply at the time. The invaders arrived when there were also fears of French threats to the western border and at the height of the campaign against the Catholic Church known as the *Kulturkampf*, prompting one anti-clerical to lump phylloxera and the Colorado beetle together with the Jesuits and 'other enemies of the Reich'.[248] This was a case where language that elided the distinction between human and non-human species had a purpose. Catholics were dehumanized as a prelude to their persecution, just as Jews began to be referred to as a 'bacillus' or as 'vermin' by followers of the new, pseudo-scientific anti-Semitism that arose in Germany at the end of the 1870s.

Other species – algaes, fish, molluscs – were carried into German waterways, like the zebra mussel in the Rhine, where they established themselves in already damaged ecosystems.[249] These problems became more severe after the invention of the ballast tank in 1840, which sucked in species promiscuously and released them thousands of miles away. Ballast tanks came into general use around 1880, intensifying what one writer has called the 'ecological roulette' of aquatic invasions.[250]

Another concern appeared on the horizon in the years after mid-century. The cultivation of moorland, the corsetting of rivers within a small part of their floodplains, the draining of ponds and marshes at an accelerating pace, all prompted the question: was Germany 'drying out'? Perhaps there were dangers in draining wetlands remorselessly and speeding water from catchment basin to ocean. The result might be lower water tables, with long-term effects on climate, wildlife and human convenience. This issue was starting to be raised in several countries in the 1850s and 60s, most notably in a great landmark work by the New Englander George Perkins Marsh, *Man and Nature*, first published in 1864.[251] Jacques Babinet was asking similar questions in France. So were people in German-speaking Europe, from the Austrian Gustav Wex to botanists concerned about falling water tables along the Upper Rhine after Tulla's corrections.[252] Perhaps the closest German analogue to Marsh was the Bavarian botanist Karl Fraas. Like Perkins, he had lived around the Mediterranean and pondered the fate of once flourishing agricultural lands. This led him to worry along similar lines about the damaging human impact on climate and the environment. In 1847 Fraas published *Climate and Plant World over Time: A Contribution to History*. One of his enthusiastic readers was Karl Marx, who wrote to Engels in 1868 that Fraas had demonstrated how bourgeois civilization 'left deserts in its wake'.[253] But it was not until the early twentieth century that concern about Germany turning into a 'steppe' land became more widely and urgently voiced.

Man and *nature* was the title of George Perkins Marsh's book. When his German contemporaries sounded the alarm about the consequences of human arrogance it was also 'nature', not 'the environment', that they invoked. But nature did not mean the same to everyone; it was the common thread linking people who held otherwise very different views. Some saw nature as a source of revealed truth, a spiritual force to rival religion. Heribert Rau's *The Gospel of Nature* was their holy book. Rau followed Rousseau, Goethe and other pantheistic writers in emphasizing the need for reverence towards nature as a life force. At no other point in the nineteenth century did this view strike such chords in Germany as it did in the 1850s and 60s, when it was a reaction to the materialism of scientists and others who viewed the natural world as nothing more than a series of physical forces. Those who instead saw nature as a 'temple' enjoyed a solid institutional basis: in journals like *Nature*; in the Humboldt societies established in 1859, the centenary year of Alexander von Humboldt's birth; and among scientists exploring the interdependence of species, whose holistic categories were very similar to the oneness-with-nature emphasized by Rau. Darwinism was an important stimulus to those who saw nature in this way, and it followed that they in turn were often sceptical of organized religion. Many belonged to heterodox groups: Protestant 'friends of the light', 'German Catholics' who had broken from Rome. Haeckel called for a 'simple religion of nature' as an alternative to the teachings of the Christian churches. In fact, he suggested that the non-anthropocentrism of ecological ideas had more in common with Buddhism than with the Christian emphasis on humankind as the crown of creation, distinct from and superior to other species.[254]

Yet orthodox Christianity also provided a basis for lamenting what was being done to nature by impious humankind. Whatever the Book of Genesis said about 'subjugation' and 'dominion' over nature, there were other strands of thought in the Christian tradition.[255] They were expressed in Franz von Kobell's strictures against those who behaved as if they could improve on creation. The ornithologist Carl Theodor Liebe echoed him: God had created plants and animals as well as human beings; all His creatures were therefore worthy of respect.[256] These were arguments from the principle of final causes: every creature in the universe had a reason to exist and a place in the divine plan. That such arguments were being made in the 1850s or 1870s will surprise only those who believe that German intellectual life had become thoroughly 'secularized' by the middle of the nineteenth century, when in fact one in every six published books was still a work of theology. Protestant and Catholic conservatives were especially repelled by the age of progress and 'materialism'. In mourning lost nature, they mourned for a world in which everything they treasured – ideas and social relations as much as familiar landmarks – seemed to be at risk.

In 1880 the conservative music professor Ernst Rudorff published an article called 'On the relationship of modern life to nature'.[257] It was prompted by his opposition to a proposed funicular railway for tourists by the side of the Rhine at Drachenfels, but went far beyond that. Rudorff savaged the instrumental attitude towards nature that he believed to be a symptom of degraded contemporary culture. He indicted the trivializing effects of tourism; he also attacked the technocratic urge to sacrifice beauty to utility by straightening every stream and destroying every nesting place for birds in the pursuit of profit. Rudorff's jeremiad, rooted in a deep dislike of modern life, was largely concerned with landscape aesthetics, although recognizably ecological concerns also peep through, as they do when Rudorff argues that river regulation actually increases the risk of floods. His article marked the symbolic beginning of the modern German nature conservation movement, with its emphasis on protecting an authentically native landscape. Only in the late nineteenth century did organizations dedicated to this task emerge in middle-class Germany, thanks in part to Rudorff's efforts. But the decades before 1880 were also saturated with the sense that something was being lost. If Rudorff stood at the beginning of a new movement, he also drew on the earlier writings of Wilhelm Heinrich Riehl, an art historian by training who became a pioneering ethnologist. Riehl, like Rudorff, hated tourists and loved wetlands. In other words, he combined views that we assign to different political camps. Riehl was a conservative who disliked industrialization, the cult of progress and the disappearance of patriarchal values. Yet his criticism of 'geometrical' waterways and pleas for the preservation of 'wilderness' were taken up by ecologically-minded botanists and have led some to claim him as a forerunner of the modern Greens.[258] This political ambiguity would run through the nature conservation movement in Germany.

The contemporary feelings of loss that humans projected onto nature were not just part of a narrowly conservative, 'anti-modern' backlash. The sentiment pervades the literature of the decades after 1850. It was precisely then that writers like Adalbert Stifter, Theodor Storm, Wilhelm Raabe and Theodor Fontane began to describe natural landscapes with a new precision, as if mindful of their precariousness.[259] Awareness of fragility and loss is explicit in Fontane's travel writings on Brandenburg. We encounter it repeatedly when he describes the change underway in the marshlands he so often visited, writing about them as if they shared his own melancholy. 'The Brieselang is a declining power, losing its terrain as it loses its character', he tells us; the Havelland in December, when it looked more like its former self, 'dreams once again of the old days'.[260] And so Fontane travelled on, through the Wustrau and the Oderbruch, bitter-sweetly recording places and species that were disappearing or had already disappeared and the green fields and meadows that took their place. They were fruitful, these 'green lowlands', 'green expanses', 'green carpet', but the new green was sometimes 'monotonous'.[261]

Fontane was no anti-modernist, but an urbane and well-travelled city dweller who accepted that the world changed, yet still allowed into his writing a sense of pathos for lost worlds. So, too, Wilhelm Raabe. In one of his later novels, *Stopfkuchen*, the narrator returns to an old haunt:[262]

> When I came to look I remembered there used to be a pond, or rather a swamp, off to the right of Red bank road, some four of five hundred square metres in size. It wasn't there.
>
> It once teemed and thronged with the dark wonders of nature, and now they had converted it into a moderately fertile potato field, useful no doubt, but the place was prettier before and more 'instructive' too. The least I owed to the frog pond, as we called it, was to look around for it with surprise and to be very sorry not to find it. Such a good acquaintance, such a good old friend! So full of sweet flags, reeds, cattails, frogs, snails, water beetles, with dragonflies whirring over it and butterflies hovering, and willows all around it . . . 'God knows, they could have left it as it was. And they should have', I grumbled . . . 'They didn't have to have those few extra sacks of feed for themselves or their stock'.
>
> But they thought they did, and there was nothing you could do about it now. I just had to square myself with the loss.

The pathos registers all the more strongly because of the narrator's sense of resignation, and the light irony about 'Mother Nature' that precedes his description.[263]

There are ironies inherent in every contemporary account of lost nature. The prospect of loss sharpened the eyes of the observer. In words or paintings, occasionally with cameras, they framed pictures of landscapes that were threatened – rather as the Oberahneschen fields in the Jade Bay became the object of passionate attachment, the more they slid beneath the water.[264] More ironic still, familiarity with disappearing wetlands and species owed much to the new communications that heralded their demise. The more widespread travel became, the more travellers sought out the 'unspoiled'. And it was the railway and steamship that took Fontane to the Brieselang and Havelland, just as it was the ocean steamer and the train that carried Raabe's Eduard back from a successful farming career in South-West Africa to investigate the places of his youth. Lost waterlands were never so prized, or so familiar, as they were at the moment of their disappearance. Some years later that great friend of the moors, the Worpswede painter Otto Modersohn, observed that 'nature' should serve as a teacher, then added that the idea came to him 'on the bridge that leads over the canal'.[265]

How 'natural' was the nature viewed from the bridge that leads over the canal? What a Modersohn or a Fontane recorded was, of course, a snapshot: a picture of nature at a given moment. The moorland celebrated and captured for posterity by the artists and writers at Worpswede had been fundamentally altered by human interventions for at least 150 years. The same was true of the moors painted by the Bavarian artists' colony at Dachau.[266] The problem was inescapable. The clergymen and botanists who counted species and lamented their declining numbers were also taking snapshots of one phase in a longer transition. The abundance whose loss they deplored (the 'before' of the 'before and after') might actually be the product of former human activity, like the birds and other species that lived in the hedgerows of the geest. The natural was sometimes an overgrown relic that had acquired the patina of age.[267] Riehl and his successors in Germany used the term 'wilderness', but there was no true wilderness in Germany; there were only historical landscapes that had been more or less intensively used by humans for their own changing purposes.[268] What can be said of the 'golden age' after the middle of the nineteenth century, whether we look at the North Sea coast, the moors of the north-west, or river valleys and wetlands anywhere in Germany, is that those uses became more intensive. They were also more destructive than earlier human interventions, although less destructive than what would follow. That is why Modersohn's moors were 'denatured' compared with what a snapshot would have shown a hundred years earlier, yet still depict a landscape that has since almost entirely disappeared.

DAM-BUILDING

In the Wonderland of Technology

In 1911 the city fathers of Brüx, a German town in north-western Bohemia, decided to build a drinking water reservoir. The retaining wall was completed on 26 June 1914. Two days later Archduke Franz-Ferdinand was assassinated at Sarajevo and the festive inauguration never took place. Celebration had to await publication of a book by two local engineers on this symbol of 'unstoppable progress'.[1] The same fate overtook a much larger construction project in the hills of what is now Hessen, but was then the borderland between Prussia and the principality of Waldeck. The waters of the Edertal Dam stretched for seventeen miles, covering a valley floor where three villages and scores of farms had once stood. Even today the third-largest dam in Germany, the Eder's 200 million cubic metres of water made it the largest European dam of its time when six years of construction came to an end in 1914. The Kaiser and his wife, the Prince and Princess of Waldeck, leading figures from the worlds of business, politics and culture, all had accepted invitations to the grand opening. But it had been scheduled for 15 August 1914 – two weeks after the war began.[2] The architects of the Eder Dam, like those in Brüx, were robbed of their celebration, consoled perhaps by the fact that the most eminent guests had already visited the site, the Kaiser and his wife twice, in August 1911 with the Princess Viktoria Luise and a picnic party that filled six cars, and again the following year, when they spoke with the engineer in charge of construction before taking tea.[3]

We have a fairly good idea of the form festivities would have taken at the Eder Dam, for the opening of two other major dams had recently been celebrated. In July 1913 the Möhne Dam near Soest was formally inaugurated; eight months before that the Kaiser attended the dedication of the Mauer Dam on the River Bober in Silesia. By then, scores of similar ceremonies (the town of Remscheid contrived to celebrate its Eschbach reservoir on no fewer than five occasions) had established a familiar routine of speeches, songs, toasts, festive meals, flags, fireworks and Bengal lights. Where the waters of the artificial lake were large, festively adorned motor boats became part of the staging.[4] The sentiments expressed on these occasions were typified by the doggerel with which the architect of the Sengbach Dam formally handed it over to the town of Solingen in May 1903:[5]

> Reward all the care that has gone into you,
> Fulfil all the wishes that people have had,
> Immutably firm on foundations of rock
> Spread lasting blessings on the Bergisch land!

Not much has been lost in translation.

The verse sounded a note that would not have been out of place at the ceremonies to celebrate the reclaimed Oderbruch or Tulla's new Rhine. The rhetoric of the occasion turned each new dam into another episode in the long-running struggle of man against nature. The gentler version of this amounted to saying that nature itself had created many natural mountain lakes; and where it had not done so, there were rocky basins that needed only to be 'completed by the hand of man'.[6] The more common version was frankly antagonistic towards nature. To dam a river was 'to place shackles on a gift of nature and make it useful for our purposes', 'to compel natural forces to serve the economy', 'to force the unregulated hydrological cycle of nature into ordered channels', to ensure that the energy locked up in mountain streams was 'tamed and applied usefully', and so on through dozens of variations.[7] To force, compel, shackle and tame: these are the terms you apply to a dangerous enemy. Just as the struggles against the Oder and Rhine had been cast in military terms, so the dammed valleys became 'great battlefields'. That was the term used by Ernst Mattern in his 1902 book on dams. Schiller, he reminded readers, had written about fire: beneficent when under human control, terrible when left to run free. The same was true of water.[8] Writing a few years later, Jakob Zinssmeister was impatient with critics of the dam-builders' incursions into nature:

they seemed to have forgotten that 'in the end, mankind is after all there to dominate nature and not to serve it'.[9]

These expressions of human mastery were familiar enough. But the age of dam-building also elicited novel reactions. Draining moorland or changing the course of a river also transformed the landscape, of course, but less starkly or dramatically than these new symbols of human domination. Novelty was part of the appeal. Looking back in 1913, an anonymous writer recalled that even the modestly sized early dams 'excited more wonder than today's structures that are ten or twenty times larger' because they were 'the first of their kind'.[10] That was true. But size also mattered; it altered the response. As dams bulked up in the decade before the First World War, commentators fell back again and again on the same set of adjectives. They were 'colossal', 'mighty', 'gigantic'.[11] Karl Kollmann visited the construction site of the Urfttal Dam in the Eifel just before it was completed in 1905, and described his impressions for readers of the family magazine *Over Land and Sea*. Kollmann was awestruck from a distance as soon as he saw how 'a giant wall rose from the floor of the valley, half the size of Cologne cathedral'. Closer inspection revealed the building of the 'giant cascade' and the 'colossal wall'; from the top the workmen looked like ants and the author felt dizzy. Thousands of future visitors would witness 'a magnificent miracle of modern technology'.[12] Even before it was finished this came to be known as 'the giant dam', thanks in part to an illustrated booklet by V. A. Carus: *Guide to the Area of the Giant Dam between Gemünd and Heimbach in the Eifel*.[13] The idea that this was a new breed of giants turns up often enough in the literature to suggest a belief that only mythological comparisons could do justice to the sense of wonder. The dam wall was often likened to a giant cyclops' eye. Hermann Schönhoff began an article on the Möhne Dam with a playful reference to the giants who, in popular lore, had shaped the land. Now it was the 'gigantic structure', 'the most enormous dam in Europe' that strode across the landscape, a 'giant work of the German spirit of enterprise'.[14]

Some found this kind of braggadocio unseemly. They were to be found, predictably, among the ranks of humanist academics, the professors against whom Jakob Zinssmeister directed his darts, but they also came from within the engineering world. At the very moment when the era of modern German dam-building was getting underway, Adolf Ernst published a book called *Culture and Technology*. A professor of engineering at the Stuttgart Polytechnic (he was a specialist on lifting devices), Ernst distrusted modern technological hubris. The conclusion that 'one-sidedly educated people draw from the partial domination of natural forces' was dangerous; it was wrong to believe 'that we are now actually on the way to becoming the lords of creation, or at least that the natural sciences together with technology are pursuing this fantastic goal'.[15] Ernst was not the only insider to condemn a narrowly materialist vision. Hans-Liudger Dienel has even argued that in this period engineers were actually less arrogant than others, such as natural scientists. Hydraulic engineers, for example, had learnt first-hand about the danger of hubris and were inclined to approach nature intuitively rather than see it as a mere object.[16] There are indeed some signs of this in contemporary debates, for despite the advent of larger, more sophisticated river models – like the pioneering river laboratory established in the 1890s by Hubert Engels at the Dresden Polytechnic – it was obvious that many aspects of river mechanics, including turbulence and sediment deposition, remained frankly mysterious.[17] The more self-critical, at least, were prepared to accept that even engineers could make mistakes when they tried to impose order on complex systems.[18]

But this was still a minority view. Nature was usually seen as a servant or an enemy.[19] That was the uncompromising attitude of men like Peter Engelmeier and Eberhard Zschimmer, who were trying to put technology on a philosophical footing in these years, and of most who toiled in the workaday world of engineering. Engelmeier was a Russian engineer who worked in Germany and wrote in German. The author of a manual for inventors and a critique of Leo Tolstoy's back-to-nature views, he believed in 'the empire of technology' because this was 'the spring in the great world clock of human development'. Zschimmer, professor of engineering at the Karlsruhe Polytechnic, Tulla's old stamping ground, argued in *The Philosophy of Technology* (1914) that the aim of technology was to achieve human freedom through material mastery and escape from the constraints of nature.[20] These are also the views we find expressed in most of the hundreds of contemporary books, pamphlets and articles on dams written by working engineers. That, at any rate, is my conclusion after reading more than 200 of them. We know that these works were written by engineers because, this being Germany, their titles and qualifications appeared where we might expect a first name. Their no-nonsense prose suggests pride in the social utility of dams and little in the way of doubts.

From Abshoff to Ziegler, these men belonged to a buoyant, expanding profession. At the time of its fiftieth anniversary in 1906 the Association of German Engineers boasted 20,000 members.[21] A few years before that, Professor H. F. Bubendey published an article in the Association's journal on 'The Methods and Objectives of German Hydraulic Engineering at the Beginning of the Twentieth Century'. He pointed to the contrast between 1900 and 1800: where once there had been a few 'men of genius', now there existed a 'cadre of trained engineers'.[22] Germany's internationally respected polytechnics were granted the right to issue doctorates in 1899, and by 1911 were turning out 11,000 students a year.[23] The days were long past when a Rothschild could joke that 'there are three ways of losing your money: women, gambling and engineers. The first two are pleasanter, but the last is the most certain'.[24] As Peter Engelmeier confidently noted in 1894, 'our professional colleagues are climbing ever higher up the social ladder'.[25] He was right: no one believed any more that engineers were rackety or dubious figures.

Some, it is true, believed that they lacked the broad vision of the humanistically educated. But the fierce contemporary debates about education, and jibes like the one delivered by Catholic political leader Ernst Lieber in parliament ('the better the engineer, the narrower his view'), only reinforced a mood of professional assertiveness.[26] One sign of that was a new willingness to appropriate the language of the humanists. They were not, engineers insisted, merely purveyors of hardware. What they did was creative, it embodied spirit, or *Geist*; engineers, too, were the guardians of culture. Of course, this was a way to fend off criticism like Lieber's, but it was at least as much about staking a claim. The magic word was culture. Books and articles about dams argued not just that these huge new structures tamed and shackled nature, but that they were 'cultural works'.[27] It was the culmination of a trend that was evident well before the war when, in 1922, the journal of the Association of German Engineers renamed itself *Technology and Culture*.

Were the experts who shared their enthusiasm for dam-building addressing a larger public? In many cases we are obviously dealing with engineers talking to other engineers. The numerous articles about dams published in *Dingler's Polytechnic Journal*, *Uhland's Technical Weekly*, *The Hydraulic Engineer* and two dozen similar publications were likely to be read only by engineers, officials, scientists and businessmen. They

did not reach out to a broader middle-class public of lawyers, professors, teachers, clergy and doctors – with the sole exception of a major
debate that took place over the quality of reservoir drinking water.
They certainly did not address the large lower middle-class readership of clerks and minor officials who were becoming avid consumers
of popular works on science, technology and a thousand fads like
'electro-culture'.

This larger audience was addressed elsewhere. Plenty of sprightly,
non-technical articles about dams appeared in publications like *The
Review*, *Social Review*, *Prometheus*, *Old World and New*, *The
Philosopher's Stone*, and in the mass-circulation weeklies *Over Land and
Sea* and *Die Gartenlaube*. Similar pieces also appeared from time to time
in the supplements of daily papers and in regional journals. The typical
article described a single dam, usually the latest. There might be some
mention of Mesopotamia or Egypt, to set the scene, but the emphasis
fell squarely on the future benefits that would flow from a modern technological marvel. These were the articles through which the vocabulary
of 'huge' and 'giant' ran like a red thread. What also ran through them,
animating the physical description of the dam and its setting, was a sense
of the thrill of the new, the excitement of the spectacle.

These authors were, to borrow John Staudenmaier's phrase, technology's storytellers. They presented a seamless past and a sunny
future.[28] Some were engineers who had turned their hand to writing
for a wider audience, others humanistically educated men who had
developed a passion for technology that they wanted to share. A good
example of the type is Dr Richard Hennig of Berlin. Hennig wrote
widely before the First World War on dam-building and the harnessing
of water-power in Germany and its African colonies.[29] He also
published a *Book of Famous Engineers* in 1911 for 'mature youths
and adults', devoting one chapter to a celebrated German dam-
builder.[30] The book reminds us that the lives-of-the-engineers genre
was in its hey-day, and that youth was a major target. Hennig's
publisher, Otto Spamer in Leipzig, had many popular science series
aimed at young readers. Another author who divided his attention
between adult and young readers was Hans Dominik. He wrote on
feats of hydraulic engineering in *Die Gartenlaube*, and published a
book in 1922 called *In the Wonderland of Technology: Masterpieces
and New Achievements that Our Youth Should Know*.[31] Here the
Eder and Möhne dams took their place alongside motor vehicles,

planes and radio in 'our proud era of technology'. They were achievements that 'elevate our century high above preceding epochs and give
us firm hope that humanity, notwithstanding passing trials and tribulations, is moving inexorably forward to a higher goal and a higher
stage of development'.[32] 'Trials and tribulations' is a rather casual
way of describing the impact of the First World War, and as we shall
see the war affected many aspects of German dam-building. But
Dominik resembled other writers who continued, into the 1920s and
30s, to tell the story of German dams in the heroic, inspirational
mode.

The historian David Nye used the phrase 'American Technological
Sublime' to describe the intense impact on contemporaries, the sense
of awe, produced by structures like the Hoover Dam.[33] It is a subject
with a considerable pedigree in American history.[34] Nye insists, however,
that this was an example of American exceptionalism: the European
capacity for awe and wonder remained stuck in the age of Immanuel
Kant and Edmund Burke; it never made the leap into modern times,
never developed as it had in America into a willingness to celebrate the
human domination of nature. This is about as wrong as it is possible
to be about a subject. Although in Germany, as in America, there were
also sceptics, abundant evidence shows the attraction of new technological wonders. Crowds gazed at the tunnelling work for Berlin's underground railways, rapturously followed every journey of the Zeppelin
airship, cheered the maiden voyage of great ocean liners like the
Hamburg-Amerika Line's *Imperator*.[35] Franz Bendt told readers of the
Gartenlaube in 1906 that 'the technical arts have lent modern times
their colouring and given them a large part of their content'.[36] A
humanist professor, Friedrich Paulsen, recorded the same trend with
more resignation than enthusiasm: 'The thoughts of the peoples are not
directed to literature or aesthetics, but to the subjugation of natural
forces and the conquest of the earth. That is already having repercussions on the minds of the young. Can we regret it? And would it help
us if we did?'[37]

Dams have celebratory inaugurations just as Zeppelins make maiden
flights and ocean liners maiden voyages. The difference is that the dam
remains in place, to be described – and to be visited. When *The Review*
ran an article in 1904 on the Urfttal Dam, the editor added a complaint
about traditional guidebooks:

It is time that guidebooks like Baedeker and Meyer stopped directing their attention one-sidedly to a few broken-down walls of modest historical interest or faded frescos by unknown masters. – In the realm of guidebooks a fundamental transformation is called for corresponding to the changed interests of our time.

'Artworks of technology', like the Urfttal Dam, deserved their due, and the editor directed readers' attention to V. A. Carus's book on the 'giant dam'.[38] As things turned out the writers of articles and guidebooks led, the public followed. Dams attracted large numbers of visitors from the start. The first generation of local dams were accessible on foot or by local transportation; the more distant giant dams could be reached by well-advertised rail links and later by car.[39] They became destinations for thousands, even tens of thousands a year. Experience had taught, said W. Mügge from the perspective of 1942, that few engineering structures attracted so many visitors.[40]

Why they went and what they took away from their visits is harder to say, but the evidence suggests two answers. There was, on the one hand, the sense of awe that writers note again and again – the intense, spellbinding experience. Some of the postcards sold at dams reinforced their association with the novel and the thrilling. A 1920s postcard of the Glörtal Dam of the future shows the sky above it crowded with aircraft, hot-air balloons, Zeppelins and a futuristic monorail.[41] This is no isolated instance of an association between dams and aviation as twin marvels. In a 1938 issue of the National Socialist publication *Volk und Welt*, the aviator and balloonist W. Abercron praised dams from the opposite perspective, because they presented an aerial view of great new expanses of water carved through by motor boats.[42] Even for those with their feet still firmly on the ground, each newly opened giant dam was a fresh opportunity for wonder. But dams also offered more mundane pleasures. That is the second part of the answer to what visitors took away from their visits. Leo Sympher pinned it down neatly. The Eschbach Dam 'became a true place of pilgrimage for the friends of dams', but for most it was a 'widely visited place of recreation'.[43] The immediate success of Eschbach as a venue for 'excursions' established a pattern.[44] The new artificial lakes attracted hikers and anglers; when there were no restrictions (as there were supposed to be at drinking water reservoirs) they also proved popular with boaters in summer and ice skaters in winter. Big dams like the Urfttal, Eder and Möhne (the largest lake in the western provinces of Prussia) drew even greater numbers of tourists who took steamer trips, patronized refreshment stalls and bought picture postcards.[45]

This was a long way from Hans Dominik's wonderland of technology, but the distance that had been travelled told its own story. The accretion of tourist kitsch at German dams was like the process that transformed the thrill of the original Zeppelin flights into pictures of Count Zeppelin on cigars and boot polish.[46] Wonder had been turned into a commodity, the taming of the elements miniaturized into a likeness on a box of cigars or a holiday postcard from the Möhne. If one hallmark of the conquest of nature is that its achievements came to seem self-evident, this is a measure of how far modern German dam-building had come from its dramatic, but uncertain beginnings.

Otto Intze: 'Grand Master' of German Dams

Damming rivers is as old as civilization. The usual aim was to capture the annual floodwaters so that they could be released gradually for irrigation. It was a German explorer, Georg Steinfurth, who uncovered one of the oldest in 1885: the Kafara Dam at Helwan, twenty miles south of Cairo, built around 2600 BC to retain floodwaters from the eastern mountains.[47] Modern German dam advocates often expressed admiration for the achievements of ancient Egypt, Assyria and China, which added history's seal of approval to the technocratic enthusiasm of the present.

The history of dams in German-speaking Europe was much more abbreviated, but still stretched back some seven hundred years to the Pfauernteich in Lower Saxony, built some time before 1298. Some 200 metres long and ten metres high at its highest point, the dam stored water for use by local industries. More or less modest structures serving similar purposes were built throughout the early modern period. But the first important era of German dam-building began in the 1480s and continued over the next three hundred years. That was when dams were built in the central mountain areas of the Harz and Erzgebirge to create a head of water for the mining industry. The water-power they generated allowed mine-shafts to be drained so that silver, tin and copper could be extracted from the earth. It also powered local stamping mills. Dutch hydraulic specialists like Willem de Raedt had a large part in all this. The dams were numerous (more than a hundred in the Harz), and the most important of them, like the Untere Hartmannsdorfer in the Erzgebirge (1572) and the Oderteich in the Harz (1720s), were very imposing, storing three times as much water as the earliest structures built in the modern era of German dam-building centuries later. They were also sophisticated: the Oderteich was made out of granite blocks and featured outlet pipes (they were made of oak) built into the dam. The theoretical understanding of dams was well advanced by the eighteenth century, when publications already outlined what would become the standard thinking on orography – calculations based on the principle that it was best to choose a deep, narrow valley as a site, so that a relatively narrow structure retained a large body of water at reasonable cost.[48]

Although some historic dams were operated into the age of modern industrialization, steam provided a more convenient source of power for draining mine shafts. The famous Saxon mining school at Freiberg in the Erzgebirge did not lose its reputation for originality in other fields, but the baton of modern thinking about dams passed to the British and, above all, the French. From Chazilly (1837) and Grosbois (1838) to Bouzey (1881) it was in France that the signature new masonry dams of the nineteenth century were built, and it was French engineers like de Sazilly and Delocre who wrote the most important theoretical work on constructing these thinner gravity dams to withstand the pressures they placed on materials. Like other pioneers, the French paid a price for being in the vanguard. Design problems became apparent at Chazilly and Grosbois; Bouzey had to be rehabilitated twice in the 1880s, before collapsing in 1895.[49] French engineers designed plenty of dams that did not fall down, but it was against this uncertain background that the modern epoch of German dam-building began. It was initiated by a project with a French connection.

In the Vosges mountains of Alsace, valleys that face east receive less rainfall than those facing west, the pattern common across Europe because of prevailing winds which bring low-pressure systems in from the Atlantic. The water that does drain down those steep valleys – and we are still talking about 2m (79") of precipitation a year – flows with an irregular rhythm common to mountain streams everywhere. Periods that produce sudden torrents (in this case from October to December, and during summer storms) alternate with periods when the flow is a mere trickle. The ratio between high and low water, between hydrological feast and famine, is around 400:1 in streams like the Doller.[50] This is part of a natural cycle; but that cycle became more extreme in modern times because of deforestation in the high valleys, for the trees and their root systems had served as a water-storage system that equalized the seasonal flow. Building dams was another instance of providing a substitute for natural mechanisms destroyed by earlier human actions. To create a more even flow of water for valley dwellers who depended on it to irrigate their fields or drive mill wheels, French engineers drew up plans in the middle of the nineteenth century to dam these uncooperative streams, building on the success already achieved by raising the level of natural lakes. But a combination of financial problems, squabbles among users, and the fears expressed by those who would live in the shadow of the dams meant that nothing had happened before Alsace became part of Germany in 1871.[51]

The new administrators of the 'Reich Lands' wanted to be seen to be doing something for their reluctant new subjects. By 1881, plans had been drawn up for a series of dams across the valleys of the Doller and the Fecht. Construction began two years later and the first dam at Alfeld was completed in 1887. Four more followed, and a final dam in the Lauch valley completed the project in 1894. The state met the costs, which came to just over one million Marks, offset by a voluntary contribution of 160,000 Marks by textile businesses that stood to benefit.[52] For whatever reason, whether it was their location on formerly French soil, or the fact that (unlike most early German dams) they were publicly financed, or because the project was relatively self-contained, these dams occupy a rather marginal place in the canonical story of modern German dam-building. They are not even mentioned by many writers.

The Alsatian dams were in fact both typical and atypical of what would follow. They were typical first of all in their geographical location. The work of draining marshes, rectifying major rivers and colonizing moors took place on the lowland plains; dams were built in the high upland valleys. It was not the major river arteries whose water was impounded, nor even the secondary rivers that drained into them, but the tributaries of those secondary rivers. In Alsace, it was the Doller and Fecht, tributaries of the Ill (which eventually joined the Rhine). Later dams would be built on the Möhne, not the Ruhr; the Eder, not the Weser; the Roer, not the Mosel. And what began in the Vosges continued in other mountainous areas of Germany: in the Sauerland

and Bergisches Land, the Eifel, the Harz and Erzgebirge. The Alsatian dams were typical in another, quite different respect: they were an attempt by the state to broker a compromise between conflicting interests, in this case the agricultural and industrial water-users who were locked in 'bitter dispute'.[53]

Conflicts over water rights would drive and shape the process of German dam-building everywhere. The outcome of that conflict in the Vosges was one of the things that made the Alsatian dams atypical. The evidence suggests that the dams proved very successful and met local expectations, which was not the case everywhere. It helped that there were no private investors looking to recover the high initial costs. The new structures played a role in keeping people in the Doller and Fecht valleys at a time when neighbouring valleys were becoming depopulated. Industrial and agricultural users also shared the water with a degree of harmony that would have surprised earlier observers, and that stood out against the generally embittered agrarian–industrial relations in Germany during the last decades of the nineteenth century.[54] But it was precisely those fraught relations, as industry and commerce gained a dominant position in the German economy, that pointed to the future of German dam-building. That, more than anything else, was what made the dams in the Vosges atypical. They were the first and last in Germany to be constructed with agricultural irrigation as a major goal. The pattern of future dam construction would make them appear, in retrospect, as an anomaly.

It was the needs of the booming industrial region in Rhineland-Westphalia that led to a new era, the 'golden decade' of dam construction in the 1890s.[55] And it was the mountain valleys that lay above the industrial towns of the Ruhr and Wupper that were, in Ernst Mattern's phrase, 'the cradle of modern German dam-building'.[56] The first great symbol of the new era was the Eschbach Dam that provided Remscheid with drinking water. Remscheiders had drawn their water historically from wells, springs and cisterns. But a growing population (it doubled between 1850 and 1875, then doubled again by the 1890s) created acute problems. In dry years people raced down the valley before dawn to scoop up with their pails whatever brackish water had accumulated overnight, or paid high prices to the owners of favourably situated private wells. After heated debates in the local council about the costs, Remscheid decided to follow more than 120 other German towns and establish a central waterworks.[57] It began operations in 1884, pumping groundwater and diverting surface water from nearby streams. But the number of users grew and their consumption grew even faster. The waterworks reached the limits of its capacity after just three years. Experts had warned about this in advance; in fact more 'forward-looking' figures on the council were banking on failure because it gave them an opportunity to present their own preferred solution: a reservoir. Rejected earlier on financial grounds, this proposal now went ahead.[58] Begun in May 1889 and completed in November 1891, the Eschbach Dam compounded over one million cubic metres of water. It was the first of its kind in Rhineland-Westphalia and the first in Germany built to provide drinking water. A diorama of the reservoir would later be installed at the German Science Museum in Munich.[59]

The Eschbach Dam was a milestone. Looking back in 1909, Richard Hennig saw it as the real start of a 'movement'.[60] Even during construction the site was crowded with visiting engineers and municipal officials.[61] The dam was widely written about; and when it went into operation without mishap this helped to dispel some (not all) of the fears and uncertainties associated with masonry dams.[62] For it is worth remembering that as late as 1898 a writer in *The Review* still felt obliged to explain to general readers the nature of dams (it was, he claimed, 'so tremendously simple' that it could be done in three sentences – three very long sentences, as it turned out).[63] Eschbach was the proof that it could be done, the 'model' that made it easier for later dams to be built. And built they were. By the early twentieth century imitators were 'shooting up like mushrooms' in the catchment basins of the Ruhr and Wupper.[64] Heavily populated central German industrial areas followed suit. The need was greater there than anywhere, because the water table had been so lowered by mining and by heavy domestic and industrial use. Industrial pollution of surface water also limited its domestic use. Damming the water of upland streams was a more attractive alternative than tapping deeper groundwater that was expensive to pump.[65] The Einsiedel reservoir opened in 1894, the first of five that would serve Chemnitz and Zwickau. Dozens more followed in Saxony and Thuringia, which came to depend on reservoir drinking water more than any other region in Germany.[66]

The fingerprints of one man were all over the early dams. He designed Eschbach and almost all the other first-generation reservoirs in Rhineland-Westphalia; he was a consultant elsewhere. By the time he died in 1904, twelve of his dams were in operation, ten were under construction and twenty-four more were later built from his blueprints. The man in question was Otto Intze. He was memorialized by a plaque on the crown of the Hennetal Dam near Meschede on the Ruhr, one of his creations, just as Tulla was commemorated on the banks of the Rhine at Karlsruhe.[67] The comparison is reasonable. Intze was at least as important within his sphere and arguably more original. Richard Hennig included him in his *Book of Famous Engineers*, alongside Nobel, Marconi and the Wright Brothers.[68] A chorus of writers then and later agreed that Intze was the 'doyen' of dam-building in Germany, the 'grand master', the 'past master', the 'trailblazer', the 'pioneer'.[69] So great was his impact that it overshadowed what had come before. In the words of Leo Sympher, a leading dam architect of the next genera-tion: 'The significance of the dams designed by Intze and built by him or with his assistance is so great that everything which had been achieved in this field earlier receded in importance, in fact was almost forgotten'.[70]

Otto Adolf Ludwig Intze was born in May 1843 in the sandy flat-lands of Mecklenburg, about as far away as it was possible to get from the green and rainy valleys of the west where he later made his name.[71] His father was a doctor in the small town of Laage, his mother a huntsman's daughter. Adolf went to a non-classical secondary school in Güstrow, then spent two and a half years working in the Baltic as a draughtsman for the English company that was building the Riga–Dünaburg railway. Still only nineteen, he returned to Germany in 1862 to study at the Polytechnic Institute in Hanover, graduating with distinction four years later. Intze taught briefly at the School of Civil Engineering in Holzminden, then took a position in 1867 with the Hamburg department of hydraulic engineering, roads and bridges. Three years later, still just twenty-seven, he accepted a chair of civil engineering at the newly established Aachen Polytechnic. During the brief span of 1866–70, while Germany was being unified, the preco-cious Intze progressed from prize-winning student to full professor. He would stay in Aachen for the rest of his life, combining the role of cele-brated academic (he later served as dean) with a busy architectural engineering practice.

Intze was active on many fronts. He designed and oversaw the building of laboratories on the Aachen campus. In private practice he designed industrial buildings in Germany, Russia, Sweden and Chile, which engaged his interest in the problem of earthquake-proof constructions. He was an expert on the use of iron and steel as building materials, and his books on the subject included one co-authored with Friedrich Heinzerling that became a standard work. In the early 1880s he also designed a new type of flexible, lightweight steel water- or gas-holder. Over the following twenty years more than 500 Intze water towers (Reich patent number 23187) were built in Germany alone.

Intze's on-site work with water tower construction took him to the Sauerland, Bergisches Land and Eifel, where most of his celebrated dams would be built. But his interest in the theory and practice of dam-building predated that. The first of hundreds of lectures on the subject was delivered to the Lower Rhine and Westphalian Association of Architects and Engineers in 1875: 'The Purpose and Construction of so-called Dams'.[72] In Germany they were still 'so-called' in 1875; but not elsewhere. Intze studied classic Spanish dams; he also visited the new Gileppe Dam in the Belgian Ardennes, just across the border from Aachen, which began operating in 1876 and had a self-consciously monumental character – it was capped by the 43-foot-high stone lion, symbol of Belgium, that stood regally on the crest.[73] In neither case was Intze impressed. The work of French engineers impressed him more, despite their misadventures. Visiting the World Exposition of 1878 in Paris on behalf of the Prussian Ministry of Public Works, Intze examined the dam designs exhibited there and returned proclaiming that Germany could aspire to French achievements. The Vosges dams, which Intze inspected while they were under construction and admired, reinforced this opinion. By then he was himself actively planning, propagandizing and building.

Intze placed 'ancient knowledge on a modern scientific and technical basis', according to Richard Hennig.[74] What he actually did was to apply in Germany the slimmed-down masonry gravity dam pioneered by de Sazilly and Delocre in France. This minimized the size, amount of materials and therefore the cost. The technique was refined by engineers like W. J. M. Rankine in Britain and Edward Wegmann in the USA, where it became the standard form used by large metropolitan water systems at the end of the nineteenth century, like the Croton Dam in New York and the Cheeseman Dam in Denver.[75] Their slimline design was an aspect of the Alsatian dams that Intze admired. His own calculations on stresses produced a similar profile: the typical Intze dam is an elegant masonry structure with a curved axis. His dams did have distinctive features, however: the wedge-shaped earth embankment on the upstream side (the 'Intze wedge'), designed to give extra protection against water seeping under the dam wall, the thick coating of bitumen waterproofing he employed, and the 'Intze mixture' of mortar composed of trass, lime paste and Rhine quartz sand. He insisted, wherever possible, on the use of locally quarried stone, and emphasized the careful measurement of precipitation and water discharge rates in each catchment area, often using equipment of his own design. These technical accomplishments explain why present-day engineers credit Intze with initiating the 'modern era' of dam-building in Germany, labelling everything that came before as 'pre-Intze'.[76]

Intze's reputation as the 'true motor of modern dam-building in Germany' rests even more on the extraordinary energy he brought to the cause.[77] The structures themselves fostered confidence. But Intze's 'tireless agitation' also helped to 'dispel the still widespread concerns about the accumulation of such powerful masses of water behind artificial dams'.[78] He examined recent dam breaches in the USA and Europe, pointing out how they were the result of bad design, poor materials, irresponsible engineers, or all three.[79] He argued that dams were necessary and could be safely built. In public lectures and through his writings he engaged in an 'intensive labour of enlightenment'.[80] Intze had a gift for 'lively propaganda'.[81] But the key to his success was the high standing he enjoyed with many different groups. An active member of the Association of German Engineers, he was the undisputed expert on dams among his peers. His most important collaborators and pupils – Bachmann, Mattern, Link – would continue his zealous advocacy and take Germany into the age of concrete dams in the 1920s and 1930s.[82] Intze's name also became known to the public. He was 'the most respected hydraulic engineer in Germany', claimed a *Gartenlaube* article in 1897.[83] At the same time, Intze was well connected within the political and economic elite. Elevated in the 1890s to the rank of Prussian Privy Councillor, he became a member of the Prussian Academy of Architecture and had a seat in the Prussian House of Lords. On three different occasions he delivered private lectures to Kaiser Wilhelm II, who was always fascinated by technical novelty, whether the subject was cars, battleships or dams.[84] By then Intze, confident and every inch the patriarch in appearance (with his beard and high forehead, he looked uncannily like Charles Dickens), was a prominent establishment figure.

But his earliest enthusiasts came from a very different background. They were the owners of small industrial concerns that used water-wheels as their source of energy. That is the greatest paradox of Intze's achievement: the prophet of a bold new technology got his start by suggesting ways to prop up a dying form of production. For centuries, in every upland region in Germany, water-wheels had been used to saw wood, full cloth, push bellows, raise hammers and crush metal.[85] In the Bergisches Land and the Sauerland, small textile and metal-working businesses were clustered along the fast-flowing streams. The Wupper was once described as the 'hardest-working river in Europe'.[86] We often overlook how long this early form of industrialization survived into the age of coal and steam. At the beginning of the 1860s there was still one water-powered mill for every thousand inhabitants of Prussia; in some parts of Germany water-power generated more energy than steam as late as the 1870s.[87] But the writing was on the wall by then, especially for small industrialists on the Wupper and tributaries of the Ruhr. The Moloch of the Ruhr heavy industrial district, founded on coal, powered by steam and closer to transportation, was threatening to drive the water-wheels of the upland valleys out of business.[88] In these circumstances, the problem that those water-wheels turned very slowly, or stopped altogether, in the 'dead water' of summer was more than an irritant.[89] It threatened the livelihood of whole valleys.

Even before Intze created the Eschbach reservoir, he had been approached in the 1880s by several small businesses in the Wupper, Lenne and Ennepe valleys. He proposed building dams to equalize the flow of water through the year, to keep the wheels turning. The owners of modest textile and metal-working mills were enthusiastic about the prospect of a 'flanking manoeuvre' to staunch the flow of production and jobs to the Ruhr.[90] But it took over a decade to realize Intze's solution. The most difficult problem that caused the delay was how to spread the costs among those who were expected to benefit from a dam, but refused to contribute to its financing. Without an answer to the free rider question, dam projects were likely to remain on the drawing board.

The creative solution, urged by several local officials and strongly backed by Intze in the face of resistance from some ministers in Berlin, was a change in the law. In May 1891, existing Prussian legislation designed to assist local agricultural cooperatives by compelling all potential beneficiaries to participate was extended to dam projects in the Wupper catchment area. (It was later extended to other rivers.) The result was the formation of the Wupper Valley Dam Association. Its members were small- to medium-sized businesses that used water-power and local waterworks, sharing the costs and the benefits. The Association sponsored a series of Intze-designed dams in the Wupper basin during the 1890s.[91]

The situation was more complex on the Ruhr, where many different interests fought over an uncertain supply of water. There was good news and bad news. The good news was that the Ruhr carried a heavy volume of water in proportion to its catchment area – comparable, in fact, to Alpine streams – because of the heavy rainfall in many tributary streams in the Sauerland. The bad news was a tremendous seasonal variation between high and low water, greater than generally found on rivers that drained the central German highlands. Upland deforestation had intensified the extremes.[92] As on the Wupper, owners of small water-powered concerns found their competitive disadvantage against big business compounded by hydrology. Those unfortunate enough to be situated on the Lower Ruhr, at the end of the water chain, also suffered from the huge volumes of water being extracted from the Ruhr by urban waterworks, mines and heavy industry. For it was the combined effects of their actions that created a general water crisis in the Ruhr at the end of the nineteenth century. In extreme cases of summer low water it was possible to ford the river in some places without getting your feet wet. It could even happen that, at the point where the Ruhr emptied into the Rhine, the flow was temporarily reversed so that Rhine water ran up the Ruhr. One of the less familiar achievements of German industrialization was its ability to make water run uphill.[93] How had it come to this? The Ruhr increasingly bore the burden of supplying water for the entire region. The Wupper was heavily polluted, industry turned the Lipper effectively into a salt-water stream, and the Emscher had already been 'sacrificed' as the designated victim river that carried effluent out of the industrial belt.[94] Nor was that all. As the coalfield in what is usually called the Ruhrgebiet extended further north of the River Ruhr, mining created more difficulties by lowering water tables. So it was not just users on the Ruhr itself who drew down water levels. Waterworks serving towns on other rivers pumped startling volumes of groundwater from the Ruhr valley that disappeared for good, as much as three-quarters of the total by the 1890s. The direct extraction of water from the Ruhr by the mining, metallurgical and chemical industries, for cleaning, cooling and processing, was even heavier.

The Krupps in Essen, who needed water for thirsty factories and thirsty workers in their new industrial settlements, were just the most familiar face of a larger crisis.[95]

Dams were supposed to be the solution to this crisis. Thanks to the 1891 law the first two reservoirs in the Ruhr basin were built over 1894–6. They dammed the valleys of two tributaries, the Füelbecke and Heilenbecke. Both structures were designed by Intze, and they were small in every way: small dams, financed by small cooperatives that joined the interests of small wire-mills and hammer-mills with those of small municipal waterworks. This model would no doubt have spawned more of the same in the future. But events had already started to unfold a few years earlier that would lead to a sustained programme of dam-building in the Ruhr, dams that were larger and funded on a very different basis. Once again it was disgruntled 'little men' who set things in motion. In the early 1890s the local Prussian administration in Düsseldorf started to hear complaints from the operators of water-powered mills on the lower Ruhr who said that the appetite of the waterworks was damaging their businesses. They asked government to restrict the volumes of water removed, or ensure that equivalent amounts were restored to the river through dams built higher up in the Ruhr basin.[96] It was predictable that Intze would be asked for a specialist opinion by the local administration, even more predictable that he strongly endorsed the proposal to build dams. He also recommended that the various parties be brought together to secure the long-range water needs of all.[97]

That was how things stood for four years. The Prussian authorities, anxious not to incur costs and aware of the tangled water-use rights involved, canvassed opinion but took no steps.[98] The rainy years in the middle nineties made the dilemma temporarily less acute (although the amounts of water permanently removed from the Ruhr continued to rise). Then, in 1897, two small business owners on the lower Ruhr who depended on water-power, Johann Scheidt in Kettwig and Hermann Vorster in Broich, began legal action against the town of Dortmund and its waterworks. It was a test case. The upper, unnavigable part of the Ruhr fell under private river law: no permission was needed for a waterworks to use available water, especially as it was groundwater, not river water, that was being pumped. The supply of water to towns was also deemed to be in the public interest and could not be legally limited by the state. This private-public one-two punch was Dortmund's

MAP 6 *Major areas of dam-building in unified Germany.*

Areas of dam-building
1 The Vosges
2 The Eifel
3 The Sauerland and Bergisches Land
4 The Harz
5 The Erzgebirge
6 The Riesengebirge
7 The Bavarian Alps

0   100   200 km

defence. But the plaintiffs pointed to a clause in private river law that required water removed from one stream to be returned to the same stream, a stipulation many waterworks were flouting; and they further argued that the groundwater pumped by Dortmund led inevitably to a drawing down of the river itself. The court found in favour of the plaintiffs, and Intze (who supported their arguments) was called as an expert witness to assess damages. But the legal proceedings were overtaken by events, for administrators who had been nervously following the case decided that it was time to bring the parties together.[99]

In the summer of 1897, the senior official in the Düsseldorf district that covered the Ruhrgebiet, Freiherr von Rheinbaben, convened a meeting in Hagen. Present were his counterpart from the Arnsberg district, representatives from the major Prussian ministries involved, and Intze, who restated his view that a dam-building programme was necessary, argued that the major water-users should bear the cost, and agreed to prepare a memorandum. A further meeting followed at Essen in January 1898, also chaired by Rheinbaben, which brought together all the conflicting interests. By adroit use of carrot and stick, Rheinbaben gained general agreement to Intze's grand design: the building of reservoirs as part of a programme to raise water levels along the whole length of the Ruhr. Most of the funding would come from the waterworks and big industrial users, although Intze's sunny forecasts led small business owners to accept a share of the costs. The Ruhr Valley Reservoirs Association, the *Ruhrtalsperrenverein* or RTV, was founded in April 1899.[100] The RTV joined the alphabet soup of other powerful interest groups (BdI, BdL, CVdI, HB, RHV) that straddled the zone between economics and politics in the Kaiser's Germany. Intze himself has been called 'the father of the Ruhr Valley Reservoirs Association'.[101]

The organization injected a new tempo into reservoir building. Seven more went into operation in the years 1904–6, all designed by Intze. They were built by local associations, funded by the RTV. The local groups resembled their counterpart on the Wupper, bringing together owners of small saw mills, hammer mills and paper mills, sometimes joined by a municipal waterworks.[102] The return for the larger users on the Ruhr who provided most of the funding through the RTV came from the effect of these dams in maintaining water levels downriver. By 1904, however, the Association had already decided to build dams in its own right – larger dams – and its statutes were changed accordingly. The first fruit of this change in direction was the Lister Dam (1912). Its twenty-two million cubic metres of storage capacity made the Lister the largest reservoir built in the Ruhr basin. But only for a year. It was eclipsed in turn by the Möhne, begun in 1908 and completed five years later.[103] This huge new structure in the far north of the Ruhr basin compounded 130 million cubic metres of water, more than the combined capacity of all of the score or so reservoirs previously built in the Ruhr and Wupper region.[104] It was also a kind of tribute to the former 'grand master'. Intze's star pupil, Ernst Link, left the Prussian administration in 1904 to work full-time for the Ruhr Valley Reservoirs Association, where he was responsible for the construction of the Möhne Dam.[105]

Flood Protection, Navigation and 'White Coal'

Just a few weeks after Freiherr von Rheinbaben took the first steps that led to the founding of the Ruhr Valley Reservoirs Association, hydrological problems of a very different kind made themselves dramatically felt across eastern and central Germany. Here it was not a question of too little water, but too much. Torrential rainfall fell over 28–30 July 1897, bringing floods to Silesia, Saxony, Anhalt and Brandenburg, as well as Austria and Bohemia. The heavy loss of life and property in so many places simultaneously 'gave these catastrophic floods the character of a national disaster'.[106] The floodwater came from swollen streams in the central highlands where Silesia, Saxony and Bohemia come together, streams that feed the Oder and Elbe. It was on these river systems that the devastation was worst, although many mountain streams in the Austrian Alps also broke their banks and Kaiser Francis Joseph's favourite summer retreat, Bad Ischl, was cut off for days. These were summer flash floods, not the result of the slow spring snow-melt, which made their onset less predictable. In many places the floodwaters arrived in the middle of the night, adding to the loss of life. The press went into disaster mode, filling its columns with stories of drowned victims and others rescued only after eighteen or twenty hours spent clinging to a roof or tree, waving white handkerchiefs as distress signals. Then there were the heroic rescue attempts that failed, where the waters claimed 'fathers and breadwinners and mocked the tears of widows and orphans'.[107] Bridges, roads, railway lines and factories were swept away, mud and stones deposited on unharvested fields. On the Bober, a tributary of the Oder, these were the highest floodwaters seen in a hundred years, with effects that were felt as far downstream as the middle Oder valley. In Spindelmühle on the Upper Elbe the river found its way back into the old bed from which it had been expelled by river regulation, to the dismay of a hundred guests at the hotel 'Zum Deutschen Kaiser', one wing of which collapsed and killed a cellar-boy. Downriver, the cresting water threatened Dresden, where the annual Volksfest was cancelled.[108]

The *Gartenlaube*, like other German papers, collected readers' money for flood victims and publicized the national relief committee formed in Berlin. It also insisted that something be done to prevent a recurrence. Controlling the wind and rain was impossible: but surely it was possible to go into the mountains and build water retention basins that could prevent, or at least ameliorate, future floods?[109] This idea was not simply plucked out of the air. The incidental advantages of dams for flood protection were an implicit part of the calculation in all the early dam projects. Intze himself laid considerable emphasis on this aspect. The 1897 floods brought flood-protection to centre-stage. Intze wrote directly on the issue.[110] The Kaiser, keen to be seen doing something, made the flood question a personal initiative and had Intze lecture to him privately on the remedy. The remedy, of course, turned out to be building dams.[111] The Prussian Flood Protection Law of 1900 foresaw a series of them in the Silesian mountains, on turbulent tributaries of the Oder. The first, designed by Intze, was constructed at Marklissa on the Queiss, begun in 1901 and completed a year after Intze's death in 1905; a second followed at Mauer on the Bober. Eventually a string of fourteen dams would dot the Queiss, Bober, Katzbach and Glatzer Neisse, financed jointly by the Prussian state and the province of Silesia.[112]

Intze's personal briefing of the Kaiser and active role in the Silesian flood-protection programme probably had a good deal to do with his appointment as Privy Councillor and elevation to the Prussian House of Lords. He evidently considered it one of his major achievements. The Silesian dams featured in the text he wrote for a photo collection on dams displayed by the Prussian Ministry of Public Works at the 1904 International Exposition in St Louis; they were there again in the last lecture he ever gave, in February of the same year.[113] By then Intze could witness yet another celebrated work nearing completion, the 'giant' Urft Dam, a major purpose of which was to minimize flooding in the Rur (or Roer) and Urft valleys. Like the Marklissa Dam, it was completed in 1905.[114] By the early years of the twentieth century, Intze was sought after everywhere as the man with the answer to raging floodwaters. He accepted an invitation from the Austrian government to design dams in Bohemia, where the 1897 floods had been just as destructive. His designs led to a series of dams intended at least to blunt the impact of future floods; and his celebrity presence left such an impression on the young Bohemian engineer Viktor Czehak, who worked under him on three of the dams, that he was still proudly citing the connection thirty years later when called in himself as an expert to comment on a dam that had gone horribly wrong.[115] Other areas that had suffered in 1897 also showed an interest in the Silesian model, so that in Saxony arguments about flood-protection now played a larger part in the debates about dam-building.[116]

No other purpose served by dams did so much to foster the idea that they represented humans 'doing battle' with nature. Richard Hennig's biographical sketch of Intze opens on exactly this note. Modern civilization had been able to control or tame many elemental natural forces, including lightning, fire and epidemic disease. It was still power-less before others, like floods; but humankind was learning to render even these 'unbound forces of nature' harmless, and one 'miraculous means' of doing so was the dam. Readers were then introduced to 'the man who in modern times contributed more than any one else' to this development.[117] In starting his sketch this way, Hennig took his cue from Intze. For in laying the foundation stone on the Marklissa Dam in 1902, Intze chose his metaphor deliberately and used it twice:[118]

> It is necessary when dealing with rivers that carry large masses of water . . . to present the water with a battleground so chosen that the human comes out the victor. This battleground against the forces of nature should be the creation of large reservoirs . . .

But was this a battle against the forces of nature? In some ways the answer is obviously yes. The floods were produced by the interaction of topography, hydrology and meteorology. Here were mountain streams that drained from central highland ranges: the Erzgebirge, Riesengebirge, Isergebirge. And here also was one of the Continent's most notorious low-pressure corridors, *Zugstrasse Vb* as German mete-orologists called it, which led northerly and north-westerly depressions across Europe every summer, producing cloudbursts on exposed moun-tain-sides. The high summer precipitation totals in the Oder basin were a familiar story. The outcome was as unwelcome as it was hard to fore-cast; but what could be more natural?[119]

Yet we can point to at least three ways in which the floods were a result of human actions. The cumulative effect of deforestation caused the water from the cloudbursts to tumble more quickly down the valley. That was as true in the central highlands as it was in the Eifel and the Ruhr further west. The impact was all the greater because river regu-lation channelled the water more swiftly downstream. And the damage was magnified because those regulated channels encouraged denser human settlement on the river banks. That is why once-in-a-century floods were happening every few decades. On the Bober, almost no major floods were recorded before the late eighteenth century; then there were four in the nineteenth century.[120] What is remarkable is how many contemporaries were willing to point out the all-too-human causes of flood catastrophes. These were not sceptical conservatives keen to point up the price of progress (some of them weighed in, too), but writers who had their eyes firmly pointed towards the future and were committed to dam technology.[121] Consider just two of the many writers who outlined the case for dams-plus-reforestation as the solution to earlier errors. P. Ziegler wrote a devastating critique of the 'disadvan-tageous effects' created by deforestation and river regulation. He then suggested that, since it was 'impossible to return to previous circum-stances', building dams on mountain streams was the only way of making good the damage.[122] The views of Professor H. Christian Nußbaum were equally unequivocal. This was a man who wanted a massive state programme to dam every river valley that could be dammed (his budget calculations in 1907 went up to the year 2012), because this was an 'obligation' of the state given the way that defor-estation and river regulation had created such a 'deplorable state of affairs'.[123] By the beginning of the twentieth century, in other words, prominent hydraulic engineers had identified the unwitting human causes of flood disasters and now saw dams as a means of undoing yesterday's mistakes.

When Ziegler said that it was impossible simply to turn the clock back, he included modern river navigation as something that could not be reversed. The interests of navigation featured in most calculations about the benefits of dams. That is no surprise. A major reason for using dams to even out river flows was to maintain minimum water levels in summer – the holy grail of shipping interests. After all, German governments spent a fortune – as much as 1.5 billion Marks between 1890 and 1918 – on improving inland navigation. Rivers were deepened to accommodate ships laden with up to 600 tons (over 1000 tons on the Rhine); new canals were built to the same dimensions.[124] Like much else about the German economy, the 'canal age' came late. Britain had enjoyed its classic canal age back in the eighteenth century, the United States earlier in the nineteenth. On the Continent the French were the nineteenth-century leaders in canals as well as dams. But by dint of sustained investment, Germany bucked the trend elsewhere (including Britain, the United States and France) that saw freight moving inexorably onto rails. Inland shipping not only increased sevenfold from 1875 to 1910; it did better than hold its own with rail.[125] Supporters saw this expansion 'on a scale undreamed-of' a few decades earlier as a root cause of German economic growth.[126] It was a symbol of German industrial dynamism in a period that saw Germany overtake Britain as an economic power house.

There was historical precedent for using impounded water to aid navigation. Upland streams had long been dammed to create a head of water on which logs could be floated – with disastrous unintended consequences, for rafting timber was a prime instance of the deforestation that caused flooding.[127] But the modern models were foreign. Many nineteenth-century French dams were designed to help shipping. American engineers built dams on the Upper Mississippi for the same reason.[128] Just as the drinking water reservoir was an alternative to the arduous task of pumping groundwater, a reservoir that released top-up water into a river seemed preferable to the dredger's thankless 'labour of Sisyphus'.[129] In a cycle like the one that led eventually to the building of anti-flood dams, the top-up water was sometimes needed to undo the effects of previous river regulation that led streams to scour their beds, as Tulla's Rhine had done.[130] Canals created special problems because of their wasteful ways. Water slopped out of the canal and was lost every time a ship moved through a lock.[131] Canals had to be supplied with water by rivers, which meant that the rivers needed to be supplied from somewhere else.

That was the main aim of the Eder Valley Dam completed in 1914, the largest built in Germany before the 1960s. The idea of building a dam at this site had been canvassed earlier as a means of preventing floods on the Eder, a tributary of the Weser. But it was the expected benefits to navigation that tipped the balance in favour of the project.[132] At the centre of the argument stood the so-called Mittelland canal, which would eventually link the Rhine-Ruhr in the west with the Elbe in the east. First introduced into the Prussian parliament in 1886, the proposal to construct a Mittelland canal was one of the most contentious political issues of the era, vigorously supported by German industry and shipping, just as vigorously opposed by German agricultural interests in the east, which feared easier access for cheap foreign foodstuffs and a further loss of labour to industry. Both sides saw it as a 'struggle for life and death'.[133] The canal became the great symbolic issue in the raging debate about the inevitability and desirability of Germany's transition from an agricultural to an industrial state.[134] Ultimately, the agrarian rearguard action failed. In 1905, a measure was approved to extend the canal system eastwards. The Eder Valley Dam was an integral part of the plan. Together with the smaller Diemel Dam, its 200 million cubic metres would replace water in the Weser that were needed to feed existing stretches of the Rhine–Ems–Weser canal and its extension on to Hanover.[135] None other than Otto Intze had advised the Prussian government that only the Eder Dam could achieve these goals.[136]

The Eder, the ultimate 'giant dam', served as the symbol of two very large ideas. It was a key to rectifying an inconvenient geographical reality: that the North German plain spread out from west to east, but was full of rivers that flowed from south to north. And, as a necessary adjunct to the Mittelland canal, the Eder gave physical expression to the ultimate triumph of Germany's 'industrial' future over its 'agrarian' past.

Each of the great German pre-war dams – the Urft, Möhne and Eder – provided an additional ingredient x. The Urft offered flood control plus x, the Möhne water for the Ruhr plus x, the Eder water for navigation plus x, and x was the same in every equation: hydro-electric power. In the decade when those three dams were completed (1905–14), no aspect of the new technology aroused such fervour. In the professional world, new publications appeared with titles like *The Turbine* and *White Coal*. A new volume was added to the *Handbook of Engineering Science* on 'The Harnessing of Hydro-Electric Power'.[137] The message soon reached a wider audience. J. L. Algermissen still worried in 1906 that there were readers of the *Social Review* unfamiliar with the term 'white coal' to denote hydro-electric power.[138] Two years later Theodor Koehn enthused that 'the whole population is beginning to interest itself in the question of the quickest and best way to exploit hydro for the common good' – hyperbole, no doubt, but understandable given the seemingly endless stream of articles on this vaunted energy of the future.[139] The century of steam had given way to the century of electricity, and white coal would be the key.[140]

There were many arguments for tapping the 'capital from the mountains'.[141] One was concern about future energy sources. Coal consumption had increased dramatically and reserves were finite, like those of oil. Coal prices were rising fast and users sometimes held hostage by suppliers. Hydro, so its advocates claimed, was not only available in areas of Germany that lacked coal deposits: it was an inexhaustible, renewable form of energy that was not subject to political vagaries. It offered a 'powerful, continuous, cheap form of energy independent of strikes, coal syndicates and petroleum rings' and was destined to be 'the main energy source of the future'.[142] In the past, hydro had been associated with the great drawback of all water-power: it could only be exploited on the spot. In the 1870s an engineer calculated that this inflexibility made a unit of hydro-power worth only half as much as a comparable unit of steam power. But the calculation had changed by the beginning of the new century.[143]

The turning point can be precisely dated to 24 August 1891. That was when the 36-year-old Bavarian engineer Oskar von Miller, who would become Germany's most important advocate of hydro, demonstrated for the first time that power could be generated in one place and used in another. Electricity was produced at a plant in Lauffen on the Neckar and transmitted overland to the Electro-Technical Exposition taking place more than a hundred miles away in Frankfurt, where it was used to run electric lights (and an artificial waterfall). The dramatically staged demonstration had the desired effect. Theodor Koehn later wrote that 'a new epoch in the application of hydro-power had begun'.[144] Meanwhile, turbine technology, based on principles first outlined by scientists who included Daniel Bernoulli and Leonhard Euler, advanced rapidly in the nineteenth century. Engineers like Benoit Fourneyron (France), Carl Henschel (Germany), James Francis (Britain), Lester Pelton (United States) and Viktor Kaplan (Austria) were engaged, not in reinventing the wheel, but in reinventing the water-wheel. By the 1890s the gains in efficiency were enormous.[145]

But who would exploit them? There was more than a hint of Darwinian economic struggle in the arguments put forward by German enthusiasts. Hydro was a 'national asset'; Germany could not afford to be left behind.[146] Our old friend Richard Hennig warned about 'sharp competition looming with some newly rising countries whose economic future looks very favourable thanks to an abundance of hydro-power'.[147] Foreign successes were all around. Switzerland was often singled out for moving quickly to exploit Alpine resources ('the Eldorado of European hydro-electric power') and the Swiss Rhine.[148] Others pointed to Italy and Scandinavia.[149] Then there was the United States. Germans were mesmerized by the giant hydro-electric plant in Niagara Falls ('Niagara in shackles') that began operations in 1895.[150] The more discerning also looked enviously to California, the true home of American long-distance transmission, where the Pacific Gas and Electric Company of San Francisco began exploiting hydro from the streams of the Sierra Nevadas in the 1890s.[151] American output was on a wholly different scale: Niagara Falls produced twice as much power in 1905 as all of Germany's installations combined.[152] Europe offered a more realistic yardstick. German writers loved to present tables showing how the country stacked up against its competitors, although Ernst Mattern complained that statistics were copied from one article to another without much critical scrutiny.[153] Still, rough as they were, the numbers showed that Germany actually came out of the comparison well. Before the war it was exploiting around a fifth of available hydro, second only to Switzerland.[154]

The heartland of German hydro-electric power was the coal-poor south. Bavaria led the way before 1914, although the most ambitious undertaking in the state was still on the drawing-board. Conceived by Oskar von Miller, it involved harnessing the waters of the Walchensee and making the electricity available to the Bayernwerk, a state-wide grid. Begun in 1918, the project came on line in 1924.[155] Württemberg, where Miller had one of his earliest successes delivering hydro-electric power to the town of Heilbronn, also had projects underway. But they were modest compared with the programme in neighbouring Baden. If Bavaria had the largest resources of hydro-electric power in the south, Baden had the greatest in proportion to its size and population – comparable indeed to Switzerland, which in many ways it resembled socially and politically. The greatest single resource was the energy to be won from the Rhine, alone or in partnership with the Swiss. This, as one Karlsruhe engineer boasted, was the 'true Rhine Gold'.[156] There were also proposals to tap the power of the Murg and Kinzig. The Rhine, Murg and Kinzig – these were the places where Tulla had been active a century earlier. Now the engineers were altering the rivers once again with a different purpose in mind.[157]

A distinctly south German note of defiance sometimes sounds through the enthusiasm for hydro. When Oskar von Miller talked about its contribution to 'the struggle for economic existence', he meant Bavaria's struggle, not Germany's.[158] Similar sentiments were expressed in Baden, self-conscious about being tucked away in the 'south-west corner' of the country.[159] Reich proposals to increase the tax on electricity by a 'Prussian' finance minister raised southern suspicion; one writer even foresaw an economic struggle between north and south.[160] It is tempting to go further. The socially utopian tone of many southern arguments for hydro seems to reflect liberal south German distinctiveness, from the dislike of 'monopolies' and 'coal barons' to the belief in bringing the benefits of electrification to peasants and craftsmen.[161] After all, in Württemberg it was the People's Party, most progressive of all German liberal parties, that made the running over hydro.[162] And it was from the south that the loudest calls came to take hydro-electric power into public ownership (as the Swiss had done), to prevent it from falling into the hands of vested interests.

The argument is intuitively attractive, confirming all our prior ideas about the different Germanys north and south of the River Main. In reality, though, the cause of hydro had utopian undertones in every part of Germany. 'White coal' was cheap, clean, hygienic and modern, not like smoky, sooty coal.[163] (There are many parallels with the enthusiasm for nuclear power in the 1960s.) Even the measurement of energy in kilowatt hours seemed like a symbolic break with the old and outmoded ('There is . . . something wrong when an engineer has to measure the prospects of a hydro installation on the basis of what a horse costs'.[164]) Perhaps more than anything else, in north and south alike, cheap hydro-electric power was presented as the answer to Germany's social problems. A chorus of voices claimed that it would help the 'little man' – the craftsman and domestic worker – against big business, arrest the drift to the cities by fostering decentralized production, provide a substitute for the rural labour shortage, and reduce divisions between town and country.[165] It was a chorus in which some Social Democrats sang along.[166] No wonder that sober voices warned of 'effusive hopes', 'boundless' enthusiasm, even 'megalomania'.[167]

With Mastery of the Water Comes the Opportunity for Conflict

It was not just hydro-electric power that prompted utopian thoughts: the whole dam-building project had a visionary quality. Dams were, after all, supposed to irrigate fields, store drinking water, turn mill wheels, protect people from floods, help inland navigation, and provide electricity. Could they really do all this? Could any given dam play so many roles at once? Certainly it could, said the experts. Intze always stressed the all-purpose versatility of the dam – one writer called it a 'red thread' in his work – and he was followed by the standard authorities.[168] For P. Ziegler, there was 'hardly a major water-resources issue' that could be solved without considering the dam, which he called a 'partner' to the many different enterprises.[169] No one, it is true, denied that tricky issues arose on the ground. Building a dam meant a basic change in local hydrology and always affected existing water-use rights upstream and down. How to balance the interests of existing fishing or milling or agricultural concerns against the future benefits of a drinking-water reservoir or power plant? Who received compensation, how much and from whom? Ziegler paid more attention than most to these 'antagonistic interests'. As he wrote, 'with mastery of the water comes the opportunity for conflict'.[170] A growing body of literature tried to refine the valuation of existing properties on water-courses, according to whether they were developed or undeveloped, bought, rented, inherited or acquired by auction.[171] And it is no coincidence that dam construction led not only to the 1891 revision of the Prussian law on cooperatives, but to wholesale revision of water laws. Every major state rewrote its laws in these years: Baden (1899, 1908), Württemberg (1900), Bavaria (1908), Saxony (1908), Prussia (1913).

This provided a legal basis for resolving questions of individual compensation, including the compensation paid to those most dramatically affected by dams: the inhabitants of valleys that were flooded. It proved much harder to balance the interests of would-be beneficiaries, for these were not really complementary at all. Drinking water reservoirs had hygienic requirements that complicated other uses, or caused extra costs if they were taken into account. Agriculture had an urgent seasonal need for summer water; but so did other users, leading to arguments about who had priority. Meanwhile, any dam designed to create a head of water for power generation ran into difficulties with the shipping interest, which wanted an even flow. Perhaps most intractable of all was the question of how to reconcile flood protection with other needs, especially the power generation that was supposed to pay for these installations (or at least offset their cost). Keeping a Silesian reservoir half-empty to receive floodwaters that might or might not come was financially problematic; not doing so defeated the original purpose.[172]

As the different parties jostled for advantage the state was drawn into the conflict. It could hardly be otherwise, because dam construction cut across the line between public and private interests at so many points. Changes to the flow of water on the private (unnavigable) stretches of a waterway were bound to have effects on the public (navigable) stretches downstream. Building a large dam like the Möhne or Eder meant moving public roads, railway track, even stations that would disappear under water. Then there was the key question: who would finance these great capital projects? For the state, fiscal prudence (and, in the early days, concerns about a new technology) had to be balanced against the claims of economic growth. As dams became an object of national prestige, the opportunity to wave the flag at international expositions also had to be added to the equation.[173] In the end, German states and provinces footed the cost when a dam was intended to serve the 'general interest', which meant flood protection and improved navigation, while the municipalities generally financed drinking water reservoirs. Dams designed to create water-power for local businesses or built to serve the larger purposes of the Ruhr Valley Reservoirs Association were left to the interests concerned. And dams to generate hydro-electric power were built by a motley assortment of states, municipalities, private companies and mixed partnerships.[174] But even where dams were built with private money the state played a role, even if some engineers did mutter about the millstone of 'bureaucratic' and 'legalistic' officials.[175] The state brought the interests together (as it did in the Ruhr), guaranteed loans, seconded officials and proved remarkably cooperative about moving roads and railways – and people – when asked.[176]

Another potential conflict shaped modern German dam-building. That was the tension between large and small. Did it make sense for small groups of small producers to build small dams in side valleys of the Wupper, when greater returns could be achieved by a more ambitious project? Many engineers felt that local dams were a wasteful use of a precious resource. Ernst Mattern was not alone in deploring the random, 'disorderly' harnessing of water-power in the early stages of the movement.[177] Georg Adam argued that local exploitation of water-power by wheel-driven mills was haphazard, almost 'accidental'.[178] The arguments were, if anything, fiercer when it came to hydro. Oskar von Miller led the pack of those who feared that the fruits of large-scale projects (he was thinking especially of the Walchensee) were being jeopardized by small, piecemeal projects.[179] The cast of mind behind these criticisms was well expressed by Mattern:

> The gaze of the engineer must free itself from petty everyday tasks and boldly lay down a direction for the development of hydro-electric power over years and decades, one that will not shackle its free development and creativity.

What was needed was a 'large-scale plan'.[180] Centralized, organized, above all rational: these were the words that turned up again and again in pre-war works calling for greater planning of water resources.[181] To these impatient technocrats, small was anything but beautiful.

What emerged from this complex play of forces? Looking back from the late 1920s, a clear pattern had emerged. By then, forty years after ground was first broken at Remscheid, the construction of dams had assumed an 'extraordinary scale': nearly ninety had been built and three dozen more were planned.[182] Beyond the fact that they were now being built in every region of Germany, what stands out most is the shift in the primary motives for building them. Plenty of writers still intoned the mantra that dams could serve (and reconcile) many different interests. But the winners and losers were obvious.

The owners of small water-powered mills were losers. Consider what happened in the valleys of the Wupper and Ruhr, where the dam movement had its start and disillusion followed close behind. The hopes placed in the new technology as a saviour against big business in the Ruhr coalfield turned out to be misplaced. The dams were built too small, the flow of water was less than promised and still dried up completely in summers with low rainfall. Intze had miscalculated.[183] This altered the economics of the dams, causing resentment over the high costs being paid for the water. The Ruhr Valley Reservoirs Association was meanwhile too busy raising capital for undertakings like the Möhne to provide help to the small dams it had initially co-funded. Pleas to the government and lawsuits were the result.[184] The situation did not improve after the war; in fact dams built mainly to provide water-power were gradually turned over to other purposes in the 1920s, usually drinking water.[185]

Agriculture fared no better. This was a sign of the declining power of agrarian interests in the new industrial age, one reason why its polit-ical representatives made so much noise. The Vosges dams remained a solitary instance in Germany where irrigation was a primary purpose. This contrasted strongly with other countries in the temperate zone: neighbouring France, or the United States. More arresting still was the contrast between promise and reality. Almost every dam project included a section devoted to the agricultural benefits. These almost never mate-rialized. Landowners living below the Ennepe Dam had previously used river water for irrigation; after the dam was built they were forbidden to use reservoir water.[186] The Urft Dam was advertised as a boon to agriculture; but that part of the scheme was never put into effect. Even the Eder Dam, a rare case in which water was provided to peasant fields, irrigated a smaller area with worse results than landowners had enjoyed before. All in all, dams provided the water for just two per cent of the irrigated area in Germany.[187] Even those pro-agriculture writers and organizations not opposed to dams as the creatures of industrial or shipping interests became highly critical. Their reward was to be lectured on how agriculture should wean itself off tariffs and embrace dams. It was, said critics, 'cutting off its nose to spite its face', too 'slow-moving' and lacking 'the necessary enlightenment' to seize its opportunity.[188]

No doubt agriculture was addicted to tariffs, and it certainly turned complaining into a political way of life. But here, at least, it had some-thing to complain about. Kurt Soergel's careful study in 1929 justified his acid comment that while dam promotion was 'extraordinarily generous with promises of jam tomorrow', the actual balance sheet for agriculture had been largely negative.[189] It was not just irrigation. Promises that raised groundwater levels would benefit cultivators also turned out to be hollow: agriculture needed 'fine regulation' of water whereas dams used water 'crudely', with results that were at best mixed. Flood protection, on the other hand, represented a genuine benefit to agriculturalists, although it also created some new problems.[190]

It speaks well for Soergel's fair-mindedness that a pro-agrarian stance did not lead him to a wholly negative view of dams and flood protection. His restraint was all the more impressive given the wild claims from enthusiasts that dams could make flooding 'a thing of the past'.[191] In fact, however much such claims may have contributed (understandably) to the early popularity of dams, there were sceptics right from the start. Some took the old view that river regulation remained the best solution to floods; others expressed the more 'modern' view, already emerging before the war, that people who settled in low-lying floodplains were asking for trouble and dams would not get them out of it. (Still, it was perhaps unwise to write as frankly as J. L. Algermissen did about people 'in the east of Germany' becoming used to 'wailing' and 'passing round the collection box' – especially for a writer from Cologne, because Rhinelanders would soon become experts at this.)[192] The doubters included engineers, geographers and the meteorologist, Karl Fischer, who observed nastily that the huge practical problems were unlikely to 'halt the victory parade of dam-building'.[193]

Even in 1918 many would have challenged Splittgerber's claim that dams had been a 'great success' in flood-protection.[194] Scepticism hardened in the 1920s, when flooding recurred in east and west. The effectiveness of existing dams varied: the Eder was very successful, dams on tributaries of the Wupper basin were not, and those in the Ruhr basin, Saxony and Silesia had a mixed record.[195] Silesia was the real test case. Intze's dams seem to have had some effect during the 1926 floods.[196] But the 'destruction' of that year still made one former collaborator of Intze's doubt whether a 'satisfactory solution' could ever be achieved.[197] Bachmann wrote a devastating critique in 1927 that laid out the problems. Dams could not be built everywhere, and building at one location left another area less protected. The dams actually built on the Bober and Queiss could not hold back more than a quarter of the largest floods. The real difficulty was that protection against smaller-scale, more frequent high water ran at cross-purposes with the original aim of providing protection against infrequent, catastrophic floods. These often arrived when the reservoir was already full – unless it had been hurriedly emptied in a controlled discharge that itself caused severe damage downstream and led people to fear the warning klaxons.

Underlying all of these problems was the fact that an empty dam produced no electricity. Safety or economic return? That conflict applied everywhere that dams claimed to offer flood protection, although meteorological and hydrological conditions on the Oder tributaries made the dilemma especially acute.[198] Bachmann's scepticism was deep and lasting. In 1938 he was still assailing the optimists: the problem of floods was 'not so easy to solve as it appears'.[199] His conclusion was the same one reached by modern experts in risk assessment: 'Using dams as a structural measure of flood control is problematic'.[200] This view had acquired sufficient weight in interwar Germany to dampen enthusiasm for new flood-protection dams. Perhaps it is a sign of how established the view has become today that modern admirers of Intze have suggested even he was cautious about recommending dams for this purpose. If so, he certainly had on odd way of showing it.[201]

As the reasons for building dams shifted, shipping was one of the winners. It had long been a powerful interest. Before the war the shipping lobby had succeeded, with support from agriculture, in blocking a plan devised by Intze to build hydro plants on the Deime and Pregel rivers in East Prussia, fearing adverse effects on navigation – a rare instance when Intze failed to get his way.[202] The Eder Dam was the shipping interest's great pre-war monument. Similar projects followed in the Weimar Republic. The largest was the Bleiloch Dam on the River Saale in Thuringia, built in 1925–32 and even larger than the Eder at 215 million cubic metres. It is not without symbolic significance that the dam was originally proposed pre-war as a flood-protection measure, but reconfigured in the post-war years as an aid to navigation. The Bleiloch augmented the water of the Elbe and sections of the Mittelland canal.[203] The Ottmachau Dam on the Neisse was built in the same years, to feed additional water to the Oder in the interests of Silesian industry. Only half the size of the Bleiloch, it was still larger than all but a handful of German dams. The Ottmachau was built despite strong opposition from the people whose land was flooded to make it possible, and from the Prussian ministry of agriculture.[204] The water from these dams was expensive, especially Ottmachau's. It cost 100,000 Marks a day to maintain the desired minimum water level on the Oder.[205] Even then, one critic judged their impact 'extraordinarily small', raising water levels 'no more than a few centimetres'.[206] In the best case – the Eder Dam – it was more like fifteen centimetres, which made a difference.[207] But even supporters felt that these dams had been less successful than expected in improving navigation. The only answer they could come up with, implausible though it sounds when the Eder, Bleiloch and Ottmachau dams already had a combined capacity of 500 million cubic metres, was to find still more water for Germany's thirsty rivers and canals.[208]

The thirst of growing industrial cities was also insatiable. More and more dams were built through the 1920s and beyond to satisfy the dual demand for water: to drink, and to use in production processes. That was not how things were supposed to turn out. Early enthusiasts promised a solution to water shortages, not a perpetual construction programme. Catchment areas that struggled to provide drinking water for 10,000 people would, so it was claimed, support cities of a million; a town that drew its supply from a reservoir would 'never suffer a water shortage'.[209] Never, in most cases, meant ten to fifteen years, less if a very dry summer intervened. The town of Lennep built a reservoir in 1893; eight years later it had to be enlarged. Remscheid's Eschbach reservoir was still expected in 1902 to suffice 'for a long time ahead'; six years later ground was broken on the new Neye Valley reservoir. Just eleven years elapsed between the completion of Barmen's first reservoir and the construction of a second.[210] The story was the same everywhere, before and after the war. And each new dam was bigger than its predecessor.[211]

'Constantly growing demand', as the director of the Chemnitz waterworks called it, was driven by rising urban populations, more towns going over to centralized water supply, and more of them becoming hooked on reservoir water.[212] Less obviously, the calculations that underlay the first generation of reservoirs turned out to include many rough and ready estimates, invariably too optimistic. Intze again led the way.[213] Nowhere, moreover, was the suggestion made by reservoir opponents in Barmen, to install meters, taken up.[214] Proud city fathers were more likely to salute the effect of reservoirs 'in weaning the population from thrifty water use'.[215] There is no mystery about rising non-domestic demand in an increasingly industrialized Germany, since it took as much as 3000 litres of water to wash every ton of coal and up to four times that to produce a ton of pig iron. French occupation of the Ruhr and the 1929–33 depression showed how critical industrial users were, for water consumption dropped sharply on both occasions. Less obviously, the almost universal decision not to invest in separate domestic and industrial water delivery systems (the town of

Euskirchen, anomalously, did) had important long-term implications for water supply, arguably adding to both cost and waste.[216]

The Ruhr is the classic case of rising demand driving the search for new and bigger dams. It still bore the double burden of large-scale industrial and domestic use, especially as drinking water came to be withdrawn directly from the river and infiltrated back into the ground as 'pseudo-groundwater'.[217] In 1897, 135 million cubic metres was withdrawn from the river, by 1913 it was 455, by 1929 668, and after the depression the volume spiked steeply upwards again, to a billion cubic metres a year in 1934.[218] As a result the Ruhr Valley Reservoirs Association was always running to stand still. The Möhne Dam was supposed to fix the problem; but by 1921 (a dry year) the Association was back where it started, and the Sorpe Dam was built (1926–35), but even before it was ready another drought year prompted plans for a new dam on the Lower Verse, eventually completed after the Second World War. By then, thoughts were already turning to the construction of yet another major reservoir.[219]

But it was white coal that became the number one reason for dam-building after the war.[220] Electricity consumption more than quadrupled from 1913 to 1927, but forty per cent of German coalfields had been lost under the Versailles Treaty. Brown coal (lignite) made up some of the difference, but hydro-electric power became decisive. In addition to the low-head power plants on the Rhine and other rivers, new hydro-electric dams appeared all over Germany: in Bavaria, the Black Forest, Silesia, even in the sandy Prussian east, where landfill dams were built on the Stolpe, Radue and Rega. While hydro was still bruited as the friend of the little man (and now, as the 'housewife's best helper'), the rosy dreams of pre-war years failed to materialize.[221] The economics of rural electrification meant that the power was not in fact cheaper, even where it was available.[222] As for the craftsmen, they were encouraged to invest in electric motors, which was good business for the electricity suppliers; but when depression hit they found themselves overexposed and indebted. For these members of the small-business *Mittelstand*, the problem was not – as so often argued – that they were 'backward-looking', but that they were too forward-looking.[223] Their fate was like that of the small industrialists in the Wupper basin who trusted Intze's calculations.

Two other pre-war aspirations – the hopes placed in public ownership, and in 'south German' hydro – were also confounded. A 1919 proposal to socialize electricity on a German-wide basis was never implemented in the face of resistance from existing owners, public and private. What happened instead was the creation of a series of powerful combines to organize electricity supply. They included public and private firms, and hybrids, like Rhenish-Westphalian Electricity of Essen (RWE).[224] Whether this set-up more closely resembled the 'planned capitalism' advocated by Walter Rathenau before the war, or the 'German socialism' advocated by Werner Sombart after it, is an open question (assuming there was, in practice, much difference).[225] Critics of hydro dams continued to blame 'the present-day form of our capitalist economy', as if control over electricity had in fact fallen into the hands of Germans who resembled the 'American monopolists' so often demonized before 1914, even though the ownership structure of the German industry belied the charge.[226] That said, it would be hard to find a better example of a home-grown monopolist than Hugo Stinnes, the man who put together RWE. And RWE, like two other, publicly-owned companies based in Prussia, pursued an aggressive expansion policy into the south – so aggressive that in 1927 a demarcation agreement had to be negotiated between them: the 'electrical peace'. The aim behind this business aggression was to add southern hydro to northern, coal-based electricity, so that power could be 'wheeled' from one part of the system to another, depending on the season.[227] The success of that strategy mocked the hopes that southerners had once placed in hydro. By the end of the 1920s the vast hydro-electric resources of Bavaria and Baden belonged to combines based in the Ruhr or Berlin.

The Impact on Environment and Landscape

Germany entered the era of high dams before the First World War. In the 1920s and 1930s their numbers grew, with construction of the Bleiloch, Niederwarthe, Sorpe, Soese and Schwammenauel. All were, by the classification of 1930, 'high dams' in the range 60–100 metres. But only just: the largest German dams were almost all 60–70 metres high. Modest by world standards, they came to look more modest with the passage of time. The register of the International Committee on Large Dams (ICOLD) contains many very high dams (over 100 metres) in North America, the former Soviet Union and the Third World. These have no German counterparts. The difference in capacity is even more striking. The Hoover Dam (1936) impounded almost 200 times as much water as the Eder or Bleiloch. When it comes to the great signature dams of the 1950s and 1960s, the Kariba, Volta and High Aswan, the multiple is closer to 800.[228] Some Germans were mindful even before 1914 that their domestic 'giants' were in fact Lilliputian. The USA and the earlier, British-built Aswan Dam usually provided the yardstick, and the comparisons were always wistful.[229] More than one writer, Richard Hennig among them, looked to the African colonies as a place where Germans too might build very large dams, until defeat in the First World War removed that possibility.[230] The Aswan continued to be viewed with great respect through the Third Reich.[231] In retrospect, however, by not building the gigantic structures that came to define twentieth-century dam-building, as well as by reason of its climate, Germany was spared their most catastrophic environmental conse-quences. These costs, like the dams themselves, were of a lower order of magnitude in Germany, but certainly not negligible.

Over the last decades evidence has mounted on the adverse effects of large dams. Take the Aswan, designed to control the Nile flood, allow its waters to be used more systematically for irrigation, and generate electricity. It achieved these things, but with dreadful unin-tended consequences. To replace the silt that no longer came down the Nile, electricity from the dam went to manufacturing chemical fertil-izer, which produced its own side-effects in the form of run-off. Impounding such a huge body of water (its surface area is twelve times larger than Lake Constance) led to high levels of evaporation. Salinization, the scourge of all irrigation regimes, became worse without the regular flushing provided by the annual flood, while Egypt's irri-gation canals became a breeding ground for the snails that carry schis-tosomiasis, a disease of the liver, intestines and urinary tract that now affects whole populations. Deprived of silt, the Nile delta shrank, depriving the Mediterranean of nutrients, which destroyed the sardine and shrimp fisheries. This was hardly the 'everlasting prosperity' that had been promised.[232] The same dismal story, with local variations, unfolded in country after country. As if that were not enough, the last thirty years has brought persuasive evidence that dams are not only vulnerable to earthquakes but cause them. Arguments about reservoir-induced seismicity began in the late 1930s; UNESCO has recommended seismic monitoring of dams since 1973. At least 90 cases have been

recorded world-wide, usually linked to the initial filling and occasionally to the rapid drawing-down of the reservoir water.[233]

Some of these problems are more remote from German experience
than others. Induced seismicity is not remote, at least in the sense that
quite small dams have triggered earthquakes, and have done so in neighbouring countries, including the Swiss, French and Italian Alps. Not
all of these areas were seismically active before. However, no case has
so far been recorded within German borders.[234] Nor did Germany
experience the problems of salinization and sickness associated with
huge, dam-based irrigation projects, because irrigation played such a
marginal role in the construction of German dams. Agriculture may
have been short-changed, but being a 'loser' was actually a blessing
because the local, small-scale irrigation practised in Germany proved
more sustainable – as some contemporaries astutely predicted when
they pointed to the disasters of over-watering in the American West.
Evaporation did occur, but at levels (around five to ten per cent) lower
than those recorded at dams in arid countries. Any evaporation meant
a loss of valuable water; it also produced local climate changes.[235] That
worried some critics at the time.[236] In fact, climatic alteration proved
to be largely benign, moderating temperatures and benefiting vegetation. Mists prevented frost in the cold season; dew provided moisture
at times of low rainfall.[237] Ironically, the mists once deplored on the
Upper Rhine plain were now welcomed in upland valleys. The irony
extends further: by creating artificial lakes, dams tempered the long-
term effects of German land being dried out by river regulation and
the draining of thousands of natural lakes, moors and marshes.[238] In
another way, however, building dams contributed to that process of
desiccation. Some projects called for diverting water from one river
basin to another via tunnels bored through rock. An unanticipated
consequence was that the tunnels siphoned off water from the areas
above them, lowering water tables. The problem was especially serious
in the Harz mountains and led to the abandonment of one early twentieth-century project – not on environmental grounds, but because large
compensation claims were feared.[239]

What about the impact of dams on the flow of water downstream?
In Germany, too, silt collected behind dam walls: all dams defeat their
own purpose in the end. This accretion generally occurred much more
slowly than in African, American, Asian (or Spanish) dams.[240] But there
were some exceptions, from the Wupper to the Alps, where the rate

was higher. Then the potential loss to agriculturalists operating downstream was increased, although there was less to lose thanks to river regulation.[241] Every dam alters entirely the downstream dynamics of river flow and sediment deposition. In Germany the most serious effects were like those that occurred on Tulla's regulated Rhine. Lightened of the debris and sediment left behind the dam wall, rivers scoured their beds, lowering the water table and killing vegetation. Some Bavarian rivers experienced *Sohlendurchschlag*, when the stream pierces its own bed, cuts suddenly through permeable rock and drops by metres at a time – a hydrological China Syndrome.[242] The ultimate downstream effects of dammed rivers are felt by the seas and oceans that receive them, inevitably so when a sixth of global discharge comes from such rivers, and especially so when the river is large (like the Nile) and the sea is small (like the Mediterranean). In Germany, the dammed rivers almost all drain into the North Sea or the Baltic, the Mediterranean of the north.[243] Their impact would be worth studying, for we know that the 240 dams in Scandinavia, by altering the seasonal flow of fresh water into the Baltic, have affected the former exchange of fresh and salt water between the Baltic and the North Sea.[244]

Judged against the worst cases, from the Volta to the Dnieper, the adverse environmental impact of German dams was modest. The climate was different, the dams were smaller. But they still constituted, in Jürgen Schwoerbel's words, a 'massive disturbance of the morphology and ecological structure' of the rivers concerned, with effects on the whole river basin.[245] The changes were most strongly felt at and around the dam site. Contemporaries spoke of a 'violent . . . transformation'; the conditions of life 'changed from top to bottom'.[246] How could it be otherwise? The reservoir basin was scraped, dynamited, drilled and sealed. Stripped of trees, plants and humus, it resembled a 'cracked, patched and knotted bathtub'.[247] The tub was then filled with water. What resulted was something that looked like and was usually called a lake, but was not. Reservoirs shared a few characteristics with their natural cousins: the wave oscillations known (from the French word) as *seiches*, and their impact on the local micro-climate.[248] But the differences were greater than the similarities. The deepest point of a lake is near the middle; in a reservoir it is right behind the dam wall. Reservoirs have a different temperature structure and undergo much more frequent changes of water level (the same happens to natural lakes, like the Walchensee, when they are harnessed to produce power). This last difference is decisive, for it means that a typical 'terracing' effect is gradually produced; there is no firm riparian zone where flora and fauna can establish themselves.[249]

Life in the water was different, too. Reservoirs arrived in Germany about the same time that limnology, the study of lakes, emerged as a discipline. August Thienemann examined both natural and unnatural lakes. A naturalist who became an important figure in early ecological thought, Thienemann pioneered new ways of thinking about the relationship between the living community (Germans called it the biocoenosis) and the habitat, or biotype.[250] He showed that the reservoir was a quite novel body of water, a biotope that favoured species able to adapt to changing conditions.[251] The reservoir, in other words, had the same effect as Tulla's newly engineered Rhine. In both cases fish proved to be eloquent witnesses to change. Local studies showed that new conditions – variations in water temperatures, water levels, breeding conditions – led to rapid turnovers of dominant species, inside reservoirs and downriver. Pike and perch disappeared below the Eder Dam, grayling below the Diemel. That was one outcome of engineering German rivers. There were two others. Dams were, of course, a major obstacle to migratory fish, already facing serious decline. And reservoirs turned out to be not quite the boon to fishing that was promised. They brought an initial bounty, but at the expense of fish along other stretches of the same river. Then reservoir stocks themselves often fell and were kept up only by fish-farming, a story that became all too familiar at dams around the world.[252]

Thienemann helped to identify the now familiar distinction between healthy oligotrophic waters (low in nutrients, high in oxygen), and undesirable eutrophic waters, where the richness of organic or mineral nutrients leads to the growth and decay of algae that deplete the oxygen content. These processes remained obscure in the classic age of German dam-building, even to leading naturalists. Thienemann himself first used the terms oligotrophic and eutrophic, coined by a Swedish botanist, in 1921.[253] Today they feature prominently in reports on German reservoirs, because many have become eutrophic, even hypertrophic. That is the result of household waste and agricultural fertilizer finding their way into the water, with especially severe consequences in shallow reservoirs. There, above all in the Wupper basin and in Saxony, cloudy water and blooming algae signal serious problems. Of course, natural lakes can and do become eutrophic as well; but reservoirs are more vulnerable, especially when they are drawn down. And so fish stock are no longer determined by economic or recreational needs, but by the effort to use 'biomanipulation' to repair the damage. The hope is that by nurturing those species that feed on smaller zooplankton, the proportion of larger plankton can be increased and water quality thereby improved. Trout and minnows are the white knights of this ecological engineering, whereas a preponderance of the cypriniden species – roach, bream and pike – often signifies a watery world that is out of joint.[254]

The ecological effects of damming rivers were not all negative. New marshland formed at the entry to reservoirs, creating a valuable niche. Water-dwelling insects benefited from a new habitat. One entomologist who roamed the lands around the Wupper Valley dams reported enthusiastically in the early 1930s on the rich insect life. His greatest rapture was devoted to finding the rare maggot *Arricia erratica* in some horse excrement near the Bever Dam, but the main cause of his enthusiasm was the huge increase in beetle numbers in the decades since the dams were built. Beetles benefited from an environment of moisture, mud, stones and moss, thriving on the jetsam of stalks and fibres washed up on the shore and awaiting them when they emerged from winter quarters.[255] But it was birds that were most obviously attracted to the new bodies of water. Naturalists recorded wild ducks, herons, ospreys, gulls, kingfishers, lapwings. Occasionally a breeding pair would be spotted. Many reservoirs were and are alive with birds in spring and autumn, as they became a part of the flyways followed by migratory species.[256] Only those who expect human interventions to bring nothing but disaster for the environment will be surprised by this paradoxical outcome. After all, even a true environmental disaster like the Salton Sea – a toxic waste in the middle of the California desert, the result of a piece of river engineering that went badly wrong – has become a major stop on the Pacific flyway. It contains more bird species than any other site in America.[257] German reservoirs likewise became unintended sanctuaries, and not just for birds. This was not at all what Intze had in mind; but commentators soon noticed that the land around the new structures made excellent nature conservation areas, a concept already being popularized before the First World War.[258] By the 1930s this was a commonplace, and today the ecological management of reservoir surrounds is as unquestioned as the 'greening' of the dams themselves.[259]

But the values of the present should not be equated with the arguments of seventy years ago. Back when the first dams were built, and for decades afterwards, even the critics rarely argued in ecological terms.[260] Nature: *that* was the thing. And what a burgeoning nature conservation movement complained about was that dams threatened 'beautiful', 'natural', 'romantic' areas.[261] Uncultivated and 'unspoiled', these were – like the Saale valley before the Bleiloch Dam was built – 'pearls of scenic charm', so that 'a piece of landscape of indescribable beauty is perishing'.[262] It was nature as idealized landscape that the critics wanted to preserve. When they complained about a future land-scape dominated by the powerful horizontal line of the water, the under-lying aesthetic judgement was evident. It was even more obvious in lamentations about the 'pleasure-seeking mobs' the reservoirs would attract. Arno Naumann was right to describe conservationists like himself as 'guardians of aesthetic landscape values'.[263]

If we ask why they ultimately succeeded in guarding so little – or, to put it another way, why it was not until the 1980s that dam pro-jects were actually stopped in Germany – then two answers suggest themselves. The first is that only in a different society that had learned to talk about the limits of growth, and when evidence of the environ-mental problems caused by dams was available, could opposition be decisive. The second answer is that defence of the landscape on aesthetic grounds was always highly subjective. It lacked clear principles, could even be used to justify the selective destruction of nature. So, for example, a prominent conservationist like Paul Schultze-Naumburg was willing to sacrifice parts of the landscape that he judged superfluous to aesthetic requirements ('where one walks for many kilometres through unchanging scenery, it cannot be regarded as an irreplaceable loss if a certain part of this same valley is turned into a reservoir').[264] Engineers could live with that. Even hard-nosed prophets of progress like Emil Abshoff and Ernst Mattern expressed confidence that the economic future could be secured while sparing 'poetry-rich valleys' and the 'beauties of nature'.[265] Another engineer, defending the Walchensee project against conservationist critics, conceded that some 'intrusive' engineering projects impinged upon the 'majestic wilderness'. But this 'sacrilege against the precious gift of natural beauty' was not inevitable: things could be managed so that 'the scenic landscape is preserved wherever possible'.[266]

The outcome was predictable. A consensus emerged that dams were not an offence against landscape values if they merged harmoniously into their surroundings. The Möhne 'fitted itself wonderfully into the natural scenery'; the same claim was made in almost identical words for the 'rare harmony' achieved by the Wupper dams.[267] Similar formulations can be read again and again.[268] 'Adaptation' to local landscape was emphasized in the competitions to determine who would design the architecture of the dams (as distinct from their engineering construction), which attracted seventy-two entries in the case of the Möhne.[269] There were differences on questions of detail, but there was also plenty of common ground: architects should be involved from the beginning, not brought in at the end to prettify the structure; ornamentation was to be avoided; the dam should not try to disguise its artificiality, but should be sensitive to the natural surroundings.

National Socialism added several crotchets of its own: dislike of concrete as a building material (this was a *bête noire* of Hitler's), hostility to modernist functionalism, opposition to anything that was 'alien' to a 'natural German landscape'.[270] But the broad thrust of Nazi thinking, with its dislike of ornamentation, praise for 'authenticity', and emphasis on harmony betwen dam and natural setting, built on a consensus that already existed by the 1930s. That consensus made aesthetic judgements about the landscape central to debates between dam-builders and conservationists, thereby shifting the question from 'should we build?' to 'how should we build?'

Defining the question of dams and nature in that way opened the door to something else. What if the creation of reservoirs not only spared natural beauty but actually enhanced it? It comes as no surprise that this view was put forward at a meeting of the German Reservoirs Association in Hanover, and by other interested parties.[271] But it clearly had a wider purchase, beginning with conservationists like Schultze-Naumburg.[272] In fact so widespread did this view become that we find medical men issuing rather impatient reminders that, however much drinking water reservoirs might add to the beauty of the landscape, it was not why they had been built.[273] Arguments that reservoirs improved on nature always drew attention to the new body of water, especially in areas that lacked natural lakes. Where critics saw a crude horizontal line that dominated the eye, enthusiasts saw a 'majestic' body of water that allowed for the play of light and mirrored the surrounding hills.[274] This might be called the genre of reservoir-romanticism, and it was often found in the pages of cosy *Heimat* journals.

A typical article described the Bever as 'one of the most romantic reservoirs in the Bergisch land'. It was printed alongside a photograph of the Brucher valley reservoir showing clouds and trees reflected in the water at dusk, and captioned 'Evening on the Brucher Valley Reservoir'.[275] A short story in the same monthly, the *Bergische Heimat*, even has the title 'Reservoir Romanticism'. As Jean Pauli's story opens, the reservoir is 'a wonderful picture of quiet and peace'. From the light glimmering on the water at sunset to the sound of evening church bells, no cliché is left unused. Pauli's hero finds himself unable to leave because 'it's so paradisically beautiful, so solitary and quiet'. Drawn to the water, he goes out in a boat and sees a heron, then – can it be? – two mermaids. But they are actually two wholesome young women bathing. After much laughter the three go off 'home through the moonlight', singing.[276]

Drowned Villages, Broken Dams

The golden rule of reservoir aesthetics was that the valley should not look 'drowned'.[277] But drowned is exactly what they were, of course – 'drowned beauty', as Rudolf Gundt described the former Saale valley beneath the Bleiloch reservoir.[278] It was possible to argue about whether the new landscape was more or less beautiful. There was no denying that people had once worked the fields and lived in the farms that now lay under water. The men and women forced from their homes in the drowned valley have proved an irresistible subject for novelists. There are examples from England, France, Belgium, Austria and Czechoslovakia.[279] The most original of them casts beetles, ants and crickets in the leading roles. Dr Ernst Candèze's *The Dam: The Tragic and Adventurous History of an Insect People* was the work of a Belgian and dealt with the impact of the Gileppe Dam. Translated into German in 1901, it went through three editions by 1914.[280] With its cast of anthropomorphized insect characters, the book gently satirized human pretensions to mastery from the perspective of the victims.

As *The Dam* opens, the diving beetle and bon viveur Phili Karpfenstecher and his earnest friend, the long-horned beetle Weber, are discussing why the water has disappeared from their once green valley, turning it into a 'waste land'. An assembly of insects decides to send a party up the now rocky riverbed to investigate. After many misadventures with human and other predators, the surviving members of the group discover the problem: a giant wall across the valley. Joseph Joachim Geiger meets a fellow grasshopper from the district and learns how the indigenous black ants, processionary caterpillars and crickets were 'driven out of their homes' by the great flood that occurred after the men finished building the wall.[281] A pair of elderly crickets fill in the rest of the terrible story. (They had faced the rising waters 'like Philomen and Baucis', we are told, but in this version of the *Faust* story they survive.[282]) Two weeks after setting off the insects return home with the bad news that 'human arbitrariness' has deprived them for ever of water. Since litigation is fruitless (a cockroach speaks bitterly about how humans use their laws against the weak), the only alternative is Weber's suggestion: mass emigration. As the book ends, the insects are planning to resettle on the slopes high above the reservoir.

Candèze's insects experience the cycle of events and emotions common to every novel about the coming of the reservoir: anxiety, disruption, disbelief, resignation, destruction, expulsion. The moment when it all begins is the arrival in the village of strangers carrying briefcases, maps and measuring equipment. Candèze has this 'fateful' moment narrated by his pair of elderly crickets, whose idyllic musical evenings stand in contrast to the noisy activity of the outsiders. Ursula Kobbe's *The Struggle with the Dam*, set in the late 1930s, also describes the consternation caused by the 'foreign guests' who put up at the *Hussar* in the Tyrolean valley of the Bluntau. These fictional accounts tally closely with what we know about the first appearance of officials in the Eder valley.[283] What followed in the Bluntau was much more intrusive, as the valley 'completely changed its appearance and became one big construction site'.[284] That meant men and machines. Villagers in the Eder valley were reportedly unsure which they found more astonishing, the 'army' of workers who spirited the work to a conclusion 'like kobolds', or the giant machinery.[285] Even before 1914 major dam projects went out for tender to Germany's largest civil engineering companies. They used heavy equipment like excavators, stone-breakers, steam-driven winches and locomobiles; concrete mixers, tip-up trucks, conveyor belts and cranes arrived on site in the 1920s. Companies usually installed their own generators as well. Noise was a constant. Nothing was louder than dynamiting, and in the Eder valley it sounded from 10,000 shot-holes packed with 24,000 kilos of Astralit explosive. A familiar local geography was turned upside down. As old landmarks were levelled, the valley floor was now dominated by the light rail track and the piles of building materials it decanted, attractive only to local children.[286]

Up to 1000 men at a time worked on the Möhne, Eder and Urft dams; even the smaller Neye project employed 800. Many, in some cases most, were foreign workers: Bosnians, Croats, Poles, Czechs, and the ubiquitous Italians, the skilled masons. Temporary townships of barracks and canteens were built for them, larger than the long-established villages scheduled for destruction.[287] The 'foreign, brown workers' were no longer available after the war, which was one reason why fewer masonry dams were built.[288] But earthfill and reinforced concrete dams still required huge numbers of labourers. Well over 1000 worked on the Agger Valley Dam. From the late 1920s these were usually drawn from the swollen ranks of the unemployed.[289] Were there tensions between villagers and workers? It might have been expected. Even if the construction crews did not have the evil reputation of, say, the canal diggers, these were young men far from home looking to relax after their eleven-hour shifts. In Ursula Kobbe's novel the construction workers drink and shout in the local inn, and a local servant girl is abandoned with child by an Italian Lothario. But the sheer scale of the workforce in the Eder and Möhne valleys probably made them more self-sufficient than their fictional counterparts in the Bluntau valley, reducing interaction with locals.[290] The use of unemployed German labourers also suggested potential flash-points. After all, in the depths of the depression rural Germany was terrified by stories of unemployed gangs making night-time raids into the countryside, stealing the beets and cabbages from the fields. But these were men who now had jobs, and they often travelled back to their homes over the weekend by special trains. If there were fears and tensions locally, they have not found their way into the record.

Resignation seems to have been the prevailing mood in the villages destined for destruction. German rural communities were not, in a general way, politically passive in the Kaiser's Germany or the Weimar Republic. Agricultural crises and disputes with urban interests triggered many protest movements, even direct action. And faced with a group that was small and unpopular, gypsies for example, German villagers showed repeatedly that they were willing to use force to drive 'outsiders' from the district. But there were no such episodes directed against construction workers or officials. There was some parliamentary protest in Waldeck against the Eder Dam's displacement of people, and there was popular opposition to the Ottmachau Dam in the 1920s.[291] On the rare occasion when a dam project was overturned, however, it was not because of local protest but because of ministerial concerns about cost or the loss of prime agricultural land.[292] The one exception proves the rule. In 1925 the electricity combine RWE announced a plan to dam the Our valley on the Germany-Luxembourg border, displacing 1000 people, mostly Luxembourgers. There was outrage at the proposed 'sacrifices for the German economy'. Negotiations dragged on until RWE gave up four years later. The dam was not built until the early 1950s, on a smaller scale and in very different political circumstances. The Our valley received its stay of execution when Luxembourg national sensibilities were ruffled, and because the original plan called for the disappearance of Vianden, 'the pearl of the Grand Duchy' and a popular tourist destination.[293]

Nothing like this held up the flooding of ordinary German valleys by Germans. Eloquent works were written to mourn what was about to disappear, like the villages in the Edertal with their homes, churches and history – a convent, a twelfth-century letter of protection from the Archbishop of Mainz. There is no mistaking the sense of loss and pathos in these accounts, usually written by educated men who lived outside the valley but knew it well. They found it hard to bear what was happening, but they accepted the official view that a painful sacrifice was necessary for the larger good. 'Mother Germania needs this little spot of German earth to benefit thousands, perhaps millions of her children', wrote the clergyman Carl Heßler from Kassel. That was the consolation.[294] The language of sacrifice permeates these writings; the lost villages are even portrayed as a kind of oblation or votive offering to the dam.[295] Men like Heßler and H. Völker wrote as memorialists, not advocates of resistance. Their tone was fatalistic: 'But it has to be!', 'Alas, there is no alternative'. Völker's account of the 'doomed' Eder valley is shot through with the sense of inevitability, for the villages and fields were going to 'disappear on the command of authority'.[296]

The command of authority – that was the point. No public enquiries preceded these projects, and the power of compulsory purchase was available to use against owners reluctant to negotiate the sale of their land. As dams grew larger, the valleys they flooded contained more villages and agricultural land. What conflict there was between dam-builders and locals revolved largely around the question of compensation. Acquiring the land was a major component of the overall cost.

According to one expert, it could run to a quarter of the total.[297] The figure was sometimes higher than that. The nine million Marks spent in the Eder valley made up forty-five per cent of the total cost; it was not much less in the Möhne.[298] Some projects went over budget because of land acquisition costs, the reason why efforts were sometimes made to conduct the initial surveys 'discreetly' in order to avoid driving up prices.[299] Mutual mistrust poisoned negotiations. Dam-builders found landowners greedy; landowners believed the evaluation process was rigged against them, a view some local officials shared. It is a measure of the discord that compulsory purchase was eventually used to acquire nearly a quarter of the land in the Möhne and Ennepe valleys, and this in turn spawned many lawsuits.[300]

The proceeds were designed to allow for resettlement of those 'forced to leave their native soil'.[301] The numbers were substantial: 700 from the Möhne valley, 900 from the Eder valley, 950 from the Saale valley. The best evidence on who they were and where they went comes from the Eder. Three villages there disappeared completely, Asel, Berich and Bringhausen, plus parts of two others.[302] Construction began in 1908, and the inhabitants were given three years to leave. When the clergyman Carl Heßler wrote the first edition of his book on the valley in 1908 he dutifully recorded the names, occupations, number of family members and intended future homes of everyone in the three villages. Most were peasants, agricultural labourers or workers, with a sprinkling of craftsmen, innkeepers and minor officials like teachers or policemen. Bringhausen included a musician and two female paupers. At that stage the word 'undetermined', or a question mark, appeared in the future-home column against most of the names, although not in the case of the smallest village, Berich. Its inhabitants had already decided to re-establish the village elsewhere.[303] At some point the same decision must have been made in the other villages, for New Asel and New Bringhausen were built overlooking the future reservoir. It is nonetheless striking how widely dispersed the future homes of the former inhabitants would be, across nearby Waldeck and Hessen and as far away as Saxony and Westphalia. Some bought 'settlement' farms in the eastern province of Posen, although no one seems to have taken up the suggestion offered by the dam-builder Leo Sympher that there were fine prospects in the German colonies.[304]

Villagers began to leave the valley as early as 1908; others followed in the spring and summer of 1909. Then it was time for the last rites, the stiffly posed photographs in front of half-timbered farms and the final farewell party for those who remained. Bringhausen held its in midsummer 1910: 'It was with deep melancholy that the old people in particular thought of the hour, rushing ever nearer, that would finally separate them from house and farm, home and hearth'.[305] The dead had already been dug up from the graveyards and reburied in their new resting places. They were followed by the living, who carried parts of their old churches to the re-founded villages as a token of continuity. Was the leaving made easier by the knowledge that the valley had been steadily losing its population for decades? Or was it made harder by the knowledge that their expulsion was happening 'at a time of the most profound peace in Germany'?[306] This was suggested by Ludwig Bing, who remembered his own boyhood in the valley; but he was looking back from 1973 and the experience of two World Wars.

It takes years to build a large dam, and years more to fill the reservoir after it is built. Doomed valleys die a slow death, which adds to the poignancy. H. Völker wrote his book on the Eder as the valley waited for the waters to rise, and an awareness of what was soon to come forms its plaintive leitmotif. Those who have not yet found a new home must hurry, he writes, before the waters close over their old homes. A little later he notes that, below Herzhausen, the lake has already become quite wide, although still shallow. Later still, after recounting some local history, he returns obsessively to the subject: 'Not much longer now, and a lovely, perhaps the loveliest part of the Eder valley will disappear from the earth; a huge lake will swallow it up and waves will lap against the hillsides and rocks. Then the wanderer will often meditate on earlier times'.[307] The wanderer makes several appearances in these pages, invited to savour the valley while there is still time, or to visit Wilhelm Lösekammer's inn at Berich and imagine the lake waters two metres higher than the top of the ancient two-storey building. The reader understands the emotional power of this long moment suspended in time, its special fascination. At Vianden, after the plan to dam the Our had been announced, it was reported that Cooks Tours would be organizing trips. 'For who would not want to see a town that was about to disappear off the face of the earth, drowned, slowly, a centimetre at a time?', asked a local newspaper.[308] But Vianden was already well-known to tourists. The sad irony of the Eder valley, as Völker recognized, is that it was little known or visited. It was the dam itself that had brought new life and people, in the form of construction workers, and it was the reservoir that would soon cause 'a renewed stream of people to pour into this romantic valley'.[309]

It took a long time to fill a valley with water, but it took even longer to dispel anxieties about a dam-breach. Just as the ruins of churches and homes reappeared above the surface of a reservoir during a very dry summer, so each newly reported case of a failed dam caused fears to resurface.[310] For dams were like other new technologies: the sense of wonder and the shiver of fear were two sides of the same coin. Exceptional size (like exceptional speed) intensified both emotions.[311] There is plenty of evidence that these fears existed, not least in the writings of engineers who insisted they were groundless.[312] Anxiety was fed by popular articles and the conservation movement. The emphasis that so many early enthusiasts placed on the long history of dams may have been intended as a kind of balm. Whether the long view offered reassurance is another matter. More than 2000 dam failures have been recorded in human history. As Richard Hennig wrote in 1909, the history of dams was the history of dam failures.[313] Germany's entry into dam-building took place against a background of spectacular nineteenth-century collapses. The Puentos Dam in Spain failed in 1802, killing over 600; Britain suffered a series of disasters in the mid-Victorian years, culminating in the collapse of the Dale Dyke Dam near Sheffield in 1864, when 250 died; problems with insecure dams in metropolitan France were followed by the failure of the Algerian Al Habra Dam, with the loss of 200 lives; and the collapse of the South Fork Dam in Johnstown, Pennsylvania in 1889 left a death toll of more than 2000 (it was recorded as 4000 and 5000 in two different German accounts). The Johnstown disaster could hardly have come at a worse time for German engineers. The same was true of the Bouzey gravity dam on the French Mosel, which was built in 1881 by two of France's most celebrated practitioners and collapsed fourteen years later.[314] These disasters occurred during the heroic first decade of German dam-building. Then, even as construction of the Eder and Möhne was underway, the collapse of yet another dam in Pennsylvania (in the Austin valley) made lurid headlines, another gravity dam just like the Eder, the Möhne and their German predecessors.[315]

Intze and his colleagues were sensitive to public anxiety. They had a number of responses. The first was that the unprecedented level of technical knowledge gave grounds for complete confidence; failures occurred only because of shoddy construction. There was much truth in this, as enquiries into failures like Johnstown and Bouzey showed. It was also true that many collapses had involved earthfill dams, widely used in Britain and America but not in Germany (where this chequered history created a strong prejudice against them). But the state-of-the-art argument was also rather disingenuous. The years on either side of 1900 saw exceptionally heated debate among civil engineers about the principles of gravity dam construction as they had evolved over the previous fifty years. Contemporary critics argued that stress calculations did not take into account uplift forces, shear stresses and problems with the elasticity of masonry structures.[316] These strictures would later be fully accepted. Here we have another example of something that runs through the history of the Oder Marshes and Rhine regulation. When a generation of engineers insists on the unprecedented knowledge of the present, it does so as if an earlier generation had not made exactly the same claims. Sometimes we even find the same individuals repeating the same mantra. In 1929 Ernst Mattern looked back on the forty-year history of German dam-building and admitted that problems of uplift and shear had 'mostly not been taken into account' in the early days. The Mattern of 1929 blithely acknowledged the earlier 'imperfection', 'limited knowledge', 'approximate processes of calculation' and 'theoretical inadequacies'. The danger that a gravity dam might 'slide' had, he conceded, 'not always been sufficiently recognized'.[317] The Mattern of 1902 had naturally given no hint of any such shortcomings, arguing that although dam-building in Germany was 'still young' the state of engineering expertise warranted 'complete confidence'.[318]

Looking back, Mattern also suggested that earlier engineers had compensated for their lack of theoretical knowledge, where this applied, by designing conservatively. That was true; but it was also true that the deliberate over-engineering of dams – making them more solid than theory said they needed to be – had as much to do with allaying public fears as it did with caution or modesty. That was very evident in Silesia. Almost the entire community of specialists in Germany regarded the Marklissa Dam as over-built, including its designer, Intze. They blamed this on an anxious public. Intze complained that extra strengthening of the crown had been done 'out of exaggerated regard for the fears of the population'; it was 'the nervousness of the Silesian population' that made him reinforce the structure to meet imaginary dangers.[319] Engineering colleagues joined the chorus. One agreed to blame 'the fears of the Silesian population'; a second thought that 'exaggerated caution had been shown'; a third claimed testily that, 'however grave the responsibility for the safety of a dam', Marklissa was one of 'many cases' where popular fears had led to 'excessive safety measures'.[320] The view that an ignorant public had to be mollified was not unique to Germany. Frederick Haynes Newell, head of the US Reclamation Service (later the Bureau of Reclamation), said that his agency favoured solid dams because of a 'desire not only to have the works substantial but to have them appear so'; plans were prepared with a view 'to being not merely safe but looking safe'.[321]

We should therefore qualify Mattern's claim that a prudent modesty alone caused early German dam architects to over-design their structures. But he was right about something else: the painstaking care devoted in Germany to every stage of the construction process. This extended from the initial surveying through the excavation of foundations to the quality-control exercised over materials. Even had there been any inclination to cut corners, close state supervision would have made it hard. This was impressively thorough in Prussia, perhaps even more so in Saxony. Supervision began with the initial plans and continued through the testing of materials and on-site inspection. Nor did it end when the structure was completed. Germans were pioneers in the construction of observation passageways from which operation of the dam could be monitored, and the inspection regime was set out in the *genaue Vorschriften* – the precise regulations – for which the German bureaucratic state was often satirized.[322] This rigorous regimen bred hubris, however, and it was what lay behind another common response to public anxiety by engineers: not 'it can't happen in this day and age', but 'it can't happen here in Germany'. National sensibilities were strongly engaged over the issue of dam safety, as they were on the larger question of dams as prestige structures. The fierce professional arguments waged in the early twentieth century over types of dam construction (earthfill, gravity or arch) and preferred materials (masonry or concrete) readily assumed a nationalist colouring. Sometimes it was glancing, like Kurt Wolf's 1906 comment that 'the dam walls built by today's engineer, in particular the German, are so safe that one can have complete confidence in their solidity'.[323] On other occasions the edge was more explicit, as it was in some sharp exchanges between German and French engineers. The French saw the Germans as stolid and slow to innovate; the Germans thought the French overly prone to 'theorizing'.[324]

From the German perspective, the sharpest contrast was between themselves and the Americans. The German critique had an element of European distaste for what was happening on the lawless margins of the civilized world. Just as British engineers found it a 'blood-curdling sensation' to view Australian dam profiles, Germans expressed themselves aghast at American practices. We get a taste of this if we look at what German engineers wrote about the collapse of the Austin Valley Dam in 1911. No commentator then or later would have disagreed with their conclusion that the dam suffered from poor design, bad location, shoddy materials and inadequate oversight. It is the tone that warrants attention: the 'indescribable irresponsibility' that had led to the collapse, the 'unforgivable', 'hardly credible' failure to attend to warning signs. As Ernst Link wrote with a kind of pained incredulity: 'Today the situation in most states of the Union is such that private individuals or companies can build dams when, where and how they want, which is hard for us in Germany to imagine'.[325] Just six days after the Austin Valley disaster two dams collapsed on the Black Falls River in Wisconsin. Operated by the La Crosse Water-Power Company, they had been poorly constructed with grossly inadequate spillways, so that a period of heavy rain was enough to sweep them away. A sarcastic engineer in Berlin (his name was Paxmann) enumerated the steps not taken, and concluded tartly: 'All these safety measures naturally require . . . larger or smaller sacrifices in costs and construction time'.[326] There was some recognition of the American role in 'pioneering the construction of bold dams', but Germans felt this was more than outweighed by the lack of regulation. This is reminiscent of Max Weber, writing with genuine admiration about the dynamism of an American capitalism unconstrained by bureaucracy, yet repelled by the casualness over human costs. American companies, he concluded, simply found it cheaper to compensate accident victims than to follow restrictive safety measures.[327] After the First World War the self-regard of German engineers was joined by self-pity, the lament that 'people abroad, especially in France, England and America, know – or want to know – little about German water resources management and our dam-building'.[328]

By the end of the twentieth century that was a part of history. German self-pity had disappeared, along with its cause. Even a residual distaste for America's Darwinian capitalism hardly applied to dams, for US dams were now being taken down on environmental grounds and the safety inspection regime was exemplary. What American safety inspections uncovered was worrying, however. A programme of check-ups in 1977–82 found that 300 out of the 900 dams inspected were 'unsafe', more than a third of them seriously.[329] So how safe were and are German dams? Built to last for hundreds, even thousands of years, many have mocked that confidence. Sites turned out to be geologically less than ideal, sometimes because they were chosen for other reasons, like cost. Folds of soft permeable rock like limestone were intercalated with hard schist, with the result that water seeped through. Over time water also wore away the mortar in masonry structures, threatening the dam wall unless treated. Finally, dams built by Intze and others before 1914 neglected uplift forces, pressures that make a dam ride up on the Archimedes principle 'like a boat on the water' and reduce the effective weight of the wall. In gravity dams, where size not shape is the key to solidity, this can have serious consequences. It is, in the words of one modern specialist, a 'congenital defect'.[330]

Some dams needed attention almost as soon as they went into operation, like Intze's Lingese Valley Dam and the Tambach Dam that served Gotha. The Thuringian dowser, Eduard Döll, went on the Central European reservoir circuit as a proven expert in finding water where it was not supposed to be found, so that its source could be sealed up.[331] Subterranean streams and seepage were tackled in the early years with thousands of bags of Portland cement. Power-grouting was used later to address problems of seepage and eroded mortar. Some dams were beyond repair. The Henne Dam, opened in 1905, was permanently closed in 1949 because the wall was unstable; others had their water levels radically lowered and were used only for leisure purposes.[332] Over the last two decades costly rehabilitation work has been necessary on many older dams: anchoring walls, injecting liquid cement into walls and bedrock, repairing crowns, constructing new outlets and spillways. The true extent of the structural shortcomings was not publicized by officials, 'no doubt in order to avoid panic', in the words of one critical engineer.[333] No technology offers complete safety. Systems analysts calculate that one dam wall in 200 will fail within seventy years of operation. Dams collapsed around the world right through the twentieth century, 200 in all, thirty-three in the USA alone in the years 1918–53.[334] Through a combination of conservative design, careful construction, rigorous inspections and good fortune, no German dam has failed since the modern era of dam-building began over a century ago. Except in war, that is, when deliberate destruction was the cause.

The vulnerability of dams in war-time was an old fear. Rumours raced through Germany in 1914 about poisoned reservoirs; even before that there were concerns that dams might be sabotaged.[335] The First World War and the international tension that followed dispelled any remaining innocence in Europe. A plot to destroy the Bluntau Valley Dam and power station is a central plot element in Ursula Kobbe's *The Struggle with the Dam*. In the Czechoslovakian border town of Vranov (formerly Austrian Frain), plans of the 1923 dam were kept secret 'for military reasons'. The danger of sabotage was one of the reasons given by local citizens who objected to the proposed Our valley reservoir on the German–Luxembourg border. (A captain in French military intelligence, code-named 'Pollux', saw the dam as a Nazi plot and the possible base for a future invasion, although his superiors remained unpersuaded.)[336] Air power greatly increased the vulnerability of dams. They were all too visible from the air, a tempting target. General Franco tried to destroy the Ordunte Dam near Bilbao during the Spanish Civil War. There were German proposals to attack the Aswan Dam during the Second World War, and the Red Army did blow up the Dnieper Dam as it retreated in 1941.[337] Three years later the string of dams in the Eifel assumed strategic significance for the 1st US Army marching on the Rhine, which was determined to destroy or capture them to prevent their waters being used as a weapon against American soldiers. Hence the heavy bombing and fierce fighting in the Urft and Rur valleys.[338]

German authorities before the Second World War had anticipated possible attacks. When the Pirna Dam was being planned in 1935, models were used to simulate the effect on Dresden, only ten miles away, if the structure were blown up. The experiment was apparently satisfactory, and the threat never materialized.[339] Dresden would perish through fire, not flood. The flood came elsewhere. In the early hours of 17 May 1943, Lancaster bombers from 617 Squadron based at RAF Scampton in Lincolnshire carried out attacks on three major German dams. Operation Chastise landed direct hits on the earthfill Sorpe Dam without breaching it, but the attacks on the Möhne and Eder succeeded. Both were nearly full. Water poured through the breaches at a rate of more than 8,000 cubic metres a second, many times the rate of any previously known natural flood, producing a wall of water whose effects were felt hundreds of miles away. The Möhne floodwaters, when they reached the Rhine twenty-five hours later, raised the level of the river by four metres. In Kassel, forty miles away from the Eder Dam, the floods arrived at 10.00 in the morning and rose until 3.00 in the afternoon, to a level far above that reached in the great flood of 1841, before the water began to subside at 5.00 p.m.[340]

When German armaments minister Albert Speer flew over the two valleys the following dawn he saw terrible scenes of destruction. In the Eder valley homes and barns were destroyed, topsoil was washed away and deposited as mud in splintered buildings. The human toll was forty-seven lives, mainly in Affoldern, Giflitz and Hemfurth which lay just below the dam wall. Hundreds of animals also perished: the cattle lowing during the flood and their carcasses strewn across the valley the next day were things that many witnesses remembered with special horror, rather as dead horses remained in the mind's eye of so many First World War veterans. The impact of the flood was even greater in the narrow Ruhr valley. A thousand homes were destroyed or damaged, as well as dozens of factories, bridges and power plants. More than 6000 animals were drowned, and the floodwaters took 1284 human lives. Over 700 of them were Russian women who worked in Neheim-Hüsten as slave labour in the munitions industry. The British government and press presented the outcome as a triumph that had crippled the industrial Ruhr, a 'titanic blow' as the *Illustrated London News* called it.[341] Enlarged photos of the damaged Möhne Dam were dropped over Germany. The National Socialist authorities drafted in thousands of workers from other construction projects, and the dams were rebuilt within the year. The German press was initially told to play down the story, out of fears for morale, although news spread quickly. But the attack was also pressed into propaganda service. Göring attacked the 'criminal terrorism' of the RAF; and the inspiration for bombing the dams was attributed to a Jewish émigré in London.[342]

RACE AND RECLAMATION

A Grey-Dark Wilderness

In the 1930s the Pripet marshes straddled the border between Poland and the Soviet Union. They covered some 100,000 square miles and formed (as they still do) the largest wetlands in Europe. The region was dominated by marshes, moors and lakes that were on their way to becoming moors, a landscape of willows and reeds interspersed with sandy dunes and forested belts of pine, birch and alder that gave the area its Polish name Polessia, or 'woodlands'. Tributaries of the River Pripet like the Stochod, the 'river of a hundred ways', drained down from the surrounding heights into a shallow basin. These meandering streams gave the whole area its character. In March and April ice-jams and waters swollen by snowmelt caused their shallow banks to overflow, flooding the land all around. The result was a waterworld much like the Oderbruch before it was drained, but on a vastly larger scale. Wolves and wild boar lived in the wooded areas, wild ducks and wild geese filled the sky, mosquitoes enjoyed a perfect breeding ground. A few wood-fired steamships travelled up and down the larger rivers like the Pripet and Horyn from their base in Pinsk, carrying passengers or towing giant rafts, but navigating the smaller channels was possible only with a flat-bottomed boat. Travel in many parts of the Pripet marshes had to await the onset of winter, which froze the shallow lakes and waterways.[1]

Some visitors in the 1930s were entranced by what they saw. One was the American geographer Louise Boyd, who made a trip there while attending the International Congress of Geographers at Warsaw in 1934 and wrote an account strongly tinged with romantic attraction to the

'wild solitude' of the marshes. She was impressed by the 'great silence
– a silence broken only by the occasional swish of canoe paddles or
the rare whistle of a steamer', and interested enough in the people who
lived there to write admiringly about their resourcefulness and local
knowledge.[2] Martin Bürgener, a German geographer from Danzig, was
made of sterner stuff. His book on the Pripet marshes came out in
1939. Bürgener was not entirely immune to the beauty of a region
where he had travelled extensively in the mid-1930s. But when he
described it as 'one of the least developed and most primeval areas of
Europe', this was not intended as a compliment.[3] What Bürgener saw
in this 'grey-dark wilderness' was a series of problems: anarchic waterways, insects and vermin that were uncontrolled, an unstable economy
based on hunting, fishing or primitive agriculture, and a population
'vegetating in hopeless apathy'.[4] This, after all, was the Urheimat or
original home of the Slavs – or so, at least, the German Slavicist Max
Vasmer had proved to the satisfaction of many German scholars of the
time, Bürgener among them.[5] That the Slav race supposedly hailed from
this 'wilderness' was no trivial claim in the politically charged scholarly debates of the interwar years, for it buttressed another, even more
dubious argument: that the fair-skinned, blue-eyed Teutonic tribes, the
direct antecedents of modern Germans, had been the first to place their
benign stamp on the lands of the North European Plain back in the
later Neolithic Age. This Urgermanen theory, which began its influential career at the hands of archaeologist Gustav Kossinna forty years
earlier, had also become German conventional wisdom by the 1930s.
Its central argument slotted smoothly into Bürgener's account of the
Pripet marshes. On his reading of the land, only in a few spots where
vestiges of early 'Teutonic' influences remained was there any relief
from the 'chaotic' pattern of settlement, only where later German
colonists had tilled the soil were signs of an 'exemplary' husbandry to
be seen.[6]

 If Bürgener saw problems, he also proposed solutions. These drew
on the familiar repertoire of modern German hydrological ambitions,
and they were radical. He proposed that the Pripet, together with its
tributaries, should be regulated. When proper drainage ditches had been
dug, alluvial land in the river valleys could be used to create a cattle
and dairy agriculture to rival those of Holland or Denmark. Reclaimed
marshes would support crops; peat dug from the moors would provide
a valuable source of energy. Brushing aside concerns about lowering

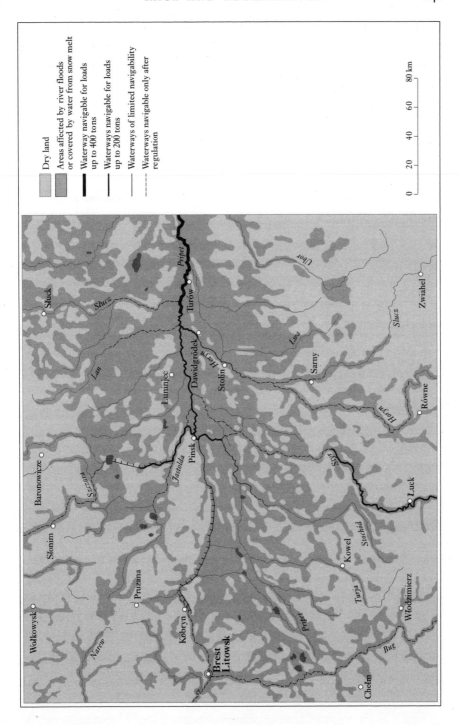

MAP 7 *The Pripet Marshes.*

the water table, Bürgener pointed instead to the glowing prospects. 'We can assume without hesitation', he asserted confidently, 'that the real end result of a comprehensively executed improvement of Polessia would be to increase the agriculturally usable area by at least five million acres'.[7]

Who or what stood in the way of this grandiose vision? Bürgener identified three obstacles: Slavs, Jews and the Polish state. Running through his book was a racially based assumption that the Slavic inhabitants of the Pripet marshes were feckless and passive, marked by 'complete helplessness' and a 'born incapacity for true husbandry', incapable of shaping their own environment.[8] This was a well-worn idea, a familiar nineteenth-century stereotype that distinguished between 'manly' and 'active' Germans, 'passive' and 'feminine' Slavs. Even the idea that marshes formed a kind of testing ground in which the masterful German triumphed over the slothful Slav had long been a cliché. Nearly eighty years before Bürgener was writing, the most celebrated German historian of his time, Heinrich von Treitschke, described how the Teutonic Knights engaged in 'arduous struggles with the vagaries of the Vistula'. As he told the story:[9]

> A seemingly impenetrable thicket grew above the reeds on the wide marshes between the backwaters of the Vistula and Nogat, until, every spring, came the terror of the country – the freshets that followed the break-up of the ice. Foot-messengers announced the approach of the enemy, which was all the more alarming because it was slow, but at length the extensive forests were submerged . . . [T]he Order . . . by directing the labour of several generations, tamed the mighty river. A chain of dikes was built across the land, and they were safeguarded by a strict dike law, which was enforced by peasant dikegraves and inspectors.

Thus reclaimed and protected, the raised land on the Lower Vistula had been transformed into a rich granary; Frederick the Great was merely returning the land to its earlier German glory with his drainage projects in West Prussia after the partition of Poland in 1772, for 'just as the first German conquerors once rescued the cornlands of the *Werder* from the torrents, so now the industrious Netzegau arose out of the swamps alongside flourishing Bromberg'.[10]

Treitschke's triumphal generalizations continued to be read by the general public into the twentieth century. So were those of Treitschke's contemporary, the now obscure Max Beheim-Schwarzbach, who drew an equally poetic contrast between the 'new green of German industriousness' and the 'swamps and marshes' of the Poles.[11] After the 1870s, when hundreds of books appeared on Hohenzollern colonizers and their medieval predecessors, the distinction became a commonplace, a mental framework for seeing the east. The German tended crops and animals; the Slav lived by fishing in the watery *Kietz* settlement. 'Woodland and swampland' yielded to the 'advanced outposts of German cultivation' as a result of 'planned drainage measures and dike-building'; the 'unhealthy, remote marshy and watery wasteland' of the Slavs was transformed by the 'long, unflinching work of the settlers' into the 'resplendent green of the flourishing meadows'.[12] Local studies of past German colonization were stitched together by prominent historians with an interest in popularization (Karl Lamprecht before the First World War, Karl Hampe and Hermann Aubin after it) to create a dominant idiom of German superiority. What they wrote found its way into the accounts of German travel writers, who assured readers that Germans in the east had historically been *Kulturbringer und Befruchter*: they had brought 'culture' (meaning green fields and meadows as well as towns and guilds), and this had made the land fertile.[13] A bloated fictional genre of books about eastern colonization told the same heroic tale through crudely stereotyped characters.

More considerable works of literature sounded the same note. One was Gustav Freytag's *Soll und Haben*, first published in 1855 but a bestseller well into the twentieth century, whose chapters on nineteenth-century Posen offered readers a series of contrasts between Polish wasteland and ordered German cultivation. When Anton Wohlfarth first travels into Posen he is confronted by 'wilderness': a sandy and monotonous plain pock-marked by standing pools of water. At the run-down estate he has come to administer only a few beleaguered German families have planted trees and created fenced-in gardens. Even as he organizes physical resistance against the threatening Poles (the action is set during the 1848 revolution), Anton sets out to repeat the colonizing deeds of earlier Germans in the east who had 'dug ditches through the moor and planted people in empty land'. And this is what he looks back on with satisfaction when he returns to the German heartland: 'He had succeeded in bringing about the green shoots of new life in uncultivated areas; he had helped to found a new colony of his own people'. Anton is helped by the aristocrat, Fink, who conceives a bold plan to divert a stream and thereby 'transform the barren sand into green meadowland' – a vision realized by German engineers and dozens of German volunteers who conjure up 'water and green meadows in the wilderness' with their picks and shovels when they are not helping to fight off unruly Slavs.[14] The colour-coding was an intrinsic part of how Germans came to read the landscape. The Slavic colour was grey, the German colour always green.[15] These stereotypes belonged to the unspoken assumptions of Martin Bürgener's generation.[16]

The cliché of the marsh-dwelling Slav was already shot through with racial contempt. So was the 'Slav flood', a term suggesting both hostility and fear, and one that had become ubiquitous in educated middle-class Germany before the First World War.[17] But Bürgener, a child of his time, went a step further. He drew on the prolific racial theorist of the 1930s, Hans Günther, in casting the Slavs of the Pripet marshes as typical 'short-headed' or 'eastern Baltic' types, hence by definition 'lacking by themselves the strength or capacity to extend their *Lebensraum*'.[18] This was the pseudo-scientific racism of National Socialism, which insisted that blood-lines were decisive. The landscape was a 'mirror of *völkisch* culture', in the words of another geographer, Wilhelm Grotelüschen.[19] That was clearly the view taken by Bürgener, a typical product of the 'great intellectual sea-change' that German geography underwent in the 1930s.[20] Geographers quickly adopted the National Socialist vocabulary of blood, soil, living space and – above all – race. Bürgener may have exercised more restraint than some colleagues – unlike Hans Schrepfer, he never cited Hitler as an authority on race and environment. But the provenance of his views on the Slavs of Polessia is plain enough in the suggestion that 'a conscious containment of the degenerate fecundity of this inferior-race population would be something to consider'.[21] This one remark, packed with loaded terms, offers a textbook example of how Bürgener fused Nazi racial thinking with older racial stereotypes. The reference to fecundity recalls the long-standing identification of Slavs as 'swamp-dwellers', an association that carried strong sexual undertones (prostitutes were 'flowers of the marsh', denizens of 'marshy ground' and 'swamps').[22] When Bürgener writes about 'containment' he uses the word *Eindämmung*, the term usually applied to damming or diking a threatening body of water, which calls to mind the 'Slav flood'. But his use of the term in connection with 'degenerate fecundity' and 'inferior-race population' has a modern, pseudo-scientific and decidedly threatening Nazi ring to it. It reminds us of Hitler denying the incurably ill a right to life, and adding that this would also 'erect a dam against the further spread of sexually transmitted diseases'.[23] Old-style bigotry and new-style racial thinking come together when Bürgener uses words like sluggish, chaotic and anarchic to describe both land and people. In these less than subtle ways, readers were prepared for the idea that it was not only the waterways of the Pripet marshes that needed a *Säuberung*, or cleansing.

Subtlety disappeared entirely when Bürgener turned to the Jewish population of the area. This was around ten per cent of the total, largely concentrated in towns and villages. Bürgener described them as a 'parasitical minority that was alien to the landscape', a 'foreign body' that lived off its host.[24] This kind of language and thinking was, of course, routine in German writing by 1939. It tended to be especially vitriolic when applied to so-called *Ostjuden*, or eastern Jews. These, after all, were the Jews who, even before the First World War, had been permitted to cross Germany from Russia to Bremen en route to the New World only if they travelled in sealed trains.[25] And, since 1917, the eastern Jews had been blamed by much of nationalist middle-class Germany for spreading the 'bacillus' of communism. German interwar writers on Poland (with the rare exception of an Alfred Döblin, who began to rediscover his own Jewish identity on a visit there) rang the changes on the terms 'parasitical' and 'alien'.[26] Sometimes this was all-pervasive, like the anecdotes and descriptions in Kurt Freytag's travel book on the east. In other cases an author might nod more briefly at the 'foreign body' within the Polish state, like Rolf Wingendorf. For economist-demographers like Theodor Oberländer and Peter-Heinz Seraphim, racial stereotypes of the *Ostjude* were closely linked to Polish 'over-population' and agrarian problems.[27] Bürgener's book is closest to those of Oberländer and Seraphim. It has an obvious 'scholarly' agenda – Jews stand in the way of 'improving' the Pripet marshes – yet it argues the case with descriptions so vicious that they make the author sound as if he has become quite unhinged. In passages that are surely designed to evoke a shudder of horror in readers (and succeed in horrifying us, although for different reasons), this monograph published by the oldest geographical journal in Germany conjures up scenes that would have fitted well into the National Socialist propaganda film, *Der ewige Jude*. In the alleyways on their front steps 'sit greasy, unkempt women whose forms ooze with fat', who 'hold their adolescent brats over the street ditches to do their morning business'.[28] Where Louise Boyd found the Jewish market at Pinsk 'kaleidoscopic' and festive, Bürgener sees only filth and disorder in the 'Jerusalem of Polessia'. And so the hate-filled descriptions keep tumbling out: Jews as the 'beneficiaries of work done by others' and Jews with their 'oriental ways', Jewish 'greasy jackets' and unwashed feet, Jewish tradesmen carrying 'tattered cardboard boxes dappled with the fat running out of them and huge, disorderly bundles wrapped in newspapers printed in Hebrew', Jews whose very names inspire the author with contempt ('Chaim and Moshe and whatever else they are called').[29] This racist bile may seem a long way from grand projects of improvement, but the distance is really not that great. When Bürgener summarizes the needs of the Pripet marshes, we find a long sentence that begins with drainage schemes and ends with 'an organic solution of the Jewish question'.[30]

It is impossible to read Martin Bürgener's comments on Slavs and Jews without thinking about what would happen – and happen in the Pripet marshes – just a few years later. Exactly the same is true of his strictures on the Polish state. The Pripet marshes had been a part of the Tsarist empire from the Polish partition of 1772 until the First World War, when they formed the terrain over which the celebrated Brusilov offensive of 1916 was launched. After the Russian revolution the area was disputed between Polish and Bolshevik forces until, in 1921, it was ceded to Poland under the Treaty of Riga. War had left its traces all over the land. In the 1920s an international group of Quakers doing relief work on the River Stochod in southern Polessia regularly encountered barbed wire running through the marshes and lines of old trenches. Sand was slowly filling the trenches, thick vegetation covering up the wire. But the changing course of the waterways periodically uncovered mounds of bones, and there were stories about deep pools containing 60-pound pike that had fattened on wartime corpses.[31] These eastern areas of the new Poland extended well beyond the Curzon Line originally laid down by the Western Powers at the end of the war. They remained disputed land, a border zone where the Polish state was nervous of its neighbours and its national minorities.

Bürgener's main interest lay in what Warsaw had done with these eastern border lands – or not done. In taking Poland to task for its sins of omission in the Pripet marshes, he served up a cocktail of racial contempt, political resentment and geopolitical fantasy. It was a toxic combination. There were undoubtedly many shortcomings to Polish hydrological efforts in Polessia, if the objective was systematic drainage (and that was indeed Warsaw's stated policy).[32] A first drainage initiative had been launched in the 1870s, under Tsarism, but these Russian works were not at first continued in the new state. An office of agricultural improvement was established at Brest-Litovsk in 1928, but it operated with a modest budget and had few results to show ten years later. By then, many of the drainage ditches dug by Russian engineers had already silted up. For Bürgener, this was a sorry catalogue. Like the slow pace of river regulation on the Polish stretches of the Vistula (a criticism that appears with the regularity of an obsession among German interwar writers), it was taken as evidence that justified a radical conclusion: 'Poland is not equal to the task of eastern colonization'.[33] There was, so his argument ran, a 'natural law' that the line of settlement always moves to incorporate areas that are not truly settled, in Europe a line that moved from west to east; but Warsaw had failed the challenge of the *Drang nach Osten* and the Pripet marshes remained 'dead space' unconnected to core Poland, 'dead flesh on the body of the Polish state'.[34] Drainage and settlement were once again inseparable from race: Poland had failed to plant Polish colonists or impose its will on an area dominated ethnically by Ukrainians, Belorussians and Jews. As the argument unfolds, it becomes evident that Bürgener is really outlining something else. He is painting a picture of what a proper colonizing people would do, a people mindful of its 'mission' in the east, a people committed to a comprehensive reclamation of the marshes, a people bold enough to recognize that this meant finding a 'biologically correct solution' for its Slav population as well as an 'organic solution' to the 'problem' of its Jewish inhabitants.[35] It was clearly not the Polish people that Bürgener had in mind.

There was an obvious political dimension to this. Like virtually every German who wrote about Poland in these years, Bürgener had one eye on the western border lands – the 'lost' German territories in Posen, West Prussia and Silesia, and the Polish corridor that separated East Prussia from the rest of Germany. This would be an especially sore point for a Danzig German. So when Bürgener claimed that Poland had neglected its territories in the east because of its zeal to assimilate new 'German' land in the west the political point-scoring was plain.[36] Here was another opportunity to question the competence, even the legitimacy, of the Polish state, an indirect way of pointing to the Polish 'dismemberment' of Germany. Bürgener was following in the footsteps of the countless pamphleteers, politicians, travel writers and historians who had been hurling their resentment at Poland for twenty years and calling for revision of the Versailles Treaty. And at some point, almost every one of these would take up the by now familiar theme, complaining to the world that it was Germans who had cleared forests, drained marshes, regulated rivers, created fields and pastures – Germans, in short, who had created a 'garden' that the Poles were now reducing to rack and ruin. As Erich Gierach exuberantly put it, 'the citizenship certificate of the Germans in the east is not a yellowing parchment . . . but the laughing meadows and flourishing fields that they have wrested from a wild nature'.[37] These were self-serving arguments designed to buttress German claims on land, but they also expressed a deep-seated German fantasy about colonization in the east.

An implicit threat to Poland runs through Bürgener's book. He tells readers that the future of the Pripet marshes, economically and ethnic-ally, is 'no longer just an internal problem of the Polish state, but already a pan-European question'.[38] It is the same argument we find in the books on Poland written by Oberländer and Seraphim. Again, the line of thought reflects the politics of the day: German ambitions in the east and hostility to the vulnerable independent states that lay between it and the USSR. But it also reveals the dominance of geopolitical thinking in Germany during the 1930s. The most obvious sign of this was the use of the term *Raum* or space (*Lebensraum*, *Grossraum*, *europäischer Raum*), to the point where it became emptied of meaning. The geographer Walter Christaller, something of an outsider in his disci-pline, wrote scathingly about the mythologizing of this 'fashionable' word: 'Precisely because space has become a longing of our time . . . it seduces even scholars into wanting to use the slogan "space" to explain and cover everything'.[39] He continued:

> People have become too easily satisfied with slogans about the power that is to be found in a space, or that emanates from it, about the narrowness of space, the domination of space, the magic of space. Space is not a sorcerer or a supernatural being.

Bürgener's closing pages certainly suggest some of the over-wrought and quasi-mystical thinking described by Christaller. He spins a dream of the east European *Raum* of the future. Polessia, we are told, stands at the crossroads between east and west, north and south. Undeveloped, it was a barrier to communications between the Baltic and the Black Sea, and beyond that to the Levant, East Africa and India. The Pripet marshes were the key to establishing both river transportation and a land bridge that would connect Danzig, Riga and Memel to the granary of the Ukraine, the industry of the Donetz basin and the oil of the Caucasus. If he had only added a few of the large, dynamic-looking arrows that Nazi planners liked to place all over their maps, Bürgener's grand design would have fitted perfectly into the German General Plan for the East put together over the next few years.[40]

Why had this 'liberating' developmental vision not been realized? Bürgener had the answer ready: it had been impeded 'solely because of the unnatural political organization of European, and especially East European space'.[41] This was an ominous observation, and a prophetic one. In the same year that his book appeared, the East European space in question was radically reorganized. On 23 August 1939 National Socialist Germany and the Soviet Union shocked the diplomatic world by signing a non-aggression pact. Its terms included a secret agreement on how Poland was to be divided up. On 1 September Germany invaded from the west, followed just over two weeks later by the USSR from the east. By the end of the month Poland had been overrun and parcelled out by the two powers. Each brutally set about the task of transforming its new territory. Polessia fell on the Soviet side of the new border. Not until 1941 would the region feature once again in German plans. When it did, the Pripet marshes became a place where Martin Bürgener's arguments were followed to their genocidal conclusion.

Race, Reclamation and Genocide

After the rapid success of the Blitzkrieg campaign the Polish territory that fell to Germany was itself divided into two roughly equal parts. The western areas were annexed to the Reich as the Gau Posen (later renamed the Gau Wartheland) and the Gau Danzig-West Prussia, with what remained being added on to two existing German provinces. These 'incorporated' lands, which contained mainly Catholic or Jewish Poles, pushed the borders of Germany far beyond the territories 'lost' to Poland after the First World War. Everything that lay between this newly engorged Reich and the line of demarcation with the USSR – an area

that contained about ten million people, and included Warsaw – was
named the General Government of the Occupied Polish Areas. A rump
Polish state under complete German control, it was run from the historic
castle in Cracow by the Nazi lawyer Hans Frank. The General Government was intended to serve the Reich as a source of labour and raw
materials, and as a dumping-ground for racially 'undesirable' elements
from Germany.[42] At the beginning of October 1939, head of the SS
Heinrich Himmler was entrusted by Hitler with the task of 'strengthening Germandom' (Himmler promptly dubbed himself Reich
Commissar for the Strengthening of Germandom, and the title was
never questioned). There were two main elements to this commission.
On the one hand, Himmler was asked to bring back ethnic Germans
from abroad and to plan agricultural settlements in the newly acquired
lands for them and for citizens of the 'Old Reich'. He was also charged
with eliminating the 'harmful influence' of 'alien' elements who constituted a 'danger' to Reich and Volk. The special focus of this author-
ization was, once again, the newly incorporated lands, where the 'alien'
elements in question actually formed the majority of the population.[43]
This double mandate set in train a programme for wholesale population transfer and racial engineering in the east.

Contemporaries often talked about the *Ostrausch*, the intoxication
of the east. The term became so familiar that some National Socialists
used it ironically. You could find the intoxication among the journalists who travelled from the 'Old Reich' to view the fruits of German
military success, and you could find it also among the thousands of
young women – students, leaders from the League of German Girls,
kindergarten teachers, school assistants – who went east to do their bit
for the national cause, sometimes achieving a degree of authority that
contrasts sharply with our familiar idea of women in Hitler's Germany.[44]
But the sentiment was perhaps most strongly felt among the young male
officials and experts who were promoted beyond anything they could
have expected at home and presented with seemingly unlimited opportunities to put their ideas into action. That was true whether they were
physically posted east, or travelled around there – like Frederick the
Great's troubleshooters nearly two centuries earlier – from their offices
in Berlin. The sense of having the world at their feet was nowhere more
evident than among the planning officials who worked in Himmler's
Commissariat for the Strengthening of Germandom. Konrad Meyer,
their chief, used the image of 'virgin land' to describe the newly

MAP 8 *Germany and Eastern Europe at the end of 1941.*

incorporated areas. So did the village-planner Herbert Frank.[45] Erhard
Mäding, one of the two officials responsible for overall landscape planning, thrilled to the idea that he was writing on a *tabula rasa*: there
was 'no precedent for the reshaping of the eastern landscape'.[46] The
other, Heinrich Wiepking-Jürgensmann, addressing a group of young
Germans on the 'urgent tasks' that awaited them in the German east,
predicted a glorious 'spring-time' for landscape planners that would
'surpass everything that even the warmest hearts among us has ever
dreamed of'.[47] Friedrich Kann enthused that the expansion of German
'living space' presented opportunities 'of a magnitude never before seen
in history'.[48] Intoxication seems almost an understatement for rapture
on this scale.

The first thing that is bound to strike anyone who reads through
German proposals for the eastern landscape of Europe is their sheer
range. The members of Konrad Meyer's team were not interested in
piecemeal change; they wanted to alter the land in its entirety. In the
grandiose phrases that recur in the planning documents, they were
concerned with 'total planning', 'comprehensive measures', 'reshaping
the landscape', the 'organic design of space'.[49] A number of keywords
studded these proposals. One of them was *Aufbau*, the everyday term
for construction which rapidly became a piece of Nazi jargon in the
phrase 'the work of construction in the east'. Another was *Gestaltung*,
meaning 'shape' or 'design'. In prose that captures perfectly the leaden
Nazi house style, Artur von Machui praised the term 'shaping the land'.
Why? Because 'with the word "shaping" it expresses a comprehensive
creative will, a universal active element'.[50] Erhard Mäding managed to
use *Gestaltung* or its derivatives no fewer than twenty-one times in one
three-page article.[51] The word was a talisman, not unlike *Raum*. It
signified an ambition to design the whole landscape of the east in the
German image. This took in roads, rail links and waterways. The grand
design embraced everything from the location and layout of new villages
(main villages and 'satellite' villages), to the farmhouses, farm buildings and communal facilities within them and the fields and pastures
beyond them. Whether the planners were using time and motion studies
to design the model farmhouse kitchen or applying central place theory
to determine the site of new settlements, prescribing the shape of fields
(no acute angles below 70 degrees!) or insisting that tree and shrub
plantings be aligned on north–south and east–west axes, improving
drainage ditches 'clogged with weeds' in the Warthegau or commis-

sioning soil maps for the whole of eastern Europe between the Arctic
and the Caspian Sea, nothing was apparently too small or too large to
escape their attention.[52]

The ultimate objective was to create a landscape suitable for the
incoming Germans. What did that mean? Here were the 'rules for the
shaping of the landscape' that went out under the Himmler signature
in 1942. The relationship with nature was a 'profound necessity of life'
for Teutonic-German man, so that the landscape laid waste by people
of 'alien race' had to be reordered accordingly:[53]

> In his old homeland and in the areas that he colonized through his racial
> energy and formed in the course of generations, the harmonious picture
> of farm, town and garden, settlement, field and landscape is a mark of
> his being. The way that fields are divided and bordered by woods, copses,
> hedges, bushes and trees, the natural use of land and water and the greening
> [Grüngestaltung] and the settlements are defining characteristics of German
> cultivated landscapes . . . If the new living spaces of the settlers are there-
> fore to become a new home, the planned and close-to-nature design [Gestal-
> tung] of the landscape is an essential precondition. That is one of the
> foundations for the securing of Germandom. It is not enough to settle our
> race in these areas and eliminate people of an alien race. Rather, these
> spaces have to take on a character that corresponds to the nature of our
> being . . .

The truly German landscape would be lively, differentiated, clean and
ordered; above all it would be 'healthy'.[54] Here was the link, the biological link, between land and people. Heinz Ellenberger, whose two areas
of expertise were German farmhouse forms and the mapping of vegetation, summed it up in a phrase of terrible, vacuous simplicity:
'Germandom and Landscape – Blood and Soil!'[55] It could stand as a
motto for the planners who worked to realize the fantasies of the Reich
Commissar for the Strengthening of Germandom.

Himmler's primary source of 'settlers' was to be provided by the
ethnic Germans living in areas that fell under Soviet control after 1939:
the Baltic, Polish Volhynia and south-eastern Europe. Through 1939–40
a huge logistical effort by the SS and party organizations brought half
a million ethnic Germans 'home to the Reich', their farms and businesses bartered by the German government against future supplies of
grain and oil. They brought with them their household effects and many

illusions about a Third Reich they had seen only from a distance. The first groups of Estonians and Latvians steamed out of Riga and Reval in autumn 1939 on ships belonging to the Nazi Strength through Joy leisure organization. Arriving in Stettin, Memel, Danzig and Gdynia (now renamed Gotenhafen), they were met by the sound of loudspeakers that boomed out sentimental songs about the flowers of the heath and by uniformed members of the League of German Girls who handed out bread rolls, before being transferred to reception camps, then to long-stay observation camps where they were screened and categorized according to their racial make-up.[56] It was in connection with this movement of people that the first systematic mass killings occurred, when at least 10,000 mental patients in psychiatric hospitals around the port cities of Danzig, Stettin and Swinemünde and then at inland sites were murdered using mobile gas vans to create space for transit camps.[57]

The winter of 1939–40 saw the more dramatic arrival – dramatic enough to provide propaganda minister Josef Goebbels with film material – of 135,000 ethnic Germans from Volhynia and Galicia, evacuated overland in almost a hundred trains and 15,000 carts. Himmler himself greeted the first Volhynian German cart as it crossed the bridge on the River San at Przemysl in January 1940 amid falling snow.[58] They were followed in turn by 50,000 Lithuanians, a second wave of Estonians and Latvians, then in autumn 1940 by 130,000 ethnic Germans from Bessarabia and Bukovina, travelling overland or on rented Danube steamers. Altogether, some half million Germans were 'brought home' and passed through the 1500 camps run by the Ethnic German Liaison Office (they included former summer camps, sanatoriums, abandoned factories and confiscated church property), where they fretted and waited for the results of the 'processing' by white-coated doctors and 'racial experts' that would determine if they were in fact German enough and, if so, whether they would receive the colour-coded card marked 'O' (for *Ost*, meaning that they had the racial stock suitable for settlement in the east), or one bearing the 'A' that denoted assignment as labourers in the 'Old Reich'. The word universally used to describe this process was another of the hydraulic metaphors that featured so prominently in the repertoire of Nazi euphemisms, in this case *Durchschleusung*, the term applied to a ship being passed through a lock.[59] Eventually around a third of a million were settled in their new 'homes'. Fully 70 per cent ended up in the newly formed Gau Wartheland. The farms, homes and businesses into which they moved were the farms, homes and businesses of Catholic and Jewish Poles. 'Resettlement' was made possible only by the violent expulsion of the original owners, without compensation.

German violence and brutality hardly began with Himmler's resettlement project. German victory in 1939 had been accompanied by round-ups and the killing of as many as 10,000 civilians in September and early October. These were aimed at likely opponents of the new regime and at the Polish 'intelligentsia': teachers, students, writers, priests, professionals, aristocrats. The violence included random killing sprees vaguely linked to 'retaliation' for the German civilians killed by Poles in Bromberg on 'Bloody Sunday', the day that war broke out. Jews were assaulted and killed in every major Polish city, shot and burned alive in synagogues and other buildings. The terror caused shame among some Wehrmacht officers and even prompted a few to complain openly.[60] What the programme for the strengthening of Germandom did was create a driving force that led to the continuing, relentless expulsion and 'evacuation' of Catholic and Jewish Poles. In towns they were rounded up in makeshift camps. In the countryside SS and police officials, assisted by young ethnic Germans, would surround a village at night and give the inhabitants forty-five minutes to leave their homes with a minimum of personal belongings. Peasant families were ordered to drive their carts to the nearest market town, where they were placed behind barbed wire while the cart was used to carry incoming 'settlers' to the evacuated farm. If things went smoothly, a column of German cleaning women would have preceded them to remove the evidence of hasty departure, but often the incomers found unmade beds and the remnants of a hurried meal still on the breakfast table. In some cases lorries were used to carry Germans out to a farm from which a Polish family was forcibly evicted as they watched, or averted their gaze, before the same vehicle carried the true owners away. The beneficiaries registered their good fortune, according to background and ideological conviction, with reactions that ranged through satisfaction, complacency, denial, and guilt.[61] Whatever feelings of shame (or nervousness) there might have been, resettlement brought 'an extraordinary leap forward' in material circumstances, as one Latvian put it. But while, in the euphoric words of another Baltic German, 'the swastika waved over the gables of houses that have become bulwarks of the German peasantry in the recovered east', the displaced inhabitants were forced further east with a suitcase and twenty Zloty.[62]

Further east at this stage could only mean one destination: the General Government. Himmler's aim in autumn 1939, reiterated throughout the following year, was to remove all Jews from the annexed areas (around 550,000), plus as many Poles as needed to be 'evacuated' to make room for ethnic Germans, at least a million people in all. Himmler, Reinhard Heydrich and his chief deputy Adolf Eichmann drew up a series of short-term and interim plans to transport these unwanted human beings across the border to the General Government. The first goods trains travelled east in December 1939. By March 1941 this barbarous traffic had decanted as many as 400,000 people into Hans Frank's domain, where in the course of 1940 Jews were ghettoized to make room for Poles who had themselves been uprooted to make room for German settlers. ('Making room' is a direct translation of the German word *Platzschaffung*.) Yet the numbers transported remained, at every stage, well below the ambitious targets. The reason was partly logistical: there were shortages of rolling stock, which was also needed to move ethnic Germans around and to ship other Poles west to work as forced labourers in the Reich. But the bottleneck was also political, because from the start Frank did everything he could to impede this dumping of destitute humanity into the General Government.[63]

This had nothing at all to do with humanitarian scruples. Frank and his subordinates objected to the practical 'problems' caused by transportations that were often chaotic, changed at the last minute and might be shuttled around for as long as eight days before reaching their destinations, with predictable results when they did. At the end of 1942, in a speech to close colleagues, Frank recalled those earlier days in self-pitying words:

> Then there came the fantasies of resettling hundreds of thousands of Jews and Poles in the General Government. You will remember these terrible months, when goods trains rolled into the General Government day and night, fully laden with people, some wagons full to the top with bodies. That was a dreadful time, in which every district head, every rural and municipal official was busy from early morning until late at night coping with this incoming wave of elements who had become unwanted in the Reich and whom they suddenly wanted to expel.

The General Government, in short, was treated as a 'dung hill into

which you could sweep and shove all the filth of the Reich'.[64] Frank
was ambitious to turn his territory into an economically productive
area, not a peripheral dumping ground, a view in which he was
supported by Göring and even by senior SS personnel within the General
Government, who saw the 'problems' on the ground created by the
policy of their boss in Berlin.

There were periodic showdowns in 1940. As further waves of ethnic
Germans were repatriated and languished in camps, Himmler wanted
to ship out more Poles – and because the farms designated for Germans
were to be more spacious than the existing units, that meant two or
three Poles had to be evacuated for every incoming German. The Reich
Commissar for the Strengthening of Germandom also wanted to set
aside land for former front soldiers and remove 30,000 Sinti and Roma
from the Reich. Above all, the long-term plan was still to remove all
the 550,000 Jews from the annexed areas, although the priority given
to seizing farmland for ethnic Germans meant that Poles made up the
great majority of those actually shipped to the General Government,
while Jews in the Gau Wartheland were ghettoized, notably in Łódź.
But Frank and his underlings dug their heels in, bolstered by Göring's
support and Hitler's tacit acceptance that the General Government had
developed into something different from what it had been in October
1939. Plans for a Jewish 'reservation' near Lublin on the River San
were abandoned, and the tempo of human transports east was periodically scaled back. While Goebbels mocked the frustration of
Himmler's grand design, Hitler presided over a series of inconclusive
crisis meetings in Berlin.[65]

Quick victory over France briefly appeared to offer a solution to the
impasse. It opened up a possibility first raised, ironically enough, by
an anti-Semitic Polish government in the 1930s and subsequently
discussed in Nazi offices concerned with 'Jewish policy': that the Jews
might be transported to the island of Madagascar. This was a prospect
that enjoyed support from all sides. For Hitler as well as Heydrich and
Eichmann in the Reich Security Main Office it would be a 'comprehensive solution of the Jewish question', as Eichmann put it in July
1940, and this at a time when more and more Jews were falling under
German control.[66] It was equally welcome to Himmler for the same
reasons, and it addressed his immediate 'problem' in the annexed areas,
where he was under pressure from Gauleiter who were calling for 'their'
Jews to be removed. The proposal was also attractive to Hans Frank

as an opportunity to be rid of the large numbers of Jews within the
General Government – some 1.3 million at the outset, although that
number had already been reduced by the high death-rates in the ghettoes. Through the summer of 1940 plans were made, reports commissioned, and discussions took place with the army and Foreign Office.[67]
It hardly needs to be said that implementation of the Madagascar plan
would have meant high death-rates by attrition, and it was intended
to. In the event it was stillborn because it presupposed German control
of Mediterranean sea lanes, and that possibility was removed by the
failure to defeat Britain in 1940. The Madagascar plan left behind a
legacy of thinking in terms of a 'territorial final solution' (Heydrich),
one that involved resettlement 'to an area not yet determined', in the
phrase used by Eichmann in a briefing paper for Himmler in December
1940.[68] It appears that around the beginning of 1941, Hitler specific-
ally charged Heydrich with drawing up plans for 'evacuating' all Jews
who fell within the areas of German control – a successor to the
Madagascar plan. And that is where the Pripet marshes came back into
the picture.

In the early months of 1941, the Reich Security Main Office and
Reich Commissariat for the Strengthening of Germandom continued
to work on their plans; so did Göring and the Wehrmacht. It was
evident that the 'area not yet determined' would be somewhere in the
east, for pushing Jews (and Poles) further 'to the east' had always been
the default position. But the General Government could no longer be
regarded as a long-term destination, even though transports continued
through February. Frank was not the only obstacle. As preparations
began for the attack on the Soviet Union – Hitler signed directive
number 21 ('Barbarossa') on 18 December 1940 – the Wehrmacht
weighed in with strong objections. Pushing more people into the
General Government threatened to cause disruption and divert precious
railway resources needed for troop mobilization. That was why the
transportation of people into Frank's domain was finally called off in
March 1941. But if the pending attack on the USSR closed one door,
it opened another. Those great open spaces behind the Soviet border,
so often mentioned in popular German novels about the 'next war' as
a place to which the defeated Polish people could be 'dispersed', offered
potential sites of Jewish 'resettlement'.[69] To think in these terms was
to imagine, on a huge scale, what Eichmann had actually implemented
on a small scale in the Nisko plan of October 1939, when several

thousand Jews from Vienna and the Protectorate of Bohemia-Moravia were transported to the Lublin district on the eastern border of the General Government with promises of settlement and retraining. When they arrived, the young and fit were ordered to build camps and dig drainage ditches, the rest were marched across sodden meadows in the pouring rain to the River San and told to cross into Soviet territory or be shot. This improvised, uncoordinated scheme was quickly called off when Himmler decided that 'finding space' for newly arrived ethnic Germans had to take priority over expelling Jews from Vienna and the Protectorate.[70]

Eighteen months on, through the spring and into the summer of 1941, the 'territorial solution' in the east contemplated by Eichmann, Heydrich and Himmler came to mean somewhere beyond the current Soviet border, land that would become available to Germany after the expected quick victory over the Red Army and the collapse of Bolshevism. The two places usually mentioned were the Arctic Sea and the Pripet marshes.[71] In the spring of 1941 the Planning Department of the Commissariat for the Strengthening of Germandom, headed by Konrad Meyer, commissioned a report from the Reich Office of Regional Planning on the areas bordering the General Government. In the report the Pripet marshes were described as 'arable land yet to be cultivated'.[72] There is no doubt that – like the Madagascar plan before it – the idea of forcing Jews to 'settle' and perform forced labour here, or in the Arctic Circle, was an intentionally genocidal proposal.

While the offices of the SS planned ahead for life after the defeat of the USSR (and this was just one small part of the repeatedly updated General Plan for the East overseen by Konrad Meyer), Hans Frank was developing plans of his own. In March 1941, the same month in which inbound transportations finally stopped, Hitler assured Frank that his territory would be 'free of Jews' in the foreseeable future and held out a vague prospect that the General Government might be extended eastwards. Frank began to lay the ground for incorporating the Belorussian area that contained the Pripet marshes, to which Jews in the General Government could be deported.[73] It is unclear whether he knew of the similar plans being hatched within the SS, although it seems unlikely that he was ignorant of them given his frequent visits to Berlin during the spring and early summer.[74] It was in July, during the heady days when the German advance through the USSR seemed unstoppable, that Frank and his team of youthful economic experts made their big push to bring the Pripet marshes within the General Government. At a meeting on 18 July, Hansjulius Schepers, Director of the Office of Regional Planning in Cracow, was asked by Frank to prepare a paper by the following day to support an extension of the General Government eastwards: 'Our aim is that the area of the Pripet Marshes and the Bialystock area be incorporated into the General Government. The Pripet Marshes would provide an opportunity to enlist labour on a large scale to contribute productively to reclamation work'.[75] On the 19th Frank wrote to Hans-Heinrich Lammers, Chief of the Reich Chancellery, making his case. He enclosed Schepers' paper on the 'colonizational tasks' in the Pripet marshes and informed Lammers that Schepers would be making an oral presentation on the subject in Berlin.[76] It is not known whether he did, but it is clear that Schepers' paper and an article published in the *Zeitschrift für Geopolitik* shamelessly plundered Martin Bürgener's book. Schepers depicted a 'primitive' hunter-gatherer economy in which 'nature remained the absolute master of the people in this area', and trumpeted the opportunities presented by nearly three million acres of peat moor: 'In a 100-year programme of exploitation 2 million tons of peat could be extracted here annually'. The numbers and the unclouded optimism were straight out of Bürgener.[77]

Another young tyro in Cracow (he was just twenty-eight, to Schepers' thirty-two) was also enlisted in the cause. Helmut Meinhold was a senior economic planner and population expert in the Institute for German Work in the East. He enthused after his arrival in early 1941 about being able 'to create something new on the basis of my own abilities. That is extraordinarily exciting to me'. The east seemed to him – as it did to Erhard Mäding – like a *'tabula rasa'*.[78] Meinhold wrote a memorandum in July on 'The Enlargement of the General Government', along with an article on the General Government as a 'transit land'. Meinhold, too, noted the Pripet marshes as a place where Jews (and Poles) could be used in reclamation work, while painting a larger picture of how the area, if developed, would serve as a key transportation link between east and west, north and south – a further (unacknowledged) nod to Bürgener.[79] Yet another contemporary contribution to debate about the Pripet marshes came from Richard Bergius, who examined the technical problems of draining them, contrasting past failures with the successes in the Po valley and the Pontine marshes achieved by 'the rising Italy of Mussolini'. The topographical problems in Polessia would be formidable, Bergius conceded, even with the construction of peripheral canals and the use of powerful pumps, so that 'for the agricultural hydrotechnician the question of improving the Pripet marshes presents a difficult but laudable task'.[80] This issue was central to Frank's claims on the area. As he wrote to Lammers: 'In its present state the region has minimal value, but with a thoroughly implemented programme of drainage and reclamation, considerable value can undoubtedly be extracted from it. I am suggesting that this area be included, primarily because I believe it is possible to engage certain elements of the population (especially Jewish ones) in productive activity that serves the Reich. You are well aware that in this regard I cannot complain of shortage of labour'.[81] The brutal sarcasm of the last line was characteristic of Frank. So was the utter disregard for Jewish life that his letter displayed. Frank's public and private utterances were at one in their expressions of hatred for 'this mishmash of Asiatic progeny'.[82] In this he was no different from Himmler or Heydrich, for their political power struggle was not marked by any ideological differences when it came to Jews.

What their rival schemes for the Pripet marshes also suggest is a powerful mental connection between race and reclamation. It was the same reflex that led Martin Bürgener just a few years earlier to talk of 'diking' the Slavs, and Theodor Oberländer to call for agrarian reform in Poland that would act as a 'drainage canal' to draw off the surplus rural population, Polish and Jewish.[83] One of Konrad Meyer's planning staff, Herbert Morgen, returned in 1940 from a visit to the newly incorporated areas on the Warthe with contempt for Polish neglect of hydrology: 'The Poles have done practically nothing in the area of river regulation. The Warthe and Vistula are silting up and extensive flooded areas can be found everywhere'.[84] The motif is one we encounter again and again among those who felt themselves charged with reshaping the physical and ethnic landscape of the east. Here, for example, is the planner Erhard Mäding, blasting the 'sterile wasteland and degraded areas' inhabited by Poles, 'concealed by vapours and gases, permeated by nauseating waterways, so that one believes oneself in a grey and eerie landscape of the underworld, not in a place of earthly human habitation', a world removed from the green garden created by German 'higher culture'.[85] Mäding's fellow landscape designer, Heinrich Wiepking-Jürgensmann, struck the same note in a 1942 article written for the SS journal, The Black Corps. His starting point was the 'watery wasteland' of the North European Plain created after the last Ice Age. The retreating ice had then revealed how 'the spirit and energies of the human races are distinguished from each other in the landscape with the sharpness of a knife'. The parasitical, locust-like peoples of the steppe were too indolent to preserve their soil by stopping the floods that washed it away or the winds that covered it with sand, whereas the Germanic race 'consciously shape[d] the surface of the earth, the soil, the hydrological cycle and, in so far as it is possible, the climate, too'. They had allowed their fruitful black earth to become parched and ruined; 'we have diverted rivers, built highly fruitful polders below the surface of the sea, drained marshes and moors . . . until we have given the landscape a human imprint, our own countenance'.[86] This racial taxonomy allowed Slav 'indolence' and Jewish 'parasitism' to be read off from the landscape and contrasted with the healthy German instinct for settlement. It was a bedrock of Nazi thinking. Late in the war, Gerda Bormann wrote to her husband, who was Chief of the Nazi Party Chancellery and Secretary to the Führer, telling him about a speech she had heard by a local Kreisleiter called Stedde. She reported Stedde's conventional racial typology (German peasants, nomadic Slavs, parasitical Jews), and added: 'We must stand firm, said the Kreisleiter, like a strong dike; if we did not the flood would sweep our cultivated lands away and destroy all that our ancestors had created'.[87]

One of the most remarkable examples of this link between race and diking or reclamation came from Reinhard Heydrich – remarkable because Heydrich is usually regarded as the embodiment of 'sober, rational, technocratic coldness'.[88] In his first speech as the newly appointed 'Reich Protector' of Bohemia-Moravia, he chose the following metaphor to describe the German racial task in the east:

These are spaces that one should in reality deal with like the diking of new land on the coast, by building a protective wall of peasant protection (*Wehrbauern*) well to the east in order to seal this land off once and for all from the storm floods of Asia, then subdividing it with transverse walls so that we gradually reclaim this earth for ourselves, then far away on the margin of the true Germany, which was colonized by German blood, we slowly lay down one German wall after another so that, working towards the east, German people of German blood can carry out German settlement.

These 'polders' would begin in Bohemia-Moravia, then extend to 'Greater Polish space', finally to the Ukraine.[89] The connection between race and reclamation, with its dehumanizing view of non-German races, could hardly be clearer.

The projected plans to drain the Pripet marshes had an additional, more explicitly murderous component: the 'natural wastage' that would be achieved by forced labour. This was another constant in Nazi thinking that cut across other differences. It was a matter of consensus at the time of the Madagascar plan and remained so when the German focus shifted to 'the east'. Forced labour was instituted in the General Government in October 1939. It was stepped up in 1941 in both ghettoes and slave labour camps where Jews toiled with grossly inadequate food, shelter and rest. In Frank's gloating words of 22 January 1941: 'As long as the Jews are here they will work, although certainly not in the way they have in the past'.[90] It is true that by the summer, economists in the General Government, with their eyes on 'output', concluded that Jewish slave labour in the given circumstances was 'unproductive'.[91] But it is also true that local ghettoes were operated in many parts of the east long beyond the point when the decision had been made to kill all European Jews. They were maintained precisely because their production was appreciated. That happened in Bialystock and even in Łódź, which lay within the Gau Wartheland that Himmler wanted to 'Germanize'.[92] Nor was it just Jewish ghetto labour that was still being exploited. Beginning in September 1941 and continuing through early 1942, Jewish forced labour was used to construct the *Durchgangstrasse IV*, a road and rail connection that would run from Lvov in Galicia to the southern Ukraine to support the Eastern Front and provide a future axis of German settlement from Poland to the Crimea.[93]

Even more than road construction, marshlands seemed to draw the National Socialist gaze as places where Jews could be worked to exhaustion or beyond. During a tour of inspection in November 1939 with Frank's deputy, Arthur Seyss-Inquart, SS Brigadier-Colonel Schmidt pointed out that an area along the demarcation line on the River San 'with its very marshy character could . . . serve as a Jewish reservation, a measure that could possibly lead to a heavy decimation of the Jews'.[94] The slave labour camps and ghetto work-brigades in the General Government were often engaged in river regulation and land reclamation projects. And that was true at the dark heart of the SS empire, in Auschwitz. The camp was constructed on the marshes of Upper Silesia. Its commandant Rudolf Höss described how, during a visit at the beginning of March 1941, Himmler ordered him to build it up as the great concentration camp in the east and 'in particular to put the prisoners to work on the largest possible projects of agricultural improvement and thereby make the entire marsh and floodplain area of the Vistula productive'.[95] When Primo Levi later called Auschwitz 'the ultimate drainage point of the German universe' he had thought himself into the heads of his persecutors, for whom drainage was both metaphor and reality.[96]

Murderous intentions marked the thinking of all the leading National Socialist actors when they drew together the threads of race, reclamation and forced labour. The 'natural decimation' of the Jews, as Heydrich called it at the Wannsee Conference in January 1942, was actively sought.[97] But the output produced by slave labour, directly or indirectly, was not just an afterthought. The subjugation of Poland and the expected destruction of the Soviet Union were driven by many different motives. They included the drive for 'living space', a brutal racial utopianism built on contempt for 'inferior' races, and a sense of geopolitical destiny. But hard to separate from those motives was another: the prospect of plunder, the opportunity to seize and exploit the resources of the east for German benefit. This was Hitler's view, and it was common ground among German agencies with a stake in the east: Gauleiter in the annexed territories, Göring's Office for the 4-Year Plan, Alfred Rosenberg's East Ministry, the Todt Organization that built *Autobahnen*, private companies brought in to run monopolies, Wehrmacht quartermasters, the General Government and the wide-ranging SS empire. They fought over nuance, over tactics and especially over jurisdiction, but not over the central idea that the east would provide Germany with food, fibres, energy, settlement land and forced labour. This emphasis on productive output was quite openly expressed. Hitler, in mid-July 1941, insisted that the peoples of the east had 'to serve us economically'. He likened the east to a large cake; the German task lay in 'dividing up this large cake, so that we can first of all dominate it, secondly administer it, and thirdly exploit it'. The ineptness of the simile does not make the intention any less clear or chilling. Goebbels, a more polished phrase-maker, called the conflict in Russia 'a war for grain and bread, for a fully laden breakfast, lunch and dinner table'.[98] For Gauleiter Arthur Greiser the task of the Gau Wartheland was to produce 'grain, grain and more grain'.[99] And one of the things that runs through the thirty-eight doctored but still self-incriminating volumes of Hans Frank's work diaries is the pride he took in the productive output of the General Government – the 600,000 tons of grain and 300 million eggs sent to the Reich in one year, the thousands of tons of fats, vegetables and seed, the vast amount of provisions delivered to the Wehrmacht. The territory he administered had, as Frank immodestly put it, 'achieved a miracle'.[100]

In the spring and summer of 1941, therefore, the temporal hinge of both the war and the Holocaust, the planners in the SS and General Government, had come up with grand designs for draining the Pripet marshes. Their proposals combined dogma (the mental connection between race and reclamation), forced labour that would surely lead to the desired 'natural wastage' of Jews, and the prospect of German mastery over an area that the experts insisted was potentially productive and a vital geopolitical crossroads.

It never happened. Instead, the marshes became a site of direct killing rather than murder by attrition. In mid-August Otto Rasch, who commanded *Einsatzgruppe* C, one of the four special mobile units under SS control, was still arguing that 'the superfluous Jewish masses can be excellently exploited and used up, namely by cultivating the great Pripet marshes'.[101] But his thinking was already out of date.[102] Two weeks earlier, the head of the SS had ordered something very different. Asked by a senior SS figure in the area about carrying out a possible 'liquidation operation' against purported partisans, Himmler visited the town of Baranovitchi on the northern edge of the Pripet marshes on 31 July. The following day he issued a radio message: 'Express orders from the Reichsführer-SS. All Jews must be shot. Drive Jewish women into the marshes.' Hermann Fegelein, commanding an SS cavalry brigade, later reported that the water proved too shallow for drowning the women, but by the middle of August the brigade had killed 15,000 people between Baranovitchi and Pinsk, 95 per cent of them Jewish. In some places they killed only men, in others men, women and children.[103] The German Army bore no direct responsibility for these murders, but it was complicit in what was done because Wehrmacht officers gladly accepted that Jews of all ages and both sexes served as links between partisan groups.[104] The complicity of the Wehrmacht in what happened in the Pripet marshes that August was just one local instance of a larger barbarization of the army in the wake of Operation

Barbarossa – its tolerance of the SS *Einsatzgruppen*, its acceptance of the 'commissar order' to kill captured 'political commissars' from the Red Army, its murderous maltreatment of Soviet POWs (over one and a half million of whom had died by February 1942), its combing-out operations against partisans that went far beyond the dictates of military security, all of these 'justified' as part of a struggle against 'Judeo-Bolshevism'.[105]

The autumn of 1941 was the decisive moment in the evolution of the Holocaust. The tempo of *Einsatzgruppen* killings increased, plans were made to expand Auschwitz and build other death camps, experiments with mobile gas-vans were made at Chelmno in early December. Even as the machinery of destruction was being put in place, 'driving people into the marshes' continued to be used as a euphemism for death. It recurred in Hitler's monologues that autumn. Two occasions stand out. On 25 October he raged about the Jews ('This criminal race has the two million dead of the World War on its conscience; now again hundreds of thousands. Don't anyone tell me that we can't send them into the marshes!'), comments usually taken as evidence that Hitler was well aware of Himmler's 1 August order from Baranovitchi.[106] Less than two weeks later Hitler returned to the subject in the course of expressing his habitual contempt for 'illogical professors': 'In two thousand years they will maintain that we came out of the swamps, when they grub around to explain the origin of those who live in the Ukraine, whereas in fact we drove the original inhabitants into the Pripet marshes in order to settle the fruitful fields ourselves'.[107] In neither case is the meaning of 'drive into the marshes' hard to decipher. By 1942 the idea of land reclamation was no more than a fiction, as it was in the case of the 3000 Jews transported that summer from the East Galician town of Drohobycz to the death camp in Bełżec, ostensibly because they were 'needed for the reclamation of the Pripet marshes'.[108] Even with the cover story in place, these were shipments of people that the men doing the shipping were 'not supposed to talk about'.[109]

Conservation and Conquest

The Pripet marshes served as both a place of killing and a cover for killings in the camps. That much is clear. It is less clear why the project to reclaim the marshes was called off. It is not as if the construction of the extermination camps completely closed the door on Jewish slave labour, or murder by attrition. Jews were still being worked to death building the *Durchgangstrasse* IV, and the Chelmno extermination camp was built to kill 'unproductive' Jews from Łódź even while the ghetto remained 'productively' in operation. The likeliest explanation is that Hitler himself vetoed the reclamation project. And his reasons? Because the Pripet marshes provided ideal terrain for military manoeuvres, but also because draining them might adversely affect the local climate and lead to *Versteppung*, or desertification. It is the most probable explanation, but not provable beyond a doubt. As with so many decisions that lead back to Hitler, there is no unbroken paper trail and we have to proceed by inference. Hitler spoke about not wanting 'to conquer the marshes' in August and again in September, but he did so only in vague terms (this, again, was typical).[110] And the matter is further complicated by the fact that even more grandiose schemes to drain the Pripet marshes were resurrected in 1942–3, by the planner Gottfried Müller in the Reich Commissariat Ostland and by Arthur Seyss-Inquart, once Hans Frank's deputy in the General Government, by then Governor of the Occupied Netherlands. Both proposed the mass deployment of Dutch colonists to reclaim and settle Polessia, proposals that retained some of the technocratic utopianism of the projects in 1941, although now they were being formulated against a background of increasing partisan activity in the marshes.[111]

But if we accept that Hitler stopped the initial project in 1941 at least in part on environmental grounds, then this raises a question about the balance between the conquest of nature and nature conservation in National Socialist policy, and how each was connected to race and military conquest. Were the National Socialists really environmentalists under the skin, murderous forerunners of the present-day Greens? And, if so, was there some kind of perverse connection between genocide and ecological sensitivity that made Nazis eager to save the wetlands and the forests while they planned the destruction of fellow humans who lived in them?[112] There is a genuine conundrum here. The solution to it lies in German views of the east.

There were many undeniable affinities beween German nature conservationism and National Socialism. They had a common dislike of the big city and 'cold' materialism, emphasized the virtues of the 'organic' and 'traditional', blamed an unbridled liberal capitalism for threatening the beauty of the landscape, and even agreed on a number of pet dislikes

– concrete because it was an un-German building material, advertisements that 'disfigured' the countryside, the planting of 'non-native' trees and shrubs. This shared hostility to the 'alien' hinted at more sinister common ground. Nature conservationists often espoused the anti-Semitism that was widespread among conservatives in the Weimar Republic, and some of the most prominent (Walter Schoenichen, Hans Schwenkel) wrote in unabashedly racial-biological terms about a German Volk supposedly rooted in its native soil and at one with nature but threatened by urban 'rootlessness'. Another well-known figure in the movement, Paul Schultze-Naumburg, was elected to the Reichstag as a member of the Nazi Party in 1932. Most leading nature conservationists welcomed Hitler's coming to power the following year.[113]

The enthusiasm was a result of what they shared with the Nazis, but also of what they believed – with some reason – that the Nazis shared with them. Take, for example, Walther Darré, the former pig breeder who became 'Reich Peasant Führer' and Minister of Food and Agriculture. When Darré was not denouncing the threat posed by 'Jews, Coloureds, criminals and the mentally defective' to the German racial stock, he was advocating self-sufficient organic farming and the virtues of an 'economy that satisfied needs'.[114] Economic decentralization, outlawing chemical insecticides, measures to protect animals, birds and forests – these were causes Darré shared with leading 'blood and soil' National Socialists, among them Heinrich Himmler and Hitler's deputy, Rudolf Hess. Himmler, Hess and Goebbels were all vegetarians; other figures in the party were drawn to the possibilities of wind and solar energy. In Alwin Seifert, a former garden architect and protégé of Fritz Todt, who ran the autobahn programme, the Nazis even had a gadfly figure who spoke the language of the emerging ecological movement.[115] Then there was Germany's foremost vegetarian and friend of nature. The Führer's diffuse views and shifting enthusiasms were in many ways typical of Nazi thinking about nature. But there were some constants. Hitler often expressed respect for nature as the primary site of a 'struggle for existence', misapplying Darwinian ideas within a racially based world view. His view of animals combined this fixed idea (respect for the 'predatory' species) with a cloying sentimentality.[116] Hitler assured the veteran bird protection leader Lina Hähnle ('mother of German birds') that he would 'extend his protective hand over the hedgerows' and 'wished for stronger bird protection'.[117] There were actions as well as words, a burst of National Socialist legislation during their first two and a half years in power.

Between April and November 1933 laws were passed on animal slaughter and cruelty to animals, then a comprehensive law on animal protection. The first of these (aimed at ritual slaughter) was, it is true, a long-standing demand of hardline German anti-Semites going back to the 1880s. But the measures taken as a whole set new standards. Much stricter limits were placed on the use of animals in scientific experiments and the law against the mistreatment of animals was strengthened by substituting the phrase 'unnecessary cruelty' for the previous 'deliberate cruelty'.[118] A new law followed on the protection of woodlands in January 1934. Then, in 1935, came the pathbreaking Reich Law on the Protection of Nature, which long remained the basic legal framework for nature conservation in both post-war German states.[119]

How impressed should we be with all this activity? The conservationist Hans Klose, who helped to draft the 1935 legislation, later boasted about the 800 conservation areas registered by 1940. But at least half of them already existed (under earlier Prussian law) before the Nazis came to power.[120] The Reich Office for Nature Conservation was understaffed and much of the work fell to unpaid local commissioners, usually retired officials or teachers, who tried to resist incursions into their protected areas by commercial interests and planning bureaucracies without powers of enforcement and often without typewriters or clerical assistance. They were simply overwhelmed.[121] The Weustenteich on the Woltermannsberge in north-west Germany is an example of what could happen. A wetlands area rich in bird life, it became a protected area in 1936. By 1943 its 50 acres had been completely destroyed by the natural-gas industry.[122] Conservationists were frequently not consulted even over major projects. Precept and practice were at odds in other ways, too. While National Socialism enlarged the place of nature and landscape conservation in school curricula, large dams continued to be built to generate hydro-electric power and the *Autobahn* programme was launched. In both cases the role of conservation was marginal and aesthetic. It was supposed to ensure that these structures 'blended into the rhythm of the landscape' as harmoniously as possible.[123] Environmental concerns were trumped by military needs and the priority given to economic plans that provided the sinews of war. That was especially true after 1936, under the Four Year Plan presided over by Hermann Göring. For it was Göring, of all people, in a double role that practically defines conflict of interest, who was simultaneously charged with priming the economic pump and protecting nature. When the interests of conservation and industry collided, as they so often did, it was invariably the former that gave way.

There was, if anything, an even sharper conflict between conservation and the aim of bringing land into productive use. The outcome was just the same. For land reclamation, or 'inner colonization', was central to Nazi policy. The tempo of land reclamation had already increased after 1919, following German territorial losses under the Versailles Treaty. It accelerated again in the Third Reich. Marshes and moors were drained; land was reclaimed from the North Sea. In 1936 a writer for the *Gartenlaube* described this renewed struggle between man and sea in the political vocabulary that was now expected:

> If it is even more necessary today than it was before to extend the cramped borders of the homeland for a land-hungry people that wants to colonize, with peaceful weapons, with perseverance and hard work, then here is the place to do it and with the trusty methods of dike-building.

What was different now was the pace at which land was 'wrested from the sea'. In Schleswig's Tümmlau Bay you could see how 'strong, weather-hardened people are working . . . pickaxe and spade rise and fall in rhythm, the crown of the dike rises higher'. As many as 900 men worked on the reclamation project that produced the Hermann Göring Polder.[124] Three years later Hans Pflug reported on the great moor drainage projects of the Emsland in similar, ideologically loaded language:[125]

> Just the word Emsland has come to stand for the programme of economic and political reconstruction in Germany. Living in the wasteland of the moors in remote camps doing hard physical labour is not easy, but the differences between the cohorts of working men dissolve through work, and one day fruitful fields and meadows will have been created out of uncultivated wasteland.

This was the old epic of wresting land from nature, dressed in new political clothes and put to energetic propaganda use by the National Socialist regime.[126]

The institution that performed most of this work was the Reich Labour Service. Established in 1931 by Chancellor Heinrich Brüning to counter mass unemployment, it was expanded by the Nazis via the quasi-conscription of young men into an institution that was 340,000 strong by 1939. The Labour Service was now expected to foster 'Volk community'. In the words of its 'Führer', Konstantin Hierl, working on the earth of the homeland would 'create the new man of the National Socialist type, bringing the blood and soil of our Volk back in touch with one another'.[127] This was the utopian aim of arresting the German flight to the cities and encouraging rural colonization, as expounded by party economic theorists like Gottfried Feder and Franz Lawaczek. It permeated the ideology of the Labour Service, right down to its authorized songs. The first verse of one of these ran as follows: 'God bless this work and our beginnings, God bless the Führer and these times. Stand by our side as we reclaim new land, make us ready at every hour to serve Germany with all our thoughts'. In another, workers sang: 'Our spades are weapons of honour, our camps are islands in the moor, we are creating fields out of wasteland so that the land of our fathers will be increased and the homeland preserved from hunger'.[128] Two things shine clearly even through this cloudy language. One was the Nazi insistence that inner colonization was necessary because Germany was cramped for 'living space' compared with other nations, a *Volk ohne Raum* – a people without space – in the phrase popularized by Hans Grimm's notorious bestseller of 1926. The other driving force was the need to maximize food production, especially as agricultural land was being steadily lost to industry, the autobahn programme and military manoeuvres. The Nazi policy of economic self-sufficiency made the food supply even more critical during the approach to war.[129]

Achieving these aims meant sacrificing wetlands. While nature conservation was starved of funds, the Labour Service received almost a billion Reichsmarks in 1934–7 alone. Another billion was budgeted for 1937–40 under the Four-Year Plan, which aimed at reclaiming five million acres.[130] This feverish activity led to huge incursions into still uncolonized areas. In the Oldenburg high moors the Labour Service ran six work camps, and those who lived in them were largely responsible for the fact that remaining uncultivated moorland in Oldenburg fell by a third in the ten years after 1934. Further south, in the Gau North Westphalia, the 10,000-acre White Fen Moor was drained and the valleys of the Ems and Lippe were transformed by river regulation. In Saxony-Anhalt, the draining of the Drömling Moors begun under Frederick the Great was largely completed under Hitler.[131] Small wonder that conservationists felt disappointed, even betrayed. They 'wept tears of blood', one of them later wrote.[132] A man like Walter Schoenichen accepted with glum resignation that dams had to be built and high-tension electric cables strung across the land, because business needed energy: conservationists did 'not in any way want to put a spoke in the wheel of industry', as he helpfully remarked.[133] But Schoenichen was passionately attached to 'the magic of the wilderness' and found it harder to bear the loss of wetlands and the regulation of rivers. The drainage ditches and straightened waterways the Reich Labour Service left behind were nothing but a hateful 'geometrizing and concreting of the German landscape'.[134] It was a common lament. Conservationists wrote articles and fished into the rummage bag of Hitler's sayings to find 'Führer-words' that seemed to back them up – which was not hard, given Hitler's propensity to express himself often and vaguely on everything under the sun. Some then directed their pleas direct to the Führer.[135]

These wholesale reclamation and regulation projects even caused a new word to enter the German language: *Versteppung*, or desertification. The basic idea, that hydrological manipulation was lowering the water table, had been around since the end of the nineteenth century, but the scientific warnings grew more urgent after the First World War, as a sharpened sense of water as a precious national resource was joined to ecological concern. In his 1922 book, *The Dangers of Desiccating Our Country*, the geologist Otto Jaeckel predicted a dark future if things went on in the same way. A 'general drying out' would follow and future generations would have to live with the results, when 'most of our meadows will have been transformed into arable, the remaining moors and lakes turned into meadows, and a large portion of our fields will have dried up'.[136] So the idea was not new. But the term *Versteppung*, with its negative 'eastern' undertones that hinted at the 'Asiatic' steppe, was. The word still had no place in the dictionary in 1934. The person who put it there was Alwin Seifert, head of the team of thirty 'landscape advocates' working under Fritz Todt to make the *Autobahnen* environmentally sensitive through natural curves and native plantings. Seifert was a cultural conservative with an informed interest in ecology. Prompted in part by the American dust bowl of 1934, Seifert first dropped the spectre of *Versteppung* into a speech before a gathering of Badenese conservationists in 1936. Later the same year his article on 'The Desertification of Germany' appeared in an engineering journal. It caused a sensation, thousands of offprints were requested, and the article was reprinted twice in more accessible collections.[137]

Seifert warned about a dust bowl in Germany if human actions continued to lower the water table. His article had plenty of criticism for the liberal capitalism of the Weimar Republic and its 'mechanistic' conceptions of nature; but Seifert was just as harsh in condemning the record of the Reich Labour Service. That was what made his intervention potentially explosive. A vigorous debate ensued. Bavarian Film Productions even wanted to make a version of Seifert's warning under the title 'Nature's SOS'. Politicians, engineers, meteorologists and Labour Service leaders weighed in critically. Seifert was accused of ignorance, exaggeration and 'metaphysical' thinking; even some sympathizers thought Seifert too alarmist.[138] But there was also support from traditional nature conservationists, as well as from geologists and ecologists like August Thienemann, one of six university professors to issue a statement that Seifert's article had 'expressed thoughts and apprehensions that the undersigned have harboured for years'. 'Wild Alwin' (as he was nicknamed by hostile engineers), stubborn and sure of his cause, pressed on.[139] Although he was not successful, Seifert was covered politically by two fellow Bavarians, Rudolf Hess and Fritz Todt.[140] In the event he would survive even the loss of these two mentors, when Hess made his mysterious plane journey to Scotland in May 1941 and Todt was killed in a plane crash nine months later.

By then the situation had changed. Until the war, however much conservationists warned about desertification and dust bowls, their voices remained marginal. The claims of nature had to yield before the twin imperatives of 'living space' and the 'battle for production'. The conquest of vast new territory in the east changed the equation. German agricultural experts now wrote routinely about the 'agrarian reordering' of Europe.[141] Just as control of Austria and Norway opened up prospects of a hydro-electric bounty, so Poland and the USSR would provide land for settlement and food production.[142] The east was a safety-valve. The conservationists Kraus and Münker, writing in the journal *Naturschutz* in 1941, urged reconsideration of moor-reclamation at home now that Germany had some 'elbow-room' further east; Walter Schoenichen spoke of the opportunity to 'ease the burden' on the 'old civilized countries'.[143] It was precisely at the moment when plans were being made for the invasion of the Soviet Union and the possible future of the Pripet marshes, in February 1941, that Hitler issued his moor edict, informing head of the Reich Chancellery Lammers that he wanted existing German moorlands to be preserved because they had favourable climatic effects, 'the more so as this war has brought us new forest and arable land in abundance'. Alwin Seifert, who found out about this apparent moratorium from Fritz Todt, was delighted; so were other old conservationists like Hans Schwenkel.[144] As things turned out, the ministries of agriculture and economics responded negatively. One flatly denied that draining moors had any adverse hydrological or climatic effects; the other insisted that peat was an essential raw material. The issue finally died the following year, amid rumours that the edict (never made public) had been withdrawn.[145] But the debate brought home the linkage between war and wetlands, and it showed that Hitler was open to arguments about *Versteppung*.

Conquest in the east made it possible to think about relaxing the 'battle for production' at home. It even led the conservationist Walter Schoenichen to imagine the creation of large national parks in Austria and German-dominated eastern Europe, a prospect that also appealed to the Austrian-born Arthur Seyss-Inquart. Call it 'nature conservation imperialism'.[146] A celebrated example is Hermann Göring's interest in the heath and woodland area of Polish Bialowies, where the Reich Master of Hunting salivated at the prospect of bison to be hunted while the overlord of the Four Year Plan was drawn to the sawmills and turpentine factory.[147] Which gained the upper hand, here or in the Pripet marshes, lay entirely in the hands of the masterful occupier. The luxury of environmental deliberation on this scale was, like genocide, a by-product of conquest.

German planners in the east always maintained that they wanted to balance modern economic needs with the claims of nature. Konrad Meyer, writing the introduction to a 1943 interim volume on *New Village Landscapes* in the incorporated eastern areas, called for a synthesis of 'tradition and revolution, nature and technology'.[148] Both elements left their traces in the planning documents. The attraction exercised by technology is unmistakable. A self-consciously modern strain ran through this work. Erhard Mäding expressed the impatience felt by many planners with the romantic attachment to an 'idyllic' idea of landscape. The romantic landscape was all very well, argued Mäding, but it often hid problems of ageing and decay. The work in the east aimed at something different:[149]

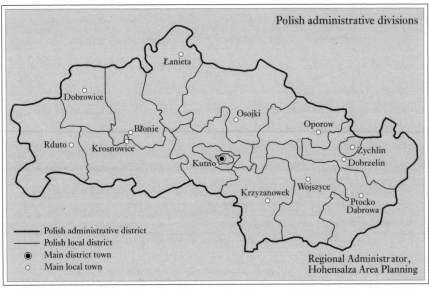

Polish administrative divisions

Łanieta

Dobrowice

Osojki

Oporow

Błonie

Żychlin

Rduto   Krosnowice

Dobrzelin

Kutno

Krzyzanowek   Wojszyce

Ptocko
Dabrowa

—— Polish administrative district
—— Polish local district
◉ Main district town
○ Main local town

Regional Administrator,
Hohensalza Area Planning

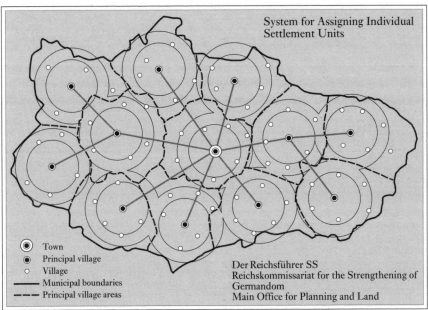

System for Assigning Individual
Settlement Units

◉ Town
◉ Principal village
○ Village
—— Municipal boundaries
--- Principal village areas

Der Reichsführer SS
Reichskommissariat for the Strengthening of
Germandom
Main Office for Planning and Land

MAP 9 *The Polish district of Kutno with its lack of 'rational' order
in German eyes, and the planners' alternative, based on central
place theory.*

The consciously designed landscape will be less idyllic and simpler in its lines, colour values and forms. It will also be larger in scale. Unlike the old cultivated landscape, it will no longer have the look of something that is almost the product of nature. It will . . . allow one to recognize that it is to a large degree a product of the human mind, a cultural form, yes a work of art.

Herbert Frank struck a similar note when he said that the planners were still trying to perfect the 'clear new forms' required by the challenge of rural settlement in a technological age, then cited the design of autobahnen and bridges as models to be followed.[150] Konrad Meyer's office mobilized experts of every kind in pursuit of this technocratic vision: engineers, architects, regional planners, geographers, sociologists, demographers, soil specialists, foresters, botanists, plant geneticists.[151] There was virtually no limit to their visions of the modern east. Autobahnen would anchor German settlements from Leningrad to the Caucasus, with rural electrification to power their milking machines. Institutes of tropical medicine would test new means of eradicating malarial mosquitoes, while a programme of planting and water management created a modern means of 'climate control'.[152]

Hydrological projects had a key role. Heinrich Wiepking-Jürgensmann told an interviewer from *Odal* (this was the *Monthly Magazine for Blood and Soil*) that 'water discharge is one of the most important spheres of work' because it affected so many other things. In the interview he noted the need to regulate rivers, dig or repair drainage ditches, and build reservoirs.[153] Improving the navigability of rivers was another staple of the planners. Martin Bürgener was one of the experts who contributed proposals for the Vistula valley.[154] Irrigation, which so often aroused the visionary gleam, also had its champions. Remarkable increases in fruit crops were predicted in areas like the Ukraine on the basis of highly suspect statistics.[155] Last, but certainly not least, new sources of hydro-electric power were always being sought. One of the principal tasks that Fritz Todt took on when, in July 1941, Hitler added the post of Inspector-General for Water and Energy to his other responsibilities, was to tap the energy resources of occupied territories to help the German armaments industry.[156] The General Government also embarked on a full repertoire of hydrological projects as soon as water management came under German control in October 1939. There were plans for regulation, reclamation, irrigation, flood protection and the exploitation of hydro-electric power from the Carpathians. We can follow their progress through Hans Frank's desk diary, as the General Governor listened to reports about what was happening on the banks of the Bug and Vistula, or visited the Roznow Dam completed in September 1941, even as construction was going on at Belzec, Sobibor and Treblinka.[157] When, in October 1943, Frank and his advisors were treated to a progress report on what had been achieved since 1939 (575,000 acres drained, 140 miles of new dikes, 700 miles of river regulated, 2250 miles of drainage ditches dug, the Roznow Dam on line), the report was delivered by Josef Buhler, Frank's representative at the Wannsee conference the previous year.[158]

The east served as a German laboratory. Like the overseas colonies of Britain and France, it was where new ideas could be given a trial run. That was certainly how settlement planners saw things, believing that new kinds of village layout, building materials or landscape design would eventually be exported back to the 'Old Reich'.[159] But if the east was a laboratory, it was one where conservationist ideas were also tested. This was the other half of Konrad Meyer's proposed synthesis of nature and technology. The extensive writings of Wiepking-Jürgensmann and Erhard Mäding, the two men most closely associated with overall landscape planning in the new east, suggest that both believed strongly in a fusion of the two elements. They thought that a truly German landscape would be both modern, in the sense that it reflected the latest scientific and technological advances, yet also close to nature. Wiepking praised the German race for building polders and diverting rivers throughout history, but insisted that this shaping of the earth had been achieved in harmony with nature, to which the Germanic race felt a special duty: 'In this Faustian yearning we performed our great deeds, created our world, in which as Goethe once said we live alongside and among the plants and animals'.[160] Mäding argued along exactly the same lines and even used some of the same examples. Germans in the past had tamed the marshy 'wilderness', but done so 'in a harmonious relationship with the natural life of the landscape'; that was now the task in the east, where the land was being shaped in accordance with the 'living world'. The result? German planners 'follow nature and harvest the reward of a greater mastery over it'.[161] That 'double' perspective is the reason why the words *Landschaftspflege* or *Landespflege* recur throughout the planning documents. They denote a concern for the landscape that embraced both 'design' and 'conservation'.[162]

The evidence of environmentally conscious thinking is all over the plans, not just in the proposals to set aside conservation land in every village and establish a conservation area in every district, but in the larger governing principles. The obsessive concern with planting and afforestation, the horror of agricultural monocultures, Himmler's injunction to 'weigh carefully all the effects' of hydrological projects – all were designed to counter soil erosion and the spectre of 'desert-ification' that Seifert had conjured up.[163] The same thinking lay behind the Large-Scale Green Plan to convert arable land into pasture on poor soils and hillsides with steep slopes. For it was a matter of faith that the German peasant 'needs a green village and hates, because he fears, the sandy steppe'.[164] Observing all this, the conservationist Hans Schwenkel was moved to complain in 1943 that while afforestation and other measures against soil erosion were being planned in the east, woods and hedgerows 'continue to be destroyed in the Old Reich'.[165]

Schwenkel had a point. The conquered spaces in the east were supposed to provide a reprieve for the relentless pressure on land in Germany. Instead, the east had primacy, as Himmler's planners devoted themselves to designing utopian landscapes whose principles would only later be applied to the Old Reich. As it turned out, they were never applied in the east either, because the changing fortunes on the eastern front ensured that few of the plans ever left the drawing board. All that the settlement experts had to show for their efforts were a multitude of written documents, a small number of scale models, and an even smaller number of actual model villages. It is therefore impossible to know how the 'synthesis' of nature and technology would have worked itself out in practice. But it is hard to believe that the 'harmony' the planners liked to invoke would have survived implementation of their ideas on a large scale. Environmental notions would probably have gone the way of Hitler's enthusiasm in 1942 for decentralized, wind-powered energy generation as an alternative to the electrical grid, an idea that came to nothing because energy needs were so urgent and Hitler lacked the sustained interest to press the issue, just as he had over the moors decree.[166] The Large-Scale Green Plan was at odds with the demand for 'grain, grain and more grain'; afforestation programmes favouring deciduous species ran against pressures to strip the forests for timber and plant fast-growing species. In both cases the planners' ideas would have encountered opposition from those who placed a premium on output, whether the Wehrmacht, Göring's office, industrial interests or the Gauleiter of newly incorporated territories.[167] For the same reason, an ambitious objective like the monitoring of hydrological projects would have been hard to implement – very much harder, for example, than Himmler's smug little plan to introduce nesting storks into concentration camps.[168]

Konrad Meyer's staff led a doubly sheltered life: first, because they worked under the powerful protection of Himmler, secondly because none of their favoured nostrums ever faced the acid test of reality. Only occasionally did they register the gap between aesthetic aspirations to mould the landscape as a 'total spatial work of art' (Mäding) and the cold logic of economic exploitation.[169] But their plans were divorced from reality in even more fundamental ways. They almost never stopped talking about landscapes, but had little to say about several awkward questions. How could the Nazi theory be squared with the fact that Poland and the USSR had built wind-breaks and taken other measures against soil erosion, as the maverick Alwin Seifert was candid enough to point out? No answer.[170] And what if ecologically-minded forestry officials in the General Government warned (as they did) about the dangers of deforestation and *Versteppung*, years after Germans had taken control? The answer here was to fall back on the argument that it would take a long time to make good the ravages of Polish 'misman-agement'.[171] But the most difficult question was the one raised by Seifert, Schwenkel, Schoenichen and other conservationists: Why, if the ideal of the 'green village' was in the very blood of the German peasant, had the danger of *Versteppung* appeared in the 'Old Reich'? This could not be ignored or argued away, and the answer the planners usually gave is that there were indeed structural problems in the Reich ('excessive' urbanization, too many small peasant families, rural attitudes left over from the era of 'capitalist materialism'), but that eastern settlements would provide the solution. This, of course, made a mockery of the purported connection between race and landscape. It also threw an even greater symbolic weight on the plans for the east as the ultimate fount of 'renewal' for the whole German Volk.

The people who lived in the east raised even more difficult questions. Himmler's storks are a reminder that the conservationist strand in plan-ning, no less than the technocratic strand, rested on thoroughly racist, murderous foundations. Both were part of a larger genocidal programme. The model village constructed in the Upper Silesian district of Saybusch could be built only because more than 17,000 former Polish inhabitants had been removed.[172] Auschwitz was the focus of model reclamation projects before it became the quintessential site of industrialized killing. Calling the occupied land of the east 'disorderly' or 'sick', branding it as either foetid swamp or barren steppe, always too wet or too dry, was a way of denying the right of its inhabitants to live there. That was also the effect of repeated German references to the east as *tabula rasa* or 'virgin land'. These remarkable euphemisms show how the occupiers had mentally removed the true inhabitants from the landscape. Claims that the east was both 'empty' and the place where the German race could 'renew' itself came together in another sustaining myth: that the European east was a perennial German frontier, a source of Volk energy. Like other National Socialist ideas (and like other frontier legends), this one was partly historical-racial, partly political, and wholly problematic. It was none the less potent for that.

The Mystique of the Frontier and the 'Wild East'

'The Volga must be our Mississippi'. That was Hitler in the autumn of 1941. He had been fascinated since he was young with the American frontier, and it showed up as one of his obsessions in the years after the attack on the USSR, a theme that peppered his monologues.[173] 'Europe – and not America – will become the land of unlimited opportunities', he insisted on another occasion. Or, again, after a typical rant about mechanized and mongrelized contemporary American culture, this: 'But the Americans have one thing that is becoming lost to us, a feeling for the wide open spaces. Hence our longing to extend our space'. Germans had lost this feeling, but it would return: 'For where would we be if we did not have at least the illusion of the vastness of our space'.[174]

Hitler spun his fantasies partly from what he had read in Karl May. He was not alone, nor was Karl May the only German author writing about the American frontier who entered the German imagination, although he is the most famous.[175] May's predecessors included Henriette Frölich, Charles Sealsfield, Julius Mann, Johann Christoph Biernatzki, Balduin Möllhausen and Otto Ruppius, not forgetting the prolific and still widely read Friedrich Gerstäcker, author of adventure stories like *The River Pirates of the Mississippi*.[176] The American frontier also cropped up in unexpected places. Theodor Fontane told readers of *Rambles through the March Brandenburg* that after a rain-drenched boat journey across the Wustrauer marshes, he and his companion felt 'as if we had travelled over the Kansas River or a prairie "far in the west"'. Gustav Freytag's *Soll und Haben*, in a plot progression overlooked by later commentators, fixated on the novel's anti-Semitic depictions of Breslau, has a character (the aristocrat Fink) who first discovers himself on the American frontier before helping the hero Anton to bring the green of German culture to the Polish 'wilderness'.[177] Freytag's bestseller is a reminder that when German literature travelled to the western frontier its subject was still Germany as much as America. The American frontier was a mirror, often a distorting mirror. The many fictional works, travel accounts and advice books for would-be immigrants (like Gerstäcker's *To Amerika!*) also reflected Germans' interest in a country to which over four million of them went in the course of the nineteenth century.[178] In National Socialist literature the sturdy deeds of German emigrant-settlers were recounted with pride (and a good deal of invention), but also with expressions of bitterness that vigorous members of the Volk had been 'lost' overseas because Germany lacked the 'living space' to keep them.[179] That was another of Hitler's favourite topics, and it brings us to a second conduit through which the mystique of the frontier became a fixed idea among National Socialists.

There is one famous frontier thesis in history: Frederick Jackson Turner's argument, first expounded in 1893, that the pioneers' engagement with the wilderness and the special character of frontier life decisively shaped American values and institutions. US historians have chipped away at Turner's thesis ever since, undermining many of his claims, but more than a century later it remains a reference point in arguments about the American West. That is Turner's significance in the USA, which is public and political as much as academic.[180] But the idea of the frontier also had broad public resonance in Europe, certainly in Germany. Turner's thesis not only interested contemporary Germans; it owed something to their work. Turner was indebted to the writings of Friedrich Ratzel on the influence of geography on history, and he later collaborated with Ratzel's American student, Ellen Churchill Semple. For his part, Ratzel, who originated the term living space, credited Turner with showing the dynamic effects of American westward expansion.[181] The American experience (or an imagined version of it) left powerful traces in German thinking because the American west seemed such an obvious analogue to the German east. In 1893, the same year that Turner first presented his ideas, the economist Max Sering wrote a book on German 'internal colonization of the east', the attempted Germanization of Polish areas in eastern Prussia underway since the 1880s. Like Ratzel, Sering had visited the USA. His book repeatedly held up North American settlers as exemplars of hardy enterprise, a model for Germans on their eastern frontier.[182] Sering's well-known contemporary, Gustav Schmoller, explicitly compared the German east with the American west. Another great public figure, the sociologist Max Weber, did so implicitly.[183] The fascination with America's open frontier continued through the post-war years. We find it in Theodor Lüddecke's celebration of America's 'endless expanses' ('American space calls for unswerving activity. It wants to be conquered'), and in Otto Maull's admiration for the 'creative power of the conquering white race'.[184] The common thread of fascination was still the link between the idea of the frontier and the German east. That was what bound together the advocates of geopolitical thinking who gathered around Karl Haushofer, Martin Bürgener's generation of geographers, and pedlars of undiluted racial thinking like Ludwig Clauß, who raved about the 'Nordic will to space' and the 'Nordic gaze' ('it strides out into space and distance; it shapes').[185]

The German frontier was in the east. But *when* was it? The short answer was that its great days lay in the past and the future. For Germans before and after the First World War, the present was a bitter disappointment. In the decades before 1914, Germany appeared to be losing the Darwinian struggle with the Poles even within its own borders. Hence the frustration felt by Sering, Weber and so many others at the failure of the 'Germanization' campaign to turn back the 'Slav flood'. Military success on the eastern front in 1914–18 made Germany the temporary master of millions, holding out the tantalizing prospect of future German domination and settlement before the post-war settlements pushed the borders even further back.[186] It was out of the bottomless resentment this created, the feeling of sheer unfairness, that the idea of the eastern frontier was asserted more powerfully than ever after 1918 to justify German territorial claims. Its champions dwelt on two periods of the past: German eastern expansion between the eleventh and fourteenth centuries, and later Habsburg and Hohenzollern colonization of the east. Contemporary concerns were projected back in time as writers with one eye on the present peopled medieval and early modern Europe with vigorous German pioneers pushing back the frontier of civilization. An idealized German *Drang nach Osten* was mentally spliced with an equally idealized American frontier society to create a hybrid – an emotion-laden narrative that served as an argument for overturning the Versailles Treaty and 'restoring' German influence in the east.

This found expression in works of every conceivable kind, scholarly and popular. The flavour is captured by Erich Keyser, writing in the notorious essay collection *German Settlement Land in the East*, which brought together historians, archaeologists, geographers and ethnographers to assert German moral claims over wide swathes of eastern Europe. For medieval German settlers, wrote Keyser, the east that they made their own was 'the land of their longings, as America was in modern times for so many who were tired of Europe, because here, far away from the narrowing constraints of the motherland, not only did a better income beckon the hard-working poor man but capital brought from home could be profitably invested in acquiring land and growing corn'.[187] A key element in the mystique of the frontier was the belief that freedom and opportunity attracted bold spirits, willing to work hard and sacrifice. Pioneers and the frontier spirit spilled into the work of medievalists.[188] The eighteenth century received the same treatment. In his 1938 book on Frederick the Great's colonization and its 'legacy' for the Third Reich, Udo Froese argued that the settlers had been defined by their 'pioneer spirit'; Frederick's work 'would have meant nothing if, like the medieval settlers, they had not been animated by the spirit of conquest, which made the narrowness of their homeland unbearable and moved them to strike out and express their will to live in the wide open spaces of the German East'.[189] Ekkehart Staritz struck a similar note in *The West–East Movement in German History*: If the east had been the 'paradise' sometimes advertised, the race would have 'gone under, suffocated by good living and indolence'; conditions required frugal, industrious settlers, happy to 'sacrifice and eat their bread in the sweat of their brow'.[190] The frontier spirit can be tracked through travel books of the 1920s and 1930s (German settlers in Latvia were 'pioneers' in the 'wide open spaces' of the Baltic), and it provides the master-plot in the genre of 'settler novels' like Hans Venatier's best-selling *Vogt Bartold*. His intrepid German settlers in thirteenth-century Silesia feel as if they are 'living on the edge of the world' as they look down on the Polish plain at the 'endless land of the east'; they have to cope with many tribulations, yet eventually succeed in taming the 'wilderness'.[191]

After 1933, this ideal of the hardy settler type was a staple of Nazi party organizations, disseminated through school lessons, songs and approved works of literature, history and race. It also pervaded the thinking of Nazi leaders. For Hitler, German successes of the twelfth century would repeat themselves in the east 'as in the conquest of America', the new eastern frontier creating a 'sturdy stock' that would prevent Germany sinking into 'softness'.[192] Himmler had held views like this from his youth and later made sure they were central to SS education. Konrad Meyer echoed the same sentiments when he wrote that in future the 'America' of the Germanic peoples would no longer lie across the ocean, but in eastern Europe: the 'tasks and obligations' there would issue in a return to the heroic past.[193] Hans Frank, addressing a 1942 party rally in Galicia, indignantly rejected the idea that Germans in the east sat back and smoked cigars (even if some people in the 'Old Reich' found that idea attractive): the General Government was not a colony, but space for settlement, 'and however far to the east the settlement zone stretches there will always be German people, German personalities, German men and women who work from morning till night, who are therefore healthy and strong and determined to defend their farms'.[194]

I called the mystique of the frontier a sustaining myth. Did those who espoused it believe what they were saying? There is no simple answer. There were, of course, opportunists: entrepreneurs who grew fat on the east, technocrats entranced by their opportunities. They were the people most likely to become impatient with the official settlement ideology if it cut across their interests. Among top party leaders, Göring rarely disguised his lack of interest in Himmler's grand design, and Goebbels exercised his sarcastic tongue at the expense of the Reich Commissar for the Strengthening of Germandom. Hitler and Himmler, on the other hand, were true believers; so were the upper echelons of the SS, and so were others (like Alfred Rosenberg) with major responsibilities in the east. It is harder to come to a conclusion about the historians who did so much to construct this justification for a new German *Drang nach Osten*. Their intellectual labour certainly conferred status and professional advantages, like the spoils of looted libraries or Hermann Aubin's opportunity to use his position at the Institute for German Work in the East to surround himself, in true German profes-

sorial style, with former associates from Breslau.[195] (The Breslau historical mafia in Cracow resembled the Hamburg mafia of economists
around Walter Emmerich.[196]) Yet many seem also to have swallowed
their own arguments. Aubin, for one, was actively engaged in fostering
interest in the German east among students and the general public well
before 1933.[197] If the frontier myth was a legitimating ideology it was,
to use J. G. Merquior's terms, both a veil and a mask.[198] What bound
all the occupiers together was an absolute belief in German racial superiority and their right to dominate eastern Europe. Beyond that, we find
a variety of attitudes to the idea of heroic settlers on the frontier. For
some it was a true driving force, for others an irrelevance or a useful
fiction if it did not get in the way of hard-headed economic and political aims, while yet others moved between these positions.

Two of the more cynical Nazi leaders illustrate the ambiguities.
Goebbels certainly mocked Himmler on occasion, and viewed the
settlement plans through the optic of their propaganda potential, but
his diaries suggest emotional identification as well. Writing in March
1940 about the film he was currently having made on the ethnic
Germans' resettlement, he expressed admiration for the subject as well
as the cinematic effects: 'Lorenz shows moving scenes from the trek
of the Volhynian Germans. It truly is a magnificent modern migration of peoples'. Later in the same year, he commented without irony
on a top-level meeting: 'Himmler reports on the resettlement. He has
already achieved much, but more remains to be done. So let's get on
with it, for we have to settle the empty spaces in the east'.[199] Hans
Frank's position was also anything but transparent. When he insisted
that the General Government was a land of settlement, not a colony,
this was a complete about-turn from earlier claims that the value of
his fiefdom consisted precisely in its 'colonial character', that it was
a 'protectorate, a kind of Tunis'. Why the change? Until the victories
in the west in 1940, Frank was looking for any argument that would
justify the General Government as a place of economic development,
not a dumping ground. Then he acquired Hitler's approval to earmark
it as part of the frontier designated for 'Germanization', a change
symbolically marked when the phrase 'for the occupied Polish territories' was dropped from the formal title of the General Government.
Once Frank had received the green light from Hitler he could indulge
in the fantasy closest to his heart, that one day the Vistula valley
would be as German as the Rhine valley – more so, in fact, because

it would have been won by new settler deeds. But when would this happen – in fifty years, a hundred? No time-scale was ever set; it would happen some time 'after the war'. Did Frank himself believe, when he addressed members of the Hitler Youth and League of German Girls in June 1942, that the General Government would become their 'true home' as they 'formed the strong roots of a new German living space'?[200] In the short time that actually remained to the German occupiers, the reality was that the General Government continued to be a colony based on economic exploitation of the crudest kind, a criminal enterprise riddled with corruption and cronyism. If it attracted competent technocrats like Helmut Meinhold and Walter Emmerich, it was also the sort of place where you sent an official like Rudolf Kiepert from the Berlin branch of the Ethnic German Liaison Office, relieved of his duties in 1943 for financial and sexual impropriety and exiled to Cracow.[201]

The gap between rhetoric and reality that exists in all political systems was especially wide under National Socialism. The frontier farmers offer a prime example. They were supposed to be a source of national renewal because they were the 'better Germans' – young, robust, rich in children, closely tied to the soil. Yet the Baltic Germans, the first to be brought back to the Reich for resettlement in the east, failed in every way to meet this profile. Relatively aged, they had smaller than average families and were top-heavy with lawyers and pharmacists. The Bessarabian Germans also diverged to an uncomfortable degree from the ideal.[202] Small wonder that public propaganda liked to concentrate on the Volhynian Germans in their wagons, 'farmers who struck out years ago into the wide-open spaces of the east'.[203] But that was only half of the story. Public statements, newspaper articles, songs – all presented the resettlement of the east in archaic terms, as a great trek entirely innocent of modern technology. The truth was that the settlers were usually moved into their new homes by rail or lorry; and if Himmler's long-term fantasies for the east had ever been translated from Konrad Meyer's drawing board into reality, the millions of new settlers would have been placed, as we have seen, in landscapes planned down to the last manure pile and labour-saving kitchen. Planners, contemplating the vista of settlement 'secure points' strung out along future rail and autobahnen links that cut across eastern Europe to the Baltic and the Crimea, called this the 'bowling-alley system'.[204] This futuristic utopia, built around central places, concentric rings of villages and arterial roads, resembled a vicious caricature of Frederick the Great's colonization, with its careful geometrical settlements. It did not at all resemble Vogt Bartold's thirteenth-century Silesia or the overland trails stretching west from Missouri a hundred years earlier.

The position of the future settlers was just as far removed from the rhetoric of vigorous pioneers. That is true in two senses. Settlers were, of course, beneficiaries of a brutal occupation regime that gave them land and resources seized from others. When incoming families were posed for photographs that showed them surrounded by flowers, cake and coffee (as well as a picture of the Führer and a copy of *Mein Kampf*), the picture told a story of Germans enjoying their status as members of the 'master race'.[205] But the price they paid was complete lack of autonomy. Starting with the experience of being shuttled through the camps bearing numbered tags, examined, sorted and (if approved) handed blue-coloured documents assigning them to the east, through to the final stage of being decanted into farms where they had no tenure, dependent on the SS for equipment and materials, their house-keeping, child-rearing and 'morale' closely monitored by volunteers from the Settlement Research Unit, the settlers were treated like laboratory rats, systematically deprived of the one quality that was central both to the frontier myth and to what German advocates of 'inner colonization' had always said was essential – self-reliance. Himmler could hardly have been more clear on who was in charge, telling resettlers that the Third Reich was the 'giver' to whom they owed everything: the security of a new home, a future for their children, and the joy that came from being able to live in the Volk state of the Führer. This, he added ominously, 'obliges the homecoming Germans to adapt themselves organically to the order and discipline of the Greater German Reich'.[206]

The ethnic Germans had no choice about going east. Those who lived in the 'Old Reich' did; they could vote with their feet. Did the mystique of the eastern frontier strike chords within Germany? Were settlers likely to come forward in sufficient numbers? Most Germans probably warmed to the epic stories of past German deeds on the frontier, told in schoolbooks, popular histories, settler novels and party propaganda. After all, these flattered the belief in German superiority, which most people took for granted. That did not mean they necessarily wanted to be part of the new frontier themselves. 'Inner colonization' even within the borders of Germany had not always been successful in the past, its advocates often critical of the 'settler material' that presented itself. Now the task defined by the Reich Commissar for the Strengthening of Germandom was dauntingly large. The General Plan for the East calculated that 3,345,805 settlers would be needed in all over a period of twenty-five to thirty years. Set against this maniacally precise number, the Plan identified on the other side of the ledger a pool of potential settlers approaching six million, two-thirds of whom would come from the 'Old Reich'.[207] Hitler was upbeat about attracting them, as well as 'Germanic' settlers from other parts of Europe like Scandinavia and the Low Countries. He told a circle of captive listeners one evening in September 1941:[208]

> If I offer [the peasantry] land in the east a stream of humanity will set off there, for the landscape the peasant finds beautiful is one that is productive. In twenty years European emigration will be directed to the east, not America.

Himmler also looked forward to the happy time when German settlers had tamed the 'endless primeval forest' and 'sanded up rivers' of the black earth zone and turned it into 'a paradise, a European California'.[209] Hans Frank entertained similar visions.

Yet even the authors of these future fantasies seem to have harboured doubts. There is an interesting formulation in *Mein Kampf*, when Hitler writes that the German people would have to be 'brought to recognize' that its future lay in 'the arduous work of the German plough'.[210] The phrase hardly suggests confidence, and a nagging unease would persist even during the years of greatest wartime optimism. Concern that Germany might be too 'soft' runs as a counterpoint through the pronouncements of Hitler and Himmler. That, of course, was the whole point of settling the eastern frontier with pioneers: it was supposed to rejuvenate the Reich. But what if the population of the Reich failed the challenge? Doubts of this kind surfaced in other places. In 1942, Artur von Machui wrote an article on 'shaping the landscape' in the east. At first glance it is full of upbeat, bombastic jargon; on closer examination it reads more like a catalogue of obstacles. After the war, German youth and others would have to be 'summoned' to go east and the peasantry 'released' from its stubborn ways in order to 'liberate energies for this greater space'. But this would require 'education, order, direction', because a century of false development had made German rural society too comfortable, too attached to 'fossilized tradition'. And so Machui goes on, noting everything that would have to change – work standards, family patterns, old habits – if the east were to receive the 'great stream of unconstrained Volk energies' it needed.[211] He makes it sound like a task that is unlikely to be fulfilled. At exactly the same time, Hans Frank was advocating 'training in public speaking for "eastern fanatics" who can make propaganda for the east in the Reich'.[212] As so often with Frank, we hear the sound of eastern self-pity, a suspicion that the 'tasks of the east' were not properly appreciated by the rest of Germany.

This kind of aggressive self-pity was commonplace in the east. It was part of the pathos of the frontier myth – being far from home and vulnerable, yet sticking it out. The sentiment (and sentimentality) is well captured in a diary entry of the young Heinrich Himmler in 1919: 'I work for my ideal of German womanhood with whom, one day, I will live my life in the east and fight my battles as a German far from beautiful Germany'.[213] Women as well as men had a place in National Socialist fantasies of eastern settlement, just as matriarchs as well as patriarchs had a place in countless narratives of toiling eastern settlers in the past, building a German future generation by generation. In the 1940s, young and unmarried German women also played a key role in the east, monitoring ethnic German resettlers on behalf of the Settlement Unit or working as teachers and journalists. They even formed their own networks.[214] For all that, the pathos of the frontier had a strongly masculine quality. Like the Pan-Germans forty years earlier ('we men who feel most German'), Himmler's generation liked to cast themselves as 'bulwarks' or 'fortresses' in the hostile east.[215] But sometimes doubts arose in even the staunchest male on the frontier; indeed, the frisson of danger was part of the pathos. Hermann Voss, Professor of Anatomy in the new Reich University of Posen, thrilled to what he called 'wild eastern stories', but he also confided to his diary: 'Yes, the "wild east" is nerve-racking. One day it will devour us'.[216]

What made the 'wild east' wild? One answer was: the inhospitable environment. In a phrase from one of the many Nazi songs that glorified the wagons rolling east, this was 'alien wilderness'.[217] It was not only völkisch songsmiths (and landscape planners) who saw things this way. So, routinely, reflexively, did low-level officials, visitors, soldiers. One of August Haussleiter's novels of the eastern front gave stylized form to the cliché, presenting the German soldier as a 'Robinson Crusoe in the wilderness . . . in the desolation of these plains, swamps and forests'.[218] But if the environment was hostile, so were the people who lived there. In this distorted view of the world the indigenous inhabitants were written off as 'history-less peoples', not true Europeans, 'nomads' rather than tillers of the soil. And Germans projected on to them the qualities to be expected of wild people or 'savages': passivity, a childlike nature, above all cunning, cruelty and undying hatred for the 'superior' race. They cast them, in short, as Indians.

Indian Wars

In October 1941 Hitler went on a typical rant about Germans creating gardens, fields and orchards in the desolate east. There was, he argued, no need for Germans to feel any pricks of conscience about those who lived there: they were inferior, and the land had to be dragged out of its lethargy. Hitler underlined his point with a startling analogy: 'There is only one task: To set about the Germanization of the land by bringing in Germans and to regard the indigenous inhabitants as Indians'.[219]

This frontier motif was an old one. Frederick the Great had compared the newly acquired Polish West Prussia unfavourably with Canada and likened the 'slovenly Polish trash' who lived there to Iroquois.[220] In the Warthe marshes, reclaimed under Frederick's direction, even the names told the story. When Slav fisherpeople gave way to German farmers, when the watery *Kietz* was replaced by the geometrical German village, the new settlements were given names like Florida, Philadelphia and Saratoga.[221] The German equation of Slav with Indian persisted through the nineteenth century, becoming a 'favourite theme of Prussian politicians'. As one of them argued, the Poles – like the 'American redskins' – were doomed to ruin; just as New World Indians were being pushed back into the 'everlasting wilderness' where they slowly perished, so Poles were 'pushed out of towns and landed properties as they yielded to Prussian civilization'.[222] The comparisons were indirect as well as direct. Reading the historical romances of bold German settlers in eastern Europe, it is not hard to decipher who the cruel and treacherous natives are supposed to be, making forays from primitive huts in their marsh and forest retreats to steal cattle, burn homesteads and threaten the bearers of a superior culture.[223] No wonder the Polish writer Ludwik Powidaj, in an 1864 article on 'Poles and Indians', traced the fate of American Indians and asked: 'What Pole will not see the situation of his own country?'[224]

The equation of the two groups in this negative sense is open to an objection. Julius Mann's *The Settlers in America* may have been typical of a whole genre in claiming that 'the savages have to retreat into ever more distant areas faced with the superiority of civilized Europeans'.[225] But there was another German way of seeing Indians that was much more positive. In the first half of the nineteenth century, we find German upper-class travellers to America who viewed the aboriginal population through a Romantic prism. Like the French aristocrat Chateaubriand, they looked for and found the 'noble savage', a standing reproach to the crass commercialism of emerging American democracy. Some even detected similarities between Indians and ancient Teutons.[226] Writers who adopted this position, novelists as well as travellers, often criticized the Indian policy pursued by frontier heroes like Andrew Jackson. Karl May would popularize this romantic view at the end of the nineteenth century in works like *Winnetou*, in which the German hero learns that the true noblemen are Indians like his friend Winnetou while the Yankees are untrustworthy opportunists.[227] Since Karl May was an author Hitler read and re-read throughout his life, this surely makes National Socialist views of east European 'Indians' seem more perplexing.

The appeal of Karl May was partly, of course, that the noble Indian provided a stick with which to beat the Anglo-Saxons for their 'hypocrisy'. In just the same way, Nazi writers felt no inhibitions about criticizing American slavery, despite an utter lack of sympathy for actual Black Americans – indeed, the *Verniggerung* of American society was a predictable constant in National Socialist criticism of the USA. Karl May's appeal was broader than that, however. The supposed nobility that the German hero shared with Winnetou played on an old German theme, a cliché among cultural conservatives, that Germans were superior to prosaic, money-grubbing Anglo-Saxons. Readers were presented with an idealized alternative to everything they hated about 'Americanism' (and the spectre of Germany becoming 'Americanized') – the dominance of business, the cult of material success, mechanization, teeming cities, the absence of culture or soul.[228] These were the common stereotypes of America in the Third Reich; Hitler's monologues were filled with them. And the alternatives to a hated reality? The idealized noble savage was one; the no less idealized frontier spirit was another.

Hitler, as so often, wanted to have it both ways – to carry on reading Karl May, then tell his acoloytes that Poles and Ukrainians should be treated like Indians. Popular Nazi writers did the same when they wrote about German colonists in America, suggesting that they had had a closer relationship with Indians yet celebrating German colonists' 'heroic deeds' in defending the frontier in the Mohawk Valley and the Carolinas.[229] But the two myths could not be combined, and it was the frontier that ultimately proved the more seductive of the two. It offered a powerful story about how German society could be rejuvenated through settlement, and a way to rationalize displacing the 'history-less peoples' – the *Stämme*, or 'tribes' – who stood in the way.[230]

To speak of Indians was to contemplate extermination. Here is Hans Frank, addressing a 1942 party gathering at Lemberg (Lvov) in the sarcastic-brutalist style that made him stand out even among leading National Socialists:[231]

> I am not speaking about the Jews that we still have here; we shall also deal with these Jews. Today, by the way, I have not seen any at all. What does that mean? After all, this is supposed to be a town where there were thousands and thousands of these flat-foot Indians – and there were no more to be seen. I hope you haven't done something bad with them? (Loud laughter)

Hitler, speaking in a smaller circle the previous year, was more matter-of-factly cynical. He had, he claimed, never heard of a German eating a loaf of bread and worrying whether the land that produced it had been conquered by the sword. 'We also eat Canadian wheat and don't think about the Indians', he added – a nod, perhaps, but no more than a nod, to Karl May's *Winnetou*.[232] These were the attitudes Nazi leaders brought with them to the 'wild east'. When German policies encountered resistance, this simply reinforced their prejudices. Slavs and Jews, cast as Indians, were only proving that that was what they were. 'There is a struggle here with the partisans as in the Indian Wars in North America', said Hitler in August 1942. Three weeks later he boasted that partisan bands would be 'strung up'; 'this will become a real Indian War'.[233] There were indeed parallels. In the German east, as in the American west, the conquerors visited dispossession and genocide on indigenous peoples, all the while proclaiming their mission to 'civilize' the land; then they attributed 'hatred' and 'primitive cruelty' to their victims. The processes were nonetheless very different: one protracted, the other concentrated on just a few years. The outcomes were different, too. Goebbels may have filmed the resettlement of the Volhynian Germans, but he never had the opportunity to film 'How the East Was Won'.

In 1941 Hitler was still talking about 'Indians' in connection with growing wheat; the following year the context was partisan activity. This shift reflected what was happening on the ground. Whereas in 1941 the rounding up of alleged partisans was often a cloak for the outright murder of Jews, by 1942 and 1943 armed resistance had become more formidable. Changing military fortunes on the eastern front provided much of the impetus for the growth of partisan activity, because of the psychological effects as well as the increasing assistance that the Soviet Union provided to the anti-German resistance. The Battle of Stalingrad in 1942–3 and the Red Army counter-offensive that followed had the same effects in the east as the successful Normandy landings of 1944 had in the west on French resistance. German policy also created partisans. Jewish round-ups and the liquidation of ghettoes led the small minority of Jews who were able to escape, especially younger ones, to take their chances in the forests and marshes. Joining them were Poles, Ukrainians and Belorussians fleeing the increasingly savage German policy of rounding up forced labour for the Reich. The occupiers turned the screw in 1942–3, surrounding and shipping off crowds who had gathered to listen to music in the towns, stripping whole villages of everyone of working age (and many who were not). Altogether as many as 1.5 million people, one in forty of the population, were deported to Germany from the Ukraine alone. There was a direct correlation between deportations and the growth of partisan numbers.[234] The brutal expulsions that preceded German settlements also created a class of the dispossessed with nothing left to lose. A classic example was the violent 'desettlement' of more than 100,000 Poles from the Zamość district of the General Government over the winter of 1942–3, which led almost immediately to revenge attacks on German settlers. As the local German administrator noted bitterly, the resettlement policy had turned the Polish population into 'bandits'.[235] This was one of many flashpoints in the conflict over tactics between the SS architects of German settlement and Hans Frank, whose short-term priority was Polish acquiescence in German rule.

Insecurity became a growing problem throughout the German-occupied east. 'On long lonely stretches and when travelling at night, it is prudent at the moment to carry a weapon', warned the 1943 Baedeker guide to the General Government.[236] As the threats to German life and property mounted, they brought home just how thinly spread and vulnerable the German conquerors actually were. That was true of railway, postal and forestry officials who worked far away from the relative safety of the towns; it was even more true of the resettlers, despite Himmler's boast that Poles and others would never be able to touch them. Olrik Breckoff, a Lithuanian German whose family was 'resettled' in Posen, recalled fifty years later how his uncle always carried a gun in 'troubled areas' and the children were warned to stop playing in the local woods, which now contained partisans as well as cranes.[237] The *Wehrbauer* – the farmer with a gun – played an integral part in Himmler's fantasy of taming the 'wild east', and the propaganda message was still being pumped out to 'resettlers' through 1944.[238] But settlers were unable to defend themselves, and soon the German army and security forces also found it impossible to protect even 'secure points' like Hegewald, the island of German settlement in the Ukraine. From 1943 onwards, as the Red Army advanced and partisan activity mounted, German settlers were pulled back to the west, from the Ukraine and Byelorussia, then from Galicia, finally from the Vistula valley and the newly-incorporated areas.[239]

Forests and marshes were the obvious destination for those fleeing German authority, and a natural base for partisans. Like the mountains that sheltered the resistance in Greece and Yugoslavia, they offered ideal terrain for concealment, a place from which to venture out on raids against German soldiers, munitions stores and railway communications. By 1943 the marshes and woodlands became a gathering point for escaped Jews, young men evading deportation, former auxiliary policemen who had deserted, communists, Polish and Ukrainian nationalists, criminals and Soviet experts who were parachuted in with weapons and supplies. The Pripet marshes were a centre of resistance. Martin Bürgener had recognized that the undrained marshes were strategically 'easy to defend and hard to conquer'.[240] He was thinking of orthodox military engagements, but the point applied with even greater force to partisan warfare. Polessia was also an area where a steady stream of partisans was created as an unintended consequence of German brutality. Bernhard Chiari has brilliantly reconstructed how this occurred stage by stage at the local level. In the composite village he calls 'Šmakoviči', situated twenty-five miles from Baranovitchi in the northern marshes, each round-up of Jews, each attempt to exact forced labour for the Reich, each family reduced to penury, each local auxiliary policeman placed in an impossible position by German demands, led more people to melt away into the underground. Military reprisals had the same effect. In Chiari's words, German soldiers and civilian administrators 'opened the Pandora's box of hostility'.[241]

From the winter of 1942–3 there were repeated 'cleaning-up' efforts by Wehrmacht and SS cavalry in Polessia, but with unimpressive results. Even the supposed successes were ambiguous. Operation February, mounted by Bach-Zelewski's SS cavalry in 1943, executed over 7,000 people accused of harbouring partisans and nearly 4000 fugitive Jews; but claims that 2200 partisans were killed in action seem dubious given the small numbers of German casualties and captured weapons. At any rate, in spring 1943 Himmler was forced to evacuate 10,000 ethnic Germans from Belorussia because their safety could not be guaranteed by SS, police and army.[242] At the beginning of that winter the Wehrmacht still believed that with sufficient numbers it could surround and destroy partisan units, but officers on the ground came to recognize that the mobility of irregulars made this impossible and combing-out operations were scaled back.[243] The terrain itself could hardly have been more psychologically hostile to the German forces. These, after all, were the 'feared Pripet marshes', as Richard Bergius called them back in the heady days of 1941.[244] The resurrection of plans to drain the marshes in 1942–3, through the large-scale deployment of Dutch labour, was closely linked to the strategic situation. But nothing came of these pipe-dreams.[245] Instead, Germans who ventured into this waterland found themselves faced with the very spectre that hundreds of novels, histories and nationalist tracts had conjured up – of coming under attack by indigenous inhabitants who then retreated from the 'superior' race into the swamps and forests. Once it had happened to the Teutonic Knights; now it was happening to the Wehrmacht. For ordinary German soldiers the Pripet marshes were 'a mysterious, unfathomable wilderness that imbued them with fear'.[246]

Military intelligence estimated in June 1943 that some 45,000 partisans were operating in Polessia; by October they put the number at 76,000. The Pripet marshes contained some of the largest formations anywhere in eastern Europe. They included well-equipped groups of battalion strength (about 800 people), like the partisans led by the Ukrainian communist Sydir Kovpak. Most were smaller, local collections of resisters, among them around 4000 members of Jewish or part-Jewish partisan groups.[247] These groups were given fictional life in Primo Levi's novel, *If Not Now, When?* [248] He knew the Pripet marshes well from spending two months in the region during the long, circuitous journey home from Auschwitz described in *The Truce*.[249] That surely explains his feeling for the land and the links between the vegetation of the marshes and resistance – the fact, for example, that winter is the hardest time for partisans, when the cover of foliage has gone, lighting a fire is dangerous, and the ice makes it easier for motorized soldiers to travel. At the beginning of *If Not Now, When?* the Jewish partisans Leonid and Memel are walking in search of Novoselki, the 'republic of the marshes', in July 1943:[250]

> The path was broken more and more often by shallow ponds, which obliged them to make exhausting detours. The water was clear, unmoving, smelling of peat, with thick, round leaves floating on it, fleshy flowers and an occasional bird's egg . . . the horizon surrounding them had never been so vast throughout their journey. Vast and sad, steeped in the intense, funereal odour of the canebrakes.

These were the Pripet marshes which, along with their inhabitants, Martin Bürgener had described with such venom in 1939. Just four years later, still undrained, they were a site of survival and resistance.

LANDSCAPE AND ENVIRONMENT IN THE POST-WAR GERMANYS

The Garden of our Hearts: The 'Lost Lands' in the East

When he was well into his nineties and almost blind, Daniel Sprem-berg would stand outside the family farmhouse and stare dimly towards the object of his contempt. If his great-grandson was at hand, he would commandeer the youthful eyes: 'Boy, look over there and tell me if the sails of the windmill are turning!' The news that they were motionless gave the old man pleasure. The Lord had sent no wind today. Perhaps – a forlorn hope – the local landowners had decided to give up new-fangled arable farming and return to the 'golden-footed sheep'.[1] For Daniel Spremberg was a shepherd, and sheep were the main business of Gennin when he first acquired the 750 acres of land on the slopes of the Warthe valley in 1778. By the beginning of the new century, however, his son-in-law August Wilhelm Künkel had turned the world of Gennin upside down. Land went under the plough and sheep were relegated to the margins. The building of a mill in the 1840s, to grind neighbours' corn as well as their own, was the final insult.[2]

The episode of the mill plays an important part in Hans Künkel's history of the family, written in the 1950s and published posthumously. Künkel was born near Landsberg on the Warthe in 1896. After serving in the First World War he spent most of his life as a teacher. In 1946, ten years before his death, he was ordained as a Protestant minister and continued his vocation by founding and running a school for orphans in Wolfenbüttel. He also wrote throughout his adult life: works of popular psychology that dealt with fate and the stages of life, histor-ical novels and *Heimat* fiction that celebrated his native landscape.[3]

These interests came together in his family history. Künkel's saga of generational change is about the arrival of 'new times'.[4] The mill, a metalled road, the railway on which passengers with bored faces raced through a countryside they no longer understood – these serve as symbols of a new age. So does Berlin, the hard-driving capital that lay across the Oder to the west. As communications made the world smaller, 'no one could live apart in the green pastures of the eighteenth century'. Künkel's elegy to a lost age condemns the gospel of profit for changing the relationship of humans to the land. 'Now', he says – meaning the late nineteenth century – 'the earth was to be exploited instead of served'.[5] Three characters in the book stand at an oblique angle to this brave new world. One is Daniel Spremberg, the blind patriarch who lived on beyond his time; the other two are Künkel's grandparents, members of the Protestant sect known as the Herrenhüter. But the central character is the land itself. The earth of Gennin represents continuity, permanence and the rhythms of nature. It persists through the vagaries of politics, war and counter-marching armies. The land survives when the nearby fortress of Küstrin falls to Napoleon and the local village is razed by French soldiers; it is there when Hermann Künkel returns from Bismarck's wars; and it offers solace when the author himself returns from the First World War with a missing arm. Hans Künkel takes his stand with those family members who believed that one should 'live oneself into the land'.[6] Treat the earth with respect and you can be redeemed.

There is nothing very original about this story of expulsion from paradise and loss of innocence. In its modern form, for the last two hundred years at least, the arc of the narrative has become familiar. But the story is less straightforward than it seems at first. Künkel's narrative begins in the same time and place that this book began – in the wet, wild places of the Oder and Warthe Marshes before they were drained in the eighteenth century. For August Wilhelm Künkel came originally from the former Oderbruch fishing village of Alt-Mädewitz, before he turned his back on a fishing family still unreconciled to the new world created by Frederick the Great's reclamations. And it was on the slopes above the newly reclaimed Warthe valley that he settled, where the Gennin estate owned meadows. We might expect his great-grandson Hans Künkel to be sympathetic to these lost worlds, and he is – up to a point. There are wistful, somewhat conventional descriptions of the reeds and lianas, the fish and wild birds that disappeared.

But that is only half the story. Künkel also has positive words for the new greenery, the arable and grazing land, created in the former marshes. It is Gennin, after all, not the wetlands once inhabited by wild duck and wild boar, that provides the emotional centre of this family chronicle. The worm in the bud for Künkel was not the reclamation of the eighteenth century but the heedless 'materialism' that came later. Like so many writers on German nature and the German homeland, especially conservative writers in the twentieth century, Künkel celebrates an 'unchanging' landscape that was not really unchanging at all.[7] A poignant moment in the book brings this home to the reader. There was one meadow at Gennin that became Künkel's favourite retreat when he returned home wounded from the trenches. Triangular in shape, it was rich in wild flowers and butterflies and well shaded by trees, a piece of land that became a symbol of healing. And how had this strangely shaped meadow been created? By the criss-crossing lines of the drainage ditches dug when the Warthe Marshes were drained.[8] We are reminded of Otto Modersohn, invoking nature as a teacher while he stood on the bridge that led over the canal.[9]

Künkel's version of paradise lost carries an ambiguity we have seen throughout this book. What makes it even more ambiguous is the fate of German lands in the east after 1945 – the 'lost lands'. By the time he wrote his family history, Künkel had fled west with his 91-year-old mother and the German Warthe had become the Polish Warta. Künkel himself says almost nothing about 1945: he died before he could bring the story up to the Second World War. It is the editor who tells us about the fleeing mother and Künkel's loss of two sons in the war (although not about his contribution to a 1939 book honouring Hitler's fiftieth birthday); and it is the editor, a law professor from the Göttingen Research Group devoted to preserving the memory of the German *Heimat* in the east, whose introduction refers explicitly to a homeland 'that stands today under Polish administration'.[10] Yet the sense of this loss permeates the book. Künkel and his mother were just two of the twelve million Germans who either fled before the Red Army or were expelled from their homes in eastern and south-eastern Europe between late 1944 and 1948. Hundreds of thousands died (some put the number as high as 1.5 million).[11] Most of the refugees and expellees found their way into the western zones of what would soon be a divided Germany, where they made up a good quarter of the population. These 'new citizens' were a formidable presence in the young Federal Republic. Their

Landsmannschaften, organizations that cultivated the collective identity of East Prussians, Silesians and Sudeten Germans, were courted by politicians, especially by Konrad Adenauer's Christian Democratic Union. Through political lobbying, at annual gatherings, in exhibitions and a welter of publications, they asserted a claim on the 'lost lands'. There was a grim irony here: never before had Germans living in the Rhineland or Bavaria been presented with such a vivid image of the German east. Thanks to the feverish efforts of refugee professors, schoolteachers, clergy, journalists and *Heimat* enthusiasts, the Germany that lay east of the Oder and Neisse rivers became truly familiar to fellowcountrymen only after it was no longer German.[12] That was Hitler's unwitting, paradoxical achievement.

The German east remembered by refugee writers was an idealized land, frozen in time. Red-brick Gothic churches and the fortresses of the Teutonic Knights belonged to their shining image of the east; so did the landscape from which those towers of Germandom rose.[13] But what kind of landscape: the natural or the cultivated, the raw or the cooked? Like Hans Künkel, most refugee writers served up an ambiguous combination. They evoked the natural beauty of lakes and forests, the breakers and dunes along the Baltic coast, winter snows and the sweet-smelling linden trees in spring, the bison and elk of East Prussia. But they always emphasized that Germans had tamed the land and made it fruitful. When Paul Fechter tried to conjure up the 'magic' of the eastern landscape he juxtaposed the wild Drausensee (a 'paradise for birds') and the 'wide, green, flat Dutch landscape of pastures' on the Lower Vistula.[14] Karlheinz Gehrmann made the point more directly, writing about East Prussia in the 1951 anthology, *German Homeland without Germans*. The 'miracle' of the German relationship with the land was that 'East Prussia became cultivated land yet remained entirely nature. Here civilization and the natural existed side by side without one damaging the other'.[15] The sustaining myth of the German east lived on, in other words, and the refugee writers who tended the flame still wanted it both ways: Germans had a special feeling for nature, but they also had a special talent for shaping the land. The second of these arguments, no less dubious than the first, was more important when it came to asserting German claims in eastern Europe. And so these post-war writers recycled a familiar story, little changed since the 1930s (or indeed the nineteenth century), which told how Germans had found a 'wilderness' and made it bloom. Even the colour-

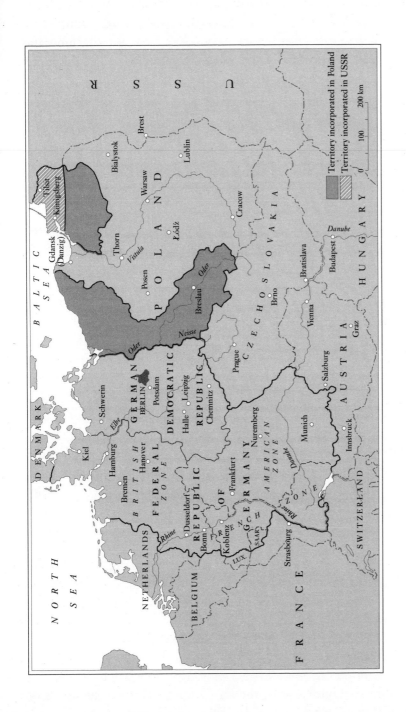

MAP 10 *Divided post-war Germany and the 'lost lands'.*

coding was the same: the 'uniform grey' transformed by the industry of German settlers into 'sparkling colours' and living green.[16] The German east had once been a green garden; now for the homesick refugees it was 'the garden of our hearts'.[17]

No one endowed these sentiments with more pathos than the East Prussian poet Agnes Miegel; and there is also no better example of how politically compromised the sentiments were. Born in Königsberg in 1879, Miegel first made her name as a writer of lyric verse. Her poetry, short stories and essays expressed a powerful feeling for her native landscape that was infused with a sense of history – the history of the Teutonic Knights and German settlers, like the Salzburgers who were among her own family's forebears.[18] Agnes Miegel saw herself as a child of the 'green plain', a recurring motif in her work.[19] The autobiographical essay 'Greeting of the Towers' is a hymn to the 'fresh green' land. It lovingly evokes the drainage canals along the River Pregel, the barns and bridges, a mill race and the blooming apple trees seen during a family walk at Whitsun. Watching her parents bathed by the setting sun she 'felt curiously at one with the earth and the sun and the sweet-smelling May-like green land'.[20] By the time she wrote this in 1936, Miegel had accepted an invitation to join the Prussian Academy of Sciences, purged after the Nazi seizure of power, and was hosting visiting groups of Hitler Youth at her East Prussian home. She later contributed, like Hans Künkel, to the book honouring Hitler's fiftieth birthday, became a Nazi party member and gave poetry readings in the new German Warthegau. Miegel may have been politically innocent, as her defenders later insisted, but her work fell squarely within a tradition that celebrated the fertile German landscape of the east as a product of cultural superiority.[21] The notorious poems of the 1940 wartime volume, *Eastern Land*, were not so out of line with what had come before:[22]

> The wind sings the eternal song of
> The green eastern land, the song of the fate-driven
> Divine mission:
> To be a bulwark and a dike in the unending plain

After her flight to the west Miegel became 'Mother East Prussia', a celebrated guest at meetings of the East Prussian *Landsmannschaft*. In works like 'In Commemoration' and 'There was a Land' she mourned and celebrated the 'green *Heimat* land' as a place of peace and fruit-fulness.[23] It was exactly the idealized image that the expellee organizations cultivated – as if all had been pastoral harmony until the Red Army marched west, as if the mass flight of Germans had fallen out of a clear blue sky.

The message was clear: Germans were victims, like the once fertile land they had created. 'There Was a Land', the work most frequently anthologized in refugee publications, was the classic expression of this:[24]

> O, cold blows the wind through empty land
> O, more gently blow ashes over dust and sand
> And the nettles grow high on the ruined door
> Even higher the thistles on the edge of the field.

The idea of a landscape decaying after the expulsion of the Germans was a commonplace in this literature. In Wolfgang Paul's poem, 'Refugees', a young couple leave the keys of their farm lying in the beet field and flee to an unhappy life in the west; meanwhile a 'jungle grows in the land'. Karlheinz Gehrmann describes the return of wilderness in the lost lands, as the steppe advances westwards, rivers sand up, dikes break and lowlands flood.[25] The flood, long-standing German image of Slav disorder, was a favourite metaphor. 'O, you drowned world!', lamented Herbert von Hoerner; 'All this is like a completely drowned world' was the opening line of Joachim Reifenrath's 'Deserted Village'.[26] Perhaps it was the same mental reflex that led both Paul Fechter and Agnes Miegel to write about the 'drowned' medieval town of Truso.[27]

It is often said that the fate of German refugees from the east was a taboo subject in the Federal Republic. That hardly squares with the political influence and generous public funding their organizations enjoyed. Hundreds of memorials dotted West Germany; scores of roads and schools were named after Agnes Miegel alone.[28] The *Landsmann-schaften* themselves were quick to charge that they were being ignored; or they complained about the hypocrisy of western leaders who preached human rights but ignored the rights of German expellees. Yet the language of human rights coming from these groups carried more than a trace of hypocrisy. It sat uneasily with long-standing German claims to the east based on ethnic or cultural superiority, all the more so when post-war writers continued to describe a paradisal landscape destroyed by 'Asiatic' invaders. What undermined the moral claims of expellee organizations was a stubborn determination to look at history with one eye closed. They constructed a victimology in which 'expulsions', 'terror' and 'brutality' were things that had happened only to Germans.[29] Social change and the *Ostpolitik* of the Willy Brandt government in the early 1970s made the *Landsmannschaften* a more marginal presence in the Federal Republic. But, hermetically sealed off within their own milieu, refugee and expellee organizations changed very slowly. One of the influences from which they sealed themselves off was the very different kind of memorializing of the German east being done by writers outside the official organizations. These writers – they included major figures like Günter Grass, Horst Bienek, Peter Härtling and Siegfried Lenz – were just as mindful of what had been lost. But their works carried greater moral weight because they recognized German crimes in the east, the reasons behind the mass flights and expulsions. The eastern landscapes they depicted carried more conviction, too, because these were not timeless tableaux in which Germans interacted with nature and other peoples were excluded, but landscapes that did justice to a complex ethnic and linguistic reality. The official organizations ignored these works or mounted campaigns against them. They had good reason to react so allergically, because the 'other' refugees challenged their frozen world of memory. This was a literary and political argument. Pre-war Danzig and its hinterland as they appear in the novels of Günter Grass – alive with diverse cultures that bleed into each other, a world removed from the sentimentalities of *Heimat* – were as much a reproach to expellee spokesmen as Grass's accusation that they were guilty of 'lies and cynicism towards elderly people who could not feel at home in the west'. This 'fractured landscape of memory' persisted through the old Federal Republic.[30]

Shortly before the world changed in November 1989 a collection of historical photographs and postcards appeared. Heinz Csallner's *Between Vistula and Warthe* is an example of how the authorized memory of the German east, frozen for decades, had started to thaw, but unevenly, like one of those eastern rivers in spring the refugees so often wrote about. An unreconstructed world view coexists awkwardly in Csallner's book with gestures towards candour. His introduction devotes space to 'racial madness' and the treatment of Jews and Poles, but only four lines, which are immediately balanced in the moral scales ('the Germans have paid for this with huge sacrifices, their homeland, their past has been largely extinguished'). He is sensitive to the negative associations of the term 'Warthegau' for Poles. But he uses the term anyway on the grounds that Germans had a long history in the area; then his only map shows the National Socialist 'Reichsgau Wartheland'.[31] *Between Vistula and Warthe* is an understated but unmistakable celebration of German cultural achievements – Frederick the Great's reclamation of the Netze and Warthe valleys, thriving towns and flourishing villages like Helldorf in the Netzebruch ('one can see in this picture what "*Heimat*" means'), steamers on the Warthe. Steamships and bridges, symbols of a world made over by German technology, appear in many pictures. One shows the bridge over the Vistula at Leslau, with a caption suggesting that the view from the bank of the river 'probably enthused many new settlers'.[32] Other pictures of bridges have captions informing readers when they were destroyed by Poles, but not why.

That was 1989. Reunification the following year brought German recognition of the Oder–Neisse line; the Soviet Union disappeared the year after that. The post-war world that had given rise to the expellee organizations changed, and they changed in response. The language of their founding charters was revised, exchanges were initiated with countries where the former 'homeland' lay, especially Poland. Publications placed the expellees' sufferings in historical context and monuments honoured the victims of Germans as well as German victims. (This had long been true when it came to the west, where commemorations of bombed-out German cities were careful to include pictures of Rotterdam and Coventry.) The shift 'from confrontation to cooperation', as the *Landsmannschaft* Vistula-Warthe called it, was evident when the 50th anniversary of mass flight came around in 1995.[33] These organizations had once shaped, or misshaped, the collective memory of refugees and expellees. Now the organizations moved on. But many individuals found the adjustment hard. An American researching a book on Prussia spoke in the late 1990s to one former expellee who lived in the Rhenish Palatinate. The man, nearly eighty, sat in his modern bungalow and explained what his former homeland meant:[34]

> To plant your feet in the ground, to know it's yours and that the beautiful fields and the woods so carefully tended are only that way because your family *made* it that way – that is my idea of a homeland . . . Always, always prepared to die for it! That's what Prussia means to me. The land out there has been a sponge for my family. It soaked our sweat and our blood and it bloomed like an oasis in the desert.

The motif of blood sacrifice was a remnant of National Socialist ideology; that Germans had greened the wilderness was, as we have seen, an idea with a much longer pedigree.

The retired teacher Helmut Enss was also close to eighty when, in 1998, he published a book about Marienau, his native village on the Lower Vistula.[35] It is what is usually called in Germany a *Heimatbuch*: a labour of love that is more chronicle than history, an omnium-gatherum of documents, historical snippets, local lore, lists, descriptions of farms, personal recollections and photographs. There are countless books like this devoted to German towns and villages, often written by retired teachers. What makes this one stand apart is that Marienau ceased to be German more than fifty years earlier and the author had not seen the village since. The original impetus for *Marienau* came from reunions in the west that brought surviving villagers together. It is a melancholy book about a lost homeland, a product of desk-top publishing that might have been written in the 1950s.

Marienau was a village of the delta, part of that fertile green landscape described by Paul Fechter where the wealthy farmers – rather like those in the reclaimed Oderbruch – had a reputation for enjoying the good things of life.[36] As it happens, Fechter knew Marienau well. As a young man in the 1890s living in nearby Elbing, he often visited with friends, one of whom had an uncle and cousin in Marienau. In the summer they walked, admiring the fat pastures and rich farmland between the drainage canals. In winter they went by train, which had just reached the village. Why go there in winter? Marienau had a well-regarded country inn and Fechter could vouch personally for the generous amounts of food and drink consumed there – it was 'the old east in its purest form'.[37] Enss describes how the village reached this state of prosperity, and the story he tells is familiar: patient medieval dike-building that turned the lower reaches of the Vistula into the 'garden of God', neglect and floods under Polish overlordship, the coming of Dutch settlers who cultivated the marshes once again, the Polish partition of 1772 that returned West Prussia to ordered Prussian ways.[38] Heinrich von Treitschke would have recognized the framing narrative. He had, after all, done a great deal to establish it through his own writing. Treitschke would also have approved how Helmut Enss carried the story on through the nineteenth century, pointing to the new security that river regulation brought to the delta villages under Bismarck's Prussian–German state. The existential threat to villages like Marienau was flooding. By 1900 it was finally 'exorcised', or so it seemed.[39]

Then this world – as a German world – came to an end. Enss plots the stages of its dissolution: the Treaty of Versailles that placed the villages of the delta under the Danzig Free State, a brief 'return to the Reich' after the Polish campaign in 1939, then the changed fortunes of war on the eastern front, and finally flight. It would be hard to read these painstakingly gathered accounts of divided families, lost loved ones, abandoned homes and blank despair without feelings of sympathy. Suffering is indivisible; it is not made less real by the prior suffering of others. But should there not be some acknowledgement of that other history, and its connection to the world torn apart in 1944–5? There is no German racial persecution in this book, there are no camps, no Poles or Jews are murdered. There is only a Germany that goes to war when frustrated beyond endurance by Polish intransigence, then attacks Russia in self-defence. Here the frozen memory has not thawed. The very last page of the book quotes one of Agnes Miegel's post-war poems.[40] The lines are especially appropriate to a delta village like Marienau, although the dominant metaphor was one that had become second nature to Germans throughout the east:

I am in a land that has remained German,
  Gone is the homeland and my tribe,
  Which kept watch on the threatened dike.

The dikes did break at the end of the war, but it was Germans themselves who broke them. In March 1945 the Wehrmacht destroyed the dikes on the Vistula during its retreat, flooding the delta to a depth of four feet. For well over a century the dike or dam against the 'Slav flood' had signified German racial superiority, but also German anxiety. Now circumstances required the use of 'flood against flood', as Helmut Enss put it. The breach in the embankment that would once have been a 'curse' became a 'blessing' because it 'held back the murdering and violating horde'.[41]

The 'Economic Miracle' and the Rise of Ecology

One of the millions who fled west at the beginning of 1945 was Countess Marion Dönhoff, by horse from her family's estate in East Prussia. Later the highly respected publisher of the liberal weekly, *Die Zeit*, Marion Dönhoff had no illusions about what had caused the catastrophe of 1944–5. She and her circle were contemptuous of National Socialism. A close friend from a neighbouring East Prussian family, Heini Lehndorff, was killed for his part in the July plot against Hitler. Her spare, unsentimental description of the flight west recalls how local Nazi officials, right up to the moment when civilian administration collapsed, impeded preparations for departure that might have saved German lives. Realism also governed Dönhoff's reactions to the homeland she mourned. In a preface to her book, published in 1962, she described coming to the painful conclusion that there was no alternative to accepting that the lost lands were truly lost:[42]

> I chose the painful sacrifice of the affirmative yes where a no would have meant revenge and hatred. I cannot believe that the highest measure of love for the homeland expresses itself in remaining mired in hatred towards those who have taken possession of it and defaming those who support reconciliation. When I think of the forests and lakes of East Prussia, the broad meadows and old avenues of trees, then I am sure they are still as incomparably beautiful as they were when this was my home. Perhaps this is the highest measure of love: to love without possessing.

Landscape plays a very important part in this book, as it does in her later memoir, *A Childhood in East Prussia*. In the memory of flight it appears at one point in a striking, unexpected way. Dönhoff recalls a moment when 'very slowly, at slow-motion speed – as if the pictures intended to imprint themselves one more time – the East Prussian landscape passed by us like the stage set of a surrealist film'. In historic towns like Elbing and Marienburg, against a lit-up sky and the sound of the guns, the thousands of refugees resembled costumed extras in a giant drama.[43] The feeling of saying farewell to a landscape, and a landscape that suddenly assumed a surreal quality, is one that we find in other accounts of flight.[44] The chaos of total defeat offered many surrealistic sights in 1945, images that mocked or inverted any idea of 'mastery' over the natural world. The pleasure steamers that once belonged to the Nazi Strength through Joy organization, ships that just a few years earlier had carried ethnic Germans triumphantly 'back to the Reich', were now pressed into service lifting refugees to safety from Baltic ports. Many ended up at the bottom of the sea, like the *Wilhelm Gustloff*, sunk with the loss of 9000 lives – six times the death-toll of the *Titanic*.[45] By May 1945 ports and dock installations were in ruins across Germany. Wilhelmshaven, created out of the mud by the Jade Bay only ninety years earlier, was levelled by bombing that destroyed not only the harbour and shipyards but schools, hospitals, churches, town hall and library. Nearly 37,000 dwellings were damaged and 500 civilians lost their lives.[46] In bombed-out towns across Germany the water supply collapsed and women stood around emergency stand-pipes waiting to fill their pails; but there was water where it was not wanted, in bomb craters and flooded cellars that the homeless converted into temporary quarters.[47] 'Only the rivers were whole', says one of John le Carré's characters, remembering these years.[48] But that was not true, either. Germany's great river arteries were blocked in 1945. They were still crammed with the debris of sunken boats and the bridges blown up by the retreating Wehrmacht, which created – perhaps most famously in the buckled Hohenzollern bridge at Cologne – enduring images of a world turned upside down. The bridges had 'dropped to their knees in the water', wrote Max Frisch in his diary.[49]

The landscape of rubble and shattered infrastructure stayed in the minds of those who witnessed it. Memories of helpless exposure to the elements drove post-war reconstruction and help to explain the importance attached to satisfying material needs, at whatever cost to the natural world. But the abjectness of defeat and destruction also pulled people in the opposite direction. It led them to seek solace, and one of the places where they found it was in nature – the idealized natural world of the local *Heimat*. After German cities had been reduced to rubble, 'nature and landscape alone remained as an essential basis of our existence'.[50] As this plaintive comment suggests, identification with the landscape and 'healing earth' had another psychological function: it allowed Germans to see themselves as victims.[51] That was true, anyway, in the western part of what soon became a divided Germany. Whether it was also true in the eastern part is harder to tell. The new regime there did its best to suppress popular attachment to *Heimat* or nature, both of them anathema to a centralizing, self-consciously anti-fascist and modern state. What evidence there is suggests that the sentiments persisted anyway, but underground.[52] They were certainly not buried in the west. There, the two responses to the prostration of 1945 – a longing for material security on the one hand, an idealization of nature on the other – sounded as point and counterpoint through the post-war years. Nowhere were those conflicting emotions more evident than among the millions of refugees from the 'lost lands' of the former German east.

A majority of refugees settled in the western zones of Germany, the future Federal Republic, where they played a very important part in the heady boom of the 1950s and 60s that goes by the name 'economic miracle'. Never in modern German history had economic growth rates been so high, never had German rivers and wetlands changed so much or so quickly. A process underway for two centuries speeded up under the pressure of reconstruction and the drive to prosperity. Refugees themselves were a prime reason for one aspect of this transformation: the final disappearance of untouched moorlands. In the past these had been reclaimed under the banner of 'inner colonization' as an antidote to the social question; then they were supposed to be the salvation of the 'Volk ohne Raum'. Now, in a movement of population that combined features from both of these earlier epochs, moorland cultivation was to be the safety-valve for refugees and expellees – often very unpopular with locals – who had been decanted into rural areas of western Germany like Lower Saxony and Bavaria. These numbered a quarter of a million in Oldenburg, which became part of Lower Saxony, approaching one in three of the population.[53] What remained of the high moors in north-west Germany were ploughed under to provide new homes for Silesians and Pomeranians. The first six settlements were already established by 1950; many more followed under the Emsland Plan. As Aschendorfmoor, Wesuwermoor, Sustrumermoor, Hesepermoor, Walchum and the rest took shape, filling the gaps left by earlier settlements, the area of intact moorland in Lower Saxony shrank to just three small, isolated remnants.[54]

The immediate post-war fate of the moors reflected the times. Moorlands were a source of desperately needed land; they also provided food and fuel until regular supplies of both were restored. The longer post-war history of former moorland areas was different, but no less emblematic of new times. Peat production, where it continued, was increasingly mechanized and the product sold as garden peat-litter or as insulation material, no longer as fuel. Elsewhere ploughs turned up the sand beneath the surface of the moor to create arable land that depended on artificial fertilizer.[55] That was the story, in microcosm, of agricultural production throughout the Federal Republic, even in already fruitful areas like the Upper Rhine plain: mechanization on larger holdings that could take advantage of it, wholesale changes to the existing drainage system, more intensive cultivation, more irrigation, more chemical fertilizer and insecticides. The good news was that a shrinking agricultural sector supported a growing urban population. The bad news was a proliferation of streams transformed into concrete culverts, and – less visible but more dangerous – nitrates that ran off into waterways and seeped into the groundwater. This was the long-term price the Federal Republic paid for its well-stocked supermarkets, the other side of that 'Well-Being for All' successfully invoked by Economics Minister Ludwig Erhard during the 1957 election campaign.[56]

Artificial fertilizer was just one source of the growing pollution problem in West German waterways. Metal sediments were a by-product of booming industry; so were toxic chemicals. The foam stood twelve feet high in some canals. Oil spilled into rivers and coastal waters; household waste contributed ammonia and phosphates. Even minor streams felt the effects. A long-term study of the Moldau, which rose in the Odenwald and flowed eventually into the Upper Rhine, shows how the burden of agricultural, household and industrial pollution had destroyed the self-cleansing capacities of the stream by the end of the 1960s. It was the same story everywhere. The fish-kills ended in Bavarian rivers only because there were no more fish to kill.[57] The same problem eventually overtook the major rivers that had to carry this toxic load to the sea. Even in the 1950s the salmon catch in the Rhine was down to a few thousand a year (it was still 160,000 before the First World War), and the few remaining fish were unsafe to eat. By the early 1970s the river that flowed through the romantic gorge below Bingen was dirtier and more polluted than it had ever been, although not quite as loaded with toxic effluents as the water that finally crossed the Lower Rhine plain into the Netherlands. For years it had been complacently assumed that the river would be able to dilute the agricultural run-off and industrial waste produced by installations along its own banks or flushed down tributaries like the Neckar, Main and Ruhr. That fond hope could no longer be sustained. Over long stretches, the Rhine was close to being biologically dead.[58]

A quarter-century of heady growth preceded the first OPEC oil shock that hit the Federal Republic in 1973–4. It stretched water resources to the limit. The engineering measures that had been turning German rivers into organic machines since the nineteenth century continued, but the tempo was faster. That meant further stream-bed regulation, additional hydro plants on rivers where they already existed and their introduction on previously unregulated (even if hardly pristine) rivers. One of them was the Mosel, canalized in 1956–64 following a treaty between France, Luxembourg and the Federal Republic. The new river contained thirteen new locks and dams, which allowed 1500-ton ships to navigate it year-round and generated energy from eleven hydro-electric plants along the German stretch. The price was 770 million Deutschmarks, but that did not include the unquantifiable cost of pressing the Mosel into a 'technical straitjacket' (Heinrich Menke) or the negative impact on local flora and fauna.[59] The remaking of the Mosel was an instance of two pressures on German water resources. One was the navigational imperative, for inland shipping accounted for a quarter of transportation in the Federal Republic by the 1980s.[60] The drive for further river regulation was especially strong on waterways that formed part of the larger west European network. (This could and still can be most simply observed by sitting at the side of the Rhine and noting the number of Dutch- or Swiss-flagged vessels.) The second underlying problem was that energy use grew much faster than the population, driven by industrial demand and households that came to depend on appliances like washing machines, driers and dish-washers. One response was increasing the supply of hydro-electric power from the Bavarian Alps, the Black Forest and the rivers of the plain, even though 'white coal' was no longer seen as the quasi-magical techno-logical fix that had fired the zealots in earlier years.[61] Nuclear energy now assumed that mantle, drawing praise – ironical in retrospect – from 1950s conservationists who painted it as an alternative to destroying the natural beauty of mountain valleys.[62]

Not that dam construction ceased; it actually went on at a pace never seen before. The years on either side of 1900 may have been the classic age of German dam-building, but measured simply in numerical terms the real golden age came in the three decades after 1950. Most new dams provided either energy or drinking water. They included some of the largest ever built in Germany, like the Rosshaupten Dam on the Bavarian Lech (1954) and the Bigge Valley Dam in the Sauerland (1965), which forced the relocation of 2500 people.[63] Even then, reservoirs provided only an eighth of the Federal Republic's drinking water. Other sources had to be tapped to supply the thirsty conurbations. For the 3.5 million people in the Rhine-Main area that meant piping in water from the Hessian Ried, the Spessart and the Vogelsberg, upland areas with large reserves of groundwater – until they were drawn down on such a scale that, as happened in the Hessian Ried during the 1970s, heavy pumping and a series of dry summers led to subsidence. In some places the ground fell by as much as twelve feet, with damage to agriculture, forests and buildings estimated at fourteen million Marks. What to do? Plan A had been a new reservoir in the Taunus mountains, but that was blocked by protesters. Plan B, pumping groundwater out of the Hessian Ried, had made the earth move. Plan C, equally controversial, was to invest a third of a billion Marks in a water-purification plant by the Rhine at Biebesheim. Its output would be piped uphill and trickled back into the earth to maintain groundwater levels in the Hessian Ried, which in turn would allow extra pumping there during dry conditions in order to 'spare' the Spessart and Vogelsberg.[64]

This saga points in two directions. It points back, on the one hand, to a long history of unintended consequences in hydrological engineering. This book has been full of examples, from the Oder to the Rhine. Anti-flood measures that brought new flood risks, 'corrected' rivers that unexpectedly scoured their beds, dams that had unanticipated side-effects, water tables that fell catastrophically – all had a place in the catalogue of engineering own-goals. But the series of water-supply problems that afflicted the Rhine-Main area also pointed forward to something new: serious opposition. Every proposal of the water engineers, whether a reservoir in the Taunus, pumping stations in the hills, or the purification plant on the Rhine, attracted criticism and alternative suggestions (they included water conservation, and separating the supply of drinking water from water destined for other purposes). This was no isolated case, nor was the timing of this particular controversy coincidental. It was in the 1970s, the most reviled and underestimated of all post-war decades, that the German – or at least the West German – way with water began to change.

The concern itself was not new. Water pollution aroused controversy from the earliest post-war years, especially when major fish-kills were captured in dramatic photographs. An Alliance for the Protection of German Waters was founded in 1951, and alarm was voiced about what was happening long before the weekly newspaper *Die Welt* announced that the Rhine was 'Germany's largest sewer'.[65] River regulation and new hydro projects also drew opposition. Nature conservationists in Bavaria fought running battles with the powerful energy combine BAWAG. The indefatigable Otto Kraus, who led local conservationists for nearly two decades, later boasted about forcing the abandonment of a dozen projects in Bavaria alone, although – a recurring pattern everywhere – the best they could often achieve was to delay or scale down the original proposals. The canalization of the Mosel attracted opposition from conservation, fishing and tourist groups (joined by the railways, which feared the competition), and together they extracted some modest concessions.[66] Wetland reclamation and excessive groundwater pumping were less immediately obvious than dead fish or geometrical rivers, but their effects on water tables did not go unremarked or unpublicized. The long-running theme of a threatened *Versteppung*, or 'desertification', remained alive. Anton Metternich warned that 'the desert threatens', Erich Hornsmann raised the alarm that the most basic element of life was becoming a 'commodity in short supply'.[67]

The 1950s were a patriarchal, conservative decade in the Federal Republic, but not at all complacent where the natural world was involved. It was, in fact, the critics' conservatism that made them alarmed. They disliked the 'domination' of nature as much as they disliked communism or American rock and roll. Their anxieties about the natural landscape fitted neatly into broader concerns: defence of the family, defence of the German *Heimat*, defence of the 'Christian West' against crass materialism and Soviet 'totalitarianism'. Opposition to the dark side of the economic miracle was often couched as a conservative critique of technological hubris ('a frenzy of arrogance', in Anton Metternich's words).[68] It is no surprise that the idealized image of a sustaining German landscape remained a central point of reference. The nature conservation societies that built up membership steadily in the years 1955–65 liked to argue that landscape despoliation was evidence of an overly 'mechanized', 'Americanized', 'mass' society. A spate of books in the 1950s cast this message in apocalyptic religious terms: Hornsmann's *Otherwise Collapse (The Answer of Nature to the Abuse of Her Laws)* (1951), Anton Böhm's *The Devil's Epoch* (1955), Günther

Schwab's *The Dance of the Devil* (1958).[69] The culturally conservative slant of this critique highlights the lines of continuity that run back to the years before 1945. Some of the Cassandras kept dubious political company (Schwab was close to the neo-Nazi NPD in the 1960s), and there is no denying the reality of an 'avocado syndrome': green on the outside, but with a 'brown', or Nazi, kernel.[70] A remarkable number of conservationists active in the Third Reich simply resumed their activities after the war without self-reflection or expressions of regret. If they publicly regretted anything, it was that things had been better before the war when well-informed men of goodwill like themselves had (so they claimed) enjoyed more influence and been allowed to do the work of protecting nature without tiresome political debate. Their writings and speeches reek of barely disguised authoritarian leanings, with more than a few examples of views that had been carried straight over from the 1930s. The Chairman of the Association of National Parks boasted that these had an important 'Volk-biological' role because the soil of the homeland was essential to the vitality of the race. Most of these men (and they were almost all men) looked back fondly on the 1935 Reich Nature Conservation Law as an exemplary piece of 'apolitical' legislation. Among the incorrigibles was old friend Alwin Seifert, who emerged from the process of de-Nazification to resume his career as a landscape architect and conservation advocate, a leading critic of Mosel canalization (among many other causes), and the author of a 1962 autobiography to which he gave the serenely self-satisfied title *A Life for the Landscape*. The previous year, Seifert was among the prominent figures who gathered by Lake Constance to issue the Green Charta of Mainau, a landmark document – at least, so it seems in retrospect – of post-war West German environmental thinking.[71]

The dubious political background of many conservationists does not invalidate everything they had to say, nor should it lead us to overlook the fact that their arguments often had a strong, well-founded ecological component. The threat of dust-bowls was no less real because it was Alwin Seifert who warned about them.[72] Seifert, Klose, Kraus and other survivors from the conservationist movement of the Third Reich were not, anyway, the only West Germans sounding the alarm in the 1950s and 60s. Directly affected economic interests like fishing and tourism raised their voices. Many scientists did the same: geologists, botanists, zoologists. They played an important part in the 'ecologization' of the conservation movement, even in the early years of the

Federal Republic when the defenders of nature-as-German-homeland remained so numerous. Among the scientists was August Thienemann, the hydro-biologist who wrote from the ecological perspective he had been advocating for fifty years when he urged that every stream be treated as a 'unitary whole, a branch of nature, a "microcosm", a world in miniature bound to the surrounding landscape by inherent mutual influences.'[73] Political leaders also stirred themselves. An all-party working group was formed in 1952, local and national politicians who called for a more careful stewardship of natural resources like water. This diversity of concern was reflected in the signatories of the Mainau Charta, which also marked an early German use of the expression 'natural environment' – the term 'environment' (*Umwelt*) only came into its own during the 1960s. What seems strange, looking back, is that so much strenuous advocacy had so little public and political impact. Hornsmann and Schwab did write bestsellers, after all, anticipating the success of Rachel Carson's *Silent Spring* (1962) when it appeared in German translation. The press was meanwhile glad to publicize dramatic, visually compelling examples of ecological catastrophe. And what could be more dramatic than dead or dying salmon in the Rhine? It seems implausible to argue, as Arne Andersen has done, that a compromised past undercut the message of nature conservationists.[74] Not only was that message well attuned to other conservative concerns; it also came from a broad range of others who were not politically compromised. The probable explanation for the lack of impact is more prosaic. The social base of the environmentally alarmed was simply too narrow, the mobilization of opinion to oppose this or that project too local and ephemeral. Press interest also remained sporadic, even if some coverage (like a long 1959 article on water resources in the weekly *Der Spiegel*) was impressively detailed and serious-minded.[75] The warning voices cut too much against the grain of a still dominant belief that economic growth could continue unchecked and without long-term costs.

When that changed, it changed quickly. In September 1970 just forty per cent of the West German public claimed to be familiar with the term 'environmental protection'; by November 1971 the number had risen to 90 per cent.[76] This was like water turning suddenly into ice or steam, one of those instant transitions that sometimes occur in the human as well as the natural world. In this case it was triggered by high politics. We can even put a date on it: 7 November 1969. When the new governing coalition of Social Democrats and Free Democrats came to power that autumn, a department in the Ministry of Health was switched to the Interior Ministry headed by Hans-Dietrich Genscher. It bore the cumbersome title Department of Water Protection, Clean Air Preservation and Noise Prevention. During a meeting on 7 November a civil servant suggested renaming it Environmental Protection. Genscher agreed.[77] But this symbolic change in November 1969 was only the outward sign that more substantial issues were at stake. One of them, it is true, was party-political advantage. The liberal Free Democrats, the junior coalition partner, saw a cause they could make their own; leading Social Democrats were drawn to an issue that appealed across class lines. But it was not all calculation. Genscher took environmental concerns seriously. So did the Social Democratic Chancellor, Willy Brandt ('Environment Willy'), who had starred in a 1961 campaign against air pollution that demanded 'blue skies over the Ruhr' long before he promised new environmental laws on taking office in 1969.[78] The reforming social–liberal coalition found officials, scientists and a host of single-issue organizations primed for a political initiative, and that was what the government offered in the early 1970s. New laws gave environmental protection a much higher profile, a Federal Office for the Environment was established in 1974 and resources flowed into research. The new direction was reinforced in the public mind by parallel global initiatives. The European Council designated 1970 as the year of nature conservation. That was also when Earth Day was first celebrated in the USA and a UN conference convened in Stockholm to prepare for 1972, the World Year of the Environment. And it was in 1972 that the Club of Rome's warning about 'The Limits of Growth' appeared, quickly translated into German. The issue acquired momentum. Environmental politics in Bonn now attracted sustained media coverage and gave focus to what had previously been a lively but diffuse constituency.[79]

Environmentalism became a staple of West German political debate, in parliament, the press and in the streets. A wave of citizens' initiatives protested pollution, high-tech projects that swallowed up land and – above all – proposed atomic energy reactors at Wyhl in the Rhenish Breisgau and Brokdorf on the Lower Elbe. Former members of the student movement and extra-parliamentary left embraced the cause, having paid it no attention at all in the 1960s (none other than Che Guevara, after all, had told his children to 'study hard to be able to master the techniques that permit the domination of nature'[80]). It was a motley collection of environmentalists, Marxist groups, feminists, anarchist *Spontis*, urban communards and anti-consumerist simple-lifers that created the Green Party at the end of the 1970s. That was the decade when nature conservation was transmuted into ecological awareness and completed a rapid political migration from right to left. A series of issues kept it on the boil: nuclear power, acid rain, long-term threats like global warming, dramatic incidents like the Sandoz chemical spill near Basel, which poisoned the Rhine in autumn 1986 just six months after the Chernobyl disaster. The twenty years that followed the Brandt government's new departure saw an outpouring of books, pamphlets and fictional works devoted to environmental themes. It swept up many of the Federal Republic's best-known critical intellectuals. Carl Amery wrote about *Nature as Politics*, Hans-Magnus Enzensberger committed himself to 'eco-socialism', the artist Joseph Beuys gave his utopian hopes an ecological twist, Günter Wallraff turned from exposing the tabloid *Bild-Zeitung* to composing an environmental manifesto that condemned human 'domination' of nature. He also joined fellow-Rhinelander Heinrich Böll in calling for a 'Green popular front'.[81] The greening of the intelligentsia was only the most visible aspect of a much larger shift in sensibility, especially among the young – the young of all ages. That new sensibility could be found in the environmentalist tracts of small publishers, the songs of popular balladeers, the message of the urban 'scene' documented in alternative magazines like *Pflasterstrand*, the conversation in the student *Kneipe*, and the daily rituals of the urban living collective, or *Wohngemeinschaft*. More, perhaps, than in any other large developed country, nature and ecology became the emotionally charged watchwords around which other concerns – the threat of war, corporate power, women's rights – crystallized.

Popular environmental activism grew even as things were getting better. Federal laws and regulations, land-use planning procedures, environmental impact assessments, new opportunities to challenge large-scale projects in the courts – together, these transformed the outlook for protecting the environment. The effects on German waters were striking. Pollution declined sharply, a result of better water-purification plants, much stricter regulation of effluents and an outright ban on pollutants like phosphate-based detergent. Despite the nitrates that continued to run off from agriculture and short-term setbacks like the

Sandoz incident, the rivers of the Federal Republic became very much cleaner from the 1970s. Oxygen levels rose; insects, molluscs and fish returned. West German success in cleaning up its waters (and its air) paralleled what other affluent western societies achieved in the same years.[82] The decline of the coal and steel industries made this easier than it would otherwise have been. More impressive, perhaps, is how the Federal Republic was able simultaneously to forsake nuclear energy while scaling back hydro-electric projects, through more efficient use of existing energy resources coupled with investment in alternatives. One modest example of the latter (it produces enough energy to meet the annual needs of about fifty households) is the wind-powered generator that now sits by the Rhine at Karlsruhe just a short distance from the memorial stone to Johann Tulla, the man who remade the river in the nineteenth century.[83] Many fewer new dams were built after the 1970s: they faced the same opposition encountered by other environmentally questionable proposals – new runways and motorway extensions as well as atomic energy plants. Conscious efforts were made to 'green' the surrounds of existing dams; drinking-water reservoirs were managed with ecological objectives in mind, so that 'biomanipulation' of plankton and fish populations became a means of trying to reverse eutrophication where it had occurred.[84]

This was a form of 'renaturing'. Was it a realistic aim? What to do in the case of heavily regulated streams raised this question in acute form. The idea of turning back the clock had many potential advantages: aesthetic (removing concrete culverts and the appearance of canalization), ecological (recreating niches to which lost species might return) and practical (restoring wetland zones as retention basins for floodwaters).[85] Nor should the economic dimension be forgotten. Just as one reason for preserving the tropical rainforest habitat is the future human return from 'bio-prospecting', German advocates of ecologically restored rivers have drawn attention to the economic costs of degradation. Thomas Tittizer and Falk Krebs pointed to a 1985 calculation that the Rhine was capable of yielding an economic return sixty times greater, or more than seventeen million Marks.[86] Restoration efforts along these lines have been made on every large German river since the late 1970s; some smaller streams have been comprehensively 'renatured'. But undoing the effects of channel regulation is much harder than removing pollutants, and the outcomes more ambiguous. Aesthetic and ecological aims are often in conflict, and most ecologists doubt that 'artificial meanders' are the answer. Better to conserve than 'repair', to protect what you can and simply wait, rather than engage in misguided efforts to 'manufacture nature'.[87] Proposals to restore the wetland floodplains on a waterway like the Rhine create special problems, because the main river to which they would be reconnected, although cleaner than it was thirty years ago, flows very much faster than it did when the wetlands were originally severed. Could the new biotopes that had developed in what was once the meander zone of the river survive?[88] But the biggest problem over most stretches of every major artery is simply the limited room for manoeuvre, because human settlement, agriculture and industry have taken over so much of the floodplain beyond the straitjacketed river. The 'Salmon 2000' campaign for the Rhine and its tributaries offers an example of the constraints. Despite sustained efforts to preserve and restore breeding grounds, construct effective fish-ladders around obstacles like hydro-electric dams, and restock the river with eggs, the campaign has succeeded in restoring salmon to the Rhine basin but not yet created a self-sustaining population.[89]

That the experts – engineers as well as ecologists – debated the issues in terms of 'renaturing' and restoring wetland habitats was itself a striking example of how much things had changed. No one could be found any longer to defend the old gutter-and-downpipe approach to river engineering. The same was true of discussions about moorland, marsh and coastal mudflats, whose defenders were no longer an anguished minority. The question now was not whether to preserve, but how best to do it. By the 1980s the environmental imperative was built into West German public debate – on energy, recycling, land-use planning – to a degree that was probably unmatched in any other large developed nation (although not in smaller ones, from Scandinavia to New Zealand). The expectations of public and media had to be taken into account by all the parties. The political presence of the Greens had the same effect. There was no significant shift in environmental policy after the political sea-change that put Helmut Kohl's Christian Democrats back into power in the early 1980s, something that distinguished the West German Right from its counterparts in Ronald Reagan's USA and Margaret Thatcher's Britain. Kohl was widely mocked by the intelligentsia for his way with words; but unlike the American president he never offered up the thought that trees were to blame for pollution, nor is it possible to imagine him risking the public reaction he would have met by declaring (as the British prime minister did at the time of the Falklands crisis) that it was 'exciting to have a real crisis on your hands when you have spent half your political life dealing with humdrum issues like the environment'.[90] The environment was not to be taken so lightly in West Germany. It was prudent for a technocratic modernizer like Lothar Späth, Christian Democratic prime minister of Baden-Württemberg, to insist that the environment would benefit if the Federal Republic moved more quickly to a post-industrial, information-based economy.[91] And the Social Democratic candidate for Chancellor in 1990, Oskar Lafontaine, was prepared to make the environment a centre-piece of his party's electoral campaign that year until he and his party were overtaken by the collapse of the German Democratic Republic.

Implementing the Transformation of Nature in Germany

One side-effect of that collapse was what it revealed about the catastrophic state of the environment in the other Germany. Over 9000 lakes killed by acid rain, heavily contaminated groundwater, some of the most polluted rivers in Europe – that was one legacy of 'real existing socialism'. How had things come to such a pass? The answers are spread over the forty years of the GDR's existence, but the most important one can be found in what was done – or not done – in the 1970s. That was when the environmental history of East Germany reached a turning point and failed to turn.

Over the first twenty years of their hostile coexistence the two German states mimicked each other, as the initial burst of reconstruction after the 'rubble years' gave way to sustained economic growth – faster in the Federal Republic, certainly, but fast enough in the other Germany to create talk about a 'socialist economic miracle'. In both countries landscape and environment paid the price of pell-mell industrial growth. The ideological justifications were, of course, quite different in each case: the 'creative destruction' of free-market capitalism in the West, the heroic Soviet model of planned economic development in the East. As Marx had said (or one version of a protean Marx), the abolition of capitalism would end the exploitation of man by man, leaving humankind free to exploit nature. Or, as a Soviet planner characteristically put it in the 1960s, free to 'correct nature's mistakes', by which he meant redirecting the River Ob to create a reservoir larger than the Caspian Sea, melting the Arctic ice cap, and diverting the Japan current to warm the eastern USSR.[92] East German planners did not have the polar ice cap in their sights, but they acted in the same spirit. Otto Möller wrote admiringly in *The Transformation of Nature in the Soviet Union* (1952) about the grandiose Soviet plans of the late Stalin era. This was no abstract enthusiasm. Reinhold Lingner's 'Plan for Implementing the Transformation of Nature in Germany', put together in 1951–3, was modelled on the almost identically-named Soviet plan of 1948, with its large-scale proposals for river regulation and diversion, irrigation schemes and plans to alter local climate. Lingner's proposals were never put fully into effect, but GDR planning remained in thrall to Soviet gigantomania. We see it in the hectic construction of a new city like Eisenhüttenstadt on the banks of the Oder, the fixation on coal, iron and steel output, the stern impatience with fields and waterways that deviated from a rational norm. The collectivization of agriculture, to take an example, was designed to expropriate large landowners in the name of 'anti-fascism'; but it was also undertaken to prove that large is beautiful, that huge fields tilled by Soviet tractors and sprayed with insecticides from the air would outperform individual peasant holdings. 'No land reform without landscape reform', as the landscape planner Georg Bela Pniower put it.[93]

There is no better example than the symbolic significance accorded to dam-building. The showpiece here was the series of great dams constructed in the river basins of the Bode and Wipper, beginning with the Sosa 'Peace Dam' opened in 1952. Size was important to their advocates – the fact, for example, that the retaining wall of the Rappbode Dam was the highest and largest in either Germany.[94] The dams were an advertisement for 'peaceful construction' and the virtues of socialist planning, the realization of 'good and progressive ideas' that had been thwarted by the economic conflicts of the capitalist system.[95] Not least, however, the dams gave testimony to how human will and planning could 'tame and control the power of water'; for the objective was to 'shape the landscape according to large-scale perspectives'. In the words of engineer Christian Weissbach, 'we want not only to change nature but to make it useful and control it'.[96]

Crude centralized planning gave way in 1963 to the New Economic

System, or NöS. Like similar initiatives in Czechoslovakia and Hungary, the idea was to introduce more decentralized decision-making and market incentives via the price mechanism. After a bumpy career the NöS was wound up at the beginning of the 1970s for political reasons, after the crushing of the 'Prague Spring' in 1968.[97] Opinions differ on whether it could ever have succeeded, and if so, what the effects might have been. In one key respect, though, the New Economic System still danced to a Soviet tune, namely in its fascination with the opportunities presented by science and technology. Dieter Staritz has called it 'messianic'.[98] Of course, the 1960s saw a similar enthusiasm in the west for technology (including nuclear technology), and perhaps it should not surprise us that the rapture shown by British Prime Minister Harold Wilson for the 'white-hot heat of the technological revolution' should have been matched in the GDR by another political leader who sported artificial fabrics. But Walter Ulbricht's model, the East German lodestar, remained the USSR. It was a sign of the times that a rebuilt residential area of Frankfurt on the Oder should be named the Cosmonaut District, just as the visionary new lightweight car of the future was christened the *Trabant*, or 'satellite' – a name bought from the Swiss trademark holder with valuable hard currency.[99]

Whether under centralized planning or the reformed system of the 1960s that placed such hopes on science and technology, nature was cast in the same role. It was there to be beaten into submission. What this meant can best be seen on the ground. Heinz Glade was a journalist who knew how to tell a good story and give it the right political inflection. In the 1970s he published a series of sketches about the region along the River Oder, where he had travelled and reported regularly over the previous quarter-century. He tells readers, predictably enough, about the construction of Eisenhüttenstadt and the rebirth of Frankfurt on the Oder, not neglecting its semi-conductor industry. He has more to say about the Oderbruch, the place where large-scale modern land reclamation began under Frederick the Great. Glade nods to that past; but now, he argues, in a socialist Germany freed from the constraints of Prussian militarism and capitalist short-sightedness, the threat of flooding has finally become 'history' and collectivized agriculture has made the region bloom thanks to cooperative organization coupled with 'technical and scientific methods'.[100] Glade's collection returns again and again to the river, and to read him (or Christian Weissbach's writing on dams) is like revisiting the writers around the year 1900 who were entranced by the 'wonderland of technology', only now the enthusiasm for progress is dressed in socialist clothes.[101] Even the admiration for size is the same. The ship canal lift at Niederfinow is 'colossal', a testament to 'scientific and technical progress'; it shows how 'the spirit of human ingenuity outwitted nature'. Nature is often outwitted in Glade's account. A new polder by the Oder shows how 'man settled the struggle between land and water' to his own advantage; an ice-breaking ship carries on the 'battle against the forces of nature'; river engineering means that 'the Oder, often called wild and refractory, is tamed'.[102]

This instrumental approach had results that are all too familiar. Untrammelled industrial growth, collectivized agriculture that sprayed chemical fertilizer as a matter of pride, large drainage and reclamation projects, modern river engineering – together, they created a litany of problems that included not only pollution, eutrophic reservoirs and contaminated groundwater but soil erosion and falling water tables. Dead fish, algae, lakes closed to swimming, subsidence – these were the external signs, the things that could not be hidden. Officially, of course, these were supposed to be the evil side-effects of capitalism; they could not happen in the GDR. If by some mischance they had happened, then an elaborate apparatus was in place to stop them happening in the future. In principle (it was part of the black humour of the eastern bloc that announcements by the fictitious Radio Eriwan always began with the words 'In principle'), the East German environment was protected by an impressive legal and political apparatus. In 1970, not coincidentally the same year that the Brandt government was moving ahead in the West, the GDR introduced a comprehensive environmental policy. A Ministry of Environmental Protection and Water Management followed in 1971, fifteen years before its counterpart achieved full ministerial status in the Federal Republic. It issued a welter of guidelines, especially on water management. Productive enterprises had to include environmental considerations in their plans; implementation decrees rained down, setting out the obligations of different state bodies; scientists were co-opted.[103] Alas, it achieved next to nothing. There were some changes for the better – usage of chemical fertilizers and pesticides was scaled back from the end of the 1970s, ways were found in the 1980s to reduce water use in industrial processes, recycling was extensive – but the larger picture remained catastrophic through the final two decades of the regime. In 1989 groundwater near industrial Bitterfeld ('the dirtiest city in Europe') had a pH level of acidity measured at 1.9, placing it somewhere between battery acid and vinegar.[104]

Why this striking divergence between the two Germanys, especially at a time when the most celebrated initiative of the Brandt government, *Ostpolitik*, was bringing about more relaxed 'German-German' relations that included cooperation on environmental questions? Normalization of relations itself provides one part of the answer. GDR leaders always felt a pressure unlike that experienced by their Czech or Hungarian counterparts: the existence of another German state serving as a measuring stick. 'Catching up' or 'overtaking' the Federal Republic economically was an obsession in the Ulbricht era. When Erich Honecker took over from the deposed Ulbricht in May 1971 the sideways glances west continued, but the policy shifted. Now it was the satisfaction of East German consumer demands that took priority, at a time when increasing numbers had televisions and almost everyone could tune in to western channels and make comparisons. It is not surprising that so many GDR citizens were attracted by the lure of consumer goods, when their own economy – which reverted to more centralized planning in the 1970s – forced them to stand in queues for hours, created periodic shortages of items like toothbrushes and contrived to turn fish fingers into a luxury commodity.[105] Even as moderating personal consumption was becoming fashionable (in some circles) in the affluent Federal Republic, austerity in the name of conservation was hardly a timely notion in the GDR. It was true, of course, that the strains placed on the environment by individual consumption remained much lower in the east: apartments were smaller, cars were fewer, less packaging meant that GDR households generated only a third as much waste as their western counterparts.[106] But the policy of shoring up social stability by heavily subsidized energy and public transportation costs had environmentally negative effects. And attempts (for the same reason) to meet consumer demand while also subsidizing basic foodstuffs and rents meant starving the economy of investment capital for innovation. Investment levels began to fall in the 1970s, even as high levels of borrowing began to ratchet up the GDR's debt to the west.

The 1970s was when East Germany failed to restructure its economy, putting off the painful transition that occurred in western countries, including West Germany.[107] This non-event – Sherlock

Holmes's dog that failed to bark in the night – had huge consequences.
It may even have set in train the eventual undermining of the regime.
One consequence was the way that the decisions (or non-decisions)
of the 1970s worsened the environmental outlook. Antiquated metallurgical, textile and paper works continued to pollute the air and
water of the industrial south. The chemical industry, still up with the
world's leaders in the 1960s, was a major offender: its dreadful environmental record in the 1970s and 80s was one measure of growing
technological backwardness. The Buna plant at Halle poured
dangerous amounts of mercury into the River Saale every day.[108]
Rivers like the Mulde, Elbe and Werra were little better. The GDR's
dilemma in the global energy crisis of the 1970s had equally damaging
effects. When the USSR raised oil prices, the response was to compensate by burning more lignite – the brown coal that was the country's
major source of fossil fuel, but a spectacular producer of water-borne
pollution and acid rain. Lignite had a lot to do with the fact that 80
per cent of the GDR's surface water was designated as 'polluted' or
'heavily polluted' by the beginning of the 1980s.[109] The country's
naturally exiguous water resources (the most meagre in Europe) made
things worse. A given quantity of water would be used and re-used
for industrial purposes, as many as a dozen times in extreme cases
like the River Saale.[110]

The other dog that failed to bark in the 1970s, or barked but did
not bite, was the environmental movement. Party leaders faced nothing
like the political pressures exerted in the Federal Republic by Green
activists, because independent movements of this kind were banned or
(in the last years of the regime) faced constant harassment. That pattern
of suppression was set at the beginning. Conservation organizations
were dissolved in the Soviet Zone of Occupation and the authorities
with landscape responsibilities expressly rejected arguments – about
Versteppung, for example – associated with conservationists like Alwin
Seifert. This was understandable, given the role of men like Seifert under
National Socialism – although the GDR also employed landscape planners once active in the Third Reich, since they were the only ones available.[111] Ideologically, though, the very idea of landscape as an
expression of *Heimat* – so widespread in the post-war Federal Republic,
and a basis for early conservationist protests – was rejected by the
ruling party in the GDR. It is true that, as the regime recognized the
usefulness of cultivating a socialist version of *Heimat* identity, societies

for nature conservation were allowed; but they were as firmly under official control as organizations for anglers and ornithologists.[112] Then came the 1970s. Watershed years in the Federal Republic, they saw no comparable upswelling of environmental ideas and organizations in the GDR, only the establishment of party-controlled workplace and neighbourhood organizations devoted to 'constructive' tasks like treeplanting. The contrast was as sharp here as it was over the matter of industrial restructuring.

Official policy did not go entirely unquestioned. Dissident intellectuals took up the issue of ecology from a utopian socialist perspective. Wolfgang Harich's *Communism without Growth?* (1975), written in response to the Club of Rome report on the 'Limits of Growth', criticized Erich Honecker's attachment to western 'norms of consumption'. Two years later Rudolf Bahro's *The Alternative* called for the 're-establishment of ecological stability' and a 'move away from the exploitation of nature by material production towards the adaptation of production to the natural cycle'. Then, in 1980, the dissident scientist Robert Havemann published an essay collection. *Tomorrow: Industrial Society at the Crossroads* outlined an 'ecological crisis' that, in Havemann's view, capitalism could not and 'real existing socialism' would not address.[113] All three books came out in the West; not one appeared in the East. Haring and Havemann were persecuted for these and other heresies; Bahro left for the Federal Republic soon after his book appeared, where he helped to found the Green Party.

It is hard to assess the impact of critics whose books remained unpublished in the GDR, and hard for a different reason when it comes to a group whose findings were published: scientists loyal to the regime. Plenty of these addressed the country's environmental problems. There was, for example, a working group of the Saxon Academy of Sciences on the 'relations between social and natural processes'. It produced papers pointing out the 'unanticipated side-effects' of economic development in the form of 'damage to the environment' and 'damage to the biosphere'. Water pollution, nitrate run-off from agriculture that contaminated groundwater, loss of flora, 'fundamental changes' to the fish population because of 'inadequate protection of species' – all were noted. Geographers argued that large-scale planning had all too often overlooked the particularities of place: greater sensitivity was necessary, and the 'verbal recognition of landscape planning' ought to be translated into practice.[114] The hydrobiologist Dietrich Uhlmann was even more forthright. He began a paper given in October 1977 by carefully covering his flanks with a quotation from Engels:[115]

> Let us not flatter ourselves too much with our human victories over nature. For every such victory revenges itself on us. It is true that in the first instance each one has the results we had counted on, but in the second and third instances it has completely different and unanticipated effects, which all too often negate those initial results.

This could hardly be bettered as a warning against hubris, although it was obviously not a part of the dialectic that Soviet planners had taken to heart. Uhlmann suggested that Engels' strictures remained valid. The pollution of Baltic waters offered an example; so, in a different way, did that 'artificial eco-system', the reservoir. People often claimed that a reservoir could 'overcome the shortcomings of nature', argued Uhlmann, as if a natural eco-system had comparable aims; but it didn't.[116] Uhlmann had a special interest in reservoirs, and much of his paper was concerned with problems of contamination and eutrophication.[117] But he also touched critically on excessive use of chemical pesticides and the problem of acid rain. 'Buffer eco-systems' were inadequate to the pressures being placed on them; unsolved problems were mounting. Uhlmann called for measures – and here Karl Marx was mustered in support – to ensure 'that an increasingly intensive exploitation of natural resources does not lead to a deterioration of living conditions for future generations'.[118] Uhlmann ended as he began: 'For all the progress of science, no one at present knows precisely enough the limits of stability of the biosphere, which will have to be preserved on a world-wide scale for the protection of future generations'. It would be hard to imagine a complex chemical plant operating on the basis of trial and error, suggested Uhlmann; but that was exactly what was happening in large eco-systems.[119]

These warnings were sophisticated and urgent. It is true that the scientists concerned were all writing within an intellectual framework that emphasized material output – the 'optimum development of the conditions of social production and living conditions' (the GDR's version of 'well-being for all').[120] Environmental damage was wasteful and inefficient, ran the argument: better planning would allow unanticipated consequences to be anticipated. Whether, despite the obvious differences of language, this was really so different from the mind-set of scientists in the Federal Republic is unclear. East German scientists certainly read and cited the work of their western colleagues, German, British and American. Often they were concerned with very similar projects, whether it was precise land-use mapping or the biomanipulation of reservoirs. It was not so much their ideas that were different; it was the context of political and public debate, or the lack of it. Some of these scientists held leading posts: Dietrich Uhlmann was a member of the Scientific Advisory Board for Mathematics and the Natural Sciences.[121] And no doubt some of their strictures were heeded: chemical pesticide use was scaled back. From the point of view of the ruling party, however, their role was to provide 'constructive' advice, no more. After all, senior figures in the party knew perfectly well that pollution and groundwater contamination were serious problems. The scientists had no scope for independent activity if they wanted to keep their positions. Their papers appeared in the pages of learned journals, but open public discussion of the issues was missing. In 1982, data on environmental damage were abruptly classified because they had become so damning; official public debate on the environment was bland.[122] Worried scientists might grumble in private. One western scholar who conducted interviews in the 1980s found genuine environmentalists among the GDR intelligentsia, even a sense that they formed a group with common goals. But they remained in the closet.[123]

The one partial exception to this straitjacket was the emergence of a small grassroots movement that sheltered under the umbrella of the Protestant Church. This went back to the early 1970s, when the Ecclesiastical Research Centre in Wittenberg took up the environmental issue. It organized lectures, mounted a travelling exhibition and later published a newsletter on the 'man–nature conflict'.[124] The Church also provided a safe haven for independent activists. A degree of relative autonomy allowed it to offer protective cover to groups that would otherwise have been too vulnerable to survive. The church provided meeting places, ancient mimeograph machines, even low-level employment for environmentalists who had lost their jobs. Compared to their counterparts in the West, these groups were obviously constrained in what they could undertake. They circulated newsletters, made occasional public efforts to highlight a particular scandal. Individual members also took 'small steps' in their personal lives that can be compared to the pursuit of alternative life-styles in the West. They used fewer household chemicals, practised organic gardening, deliberately limited their own consumption. Private decisions like this could assume a public face, as they did when an ecological group in Dresden rewrote the Ten Commandments in its newsletter (the expanded Tenth Commandment read: 'We must alter our attitude towards earthly goods so that it is consistent with environmental sustainability').[125] But these organizations remained small and isolated, with little public impact, another example of the largely private satisfactions (in this case ascetic) available in the niches of a repressive society.

Environmental opposition intensified in the last years of the GDR. Many new groups were formed around 1983–4, a mirror image of the upsurge in environment-and-peace activism in the Federal Republic. Chernobyl gave further urgency to the cause. That was the year, 1986, when the Environment Library was founded in the basement of the Zion Church in Berlin, providing a home for poetry readings, concerts, talks and guest lectures by western visitors that attracted as many as 300 people. East German environmentalists extended their contacts with Green politicians and sympathetic media in the West, but also with the network of East European groups known as Greenway. In 1988 a group that called itself Arche broke away from the loose network around the Environment Library and followed a more radical course. The authorities responded to the environmental movement with carrot and stick. It tried cooptation into the officially sponsored Society for Nature and Environment. This 'bridge between party and society' gathered 60,000 members by 1986, but failed to halt the growth of independent groups. Individuals were also harassed and environmental newsletters seized, a strategy that culminated in a raid on the Environment Library in 1987. But outright repression threatened to give more publicity to environmental organizations, especially when news of it was beamed back to the GDR by western media. In the last years of the regime the Stasi moved towards a systematic policy of infiltration designed to foment divisions in the movement and sabotage environmentalism from within.

Only after the collapse of the GDR did Stasi records reveal the bitter truth. The security police had 'informal collaborators' within the Environment Library; it had even promoted the breakaway of the Arche group in 'Operation Wedge'. Stasi infiltration continued until the regime fell. Its impact was felt even longer than that, for each new revelation about Stasi dirty tricks caused disarray and weakened the environmental movement during the transition to a united Germany.[126]

EPILOGUE:
WHERE IT ALL BEGAN

In 1995 Günter Grass published a controversial novel about German reunification.[1] *Too Far Afield* folds nearly 200 years of German history into 650 pages, but at its core is a double narrative that suggests parallels between the greedy materialism that followed reunification and the speculative boom that followed German unification in 1871. The figure who links these two eras is the nineteenth-century novelist and travel writer, Theodor Fontane. *Ein Weites Feld* takes its title from the catchphrase used by one of Fontane's characters, and Grass's main protagonist is a man who identifies so closely with 'the Immortal One' that all his friends call him 'Fonty'. He is Theo Wuttke, a seventy-year-old former East German archivist and sometime lecturer for the Cultural Union, an independent-minded man who spurned advancement in the party and used his lectures on Fontane to deliver coded criticism of the first German Workers' and Peasants' State.

Grass's book is about landscape and German historical memory. He uses Theodor Fontane to show the reader how history is imprinted on the land. We follow Theo Wuttke as he travels through East Germany in the 1950s and 60s to give his lectures, or goes on hikes and steamship excursions with his daughter. And we look over 'Fonty's' shoulder as he travels mentally through the same landscape a century earlier, to the locations where Fontane set his novels and the places described with such care and artfulness in *Rambles Through the March Brandenburg*. With the grey but familiar landscape of the GDR disappearing, Wuttke/'Fonty' makes another series of journeys through the German present and the Prussian past: to Neuruppin and Neuhardenberg, to the Baltic islands and the waterland of the Spreewald. Many of these journeys are undertaken in the company of his one-time shadow and protector, the former Stasi man Hoftaller. One day they drive to the Oder in Hoftaller's Trabant, 'the incomparable cardboard car'. They want to gaze across the river at Poland and visit the scene of Fontane's first novel, *Before the Storm*, set in the Oderbruch – 'a mighty tome which, like the Oder Delta, branched off in far too many directions'.[2] From the western embankment of the river that marked the German border with the east, 'Fonty' points to places that framed German history. To the north lay Küstrin, the ruined fortress that once guarded the Oder, where the later Frederick the Great was imprisoned by his father. To the south-east were Silesia and the uplands of the Riesengebirge where the Oder had its origins. And due east lay 'the lost Vistula region'. Two old men rehearse all the familiar arguments about Germany and the east; then they argue about whether those arguments are finally over. There is no longer any eavesdropper to hear them, no human listener anyway: 'These words and more were heard by the Oder River, which was in no hurry, after a dry summer had left its water level low'.[3]

The melancholy of this eastern border river pervades recent writing on the Oder. In 1992 the photographer Joachim Richau published a book of black and white photographs of the river, full of still broken bridges and abandoned customs posts like the Zollbrücke on the northern edge of the Oderbruch (still abandoned when I cycled past it a few years later). 'Only a thin skin has grown here over the wounds of war', wrote Wolfgang Kil in the text that accompanied the book.[4] The lands on the western bank of the Oder were indeed among the bloodiest of Europe's killing fields as the final battles for Berlin were fought in April 1945. The war memorial on the Seelow Heights is a reminder of that; so are the bodies that still come to light. Erwin Kowalke, who made it his life's work to find and identify them, has recovered the remains of thousands of victims.[5] Before 1990 the Oder was melancholy in East German eyes for another reason. It marked the GDR border – not, of course, a tightly sealed border like the one that cut them off from the west, but still a reminder of their confinement, always coloured by awareness of that other border: 'Here, too', says Wolfgang Kil, 'a border landscape became a special zone that one did not enter without a trace of anxiety'. Anglers on the Polish side of the river, viewed from the great diked embankment on the German side, gave off a sense of ease and naturalness that was not to be found at home; the occasional passing barge seemed 'extra-territorial'. Concrete posts marked red-black-gold and bearing the insignia of GDR sovereignty could be found at some distance from the Oder, a tribute to the vagaries of the river. 'Anyone who went past them down to the water had to think about whether he was doing something that was not allowed. Only ducks and great crested grebes, storks and herons had no inkling of politics'.[6]

This glimpse of wild birds wheeling over a wild river is how Wolfgang Kil remembered the Oder. It is also the image of the river we find in Christa Wolf's novel from the 1970s, *Kindheitsmuster* or 'patterns of childhood', a book in which history and memory are fused with landscape as closely as they are in Günter Grass's work thirty years later. The autobiographical main character crosses the Oder to visit the town where she grew up: 'G., formerly L.' (Gorzów Wielkopolski, once the German town of Landsberg on the Warthe). On the return journey she has 'a view of the Oder River, losing itself in meadowlands and thickets of willow, an eastern river, wide, untamed, and silted up'.[7] This image of the river, untamed and 'eastern', persisted after reunification. In November 1999 Karl Schlögel published a long article on the Oder in the *Frankfurter Allgemeine Zeitung*.[8] The tone is set by a large photograph of the ruined fortress at Küstrin, a 'reminiscence of Prussia between the Oder and Warthe Marshes', now overgrown and lapped by reed-filled waters. Schlögel, like Grass, takes his lead from Theodor Fontane, whose *Rambles* described the once lively steamship traffic on the Oder and the quayside bustle at Frankfurt on the Oder. But not any more; the steamers and barges had gone, along with other claims to human mastery:

> Nature has returned to the river, from which it had been expelled by centuries of work and industry. And so today the rare chartered steamer glides through a landscape that is otherwise to be found only in eastern Europe, on the Vistula, on the Memel – on the Amazon. Herons, cranes, sea eagles and other rare creatures frolic close by. But what we have before us is not 'pure nature'. The paradise is of more recent vintage. The precondition of the new wilderness was the desolation created by human catastrophes. The advance of nature followed the retreat of humans. The wetlands expanded into the areas evacuated by people.

The image of an 'Amazonian landscape', once a familiar shorthand for the unclaimed Oder Marshes, is one the author likes so much that he uses it twice. And this by the banks of the Oder, of all places, where the history of modern German land reclamation began in the reign of Frederick the Great. If Schlögel is to be believed, we have come full circle.

But this is no wilderness, old or new. The Oder, 100 miles shorter than it was in the eighteenth century thanks to a relentless series of 'corrections', has not ceased to be a working river. It is true that traffic was severely curtailed after 1945, even after hundreds of wrecked vessels were finally removed, and the powerful German-controlled axis of trade that existed before 1939 was destroyed for ever. But the navigable Oder created largely by Prussian hydrological engineers still carried the industrial output from what was now Polish Silesia down to the Baltic port of Szczecin, the former Stettin. The river also served that East German tribute to Stalinist industrialization, Eisenhüttenstadt, built on its banks next to the Oder–Spree canal. Further downstream, on the northern edge of the Oderbruch, vessels passed between the river and the Finow canal, their movement eased by post-war dredging.[9] The stretch of the Lower Oder that most resembles the 'wild', 'untamed' eastern river described by Christa Wolf and Karl Schlögel is the one that flows alongside the Oder Marshes. Walk or cycle along it and you can see the wild birds, register the small fishing boats and a tranquillity that makes the river seem quite different from the Rhine or any other west German artery. But the only view of the Oder is from the high dike that runs along its whole length; and this more 'natural' river is in fact the Petri canal, the great cut that was made 250 years ago to drain the Oderbruch. It is an artificial waterway that has acquired a patina of naturalness with age.

Much the same could be said of the Oderbruch itself. Since reunification, the 'naturalness' has been a selling-point. The Oderbruch is an area where 'nature is still intact', according to a collection of photographs published in 1992.[10] 'Anyone who is searching for untouched nature' should visit the Oderbruch, wrote Erwin Nippert three years later; for this was 'one of the last river wetland landscapes in eastern Germany!', in fact a 'singular natural paradise'.[11] Almost every tourist pamphlet describes the yellow carpet of *Adonisröschen*, or helleboraster, that covers the area in spring, and most mention the breeding pairs of rare black storks and corncrakes. Yet these same works will also tell you that the Oderbruch was drained by Frederick the Great in the eighteenth century – although not that helleboraster is a Eurasian transplant in this 'natural paradise'. The Oderbruch today is what humans have made it. Many conservationists want to protect its natural beauty – seeing, perhaps, that 'little green space fenced off' that Karl Immermann longed for almost two centuries ago.[12] Let us see things straight, however. What is at stake here is not 'untouched' or 'intact' nature, but the question of 'renaturing' the Oderbruch – what this might mean, and how far it might go. The details are different, but the underlying issues are the same ones that confront planners, engineers, farmers, ecologists and tourist offices on the Rhine.

Only after reunification did these issues come to the fore. The Oderbruch in the GDR years was dedicated to intensive agricultural production at any price. Conservation came a very distant second. Kurt Kretschmann, who directed the House of Nature Conservation in Bad Freienwalde, was concerned largely with 'beautification': the landscaping of a chicken farm in Wriezen, the laying out of ornamental gardens on the village greens of Altwriezen and Neuküstrinchen. There was nothing here for the corncrakes and black storks; in fact Kretschmann's attachment to beautifying the landscape meant taking 'wasteland' in hand, which was why he earned the praise of a party journalist like Heinz Glade in the 1970s.[13] Things changed in the 1980s, when the ornithologist Martin Müller helped to establish a Wetlands Area of National Significance in the Oderbruch, which secured the flyways of the many migratory birds (including an estimated 80,000 northern geese) who used it every autumn and spring.[14] The waning years of the GDR also brought members of East Berlin's Prenzlauer Berg intelligentsia to the Oderbruch as permanent or part-time residents, artists and writers who were likely to sympathize with conservationist aims.[15] But it was the end of the regime that posed the hard questions. Agricultural collectives disappeared and unemployment rose. It stood at twenty-one per cent in the 1990s, more than two-thirds comprising women. Opportunities for the young were limited and the local population showed a downward trend. How would the Oderbruch reinvent itself under the new dispensation?[16]

One answer was a basic restructuring of agriculture, the bedrock of the local economy ever since the land was reclaimed 250 years earlier. This meant a decline in the areas given over to potatoes and sugar beet, an increase in those devoted to oil-producing plants and legumes.[17] Greater specialization was the hallmark of new private ownership. Others, however, saw the opportunity to make a more radical shift away from arable farming. A zone along the river could, it was argued, be given over to grazing. Behind this lay the idea of restoring riparian wetlands and joining up existing conservation areas. But the weight of agricultural interests scotched these green dreams.[18] The Action Group formed by the local districts in 1994 steered a middle course that emphasized an 'environmentally sustainable agriculture as the dominant form of economic activity', buttressed by agricultural processing industries, the encouragement of small businesses and a new service sector in which tourism would have a large place. Money from the state of Brandenburg and the EU was used to foster local crafts and make the Oderbruch more attractive to visitors. Now it was possible to travel there all the way from Berlin without setting food on land thanks to refurbished canals. Cycle paths were extended, tourist offices opened, new signage went up to assist visitors to these confusingly uniform flatlands. Buildings that had once housed tractors, symbol of Soviet-era collectivization, were converted into stables; former administrative offices became guest houses.[19]

This judicious combination of revitalized agriculture and aesthetic make-over was threatened in the summer of 1997 by an old enemy: floodwaters.[20] They came just 50 years after the last 'once-in-a-century-flood' in 1947 and exactly 250 years after the beginning of Frederick the Great's reclamation work in the eighteenth century, celebration of which was swept away by the newest Oder floods. A nineteenth-century commentator like Walter Christiani would have said that the river was 'rattling its chains'.[21] The immediate cause of the floodwaters was exceptionally heavy rain at the beginning of July in the Czech and Polish catchment areas of the Oder. Deforestation and stream regulation in these upland regions sped the passage of water down to the main river, a problem all too familiar both before and after the draining of the Oderbruch. By 10 July substantial areas of the Czech Republic and Poland were under water, thousands were homeless and thirty-nine people had died. The floods would eventually inundate 1200 towns and villages, claiming more than 100 lives. By 13 July the crest of the high waters flooded Wrocław, the former Breslau; the following day the first level of alarm was announced for areas of Brandenburg bordering the river. On 17 July the floodwaters reached Ratzdorf, the point where the Neisse flows into the Oder, and measurements showed the river at 6.2 metres, almost 3.5 metres above normal summer levels. The 'battle against the flood' in Brandenburg would continue for more than three weeks, prolonged by further heavy rain in the upland catchment area that created a second crest of high water.[22]

There were nearly 100 miles of dike along the Oder in Brandenburg, last heightened and strengthened in 1982. The dikes were in good condition, but now had to withstand water pressure that reached six tons per square metre. These were earthwork dikes that became waterlogged and in some places began to break up. Hundreds of small leaks developed and at a dozen points the dike threatened to fail completely. In two places it did. Both failures occurred south of Frankfurt on Oder, the first at Brieskow-Finkenheerd on 23 July, where a 200-foot breach of the dike soon widened to over 650 feet, followed the next day by a further collapse at Aurith. The Ziltendorf valley, from which inhabitants had been evacuated, was flooded. On 27 July the record high water reached Frankfurt, where sandbags saved the city. The Oderbruch then became the focus of attention. Because the whole area was a giant polder that lay below the normal level of the river, any major dike breach would mean that what happened in the Ziltendorf valley would also happen in the Oderbruch, but on a much larger scale. This was where much of the effort of 30,000 Bundeswehr soldiers and 20,000 civilians was concentrated in the closing days of July, where helicopters dropped sandbags into the weakened sections of dike that threatened to collapse near Reitwein in the southern Oderbruch and Hohenwutzen to the north. Northern areas of the Oderbruch were evacuated and on 31 July the dike at Hohenwutzen, partly breached in many places, was given only a one in ten chance of holding. But it did. This was the 'miracle of Hohenwutzen'. The fall-back dikes and cross-dikes desperately constructed in case the main defences failed were not needed after all, and on 9 August the 6,500 evacuees from the Oderbruch were allowed to return home.

The drama of the battle against the 'forces of nature' created two heroes: Brandenburg's Environment Minister, Matthias Platzeck, hailed as a modern-day 'dike master', and 'flood general' Hans-Peter von Kirchbach.[23] Media coverage also led to a huge outpouring of public donations, the largest ever for a domestic disaster. Nightly TV news bulletins during the three-week struggle with the floodwaters were credited with dismantling (at least temporarily) the 'wall in the mind' that still divided East and West Germans. The efforts of uniformed and volunteer helpers were given permanent recognition by a monument, Matthias Körner's 'Balance of Forces', unveiled in the Oderbruch village of Neuranft in August 1998. But beyond the sense of relief tinged with self-congratulation there was a darker side to the July 1997 events. No German lives were lost in the floods, but they left behind dead fish, temporarily contaminated water, eight million sandbags that had to be cleared away, ruined homes, waterlogged fields, and costs that ran upwards of 600 million Marks, or 300 million euros.[24] What some were calling the 'flood of the millennium' also posed hard questions for the future. How could a recurrence be prevented? Was dike-building enough?

The hero of the hour, Environment Minister Platzeck, gave an answer that could hardly have been clearer. Brandenburg was lucky; it had 'got away with a black eye':[25]

> A real catastrophe was avoided here only because 650,000 hectares were flooded along the upper reaches of the river. Without this unwitting retention, water levels would have risen considerably higher. Brandenburg's flood-threatened areas would not have had the slightest chance. We are now reaping the results of the fact that over the last hundred years the retention areas on the Oder have shrunk by 80 per cent from 780,000 to 75,000 hectares.

The flood retention zone in the national park on the Lower Oder (just downstream from the Oderbruch) had proved its value when put to the test. In the Lower Oder valley the danger had been least acute where the swollen waters were able to spread themselves; the greatest threat was where the dike ran directly along the river. Platzeck was not alone in taking this view, nor was it a position staked out only by the Greens. Shortly after the floods the Brandenburg state parliament passed a resolution that 'we have to harmonize our actions as much as possible with our natural environment'.[26] But how much was 'as much as possible'? In the immediate aftermath of July 1997 the responsible ministries of state gave serious thought to 'sacrificing' stretches of the floodplain that had been claimed for human use – the Ziltendorf valley, perhaps even areas of the Oderbruch. Certainly giving the Ziltendorf valley back to the river would have made sense, because its farmland had been damaged and its houses destroyed. The three villages in the low-lying valley could have been rebuilt at a safe distance (which was, after all, what had always been done in the past when a reservoir was deemed essential). The danger posed by future floods would have been

16. Steamships share the river with other craft on the Rhine at Cologne in this illustration from Lucy Hill's *Rhine Roamings* (Boston, 1880).

17. The festive opening of the new Remscheid Dam in June 1893.

18. Otto Intze, 'grand master' of modern German dam-building.

19. The Bleiloch Dam on the River Saale, built 1925–32.

20. The insects discover the dam wall in Ernst Candèze's *Die Talsperre* (Leipzig, 1901).

21. Artificial waterfall at the Frankfurt Electro–Technical Exposition of 1891, which powered the first overland transmission of electricity.

22. Villagers pose in front of their homes in Kleinblumenberg in September 1908, before the flooding of the Neye valley the following year.

23. The breached Möhne Dam, through which water still poured some twelve hours after the attack in the early hours of 17 May 1943.

24. German 'resettlers' in occupied Poland, 1941.

25. Three Hitler Youth gaze dreamily at a barge on an unnamed canal. This 1936 photo suggests how landscapes shaped by humans were romanticized in the Third Reich.

26. Hitler in Schleswig-Holstein to celebrate the opening of the Hermann Göring Polder.

27. Konrad Meyer (*second from left*) shows Gauleiter Fritz Bracht (*right*) a model village during the 1942 exhibition on 'Planning and Construction in the East'.

28. Alwin Seifert's collection of conservationist essays, *Im Zeitalter des Lebendigen* (Planegg, 1941), included this photo of the Vistula near Dirschau – 'a river of the steppe', as his caption calls it.

29. The Künkel family farmhouse at Gennin on the hills above the Warthe Valley, land that became Polish after 1945.

30. Agnes Miegel,
'Mother East Prussia'

31. The once powerful Prussian fortress of Küstrin in 1997, partly 'reclaimed' by nature.

removed, the pressure on other areas relieved, and all at a cost relatively low in relation to the long-term benefits.[27]

But too many obstacles stood in the way of this radical option. The
politicians feared large claims for damages if arable and building land
was converted into wetland meadows. Loss of image was also involved.
Promises had been made in the immediate crisis that people would be
returned home and the situation restored to normal as quickly as
possible. This narrowed the room for manoeuvre later. Even environmentalists were caught up in the drama of the event in ways that trapped
them in the logic of the status quo. Ecologists and conservationists
along the Lower Oder not only acted as dike 'runners' and sandbag-
fillers in the battle for the Oderbruch, which was understandable
enough; some initially spoke of an unavoidable 'natural disaster' – as
if there was anything 'natural' about floodwaters that arrived as quickly
as they did because of deforestation and mountain stream regulation,
and posed the local threat they did precisely where humans had corsetted
the Oder most tightly.[28]

What emerged from the 1997 floods was a dual-track policy of
restoring the dikes, coupled with incremental steps to tackle the flood
risk through measures more in harmony with the natural environment.
Damaged dikes were quickly repaired, then a programme was launched
to strengthen them along their entire 100-mile length in Brandenburg.
By August 2004, when the work was two-thirds complete, it had cost
around 125 million euros. The programme is expected to be finished
by 2006. The Oderbruch section of dike between Reitwein in the south
and Hohensaaten in the north is complete, although delayed in 2000
by the huge amounts of Second World War ordnance, some of it still
unexploded, that was uncovered – along with the remains of thirty-
three soldiers – when the engineers went to work ('you can't repair a
dike that is full of bombs and grenades').[29] The new dikes are designed
to withstand a 200-year flood, and a freeboard on top is supposed to
make them proof even against a once-in-a-millennium event.

The second policy track, the more 'natural' method of flood protection favoured by environmentalists, is also underway. In 2002 the
President of the Brandenburg State Office of the Environment, Matthias
Freude, announced that the dikes would be moved back from the river
in the Oder-Spree region south of Frankfurt on Oder, near Neuzelle
and Aurith, creating a wetlands area of about 1,500 acres that would
also serve as a future flood retention basin. Work began the following

year.[30] The straitjacketing of the river had now been loosened at a
second point – the first was the Lower Oder Valley National Park
downstream from the Oderbruch, praised five years earlier by Matthias
Platzeck for doing its job when deliberately flooded in July 1997 to
relieve the pressure elsewhere.[31] This environmentally sensitive
approach to flood protection has been widely recognized and practised
in recent years. Projects that restore river wetlands on ecological grounds
and to create retention basins have been supported by the EU all across
Europe from the Danube to the Netherlands. Within Germany the same
policy has been pursued in the wake of the Elbe floods.[32] In 2003 the
Federal Foundation for the Environment established 'Floods and Nature
Conservation' as one of its key projects, working with generally sympathetic state and federal authorities to 'renature' river systems as a means
of serving this dual purpose. The Foundation's pilot schemes have
spanned Germany, from Johann Tulla's old stamping grounds of the
Rhine and Kinzig in the west to the rivers of the former GDR.[33] It is
an appealing policy, undoing some of the malign effects wrought by
earlier generations of hydrological engineers and enhancing flood
protection into the bargain. As we saw in the case of the Rhine, however,
it is an approach that has its own snares and delusions, and one that
even in a country as environmentally sensitive as the Federal Republic
has to work within the constraints – the historical ballast – of what
has been created in the past.

The Oderbruch is a perfect illustration. It looks in some ways like
a green paradise, 'green' in the modern sense of environmentally friendly.
The LEADER action group formed ten years ago by local politicians
looks to develop the infrastructure in ways that are 'environmentally
sustainable', take account of ecological perspectives and develop eco-
tourism. The Brandenburg state government believes that the Oderbruch
contains areas that are 'very valuable for nature and landscape conservation' and is looking for ways to 'renature' its waterways.[34] An
example is the project commissioned in 2002 from the water consultancy firm WASY to raise groundwater levels in the Lieper polder,
designed among other things to counteract drying-out effects – no one
any longer calls this *Versteppung* – and find less obtrusive alternatives
to water-retention weirs on local waterways.[35] A five-year support initiative to foster local employment, part of the InnoRegio (Innovative
Impulses for the Regions) programme funded by the Federal Ministry
of Education and Research, emphasizes ecological policies in the

Oderbruch and builds these into its plans to work with youth there. It talks about organic agriculture, alternative energy, pilot schemes for 'environmental technologies', 'ecologically and economically appropriate community projects'. The green message shines through the clotted bureaucratic prose about communicative action structures, innovative dynamics, and local identity in an 'ever faster changing society'.[36] No wonder that BUNDjugend, a Berlin group that works to encourage environmental awareness among young Germans, sends parties to Wilhelmsaue in the northern Oderbruch to participate in seminars and earn their 'eco-licenses'.[37] And no wonder, either, that the area has become a haven for green-minded artists and intellectuals.

But this is a green paradise that has to earn its way. When Frederick the Great looked down and exulted in the greenery created when the Oderbruch was drained, or when Ernst Breitkreutz celebrated this 'green land', they were drawing on another meaning of the word green – the green garden, land that had been made fertile and productive. That is still the reality of the Oderbruch, where 87 per cent of all land is devoted to agriculture, and neither the LEADER Action Group nor the Brandenburg authorities can ignore it. As the state government notes, this is a 'historically and economically valuable cultivated landscape' with fruitful soil, and it adds: 'A renaturing of the waterways must adapt itself to the circumstances of the cultivated land that has developed here'.[38] But one effect of agricultural cultivation, most of which is not organic, has been the pollution of local waterways. The Old Oder, the network of streams that remains as a residue of Frederick's reclamation and gives the Oderbruch its character, looks idyllic; but it receives heavy doses of fertilizer run-off and household waste. The fact that the water is slow-moving and is not flushed out by the main river makes matters worse. In the early twenty-first century the picturesque Old Oder was dirtier than the Rhine. Between Seelow and Neutrebbin it had a water quality of II–III (critically burdened with pollutants), between Neutrebbin and Wriezen it improved a little to class II (moderately burdened); but from Wriezen until it emptied into the main river, the Old Oder was designated class III, or 'heavily polluted'.[39]

There was another reminder, disturbing for many, of what the area owed to its Frederician origins. From the beginning the reclaimed Oderbruch served as a laboratory. Animal species as well as people came together from all over Europe; new breeds, crops and rotations were tried out, imitating the new model husbandry of eighteenth-century

England. It was no coincidence that the pioneer of German scientific agriculture, Daniel Albrecht Thaer, should have settled in the Oderbruch, with its fields of clover, rape and caraway and its new varieties of peas.[40] The modern equivalent of this agronomic zeal is the use of genetically modified crops, and it is perhaps unsurprising that the Oderbruch should once again be the experimental site. At the end of the 1990s the owner of the TIBO agricultural business south of Bad Freienwalde, Siegfried Manthey, planted a field with genetically modified maize from the American multinational Monsanto. This was a strain of the crop injected with the bacterium *Bacillus thuringiensis*, designed to poison the corn borer, which had been eating its way through the maize fields of the Federal Republic from south to north.

The potential benefits are obvious, and even a leading scientific advocate of environmentalism like Edward O. Wilson accepts that genetically modified crops will 'almost certainly play an important role in the evergreen revolution' of agricultural production.[41] Supporters of the new technology expressed impatience with German and EU bans on transgenic crops grown for sale to the public, blaming 'eco-fundamentalists' for delaying the spread of a humanitarian marvel of science.[42] Yet there were grounds for the concern expressed by German Environment Minister, Jürgen Trittin, and the head of the Federal Office of Nature Conservation, Hartmut Vogtmann. Both asked questions that were similar to those raised by environmentalists in the Oderbruch, like the Barnim Action Group against Genetic Technology.[43] Unlike earlier forms of hybridization, genetic engineering is performed across widely different species: the results of transgenetic foods or feedstuffs are hard to predict. Unintended secondary effects, such as genes that act as allergens or carcinogens, are at least a possibility. Despite attempts to establish buffer zones, transgenes can also escape from modified crops into wild crops of the same species – from Siegfried Manthey's five-acre field of modified maize to his other 1000 acres of maize fields, or the 31,000 acres of the crop grown elsewhere in the Oderbruch. Whether transgenetic hybrids could in fact overwhelm wild varieties is unknown (the experience of past competition between hybrids and wild strains suggests not), but the question remains open. What has been established is that genetically modified maize can damage biodiversity when *Bacillus thuringiensis* is carried by the wind to plants on which the caterpillars of monarch butterflies feed, seriously reducing their numbers. It is, as always, the unintended consequences that have to be summoned by an effort of the imagination, the possible future costs that have to be set against the confident promises of the present. That is what Edward O. Wilson means when he worries that genetically modified crops might lead us to be 'trapped in a Faustian bargain that threatens freedom and security'.[44]

It is a lesson worth taking to heart in the Oderbruch, whose very existence is based on a Faustian struggle to 'bring the earth back to itself' in the eighteenth century. This is a floodplain; what humans have made of it is provisional. The landscape of the Oderbruch and the different ways of life that are lived there would not exist without protection from the river. Farmers and environmental activists, Siegfried Manthey and his opponents in the Barnim Action Group, all live in the shadow of the dike. That is why the State of Brandenburg is careful to insist that 'renaturing' the waterways can 'proceed only in small steps and in unison with flood protection'. An official survey refers to the 'total dependence of the people who live there [the Oderbruch] on the firmness of the dike'.[45] But that is not quite true, or not the whole truth. The floods that threaten the Oderbruch come from upstream, and whether or not they threaten its existence also depends on what happens to the river's swollen waters upstream. In July 1997, even the dike breaches that inundated the small Ziltendorf valley had an immediate effect in lowering water levels downriver. But the real saviour of the Oderbruch in 1997, as Matthias Platzeck pointed out, was the huge area of the Oder floodplain that the river 'reclaimed' in the Czech Republic and Poland. If the river had not been able to flow into those 270,000 acres, there is little doubt that it would have flowed instead into the Oderbruch. Engineers estimated that the high water in Brandenburg would have crested as much as six feet higher but for the flooding upstream.[46] It was only natural justice that more than half of the German charitable donations for flood assistance were passed on to Czech and Polish victims.[47]

Peter Jochen Winters has suggested that the disaster 'strengthened the feelings of community between Germans and their neighbours in Poland and the Czech Republic'.[48] This was no doubt true in immediate, humanitarian terms, but the aftermath of 1997 also created the potential for conflict. Feelings of superiority towards their neighbours across the 'German–Polish peace border' had been common in the former GDR. They were tacitly encouraged by party bosses in the era of Solidarność. Unification did not dispel the sentiments; quite the contrary. Then came the Polish response to the floods. The 'Odra 2006' programme proposed higher dikes, dredging and further stream-bed regulation to improve navigability, as well as new measures to exploit the river as a source of power. The transportation and environment ministers of Brandenburg immediately issued strong protests: the further straitjacketing of the Middle Oder would inevitably speed the water faster downstream, where the next major flood would devastate German land. Hostility to the Polish plan, which was shared by environmental groups, created a sensitive political situation. Brandenburg Environment Minister Platzeck and the then Federal Environment Minister Angela Merkel met with their Polish counterparts in the spa town of Miedzyzdroje, where they tried to resolve their differences. Platzeck referred to 'difficult discussions with the Polish side'.[49]

This was a new, ironic twist on an old story. Historically, it was Germans who liked to talk about the 'conquest of nature'. Frederick the Great had replaced Slav fishing people with German cultivators when he drained marshlands like the Oderbruch. Nineteenth- and twentieth-century Germans liked to see themselves as the dike-builders, superior to the 'feckless' Slavs who were supposedly unable to shape their own landscape, a cultural reflex that found its darkest expression in the genocidal hubris of National Socialism.[50] Traces of that old contempt survived in the anti-Polish slur, familiar to anyone who had grown up in East Germany, that labelled economic mismanagement as *polnische Wirtschaft*. Now it was Polish plans for dike-building and river regulation that fluttered opinion in Berlin because of a fear – justifiable enough – that these would make future floods more threatening to German land and lives. But perhaps this was only a variation on the old theme. For Bernhard Hummel, the 'chauvinist undertones' in the German response consisted in the unvoiced belief that German reclaimed land was ultimately more valuable than the Polish variety, which was why the latter should continue to be 'sacrificed' to save the former.[51]

There were undeniably chauvinist undertones on the German side (although not only there). But compared with the history of most of the 250 years covered by this book, what is striking about contemporary debates over the Oder – and a source of hope – is the extent to which they transcend old divisions. In a world where nation states are not the only actors, other voices can be heard. One is the international action committee 'Time for the Oder' (*Zeit für die Oder*), a coalition

of more than thirty environmental, conservation and leisure organizations in Germany, Poland and the Czech Republic. It brings together
groups in Berlin and along the German Oder with others in Wrocław,
Opóle and Jelenia Góra, Decin and Ostrava. The coalition calls for
environmentally friendly forms of flood protection, above all by 'renaturing' the river to restore riparian wetlands. It rejects 'Odra 2006'
as yet another futile technological fix that only transfers the problems
downstream and creates new ones for the future.[52] 'Time for the Oder'
ends its plea for a change of heart by urging adherence to the guidelines of another transnational organization: the European Union. There
is irony in this as well. Almost 50 years earlier, in 1956–64 it was
members of the incipient EU – Germany, France and Luxembourg –
that cooperated to drive through canalization of the Mosel against the
cries of nature conservationists.[53] Now, enlarged to the east and
committed to a very different view of river management, the EU was
a key broker in working out a more environmentally sustainable future
for the Oder valley that would break the cycle of hydrological leapfrog. Manfred Stolpe, then Prime Minister of Brandenburg, was right
when he argued in 1997 that this was a 'European challenge'.

Within the European Union, in discussions at the International
Commission on the Protection of the Oder, and in bilateral talks between
the three countries involved, the outlines of the solution have become
plain. It will not come from any one country acting alone, whether
Germany, Poland or the Czech Republic, and it will not come from
viewing the river as an enemy to be conquered by forcing it into an
even tighter and faster channel. Two sets of measures are called for.
The first and more important will have to occur in the upland catchment areas of the Oder. There was a time, a century ago, when civil
engineers like Otto Intze thought that building dams in the Central
European highlands was the solution to flooding: meeting the threatening waters on a 'battleground' of human choosing, as Intze put it.
But there was widespread and justified scepticism about this 'solution'
even in the 1920s and 30s, as we have seen.[54] Far better, it has long
been recognized, would be a successful afforestation programme that
allowed upland areas to retain much more of the heavy precipitation
that now reaches the lowland plain so quickly. Undoing the regulation
of mountain streams, another of yesterday's futures, would have the
same effect. The water from highland downpours would still cause
water levels to rise; in fact they would rise for longer. But the crest of

the high water would be lower as the river worked its way more slowly through the lowlands.

It is in the middle and lower reaches of the Oder (and of other rivers) that the second set of measures need to be undertaken: moving back the dikes or other defences in order to 'renature' some areas of the floodplain, which would be restored to riparian wetlands and serve as flood retention basins. This policy, suggested by a few people after the central European floods of the 1890s but dismissed by engineers as 'unthinkable', has become the common sense of today.[55] Moving back dikes will be very costly – *sauteuer* is the undiplomatic term reportedly used in the German Ministry of the Environment. The expectation is that the Federal Republic and the EU are likely to foot most of the bill, running to billions of euros.[56] But the technocratic pipedreams pursued in earlier generations were very expensive, too, and because their promises of security proved illusory the bills fell due again and again. The financial issue is not the only difficulty, of course. On the middle and lower reaches of the Oder, where agriculture, industry and residential property have colonized the floodplain, whose interests will be sacrificed? Once, and not so long ago, measured by the timescale of this book, it was commonplace for villages to be swept away by the changing course of a river, like the drowned villages of the Upper Rhine, just as the Oberahneschen fields slowly disappeared beneath the surface of the Jade Bay. But these were 'natural', random events. It is another matter to move back a dike and deliberately flood a village or land that has been farmed for generations. Is doing so to create water retention basins in the name of environmentally sustainable flood protection any different from deliberately flooding a valley to create a reservoir that will generate hydro-electric power?

Let me try to answer that question in some final reflections. Those 'natural' events in the past that caused villages to disappear were not always as natural as they seemed. They were sometimes an indirect result of human actions – deforestation, most obviously, or the decision by one village to transfer the risk to another village downstream by strengthening *its* defences. They were always a result of the decision to build a town or village in a vulnerable place. It was a belief that this vulnerability could be made a thing of the past and human security guaranteed that spawned the modern era of river regulation and dike building. That belief proved to be far too optimistic. Large-scale technological programmes, animated by a sense of confidence that often bordered on hubris, also had many unintended consequences, as this book has repeatedly shown. The cost and import of these consequences, for humans and the environment, is only now becoming fully apparent. The same is true of moorland colonization, dam-building, and the variety of ways in which Germans drew down their groundwater and polluted their rivers.

None of those realities makes it easier to contemplate the deliberate sacrifice of land or human settlements, even in the virtuous cause of a more sensible policy towards river management and flood protection. This book has been concerned with how people shaped their natural environment, and the landscapes created by humans acquire powerful historical and emotional associations. The history I have told began in the Oderbruch, with the drama of reclamation. Reclaiming it cost lives and ruined the health of many more, ditch-diggers and early colonists. What resulted was and is in some ways hard to justify rationally, a small, thinly populated area that lies well below the normal water level of a river that is a permanent threat to its existence. After more than 250 years, however, this new land has acquired the patina of age and with it certain claims. It is a landscape full of historical associations and the signs of human endeavour, it is the involuntary graveyard of Germans and Russians who fought there in the spring of 1945, and it is (at least to my eyes) bleakly beautiful. I would not wish it returned to the 'wilderness of water and marsh' that existed before the reclamation, even if such a thing were possible. 'Wilderness' is, of course, an eminently human idea, often a misleading one. The Oder marshes had felt the imprint of human activity long before they were 'conquered' at the command of Frederick the Great. Reclamation meant that one set of human uses was replaced by another. Now the question is whether, and how, to reset the balance. It is no Green utopian dream to believe that there is space enough for food production and nesting storks, that an environmentally sustainable agriculture can be combined with incremental steps to 'renature' some riparian zones as wetlands habitat.

It seems unlikely that the Oderbruch will be deliberately flooded as a retention basin (there are areas to the north and south that now serve that purpose), and if an environmentally sustainable flood protection policy succeeds the area will be safer than it has been in the past. But other polders in other places will have to be flooded if that policy is to succeed, and the people who live in them will feel the loss. Their insecurity will finally be removed, but only because they have been removed from their homes. It would almost certainly be no consolation to tell them, although it is true, that the policy now being pursued is not only friendlier to the environment but promises a greater degree of true security to most people who live along the Oder. And it would be equally unlikely to console them, although it is just as true, that the policy will succeed only by agreement between Germany, Poland and the Czech Republic under the umbrella of the European Union. Both of these truths should be a source of pleasure to the rest of us, however, because for most of the period covered by this book the idea that nature should be shackled held sway, and the 'conquest of nature' in Germany was all too closely linked to the conquest of others.

LIST OF ABBREVIATIONS

AAAG	Annals of the Association of American Geographers
AdB	Archiv der 'Brandenburgia' Gesellschaft für Heimatkunde der Provinz Brandenburg
AfK	Archiv für Kulturgeschichte
AfS	Archiv für Sozialgeschichte
AHR	American Historical Review
ANW	Alte und Neue Welt
AS	Die Alte Stadt
BA	Bautechnik-Archiv
BdL	Berichte zur deutschen Landeskunde
BeH	Bergische Heimat
BH	Badische Heimat
BIG	Bayerisches Industrie- und Gewerbeblatt
BSW	Bauen/Siedeln/Wohnen
BZN	Beiträge zur Naturdenkmalpflege
BzR	Beiträge zur Rheinkunde
CEH	Central European History
DA	Deutsche Arbeit
DeW	Deutsche Wasserwirtschaft
DG	Die Gartenkunst
DLKZ	Deutsche Landeskulturzeitung
DSK	Das Schwarze Korps
DT	Deutsche Technik
DW	Die Wasserwirtschaft
EH	Environment and History

EHR	Environmental History Review
EKB	Elektrische Kraftbetrieb und Bahnen
ER	Environmental Review
FAZ	Frankfurter Allgemeine Zeitung
FBPG	Forschungen zur Brandenburgischen und Preussischen Geschichte
FD	Forschungsdienst
GG	Geschichte und Gesellschaft
GI	Gesundheits-Ingenieur
GLA	Badisches Generallandesarchiv Karlsruhe
GLL	German Life and Letters
GR	Geographical Review
GSR	German Studies Review
GWF	Das Gas- und Wasserfach
GZ	Geographische Zeitschrift
HGN	History of Geography Newsletter
HM	History and Memory
HHO	Heimatkunde des Herzogtums Oldenburg
HPBl	Historisch-Politische Blätter für das katholische Deutschland
HWJ	History Workshop Journal
HSR	Historical Social Research
HZ	Historische Zeitschrift
JbbD	Jahrbuch des baltischen Deutschtums
JbN	Jahrbuch der Naturwissenschaften
JbHG	Jahrbuch der Hafenbautechnischen Gesellschaft
JHG	Journal of Historical Geography
JMH	Journal of Modern History
KJb	Klinisches Jahrbuch
KuT	Kultur und Technik
LJbb	Landwirtschaftliche Jahrbücher
MCWäL	Medicinisches Correspondenzblatt des württembergischen ärztlichen Landesvereins
MGM	Militärgeschichtliche Mitteilungen
MLWBL	Mitteilungen der Landesanstalt für Wasser-, Boden- und Lufthygiene
NB	Neues Bauerntum
NBJ	Neues Bergisches Jahrbuch
NDB	Neue Deutsche Biographie

NSM	Nationalsozialistische Monatshefte
NuL	Natur und Landschaft
NuN	Naturschutz- und Naturparke
OJ	Oldenburger Jahrbuch
PGQ	Political Geography Quarterly
PHG	Progress in Human Geography
PJbb	Preussische Jahrbücher
PlP	Planning Perspectives
PÖ	Politische Ökologie
PP	Past and Present
PVBl	Preussisches Verwaltungsblatt
RAZS	Rheinisches Archiv für Zivil- und Strafrecht
RKFDV	Reichskommissariat für die Festigung deutschen Volkstums
RTV	Ruhr-Talsperrenverein
RTW	Rundschau für Technik und Wirtschaft
RuR	Raumforschung und Raumordnung
SB	Schweizerische Bauzeitung
SVGN	Schriften des Vereins für Geschichte der Neumark
TC	Technology and Culture
TM	Technologisches Magazin
TuW	Technik und Wirtschaft
ÜLM	Über Land und Meer
UTW	Uhlands Technische Wochenschrift
VfZ	Vierteljahresheft für Zeitgeschichte
VuW	Volk und Welt
VW	Verkehrstechnische Woche
WK	Die Weisse Kohle
WMB	Wanderungen durch die Mark Brandenburg (Theodor Fontane)
WuG	Wasser und Gas
YES	Yearbook for European Studies
ZbWW	Zentralblatt für Wasser und Wasserwirtschaft
ZdB	Zentralblatt der Bauverwaltung
ZDWW	Zeitschrift der Deutschen Wasserwirtschafts- und Wasserkraftverbandes
ZfA	Zeitschrift für Agrarpolitik
ZfB	Zeitschrift für Bauwesen
ZfBi	Zeitschrift für Binnenschiffahrt

ZfdgT	Zeitschrift für das gesamte Turbinenwesen
ZfG	Zeitschrift für Gewässerkunde
ZfGeo	Zeitschrift für Geopolitik
ZfO	Zeitschrift für Ostforschung
ZfS	Zeitschrift für Sozialwissenschaft
ZGEB	Zeitschrift der Gesellschaft für Erdkunde zu Berlin
ZGO	Zeitschrift für die Geschichte des Oberrheins
ZGW	Zeitschrift für die Gesamte Wasserwirtschaft
ZHI	Zeitschrift für Hygiene und Infektionskrankheiten
ZöIAV	Zeitschrift des österreichischen Ingenieur- und Architekten-Vereines
ZVDI	Zeitschrift des Vereins Deutscher Ingenieure

NOTES

Introduction: Nature and Landscape in German History

1 Thomas Lekan, *Imagining the Nation in Nature: Landscape Preservation and German Identity, 1885–1945* (Cambridge, Mass., 2004), 74.

2 August Trinius (1916), cited in William H. Rollins, *A Greener Vision of Home: Cultural Politics and Environmental Reform in the German Heimatschutz Movement, 1904–1918* (Ann Arbor, 1997), 246.

3 Clarence Glacken, *Traces on the Rhodian Shore: Nature and Culture in Western Thought from Ancient Times to the End of the Eighteenth Century* (Berkeley, 1967), 600.

4 Reinhold Koser, *Geschichte Friedrich des Grossen*, 3 vols. (Darmstadt, 1974), vol. 3, 97; Walter Christiani, *Das Oderbruch: Historische Skizze* (Freienwalde, 1901), 46.

5 Freud, 'Thoughts for the Times on War and Death', *The Penguin Freud Library*, vol. 12 (Harmondsworth, 1991), 62, 64.

6 Walter Benjamin, 'The Work of Art in the Age of Mechanical Reproduction', in Benjamin, *Illuminations*, transl. Harry Zohn (London, 1973), 242.

7 P. Ziegler, *Der Talsperrenbau* (Berlin, 1911), 5.

8 Jakob Zinssmeister, 'Industrie, Verkehr, Natur und moderne Wasserwirtschaft', *WK*, Jan. 1909, 14.

9 Professor [Heinrich] Wiepking-Jürgensmann, 'Das Grün im Dorf und in der Feldmark', *BSW* 20 (1940), 442.

10 Goethe, *Faust*, Part II, line 11,541.

11 For an excellent recent example, see John McNeill, *Something New under the Sun: An Environmental History of the Twentieth Century* (London and New York, 2000).

12 On 'Humpty-Dumpty effects': Stuart L. Pimm, *The Balance of Nature:*

Ecological Issues in the Conservation of Species and Communities (Chicago, 1991), 258–9.

13 Wolfgang Welsch, 'Postmoderne: Pluralität zwischen Konsens und Dissens', *AfK* 73 (1991), 193–214 (quotation, 211), recapitulating the arguments of Theodor Adorno and Max Horkheimer, *The Dialectic of Enlightenment* (New York, 1972), first published as *Dialektik der Aufklärung* (New York, 1944).

14 See K. Blaschke, 'Environmental History: Some Questions for a New Subdiscipline of History', in Peter Brindlecombe and Christian Pfister (eds.), *The Silent Countdown: Essays in European Environmental History* (Berlin, 1990), 68–72; William C. Cronon, 'The Uses of Environmental History', *EHR* 17 (1993), 1–22; T. C. Smout, 'Problems for Global Environmental Historians', *EH* 8 (2002), 107–16, esp. 112, 116. Cronon and another leading American environmental historian, Richard White, have been exceptionally thoughtful in addressing this question; so, in Germany, have been scholars such as Joachim Radkau and Franz-Josef Brüggemeier.

15 Richard White, *The Organic Machine: The Remaking of the Columbia River* (New York, 1995), 112.

16 Ernst Candèze, *Die Talsperre*, translated from the French original (Leipzig, 1901). Candèze's anthropomorphized insects are not, of course, an alternative to the ecological record; but the author's skill and empathy are such that his account helpfully supplements what we can learn from other sources. On Toynbee, see McNeill, *Something New under the Sun*, xxii–xxiii.

17 Donald Worster, 'Thinking like a River', in Worster, *The Wealth of Nature* (New York, 1993), 123–34.

18 That is a central argument in Hansjörg Küster, *Geschichte der Landschaft in Mitteleuropa* (Munich, 1995). Helmut Jäger, *Einführung in die Umweltgeschichte* (Darmstadt, 1994), 229, makes this point about the *Watt*, or mudflats of the North Sea coast.

19 Henry Makowski and Bernhard Buderath, *Die Natur dem Menschen untertan: Ökologie im Spiegel der Landschaftsmalerei* (Munich, 1983), 226.

20 Becker cited in Wolfgang Diehl, 'Poesie und Dichtung der Rheinebene', in Michael Geiger, Günter Preuß and Karl-Heinz Rothenberger (eds.), *Der Rhein und die Pfälzische Rheinebene* (Landau i. d. Pfalz, 1991), 384.

21 See, for example, Götz Großklaus and Ernst Oldemeyer (eds.), *Natur als Gegenwelt: Beiträge zur Geschichte der Natur* (Karlsruhe, 1983); Joachim Radkau, 'Was ist Umweltgeschichte?', in Werner Abelshauer (ed.), *Umweltgeschichte. Umweltverträgliches Wirtschaften in historischer Perspektive: Acht Beiträge* (Göttingen, 1994), 11–28, esp. 14–16.

22 Marcus Aurelius, *Meditations*, bk. 4, sect. 43; Machiavelli, *The Prince*, ch. 25. See also Roger D. Masters, *Fortune is a River* (New York, 1999), 10–11.

23 Hans Boldt (ed.), *Der Rhein: Mythos und Realität eines europäischen Stromes* (Cologne, 1988).

24 Cited H. C. Darby, 'The Relations of Geography and History', in Griffith Taylor (ed.), *Geography in the Twentieth Century* (London, 1957), 640.

25 Ibid., 641.

26 Marc Bloch, *The Historian's Craft* (Manchester, 1954), 26.

27 Joshua Meyrowitz, *No Sense of Place: The Impact of Electronic Media on Social Behaviour* (Oxford, 1989). See also Marc Augé, *Non-Places: Introduction to an Anthropology of Supermodernity* (London and New York, 1995).

28 Georges Duby, *History Continues* (Chicago, 1994), 27, 28.

29 Hartmut Lehmann and James Van Horn Melton (eds.), *Paths of Continuity: Central European Historiography from the 1930s to the 1950s* (Cambridge, 1994); Jürgen Kocka, 'Ideological Regression and Methodological Innovation: Historiography and the Social Sciences in the 1930s and 1940s', HM 2 (1990), 130–7; Willi Oberkrome, *Volksgeschichte: Methodische Innovation und völkische Ideologisierung in der deutschen Geschichtswissenschaft 1918–1945* (Göttingen, 1993); Peter Schöttler, 'Das "Annales-Paradigma" und die deutsche Historiographie (1929–1939)', in Lothar Jordan and Bernd Korländer (eds.), *Nationale Grenzen und internationaler Austausch: Studien zum Kultur- und Wissenschaftstransfer in Europa* (Tübingen, 1995), 200–20.

30 William Vitek and Wes Jackson, *Rooted in the Land: Essays on Community and Place* (New Haven, 1996).

31 'Land und Leute' was volume 1 of Riehl's *Die Naturgeschichte des Volkes als Grundlage einer deutschen Social-Politik*, now in English as *The Natural History of the German People*, transl. David Diephouse (Lewiston, NY, 1990). On Riehl, George L. Mosse, *The Crisis of German Ideology: Intellectual Origins of the Third Reich* (London, 1966), 19–24; Celia Applegate, *A Nation of Provincials: The German Idea of Heimat* (Berkeley, 1990), 34–42, 78–9, 217–18; Jasper von Altenbockum, *Wilhelm Heinrich Riehl 1823–1897* (Cologne, 1994).

32 See Stephen Pyne, *Vestal Fire: An Environmental History Told through Fire, of Europe and Europe's Encounter with the World* (Seattle, 1997), which I draw on in Chapters 1 and 3 below. This is the fifth volume in Pyne's 'Cycle of Fire' sequence. See also Johann Goudsblom, *Fire and Civilization* (London, 1992).

33 Rita Gudermann, *Morastwelt und Paradies: Ökonomie und Ökologie in der Landwirschaft am Beispiel der Meliorationen in Westfalen und Brandenburg (1830–1880)* (Paderborn, 2000); Sabine Doering-Manteuffel, *Die Eifel: Geschichte einer Landschaft* (Frankfurt/Main, 1995); Horst Johannes Tümmers, *Der Rhein: Ein europäischer Fluss und seine Geschichte* (Munich, 1994); Mark Cioc, *The Rhine: An Eco-Biography 1815–2000* (Seattle, 2002); Rainer Beck, *Unterfinning: Ländliche Welt vor Anbruch der Moderne*

(Munich, 1993). See also the titles listed in the bibliography of Küster, *Geschichte der Landschaft*, and Norbert Fischer, 'Der neue Blick auf die Landschaft', *AfS* 36 (1996), 434–42.

34 Heinrich Wiepking-Jürgensmann, 'Gegen den Steppengeist', *DSK*, 16 Oct. 1942. See also Mark Bassin, 'Race contra Space: The Conflict between German *Geopolitik* and National Socialism', *PGQ* 6 (1987), 115–34.

35 H. H. Bechtluft, 'Das nasse Geschichtsbuch', in W. Franke and G. Hugenberg (eds.), *Moor im Emsland* (Sögel, 1979), 40–59.

Chapter One: Conquests from Barbarism

1 Koser, *Geschichte*, vol. 2, 247.

2 Hugh West, 'Göttingen and Weimar: The Organization of Knowledge and Social Theory in Eighteenth-Century Germany', *CEH* 11 (1978), 150–61.

3 Johann [Jean] Bernoulli, *Reisen durch Brandenburg, Pommern, Preussen, Curland, Russland und Pohlen, in den Jahren 1777 und 1778*, 6 vols. (Leipzig, 1779–80).

4 Bernoulli, *Reisen*, vol. 1, 31–8. Shells, especially rare and 'exotic' specimens, were highly valued by eighteenth-century collectors because they met contemporary ideas of beauty and refinement. They seized the eye, stimulated the spirit and diverted simultaneously. See Bettina Dietz, 'Exotische Naturalien als Statussymbol', in Hans-Peter Bayerdörfer and Eckhardt Hellmuth (eds.), *Exotica: Inszenierung und Konsum des Fremden 1750–1900* (Münster, 2003).

5 Bernoulli, *Reisen*, vol. 1, 26–31, 38–9. The improvements at Gusow provide the main evidence in Antje Jakupi, Peter M. Steinsiek and Bernd Herrmann, 'Early Maps as Stepping Stones for the Reconstruction of Historic Ecological Conditions and Biota', *Naturwissenschaften*, 90 (2003), 360–5.

6 Bernoulli, *Reisen*, vol. 1, 39.

7 Theodore Fontane, *Wanderungen durch die Mark Brandenburg* [*WMB*], Hanser Verlag edition, 3 vols. (Munich and Vienna, 1991), vol. 1, 550; Christiani, *Das Oderbruch*, 13. Many later writers refer back to Friedrich Wilhelm Noeldechen, *Oekonomische und staatswissenschaftliche Briefe über das Niederoderbruch und den Abbau oder die Verteilung der Königlichen Ämter und Vorwerke im hohen Oderbruch* (Berlin, 1800), 28, who refers to a 'barren swamp' and a 'wilderness'.

8 Dr Müller, 'Aus der Kolonisationszeit des Netzebruchs', *SVGN* 39 (1921), 3.

9 Anneliese Krenzlin, *Dorf, Feld und Wirtschaft im Gebiet der grossen Täler und Platten östlich der Elbe: Eine siedlungsgeographische Untersuchung* (Remagen, 1952), 10–15; Margaret Reid Shackleton, *Europe: A Regional Geography* (London, 1958), 242–63.

10 Shackleton, *Europe*, 252.

11 This engraving can be found in Matthäus Merian, *Topographia Electorat Brandenburgici et Ducatus Pomeraniae, das ist, Beschreibung der Vornembsten und bekantisten Stätte und Plätze in dem hochlöblichsten Churfürstenthum und March Brandenburg*, facsimile of 1652 edn. (Kassel and Basel, 1965).

12 See Bernd Herrmann, with Martina Kaup, *'Nun blüht es von End' zu End' all überall'. Die Eindeichung des Nieder-Oderbruches 1747–1753* (Münster, 1997), 32–5, and the discussion of Fontane on 35–40.

13 Johann Christoph Bekmann, *Historische Beschreibung der Chur- und Mark Brandenburg* (Berlin, 1751), cited in Fontane, *WMB*, vol. 1, 566.

14 Fontane, *WMB*, vol. 1, 568; Hermann Borkenhagen, *Das Oderbruch in Vergangenheit und Gegenwart* (Neu-Barnim, 1905), 8; Werner Michalsky, *Zur Geschichte des Oderbruchs: Die Entwässerung* (Seelow, 1983), 3–4; Erwin Nippert, *Das Oderbruch* (Berlin, 1995), 92; Herrmann, *'Nun blüht es von End' zu End' all überall'*, 63–4.

15 Glacken, *Traces*, 476; Norman Smith, *Man and Water: A History of Hydro-Technology* (London, 1976), 28–40. On the Dutch as settlers across northern Europe, see Max Beheim-Schwarzbach, *Hohenzollernsche Colonisationen* (Leipzig, 1874), 418, who refers to their 'extraordinary competence and usefulness in the cultivation of the soil, particularly in the improvement and draining of swamps and marshes'.

16 A New Holland was presented to Frederick William's bride Luise, another set up in the same years by Jobst von und zu Hertefeld, which later entered royal hands. These and others were known by the generic term 'Holländereien'. See Beheim-Schwarzbach, *Colonisationen*, 36–8; Jan Peters, Hartmut Harnisch and Lieselott Enders, *Märkische Bauerntagebücher des 18. und 19. Jahrhunderts* (Weimar, 1989), 18–26.

17 Kloeden's description of the Havelland marshes: Fontane, *WMB*, vol. 2, 105.

18 Fontane, *WMB*, vol. 1, 568; Christiani, *Das Oderbruch*, 34.

19 Fontane, *WMB*, vol. 1, 569; Peter Fritz Mengel, 'Die Deichverwaltung des Oderbruches', in Mengel (ed.), *Das Oderbruch*, vol. 2 (Eberswalde, 1934), 292–3; Borkenhagen, *Oderbruch*, 8–10; Herrmann, *'Nun blüht es von End' zu End' all überall'*, 65–72. On the nine major floods, 1694–1736: Heinrich Carl Berghaus, *Landbuch der Mark Brandenburg*, 3 vols. (Brandenburg, 1854–6), vol. 3, 27 (table VIII).

20 Erich Neuhaus, *Die Fridericianische Colonisation im Netze- und Warthebruch* (Landsberg, 1905), 30.

21 Noeldeschen, *Oekonomische Briefe*, 29–30; Fontane, *WMB*, vol. 1, 568–9; Herrmann, *'Nun blüht es von End' zu End' all überall'*, 72–3.

22 Gerhard Ritter, *Frederick the Great*, transl. Peter Paret (Berkeley, 1968), 26–31.

23 Leopold von Ranke, *Zwölf Bücher preussischer Geschichte*, vol. 3 (Leipzig, 1874), 127, cit. Heinrich Bergér, *Friedrich der Grosse als Kolonisator* (Giessen, 1896), 5; Rudolph Stadelmann, *Preussens Könige in ihrer Thätigkeit für die Landescultur*, vol. 2 (Leipzig, 1882), 5–6; Heinrich Bauer, *Die Mark Brandenburg* (Berlin, 1954), 128.

24 Letter from Rheinsberg, 12 Sep. 1737: Bergér, *Friedrich der Grosse*, 6.

25 Bergér, *Friedrich der Grosse*, 70; Henry Makowski and Bernhard Buderath, *Die Natur dem Menschen untertan* (Munich, 1983), 64.

26 Koser, *Geschichte*, vol. 2, 246.

27 Koser, *Geschichte*, vol. 3, 184.

28 Simon Leonhard von Haerlem, 'Gutachten vom 6. Januar 1747', reprinted in Herrmann, *'Nun blüht es von End' zu End' all überall'*, 88–121 (quotation: 107); Albert Detto, 'Die Besiedlung des Oderbruches durch Friedrich den Grossen', *FBPG* 16 (1903), 165.

29 Matthias G. von Schmettow, *Schmettau und Schmettow: Geschichte eines Geschlechts aus Schlesien* (Büderich, 1961), 379–80.

30 The Plauen canal linked the Havel and Elbe. Like the Oder–Finow canal, completed in 1746, its construction belonged to what Wolffsohn calls the 'first phase' of canal building (1740–6), which had no connection with drainage, reclamation and colonization: Seew Wolffsohn, *Wirtschaftliche und soziale Entwicklungen in Brandenburg, Preussen, Schlesien und Oberschlesien in den Jahren 1640–1853* (Frankfurt/Main, Berlin and New York, 1985), 40–2.

31 Herrmann, *'Nun blüht es von End' zu End' all überall'*, 80, 86, 122–3.

32 'Eulogium of Euler', in *Letters of Euler on Different Subjects in Physics and Philosophy Addressed to a German Princess*, translated from the French by Henry Hunter, 2 vols. (London, 1802), lxv. Hunter himself also linked Euler's name with Newton's. See Preface, xxiii.

33 Karl Karmarsch, *Geschichte der Technologie seit der Mitte des 18. Jahrhunderts* (Munich, 1872), 13–14; Robert Gascoigne, *A Chronology of the History of Science* (New York, 1987), 71–3, 421–3, 507–9.

34 *Letters of Euler*, xxxiii-liii, 187.

35 'Eulogium of Euler', xxxvi-xxxvii; Bernoulli, *Reisen*, vol. 5, 10; Roger D. Masters, *Fortune is a River*, 132. On Bernoulli and Euler, see Günther Garbrecht, *Wasser: Vorrat, Bedarf und Nutzung in Geschichte und Gegenwart* (Reinbek, 1985), 178–81.

36 *Letters of Euler*, 187

37 Text of report in Christiani, *Oderbruch*, 82–9 and Herrmann, *'Nun blüht es von End' zu End' all überall'*, 124–9.

38 Christiani, *Oderbruch*: poem reprinted on the unpaginated pages at the end of the book.

39 Photo in Nippert, *Oderbruch*, 100. On the many memorials to Frederick

in the Oderbruch – at Neuhardenberg, Letschin, Neulewin, Neutrebbin, Güstebiese, Altrüdnitz – see Rudolf Schmidt, 'Volkskundliches aus dem Oderbruch', in Mengel (ed.), *Oderbruch*, vol. 2, 111.

40 'Fragen eines lesenden Arbeiters', *Die Gedichte von Bertolt Brecht in einem Band* (Frankfurt/Main, 1981), 656–7.

41 Accounts include Fontane, *WMB*, vol. 1, 569–74; Christiani, *Oderbruch*, 36–40; Detto, 'Besiedlung', 163–72; Ernst Breitkreutz, *Das Oderbruch im Wandel der Zeit* (Remscheid, 1911), 11–26; G. Wentz, 'Geschichte des Oderbruches', in Mengel (ed.), *Das Oderbruch*, vol. 1 (Eberswalde, 1930), 85–238; Borkenhagen, *Oderbruch*, 10–12; *Das Oderbruch im Wandel der Zeit*, 14–18.

42 On the specialist 'Teichgrabers' in the eighteenth century see Ludwig Hempel, 'Zur Entwicklung der Kulturlandschaft in Bruchländereien', *BdL* 11 (1952), 73; on rising hourly rates in this part of Prussia, Neuhaus, *Colonisation*, 39–40.

43 Michalsky, *Zur Geschichte*, 5; Detto, 'Besiedlung', 167–71; Udo Froese, *Das Kolonisationswerk Friedrich des Grossen* (Heidelberg, 1938), 17.

44 Ulrike Müller-Weil, *Absolutismus und Aussenpolitik in Preussen* (Stuttgart, 1992), 107. Soldiers in the large standing army were, in fact, widely used to fill in gaps left by the shortage of police, firefighters, and customs officers, as well as acting as craftsmen and labourers.

45 Haerlem and Petri to Retzow, 18 July 1753: Detto, 'Besiedlung', 171.

46 Fontane, *WMB*, vol. 1, 547; Christiani, *Oderbruch*, 46; Koser, *Geschichte*, vol. 3, 97.

47 Fontane, *WMB*, vol. 1, 570.

48 Stadelmann, *Preussens Könige*, vol. 2, 63–72: Fontane, *WMB*, vol. 2, 103–7.

49 Frederick to East Prussian Kammerpräsident von Goltz, 1 Aug. 1786: Stadelmann, *Preussens Könige*, vol. 2, 655.

50 Neuhaus, *Colonisation*, 33. On Frederick and Frau von Wreech, Fontane, *WMB*, vol. 1, 894–907.

51 On Brenckenhoff, see August Gottlob Meissner, *Leben Franz Balthasar Schönberg von Brenkenhof* (Leipzig, 1782); Benno von Knobelsdorff-Brenkenhoff, *Eine Provinz im Frieden erobert: Brenckenhoff als Leiter der friderizianischen Retablissements in Pommern 1762–1780* (Cologne and Berlin, 1984).

52 Alice Reboly, *Friderizianische Kolonisation im Herzogtum Magdeburg* (Burg, 1940), on the Magdeburg Plain; F. Hamm, *Naturkundliche Chronik Nordwestdeutschlands* (Hanover, 1976), 103 ff., and chapter 3, below, on the Emsland; Hermann Kellenbenz, *Deutsche Wirtschaftsgeschichte*, 2 vols. (Munich, 1977–81), vol. 1, 324, on the Donaumoos.

53 Keith Tribe, 'Cameralism and the Science of Government', *JMH* 56 (1984), 163–84; David F. Lindenfeld, *The Practical Imagination: The German*

Sciences of State in the Nineteenth Century (Chicago, 1997), 11–45. A bibliography of eighteenth-century works on cameralist sciences lists 14,000 works: Magdelene Humpert, *Bibliographie der Kameralwissenschaften* (Cologne, 1937).

54 Bernard Heise, 'From Tangible Sign to Deliberate Delineation: The Evolution of the Political Boundary in the Eighteenth and Early Nineteenth Centuries', in Wolfgang Schmale and Reinhard Stauber (eds.), *Menschen und Grenzen in der frühen Neuzeit* (Berlin, 1998), 171–86; Anne Buttimer, *Geography and the Human Spirit* (Baltimore, 1993), 105.

55 Müller-Weil, *Absolutismus*, 307–15.

56 Henning Eichberg, 'Ordnen, Messen, Disziplinieren', in Johannes Kunisch (ed.), *Staatsverfassung und Heeresverfassung in der europäischen Geschichte der frühen Neuzeit* (Berlin, 1986), 347–75.

57 Hamm, *Naturkundliche Chronik*, 122.

58 Knobelsdorff-Brenkenhoff, *Eine Provinz*, 56–7, 158, emphasizes this.

59 Beheim-Schwarzbach, *Colonisationen*, 266.

60 René Descartes, *Discourse on Method and Related Writings*, transl. Desmond M. Clarke (Harmondsworth, 1999), 44; Georges-Louis Leclerc, Comte de Buffon, *Histoire Naturelle*, 44 vols. (Paris, 1749–1804), vol. 12, 14. Glacken, *Traces*, chs. 3–4, is a wonderful guide on this subject.

61 On the great fire of 1664 in Wriezen/Oderbruch, see C. A. Wolff, *Wriezen und seine Geschichte im Wort, im Bild und im Gedichte* (Wriezen, 1912), 41–2; [anon], *Aus Wriezen's Vergangenheit* (Wriezen, 1864), 3–6.

62 Stadelmann, *Preussens Könige*, vol. 2, 224–5; E. L. Jones, *The European Miracle: Environments, Economies and Geopolitics in the History of Europe and Asia* (Cambridge, 1981), 143–4.

63 Stephen Pyne, *Vestal Fire*, 203.

64 Pyne, *Vestal Fire*, 186–99; James C. Scott, *Seeing Like a State* (New Haven, 1998), 11–22.

65 Frederick to Voltaire, 10 Jan. 1776: Stadelmann, *Preussens Könige*, vol. 2, 43.

66 Ibid., 51, 57, 60–1.

67 Friedrich Engels, 'Landschaften' [1840], in Helmut J. Schneider (ed.), *Deutsche Landschaften* (Frankfurt/Main, 1981), 477.

68 Keith Thomas, *Man and the Natural World* (London, 1983), 274, for English parallels. On 'dishonourable occupations', Werner Danckert, *Unehrliche Leute: Die verfemten Berufe* (Berne, 1963).

69 Stadelmann, *Preussens Könige*, vol. 1, 172–6, vol. 2, 220–2. The number of sparrows killed added up to about 350,000 per year. Keith Thomas, *Man and the Natural World*, 274, notes that 4152 sparrows were killed in one Lincolnshire village in 1779 and 14,000 killed in a Bedfordshire village over 1764–74.

70 Franz von Kobell, *Wildanger* (Munich, 1936 [1854]), 121, 136; Makowski and Buderath, *Natur*, 132.

71 Stadelmann, *Preussens Könige*, vol. 1, 171–2, vol. 2, 81, 222–3.

72 Frederick to Kammerdirektor von der Goltz, 24 June 1786: ibid., vol. 2, 651.

73 Ibid., vol. 2, 52.

74 Barry Holstun Lopez, *Of Wolves and Men* (New York, 1978). English parallels in Thomas, *Man and the Natural World*, 40–1, 61.

75 Makowski and Buderath, *Natur*, 132; Hamm, *Naturkundliche Chronik*, 106–18; Kobell, *Wildanger*, 119–24, 139, 147.

76 Manfred Jakubowski-Tiessen, *Sturmflut 1717: Die Bewältigung einer Naturkatastrophe in der frühen Neuzeit* (Munich, 1992). See also Chapter 3, below.

77 Neuhaus, *Colonisation*, 28–9. Hamm has used similar chronicle sources for his compilatory work on north-western Germany, *Naturkundliche Chronik*.

78 Berghaus, *Landbuch*, vol. 3, 27 (table VIII); Christiani, *Oderbruch*, 28–33; *Aus Wriezen's Vergangenheit*, 11–14; Herrmann, 'Nun blüht es von End' zu End' all überall', 68–72.

79 Jones, *European Miracle*, 137–47.

80 Glacken, *Traces*, 604–6, 659–65, 670, 680–1, 688–9, 702–3; Franklin Thomas, *The Environmental Basis of Society* (New York, 1925), 230–2; Yi-Fu Tuan, *Passing Strange and Wonderful: Aesthetics, Nature and Culture* (Washington DC, 1993), 61, 68, 76–7.

81 Paul Wagret, *Polderlands* (London, 1968), 46–7; Breitkreutz, *Oderbruch*, 6.

82 Decree of 7 June 1776: Stadelmann, *Preussens Könige*, vol. 2, 81.

83 Meissner, *Brenkenhof*, 80–1.

84 Johanniter-Ordens-Kammerrat Stubenrauch, in 1778: Neuhaus, *Colonisation*, 8–9.

85 Bergér, *Friedrich der Grosse*, 10–11.

86 Beheim-Schwarzbach, *Colonisationen*, 289–97; Detto, 'Besiedlung', 180–1; Bergér, *Friedrich der Grosse*, 9–19; Reboly, *Friderizianische Kolonisation*, 10–11, 30–40, 76–7; Froese, *Kolonisationswerk*, 8–9; W. O. Henderson, *Studies in the Economic Policy of Frederick the Great* (London, 1963), 127.

87 Otto Kaplick, *Das Warthebruch: Eine deutsche Kulturlandschaft im Osten* (Würzburg, 1956), 80–1.

88 Beheim-Schwarzbach, *Colonisationen*, 369. The 2712 families (11,486 people) had total assets of just under 283,000 Taler.

89 Calculated from Bergér, *Friedrich der Grosse*, 91 (Anhang Nr. 7: 'Verzeichnis der im Jahre 1747 nach Pommern abgegangenen Pfälzer-Transporte'). I could find no correlation between the ratio of peasants to craftsmen in a given party and the wealth of that party, although the party most dominated

by peasants (which was also the smallest) had the largest average cash assets.

90 Bergér, *Friedrich der Grosse*, 90 ('Specification', Anhang Nr. 6).

91 P. Schwarz, 'Brenkenhoffs Berichte über seine Tätigkeit in der Neumark', *SVGN* 20 (1907), 46. On the assets brought by colonists, also Beheim-Schwarzbach, *Colonisationen*, 573; Neuhaus, *Colonisation*, 90; Froese, *Kolonisationswerk*, 24–5.

92 Beheim-Schwarzbach, *Colonisationen*, 330–1.

93 Bergér, *Friedrich der Grosse*, 81.

94 Siegfried Maire, 'Beiträge zur Besiedlungsgeschichte des Oderbruchs', *AdB* 13 (1911), 37–8.

95 Alfred Biese, *The Development of the Feeling for Nature in the Middle Ages and Modern Times* (London, 1905), 286.

96 Mack Walker, *The Salzburg Transaction: Expulsion and Redemption in Eighteenth-Century Germany* (Ithaca, 1992), on the earlier Salzburgers.

97 Detto, 'Besiedlung', 183.

98 Breitkreutz, *Oderbruch*, 53–7; Detto, 'Besiedlung', 180–2.

99 Carsten Küther, *Räuber und Gauner in Deutschland* (Göttingen, 1976).

100 Wolfgang Jacobeit, *Schafhaltung und Schäfer in Zentraleuropa* (East Berlin, 1961), 99–111.

101 Neuhaus, *Colonisation*, 29.

102 For example, Beheim-Schwarzbach, *Colonisationen*, 396.

103 Ibid., 371.

104 Froese, *Kolonisationswerk*, 47–8 (and photos on following pages).

105 Johannes Kunisch, *Absolutismus: Europäische Geschichte vom Westfälischen Frieden bis zur Krise des Ancien Regime* (Göttingen, 1986), 911. See also Müller-Weil, *Absolutismus*, 315–22, on the geometry of settlements.

106 Simon Schaffer, 'Enlightened Automata', in William Clark, Jan Golinski and Simon Schaffer (eds.), *The Sciences in Enlightened Europe* (Chicago, 1999), 139–48; Horst Bredekamp, *The Lure of Antiquity and the Cult of the Machine* (Princeton, 1995), 4; Carl Mitcham, *Thinking through Technology* (Chicago, 1994), 206, 289.

107 Beheim-Schwarzbach, *Colonisationen*, 446.

108 Ibid., 271.

109 H. C. Johnson, *Frederick the Great and his Officials* (London, 1975).

110 The phrase is Gerhard Ritter's, in *Frederick the Great*, 155.

111 Müller-Weil, *Absolutismus*, 267.

112 On Brenckenhoff (sometimes spelled Brenkenhoff, or Brenkenhof), see Meissner, *Brenkenhof*, and Knobelsdorff-Brenckenhoff, *Eine Provinz*. Regarding his semi-literacy, Dr Rehmann's 'Kleine Beiträge zur Charakteristik Brenkenhoffs', *SVGN* 22 (1908), 106, draws on Prussian official Johann Georg Scheffler's evidence about Brenckenhoff's lack of letters: his

painful spelling and orthography even when writing his signature, which was about the only thing he could write.

113 Koser, *Geschichte*, vol. 3, 342–3, who uses the phrase 'self-made man'. Compare the description of Brenckenhoff as an 'American type' in Hans Künkel, *Auf den kargen Hügeln der Neumark: Zur Geschichte eines Schäfer- und Bauerngeschlechts im Warthebruch* (Würzburg, 1962), 26.

114 Ritter, *Frederick the Great*, 151–3; Müller-Weil, *Absolutismus*, 267.

115 Beheim-Schwarzbach, *Colonisationen*, 275.

116 Breitkreutz, *Oderbruch*, 82–5; Detto, 'Besiedlung', 183.

117 Koser, *Geschichte*, vol. 3, 343. See also Knobelsdorff-Brenkenhoff, *Eine Provinz*, 59–63; Rehmann, 'Kleine Beiträge', 101–2.

118 Knobelsdorff-Brenkenhoff, *Eine Provinz*, 80 ('intrigues and deceptions'); Koser, *Geschichte*, vol. 3, 202, on Silesian officials being instructed to view Brenckenhoff's work in the Netze and Warthe marshes ('you will have seen there many good and useful things').

119 Knobelsdorff-Brenkenhoff, *Eine Provinz*, 79 ('keep a close eye'); Müller-Weil, *Absolutismus*, 270 ('not to place the slightest obstacle in his path').

120 Beheim-Schwarzbach, *Colonisationen*, 269.

121 Haerlem and Petri to Retzow, 15 Aug. 1754: Detto, 'Besiedlung', 174.

122 Rehmann, 'Kleine Beiträge', 111.

123 Koser, *Geschichte*, vol. 3, 342.

124 Ibid.

125 Petri to Retzow (written from Liezegöricke), 31 May 1756: Detto, 'Besiedlung', 183–4.

126 Goethe, *Faust*, Part II, lines 11,123–4. See also Marshall Berman, *All That Is Solid Melts into Air: The Experience of Modernity* (Harmondsworth, 1988), 60–5; Gerhard Kaiser, 'Vision und Kritik der Moderne in Goethes Faust II', *Merkur* 48/7 (July 1994), 594–604.

127 Goethe, *Faust*, Part II, lines 11,541, 11,563–4.

128 Fontane, *WMB*, vol. 1, 560.

129 Rehmann, 'Kleine Beiträge', 115.

130 Christiani, *Oderbruch*, 92–100.

131 Schwarz, 'Brenckenhoffs Berichte', records the crops and animals.

132 The first volume of *Grundsätze der rationellen Landwirtschaft* appeared in 1809, volumes 2 to 4 in 1810–12. In 1806, Möglin became the home of Germany's first academic institution for scientific agriculture. On Thaer, also H. H. Freudenberger, 'Die Landwirtschaft des Oderbruches', in Mengel (ed.), *Oderbruch*, vol. 2, 200–3.

133 Christiani, *Oderbruch*, 'Vorwort'; Breitkreutz, *Oderbruch*, iii, 116. On the Warthebruch as a 'blooming garden', Künkel, *Auf den kargen Hügeln der Neumark*, 32.

134 Theodor Fontane, *Before the Storm*, ed. R. J. Hollingdale (Oxford, 1985),

123–4 (first published as *Vor dem Sturm* in 1878). This is a description from later decades that Fontane has transposed to the years of the Napoleonic wars.

135 Fontane, *WMB*, vol. 1, 559–60.

136 William H. McNeill, *Plagues and Peoples* (New York, 1976), 218.

137 Fernand Braudel, *Capitalism and Material Life 1400–1800* (London, 1974), 37–54.

138 Wagret, *Polderlands*, 45.

139 Fontane, *WMB*, vol. 1, 574–81, which – like many later accounts – draws on Pastor S. Buchholtz's *Versuch einer Geschichte der Churmark Brandenburg*, 2 vols. (Berlin, 1765), which described things just as they were changing. See also Noeldeschen, *Oekonomische Briefe*, 28–37; Wentz, 'Geschichte des Oderbruches', 88–92; Christiani, *Oderbruch*, 11–25; Breitkreutz, *Oderbruch*, 3–6; Krenzlin, *Dorf, Feld und Wirtschaft*, 68–9; Herrmann, '*Nun blüht es von End' zu End' all überall*', 11–32.

140 Fred Pearce, *The Dammed* (London, 1992), 32–3. See also H. C. Darby, *The Draining of the Fens* (Cambridge, 1940).

141 Breitkreutz, *Oderbruch*, 14–15; Borkenhagen, *Oderbruch*, 16. On riots and disorders during the earlier English fenland draining, Wagret, *Polderlands*, 91.

142 Künkel, *Auf den kargen Hügeln der Neumark*, 54. Frederick's Draconian decree of June 1754 in Breitkreutz, *Oderbruch*, 15.

143 Christiani, *Oderbruch*, 40; Detto, 'Besiedlung', 198–200.

144 Noeldeschen, *Oekonomische und staatswissenschaftliche Briefe*, 69; Fontane, *WMB*, vol. 1, 565; Rudolf Schmidt, *Wriezen*, vol. 2 (Bad Freienwalde, 1932), 20–1; Herrmann, '*Nun blüht es von End' zu End' all überall*', 25–32.

145 'Fish and crabs . . .': Fontane, *WMB*, vol. 3, 578 (following Buchholtz).

146 Gudermann, *Morastwelt und Paradies*.

147 Scott, *Seeing Like a State*.

148 Schmidt, *Wriezen*, vol. 2, 21.

149 Ibid., 7, 11–12, 31. See also Herrmann, '*Nun blüht es von End' zu End' all überall*', 170–1.

150 Breitkreutz, *Oderbruch*, 36; Froese, *Kolonisationswerk*, 24; Schwarz, 'Brenckenhoffs Berichte', 60; Knobelsdorff-Brenkenhoff, *Eine Provinz*, 86.

151 'Die ersten haben den Tod, die zweiten die Not, die dritten das Brot': Peters, Harnisch and Enders, *Märkische Bauerntagebücher*, 53.

152 To Amtsrat Clausius, 1779, regarding a new colony in the Rhinluch: Beheim-Schwarzbach, *Colonisationen*, 277.

153 Breitkreutz, *Oderbruch*, 87–8.

154 The term is Alfred Crosby's: *Ecological Imperialism: The Biological Expansion of Europe, 900–1900* (Cambridge, 1986), 22.

155 See below, Chapters 3 and 5.

156 Breitkreutz, *Oderbruch*, 117.

157 Christiani, *Oderbruch*, 49–66; Borkenhagen, *Oderbruch*, 15–16, 19. On 1997 see below, epilogue.

158 Stadelmann, *Preussens Könige*, vol. 2, 52–4; Kaplick, *Warthebruch*, 14–15.

159 It happened when Frederick William I's work in the Upper Oderbruch had adverse effects on the Lower Bruch; and when Haerlem's diking of the Oder near Küstrin led to the river breaking through and creating back-up floods in the lower Warthe. Sometimes the problems were 'exported', as in improvement schemes designed to keep the high waters of the Aller from the southern and western Drömling, which created problems instead for Hanoverian and Brunswick territories: Hamm, *Naturkundliche Chronik*, 116, 120–1.

160 Michalsky, *Zur Geschichte*, 12. On the East German belief that the Oder had finally been tamed, see below, Chapter 6.

161 See *Die Melioration der der Ueberschwemmung ausgesetzten Theile des Nieder- und Mittel-Oderbruchs* (Berlin, 1847); Wehrmann, *Die Eindeichung des Oderbruches* (Berlin, 1861); Christiani, *Oderbruch*, 49–81; Mengel, 'Die Deichverwaltung des Oderbruches', in Mengel (ed.), *Oderbruch*, vol. 2, 299–389; Hans-Peter Trömel, *Deichverbände im Oderbruch* (Bad Freienwalde, 1988).

162 The second, because severe flooding also occurred in 1947.

163 Dunbar, *Essays on the History of Mankind in Rude and Cultivated Ages*, cit. Glacken, *Traces*, 600.

164 Fontane, *WMB*, vol. 1, 585.

165 Karl Eckstein, 'Etwas von der Tierwelt des Oderbruches', in Mengel (ed.), *Oderbruch*, vol. 2, 143–74; Herrmann, *'Nun blüht es von End' zu End' all überall'*, 176–80; Martina Kaup, 'Die Urbarmachung des Oderbruchs: Umwelthistorische Annäherung an ein bekanntes Thema', in Günter Bayerl, Norman Fuchsloch and Torsten Meyer (eds.), *Umweltgeschichte – Methoden, Themen, Potentiale* (Münster, 1996), 111–31.

166 Siegfried Giedion, *Mechanization Takes Command* (New York, 1948), 34–6; Bredekamp, *The Lure of Antiquity and the Cult of the Machine*, 4; Schaffer, 'Enlightened Automata', 142–3.

167 Thomas, *Man and the Natural World*, 91, 285.

168 Novalis, 'Die Christenheit oder Europa', cited in Rolf Peter Sieferle, *Fortschrittsfeinde? Opposition gegen Technik und Industrie von der Romantik bis zur Gegenwart* (Munich, 1984), 46.

169 Biese, *Feeling for Nature*, 238–45; Jost Hermand, *Grüne Utopien in Deutschland* (Frankfurt/Main, 1991), 35. The Anacreontic poets included Johann Peter Uz, J. W. L. Gleim and Ewald von Kleist.

170 Biese, *Feeling for Nature*, 251.

171 Bernoulli, *Reisen*, vol. 1, 38–9.

172 Hermand, *Grüne Utopien*, 36.

173 Götz Großklaus, 'Der Naturraum des Kulturbürgers', in Großklaus and Oldemeyer (eds.), *Natur als Gegenwelt*: 171; Glacken, *Traces*, 594.

174 Quotations from a poem of Wilhelm August Schmidt's that includes the lines:

> O dann kann ich oft im wüsten Bruch
> Oft im wilden Wald mich selbst vergessen

> Wohl mir, o Natur, dass ich mich dein
> Mehr, als über Ball und Maske freue, . . .

Schmidt lived in the Spreewald, which resembled the undrained Oderbruch and Warthebruch. See Schneider (ed.), *Deutsche Landschaften*, 51.

175 Goethe, *The Sorrows of Young Werther* (Vintage Classics, 1990), 65.

176 Ibid., 15.

177 Ibid., 49.

178 Fontane, *WMB*, vol. 2, 104–5 (quoting Klöden); Neuhaus, *Colonisation*, 8–9 (quoting Stubenrauch); Künkel, *Auf den kargen Hügeln der Neumark*, 33 (quoting the unnamed Danish professor).

179 Hermand, *Grüne Utopien*, 36. An example is Adolph Knigge's *Dream of Herr Brick* (1783).

180 Richard Grove, *Green Imperialism: Scientists, Ecological Crises, and the History of Environmental Concern, 1600–1860* (Cambridge, 1994), 314–28.

181 Glacken, *Traces*, 541–2; Grove, *Green Imperialism*, 328.

182 On this as a first 'green wave', see Henning Eichberg, 'Stimmung über die Heide – Vom romantischen Blick zur Kolonisierung des Raumes', in Großklaus and Oldemeyer (eds.), *Natur als Gegenwelt*, 217; on 'green utopias', Hermand, *Grüne Utopien*.

183 Künkel, *Auf den kargen Hügeln der Neumark*, 30.

184 Fernand Braudel, *Civilization and Capitalism*, vol. 1 (London, 1981), 69–70.

185 For example, the influential American scholar Donald Worster in *The Wealth of Nature* (New York, 1993). For views closer to the ones I am expressing, see William Cronon, 'The Uses of Environmental History'; Michael Williams, 'The Relations of Environmental History and Historical Geography', *JHG* 20 (1994), 3–21; David Demeritt, 'Ecology, Objectivity and Critique in Writings on Nature and Human Societies', *JHG* 20 (1994), 22–37; Joachim Radkau, 'Was ist Umweltgeschichte?'. The impact of chaos theory on ecology is well brought out in Pimm, *Balance of Nature*, 99–134.

186 T. Dunin-Wasowicz, 'Natural Environment and Human Settlement over the Central European Lowland in the 13th Century', in Peter Brindlecombe and

Christian Pfister (eds.), *The Silent Countdown: Essays in European Environmental History* (Berlin and Heidelberg, 1990), 90–105; B. Prehn and S. Griesa, 'Zur Besiedlung des Oderbruches von der Bronze- bis zur Slawenzeit', in H. Brachmann and H.-J. Vogt (eds.), *Mensch und Umwelt* (Berlin, 1992), 27–32.

187 The picture is reproduced, with analysis, in Makowski and Buderath, *Die Natur*, 158.

188 Neuhaus, *Colonisation*, 4.

189 Bruno Krüger, *Die Kietzsiedlungen im nördlichen Mitteleuropa* (Berlin, 1962), 109 reports on a detailed analysis of how mills had raised water levels and 'changed a part of the landscape'.

190 Makowski and Buderath, *Die Natur*, 172–3; Glacken, *Traces*, 698–702.

191 Elizabeth Ann R. Bird, 'The Social Construction of Nature: Theoretical Approaches to the Study of Environmental Problems', *ER* 11 (1987), 261.

Chapter Two: The Man Who Tamed the Wild Rhine

1 Nikolaus Hofen, 'Sagen und Mythen aus der Vorderpfalz', in Michael Geiger, Günter Preuß and Karl-Heinz Rothenberger (eds.), *Der Rhein und die Pfälzische Rheinebene* (Landau, 1991), 396–7.

2 Hans Biedermann, *Dictionary of Symbolism* (New York, 1994), 36–7.

3 For similar legends in Brandenburg, see Bauer, *Mark Brandenburg*, 57.

4 Heinz Musall, *Die Entwicklung der Kulturlandschaft der Rheinniederung zwischen Karlsruhe und Speyer vom Ende des 16. bis zum Ende des 19. Jahrhunderts* (Heidelberg, 1969), 53, 57, 69, 78.

5 Ibid., 44, 54–6, 67–8, 160–1.

6 Tümmers, *Der Rhein*, 139–40; Fritz Schulte-Mäter, *Beiträge über die geographischen Auswirkungen der Korrektion des Oberrheins* (Leipzig, 1938), 27–9, 59, 77.

7 On the geomorphology and hydrology of the Rhine: Jean Dollfus, *L'Homme et le Rhin: Géographie Humaine* (Paris, 1960), 10–32; Michael Geiger, 'Die Pfälzische Rheinebene – Eine natur- und kulturräumliche Skizze', in Geiger, Preuß and Rothenberger (eds.), *Der Rhein und die Pfälzische Rheinebene*, 17–45; Thomas Tittizer and Falk Krebs (eds.), *Ökosystemforschung: Der Rhein und seine Auen – Eine Bilanz* (Berlin and Heidelberg, 1996), 9–21; Cioc, *The Rhine*: 11–36.

8 The painting, *Blick vom Isteiner Klotz rheinaufwärts gegen Basel* (View from the Istein Cliffs Upriver to Basel) is in the Kunstmuseum Basel.

9 For superb accounts of the dynamics of river flow, see Luna B. Leopold, *A View of the River* (Cambridge, Mass., 1994); E. C. Pielou, *Fresh Water* (Chicago, 1998), 80–148.

10 I am drawing here especially on Musall, *Kulturlandschaft*.

11 Ibid., 121.

12 Ibid., 152.

13 Emmanuel Le Roy Ladurie, 'Writing the History of the Climate', *The Territory of the Historian* (Chicago, 1979), 287–91; Christof Dipper, *Deutsche Geschichte 1648–1789* (Frankfurt/Main, 1991), 10–18; Brian Fagan, *The Little Ice Age* (New York, 2000).

14 Musall, *Kulturlandschaft*, 151; Josef Mock, 'Auswirkungen des Hochwasserschutzes', in Hans Reiner Böhm and Michael Deneke (eds.), *Wasser: Eine Einführung in die Umweltwissenschaften* (Darmstadt, 1992), 176–84.

15 Musall, *Kulturlandschaft*, 120.

16 Ibid., 119, 161–2.

17 Heinrich Cassinone and Heinrich Spiess, *Johann Gottfried Tulla, der Begründer der Wasser- und Strassenbauverwaltung in Baden: Sein Leben und Wirken* (Karlsruhe, 1929), 41–2; Hans Georg Zier, 'Johann Gottfried Tulla: Ein Lebensbild', *BH* 50 (1970), 445.

18 Dollfus, *L'Homme et le Rhin*, 118.

19 Heinrich Wittmann, 'Tulla, Honsell, Rehbeck', *BA* 4 (1949), 14; Cioc, *Rhine*, 54.

20 On the early life and apprentice years, see Cassinone and Spiess, *Tulla*, 1–17.

21 Zier, 'Lebensbild', 390–3.

22 Ibid., 394.

23 Cassinone and Spiess, *Tulla*, 8–14.

24 Zier, 'Lebensbild', 398.

25 Ibid., 399.

26 Cassinone and Spiess, *Tulla*, 15–17; Zier, 'Lebensbild', 380, 406–13.

27 GLA, Nachlass Sprenger, 6: Tulla to Landbaumeister Winter, 30 Aug. 1814.

28 Cassinone and Spiess, *Tulla*, 20–32; Zier, 'Lebensbild', 417–29; Wittmann, 'Tulla, Honsell, Rehbock', 7.

29 Josef Smets, 'De l'eau et des hommes dans le Rhin inférieur du siècle des Lumières à la pré-industrialisation', *Francia* 21 (1994), 95–127, on the Niers. On the Oder, see Chapter 1, above, and Berghaus, *Landbuch*, vol. 3, 4, on the three cuts made in 1790 and 1791 by the villages of Bellinchen and Lunow (the so-called 'Lunower Durchstiche').

30 David Gilly, *Grundriß zu den Vorlesungen über das Praktische bei verschiedenen Gegenständen der Wasserbaukunst* (Berlin, 1795); David Gilly, *Fortsetzung der Darstellung des Land- und Wasserbaus in Pommern, Preussen und einem Teil der Neu- und Kurmark* (Berlin, 1797); David Gilly and Johann Albert Eytelwein (eds.), *Praktische Anweisung zur Wasserbaukunst* (Berlin, 1805). On Eytelwein's plans, see Walter Tietze, 'Die Oderschiffahrt: Studien zu ihrer Geschichte und zu ihrer wirtschaftlichen

Bedeutung', dissertation, Breslau 1906, 23–7; and for Eytelwein's influence on Tulla, see Wittmann, 'Tulla, Honsell, Rehbock', 10.

31 Johann Beckmann, *Anleitung zur Technologie* (1777). See Mitcham, *Thinking through Technology*, 131.

32 Karmarsch, *Geschichte der Technologie*, 863; Wilhelm Treue, *Wirtschafts- und Technikgeschichte Deutschlands* (Berlin and New York, 1984), 221.

33 Zier, 'Lebensbild', 383.

34 Ibid., 431–2.

35 J. G. Tulla, *Die Grundsätze, nach welchen die Rheinbauarbeiten künftig zu führen seyn möchten; Denkschrift vom 1.3.1812.*

36 Cited in Tümmers, *Der Rhein*, 145.

37 See Chapter 1.

38 Lindenfeld, *Practical Imagination*, 77–8; Wittmann, 'Tulla, Honsell, Rehbock', 7; Zier, 'Lebensbild', 427–8.

39 Tulla, *Über die Grundsätze*, cited in Max Honsell, *Die Korrektion des Ober- rheins von der Schweizer Grenze unterhalb Basel bis zur Grossh. Hessi- schen Grenze unterhalb Mannheim* (Karlsruhe, 1885), 5.

40 Carl von Clausewitz, *On War*, ed. Michael Howard and Peter Paret (Princeton, 1976), book 8, ch. 2, 591–2.

41 On the collapse of the Empire and its effects on states like Baden that bene- fited territorially, see David Blackbourn, *The Fontana History of Germany 1780–1918: The Long Nineteenth Century* (London, 1997), 61–4, 75–7.

42 H. Schmitt, 'Germany without Prussia: A Closer Look at the Confedera- tion of the Rhine', *GSR* 6 (1983), 9–39.

43 Lloyd E. Lee, 'Baden between Revolutions: State-Building and Citizenship, 1800–1848', *CEH* 24 (1991), 248–67.

44 To give just some examples of these issues from the voluminous archival record in Karlsruhe, see *GLA* 237/16806: Die Abgabe von Faschinenholz an die Flussbauverwaltung und die Bewirtschaftung derjenigen Waldungen, welche der Flussbaudienstbarkeit unterstellt sind; 237/44858: Den Bedarf an Faschinenhölzern für die Rheinbauten und Flussbauten, sowie die Bewirtschaftung der Faschinenwaldungen auf den Rheininseln und den Rheinvorlanden; 237/30617: Das Flussbauwesen, die Regulierung der Fluss- baumaterialienpreise an Faschinen, Pfählen etc, die Bestimmung der Forstge- bühren bei Abgaben der Faschinen, das Kiesgraben zum Behuf der Rheinbauten; 237/30623: Die Festsetzung und Erhebung der Fluss- und Dammbaukostenbeiträge; 237/30624: Normen zur Feststellung und Erhe- bung der Flussbausteuer und Dammbaubeiträge; 237/30802: Die an Private zu leistenden Entschädigungen für abgetretenes Grundeigentum zu Damm- bauten. Betr. Dettenheim, Eggenstein, Erlach, Diersheim, Rheinbischoffs- heim; 237/30793: Die Rheinrektifikation, insb. das Eigentum der durch künstliche Rheinbauten entstehenden Altwasser und Verlandungen. The

question of who would benefit from newly formed land was not determined until a law of 1855. See *GLA* 237/35062.

45 *GLA* 237/35060: Die Rheinkorrektionen und die Entschädigung derjenigen, denen durch die vorgenomennen Durchschnitte Güter verloren gegangen oder deterioriert worden, I. 1819–1839 is a file in which, despite the apparently narrow subject matter (prompted by a 'cut' near Daxlanden), these departments of state all expressed views.

46 Christoph Bernhardt, 'The Correction of the Upper Rhine in the Nineteenth Century: Modernizing Society and State by Large-Scale Water Engineering', in Susan C. Anderson and Bruce H. Tabb (eds.), *Water, Culture, and Politics in Germany and the American West* (New York, 2001), 183–202; Cioc, *Rhine*, 49–50.

47 Henrik Froriep, 'Rechtsprobleme der Oberrheinkorrektion im Grossherzogtum Baden', dissertation, Mainz (1953), 14–17.

48 Johannes Gut, 'Die badisch-französische sowie die badisch-bayerische Staatsgrenze und die Rheinkorrektion', *ZGO* 142 (1994), 215–32.

49 Peter Sahlins, 'Natural Frontiers Revisited: France's Boundaries since the Seventeenth Century', *AHR* 95 (1990), 1440.

50 Ibid., 1442.

51 Froriep, 'Rechtsprobleme', 17–21.

52 Ibid., 78–90.

53 Thomas Nipperdey, *Deutsche Geschichte 1800–1866* (Munich, 1983), 11.

54 Honsell, *Korrektion*; Wittmann, 'Tulla, Honsell, Rehbock', 11–12; Egon Kunz, 'Flussbauliche Massnahmen am Oberrhein von Tulla bis heute mit ihren Auswirkungen', in Norbert Hailer (ed.), *Natur und Landschaft am Oberrhein: Versuch einer Bilanz* (Speyer, 1982), 38; Cioc, *Rhine*, 51–3.

55 *GLA* 237/44858: Den Bedarf an Faschinenhölzern für die Rheinbauten und Flussbauten sowie die Bewirtschaftung der Faschinenwaldungen auf den Rheininseln und den Rheinvorlanden betr. The costs at that stage were around 100,000 Gulden a year.

56 Cassinone and Spiess, *Tulla*, 55–87.

57 Calculated from Figure 12 in Heinz Musall, Günter Preuß and Karl-Heinz Rothenberger, 'Der Rhein und seine Aue', in Geiger, Preuß and Rothenberger (eds.), *Der Rhein und die Pfälzische Rheinebene*, 55. See also Musall, *Kulturlandschaft*, 199–201; Tümmers, *Rhein*, 146.

58 Schulte-Mäter, *Auswirkungen der Korrektion*, 61.

59 On the Carolingian precedent, *Fossa Carolina – 1200 Jahre Karlsgraben*, special issue of *Zeitschrift der Bayerischen Staatsbauverwaltung* (Munich, 1993); Walter Keller, *Der Karlsgraben: 1200 Jahre, 793–1993* (Treuchtlingen, 1993); Paolo Squatritti, 'Digging Ditches in Early Medieval Europe', *PP* 176 (2002), 11–65. On the labour force engaged in Rhine rectification, Cassinone and Spiess, *Tulla*, 59: Roland Paul, 'Alte Berufe am

Rhein', in Geiger, Preuß and Rothenberger (eds.), *Der Rhein und die Pfälzische Rheinebene*, 280.

60 Musall, *Kulturlandschaft*, 154–5; Honsell, *Korrektion*, 6; Wittmann, 'Tulla, Honsell, Rehbock', 11; Traude Löbert, *Die Oberrheinkorrektion in Baden: Zur Umweltgeschichte des 19. Jahrhunderts* (Karlsruhe, 1997), 68–80; Christoph Bernhardt, 'Zeitgenössische Kontroversen über die Umweltfolgen der Oberrheinkorrektion im 19. Jahrhundert', *ZGO* 146 (1998), 297–9.

61 Zier, 'Lebensbild', 431.

62 Ibid.

63 Ibid., 440.

64 Ibid., 431, 440.

65 Ibid., 431.

66 The full title of the 1825 memorandum was *Über die Rectification des Rheines, vom seinem Austritt aus der Schweiz bis zu seinem Eintritt in das Großherzogtum Hessen*. A copy of the memorandam is included in *GLA* 237/35060: Die Rheinkorrektionen, a reminder that it was a working document, not a piece of abstract wisdom.

67 *GLA*, Nachlass Sprenger, 1, 16. On Tulla's relationship with Sprenger, see ibid., 14: Sprenger to Tulla, 28 Jan. 1824, where the young Sprenger reported on the commissions he had performed the previous year on Tulla's behalf, and (like the young Tulla before him) alluded delicately to the fact that the heavy travel schedule meant that he had exceeded his allowance.

68 Zier, 'Lebensbild', 437; Cassinone and Spiess, *Tulla*, 60–2.

69 Zier, 439–40.

70 Tulla, *Denkschrift: Die Rectification des Rheines* (Karlsruhe, 1822), 7. The same view was expressed later in the same memorandum of 1822: 'In cultivated lands the bed of the river should therefore be given one regular and unchanging course and kept within it' (ibid., 41).

71 Zier, 'Lebensbild', 429.

72 Carl Philipp Spitzer and August Becker, cited in Wolfgang Diehl, 'Poesie und Dichtung der Rheinebene', in Geiger, Preuß and Rothenberger (eds.), *Der Rhein und die Pfälzische Rheinebene*, 379, 384. On Becker and his importance for interpretation of the Palatine landscape, Celia Applegate, *A Nation of Provincials*, 39, 55–7, 79, 123.

73 Quotation from Heinrich Wittmann, *Flussbau und Siedlung* (Ankara, 1960), 20.

74 *Die Rheinpfalz*, 4 Oct. 2002.

75 Tulla, *Über die Rectification des Rheines*, 52.

76 Honsell, *Korrektion*, 71–5; Tümmers, *Rhein*, 147–8.

77 Dipper, *Deutsche Geschichte 1648–1789*, 19.

78 Schulte-Mäter, *Auswirkungen der Korrektion*, 53, 70.

79 Harald Fauter, 'Malaria am Oberrhein in Vergangenheit und Gegenwart',

dissertation, University of Tübingen (1956); Honsell, *Korrektion*, 75; Löbert, *Oberrheinkorrektion*, 53–5; Bernhardt, 'Correction of the Upper Rhine', 183. The counter-argument on the furcation zone was made by Dr Preuß during discussion at a 1977 symposium in Speyer: Hailer (ed.), *Natur und Landschaft am Oberrhein*, 45–6. It was made by earlier writers such as van der Wijck (in 1846) and the great naturalist Robert Lauterborn (in 1938): Bernhardt, 'Zeitgenössische Kontroversen', 303–4.

80 On Tulla's project and the growth of Mannheim, see Dieter Schott, 'Remodeling "Father Rhine": The Case of Mannheim 1825–1914', in Anderson and Tabb (eds.), *Water, Culture, and Politics*, 203–35.

81 Carl Lepper, *Die Goldwäscherei am Rhein* (Heppenheim, 1980); Gustav Albiez, 'Die Goldwäscherei am Rhein', in Kurt Klein (ed.), *Land um Rhein und Schwarzwald* (Kehl, 1978), 268–71.

82 Musall, *Kulturlandschaft*, 106.

83 Paul, 'Alte Berufe am Rhein', 277; Tümmers, *Der Rhein*, 142.

84 Musall, *Kulturlandschaft*, 143.

85 Ibid., 190; Schulte-Mäter, *Auswirkungen der Korrektion*, 62.

86 Lepper, *Goldwäscherei*, 76; Paul, 'Alte Berufe am Rhein', 279.

87 GLA 237/44817: Goldwaschen im Rhein 1824–1946; Tümmers, *Der Rhein*, 142–3; Albiez, 'Goldwäscherei', 271.

88 Tümmers, *Der Rhein*, 142.

89 Paul, 'Alte Berufe am Rhein', 279; Schulte-Mäter, *Auswirkungen der Korrektion*, 74–6; Musall, *Kulturlandschaft*, 236.

90 Musall, *Kulturlandschaft*, 190, has examples from around Eggenstein, Dettenheim and Neuburg.

91 Horst Koßmann, 'Fische und Fischerei', in Geiger, Preuß and Rothenberger (eds.), *Der Rhein und die Pfälzische Rheinebene*, 204; Schulte-Mäter, *Auswirkungen der Korrektion*, 47–8, 54; Paul, 'Alte Berufe am Rhein', 273.

92 Musall, *Kulturlandschaft*, 142.

93 Hans-Rüdiger Fluck, 'Die Fischerei im Hanauerland', *BH* 50 (1970), 484.

94 Anton Lelek and Günter Buhse, *Fische des Rheins – früher und heute* (Berlin and Heidelberg, 1992), 34. Forty-five represented all but two of the forty-seven species then to be found along the whole length of the river.

95 Koßmann, 'Fische und Fischerei', 205; Götz Kuhn, *Die Fischerei am Oberrhein* (Stuttgart, 1976), 21–2.

96 Jäger, *Einführung*, 202; Kuhn, *Fischerei*, 24.

97 Paul, 'Alte Berufe am Rhein', 273; Kuhn, *Fischerei*, 54.

98 Kunz, 'Flussbauliche Massnahmen am Oberrhein', 39; Kuhn, *Fischerei*, 55.

99 The price of the lease (*Pacht*) on the Herrenbach fell from 185 to 13 Guilder between 1828 and 1853; that of the Königsee near Liedolsheim fell from thirty Guilder to just one Guilder in the same period: Musall, *Kulturlandschaft*, 235.

100 Ibid., 236, on the forty-one fishermen in Rheinhausen and the nineteen in Philippsburg in the 1860s; Schulte-Mäter, *Auswirkungen der Korrektion*, 40–2, on Breisach fisher families through the 1880s.

101 Ragnar Kinzelbach, 'Zur Entstehung der Zoozönose der Rheins', in Kinzelbach (ed.), *Die Tierwelt des Rheins einst und jetzt* (Mainz, 1985), 31; Tittizer and Krebs, *Ökosystemforschung*, 27–40; Lelek and Buhse, *Fische des Rheins*, 13–23, 184–5.

102 Kuhn, *Fischerei*, 186.

103 Paul, 'Alte Berufe am Rhein', 273; Fluck, 'Die Fischerei', 477; Koßmann, 'Fische und Fischerei', 206; Tittizer and Krebs, *Ökosystemforschung*, 37–8.

104 Kuhn, *Fischerei*, 57–9, 63; Cioc, *Rhine*, 158–67; Lelek and Buhse, *Fische des Rheins*, 37–40.

105 On the zander, Lelek and Buhse, *Fische des Rheins*, 177–9.

106 Ibid., 160–3.

107 Kuhn, *Fischerei*, 79–90, 156–63.

108 Willi Gutting, *Die Aalfischer: Roman vom Oberrhein* (Bayreuth, 1943).

109 Ibid., 213.

110 I have been unable to obtain a copy of Gutting's brief memoirs, 'Sicht von oben', cited without bibliographical details in Diehl, 'Poesie und Dichtung', 381.

111 Gutting, *Die Aalfischer*, 8.

112 Ibid., 31, 56.

113 Ibid. 189, 190–1, 225. The Faustian episode is on 183–96. In Gutting's novel, *Glückliches Ufer* (Bayreuth, 1943), there is a similar emphasis on the dike that protects the 'fruitful land' of the villagers.

114 Löbert, *Oberrheinkorrektion*, 95–100.

115 Gutting, *Die Aalfischer*, 189.

116 Ibid., 188.

117 The term 'outdoor geometry' comes from the American conservationist Aldo Leopold, with Germany in mind. Cioc, *Rhine*, 167, cites Leopold's comment that all German streams looked 'straight as a dead snake'.

118 The proceedings were published in Hailer (ed.), *Natur und Landschaft am Oberrhein*.

119 Carl Zuckmayer, *A Part of Myself* (New York, 1984), 100 (first German edition 1966).

120 On Lauterborn, see Cioc, *Rhine*, 173–5 and Ragnar Kinzelbach, 'Vorwort', in Kinzelbach (ed.), *Die Tierwelt des Rheins*; on his predecessors, Georg Philippi, 'Änderung der Flora und Vegetation am Oberrhein', in Hailer (ed.), *Natur und Landschaft am Oberrhein*, 87.

121 Musall, *Kulturlandschaft*, 95; Robert Mürb, 'Landwirtschaftliche Aspekte beim Ausbau von Fliessgewässern', in Böhm and Deneke (eds.), *Wasser*, 120; Tittizer and Krebs, *Ökosystemforschung* (the subtitle of which is *Der*

Rhein und seine Auen: Eine Bilanz); Cioc, *Rhine*, 150–4. On habitat fragmentation, D. S. Wilcove, C. H. McLellan and A. P. Dobson, 'Habitat Fragmentation in the Temperate Zone', in Andrew Goudie (ed.), *The Human Impact Reader* (Oxford, 1997), 342–55.

122 Ragnar Kinzelbach, 'Veränderungen der Fauna im Oberrhein', in Hailer (ed.), *Natur und Landschaft am Oberrhein*, 78; see also Cioc, *Rhine*, 12.

123 Cioc, *Rhine*, 156–7.

124 Kinzelbach, 'Veränderungen der Fauna', 66–83. Tittizer and Krebs (eds.), *Ökosystemforschung* also emphasize the multiple, interrelated causes of the decline in biodiversity, devoting over a hunded pages to pollution alone.

125 Cited in Günter Preuß, 'Naturschutz', in Geiger, Preuß and Rothenberger (eds.), *Der Rhein und die Pfälzische Rheinebene*, 238–9.

126 Cited Philippi, 'Änderung der Flora und Vegetation', in Hailer (ed.), *Natur und Landschaft am Oberrhein*, 92.

127 Philippi, 'Änderung der Flora und Vegetation', 98.

128 Herbert Schwarzmann, 'War die Tulla'sche Oberrheinkorrektion eine Fehlleistung im Hinblick auf ihre Auswirkungen?', *DW* 54 (1964), 279–87; Egon Kunz, 'Flussbauliche Massnahmen am Oberrhein', 39; Tümmers, *Der Rhein*, 148–50; Cioc, *Rhine*, 54. Garbrecht (*Wasser*, 188) defends Tulla on the grounds that his correction was, by contemporary standards, 'bold and in principle correct'.

129 Philippi, 'Änderung der Flora und Vegetation', 89; Schulte-Mäter, *Auswirkungen der Korrektion*, 19–20, 27–38; Tümmers, *Der Rhein*, 172–4.

130 See Kinzelbach, 'Veränderungen der Flora', 67–8; Philippi, 'Änderung der Flora und Vegetation', 98–9; Musall, Preuß and Rothenberger, 'Der Rhein und seine Aue', 69–72.

131 Leopold and Roma Schua, *Wasser – Lebenselement und Umwelt: Die Geschichte des Gewässerschutzes in ihrem Entwicklungsgang dargestellt und dokumentiert* (Freiburg and Munich, 1981), 150.

132 F[ritz] André, *Bemerkungen über die Rectification des Oberrheins und die Schilderung der furchtbaren Folgen, welche dieses Unternehmen für die Bewohner des Mittel- und Niederrheins nach sich ziehen wird* (Hanau, 1828), iv.

133 Löbert, *Oberrheinkorrektion*, 43–8; Bernhardt, 'Zeitgenössische Kontroversen', 299–311; Cioc, *Rhine*, 69–72. The critical Prussian memorandum of 14 July 1826 against Tulla's proposal is reprinted in Schua and Schua, *Wasser*, 146–50. Eytelwein had been a dike inspector in the Oderbruch in 1790, five years after the major flooding of 1785.

134 Schulte-Mäter, *Auswirkungen der Korrektion*, 59–60. GLA 237/23985 has material on the rectification of the Kinzig and Rench, 1803–28.

135 Bernhardt, 'Zeitgenössische Kontroversen', 313–17; Bernhardt, 'Correction of the Upper Rhine', 192–4, 197–9; Cioc, *Rhine*, 72. On Honsell, see

Wittmann, 'Tulla, Honsell, Rehbock', 15–16, R. Fuchs, *Dr. ing. Max Honsell* (Karlsruhe, 1912), 5–6, 47–77, and Honsell's own *Die Korrektion des Oberrheins*.

136 Tümmers, *Der Rhein*, 158; Gerd-Peter Kossler, *Natur und Landschaft im Rhein-Main-Gebiet* (Frankfurt/Main, 1996), 124. Kossler, 129, also gives a dramatic example of how the side-arms retained water before they were cut off, noting the nine-metre deep pool created by the 1883 floods in the side-arm area near Stockstadt.

137 GLA 237/24112: Die Hochwasserschäden im Jahre 1844; 237/24113: Das Hochwasser im Jahre 1851; 237/30826: Die Ergänzung und Verstärkung der Rheindämme; 237/24141–55: Das Hochwasser und Beschädigungen im Jahre 1876; 237/24088–9: Die Ergänzung und Verstärkung der Rheindämme in den Rheingemeinden des Amtsbezirkes Lörrach und Freiburg; 237/24156–76: Die Hochwasserschäden im Jahre 1877; 237/24091: Die Ergänzung und Verstärkung der Rheindämme auf Gemarkung Daxlanden, Knielingen und Neuburgweier 1879–1880; 237/24177–92: Die Hochwasserschäden im Jahre 1879. 1880. – and so on through the 1880s and 1890s.

138 Kunz, 'Flussbauliche Massnahmen am Oberrhein', 47.

139 On efforts to 'renature' the Rhine and restore the Auenwald in the interests of both conservation and flood prevention, see Chapter 6 below. The epilogue discusses the same issue on the Oder.

140 Zier, 'Lebensbild', 419–20.

141 Roy E. H. Mellor, *The Rhine: A Study in the Geography of Water Transport* (Aberdeen, 1983), 22–4; Cioc, *Rhine*, 73–5; Mock, 'Auswirkungen', 186–90.

142 Cioc, *Rhine*, calls one of his chapters 'Water Sorcery'.

Chapter Three: Golden Age

1 The description of Kerst from his Oldenburg friend Theodor Erdmann. Vice-admiral Batsch called him 'hot-blooded, somewhat coarse-grained'. See Edgar Grundig, *Chronik der Stadt Wilhelmshaven*, 2 vols. (Wilhelmshaven, 1957), vol. 1, 456–7.

2 On Hinckeldey, Albrecht Funk, *Polizei und Rechtsstaat* (Frankfurt/Main, 1986), 60–70.

3 Grundig, *Chronik*, vol. 1, 456–8, 464–6.

4 See Gaebler's artful, flattering memorandum to Manteuffel in August 1852: Heinrich von Poschinger (ed.), *Unter Friedrich Wilhelm IV. Denkwürdigkeiten des Ministerpräsidenten Otto Freiherr von Manteuffel, Zweiter Band: 1851–1854* (Berlin, 1901), 233–4. On the naval enthusiasm of Gaebler's superior, Hinckeldey, Adolf Wermuth, *Ein Beamtenleben: Erinnerungen* (Berlin, 1922), 15.

5 Grundig, *Chronik*, 467–9; Helmuth Gießler, 'Wilhelmshaven und die Marine', in Arthur Grunewald (ed.), *Wilhelmshaven: Tidekurven einer Seestadt* (Wilhelmshaven, 1969), 229–30; *Festschrift: 75 Jahre Marinewerft Wilhelmshaven* (Oldenburg, 1931), 18–20; Rolf Uphoff, *'Hier lasst uns einen Hafen bau'n!' Entstehungsgeschichte der Stadt Wilhelmshaven. 1848–1890* (Oldenburg, 1995), 40–1, 56–8. On the auctioning off of the fleet, Max Bär, *Die deutsche Flotte 1848–1852* (Leipzig, 1898), 207–18.

6 Giles MacDonogh, *Prussia: The Perversion of an Idea* (London, 1994), 167.

7 'Die deutsche Kriegsflotte', *Die Gegenwart*, vol. 1 (Leipzig, 1848), 441.

8 Ibid., 442.

9 Uphoff, *Entstehungsgeschichte*, 36; Lord Napier to Earl Russell, 20 April 1865: Veit Valentin (ed.), *Bismarcks Reichsgründung im Urteil englischer Diplomaten* (Amsterdam, 1937), 522. In his August 1852 memorandum to Manteuffel, Gaebler also described the building of a Prussian fleet as a conquest ('This conquest . . . Yes, it is a conquest').

10 P. Koch, *50 Jahre Wilhelmshaven: Ein Rückblick auf die Werdezeit* (Berlin, n.d. [1919]), 5–6; Gustav Rüthning, *Oldenburgische Geschichte*, vol. 2 (Bremen, 1911), 589–90; Grundig, *Chronik*, vol. 1, 441–60; Uphoff, *Entstehungsgeschichte*, 36–40.

11 Grundig, *Chronik*, vol. 1, 475.

12 Bär, *Flotte*, 222. By this time the Crimean War was already underway, which muted reactions in Austria and abroad.

13 On the negotiations and terms, including the agreement by Prussia to resolve the long dispute between Oldenburg and the heirs of the Bentinck family over the sovereignty of Kniphausen, see 'Geschichte des Vertrages vom 20.7.1853 über die Anlegung eines Kriegshafens an der Jade. Aus den Aufzeichnungen des verstorbenen Geheimen Rats Erdmann', *OJ* 9 (1900), 35–9; Rüthning, *Oldenburgische Geschichte*, vol. 2, 590–4.

14 Theodor Murken, 'Vom Dorf zur Großstadt', in Grunewald (ed.), *Wilhelmshaven*, 178; Uphoff, *Entstehungsgeschichte*, 58–9.

15 Carl Woebcken, *Jeverland* (Jever, 1961), 15–16; Wilhelm Stukenberg, *Aus der Kulturentwicklung des Landes Oldenburg* (Oldenburg, 1989), 21.

16 Georg Sello, *Der Jadebusen* (Varel, 1903), 40.

17 Werner Haarnagel, *Probleme der Küstenforschung im südlichen Nordseegebiet* (Hildesheim, 1950).

18 Klaus Brandt, 'Vor- und Frühgeschichte der Marschengebiete', in Albrecht Eckhardt and Heinrich Schmidt (eds.), *Geschichte des Landes Oldenburg* (Oldenburg, 1987), 15–35; Johann Kramer, *Kein Deich – Kein Land – Kein Leben* (Leer, 1989), 56–8.

19 Heinrich Schmidt, 'Grafschaft Oldenburg und oldenburgisches Friesland im Mittelalter und Reformationszeit', in Eckhardt and Schmidt (eds.), *Geschichte*, 101–9; Sello, *Jadebusen*, 10–16.

20 Stukenberg, *Aus der Kulturentwicklung des Landes Oldenburg*, 22.

21 Carl Woebcken, *Die Entstehung des Jadebusen* (Aurich, 1934).

22 Sello, *Jadebusen*, 21; Adolf Blumenberg, *Heimat am Jadebusen: Von Menschen, Deichen und versunkenem Land* (Nordenham-Blexen, 1997), 19–101.

23 Sello, *Jadebusen*, 20–2; Carl Woebcken, *Deiche und Sturmfluten an der deutschen Nordseeküste* (Bremen and Wilhelmshaven, 1924), 140–2. Cf. Husum, which owed its wealth to the drowning of Rungholt in 1362: ibid., 75–6.

24 Sello, *Jadebusen*, 8.

25 Map in Dettmar Coldewey, 'Bevor die Preußen kamen', in Grunewald (ed.), *Wilhelmshaven*, 156; Woebcken, *Deiche und Sturmfluten*, 140.

26 Hans Walter Flemming, *Wüsten, Deiche und Turbinen* (Göttingen, 1957), 150.

27 Erich Heckmann, 'Überliefertes Brauchtum in einer jungen Stadt', in Grunewald (ed.), *Wilhelmshaven*, 406–8; Woebcken, *Deiche und Sturmfluten*, 195–210.

28 Jakubowski-Tiessen, *Sturmflut 1717*, 217–25.

29 Flemming, *Wüste, Deiche und Turbinen*, 154.

30 Theodor Storm, *Der Schimmelreiter* (Berlin, 1888).

31 A good example is Kramer, *Kein Deich – Kein Land – Kein Leben*. On the 'dangerous effects of natural forces' on the one hand, set against the claim that 'we can be truly proud of our modern technology' on the other, see Flemming, *Wüsten, Deiche und Turbinen*, 150, 171.

32 Karl Tillessen, 'Gezeiten, Sturmfluten, Deiche und Fahrwasser', in Grunewald (ed.), *Wilhelmshaven*, 41–64; Woebcken, *Deiche und Sturmfluten*, 30–1; Kramer, *Kein Deich – Kein Land – Kein Leben*, 29–31.

33 See Haarnagel, *Probleme der Küstenforschung* and Karl-Ernst Behre, *Meeresspiegelbewegungen und Siedlungsgeschichte in den Nordseemarschen* (Oldenburg, 1987). Heinrich Schütte's 'sinking coast' thesis, first developed in the early twentieth century, was an essential stimulus to research. See Schütte, *Sinkendes Land an der Nordsee?* (Oehringen, 1939).

34 Behme, *Meeresspiegelbewegungen und Siedlungsgeschichte*, 34–5; Heinrich Schmidt, 'Grafschaft Oldenburg', 123–4; Sello, *Jadebusen*, 10–16.

35 Küster, *Geschichte der Landschaft*, 213–21; Jäger, *Einführung*, 28–31; Dietrich Deneke, 'Eingriffe der Menschen in die Landschaft: Historische Entwicklung – Folgen – erhaltene Relikte', in Ernst Schubert and Bernd Herrmann (eds.), *Von der Angst vor der Ausbeutung: Umweltgeschichte zwischen Mittelalter und Neuzeit* (Frankfurt/Main, 1994), 61, 68. See also L. Carbognin, 'Land Subsidence: A Worldwide Environmental Hazard', in Goudie (ed.), *Human Impact Reader*, 30–1.

36 Woebcken, *Deiche und Sturmfluten*, 88.

37　Kramer, *Kein Deich – Kein Land – Kein Leben*, 72–99; Rüthning, *Oldenburgische Geschichte*, vol. 2, 97–114; Küster, *Geschichte der Landschaft*, 221.

38　Coldewey, 'Bevor die Preussen kamen', 174; Woebcken, *Entstehung des Jadebusen*, 50–4; Hamm, *Naturkundliche Chronik*, 70.

39　Sello, *Jadebusen*, 34; Kramer, *Kein Deich – Kein Land – Kein Leben*, 76–7; Walter Deeters, 'Kleinstaat und Provinz', in Karl-Ernst Behre and Hajo von Langen (eds.), *Ostfriesland: Geschichte und Gestalt einer Kulturlandschaft* (Aurich, 1995), 155–6.

40　Jakubowski-Tiessen, *Sturmflut 1717*, 242.

41　Kramer, *Kein Deich – Kein Land – Kein Leben*, 100–2.

42　The after-effects of one major flood are examined superbly by Jakubowski-Tiessen, *Sturmflut 1717*, chs 6–9.

43　Woebcken, *Jeverland*, 98; Jäger, *Einführung*, 30–1.

44　Woebcken, *Deiche und Sturmfluten*, 90–3; Küster, *Geschichte der Landschaft*, 218–19.

45　Grundig, *Chronik*, vol. 1, 52.

46　Jakubowski-Tiessen, *Sturmflut 1717*, 44–78; Woebcken, *Deiche und Sturmfluten*, 93–7; Wilhelm Norden, *Eine Bevölkerung in der Krise: Historisch-demographische Untersuchungen zur Biographie einer norddeutschen Küstenregion (Butjadingen 1600–1850)* (Hildesheim, 1984), 76–80; Rüthning, *Oldenburgische Geschichte*, vol. 2, 114–21. Kramer, *Kein Deich – Kein Land – Kein Leben*, 40, gives higher figures for the loss of people and animals.

47　Woebcken, *Deiche und Sturmfluten*, 99–108, quotation 101; Kramer, *Kein Deich – Kein Land – Kein Leben*, 40–1.

48　Waldemar Reinhardt, 'Die Besiedlung der Landschaft an der Jade', in Grunewald (ed.), *Wilhelmshaven*, 139–40; Uphoff, *Entstehungsgeschichte*, 11–29. On similar trends across the bay in Butjadingen, see Norden, *Bevölkerung*, 283–94, and on the special status of wealthy marsh farmers, Küster, *Geschichte der Landschaft*, 222.

49　Uphoff, *Entstehungsgeschichte*, 62.

50　Murken, 'Vom Dorf zur Grossstadt', 180; Uphoff, *Entstehungsgeschichte*, 60–3.

51　Coldewey, 'Bevor die Preussen kamen', 174–5; Catharine Schwanhäuser, *Aus der Chronik Wilhelmshavens* (Wilhelmshaven, 1974 [1926]), 33; Grundig, *Chronik*, vol. 1, 13–14, 438–9; Schmidt, 'Grafschaft Oldenburg', 207.

52　'Die deutsche Kriegsflotte', 450, 459–60.

53　Schwanhäuser, *Chronik*, 3.

54　Theodor Murken, 'Wilhelmshavener Kaleidoscop', in Grunewald (ed.), *Wilhelmshaven*, 371.

55　Koch, *50 Jahre*, 8–14.

56 Waldemar Reinhardt, 'Witterung und Klima im Raum Wilhelmshaven', in Grunewald (ed.), *Wilhelmshaven*, 32–40.

57 Louise von Krohn, *Vierzig Jahre in einem deutschen Kriegshafen Heppens-Wilhelmshaven: Erinnerungen* (Rostock, 1911), iii.

58 Ibid., 3–4.

59 Ibid., 17.

60 Ibid., 65; Archibald Hurd and Henry Castle, *German Sea-Power* (London, 1913), 85.

61 Koch, *50 Jahre*, 19–22; Schwanhäuser, *Chronik*, 7; Woebcken, *Deiche und Sturmfluten*, 108.

62 Uphoff, *Entstehungsgeschichte*, 80–3; Günther Spelde, *Geschichte der Lotsen-Brüderschaften an der Aussenweser und an der Jade* (Bremen, n.d.[1985]), 169; Woebcken, *Deiche und Sturmfluten*, 108; Hamm, *Naturkundliche Chronik*, 161.

63 Koch, *50 Jahre*, 16, 21–2.

64 Axel Wiese, *Die Hafenbauarbeiter an der Jade (1853–1871)* (Oldenburg, 1998), 40–1.

65 Ibid., 52–3.

66 Krohn, *Vierzig Jahre*, 64–5; Schwanhäuser, *Chronik*, 3; Murken, 'Kaleidoscop', 372.

67 Blackbourn, *Fontana History of Germany*, 205–6.

68 Wiese, *Hafenbauarbeiter*, 42–7; Uphoff, *Entstehungsgeschichte*, 89–90.

69 W. Krüger, 'Die Baugeschichte der Hafenanlagen', *JbHG* 4 (1922), 98.

70 Schwanhäuser, *Chronik*, 7–8; Wiese, *Hafenbauarbeiter*, 67–9.

71 See the tables in Uphoff, *Entstehungsgeschichte*, 202–6. A major reason for the probable under-recording is that seriously ill workers who lived locally went home to die.

72 Schwanhäuser, *Chronik*, 16–17; Murken, 'Kaleidoscop', 372; Wiese, *Hafenbauarbeiter*, 72–8, 84–8.

73 Norden, *Bevölkerung*, 106–10; Ernst Hinrichs, 'Grundzüge der neuzeitlichen Bevölkerungsgeschichte des Landes Oldenburg', *Vorträge der Oldenburgischen Landschaft* 13 (1985), 20–1; Waldemar Reinhardt, 'Die Stadt Wilhelmshaven in preussischer Zeit', in Eckhardt and Schmidt (eds.), *Geschichte*, 640.

74 Dr P. Mühlens, 'Bericht über die Malariaepidemie des Jahres 1907 in Bant, Heppens, Neuende und Wilhelmshaven sowie in der weiteren Umgegend', *KJb* 19 (1907), 56.

75 Hamm, *Naturkundliche Chronik*, 163.

76 There had been 'a great deal, a very great deal of fever', recalled Krohn, *Vierzig Jahre*, 12; the workforce had 'all too many victims', said Koch, *50 Jahre*, 12.

77 Krohn, *Vierzig Jahre*, 15–16, 27, 30.

78 To give an idea of *how* thin it was, the 858 people who lived in the Prussian-owned territory in 1861 (a larger number had spilled out into surrounding Oldenburg land) included just thirty-six families: Koch, *50 Jahre*, 38.

79 Koch, *50 Jahre*, 71; Krohn, *Vierzig Jahre*, 75.

80 Koch, *50 Jahre*, 11; Schwanhäuser, *Chronik*, 12–13.

81 Schwanhäuser, *Chronik*, 9, 28; Krohn, *Vierzig Jahre*, 67, 120, 125; Krüger, 'Baugeschichte', 98.

82 Koch, *50 Jahre*, 17; Krohn, *Vierzig Jahre*, 128; Schwanhäuser, *Chronik*, 19–20, 58, 102.

83 Schwanhäuser, *Chronik*, 37.

84 Krohn, *Vierzig Jahre*, 9, 64–5; Schwanhäuser, *Chronik*, 6.

85 Koch, *50 Jahre*, 26–9; Uphoff, *Entstehungsgeschichte*, 112–14; Rüthning, *Oldenburgische Geschichte*, vol. 2, 605; Grundig, *Chronik*, vol. 2, 193–6.

86 Koch, *50 Jahre*, 82; Murken, 'Vom Dorf zur Grossstadt', 179–80.

87 Schwanhäuser, *Chronik*, 41; Koch, *50 Jahre*, 66–7.

88 Krohn, *Vierzig Jahre*, 219; Mühlens, 'Bericht'.

89 Grundig, *Chronik*, vol. 2, 647, on Rohlfs; Schwanhäuser, *Chronik*, 86, on the exhibition.

90 Krohn, *Vierzig Jahre*, 252.

91 He said it on 23 September 1898, while inaugurating a new harbour in Stettin.

92 Wolfgang Günther, 'Freistaat und Land Oldenburg (1918–1946)', in Eckhardt and Schmidt (eds.), *Geschichte des Landes Oldenburg*, 404–13.

93 'Land und Leute in Oldenburg', in *August Hinrichs über Oldenburg*, compiled by Gerhard Preuß (Oldenburg, 1986), 39.

94 On the Ems–Jade canal: Victor Kurs, 'Die künstlichen Wasserstrassen im Deutschen Reiche', *GZ* (1898), 611–12; Hamm, *Naturkundliche Chronik*, 177.

95 Karl-Ernst Behre, 'Die Entstehung und Entwicklung der Natur- und Kulturlandschaft der ostfriesischen Halbinsel', in Behre and van Lengen (eds.), *Ostfriesland*, 7–12; Makowski and Buderath, *Die Natur*, 201–20.

96 Kurs, 'Die künstlichen Wasserstrassen', 611.

97 On the creation of high moors, and the differences between low and high moorland: Behre, 'Entstehung und Entwicklung', 30–1; Mechthild Schwalb, *Die Entwicklung der bäuerlichen Kulturlandschaft in Ostfriesland und West-oldenburg* (Bonn, 1953), 12–14.

98 E. Stumpfe, *Die Besiedelung der deutschen Moore mit besonderer Berücksichtigung der Hochmoor- und Fehnkolonisation* (Leipzig and Berlin, 1903), 52–3, 69. The next highest figure was in the Prussian province of Hanover, where moorland covered a seventh of the surface.

99 Wolfgang Schwarz, 'Ur- und Frühgeschichte', in Behre and van Lengen (eds.), *Ostfriesland*, 51–2 (with superb illustrations); August Hinrichs, 'Zwischen

Marsch, Moor und Geest', in *August Hinrichs über Oldenburg*, 35.

100 *Etwas von der Teich-Arbeit, vom nützlichen Gebrauch des Torff-Moores, von Verbesserung der Wege aus bewährter Erfahrung mitgetheilet von Johann Wilhelm Hönert* (Bremen, 1772), 82–3, 130–1.

101 Küster, *Geschichte der Landschaft*, 270.

102 Hinrichs, 'Zwischen Marsch, Moor und Geest', 35–6; Makowski and Buderath, *Die Natur*, 221–5; Hamm, *Naturkundliche Chronik*, 194; Jörg Hansemann, 'Die historische Entwicklung des Torfabbaues im Toten Moor bei Neustadt am Rübenberge', *Telma* 14 (1984), 133.

103 Angela Wegener, 'Die Besiedlung der nordwestdeutschen Hochmoore', *Telma* 15 (1985), 152.

104 The very recent one was Auricher Wiesmoor; two further fen colonies – Wilhelms Fen I and II – would be founded as extensions of existing settlements in the 1880s.

105 H. Tebbenhoff, *Grossefehn: Seine Geschichte* (Ostgrossefehn, 1963); Ekkehard Wassermann, 'Siedlungsgeschichte der Moore', in Behre and van Lengen (eds.), *Ostfriesland*, 101–7; Deeters, 'Kleinstaat und Provinz', 147, 156, 166–7; Stumpfe, *Besiedelung*, 104–33, 170–87; Wegener, 'Besiedlung', 154–6; Küster, *Geschichte der Landschaft*, 270–3.

106 Stumpfe, *Besiedelung*, 196–208.

107 Deeters, 'Kleinstaat und Provinz', 173–4.

108 E. Schöningh, *Das Bourtanger Moor: Seine Besiedlung und wirtschaftliche Erschliessung* (Berlin, 1914); Stumpfe, *Besiedelung*, 214–20, 312–19. See below for the change in Prussian thinking.

109 Robert Glass, 'Die Besiedlung der Moore und anderer Ödländerein', *HHO* 2 (1913), 335–55, the work of a local moor inspector; L. Stöve, *Die Moorwirtschaft im Freistaate Oldenburg, unter besonderer Berücksichtigung der inneren Kolonisation* (Würzburg, 1921); Stumpfe, *Besiedelung*, 274–309.

110 A. Geppert, *Die Stadt am Kanal: Papenburgs Geschichte* (Ankum, 1955).

111 L[udwig] Starklof, *Moor-Kanäle und Moor-Colonien zwischen Hunte und Ems: Vier Briefe* (Oldenburg, 1847).

112 This biographical sketch is based on *Ludwig Starklof 1789–1850: Erinnerungen. Theater, Erlebnisse, Reisen*, ed. by Harry Niemann, with contributions from Hans Friedl, Lu-Ramona Fries, Karl Veit Riedel, Friedrich-Wilhelm Schaer (Oldenburg, 1986). See also Eckhardt and Schmidt (eds.), *Geschichte des Landes Oldenburg*, 289, 299, 317, 319, 322–3, 594, 606, 891, 931, 938, 949, 958; Rüthning, *Oldenburgische Geschichte*, draws heavily on Starklof's autobiography, but without attribution.

113 Starklof, *Vier Briefe*, 40.

114 Ibid., 10–13.

115 Ibid., 37–8.

116 Ibid., 17–18.

117 Ibid., 27–8.

118 Ibid., 20.

119 Ibid., 23, 28.

120 Niemann (ed.), *Ludwig Starklof*, 170–82; Hans Friedl, 'Ludwig Starklof (1789–1850): Hofrat und Rebell', ibid., 27–35; Rüthning, *Oldenburgische Geschichte*, vol. 2, 544–6.

121 Kurs, 'Die künstlichen Wasserstrassen', 611–13; Stumpfe, *Besiedelung*, 275–9; Klaus Lampe, 'Wirtschaft und Verkehr im Landkreis Oldenburg von 1800 bis 1945', in Eckhardt and Schmidt (eds.), *Geschichte des Landes Oldenburg*, 745.

122 Tebbenhoff, *Großefehn*.

123 Starklof, *Vier Briefe*, 47.

124 Stumpfe, *Besiedelung*, 197–204 (quotation 199).

125 Cited in Stumpfe, *Besiedelung*, 219.

126 Starklof, *Vier Briefe*, 40–8; Stumpfe, *Besiedelung*, 204–6.

127 Hans Pflug, *Deutsche Flüsse – Deutsche Lebensadern* (Berlin, 1939), 61.

128 They had smaller dimensions and few *Inwieken*: Stumpfe, *Besiedelung*, 135.

129 Wassermann, 'Siedlungsgeschichte', 101, with excellent illustrations depicting canal and colony lay-outs, 103–4.

130 Stumpfe gives many examples of these problems. For a case in the Teufels Moor, to the east, where a canal was built in the mid-eighteenth century to transport peat and abandoned less than fifty years later because of the maintenance costs, see Hansemann, 'Entwicklung des Torfabbaues im Toten Moor', 134; criticism of the 'Wildwachs' of early canals in Deeters, 'Kleinstaat und Provinz', 156; and criticism of the original Hunte–Ems canal in Lampke, 'Wirtschaft und Verkehr', 745.

131 Hamm, *Naturkundliche Chronik*, 170.

132 On reservoirs and canals, see Chapter 4 below.

133 Alfred Hugenberg, *Innere Colonisation im Nordwesten Deutschlands* (Strasbourg, 1891), 359.

134 Stumpfe's comment compared the decline of Fehntjer to the decline of craft branches after the end of the guild system: *Besiedelung*, 402–3.

135 Deeters, 'Kleinstaat und Provinz', 166–7; Wassermann, 'Siedlungsgeschichte', 106.

136 Stumpfe, *Besiedelung*, 139, 142, 175; Gunther Hummerich and Wolfgang Lüdde, *Dorfschiffer* (Norden, 1992).

137 In Papenburg the numbers fell from 182 (1869) to 71 (1890) to 38 (1895) to 18 (1901); in Great Fen from 53 (1869 and 1882) to 27 (1890) to 22 (1895) to 8 (1901); in Bockzeteler Fen from 23 (1869) to 16 (1882) to 13 (1890) to 7 (1895) to 2 (1901). West Rhauder Fen was the solitary exception in this time period. See table in Stumpfe, *Besiedelung*, 252–3. Barssel, an inland port in west Oldenburg with connections to the Ems, went through

the same experience. In 1870 it still harboured forty schooners that sailed as far as the USA and the Mediterranean; just ten years later, sea-going shipping was in sharp decline: Lampe, 'Wirschaft und Verkehr', 745.

138 Kurs, 'Die künstlichen Wasserstrassen', 611.

139 Fontane, *WMB*, vol. 2, 103. Italics in original. He was referring here to the Havelland, and in calling the local peat-cutting centre, Linum, the local 'Newcastle' he was also alluding to the competition of coal.

140 Stumpfe, *Besiedelung*, 184.

141 Ibid., 252–3.

142 Schwalb says the sixteenth century: 39–41.

143 Hamm, *Naturkundliche Chronik*, 81; Wegener, 'Besiedlung', 164.

144 Wassermann, 'Siedlungsgeschichte', 107.

145 Andrew Steele, *The Natural and Agricultural History of Peat-Moss or Turf-Bog* (Edinburgh, 1826), 53–4. Steele's book is devoted to demonstrating the value of burning the moor surface.

146 On the scientific and European dimensions: Pyne, *Vestal Fire*, 168–76.

147 Wassermann, 'Siedlungsgeschichte', 109.

148 Ibid., 107–11; Deeters, 'Kleinstaat und Provinz', 166; Stumpfe, *Besiedelung*, 68–82.

149 Schwalb, *Entwicklung der bäuerlichen Kulturlandschaft*, 41; Wassermann, 'Siedlungsgeschichte', 109–11; Hamm, *Naturkundliche Chronik*, 194; Küster, *Geschichte der Landschaft*, 276; Makowski and Buderath, *Die Natur*, 230; Pyne, *Vestal Fire*, 171, 175.

150 Schwalb, *Entwicklung der bäuerlichen Kulturlandschaft*, 17–18. Taking extreme dates of late and early frosts, there were just twelve high-summer days when no frosts were ever recorded.

151 Wegener, 'Besiedlung', 158.

152 H. Schoolmann, *Pioniere der Wildnis: Geschichte der Kolonie Moordorf* (n.p., 1973); H. Rechenbach (ed.), *Moordorf: Ein Beitrag zur Siedlungsgeschichte und zur sozialen Frage* (Berlin, 1940).

153 Wegener, 'Besiedlung', 158. Ludwig Starklof's comments on the smoky, poverty-stricken huts, by contrast with East Friesland's flourishing fen colonies, reflected his negative view of existing moor colonies in Oldenburg during the 1840s.

154 Wassermann, 'Siedlungsgeschichte', 110.

155 Stumpfe, *Besiedelung*, 310–11; Wegener, 'Besiedlung', 159–60.

156 Stumpfe, *Besiedelung*, 263–74 (quotation 267).

157 Ibid., 319–32.

158 Deeters, 'Kleinstaat und Provinz', 181 (quotation); Kurs, 'Die künstlichen Wasserstrassen', 612, gives the total cost of the canal as almost fourteen million Marks.

159 Wegener, 'Besiedlung', 159–60; Stumpfe, *Besiedelung*, 333–87.

160 Fontane, *WMB*, vol. 1, 346–53. Other Fontane works in which the peat inspector appears include *Allerlei Glück*, *Frau Jenny Treibel*, *Mathilde Möhring*, *Effi Briest* and *Der Stechlin*. See the notes to *WMB*, vol. 3, 876.

161 Stumpfe, *Besiedelung*, 307.

162 Starklof, *Vier Briefe*, 37.

163 Niemann (ed.), *Ludwig Starklof*, 167–8; Friedl, 'Ludwig Starklof', 26; Lampe, 'Wirtschaft und Verkehr', 724, 745.

164 Edwin J. Clapp, *The Navigable Rhine* (Boston, 1911), 40–1; Tümmers, *Der Rhein*, 243–4; Cioc, *Rhine*, 55–8. For a contemporary description of the hazards on the unregulated Middle Rhine, see Victor Hugo, *The Rhine* (New York, 1845), 132, 141.

165 Franz Kreuter, 'Die wissenschaftlichen Bestrebungen auf dem Gebiet des Wasserbaues und ihre Erfolge', *Beiträge zur Allgemeinen Zeitung* 1 (1908), 1–20; Treue, *Wirtschafts- und Technikgeschichte*, 375; Günther Garbrecht, 'Hydrotechnik und Natur: Gedanken eines Ingenieurs', in *100 Jahre Deutsche Verbände der Wasserwirtschaft 1891–1991: Wasserwirtschaft im Wandel der Zeit* (Bonn, 1991), 32–6; Hamm, *Naturkundliche Chronik*, 165; Tietze, *Oderschiffahrt*, 7, 26–33.

166 Tietze, *Oderschiffahrt*, 14.

167 Ernst Mattern, *Der Thalsperrenbau und die Deutsche Wasserwirtschaft* (Berlin, 1902), 4.

168 Compiled from Wolfgang Köllmann (ed.), *Quellen zur Bevölkerungs-, Sozial- und Wirtschaftsstatistik Deutschlands 1815–1875*, vol. 2 (Boppard, 1989), 331, 392, 463, 531, 608, 681.

169 On rafting: Andreas Kunz, 'Binnenschiffahrt', in Ulrich Wengenroth (ed.), *Technik und Wirtschaft* (Düsseldorf, 1993), 391; Musall, *Kulturlandschaft*, 111, 145; Jürgen Delfs, *Die Flösserei im Stromgebiet der Weser* (Hanover, 1952); Makowski and Buderath, *Die Natur*, 176–7.

170 Hugo, *The Rhine*, 276. See the similar description in Michael J. Quin, *Steam Voyages on the Seine, the Moselle & the Rhine*, 2 vols. (London, 1843), vol. 2, 99.

171 Kellenbenz, *Wirtschaftsgeschichte*, vol. 2, 56, 114; Clapp, *Navigable Rhine*, 14–16; Tümmers, *Der Rhein*, 232–33.

172 Ludwig Bamberger, *Erinnerungen* (Berlin, 1899), 49–50; Clapp, *Navigable Rhine*, 23–4; Tümmers, *Der Rhein*, 230–2.

173 Kellenbenz, *Wirtschaftsgeschichte*, vol. 2, 114.

174 Victor Hugo (*The Rhine*, 277) quotes the well-known saying that the speculator in rafting should have three capitals: one on the Rhine, the second on shore, and the third in his pocket.

175 Fontane, *WMB*, vol. 1, 550–3.

176 Friedrich Wickert, *Der Rhein und sein Verkehr* (Stuttgart, 1903), 22–3, 131–2; Kellenbenz, *Wirtschaftsgeschichte*, vol. 2, 114, 189; Kurt Ander-

mann (ed.), *Baden: Land – Staat – Volk 1806–1871* (Karlsruhe, 1890)
86.

177 Hugo, *The Rhine*, 276 ('street of the priests', or *Pfaffengasse*, was an old
jibe about the Rhine); Eberhard Gothein, *Geschichtliche Entwicklung der
Rheinschiffahrt im 19. Jahrhundert* (Leipzig, 1903), 297. See also Musall,
Kulturlandschaft, 237.

178 Not quite reversed, in fact: in 1907 the volume carried upstream was double
that carried downstream: Clapp, *Navigable Rhine*, 34; Cioc, *Rhine*, 73.

179 Kunz, 'Binnenschiffahrt', 385–7.

180 Dolf Sternberger, *Panorama of the Nineteenth Century* (Oxford, 1977),
20–3.

181 On the popularity of the railway with former 'tramping journeymen', see
Blackbourn, *Fontana History of Germany*, 273; on the Oder steamer,
Fontane, *WMB*, vol. 1, 553–5.

182 Tümmers, *Der Rhein*, 226.

183 Niemann (ed.), *Ludwig Starklof*, 168, 216.

184 Emil Zenz, *Geschichte der Stadt Trier im 19. Jahrhundert*, vol. 2 (Trier,
1980), 146.

185 Fontane, *WMB*, vol. 1, 561.

186 Quin, *Steam Voyages*, vol. 2, 83.

187 Mark Cioc, 'Die Rauchplage am Rhein vor dem Ersten Weltkrieg', *BzR* 51
(1999), 48; Tümmers, *Der Rhein*, 226–34.

188 Quin, *Steam Voyages*, vol. 2, 99; Hugo, *The Rhine*, 131.

189 Lucy A. Hill, *Rhine Roamings* (Boston, 1880).

190 Ibid., 127–8. See also 169, for a more conventional account, closer to Hugo's
or Quin's, of the Rhine 'dotted with steamers'.

191 See Sternberger, *Panorama*.

192 See Wolfgang Schivelbusch, *The Railway Journey* (New York, 1979).

193 Hugo, *The Rhine*, 139; Quin, *Steam Voyages*, vol. 2, 121–2; Karl Immermann, *Reisejournal* (1833), cited in Schneider (ed.), *Deutsche Landschaften*,
331.

194 On Rhine Romanticism, tourism (and the English): Tümmers, *Der Rhein*,
248–61; Hugo, *The Rhine*, 83–4; Hill, *Rhine Roamings*, 262–3.

195 Quin, *Steam Voyages*, vol. 2, 116. This was a common view of travellers,
who believed that downstream of Cologne and upstream of Mainz 'the
river ceases to be attractive' (Hill, *Rhine Roamings*, 52)

196 Friedrich Engels, 'Siegfrieds Heimat' (1840), cited in Schneider (ed.),
Deutsche Landschaften, 335.

197 Helmut Frühauf, *Das Verlagshaus Baedeker in Koblenz 1827–1872*
(Koblenz, 1992). Baedeker divided Germany into five regions: the North
East, the North West, the South, the Rhineland and Berlin.

198 See Applegate, *A Nation of Provincials*.

199 David Blackbourn, '"Taking the Waters": Meeting Places of the Fashionable World', in Martin H. Geyer and Johannes Paulmann (eds.), *The Mechanics of Internationalism* (Oxford, 2001), 435–57.

200 Fontane, *WMB*, vol. 1, 553–5.

201 See Fontane's gently satirical account of Freienwalde in *WMB*, vol. 1, 591–2.

202 Fontane, *WMB*, vol. 1, 29–31, 871, refers to mock battles at Carwe and Tamsel respectively; Marion Gräfin Dönhoff, *Namen die keiner mehr nennt* (Düsseldorf and Cologne, 1962), 112–13, describes festivities at Hohenzollern Rheinsberg in 1750.

203 Tümmers, *Der Rhein*, 73–4. On the tourist development of Lake Constance after the middle of the nineteenth century, see Gerd Zang (ed.), *Provinzialisierung einer Region* (Frankfurt/Main, 1978).

204 H. S. Bakker, *Norderney* (Bremen, 1956); *Saison am Strand: Badeleben an Nord- und Ostsee – 200 Jahre,* catalogue, Altonaer Museum in Hamburg/Norddeutsches Landesmuseum (Herford, 1986).

205 Dönhoff, *Namen die keiner mehr nennt*, 42.

206 Tümmers, *Der Rhein*, on 'Rhine patriotism'; Irmline Veit-Brause, *Die deutsch-französische Krise von 1840* (Cologne, 1967).

207 Hans-Georg Bluhm, 'Landschaftsbild im Wandel', in *Saison am Strand*, 30.

208 H. Kohl (ed.), *Briefe Ottos von Bismarck an Schwester und Schwager* (Leipzig, 1915), 15. *Saison am Strand*, 97 reproduces a photo showing two male visitors posing proudly, guns in hand, with a woman on the arm of one, behind the bodies of six seals killed at Föhr.

209 Deeters, 'Kleinstaat und Provinz', 171–3; Hamm, *Naturkundliche Chronik*, 158, 162.

210 Blackbourn, *Fontana History of Germany*, 203, 273–5.

211 Ferdinand Grautoff, 'Ein Kanal, der sich selber bauen sollte', *Die Gartenlaube* (1925), 520.

212 Norman Davies and Roger Moorhouse, *Microcosm: Portrait of a Central European City* (London, 2002), 262.

213 Hans J. Reichhardt, 'Von Treckschuten und Gondeln zu Dampfschiffen', in *Zwischen Oberspree und Unterhavel: Von Sport und Freizeit auf Berlins Gewässern – Eine Ausstellung des Landesarchivs Berlin, 3. Juli bis 30. September 1985* (Berlin, 1985), 19, 26–8. I am grateful to John Czaplicka for bringing this to my attention.

214 Harry Schreck in the *Vossische Zeitung*, cited ibid., 42.

215 Andreas Daum, *Wissenschaftspopularisierung im 19. Jahrhundert* (Munich, 1998), 127.

216 Hermann von Helmholtz, *Science and Culture: Popular and Philosophical Essays*, ed. David Cahan (Chicago, 1995), 206–7. See also Daum, *Wissenschaftspopularisierung*, 125–9 on the 'rhetoric' of the annual meetings.

217 Ernst Kapp, *Grundlinien einer Philosophie der Technik* (Braunschweig, 1877), 138.

218 Hamm, *Naturkundliche Chronik*, 155; Kellenbenz, *Wirtschaftsgeschichte*, vol. 2, 117, 139, 279; Andreas Kunz, 'Seeschiffahrt', in Wengenroth (ed.), *Technik und Wirtschaft*, 371.

219 Kunz, 'Seeschiffahrt', 368–9; Spelde, *Geschichte der Lotsen-Brüderschaften*, 26–8, 85–8; Hamm, *Naturkundliche Chronik*, 169.

220 Ernst Schick, *Ausführliche Beschreibung merkwürdiger Bauwerke, Denkmale, Brücken, Anlagen, Wasserbauten, Kunstwerke, Maschinen, Instrumente, Erfindungen und Unternehmungen der neueren und neuesten Zeit. Zur belehrenden Unterhaltung für die reifere Jugend bearbeitet* (Leipzig, 1838).

221 Ernst Kapp, *Vergleichende allgemeine Erdkunde* (Braunschweig, 1868), 647–9.

222 Starklof, *Vier Briefe*; Blackbourn, *Fontana History of Germany*, 119.

223 Karl Mathy, 'Eisenbahnen und Canäle, Dampfboote und Dampfwagentransport', in C. Rotteck and C. Welcker (eds.), *Staats-Lexikon*, vol. 4 (Altona, 1846), 228–89 (quotation, 231).

224 Mitcham, *Thinking through Technology*, 20–4.

225 Ernst Meyer, *Rudolf Virchow* (Wiesbaden, 1956); Arnold Bauer, *Rudolf Virchow: Der politische Arzt* (Berlin, 1982).

226 Hans-Liudger Diemel, 'Homo Faber: Der technische Zugang zur Natur', in Werner Nachtigall and Charlotte Schönbeck (eds.), *Technik und Natur* (Düsseldorf, 1994), 66.

227 Frank Otto [pseud. for Otto Spamer], *'Hilf Dir Selbst!' Lebensbilder durch Selbsthülfe und Thatkraft emporgekommener Männer: Gelehrte und Forscher, Erfinder, Techniker, Werkleute. Der Jugend und dem Volke in Verbindung mit Gleichgesinnten zur Aneiferung vorgeführt* (Leipzig, 1881).

228 Carl Ritter, 'The External Features of the Earth in their Influence on the Course of History' [1850], *Geographical Studies by the Late Professor Carl Ritter of Berlin*, translated by William Leonard Gage (Cincinnati and New York, 1861), 311–56. See also the many examples in Kapp, *Vergleichende allgemeine Erdkunde*.

229 Ritter, *Geographical Studies*, 257–63, 267, 335–6.

230 His expedition formed the basis of Patrick White's great novel, *Voss* (1957).

231 Richard Oberländer, *Berühmte Reisende, Geographen und Länderentdecker im 19. Jahrhundert* (Leipzig, 1892), 28–64, quotation, 59.

232 See Felix Lampe, *Grosse Geographen* (Leipzig and Berlin, 1915), 245–51.

233 Eugen von Enzberg, *Heroen der Nordpolarforschung. Der reiferen deutschen Jugend und einem gebildeten Leserkreise nach den Quellen dargestellt* (Leipzig, 1905), 128–75 (quotation, 175); Reinhard A. Krause, *Die Gründungsphase deutscher Polarforschung 1865–1875* (Bremerhaven,

1992); *125 Jahre deutsche Polarforschung: Alfred-Wegener-Institut für Polar- und Meeresforschung* (Bremerhaven, 1993). Koldewey wrote his own accounts of the first and second expeditions, published in 1871 and 1873–4 respectively.

234 Daum, *Wissenschaftspopularisierung*, 104–5, 108–9. In Bremen, for example, the Humboldt Association was founded around 1860, the Natural Science Association in 1864 and the Geographical Society in 1876: ibid., 93, 141; Hamm, *Naturkundliche Chronik*, 176.

235 Louis Thomas, *Das Buch wunderbarer Erfindungen* (Leipzig, 1860), 3.

236 See 'Die neue deutsche Lyrik', *Die Gegenwart*, vol. 8 (1853), 49.

237 Cioc, 'Die Rauchplage am Rhein', 48–53.

238 Thomas Rommelspacher, 'Das natürliche Recht auf Wasserver-schmutzung', in Franz-Josef Brüggemeier and Rommelspacher (eds.), *Besiegte Natur: Geschichte der Umwelt im 19. und 20. Jahrhundert* (Munich, 1987), 54.

239 Ibid., 44.

240 Wilhelm Raabe, *Pfisters Mühle* (1884); Jeffrey L. Sammons, *Wilhelm Raabe: The Fiction of the Alternative Community* (Princeton, 1987), 269–82.

241 Friedrich Nietzsche, *On the Genealogy of Morals* (1887), Part III, section 9. My translation.

242 Kobell, *Wildanger*, 10, 248.

243 Ibid., 248–9; Makowski and Buderath, *Die Natur*, 236; Hamm, *Naturkundliche Chronik*, 195.

244 Makowski and Buderath, *Die Natur*, 80; Zirnstein, *Ökologie*, 181; Raymond H. Dominick, *The Environmental Movement in Germany: Prophets and Pioneers, 1871–1971* (Bloomington, IN, 1992), 53.

245 Zirnstein, *Ökologie*, 143–6.

246 Daum, *Wissenschaftspopularisierung*, 332–5 ; Zirnstein, *Ökologie*, 143–72; Makowski and Buderath, *Die Natur*, 236. On Thienemann, see Chapter 4 below.

247 Wermuth, *Erinnerungen*, 48–50.

248 Cited in Johannes Baptist Kissling, *Geschichte des Kulturkampfes im Deutschen Reiche*, 3 vols. (Freiburg, 1911–16), vol. 3, 58.

249 See above, Chapter 2.

250 J. T. Carlton and J. B. Geller, 'Ecological Roulette: The Global Transport of Non-indigenous Marine Organisms', *Science*, 261 (1993), 78–83. On aquatic invasions, McNeill, *Something New under the Sun*, 257–60.

251 George Perkins Marsh, *Man and Nature*, edited by David Lowenthal (Cambridge, Mass, 1965), Chapter IV ('The Waters'), esp. 304–10.

252 Marsh, *Man and Nature*, 310 note 31; Thomas Kluge and Engelbert Schramm, *Wassernöte: Umwelt- und Sozialgeschichte des Trinkwassers* (Aachen, 1986), 183–7. On Tulla, see Chapter 2 above.

253 Karl Fraas, *Klima und Pflanzenwelt in der Zeit, ein Beitrag zur Geschichte* (Landshut, 1847). See Zirnstein, *Ökologie*, 135–6.

254 Daum, *Wissenschaftspopularisierung*, 138–53, 193–210; Dominick, *Environmental Movement*, 39.

255 Genesis, 9:3: 'Be fruitful and multiply, and fill the earth and subdue it; and have dominion over the fish of the sea and the birds of the air and over every living thing that moves upon the earth'. On the different strands within Christian tradition, see Glacken, *Traces*; William Leiss, *The Domination of Nature* (New York, 1972), 29–35; Ernst Oldemeyer, 'Entwurf einer Typologie des menschlichen Verhältnisses zur Natur', in Großklaus und Oldemeyer (eds.), *Natur als Gegenwelt*, 28–30; Ruth Groh and Dieter Groh, *Weltbild und Naturaneignung* (Frankfurt/Main, 1991), 11–91.

256 Dominick, *Environmental Movement*, 34.

257 Ernst Rudorff, 'Ueber das Verhältniss des modernen Lebens zur Natur', *PJbb* 45 (1880), 261–76.

258 The botanist Robert Lauterborn cited Riehl on 'wilderness' in his 'Beiträge zur Fauna und Flora des Oberrheins und seiner Umgebung', *Pollichia* 19 (1903), 42–130: Preuß, 'Naturschutz', 233. On Riehl's ambiguity, see also Applegate, *Nation of Provincials*, 34–42; Dominick, *Environmental Movement*, 22–3; Lekan, *Imagining the Nation in Nature*, 6–7; Sieferle, *Fortschrittsfeinde?*

259 See Schneider (ed.), *Deutsche Landschaften*, xvii–xviii.

260 Fontane, *WMB*, vol. 2, 101–2, 108–9.

261 *WMB*, vol. 1, 351, 593; vol. 2, 101.

262 Wilhelm Raabe, *Stopfkuchen*, translated by Barker Fairley (who calls the novel 'Tubby Schaumann'): *Wilhelm Raabe, Novels* (New York, 1983), 176.

263 Ibid., 175: 'Mother Nature had seen to it that everything was nicely washed'.

264 Blumenberg, *Heimat am Jadebusen*, which deals extensively with efforts to 'save' the fields.

265 Makowski and Buderath, *Die Natur*, 226; and see Introduction above.

266 Küster, *Geschichte der Landschaft*, 274, 341.

267 Ibid., 328–30; Jäger, *Einführung*, 54; Deneke, 'Eingriffe der Menschen'.

268 Lekan, *Imagining the Nation in Nature*, 14–16, and below, Chapter 5.

Chapter Four: Dam-building

1 Josef Ott and Erwin Marquardt, *Die Wasserversorgung der kgl. Stadt Brüx in Böhmen mit bes. Berücks. der in den Jahren 1911 bis 1914 erbauten Talsperre* (Vienna, 1918), Vorwort, 54.

2 Ludwig Bing (ed.), *Vom Edertal zum Edersee: Eine Landschaft ändert ihr Gesicht* (Korbach and Bad Wildungen, 1973), 6.

3 H. Völker, *Die Eder-Talsperre* (Bettershausen bei Marburg, 1913), 7, 25.

4   Carl Borchardt, *Die Remscheider Stauweiheranlage sowie Beschreibung von 450 Stauweiheranlagen* (Munich and Leipzig, 1897), 97–9; B. [Bachmann?], 'Die Talsperre bei Mauer am Bober', *ZdB* 32, 16 Nov. 1914, 611; Hermann Schönhoff, 'Die Möhnetalsperre bei Soest', *Die Gartenlaube* (1913), 686.

5   'Die Thalsperren im Sengbach-, Ennepe- und Urft-Thal', *Prometheus*, 744 (1904), 250.

6   Dr Kreuzkam, 'Zur Verwertung der Wasserkräfte', *VW* (1908), nr. 36, 952.

7   Fischer-Reinau, Ingenieur, 'Die wirtschaftliche Ausnützung der Wasserkräfte', *BIG* (1908), 103; 'Über die Bedeutung und die Wertung der Wasserkräfte in Verbindung mit elektrischer Kraftübertragung', *ZGW* (1907), nr. 1, 4; *Festschrift zur Weihe der Möhnetalsperre, Ein Rückblick auf die Geschichte des Ruhrtalsperrenvereins und den Talsperrenbau im Ruhrgebiet* (Essen, 1913), 2; W. Berdrow, 'Staudämme und Thalsperren', *Die Umschau* (1898), 255.

8   Ernst Mattern, *Thalsperrenbau*, 99. Cf. p. 50. Mattern was quoting a little freely from Schiller's 'The Song of the Bell'.

9   Jakob Zinssmeister, 'Industrie, Verkehr, Natur und moderne Wasserwirtschaft', 14.

10 *Festschrift . . . Möhnetalsperre*, 4.

11 See O. Bechstein, 'Vom Ruhrtalsperrenverein', *Prometheus* 28, 7 Oct. 1916, 138; L. Ernst, 'Die Riesentalsperre im Urftal [sic]', *Die Umschau* (1904), 667–8; A. Splittgerber, 'Die Entwicklung der Talsperren und ihre Bedeutung', *WuG* 8, 1 Jul. 1918, 255.

12 Karl Kollbach, 'Die Urft-Talsperre', *ÜLM* 92 (1913–14), 694–5.

13 V. A. Carus, *Führer durch das Gebiet der Riesentalsperre zwischen Gemünd und Heimbach-Eifel mit nächster Umgebung* (Trier, 1904).

14 Schönhoff, 'Möhnetalsperre', 685–6.

15 Adolf Ernst, *Kultur und Technik* (Berlin, 1888), 30.

16 Dienel, 'Homo Faber', 60–1.

17 On river modelling and the Engels laboratory, see Martin Reuss, 'The Art of Scientific Precision: River Research in the United States Army Corps of Engineers to 1945', *TC* 40 (1999), 294–301. Similar models were built at the Polytechnics in Berlin-Charlottenburg, Braunschweig, Danzig and Karlsruhe.

18 See the article (originally a public lecture) by Professor Franz Kreuter of Munich (1907), 'Die wissenschaftlichen Bestrebungen auf dem Gebiet des Wasserbaues und ihre Erfolge', *Beiträge zur Allgemeinen Zeitung* (Munich) 1 (1908), 1–20, which regrets that hydraulic engineers were so reluctant to admit their mistakes. See also below, p. 203.

19 Dienel, 'Homo Faber', 61.

20 Mitcham, *Thinking through Technology*, 26–9.

21 Franz Bendt, 'Zum fünfzigjährigen Jubiläum des "Vereins deutscher Ingenieure"', *Die Gartenlaube* (1906), 527–8.

22 H. F. Bubendey, 'Die Mittel und Ziele des deutschen Wasserbaues am Beginn des 20. Jahrhunderts', *ZVDI* 43 (1899), 499.

23 Mikael Hard, 'German Regulation: The Integration of Modern Technology into National Culture', in Hard and Andrew Jamison (eds.), *The Intellectual Appropriation of Technology: Discourses on Modernity, 1900–1939* (Cambridge, Mass., 1998), 37.

24 Charles Kindleberger, *Economic Growth in France and Britain* (London, 1964), 158.

25 Mitcham, *Thinking through Technology*, 26.

26 Lieber quotation: Gerhard Zweckbronner, '"Je besser der Techniker, desto einseitiger sein Blick?" Probleme des technischen Fortschritts und Bildungsfragen in der Ingenieurzeitung im Deutschen Kaiserreich', in Ulrich Troitzsch and Gabriele Wohlauf (eds.), *Technikgeschichte* (Frankfurt/Main, 1980), 340.

27 The Eder Dam was 'a cultural work of the first order': Geheimer Oberbaurat Keller, cited in 'Einiges über Talsperren', *ZfBi* (1904), 271.

28 John M. Staudenmaier, *Technology's Storytellers* (Cambridge, Mass., 1985).

29 Richard Hennig, 'Deutschlands Wasserkräfte und ihre technische Auswertung', *Die Turbine* (1909), 208–11, 230–4; 'Aufgaben der Wasserwirtschaft in Südwestafrika', ibid., 331–3; 'Die grossen Wasserfälle der Erde in ihrer Beziehung zur Industrie und zum Naturschutz', *ÜLM* 53 (1910–11), 872–3.

30 Richard Hennig, *Buch berühmter Ingenieure: Grosse Männer der Technik ihr Lebensgang und ihr Lebenswerk. Für die reifere Jugend und für Erwachsene geschildert* (Leipzig, 1911).

31 Hans Dominik, 'Riesenschleusen im Mittellandkanal', *Die Gartenlaube* (1927), 10; *Im Wunderland der Technik: Meisterstücke und neue Errungenschaften, die unsere Jugend kennen sollte* (Berlin, 1922).

32 Dominik, *Wunderland*, 32, 33.

33 David E. Nye, *American Technological Sublime* (Cambridge, Mass., 1994).

34 Leo Marx, *The Machine in the Garden* (New York, 1965); John Kasson, *Civilizing the Machine* (New York, 1977).

35 Bernhard Rieger, '"Modern Wonders": Technological Innovation and Public Ambivalence in Britain and Germany between the 1890s and 1933', *HWJ* 55 (2003), 154–78; Peter Fritzsche, *A Nation of Flyers* (Cambridge, Mass., 1992); the articles by Joachim Radkau and Michael Salewski, in Salewski and Ilona Stölken-Fitschen (eds.), *Moderne Zeiten: Technik und Zeitgeschichte im 19. und 20. Jahrhundert* (Stutgart, 1994); Blackbourn, *Fontana History of Germany*, 394–5.

36 Bendt, 'Jubiläum', 527.

37 Cited in Zweckbronner, 'Je besser der Techniker', 337.

38 *Die Umschau* (1904), 668: editor's note.

39 Kollbach, 'Urfttalsperre'; Christiane Karin Weiser, 'Die Talsperren in den

Einzugsgebieten der Wupper und der Ruhr als funktionierendes Element in der Kulturlandschaft in ihrer Entwicklung bis 1945', dissertation, University of Bonn, 1991, 191, 194.

40 J. Weber, 'Die Wupper-Talsperren', *BeH* 4, August 1930, 313; Bing, *Vom Edertal zum Edersee*, 10; W. Mügge, 'Über die Gestaltung von Talsperren und Talsperrenlandschaften', *DW* 37 (1942), 405.

41 Kluge and Schramm, *Wassernöte*, 151.

42 W. Abercron, 'Talsperren in der Landschaft: Nach Beobachtungen aus der Vogelschau', *VuW* 6, Jun. 1938, 33–9.

43 Leo Sympher, 'Der Talsperrenbau in Deutschland', *ZdB* 27 (1907), 169.

44 Borchardt, *Remscheider Stauweiheranlage*, 99.

45 Schönhoff, 'Möhnetalsperre', 685; Russwurm, 'Talsperren und Landschaftsbild', *Der Harz* 34 (1927), 50; Weiser, 'Talsperren', 191–2; Manfred Bierganz, 'Wirtschaft und Verkehr', in *Die Eifel 1888–1988* (Düren, 1989), 597; *Festschrift . . . Möhnetalsperre*, 70; Peter Franke (ed.), *Dams in Germany* (Düsseldorf, 2001), 138–9.

46 Fritzsche, *Nation of Flyers*, 17.

47 Schwoerbel, 'Technik und Wasser', 379; Günther Garbrecht, 'Der Sadd-el-Kafara, die älteste Talsperre der Welt', in Garbrecht (ed.), *Historische Talsperren* (Stuttgart, 1987), 97–109.

48 Rolf Meurer, *Wasserbau und Wasserwirtschaft in Deutschland* (Berlin, 2000), 54–60; Martin Schmidt, 'Die Oberharzer Bergbauteiche', in Garbrecht (ed.), *Historische Talsperren*, 327–85; P. Ziegler, *Der Talsperrenbau*, 86; Norman Smith, *A History of Dams* (London, 1971), 157.

49 Gerhard Rouvé, 'Die Geschichte der Talsperren in Mitteleuropa', in Garbrecht (ed.), *Historische Talsperren*, 300–10; Meurer, *Wasserbau*, 117–18.

50 Kurt Soergel, 'Die Bedeutung der Talsperren in Deutschland für die Landwirtschaft', dissertation, University of Leipzig (1929), 39–42.

51 Martin Steinert, 'Die geographische Bedeutung der Talsperren', dissertation, University of Jena (1910), 17–18; Soergel, 'Bedeutung', 40–1; Rouvé, 'Talsperren in Mitteleuropa', 310–11.

52 Soergel, 'Bedeutung', 41–2; Ziegler, *Talsperrenbau*, 67–8; C. Wulff, *Die Talsperren-Genossenschaften im Ruhr- und Wuppergebiet* (Jena, 1908), 6–7.

53 Wulff, *Talsperren-Genossenschaften*, 2.

54 Soergel, 'Bedeutung', 39–53, Steinert, 'Die geographische Bedeutung', 66–8.

55 Axel Föhl and Manfred Hamm, *Die Industriegeschichte des Wassers* (Düsseldorf, 1985), 128; Wolfram Such, 'Die Entwicklung der Trinkwasserversorgung aus Talsperren in Deutschland', in *GWF* 139: *Special Talsperren* (1998), 66.

56 Ernst Mattern, *Die Ausnutzung der Wasserkräfte* (Leipzig, 1921), 6.

57 Beate Olmer, *Wasser. Historisch: Zu Bedeutung und Belastung des*

Umweltmediums im Ruhrgebiet 1870–1930 (Frankfurt/Main, 1998), 229; Kluge and Schramm, *Wassernöte*, 138–41. Similar constraints led to a similar conclusion in Trier: Zenz, *Trier*, vol. 2, 225–7.

58 Weiser, 'Talsperren', 53–8; Kluge and Schramm, *Wassernöte*, 140–1.

59 Borchardt, *Remscheider Stauweiheranlage*; Föhl and Hamm, *Industriegeschichte*, 132.

60 Hennig, 'Deutschlands Wasserkräfte', 232.

61 Borchardt, *Remscheider Stauweiheranlage*, 98–9.

62 Borchardt, *Remscheider Stauweiheranlage*, iv; Meurer, *Wasserbau*, 109–12.

63 Berdrow, 'Staudämme', 255.

64 Borchardt, *Remscheider Stauweiheranlage*, iii.

65 Guido Gustav Weigend, 'Water Supply of Central and Southern Germany', dissertation, University of Chicago (1946), 3–4. Sometimes, of course, groundwater sources simply dried up: Georg Adam, 'Wasserwirtschaft und Wasserrecht früher und jetzt', *ZGW* 1, 1 Jul. 1906, 3.

66 M. Hans Klössel, 'Die Errichtung von Talsperren in Sachsen', *PVbl* (1904), 120–1; Meyer, 'Bedeutung der Talsperren', 126–7; Such, 'Entwicklung', 69–71.

67 Sympher, 'Talsperrenbau', 177–8. The memorial was an iron plaque showing Intze in relief (the work of his son), surrounded by dark basalt lava and topped by a structure with three columns.

68 Richard Hennig, 'Otto Intze, der Talsperren-Erbauer (1843–1904)', in *Buch berühmter Ingenieure*, 104–21.

69 Theodor Koehn, 'Über einige grosse europäische Wasserkraftanlagen und ihre wirtschaftliche Bedeutung', *Die Turbine* (1909), 112; *Festschrift . . . Möhnetalsperre*, 13; Hennig, 'Deutschlands Wasserkräfte', 233; Josef Stromberg, 'Die volkswirtschaftliche Bedeutung der deutschen Talsperren', dissertation, University of Cologne (1932), 10, 62; Föhl and Hamm, *Industriegeschichte*, 128; Völker, *Edder-Talsperre*, 22; Kreuzkam, 'Deutschlands Talsperren', 657; Heinrich Gräf, 'Über die Verwertung von Talsperren für die Wasserversorgung vom Standpunkte der öffentlichen Gesundheitspflege', *ZHI* 62 (1909), 485.

70 Sympher, 'Talsperrenbau', 159.

71 This biographical sketch is based mainly on Hennig, 'Otto Intze'; Hans-Dieter Olbrisch, 'Otto Intze', *NDB*, vol. 10 (Berlin, 1974), 176–7; Oskar Schatz, 'Otto Intze: Zur 125. Wiederkehr des Geburtsjahres des Begründers des neuzeitlichen deutschen Talsperrenbaus', *GWF* 109, Sep. 1968, 1037–9.

72 Otto Intze, *Zweck und Bau sogenannter Thalsperren* (Aachen, 1875).

73 J. L. Algermissen, 'Talsperren: Weisse Kohle', *Soziale Revue* 6 (1906), 144; O. Feeg, 'Wasserversorgung', *JbN* 16 (1901), 336.

74 Hennig, 'Otto Intze', 105.

75 Donald C. Jackson, 'Engineering in the Progressive Era: A New Look at Frederick Haynes Newell and the US Reclamation Service', *TC* 34 (1993), 556.

76 Jürgen Giesecke, Hans-Jürgen Glasebach and Uwe Müller, 'German Standardization in Dam Construction', in Franke (ed.), *Dams in Germany*, 81; Martin Schmidt, 'Before the Intze Dams: Dams and Dam Construction in the German States Prior to 1890', ibid., 10–35.

77 Meurer, *Wasserbau*, 118.

78 Wulff, *Talsperren-Genossenschaften*, 2–3.

79 See, for example, *Thalsperren im Gebiet der Wupper: Vortrag des Prof. Intze . . . am 18. Oktober 1889* (Barmen, 1889), 4–9.

80 Such, 'Entwicklung', 67.

81 Föhl and Hamm, *Industriegeschichte*, 131. On his 'tireless activity', Borchardt, *Remscheider Stauweiheranlage*, 111; also 'Einiges über Talsperren', 271.

82 Dr Bachmann, 'Die Talsperren in Deutschland', *WuG* 17, 15 Aug. 1927, 1134; Such, 'Entwicklung', 69, especially on Ernst Link (1873–1952).

83 'Die Wasserkräfte des Riesengebirges', *Die Gartenlaube* (1897), 239–40; Hennig, 'Otto Intze', 105.

84 Hennig, 'Otto Intze', 119.

85 Kellenbenz, *Wirtschaftsgeschichte*, vol. 1, 105–7, 150–62, 252–5; Eckart Schremmer, *Die Wirtschaft Bayerns: Vom hohen Mittelalter bis zum Beginn der Industrialisierung* (Munich, 1970), 331–45. On rivers' energy-utilization, Leopold, *View of the River*, 245.

86 Hennig, 'Deutschlands Wasserkräfte', 231; Treue, *Wirtschafts- und Technikgeschichte*, 397–8.

87 On the ratio of water mills to inhabitants: Karl Lärmer and Peter Beyer (eds.), *Produktivkräfte in Deutschland, 1800 bis 1870* (Berlin, 1990), 310. In Württemberg, 53 per cent of all horse-power generated came from water as late as 1875; even in advanced Saxony the figure was still 31 per cent: ibid., 395. On the continued use of water-power in Saxony, Hubert Kiesewetter, *Industrialisierung und Landwirtschaft: Sachsens Stellung zum Industrialisierungsprozess Deutschlands im 19. Jahrhundert* (Cologne, 1988), 458–70.

88 Theodor Koehn, 'Der Ausbau der Wasserkräfte in Deutschland', *ZfdgT* (1908), 462; Wolfgang Feige and Friedrich Becks, *Wasser für das Ruhrgebiet: Das Sauerland als Wasserspeicher* (Münster, 1981), 30–1.

89 Mattern, *Thalsperrenbau*, 65; Martin Lochert, 'Zur Geschichte des Talsperrenbaus im Bergischen Land vor 1914', *NBJ* 2 (1985–6), 110–14.

90 Weiser, 'Talsperren', 34–5; Weber, 'Wupper-Talsperren', 314–15; Wulff, *Talsperren-Genossenschaften*, 7–8, 14–15; Olmer, *Wasser*, 231.

91 Wulff, *Talsperren-Genossenschaften*, 8–11; Ziegler, *Talsperrenbau*, 69;

Weber, 'Wupper-Talsperren', 313–14; *Festschrift . . . Möhnetalsperre*, 2–4; Olmer, *Wasser*, 230–7.

92 Feige and Becks, *Wasser für das Ruhrgebiet*, 20–9.

93 Weiser, 'Talsperren', 113; Kluge and Schramm, *Wassernöte*, 182.

94 Franz-Josef Brüggemeier and Thomas Rommenspacher, 'Umwelt', in Wolfgang Köllmann, Hermann Korte, Dietmar Petzina and Wolfhard Weber (eds.), *Das Ruhrgebiet im Industriezeitalter*, vol. 2 (Düsseldorf, 1990), 518–26; Cioc, *The Rhine*, 88–91.

95 Link, 'Talsperren des Ruhrgebiets', 99–101; Link, 'Bedeutung', 67–9; Feige and Becks, *Wasser für das Ruhrgebiet*, 12, 33; Weiser, 'Talsperren', 39–41; Olmer, *Wasser*, 181–246; Ulrike Gilhaus, *'Schmerzenskinder der Industrie': Umweltverschmutzung, Umweltpolitik und sozialer Protest in Westfalen 1845–1914* (Paderborn, 1995), 93–4.

96 Olmer, *Wasser*, 230.

97 *Festschrift . . . Möhnetalsperre*, 6–7; Olmer, *Wasser*, 237.

98 On the legal positions going back to the *Code civil* dating from French occupation, Dr Biesantz, 'Das Recht zur Nutzung der Wasserkraft rheinischer Flüsse', *RAZS* 7 (1911), 48–66.

99 Wulff, *Talsperren-Genossenschaften*, 16–17; *Festschrift . . . Möhnetalsperre*, 6–7; Olmer, *Wasser*, 238–9.

100 Wulff, *Talsperren-Genossenschaften*, 17; *Festschrift . . . Möhnetalsperre*, 7–11; Link, 'Bedeutung'; Link, 'Talsperren des Ruhrgebiets', 101; Splittgerber, 'Entwicklung', 257–8; Weiser, 'Talsperren', 112–17.

101 Bechstein, 'Vom Ruhrtalsperrenverein', 135–9; Cioc, *The Rhine*, 92–3.

102 Wulff, *Talsperren-Genossenschaften*, 19.

103 On the construction programme of the RTV, Wulff, *Talsperren-Genossenschaften*, 18–20; Link, 'Talsperren des Ruhrgebiets'; Weiser, 'Talsperren', 112–53; Olmer, *Wasser*, 246–62; Kluge and Schramm, *Wassernöte*, 161–8.

104 On the Möhne, *Festschrift . . . Möhnetalsperre*; Schönhoff, 'Die Möhnetalsperre bei Soest', 684–6. The capacities have been calculated from the tables in Mattern, *Ausnutzung der Wasserkräfte*, 940–3; Carl Borchardt, *Denkschrift zur Einweihung der Neye-Talsperre bei Wipperfürth* (Remscheid, 1909), 109–10; Such, 'Entwicklung', 68.

105 He was also responsible two decades later for the giant Sorpe Dam. On his role in both, see Ernst Link, 'Ruhrtalsperrenverein, Möhne- und Sorpetalsperre', *MLWBL* (1927), 1–11; Ernst Link, 'Die Sorpetalsperre und die untere Versetalsperre im Ruhrgebiet als Beispiele hoher Erdstaudämme in neuzeitlicher Bauweise', *DeW*, 1 Mar. 1932, 41–5, 71–2.

106 'Die Wasser- und Wetterkatastrophen dieses Hochsommers', *Die Gartenlaube* (1897), 571. On the impact in Bohemia, R. Grassberger, 'Erfahrungen über Talsperrenwasser in Österreich', *Bericht über den XIV. Internationalen Kongress für Hygiene und Demographie, Berlin 1907*, vol. 3 (Berlin, 1908),

230–1; Viktor Czehak, 'Über den Bau der Friedrichswalder Talsperre', *ZöIAV* 49, 6 Dec. 1907, 853.

107 'Die Wasser- und Wetterkatastrophen', 571.

108 Ibid., 572.

109 Ibid.

110 Otto Intze, *Bericht über die Wasserverhältnisse der Gebirgsflüsse Schlesiens und deren Verbesserung zur Ausnutzung der Wasserkräfte und zur Verminderung der Hochfluthschäden* (Berlin, 1898).

111 Hennig, 'Otto Intze', 115–16, 119; Berdrow, 'Staudämme', 255.

112 Ziegler, *Talsperrenbau*, vi; Mattern, *Ausnutzung der Wasserkräfte*, 996–9; Olbrisch, 'Otto Intze', 177.

113 Otto Intze, *Talsperrenanlagen in Rheinland und Westfalen, Schlesien und Böhmen. Weltausstellung St. Louis 1904: Sammelausstellung des Königlich Preussichen Ministeriums der Öffentlichen Arbeiten. Wasserbau* (Berlin, 1904); 'Die geschichtliche Entwicklung, die Zwecke und der Bau der Talsperren', lecture delivered to Berlin branch of *Verein deutscher Ingenieure*, 3 Feb. 1904: *ZVDI* 50, 5 May 1906, 673–87.

114 Intze, *Talsperrenanlagen*, 31; Meurer, *Wasserbau*, 112–14; Koehn, 'Wasserkraftanlagen', 113–14; Wilhelm Küppers, 'Die grösste Talsperre Europas bei Gemünd (Eifel)', *Die Turbine* 2, Dec. 1905, 61–4, 96–8.

115 Hennig, 'Otto Intze', 119–20; Schatz, 'Otto Intze', 1039; Grassberger, 'Talsperrenwasser', 230–1; 'Talsperrenbauten in Böhmen', *Die Talsperre* (1911), 125–6; A. Meisner, 'Die Flussregulierungsaktion und die Talsperrenfrage', *RTW*, 6 Nov. 1909, 405–8. On Viktor Czehak: Czehak, 'Friedrichswalder Talsperre', 853; 'Auszug aus dem Gutachten des Baurates Ing. V. Czehak', in *Die Marktgemeinde Frain und die Frainer Talsperre: Eine Stellungnahme zu den verschiedenen Mängeln des Talsperrenbaues* (Frain, 1935).

116 Soergel, 'Bedeutung', 103–4; Klössel, 'Errichtung', 120–1; 'Thalsperren am Harz', *GI*, 31 May 1902, 167–8.

117 Hennig, 'Otto Intze', 104–5.

118 'Ueber Talsperren', *ZfG* 4 (1902), 253 (report on Intze's address at the Marklissa Dam).

119 Karl Fischer, 'Die Niederschlags- und Abflussbedingungen für den Talsperrenbau in Deutschland', *ZGEB* (1912), 641–55; Hennig, 'Otto Intze', 114; Shackleton, *Europe*, 16, 23.

120 B., 'Die Talsperre bei Mauer am Bober', 609.

121 For an example of a conservative 'agrarian' writer, see 'Landwirtschaft und Talsperren', *Volkswohl* 19 (1905), 88–9, explicitly linking the 1897 floods in central Europe to corrections that reduced river length and speeded up flow of water.

122 P. Ziegler, 'Ueber die Notwendigkeit der Einbeziehung von Thalsperren in

die Wasserwirtschaft', *ZfG* 4 (1901), 50–1; Ziegler, *Der Talsperrenbau*, 4–5.

123 H. Chr. Nußbaum, 'Die Wassergewinnung durch Talsperren', *ZGW* (1907), 67–70; Nußbaum, 'Zur Frage der Wirtschaftlichkeit der Anlage von Stau-Seen', *ZfBi* (1906), 463. Along the same lines, see Berdrow, 'Staudämme', 256; Weber, 'Wupper-Talsperren', 314; Stromberg, 'Bedeutung', 29–30.

124 Kunz, 'Binnenschiffahrt', 385–7.

125 Ibid., 396; Kellenbenz, *Wirtschaftsgeschichte*, vol. 2, 276.

126 Hermann Keller, 'Natürliche und künstliche Wasserstrassen', *Die Woche*, 1904, vol. 2, no. 20, 873–5 (quotation, 874).

127 See above, Chapters 1 and 2.

128 Ziegler, *Talsperrenbau*, vi; Mattern, *Thalsperrenbau*, 12–13.

129 Mattern, *Thalsperrenbau*, 6.

130 Soergel, 'Bedeutung', 101.

131 Nikolaus Kelen, *Talsperren* (Berlin and Leipzig, 1931), 10. For a description of 'giant locks' in operation, see Dominik, 'Riesenschleusen im Mittellandkanal', 10.

132 Völker, *Edder-Talsperre*, 3; Emil Abshoff, 'Talsperren im Wesergebiet', *ZfBi* 13 (1906), 202–6.

133 'Zum Kanal-Sturm in Preussen', *HPBl* (1899), 453–62 (quotation, 454).

134 Bubendey, 'Mittel und Ziele des deutschen Wasserbaues', 500; Georg Gothein, 'Die Kanalvorlage und der Osten', *Die Nation* 16 (1898–9), 368–71; Georg Baumert, 'Der Mittellandkanal und die konservative Partei in Preussen: Von einem Konservativen', *Die Grenzboten* 58 (1899), 57–71; 'Die Ablehnung des Mittellandkanals: Von einem Ostelbier', *Die Grenzboten* 58 (1899), 486–92; Ernst von Eynern, *Zwanzig Jahre Kanalkämpfe* (Berlin, 1901); Hannelore Horn, *Der Kampf um den Bau des Mittellandkanals* (Cologne-Opladen, 1964).

135 Abshoff, 'Einiges über Talsperren', 90–3; Regierungsrat Roloff, 'Der Talsperrenbau in Deutschland und Preussen', *ZfB* 59 (1910), 560; Bing, *Vom Edertal zum Edersee*, 9; Völker, *Edder-Talsperre*, 3–5; Sym007, 'Talsperrenbau', 176.

136 Olbrisch, 'Otto Intze', 176–7; Abshoff, 'Talsperren im Wesergebiete', 203.

137 *Die Turbine* (1904) was based in Berlin, *Die Weisse Kohle* (1908) in Munich. Other new publications in the same year included *Die Talsperre* (from 1903), *Zeitschrift für das Gesamte Turbinenwesen* (from 1905), *Zentralblatt für Wasserbau und Wasserwirtschaft* (from 1906) and *Zeitschrift für die gesamte Wasserwirtschaft*. On the new volume of the *Handbuch der Ingenieurwissenschaften*, see Koehn, 'Ausbau', 476.

138 Algermissen, 'Talsperren: Weisse Kohle', 154.

139 Koehn, 'Ausbau', 463.

140 'Über die Bedeutung und die Wertung der Wasserkräfte', 4–8; Ziegler, *Talsperrenbau*, 6. See also Berdrow, 'Staudämme', 255, for the argument that coal and steam had perhaps been over-valued.

141 Fischer, 'Ausnützung der Wasserkräfte', 112.

142 Quotations, Ziegler, 'Ueber die Nothwendigkeit', 52; Mattern, *Thalsperrenbau*, 74. See also Algermissen, 'Talsperren', 153–4; Hennig, 'Deutschlands Wasserkräfte', 209; A. Korn, 'Die "Weisse Kohle"', *TM* 9 (1909), 744–6; S. Herzog, 'Ausnutzung der Wasserkräfte für den elektrischen Vollbahnbetrieb', *UTW* (1909), 19–20, 23–4; Koehn, 'Ausbau', 465; Zinssmeister, 'Industrie, Verkehr, Natur', 12–15; Mattern, 'Ausnutzung', 794 (which, in fact, overstated remaining German coal reserves); and – writing a few years later – Karl Micksch, 'Energie und Wärme ohne Kohle', *Die Gartenlaube* 68 (1920), 81–3, which also mentions solar, wind and tidal power.

143 E. Freytag, 'Der Ausbau unserer Wasserwirtschaft und die Bewertung der Wasserkräfte', *TuW* (1908), 401, reporting the earlier calculations of Professor H. Wiebe and his own calculations (1908) that the unit of hydro-energy was now worth 80 per cent of its steam-derived equivalent.

144 Koehn, 'Wasserkraftanlagen', 111. See also Mattern, *Thalsperrenbau*, 68; Meurer, *Wasserbau*, 105–8; Hennig, 'Deutschlands Wasserkräfte', 208–9; and Thomas P. Hughes, *Networks of Power: Electrification in Western Society, 1880–1930* (Baltimore, 1983), 129–35.

145 Mattern, *Ausnutzung*, 2–3; Koehn, 'Ausbau', 462–3; Meurer, *Wasserbau*, 71–2; Hughes, *Networks of Power*, 263.

146 'Über die Bedeutung', 8; Kretz, 'Zur Frage der Ausnutzung des Wassers des Oberrheins', *ZfBi* 13 (1906), 361.

147 Hennig, 'Deutschlands Wasserkräfte', 209.

148 Ziegler, *Talsperrenbau*, v; Kreuzkam, 'Zur Verwertung der Wasserkräfte', 951–2. On the early harnessing of Rhine energy at Schaffhausen, Hanns Günther, *Pioniere der Technik: Acht Lebensbilder grosser Männer der Tat* (Zurich, 1920), 91–119 ('Heinrich Moser: Ein Pionier der "weissen Kohle"').

149 Friedrich Vogel, 'Die wirtschaftliche Bedeutung deutscher Gebirgswasserkräfte', *ZfS* 8 (1905), 607–14; Jakob Zinssmeister, 'Die Beziehungen zwischen Talsperren und Wasserabfluss', *WK* 2, 25 Feb. 1909, 47; Koehn, 'Wasserkraftanlagen', 174–6; Algermissen, 'Talsperren: Weisse Kohle', 141.

150 Ernst von Hesse-Wartegg, 'Der Niagara in Fesseln', *Die Gartenlaube* (1905), 34–8; Koehn, 'Ausbau', 463–4; Korn, 'Weisse Kohle', 746; Kreuzkam, 'Zur Verwertung', 919.

151 Eugen Eichel, 'Ausnutzung der Wasserkräfte', *EKB* 8 (1910), 24 Jan. 1910, 52–4; Wilhelm Müller, 'Wasserkraft-Anlagen in Kalifornien', *Die Turbine*

(1908), 32–5. On California, Hughes, *Networks of Power*, 262–84.

152 Koehn, 'Ausbau', 464.

153 Mattern, *Ausnutzung*, 795.

154 Koehn, 'Ausbau', 464 (1905 figures); Kreuzkam, 'Zur Verwertung', 951 (1908); Ziegler, *Talsperrenbau*, v (1911).

155 W. Halbfaß, 'Die Projekte von Wasserkraftanlagen am Walchensee und Kochelsee in Oberbayern', *Globus* 88 (1905), 296–7; Peter Fessler, 'Bayerns staatliche Wasserkraftprojekte', *EPR* 27, 26 Jan. 1910, 31–4; Hennig, 'Deutschlands Wasserkräfte', 210; Hughes, *Networks of Power*, 334–50.

156 Kretz, 'Zur Frage der Ausnutzung', 368.

157 Koehn, 'Wasserkraftanlagen', 173; Hennig, 'Deutschlands Wasserkräfte', 209–10.

158 Oskar von Miller, 'Die Ausnutzung der deutschen Wasserkräfte', *ZfA*, August 1908, 405.

159 Kretz, 'Zur Frage der Ausnutzung', 362.

160 Hennig, 'Deutschlands Wasserkräfte', 209.

161 Kretz's 'Zur Frage der Ausnutzung' represents this stance exceptionally clearly, but is not unusual. Oskar von Miller's writings have a similar inflected social concern.

162 Kreuzkam, 'Zur Verwertung', 950.

163 See, for example, Algermissen, 'Talsperren: Weisse Kohle', 161; Herzog, 'Ausnutzung', 23–4. The argument came up often in the context of electrifying the railways: Vogel, 'Bedeutung', 611; Mattern, *Ausnutzung*, 793.

164 Fischer-Reinau, 'Die wirtschaftliche Ausnützung der Wasserkräfte', 103.

165 Borchardt, *Remscheider Stauweiheranlage*, iv; Heinrich Claus, 'Die Wasserkraft in statischer und sozialer Beziehung', *Wasser- und Wegebau* (1905), 413–16; *Die Ennepetalsperre und die mit ihr verbundenen Anlagen des Kreises Schwelm (Wasser- und Elektrizitätswerk)* (Schwelm, 1905), 39; Hennig, 'Deutschlands Wasserkräfte', 233; Koehn, 'Ausbau', 479; Kretz, 'Zur Frage der Ausnutzung', 361–8; Mattern, *Thalsperrenbau*, 69–70; Vogel, 'Bedeutung', 609–10. For a similarly utopian Swiss vision of social progress via electrification, see Emil Zigler, 'Unsere Wasserkräfte und ihre Verwendung', *ZbWW* 6, 20 Jan. 1911, 33–5, 51–3.

166 Richard Woldt, *Im Reiche der Technik: Geschichte für Arbeiterkinder* (Dresden, 1910), 47–52.

167 Mattern, *Ausnutzung*, 991 (reporting critics, not his own view); Badermann, 'Die Frage der Ausnutzung der staatlichen Wasserkräfte in Bayern', *Kommunalfinanzen* (1911), 154–5; Algermissen, 'Talsperren: Weisse Kohle', 159–60, who thought megalomania was an 'infantile disorder' of hydroelectric power.

168 Soergel, 'Bedeutung', 20–1, 23. Among those who followed, see Sympher, 'Talsperrenbau', 159; Wulff, *Talsperren-Genossenschaften*, 3–4; Nußbaum,

'Wassergewinnung', 67–8; Ziegler, *Talsperrenbau*, v–vi; Kelen, *Talsperren*, 6–11; Mattern, *Thalsperrenbau* (whose sub-title managed to mention most of the different purposes of dams).

169 Ziegler, *Talsperrenbau*, 6.

170 Ziegler, *Talsperrenbau*, 5. See also ibid., vii–viii, 57–9.

171 Jakob Zinssmeister, 'Wertbestimmung von Wasserkräften und von Wasserkraftanlagen', *WK* 2, 5 Jan. 1909, 1–3.

172 Hennig, 'Deutschlands Wasserkräfte', 233; Stromberg, 'Bedeutung', 7, 29; Soergel, 'Bedeutung', 20–1. Intze ('Ueber Talsperren', 252–4) acknowledged that there were sceptics over reconciling flood protection and other uses, but argued that the doubts were only 'partly well-founded and diminish more and more with the choice of proper dimensions for the installations'.

173 On national prestige and industrial expositions: Berdrow, 'Staudämme', 255–7; Meurer, *Wasserbau*, 125.

174 Wulff, *Talsperren-Genossenschaften*, 6–7; Klössel, 'Errichtung von Talsperren', 121; Mattern, *Thalsperrenbau*, 77–81; Ziegler, *Talsperrenbau*, 67–8; Kretz, 'Zur Frage der Ausnutzung', 361–8; Koehn, 'Ausbau', 465.

175 For example, J. Köbl, 'Die Wirkungen der Talsperren auf das Hochwasser', *ANW* 38 (1904), 510; Albert Loacker, 'Die Ausnutzung der Wasserkräfte', *Die Turbine* 6 (1910), 235. Similar views run through Richard Hennig's writing.

176 Ziegler, *Talsperrenbau*, 67–70; *Festschrift . . . Möhnetalsperre*, 6–24, 73–6.

177 Mattern, *Ausnutzung*, 931.

178 Adam, 'Wasserwirtschaft und Wasserrecht', 2.

179 Miller, 'Ausnutzung', 401–5.

180 Mattern, *Ausnutzung*, 1005. See also Vogel, 'Bedeutung', 612.

181 The term 'rational' appeared twenty-eight times in one lecture by Albert Loacker: 'Ausnutzung'. See also Adam, 'Wasserwirtschaft und Wasserrecht', 2–6; Ziegler, 'Ueber die Notwendigkeit', 58.

182 Bachmann, 'Die Talsperren in Deutschland', 1134, 1156. Others came up with a smaller number of around 60 completed dams: Ernst Mattern, 'Stand der Entwicklung des Talsperrenwesens in Deutschland', *WuG* 19, 1 May 1929, 863 (who has the lowest number); Stromberg, 'Bedeutung', 23; Soergel, 'Bedeutung', 12–14. The difference is accounted for largely by the fact that Bachmann includes a substantial number of dams with walls less than fifteen metres high if they were otherwise important.

183 Wulff, *Talsperren-Genossenschaften*, 14, 20–445; Ziegler, *Talsperrenbau*, 71–2; Weiser, 'Talsperren', 227–31; Lochert, 'Geschichte des Talsperrenbaus im Bergischen Land', 122–3.

184 See the petition of the metalworking businesses association in Hagen, cited in Wulff, *Talsperren-Genossenschaften*, 21–2.

185 Weiser, 'Talsperren', 250–64.

186 Ibid., 13.

187 Soergel, 'Bedeutung', 23, 53–60; Völker, *Edder-Talsperre*, 27. Emil Abshoff, addressing an audience of shipping interests on the effects of dams like the Eder, noted that they might provide surplus water that could be used for agriculture; but he made it clear that the main purpose of raising river levels for navigational purposes would be thwarted if there was substantial diversion of water for 'other purposes', and this should accordingly 'not occur': Abshoff, 'Einiges über Talsperren'.

188 'Landwirtschaft und Talsperren', 88–9; Hennig, 'Deutschlands Wasserkräfte', 233; Wulff, *Talsperren-Genossenschaften*, 6; Koehn, 'Ausbau', 496.

189 Soergel, 'Bedeutung', 39. He used the term 'Zukunftsmusik', literally 'future music', which could also be translated as 'dreams of tomorrow'. For an exactly parallel view from Bohemia, about agriculture's exclusion from the benefits of dams, see Meisner, 'Flussregulierungsaktion', 408.

190 Ibid., 87–135.

191 Koehn, 'Ausbau', 480.

192 Algermissen, 'Talsperren: Weisse Kohle', 145; Köbl, 'Wirkungen der Talsperren auf das Hochwasser', 507–8.

193 Fischer, 'Niederschlags- und Abflussbedingungen', 655; Steinert, 'Die geographische Bedeutung', 55.

194 Splittgerber, 'Entwicklung', 206.

195 See Weber, 'Wupper-Talsperren', 317; Bachmann, 'Talsperren in Deutschland', 1142, 1146, 1153–6; Weiser, 'Talsperren', 94–5; Stromberg, 'Bedeutung', 31–4; Soergel, 'Bedeutung', 120–35. Most of these writers discuss the major floods of 1925–6. For a more positive assessment of the role of the Ruhr and Wupper dams in holding back floodwaters in 1909, see Zinssmeister, 'Beziehungen', 45–7; L. Koch, 'Im Zeichen des Wassermangels', *Die Turbine* (1909), 494.

196 Soergel, 'Bedeutung', 127–8.

197 Bachmann, 'Talsperren', 1142.

198 Ibid., 1154–6; also Soergel, 'Bedeutung', 107–18.

199 Bachmann, 'Wert des Hochwasserschutzes und der Wasserkraft des Hochwasserschutzraumes der Talsperren', *DeW* (1938), 65–9 (quotation, 65).

200 David Alexander, *Natural Disasters* (New York, 1993), 135.

201 See Föhl and Hamm, *Industriegeschichte*, 134–5.

202 Hennig, 'Otto Intze', 118. On the other hand, during negotiations over the founding of the Ruhr Valley Reservoirs Association, Prussian officials dropped plans to use enhanced Ruhr water to feed a local canal because it threatened their main objective: Olmer, *Wasser*, 245.

203 Werner Günther, 'Der Ausbau der oberen Saale durch Talsperren', dissertation, University of Jena, 1930.

204 Stromberg, 'Bedeutung', 55–9; Mattern, 'Stand', 863; Bachmann, 'Talsperren', 1140.

205 Bachmann, 'Talsperren', 1151. The cost of water from the Ottmachau was five times as great per cubic metre as water from the Eder Dam.

206 Köbl, 'Wirkungen', 508.

207 Stromberg, 'Bedeutung', 57.

208 Ibid., 56–7; Mattern, 'Stand', 863.

209 Berdrow, 'Staudämme', 255; Steinert, 'Die geographische Bedeutung', 61. See also Kurt Wolf, 'Über die Wasserversorgung mit besonderer Berücksichtigung der Talsperren', MCWäL (1906), 633–4.

210 Albert Schmidt, 'Die Erhöhung der Talsperrenmauer in Lennep', ZfB (1907), 227–32; Weber, 'Wupper-Talsperren', 106, 318–19.

211 See the progression in the Chemnitz reservoirs, from Einsiedel (1894: 0.3 cubic metres) to Klatschmühle (1909: 0.55) to Lautenbach (1914: 3.0) to Saidenbach (1933: 22.4): Meurer, Wasserbau, 125.

212 Meyer, 'Bedeutung', 121–30 (quotation, 123); Stromberg, 'Bedeutung', 35; Meurer, Wasserbau, 127–8.

213 Kluge and Schramm, Wassernöte, 161–3.

214 Weiser, 'Talsperren', 234.

215 Ott and Marquardt, Die Wasserversorgung der kgl. Stadt Brüx, 76.

216 Kluge and Schramm, Wassernöte and Olmer, Wasser argue this point strongly. On Euskirchen, see Weiser, 'Talsperren', 234.

217 Feige and Becks, Wasser für das Ruhrgebiet, 14.

218 Link, 'Talsperren des Ruhrgebiets', 100–1; Link, 'Bedeutung', 67–9; Feige and Becks, Wasser für das Ruhrgebiet, 12, 32–3. The amount of water permanently removed from the Ruhr basin rose in proportion.

219 Link, 'Bedeutung', 69–70; Link, 'Die Sorpetalsperre', 41–5, 71–2; Weiser, 'Talsperren', 145–52. The major new reservoir was in the Bigge valley (1965).

220 Kelen, Talsperren, 6–11. See the steep upward curve depicted in Rouvé, 'Talsperren in Mitteleuropa', 323.

221 Stromberg, 'Bedeutung', 52, 55.

222 Soergel, 'Bedeutung', 137. On the economics of 'low-load' electrical supply to rural areas: Hughes, Networks of Power, 318.

223 Ulrich Wengenroth, 'Motoren für den Kleinbetrieb: Soziale Utopien, technische Entwicklung und Absatzstrategien bei der Motorisierung des Kleingewerbes im Kaiserreich', in Wengenroth (ed.), Prekäre Selbständigkeit (Stuttgart, 1989), 177–205, an article that comes out of a Volkswagen Foundation project on the introduction of the electrical motor in German industry and small businesses, 1890–1930.

224 Günther, 'Der Ausbau der oberen Saale durch Talsperren', 37; Hughes, Networks of Power, 313–19.

225 See Hard, 'German Regulation', 35.

226 Hans Middelhoff, *Die volkswirtschaftliche Bedeutung der Aggertalsperren-anlagen* (Gummersbach, 1929), 60–1. Ownership in 1928 was 57 per cent public, 29 per cent mixed public/private, 14 per cent private.

227 Hughes, *Networks of Power*, 407–28.

228 On 1930 classifications, Kelen, *Talsperren*, 16. For the dimensions of German dams, see the listing of German dams on the ICOLD register (311 out of 40,000) in Franke (ed.), *German Dams*, 466–95; Meurer, *Wasserbau*, 186. Smith, *History of Dams*, 236, has a list of the world's largest. My comparisons are based on a conversion of his measurements in acre-feet to cubic metres.

229 Hennig, 'Deutschlands Wasserkräfte', 232; Algermissen, 'Talsperren: Weisse Kohle', 139–40.

230 Koehn, 'Ausbau', 491; Bubendey, 'Mittel und Ziele', 501; Hennig, 'Wasser-wirtschaft und Südwestafrika'.

231 Abercron, 'Talsperren in der Landschaft', 33.

232 McNeill, *Something New under the Sun*, 166–73; also Edward Goldsmith and Nicholas Hildyard, *The Social and Environmental Effects of Large Dams* (San Francisco, 1984), a Sierra Club publication that is a compendium of all the possible negative side-effects.

233 Alexander, *Natural Disasters*, 56–7; Goldsmith and Hildyard, *Social and Environmental Effects*, 101–19. For a sceptical view that runs in the face of most research, see R. B. Meade, 'Reservoirs and Earthquakes', in Goudie (ed.), *The Human Impact Reader*, 33–46.

234 On the European cases, Rainer Blum, *Seismische Überwachung der Schlegeis-Talsperre und die Ursachen induzierter Seismizität* (Karlsruhe, 1975), a valuable summary as well as a case study of one Swiss dam.

235 Steinert, 'Die geographische Bedeutung', 20–3.

236 Like Professor Wilhelm Halbfaß, whose concerns were reported by Zinss-meister, 'Industrie, Verkehr, Natur', 14.

237 Steinert, 'Die geographische Bedeutung', 39–47. Meteorological stations, like the one at the Möhne Dam, confirmed this: Stromberg, 'Bedeutung', 44.

238 Jäger, *Einführung* 44–51.

239 Kluge and Schramm, *Wassernöte*, 203; Weiser, 'Talsperren', 243–4.

240 Steinert, 'Die geographische Bedeutung', 47–54; Mattern, *Thalsperrenbau*, 54–5.

241 Weber, 'Wupper-Talsperren', 37; Helmut Maier, 'Kippenlandschaft, "Wassertaumel" und Kahlschlag: Anspruch und Wirklichkeit national-sozialistischer Energiepolitik', in Bayerl, Fuchsloch and Meyer (eds.), *Umweltgeschichte*, 253.

242 Maier, 'Energiepolitik', 253. On the problem of dams and bed-scouring,

see Alice Outwater, *Water: A Natural History* (New York, 1996), 105–6. The use of the term China Syndrome is my own.

243 Almost all, because a few drain, via the Danube, into the Black Sea.

244 Raimund Rödel, *Die Auswirkungen des historischen Talsperrenbaus auf die Zuflussverhältnisse der Ostsee* (Greifswald, 2001).

245 Schwoerbel, 'Technik und Wasser', 378.

246 Arno Naumann, 'Talsperren und Naturschutz', *BzN* 14 (1930), 79; Günther, 'Ausbau der oberen Saale durch Talsperren', 11. Mügge, 'Über die Gestaltung von Talsperren', 415, writes that dams came into being 'suddenly and violently'.

247 Ziegler, *Talsperrenbau*, 97.

248 Prof. Thiesing, 'Chemische und physikalische Untersuchungen an Talsperren, insbesondere der Eschbachtalsperre bei Remscheid', *Mitteilungen aus der Königlichen Prüfungsanstalt für Wasserversorgung und Abwässerbeseitigung zu Berlin* 15 (1911), 42–3, 140–1.

249 'Die biologische Bedeutung der Talsperren', *TuW* 11, April 1918, 144; Becker, 'Beiträge zur Pflanzenwelt der Talsperren des Bergischen Landes und ihrer Umgebung', *BeH* 4, August 1930, 323–6; Edwin Fels, *Der wirtschaftliche Mensch als Gestalter der Erde* (Stuttgart, 1954), 88.

250 Leslie A. Real and James H. Brown (eds.), *Foundations of Ecology: Classic Papers with Commentaries* (Chicago, 1991), 11; Zirnstein, *Ökologie*, 159–60. Kluge and Schramm, *Wassernöte*, 169–72.

251 A. Thienemann, 'Hydrobiologische und fischereiliche Untersuchungen an den westfälischen Talsperren', *LJbb* 41 (1911), 535–716; 'Die biologische Bedeutung' (reporting Thienemann's work).

252 C. Mühlenbein, 'Fische und Vögel der bergischen Talsperren', *BeH* 4, August 1930, 326–7; 'Die biologische Bedeutung'; Soergel, 'Bedeutung', 138–9; Thiesing, 'Chemische und physikalische Untersuchungen', 264–5; Borchardt, *Remscheider Stauweiheranlage*, 96–7. On dams and fishing elsewhere, Goldsmith and Hildyard, *Social and Environmental Effects*, 91–101; and for a superb account of dams and fish on one river, the Columbia in the American Pacific Northwest, White, *Organic Machine*.

253 Zirnstein, *Ökologie*, 161–3.

254 Kluge and Schramm, *Wassernöte*, 204–5; Norbert Große et al., 'Der Einfluss des Fischbestandes auf die Zooplanktonbesiedlung und die Wassergüte', *GWF* 139 (1998): *Special Talsperren*, 30–5.

255 P. Eigen, 'Die Insektenfauna der bergischen Talsperren', *BeH* 4, August 1930, 327–31.

256 Mühlenbein, 'Fische und Vögel', 327.

257 Richard White, 'The Natures of Nature Writing', *Raritan*, Fall 2002, 154–5.

258 Splittgerber, 'Entwicklung', 207. On the nature conservation idea, Michael

Wettengel, 'Staat und Naturschutz 1906–1945: Zur Geschichte der Staatlichen Stelle für Naturdenkmalpflege in Preussen und der Reichsstelle für Naturschutz', HZ 257 (1993), 355–99, and below, Chapter 5.

259 On the 1930s: *Die Eifel* (1938), 137, cited in Heinz Peter Brogiato and Werner Grasediek, 'Geschichte der Eifel und des Eifelvereins von 1888 bis 1988', in *Die Eifel 1888–1988* (Düren, 1989), 441–3; Mügge, 'Uber die Gestaltung', 418. On the present day: Franke (ed.), *Dams in Germany*, 295, 302, 310 (on the Ennepe, Möhne and Sorpe); GWF 139 (1998): *Special Talsperren* issue.

260 Weiser, 'Talsperren', 4.

261 Klössel, 'Die Errichtung von Talsperren in Sachsen', 121; Völker, *Edder-Talsperre*, 25, 54; Arno Naumann, 'Talsperren und Naturschutz'. On the Walchensee project and the landscape, Koehn, 'Wasserkraftanlagen', 174; Hughes, *Networks of Power*, 340–1.

262 Rudolf Gundt, 'Das Schicksal des oberen Saaletals', *Die Gartenlaube* (1926), 214.

263 Paul Schultze-Naumburg, 'Ästhetische und allgemeine kulturelle Grundsätze bei der Anlage von Talsperren', *Der Harz* 13 (1906), 353–60 (quotation, 359); Naumann, 'Talsperren und Naturschutz', 83.

264 Schultze-Naumburg, 'Grundsätze'.

265 Abshoff, 'Einiges über Talsperren', 91–2; Mattern, *Ausnutzung*, 1001–2.

266 Fischer, 'Ausnützung der Wasserkräfte', 106.

267 Schönhoff, 'Möhnetalsperre', 684–5; Weber, 'Wupper-Talsperren', 313.

268 Schultze-Naumburg, 'Grundsätze', 358; Philipp A. Rappaport, 'Talsperren im Landschaftsbilde und die architektonische Behandlung von Talsperren', WuG 5, 1 Nov. 1914, 15–18; Werner Lindner, *Ingenieurwerk und Naturschutz* (Berlin, 1926), 57–60; Ehnert, 'Gestaltungsaufgaben im Talsperrenbau', *Der Bauingenieur* 10 (1929), 651–6.

269 Kullrich, 'Der Wettbewerb für die architektonische Ausbildung der Möhnetalsperre', ZbB 28, 1 Feb. 1908, 61–5; *Festschrift . . . Möhnetalsperre*, 41. Weiser, 'Talsperren', 270–3, has illustrations of the top entries.

270 Mügge, 'Uber die Gestaltung von Talsperren und Talsperrenlandschaften', 404–19 (quotation, 418). On Hitler and concrete, Martin Vogt (ed.), *Herbst 1941 im 'Führerhauptquartier'* (Koblenz, 2002), 9–10.

271 The engineer Witte argued at a 12 March 1902 meeting of the German Reservoirs Association that dams led to 'an enhancement of natural beauty': 'Thalsperren am Harz', 167–8. See also Kreuzkam, 'Deutschlands Talsperren', 660; Kelen, *Talsperren*, 11.

272 Paul Schultze-Naumburg, 'Kraftanlagen und Talsperren', *Der Kunstwart* 19 (1906), 130. A speech of Schultze-Naumburg's, also arguing that reservoirs created 'new beauty', is reported in Sympher, 'Talsperrenbau', 178.

273 Thiesing, 'Chemische und physikalische Untersuchungen', 262–3 (which

mentions Schultze-Naumburg by name); Gräf, 'Über die Verwertung von Talsperren für die Wasserversorgung', 479–80.

274 Kollbach, 'Urft-Talsperre'; Abercron, 'Talsperren in der Landschaft'.

275 Weber, 'Wupper-Talsperren', 316.

276 Jean Pauli, 'Talsperrenromantik', *BeH* 4, August 1930, 331–2.

277 Rappaport, 'Talsperren im Landschaftsbilde', 15.

278 Gundt, 'Schicksal', 215.

279 Reginald Hill, *On Beulah Height* (London, 1998); Thyde Mourier, *Le barrage d'Arvillard* (1963); Ernst Candèze, *Die Talsperre: Tragisch abenteuerliche Geschichte eines Insektenvölkchens*, transl. from the French (Leipzig, 1901); Ursula Kobbe, *Der Kampf mit dem Stausee* (Berlin, 1943), an Austrian work; Marie Majerova, *Die Talsperre*, transl. from the Czech (East Berlin, 1956); Libusa Hanusova, *Die Talsperre an der Moldau*, transl. from the Czech (East Berlin, 1952).

280 Kluge and Schramm, *Wassernöte*, 167.

281 Candèze, *Talsperre*, 205.

282 Candèze, *Talsperre*, 209.

283 Candèze, *Talsperre*, 201–2; Kobbe, *Kampf mit dem Stausee*, 33–8; Völker, *Edder-Talsperre*, 5, 28.

284 Kobbe, *Kampf mit dem Stausee*, 140.

285 Völker, *Edder-Talsperre*, 28.

286 See *Festschrift . . . Möhnetalsperre*, 42–64; Völker, *Edder-Talsperre*, 6, 23; Bing, *Vom Edertal zum Edersee*, 6; Kelen, *Talsperren*, 102–17; Kobbe, *Kampf mit dem Stausee*, 146.

287 W. Soldan and C[arl] Heßler, *Die Waldecker Talsperre im Eddertal* (Marburg and Bad Wildungen, 2nd edn., 1911), 38; Bing, *Vom Edertal zum Edersee*, 6; Völker, *Edder-Talsperre*, 7; *Festschrift . . . Möhnetalsperre*, 50; Kollbach, 'Urft-Talsperre'; Borchardt, *Denkschrift zur Einweihung der Neye-Talsperre*, 32–4, 43, 47; Föhl and Hamm, *Industriegeschichte*, 130.

288 Schönhoff, 'Möhnetalsperre', 685.

289 Middelhoff, *Aggertalsperrenanlagen*, 45; Stromberg, 'Bedeutung', 62; Naumann, 'Talsperren und Naturschutz', 80; Weiser, 'Talsperren', 99; Brogiato and Grasediek, 'Eifel', 414.

290 Although workers did live in private homes in the Eder and Möhne valleys: Bing, *Vom Edertal zum Edersee*, 6; *Festschrift . . . Möhnetalsperre*, 54.

291 Völker, *Edder-Talsperre*, 4; Bachmann, 'Talsperren', 1140.

292 Examples include a proposal for the middle Oder (see Fischer, 'Niederschlags- und Ablußbedingungen', 654), and another in the Wenne valley (see Weiser, 'Talsperren', 246–7).

293 Jean Milmeister, *Chronik der Stadt Vianden 1926–1950* (Vianden, 1976), 13–33, 127–9, 149, 164–8; Brogiato and Grasediek, 'Eifel', 336.

294 Soldan and Heßler, *Waldecker Talsperre*, 55–6. For the familiar official and

technocratic view of the necessity of 'sacrifice', see Mattern, *Thalsperrenbau*, 57; Hennig, 'Deutschlands Wasserkräfte', 233.

295 Völker, *Edder-Talsperre*, 8.

296 Soldan and Heßler, *Waldecker Talsperre*, 55; Völker, *Edder-Talsperre*, 8.

297 K. Thielsch, 'Baukosten von Wasserkraftanlagen', *ZfdgT*, 20 Aug. 1908, 357.

298 For the Eder it was 9 out of 20 million Marks (Völker, *Edder-Talsperre*, 27); for the Möhne, 8.2 out of 21.5 million, or 38 per cent (*Festschrift . . . Möhnetalsperre*, 11, 25–7); for the Mauer, 2.4 out of 8.3 million, or 29 per cent (B., 'Die Talsperre bei Mauer', 611); for the Ennepe, 750,000 out of 2.8 million, or 27 per cent (*Ennepetalsperre*, 4, 11–12).

299 Wulff, *Talsperren-Genossenschaften*, 21; Weiser, 'Talsperren', 78.

300 *Festschrift . . . Möhnetalsperre*, 25–9; Koch, 'Wert einer Wasserkraft'; Weiser, 'Talsperren', 241–2. In the Möhne valley, two of the most difficult negotiations were with aristocratic landowners, who were ultimately very generously compensated: *Festschrift . . . Möhnetalsperre*, 28–9.

301 Bechstein, 'Vom Ruhrtalsperrenverein', 138. See also Sympher, 'Talsperrenbau', 177; Schultze-Naumburg, 'Grundsätze', 357.

302 In the Möhne valley three villages also disappeared completely, Delecke, Drüggelte and Kettlersteich, along with parts of three others.

303 Soldan and Heßler, *Waldecker Talsperre*, 66, 77–9, 83.

304 Soldan and Heßler, *Waldecker Talsperre*, 66, 77–9, 83; Völker, *Edder-Talsperre*, 16–20; Bing, *Vom Edertal zum Edersee*, 7; Sympher, 'Talsperrenbau', 177.

305 Völker, *Edder-Talsperre*, 10.

306 Bing, *Vom Edertal zum Edersee*, 1.

307 Völker, *Edder-Talsperre*, 20, 26, 54.

308 Milmeister, *Chronik*, 22.

309 Völker, *Edder-Talsperre*, 28.

310 On the reappearance of ruins, Weber, 'Wupper-Talsperren', 313, 316; Weiser, 'Talsperren', 195; Bing, *Vom Edertal zum Edersee*, 2–3, 8, 28–9.

311 Rieger, 'Modern Wonders'; Ziegler, *Talsperrenbau*, 85, on the particular anxiety attached to large dams.

312 'Thalsperren am Harz', 167–8; Wulff, *Talsperren-Genossenschaften*, 3; Ernst, 'Riesentalsperre', 668; Wolf, 'Ueber die Wasserversorgung', 633–4; Kluge and Schramm, *Wassernöte*, 136–7.

313 Hennig, 'Deutschlands Wasserkräfte', 232. The figure of 2000 comes from Alexander, *Natural Disasters*, 359.

314 Berdrow, 'Staudämme', 258; Gräf, 'Verwertung von Talsperren', 485; Hennig, 'Deutschlands Wasserkräfte', 232; Meurer, *Wasserbau*, 117–18; Föhl and Hamm, *Industriegeschichte*, 129; Kluge and Schramm, *Wassernöte*, 135; Pearce, *The Dammed*, 35–6; Rouvé, 'Talsperren in

Mitteleuropa', 303–10; Alexander, *Natural Disasters*, 358.

315 'Eine Dammbruchkatastrophe in Amerika', *Die Gartenlaube* (1911), 1028.

316 Arguments summarized by Smith, *History of Dams*, 201–7, 219–21. See also the strong critique by the American George Holmes Moore on the vulnerability of wide-based gravity dams to hydrostatic uplift forces: Jackson, 'Engineering', 560, 571.

317 Mattern, 'Stand', 858–60.

318 Mattern, *Thalsperrenbau*, v.

319 Intze, 'Talsperren in Rheinland und Westfalen, Schlesien und Böhmen', 28, 36; 'Ueber Talsperren', 254.

320 Fr. Barth, 'Talsperren', *BIG* (1908), 269; Koehn, 'Ausbau', 491–2; Bachmann, 'Hochwasserentlastungsanlagen', 334. On the (near-)unanimity of the profession, Meurer, *Wasserbau*, 117.

321 Jackson, 'Engineering', 559.

322 See, for example, the Prussian decree from the Ministers of Trade and Industry, Public Works, Interior and Domains and Forestry, 18 Jun. 1907: 'Anleitung für Bau und Betrieb von Sammelbecken', *ZbWW*, 20 July 1907, 321–4; also Berdrow, 'Staudämme', 258; Mattern, 'Stand', 860; Weiser, 'Talsperren', 235; Giesecke et al., 'Standardization'.

323 Wolf, 'Ueber die Wasserversorgung', 633–4.

324 See Ernst Mattern's 'Ein französisches Urteil über deutsche Bauweise von Staudämmen und Sperrmauern' (*ZdB* 24 Jun. 1905, 319–20), which was a reply to an article by the French engineer Jacquinot in *Le Génie Civil* of 3 Dec. 1904, and Jacquinot's response, 'Über Talsperrenbauten', in the *ZdB*, 29 Sep. 1906, 503–5.

325 Ernst Link, 'Die Zerstörung der Austintalsperre in Pennsylvanien (Nordamerika) II', *ZdB*, 20 Jan. 1912, 36; also Mattern, 'Die Zerstörung der Austintalsperre in Pennsylvanien (Nordamerika) I', ibid., 13 Jan. 1912, 25–7; Ehlers, 'Bruch der Austintalsperre und Grundsätze für die Erbauung von Talsperren', ibid., 8 May 1912, 238.

326 Paxmann, 'Bruch der Talsperre bei Black River Falls in Wisconsin', ibid., 25 May 1912, 275.

327 Marianne Weber, *Max Weber: A Biography* (New York, 1975).

328 Mattern, 'Stand', 862.

329 'Prinzip Archimedes', *Der Spiegel*, 1986, no. 4, 79.

330 Ibid., 77; Franke (ed.), *German Dams*, 181, 292–5; Weiser, 'Talsperren', 146–50; Kluge and Schramm, *Wassernöte*, 201–2.

331 On the Lingese Dam, Weiser, 'Talsperren', 102–3; on Tambach and Eduard Döll, Ott and Marquardt, *Wasserversorgung der Kgl. Stadt Brüx*, 65–7.

332 Kluge and Schramm, *Wassernöte*, 202; Weiser, 'Talsperren', 75.

333 'Prinzip Archimedes', 77–9 (quotation 77, from Dr Alexius Vogel); Jürgen Fries, 'Anpassung von Talsperren an die allgemein anerkannten Regeln der

Technik', *GWF* 139 (1998), *Special Talsperren*, 59–64; Franke (ed.), *German Dams*, 181, 292–5, 302–9.

334 'Prinzip Archimedes', 79; Alexander, *Natural Disasters*, 359.

335 Splittgerber, 'Entwicklung', 209; Lieckfeldt, 'Die Lebensdauer der Talsperren', *ZdB*, 28 Mar. 1906, 167–8, which presented war – like earthquakes – as an 'external force' that should always be taken into account.

336 *Frainer Talsperre*, 5; Milmeister, *Chronik*, 17, 30–2.

337 Smith, *History of Dams*, 243.

338 Brogiato and Grasediek, 'Die Eifel', 421, 427–8, 431. For subsequent examples of dams being targeted in wartime – in Korea, and during civil wars in Mozambique and El Salvador – see Goldsmith and Hildyard, *Social and Environmental Effects*, 103–4.

339 O. Kirschner, 'Zerstörung und Schutz von Talsperren und Dämmen', *SB*, 24 May 1949, 301–2.

340 Based on Kirschner, 'Zerstörung', 277–81; Joachim W. Ziegler (ed.), *Die Sintflut im Ruhrtal: Eine Bilddokumentation zur Möhne-Katastrophe* (Meinerzhagen, 1983); Bing, *Vom Edertal zum Edersee*, 14–18, 30–1; John Ramsden, *The Dambusters* (London, 2003).

341 Ramsden, *Dambusters*, 12.

342 Ziegler (ed.), *Sintflut*, 26–7.

Chapter Five: Race and Reclamation

1 Louise Boyd, 'The Marshes of Pinsk', *GR* 26 (1936), 376–95; Martin Bürgener, *Pripet-Polessie: Das Bild einer polnischen Ostraum-Landschaft*, *Petermanns Geographische Mitteilungen, Ergänzungsheft* 237 (Gotha, 1939); Kurt Freytag, *Raum deutscher Zukunft: Grenzland im Osten* (Dresden, 1933), 84; Joice M. Nankivell and Sydney Loch, *The River of a Hundred Ways* (London, 1924).

2 Boyd, 'Marshes of Pinsk', 380–1, 395.

3 Bürgener, *Pripet-Polessie*, 9.

4 Ibid., 53, 56.

5 Max Vasmer, 'Die Urheimat der Slawen', in Wilhelm Volz (ed.), *Der ostdeutsche Volksboden: Aufsätze zu den Fragen des Ostens. Erweiterte Ausgabe* (Breslau, 1926), 118–43. Bürgener accepts the argument, quoting Vasmer and some of the many German writers who followed him (Witte, Hofmann, von Richthofen). See also Michael Burleigh, *Germany Turns Eastwards: A Study of Ostforschung in the Third Reich* (Cambridge, 1988), 29, 30, 49, 60.

6 Bürgener, *Pripet-Polessie*, 46, 59. On the *Urgermanen* theory: Gustav Kossinna, *Die Herkunft der Germanen* (Würzburg, 1911); Ekkehart Staritz, *Die West-Ostbewegung in der deutschen Geschichte* (Breslau, 1935), 25–48;

Wolfgang La Baume, *Urgeschichte der Ostgermanen* (Danzig, 1934); Wolfgang Wippermann, *Der 'Deutsche Drang nach Osten': Ideologie und Wirklichkeit eines politischen Schlagwortes* (Darmstadt, 1981), 94, 98–9, notes
that the theory also had its critics from the beginning.

7 Bürgener, *Pripet-Polessie*, 86–90 (quotation: 90), also 71, 75.

8 Ibid., 38–9, 44–6.

9 Heinrich von Treitschke, *Origins of Prussianism (The Teutonic Knights)*,
originally published 1862, transl. Eden and Cedar Paul (New York, 1969),
93–4. I have altered the translation in a few places to remove archaisms.

10 Heinrich von Treitschke, *Deutsche Geschichte im 19. Jahrhundert, Erster
Teil* [1879] (Königstein/Ts, 1981), 66. Similar comments, ibid., 45, 56–7,
76. The English term for Werder is the little-used word 'eyot'.

11 Beheim-Schwarzbach, *Hohenzollernsche Colonisationen*, 423–4, 426. His
work was quoted by a later leading Nazi landscape planner: Heinrich
Friedrich Wiepking-Jürgensmann, 'Friedrich der Grosse und wir', *DG* 33
(1920), 69–78. In his writings, Wiepking-Jürgensmann sometimes went by
his initials, sometimes by name or title; sometimes as Wiepking, at other
times by the full name. This one had the byline 'H. F. Wiepking'; I have
given his full name.

12 Otto Schlüter, *Wald, Sumpf und Siedelungsland in Altpreussen vor der
Ordenszeit* (Halle, 1921), 2, 7; Müller, 'Aus der Kolonisationszeit des Netzebruchs', 3. On the sheer volume of works: Harvard's Widener Library alone
has the better part of a hundred. Analysis of the 62 printed sources cited
by Schlüter suggests that the boom began in the 1870s and 80s.

13 Freytag, *Raum deutscher Zukunft*, 11.

14 Gustav Freytag, *Soll und Haben* (Berlin, 1855), 536–9, 681–3, 688, 698–9,
820.

15 Wiepking-Jürgensmann, 'Das Grün im Dorf und in der Feldmark', 442,
which opens with the sentence 'A German village can only ever be a green
village'. Rolf Wingendorf, *Polen: Volk zwischen Ost und West* (Berlin, 1939)
has a chapter that dwells on the 'grey' Polish landscape.

16 Rudolf Kötzschke, Lamprecht's former student and another historian with
popularizing ambitions, noted in 1926 how a 'generation earlier' the historical understanding of 'German eastern colonization' had ceased to be an
academic preserve and became a matter of public interest: Kötzschke, 'Über
den Ursprung und die geschichtliche Bedeutung der ostdeutschen Siedlung',
in Volz (ed.), *Der ostdeutsche Volksboden*, 8–9.

17 See Neuhaus, *Friedericianische Colonisation*, 4. Other examples in Helmut
Walser Smith, *German Nationalism and Religious Conflict* (Princeton,
1995), 193–4; William Hagen, *Germans, Poles and Jews: The Nationality
Conflict in the Prussian East, 1772–1914* (Chicago, 1980), 184; Roger
Chickering, *'We Men Who Feel Most German': A Cultural Study of the*

Pan-German League (London, 1984), 74–101; Wippermann, 'Deutsche Drang nach Osten', 98–9.

18 Bürgener, *Pripet-Polessie*, 56–7. Among Günther's works were two that sold in the hundreds of thousands, *Rassenkunde des deutschen Volkes* and *Kleine Rassenkunde des deutschen Volkes*. Bürgener refers to Günther in his text, but includes none of his works in the bibliography. Bürgener used Gustav Paul's *Grundzüge der Rassen- und Raumgeschichte des deutschen Volkes* (Munich, 1935) to similar effect.

19 Hans-Dietrich Schultz, *Die deutschsprachige Geographie von 1800 bis 1970* (Berlin, 1980), 205.

20 The geographer Reinhard Thom, cited ibid., 203. The racial view of landscape is evident throughout Bürgener's book; he drew especially on N. Creutzburg's *Kultur im Spiegel der Landschaft* (Leipzig, 1930).

21 Bürgener, *Pripet-Polessie*, 56–7. On Hans Schrepfer and Hitler, see Schultz, *Die deutschsprachige Geographie*, 209, and 202–28 more generally on the capitulation of academic geography.

22 See Emily Anderson (ed.), *The Letters of Beethoven*, vol. 2 (New York, 1985), 638–9; Maynard Solomon, 'Franz Schubert and the Peacocks of Benvenuto Cellini', *19th-Century Music* 12 (1989), 202. I am grateful to Karen Painter for these references. The 'marshy district' as a code for prostitution also appears in Theodor Fontane's novel *Irrungen, Wirrungen*.

23 Adolf Hitler, *Mein Kampf* (Munich, 1943 edn., 279–80), cited Gert Gröning and Joachim Wolschke-Bulmahn, 'Naturschutz und Ökologie im Nationalsozialismus', *AS* 10 (1983), 15–16.

24 Bürgener, *Pripet-Polessie*, 61.

25 Jack Wertheimer, *Unwelcome Strangers: East European Jews in Imperial Germany* (New York, 1987); Katja Wüstenbecher, 'Hamburg and the Transit of East European Emigrants', in Andreas Fahrmeir, Oliver Faron and Patrick Weil (eds.), *Migration Control in the North Atlantic World* (New York and Oxford, 2003), 223–36.

26 Alfred Döblin, *Reise in Polen* [1926] (Olten and Freiburg, 1968). As the book shows, however, Döblin remained ambivalent towards Polish Jews.

27 Freytag, *Raum deutscher Zukunft*; Wingendorf, *Polen*, 73–4; Theodor Oberländer, *Die agrarische Überbevölkerung Polens* (Berlin, 1935); Peter-Heinz Seraphim, *Das Judentum im osteuropäischen Raum* (Essen, 1938); Seraphim (ed.), *Polen und seine Wirtschaft* (Königsberg, 1937). On Oberländer and Seraphim, see the major work by Götz Aly and Susanne Heim, *Vordenker der Vernichtung* (Frankfurt/Main, 1995), 91–101, who cite other works written from a similar standpoint.

28 Bürgener, *Pripet-Polessie*, 61–2.

29 Ibid., 61–6; Boyd, 'Marshes of Pinsk', 380, 391.

30 Bürgener, *Pripet-Polessie*, 105.

31 Nankivell and Loch, *The River of a Hundred Ways*, 29, 46, 54–5, 252–6.

32 Boyd, 'Marshes of Pinsk', 395, contrasts progress on the Pripet marshes with drainage projects on the Zuider Zee and Pontine marshes.

33 Bürgener, *Pripet-Polessie*, 92, and 70–87 more generally.

34 Ibid., 91, 122. On the 'lessons' Nazi writers drew from the west–east movement in history, see Staritz, *Die West-Ostbewegung*; and Wippermann, *'Deutsche Drang nach Osten'*.

35 Bürgener, *Pripet-Polessie*, 56, 105.

36 Ibid., 122.

37 Gierach, 'Die Bretholzsche Theorie', in Volz (ed.), *Der ostdeutsche Volksboden*, 151. Almost every article in this collection contains similar arguments, e.g. those by Aubin, Kötzschke and Schlüter. See also Erich Keyser, *Westpreussen und das deutsche Volk* (Danzig, 1919), 2, 10–12; *Deutscher Volksrat: Zeitschrift für deutsches Volkstum und deutsche Kultur im Osten* [Danzig], 1/19, 13 August 1919, 154; *Mitteilungen der deutschen Volksräte Polens und Westpreussens*, 14 Mar 1919; *Westpreussen und Polen in Gegenwart und Vergangenheit*, 15; *Die polnische Schmach: Was würde der Verlust der Ostprovinzen für das deutsche Volk bedeuten? Ein Mahnwort an alle Deutschen, hsg. vom Reichsverband Ostschutz* (Berlin, 1919), 10. These pamphlets can be found bound together in Harvard's Widener Library (Ger 5270.88).

38 Bürgener, *Pripet-Polessie*, 56.

39 Cited Schultz, *Die deutschsprachige Geographie*, 226–7.

40 Bürgener, *Pripet-Polessie*, 9, 115–21, 127–8.

41 Ibid., 127–8.

42 Martin Broszat, *Nationalsozialistische Polenpolitik 1939–1945* (Stuttgart, 1961).

43 Robert L. Koehl, *RKFDV: German Resettlement and Population Policy 1939–1945* (Cambridge, Mass., 1957), 49–52; Josef Ackermann, *Heinrich Himmler als Ideologe* (Göttingen, 1970), 204–6; Rolf-Dieter Müller, *Hitlers Ostkrieg und die deutsche Siedlungspolitik* (Frankfurt/Main, 1991), 86; Bruno Wasser, *Himmlers Raumplanung im Osten: Der Generalplan Ost in Polen 1940–1944* (Basel, 1993), 25–6.

44 Elizabeth Harvey, *Women and the Nazi East* (New Haven and London, 2003), 13; Harvey, 'Die deutsche Frau im Osten', *AfS* 38 (1998), 196; Aly and Heim, *Vordenker*, 188–203 ('Herrenmensch – ein Lebensgefühl').

45 Konrad Meyer, 'Zur Einführung', *Neue Dorflandschaften: Gedanken und Pläne zum ländlichen Aufbau in den neuen Ostgebieten und im Altreich. Herausgegeben vom Stabshauptamt des Reichskommissars für die Festigung deutschen Volkstums, Planungsamt sowie vom Planungsbeauftragten für die Siedlung und ländliche Neuordnung* (Berlin, 1943), 7; Herbert Frank, 'Dörfliche Planung im Osten', ibid., 45.

46 Erhard Mäding, *Regeln für die Gestaltung der Landschaft: Einführung in die Allgemeine Anordnung Nr. 20/VI/42 des Reichsführers SS, Reichskommissars für die Festigung deutschen Volkstums* (Berlin, 1943), 55–62 reprints Himmler's *Allgemeine Anordnung* and adds commentary. The original directive is also in Mechtild Rössler and Sabine Schleiermacher (eds.), *Der 'Generalplan Ost'* (Berlin, 1993), 136–47 (quotation, 137). The directive was drawn up by Konrad Meyer, Wiepking-Jürgensmann and Mäding, with some direct input from Himmler. See Gert Gröning and Joachim Wolschke-Bulmahn, *Die Liebe zur Landschaft*, part III: *Der Drang nach Osten: Zur Entwicklung im Nationalsozialismus und während des Zweiten Weltkrieges in den 'eingegliederten Ostgebieten'* (Munich, 1987), 112–25.

47 Heinrich Friedrich Wiepking-Jürgensmann, 'Der Deutsche Osten: Eine vordringliche Aufgabe für unsere Studierenden', *DG* 52 (1939), 193.

48 Friedrich Kann, 'Die Neuordnung des deutschen Dorfes', in *Neue Dorflandschaften*, 100.

49 There is fundamental discussion of this in Gröning and Wolschke-Bulmahn, *Die Liebe zur Landschaft*. See also Klaus Fehn, '"Lebensgemeinschaft von Volk und Raum": Zur nationalsozialistischen Raum- und Landschaftsplanung in den eroberten Ostgebieten', in Joachim Radkau and Frank Uekötter (eds.), *Naturschutz und Nationalsozialismus* (Frankfurt/Main, 2003), 207–24; Aly and Heim, *Vordenker*, 125–88.

50 Artur von Machui, 'Die Landgestaltung als Element der Volkspolitik', *DA* 42 (1942), 297. For other examples (among hundreds) of the usage see Wilhelm Grebe, 'Zur Gestaltung neuer Höfe und Dörfer im deutschen Osten', *NB* 32 (1940), 57–66; Heinrich Werth, 'Die Gestaltung der deutschen Landschaft als Aufgabe der Volksgemeinschaft', *NB* 34 (1942), 109–11; M., 'Landschaftsgestaltung im Osten', *NB* 36 (1944), 201–11.

51 Erhard Mäding, 'Die Gestaltung der Landschaft als Hoheitsrecht und Hoheitspflicht', *NB* 35 (1943), 22–4.

52 Herbert Frank, 'Das natürliche Fundament', in *Neue Dorflandschaften*, 15; Paula Rauter-Wilberg, 'Die Kücheneinrichtung', ibid., 133–6; Clara Teschner, 'Landschaftsgestaltung in den Ostgebieten', *Odal* 11 (1942), 567–70 (interview with planner Wiepking-Jürgensmann); Walter Christaller, 'Grundgedanken zum Siedlungs- und Verwaltungsaufgaben im Osten', *NB* 32 (1940), 305–12; Udo von Schauroth, 'Raumordnungsskizzen und Ländliche Planung', *NB* 33 (1941), 123–8; J. Umlauf, 'Der Stand der Raumordnungsplanung für die eingegliederten Ostgebiete', *NB* 34 (1942), 281–93; Walter Wickop, 'Grundsätze und Wege der Dorfplanung', in *Neue Dorflandschaften*, 47; Franz A. Doubek, 'Die Böden des Ostraumes in ihrer landbaulichen Bedeutung', *NB* 34 (1942), 145–50.

53 *Allgemeine Anordnung Nr. 20/VI/42 über die Gestaltung der Landschaft in den eingegliederten Ostgebieten vom 21. Dezember 1942*, in Rössler

and Schleiermacher (eds.), *Generalplan Ost*, 136.

54 Examples: Konrad Meyer, 'Planung umd Ostaufbau', *RuR* 5 (1941), 392–7; Werth, 'Gestaltung der deutschen Landschaft', 109; Wiepking-Jürgensmann, 'Aufgaben und Ziele deutscher Landschaftspolitik', *DG* 53 (1940), 84; Kann, 'Neuordnung des deutschen Dorfes', 100; Ulrich Greifelt, 'Die Festigung deutschen Volkstums im Osten', in Hans-Joachim Schacht (ed.), *Bauhandbuch für den Aufbau im Osten* (Berlin, 1943), 9–13, esp. 11 (on 'Gesundung').

55 Heinz Ellenberg, 'Deutsche Bauernhaus-Landschaften als Ausdruck von Natur, Wirtschaft und Volkstum', *GZ* 47 (1941), 85.

56 See the first-person accounts by Berndt von Staden, 'Erinnerungen an die Umsiedlung', *JbbD* 41 (1994), 62–75; Olrik Breckoff, 'Zwischenspiel an der Warthe – und was daraus wurde', ibid., 142–9; also Koehl, *RKFDV*, 53–75; Wasser, *Himmlers Raumplanung im Osten*, 26–8; Jürgen von Hehn, *Die Umsiedlung der baltischen Deutschen: Das letzte Kapitel baltischdeutscher Geschichte* (Marburg, 1982); Harry Stossun, *Die Umsiedlungen der Deutschen aus Litauen während des Zweiten Weltkrieges* (Marburg, 1993); Valdis O. Lumans, *Himmler's Auxiliaries: The Volksdeutsche Mittelstelle and the German National Minorities of Europe, 1933–1945* (Chapel Hill, 1993).

57 Götz Aly, *'Final Solution': Nazi Population Policy and the Murder of the European Jews* (London, 1999), 70–6.

58 S. Zantke, 'Die Heimkehr der Wolhyniendeutschen', *NSM* 11 (1940), 169–71.

59 Stossun, *Umsiedlungen*, 111–45; Dirk Jachomowski, *Die Umsiedlung der Bessarabien-, Bukowina- and Dobrudschadeutschen* (Munich, 1984), 107–42; Koehl, *RKFDV*, 95–110; Lumans, *Himmler's Auxiliaries*, 186–95.

60 Broszat, *Polenpolitik*, 38–48; Christian Jansen and Arno Weckbecker, *Der Volksdeutsche 'Selbstschutz' in Polen 1939/40* (Munich, 1992); Arno J. Mayer, *Why Did the Heavens Not Darken? The 'Final Solution' in History* (New York, 1990), 181–4.

61 Descriptions in Breckoff, 'Zwischenspiel', 142–4; Staden, 'Erinnerungen', 64–9; Stossun, *Umsiedlungen*, 149–53; Broszat, *Polenpolitik*, 95–7; Lumans, *Himmler's Auxiliaries*, 195–6; Harvey, 'Die deutsche Frau im Osten', 206–7.

62 Hehn, *Umsiedlung*, 195; Hans-Erich Volkmann, 'Zur Ansiedlung der Deutsch-Balten im "Reichsgau" Wartheland', *ZfO* 30 (1981), 550.

63 Götz Aly, '"Jewish resettlement": Reflections on the Political Prehistory of the Holocaust', in Ulrich Herbert (ed.), *National Socialist Extermination Policies* (New York and Oxford, 2000), 59–63; Broszat, *Polenpolitik*, 100–1; Christopher Browning, *Nazi Policy, Jewish Workers, German Killers* (Cambridge, 2000), 9–13; Koehl, *RKFDV*, 121–6, 129–30.

64 Frank's report on the General Government, 9 Dec 1942: A. J. Kaminski,

Nationalsozialistische Besatzungspolitik in Polen und der Tschechoslovakei 1939–1945. Dokumente (Bremen, 1975), 89–90. The *Diensttagebuch des deutschen Generalgouverneurs in Polen 1939–1945*, ed. Werner Präg and Wolfgang Jacobmeyer (Stuttgart, 1975), 585–6, reports this end-of-year speech, but only briefly paraphrases the opening, historical part of it.

65 Aly, *'Final Solution'*, 59–79; Browning, *Nazi Policy*, 12–13; Philippe Burrin, *Hitler and the Jews* (London, 1994), 73–5; Mayer, *Heavens*, 186–90.

66 Aly, *'Final Solution'*, 92; Aly and Heim, *Vordenker*, 257–65; Browning, *Nazi Policy*, 15–17; Burrin, *Hitler and the Jews*, 77–9.

67 Christopher R. Browning, *The Final Solution and the German Foreign Office* (New York, 1978), 35–43.

68 Aly, *'Final Solution'*, 109, 125.

69 Kaminski, *Dokumente*, 5–16. In the novels, Siberia was usually the favoured destination.

70 Hans Safrian, *Die Eichmann-Männer* (Vienna and Zürich, 1993), 68–85; Browning, *Nazi Policy*, 6–7; Burrin, *Hitler and the Jews*, 72; Yehuda Bauer, *Rethinking the Holocaust* (New Haven and London, 2001), 180. Some Sinti and Roma were also among the victims of the Nisko Plan.

71 Dieter Pohl, 'The Murder of Jews in the General Government', in Herbert (ed.), *National Socialist Extermination Policies* (New York and Oxford, 2000), 86; Christoph Dieckmann, 'The War and the Killing of the Lithuanian Jews', ibid., 250; Aly, *'Final Solution'*, 171–4; Safrian, *Eichmann-Männer*, 105–12.

72 Aly, *'Final Solution'*, 176.

73 Pohl, 'Murder of the Jews', 85–6; Thomas Sandkühler, 'Anti-Jewish Policy and the Murder of the Jews in the District of Galicia, 1941/42', in Herbert (ed.), *National Socialist Extermination Policies*, 107; Thomas Sandkühler, *'Endlösung' in Galizien* (Bonn, 1996), 49–53, 110–11.

74 Frank was in Berlin on 17–18 March, 27 March, 4–5 April and 4–6 May 1941: *Diensttagebuch*, 332–3, 339, 351, 371.

75 *Diensttagebuch*, 387: 18 July 1941. See ibid., 951, for a brief biography of Schepers.

76 Ibid. (which, however, does not include text of letter); Aly, *'Final Solution'*, 175–6; Sandkühler, 'Anti-Jewish Policy', 109. Burrin, *Hitler and the Jews*, 100 assumes that Frank knew the area 'to be of scant economic interest'.

77 Hansjulius Schepers, 'Pripet-Polesien, Land und Leute', *ZfGeo*, 19 (1942), 280–1, 287. Schepers and another young economic expert who would later be involved in the Pripet marshes, Dr Walter Föhl, had both represented the General Government in a meeting at Heydrich's Reich Security Main Office on 8 January 1941: Kaminski, *Dokumente*, 84.

78 Aly and Heim, *Vordenker*, 194, 198.

79 Helmut Meinhold, 'Die Erweiterung des Generalgouvernements nach

Osten', July 1941, cited Aly and Heim, *Vordenker*, 119, 249–52; Meinhold, 'Das Generalgouvernement als Transitland: Ein Beitrag zur Kenntnis
der Standortslage des Generalgouvernements', *Die Burg*, 2 (1941), Heft 4,
24–44.

80 Richard Bergius, 'Die Pripetsümpfe als Entwässerungsproblem', *ZfGeo*, 18
(1941), 667–8 (quotation 668).

81 Frank to Lammers, 19 July 1941, cited Aly, *'Final Solution'*, 175. Just three
days after the letter to Lammers, Frank's 'discussion points' for a meeting
in the General Government included 'Entlastung durch Abschiebung von
Juden und anderen asozialen Elementen nach dem Osten': *Diensttagebuch*,
389: 22 July 1941.

82 'Whether they go to Madagascar or somewhere else, none of that interests
us. We are clear that the best thing for this mishmash of Asiatic progeny
is that they slouch back to Asia, where they have come from. [laughter]':
speech at a Nazi party reception in Lublin, 22 Jan. 1941, *Diensttagebuch*,
330. On Frank, see Christoph Klessmann, 'Hans Frank: Party Jurist and
Governor-General in Poland', in Ronald Smelser and Rainer Zitelmann
(eds.), *The Nazi Elite* (New York, 1983), 39–47.

83 Oberländer, *Die agrarische Überbevölkerung*; Aly and Heim, *Vordenker*,
96. Bürgener was familiar with Oberländer's work.

84 Herbert Morgen, 'Ehemals russisch-polnische Kreise des Reichsgaues
Wartheland: Aus einem Reisebericht', *NB* 32 (1940), 326.

85 Mäding (1943), cited Gröning and Wolschke-Bulmahn, *Liebe zur Landschaft*, 134. Compare Mäding, 'Regeln für die Gestaltung der Landschaft'.

86 Wiepking-Jürgensmann, 'Gegen den Steppengeist'. For one of many similar
statements, see Wiepking-Jürgensmann, 'Aufgabe und Ziele', 81–2.

87 Gerda Bormann to Martin Bormann, 24 Feb. 1945: *The Bormann Letters*,
ed. Hugh Trevor-Roper (London, 1945), 194.

88 Günther Deschner, 'Reinhard Heydrich', in Smelser and Zitelmann (eds.),
The Nazi Elite, 92.

89 Müller, *Siedlungspolitik*, 102. Deschner sees the speech in Prague as an
example of Heydrich's cold matter-of-factness.

90 *Diensttagebuch*, 330: 22 Jan. 1941. Also Broszat, *Polenpolitik*, 65–7; Pohl,
'Murder of the Jews', 85–6.

91 Aly, *'Final Solution'*, 167–8, emphasizes this.

92 Bauer, *Rethinking the Holocaust*, 90–1, who draws on the work of Sarah
Bender (on Bialystock) and Michael Unger (on Łódź). See also Browning,
Nazi Policy, 58–88, and Mayer, *Heavens*, 352, who stresses the role of
forced labour in mobilizing production for the war effort in the winter of
1941–2.

93 Sandkühler, 'Anti-Jewish Policy and the Murder of the Jews', 111–25.

94 Safrian, *Eichmann-Männer*, 88; Browning, *Nazi Policy*, 8.

95 Bauer, *Rethinking the Holocaust*, 165. Bauer accepts that this was not simply a retrospective 'softening' of his role by Höss, but an accurate account of an early stage in the camp's history. See also ibid., 170–1, on the persistence of the Jewish forced labour theme through August. The first systematic gassings (of Soviet POWs) took place at Auschwitz in September 1941.

96 Primo Levi, *Moments of Reprieve: A Memoir of Auschwitz* (New York, 1987), 124.

97 Mark Roseman, *The Wannsee Conference and the Final Solution* (New York, 2003), 101, 111.

98 Hitler and Goebbels cited in Manfred Weißbecker, '"Wenn hier Deutsche wohnten . . ." Beharrung und Veränderung im Russlandbild Hitlers und der NSDAP', in Hans-Erich Volkmann (ed.), *Das Russlandbild im Dritten Reich* (Cologne, 1994), 34–5, 37.

99 Volkmann, 'Zur Ansiedlung der Deutsch-Balten im "Warthegau"', 541–2.

100 See, for example, *Diensttagebuch*, 590–2: 14 Dec. 1942; Kaminski, *Dokumente*, 96. Frank even recorded with pride the quantities of vodka and cigarettes that the German monopolies in the General Government supplied to the Reich: Frank, 14 Jan. 1944: Kaminski, *Dokumente*, 99.

101 Burrin, *Hitler and the Jews*, 106–7; Sandkühler, 'Anti-Jewish Policy and the Murder of the Jews', 112; Bauer, *Rethinking the Holocaust*, 170–1; Aly, 'Final Solution', 176.

102 Mid-August was exactly the moment when new orders (to kill Jews) were reaching the leaders of the Einsatzgruppen, in a process that was quite uneven. See Alfred Streim, 'Zur Eröffnung des allgemeinen Judenvernichtungsbefehls gegenüber den Einsatzgruppen', in Eberhard Jäckel and Jürgen Rohwer (eds.), *Der Mord an den Juden im Zweiten Weltkrieg* (Stuttgart, 1985), 113–16.

103 Ruth Bettina Birn, *Die Höheren SS- und Polizeiführer: Himmlers Vertreter im Reich und in den besetzten Gebieten* (Düsseldorf, 1986), 171; Christian Gerlach, 'German Economic Interests, Occupation Policy and the Murder of the Jews in Belorussia, 1941/43', in Herbert (ed.), *National Socialist Extermination Policies*, 220.

104 On the Wehrmacht and actions in the Pripet marshes, see Jürgen Förster, 'Wehrmacht, Krieg und Holocaust', in Rolf-Dieter Müller and Hans-Erich Volkmann (eds.), *Wehrmacht: Mythos und Realität* (Munich, 1999), 955–6; Lutz Klinkhammer, 'Der Partisanenkrieg der Wehrmacht 1941–1944', in ibid., 817; Mayer, *Heavens*, 380.

105 Christian Streit, *Keine Kameraden* (Stuttgart, 1978); Omer Bartov, *The Eastern Front, 1941–45: German Troops and the Barbarisation of Warfare* (London, 1985). In addition to the strands of complicity already noted, recent work has also emphasized the close links between genocide and the provisioning of the Wehrmacht. See Christian Gerlach, *Krieg, Ernährung,*

Völkermord (Hamburg, 1998), and 'German Economic Interests, Occupation Policy and the Murder of the Jews', 210–39.

106 Burrin, *Hitler and the Jews,* 111–12; Christopher R. Browning, *The Path to Genocide* (Cambridge, 1992), 106; Ian Kershaw, *Hitler, 1936–45: Nemesis* (London, 2000), 488. Some weeks before that, in September 1941, Hitler approved a proposal by Walter Hewel, Foreign Office representative in the Führer-HQ, to deport the English on Jersey to the Pripet marshes if the Germans interned by the British in Iran were not released. In fact, British citizens from the Channel Islands were arrested and interned in the Black Forest. See Vogt (ed.), *Herbst 1941*, 54 n. 491.

107 Hitler, 5 Nov. 1941: *Monologe im Führer-Hauptquartier 1941–1944: Die Aufzeichnungen Heinrich Heims*, ed. Werner Jochmann (Hamburg, 1980), 128.

108 Martin Gilbert, *The Holocaust* (New York, 1985), 307, cited Aly, '*Final Solution*', 175.

109 See the 21 June 1942 letter of Walter Föhl, Deputy Head of the Department of Population and Welfare in the General Government, to his 'SS-comrades' in Berlin: 'Every day we receive trains with over 1000 Jews each from all over Europe, we give them first aid and accommodate them more or less provisionally or deport them further into the White Ruthenian marshes in the direction of the Arctic sea, where all of them – if they survive (and the Jews from the Kurfürstendamm or from Vienna and Pressburg certainly will not) – will be gathered by the end of the war, not without first having built some roads. (But we're not supposed to talk about it!)': Aly and Heim, *Vordenker*, 215–16, of which the above is my translation, and Aly, '*Final Solution*', 175–6.

110 The reference in the August monologue refers only to the value of the terrain for military exercises (*Monologe*, 55); on 28 September he referred to both military manoeuvres and the environmental objections (ibid., 74). In neither case are the marshes identified by name, just as Hitler did not specify further in his violent 'into the marshes' remark on 25 October.

111 Martin Seckendorf, 'Die "Raumordnungsskizze" für das Reichskommissariat Ostland vom November 1942: Regionale Konkretisierung der Ostraumplanung', in Rössler and Schleiermacher (eds.), *Der 'Generalplan Ost'*, 180, and the attached Dokument 6: Gottfried Müller, 'Vorentwurf eines Raumordnungsplanes für das Ostland, 17. November 1942', 196; Koos Bosma, 'Verbindungen zwischen Ost- und Westkolonisation', ibid., 198–214; Burleigh, *Germany Turns Eastwards*, 238–9. On the Pripet marshes and partisans, see below, pp. 294–6.

112 See Anna Bramwell, *Blood and Soil: Richard Walther Darré and Hitler's 'Green Party'* (Abbotsbrook, 1985); Simon Schama, *Landscape and Memory* (New York, 1995), 67–72, 118–19.

113 Dominick, *Environmental Movement*, 81–102; Gerd Gröning and Joachim Wolschke-Bulmahn, 'Naturschutz und Ökologie', 2–5; Burkhardt Riechers, 'Nature Protection during National Socialism', *HSR* 21 (1996), 40–7; Kiran Klaus Patel, 'Neuerfindung des Westens – Aufbruch nach Osten: Naturschutz und Landschaftsgestaltung in den Vereinigten Staaten von Amerika und in Deutschland, 1900–1945', *AfS* 43 (2003), 207; Lekan, *Imagining the Nation in Nature*, 141–54.

114 Gesine Gerhard, 'Richard Walther Darré – Naturschützer oder "Rassenzüchter"?', in Radkau and Uekötter (eds.), *Naturschutz*, 257–71 (quotation, 268), more critical than Bramwell, *Blood and Soil*; Franz-Josef Brüggemeier, *Tschernobyl, 26. April 1986: Die ökologische Herausforderung* (Munich, 1998), 155–7 (quotation, 156).

115 Thomas Zeller, '"Ganz Deutschland sein Garten": Alwin Seifert und die Landschaft des Nationalsozialismus', in Radkau and Uekötter (eds.), *Naturschutz*, 273–307; Patel, 'Naturschutz', 211.

116 Robert A. Pois, *National Socialism and the Religion of Nature* (London, 1986), 38; Boria Sax, *Animals in the Third Reich: Pets, Scapegoats, and the Holocaust* (New York, 2000).

117 Anna-Katharina Wöbse, 'Lina Hähnle und der Reichsbund für Vogelschutz', in Radkau and Uekötter (eds.), *Naturschutz*, 320.

118 Edeltraud Klueting, 'Die gesetzliche Regelung der nationalsozialistischen Reichsregierung für den Tierschutz, den Naturschutz und den Umweltschutz', in Radkau and Uekötter (eds.), *Naturschutz*, 78–88. Sax, *Animals in the Third Reich*, 175–9, prints the Law on Animal Protection as an appendix.

119 Klueting, 'Die gesetzliche Regelung', 88–101; Wettengel, 'Staat und Naturschutz', 382–7.

120 Riechers, 'Nature Protection', 47; Brüggemeier, *Tschernobyl*, 159–60. The figure of 800 may itself be an over-estimate.

121 Wettengel, 'Staat und Naturschutz', 382–9; Gröning and Wolschke-Bulmahn, 'Naturschutz und Ökologie', 11; Heinrich Rubner, *Deutsche Forstgeschichte 1933–1945: Forstwirtschaft, Jagd und Umwelt im NS-Staat* (St Katharinen, 1985), 85–6; Thomas Lekan, 'Organische Raumordnung: Landschaftspflege und die Durchführung des Reichsnaturschutzgesetzes im Rheinland-Westfalen', in Radkau and Uekötter (eds.), *Naturschutz*, 145–65.

122 Hamm, *Naturkundliche Chronik*, 232.

123 On the advocacy of hydro-electric power among Nazis like Gottfried Feder, see Henry A. Turner, *German Big Business and the Rise of Hitler* (New York, 1985), 281, and on Hitler's enthusiasm for it: *Monologe*, 53–4. On hydro-electric power, dams and the environment: Helmut Maier, 'Kippenlandschaft, "Wasserkrafttaumel" und Kahlschlag', 247–66 (Walter Schoenichen's comment about 'blending in to the rhythm of the landscape',

257). On the autobahn and Alwin Seifert's role as 'landscape advocate', Thomas Zeller, *Strasse, Bahn, Panorama: Verkehrswege und Landschaftsveränderungen in Deutschland von 1930 bis 1990* (Frankfurt/Main, 2002), 203–9; Thomas Zeller, '"Ganz Deutschland sein Garten"', 277–81; Dietmar Klenke, 'Autobahnbau und Naturschutz in Deutschland', in Matthias Freese and Michael Prinz (eds.), *Politische Zäsuren und gesellschaftlicher Wandel im 20. Jahrhundert* (Paderborn, 1996), 465–98. On the simultaneous exploitation of natural resources and rhetorical attachment to conservation, Ulrich Linse, *Ökopax und Anarchie: Eine Geschichte der ökologischen Bewegung in Deutschland* (Munich, 1986), 153–63.

124 Eugenie von Garvens, 'Land dem Meere abgerungen', *Die Gartenlaube* (1935), 397–8. On the Tümmlau Bay (and the construction difficulties) see Jan G. Smit, *Neubildung deutschen Bauerntums: Innere Kolonisation im Dritten Reich – Fallstudien in Schleswig-Holstein* (Kassel, 1983), 280–311.

125 Pflug, *Deutsche Flüsse – Deutsche Lebensadern*, 60–1.

126 Smit, *Neubildung*, emphasizes the propaganda use.

127 Patel, 'Naturschutz', 216. See also Patel's comparative study of the Labour Service and its American equivalent, *'Soldaten der Arbeit': Arbeitsdienste in Deutschland und den USA 1933–1945* (Göttingen, 2003).

128 The words in both cases were by Thilo Scheller: Hans-Jochen Gamm, *Der braune Kult: Das Dritte Reich und seine Ersatzreligion* (Hamburg, 1962), 94–5.

129 Wettengel, 'Staat und Naturschutz', 390.

130 Riechers, 'Nature Protection', 48.

131 Lampe, 'Wirtschaft und Verkehr', 757; Arno Schröder, *Mit der Partei vorwärts! Zehn Jahre Gau Westfalen-Nord* (Detmold, 1940), 140–2. A small part of the Drömling remained. It later became a natural park, helped – ironically – by the observations of birds and flora made by the future Professor Däthe while he was in the Reich Labour Service: Fred Braumann and Helmut Müller, 'Der Naturpark Drömling in Sachsen-Anhalt', *NuN* 152 (1994), 12.

132 Hans Klose, cited Gröning and Wolschke-Bulmahn, 'Naturschutz und Ökologie', 9.

133 Maier, 'Kippenlandschaft, "Wasserkrafttaumel" und Kahlschlag', 258.

134 Patel, 'Naturschutz', 216. See also Walter Schoenichen, *Zauber der Wildnis in deutscher Heimat* (Neudamm, 1935). For an analysis of Schoenichen's almost obsessive interest in 'primeval landscape', see Ludwig Fischer, 'Die Urlandschaft', in Radkau and Uekötter (eds.), *Naturschutz*, 183–205, esp. 186–7.

135 Hans Klose was one: Rubner, *Forstgeschichte*, 83–4.

136 Otto Jaeckel, *Gefahren der Entwässerung unseres Landes* (Greifswald, 1922), 12–13; Kluge and Schramm, *Wassernöte*, 183–99.

137 Alwin Seifert, 'Die Versteppung Deutschlands', *DT*, 4 (1936), reprinted in *Die Versteppung Deutschlands? Kulturwasserbau und Heimatschutz* (Berlin and Leipzig, 1938), then in Seifert's own essay collection, *Im Zeitalter des Lebendigen* (Dresden, 1941), 24–51.

138 See J. Buck, 'Landeskultur und Natur', *DLKZ* 2 (1937), 48–54, a withering attack by an engineer that culminated in the charge that Seifert neglected the most urgent needs of the 'Volk ohne Raum'.

139 See his wartime article, 'Die Zukunft der ostdeutschen Landschaft', *BSW* 20 (1940), 312–16.

140 Todt, 'Vorwort', *Im Zeitalter des Lebendigen*; Zeller, 'Alwin Seifert', 282–7; Bramwell, *Blood and Soil*, 173–4; Patel, 'Naturschutz', 215–18; Zirnstein, *Ökologie*, 205–6; Kluge and Schramm, *Wassernöte*, 191–6.

141 Hermann-Heinrich Freudenberger, 'Probleme der agrarischen Neuordnung Europas', *FD* 5 (1943), 166–7.

142 On hydro, Maier, 'Kippenlandschaft, "Wasserkraftttaumel" und Kahlschlag', 260–4; Roman Sandgruber, *Strom der Zeit: Das Jahrhundert der Elektrizität* (Linz, 1992), 212–19. Hitler on Norway and hydro: *Monologe*, 53–4 (2 Aug. 1941).

143 Gröning and Wolschke-Bulmahn, 'Naturschutz und Ökologie', 11–13; 'Politics, Planning and the Protection of Nature: Political Abuse of Early Ecological Ideas in Germany, 1933–45', *PIP* 2 (1987), 133–4; Fehn, '"Lebensgemeinschaft von Volk und Raum"', 220–1. Note the title of a 1943 article by Schoenichen: 'Nature Conservation in the Context of a European Spatial Order'.

144 Hans Schwenkel, 'Landschaftspflege und Landwirtschaft: Gefahren der zerstörten Landschaft', *FD* 15 (1943), 127.

145 Zeller, 'Alwin Seifert', 295–7.

146 Wettengel, 'Staat und Naturschutz', 395.

147 Schama, *Landscape and Memory*, 67–72; Rubner, *Forstgeschichte*, 135–6.

148 'Einführing' to *Neue Dorflandschaften*.

149 Erhard Mäding, *Landespflege: Die Gestaltung der Landschaft als Hoheitsrecht und Hoheitspflicht* (Berlin, 1942), 215, repeated in Mäding's article the following year, 'Gestaltung der Landschaft', 24. For a similar critique of 'romantic' conceptions, Walter Wickop, 'Grundsätze und Wege der Dorfplanung', 46.

150 Herbert Frank, 'Das natürliche Fundament', 11.

151 In addition to Aly and Heim, *Vordenker* and Rössler and Schleiermacher (eds.), *'Generalplan Ost'*, see Susanne Heim (ed.), *Autarkie und Ostexpansion: Pflanzenzucht und Agrarforschung im Nationalsozialismus* (Göttingen, 2002).

152 William H. Rollins, 'Whose Landscape? Technology, Fascism and Environmentalism on the National Socialist Autobahn', *AAAG* 85 (1995), 507–8;

Aly and Heim, *Vordenker*, 159; Achim Thom, 'Aspekte und Wandlungen des Russlandbildes deutscher Ärzte im Dritten Reich', in Volkmann (ed.), *Russlandbild im Dritten Reich*, 448; W. Kreutz, 'Methoden der Klimasteuerung: Praktische Wege in Deutschland und der Ukraine', *FD* 15 (1943), 256–81.

153 Teschner, 'Landschaftsgestaltung in den Ostgebieten', 570. See also Wiepking-Jürgensmann, 'Aufgaben und Ziele deutscher Landschaftspolitik', 81–96.

154 Martin Bürgener, 'Geographische Grundlagen der politischen Neuordnung in den Weichsellandschaften', *RuR* 4 (1940), 344–53.

155 See Kreutz, 'Methoden der Klimasteuerung', 275 (table), 281.

156 Franz W. Seidler, 'Fritz Todt', in Smelser and Zitelmann (eds.), *The Nazi Elite*, 252.

157 *Diensttagebuch*, 189–91 (24 Apr. 1940); 250 (11 Jul. 1940); 347–9 (3 Apr. 1941); 546 (21 Aug. 1942, visit to the Rozno Dam). See also Meinhold, 'Das General-Gouvernment als Transitland', 36–40, 44.

158 *Diensttagebuch*, 749 (26 Oct. 1943).

159 See Frank, 'Dörfliche Planung im Osten', 45; Greifelt, 'Die Festigung deutschen Volkstums im Osten', 11–12. G. Brusch, 'Betonfertigteile im Landbau des Ostens', in Schacht (ed.), *Bauhandbuch für den Aufbau im Osten*, 197, argued that experimental use of prefabricated concrete in rural construction in the east was an example of using 'modern technology' to 'create something new' that could then be used in the Old Reich.

160 Heinrich Friedrich Wiepking-Jürgensmann, 'Gegen den Steppengeist'.

161 Mäding, 'Gestaltung der Landschaft', 23–4.

162 Both Gröning and Wolschke-Bulmahn, *Liebe zur Landschaft* and Fehn, '"Lebensgemeinschaft von Volk und Raum"', note this double quality.

163 *Allgemeine Anordnung Nr. 20/VI/42 über die Gestaltung der Landschaft in den eingegliederten Ostgebieten*, 138.

164 Wickop, 'Grundsätze und Wege der Dorfplanung', 47; Wiepking-Jürgensmann, 'Dorfbau und Landschaftsgestaltung', 42–3.

165 Schwenkel, 'Landschaftspflege und Landwirtschaft', 124, a charge he repeated in an almost identically titled article: 'Landschaftspflege und Landwirtschaft', *NB* 35 (1943), 7–18, esp. 13.

166 Brüggemeier, *Tschernobyl*, 165–7.

167 See Rolf-Dieter Müller, 'Industrielle Interessenpolitik im Rahmen des "Generalplan-Ost"', *MGM* 42 (1981), 101–51.

168 Gröning and Wolschke-Bulmahn, *Liebe zur Landschaft*, 30.

169 The original was *Gesamtraumkunstwerk*: Mäding, 'Gestaltung der Landschaft', 23. Gröning and Wolschke-Bulmahn, *Liebe zur Landschaft*, 125–39, argue that the aestheticizing element in landscape planning was a rationalization of the planners' weakness vis-à-vis larger economic forces.

170 Gröning and Wolschke-Bulmann, *Liebe zur Landschaft*, 135–6.

171 As, for example, Herbert Morgen, 'Forstwirtschaft und Forstpolitik im neuen Osten', *NB* 33 (1941), 103–7. See also Rubner, *Forstgeschichte*, 136–40. On ecologically-minded articles in the General Government's own forestry journal, *Wald und Holz*, Christoph Spehr, *Die Jagd nach Natur* (Frankfurt/Main, 1994), 173–5.

172 Broszat, *Polenpolitik*, 99; Aly and Heim, *Vordenker*, 147–9. Gröning and Wolschke-Bulmann, *Liebe zur Landschaft*, 49–61 make this point powerfully.

173 Hitler wrote that as a youth he 'adopted the attitude of all those who shake the dust of Europe from their feet with the irrevocable intention of founding a new existence in the New World and conquering a new home': Alan E. Steinweis, 'Eastern Europe and the Notion of the "Frontier" in Germany to 1945', *YES* 13 (1999), 56–7.

174 Kershaw, *Nemesis*, 434–5; Hitler, *Monologe*, 70 (25 Sep. 1941), 78 (13 Oct. 1941), 398–99 (13 Jun. 1943).

175 On Hitler and Karl May: *Monologe*, 281–2, 398. On May himself, Helmut Schmiedt, *Karl May* (Frankfurt/Main, 1985).

176 Wynfrid Kriegleder, 'The American Indian in German Novels up to the 1850s', *GLL* 53 (2000), 487–98; Friedrich Gerstäcker, *Die Flusspiraten des Mississippi* (Jena, 1848). On Gerstäcker and America, see Augustus J. Prahl, 'Gerstäcker und die Probleme seiner Zeit', dissertation, Johns Hopkins University, 1933.

177 Fontane, *WMB*, 346–53 (quotation, 353); Freytag, *Soll und Haben*, 679–96 (Book 5, chapters 1, 2).

178 Friedrich Gerstäcker, *Nach Amerika!* (Jena, 1855).

179 See, for example, Adalbert Forstreuter, *Der endlose Zug: Die deutsche Kolonisation in ihrem geschichtlichen Ablauf* (Munich, 1939), 101–12, 133–9; A. Hillen Ziegfeld, *1000 Jahre deutsche Kolonisation und Siedlung: Rückblick und Vorschau zu neuem Aufbruch* (Berlin, n.d. [1942]), 39–42, 51–7.

180 See Frederick Jackson Turner, *The Frontier in American History* (Tucson, 1986), ix–xx, 'Foreword' by Wilbur Jacobs; Patricia Nelson Limerick, *The Legacy of Conquest: The Unbroken Past of the American West* (New York, 1988), 17, 20–3, 49, 71, 83, 253–4; William Cronon, *Nature's Metropolis: Chicago and the Great West* (New York, 1992), xvi, 31–54, 150.

181 Mark Bassin, 'Imperialism and the Nation State in Friedrich Ratzel's Political Geography', *PHG* 11 (1987), 479–80, 489; W. Coleman, 'Science and Symbol in the Turner Frontier Hypothesis', *AHR* 72 (1966), 39–40; Steinweis, 'Eastern Europe and the Notion of the "Frontier"', 60–1.

182 Max Sering, *Die innere Kolonisation im östlichen Deutschland* (Leipzig, 1893), 160, 166, 172–3, 180, 205, 212, 214, 230–31. On Ratzel's Amer-

ican visit, Mark Bassin, 'Friedrich Ratzel's Travels in the United States: A Study in the Genesis of his Anthropogeography', *HGN* 4 (1984), 11–22.

183 Dipper, *Deutsche Geschichte 1648–1789*, 26 (on Schmoller); Max Weber, 'Capitalism and Society in Rural Germany', in Hans Gerth and C. Wright Mills (eds.), *From Max Weber: Essays in Sociology* (London, 1952), 363–85 (a lecture on Europe and America originally delivered in St Louis).

184 Theodor Lüddecke, 'Amerikanismus als Schlagwort und Tatsache', cited Peter Berg, *Deutschland und Amerika 1918–1929* (Lübeck and Hamburg, 1963), 134; Otto Maull, *Die Vereinigten Staaten von Amerika als Grossreich*, cited Steinweis, 'Eastern Europe and the Notion of the "Frontier"', 61–2.

185 Dan Diner, '"Grundbuch des Planeten": Zur Geopolitik Karl Haushofers', *VfZ* 32 (1984), 1–28; Bassin, 'Race contra Space'; Schultz, *Die deutschsprachige Geographie*, 176–228; Ludwig Ferdinand Clauß, *Rasse und Seele* (Munich, 1926), 37, 144.

186 Immanuel Geiss, *Der Polnische Grenzstreifen 1914–1918* (Lübeck and Hamburg, 1960); Vejas G. Liulevicius, *Warland on the Eastern Front: Culture, National Identity and German Occupation in World War I* (Cambridge, 2000).

187 Erich Keyser, 'Die deutsche Bevölkerung des Ordenslandes Preussen', in Volz (ed.), *Der ostdeutsche Volksboden*, 234.

188 See Karl Hampe, *Der Zug nach dem Osten: Die kolonisatorische Grosstat des deutschen Volkes im Mittelalter* (Leipzig and Berlin, 1935; first edn. 1921), 37; Hermann Aubin, 'Die historische Entwicklung der ostdeutschen Agrarverfassung und ihre Beziehungen zum Nationalitätsproblem der Gegenwart', in Volz (ed.), *Der ostdeutsche Volksboden*, esp. 345–7. Also Karen Schönwälder, *Historiker und Politik: Geschichtswissenschaft im Nationalsozialismus* (Frankfurt/Main, 1992), 35–65; Burleigh, *Germany Turns Eastwards*, 22–39.

189 Froese, *Kolonisationswerk Friedrichs des Grossen: Wesen und Vermächtnis*, 116.

190 Staritz, *Die West-Ostbewegung*, 160–1.

191 Freytag, *Raum deutscher Zunkunft*, 154, 249; Hans Venatier, *Vogt Bartold: Der grosse Zug nach dem Osten* (17th edn., Leipzig, 1944), 147, 186, 235, 435.

192 Kershaw, *Nemesis*, 434–5; Hitler, *Monologe*, 68 (25 Sep. 1941). On medieval colonization within Hitler's earlier thinking, see also his Bamberg speech in February 1926, cited Weißbecker '"Wenn hier Deutsche wohnten"', in Volkmann (ed.), *Russlandbild*, 20.

193 Konrad Meyer, 'Der Osten als Aufgabe und Verpflichtung des Germanentums', *NB* 34 (1942), 207.

194 *Diensttagebuch*, 534, 1 Aug. 1942: Speech in Lemberg.

195 Burleigh, *Germany Turns Eastwards*, 192–3 (Aubin), 253–99 (spoils).

196 Aly and Heim, *Vordenker*, 232.

197 Marc Raeff, 'Some Observations on the Work of Hermann Aubin', in Hartmut Lehmann and James Van Horn Melton (eds.), *Paths of Continuity: Central European Historiography from the 1930s to the 1950s* (Cambridge, 1994), 239–49, and Edgar Melton, 'Comment', ibid., 251–61, and Burleigh, *Germany Turns Eastwards*. Eduard Mühle is writing a biography of Aubin.

198 J. G. Merquior, *The Veil and the Mask* (London, 1979), 1–38.

199 Goebbels diaries, 13 Mar. 1940 and 9 Aug. 1940, cited Hans-Heinrich Wilhelm, *Rassenpolitik und Kriegsführung* (Passau, 1991), 93, 99.

200 Quotations from Frank in Kaminski, *Dokumente*, 67–9, 72, 74–6, 80–1, 88. There is little doubt that Frank personally believed spurious claims about earlier 'Teutonic-Germanic' settlement.

201 Lumans, *Himmler's Auxiliaries*, 140.

202 Volkmann, 'Zur Ansiedlung', 532–3; Koehl, *RKFDV*, 99.

203 'Die Heimkehr der Wolhyniendeutschen', 169.

204 Otto Bräutigam, *Überblick über die besetzten Ostgebiete während des 2. Weltkrieges* (Tübingen, 1954), 80.

205 See Werner Zeymer, 'Erste Ergebnisse des Ostaufbaus: Ein Bilderbericht', *NB* 32 (1940), 415.

206 Volkmann, 'Zur Ansiedlung', 545.

207 Wasser, *Himmlers Raumplanung*, 58.

208 Hitler, *Monologe*, 70 (25 Sep. 1941).

209 Reichsfüher SS [Himmler], *Der Untermensch*, a 1942 brochure, cited Gröning and Wolschke-Bulmahn, *Liebe zur Landschaft*, 132.

210 Hitler, *Mein Kampf*, 742.

211 Machui, 'Landgestaltung', 297–304.

212 *Diensttagebuch*, 543 (15 Aug. 1942).

213 Diary entry of 11 Nov. 1919: Ackermann, *Himmler als Ideologe*, 198.

214 Harvey, *Women and the Nazi East*; Aly and Heim, *Vordenker*, 198–202.

215 Chickering, 'We Men Who Feel Most German'.

216 'The Posen Diaries of the Anatomist Hermann Voss', in Götz Aly, Peter Chroust and Christian Pross, *Cleansing the Fatherland: Nazi Medicine and Racial Hygiene* (Baltimore, 1994), 139, 146.

217 'Die fremde Wildnis schreckt uns nicht mit Falsch und Trug;/ wir geben ihr ein deutsch' Gesicht mit Schwert und Pflug,/Nach Ostland . . .', words by Hans Baumann (1935): Gamm, *Der braune Kult*, 69.

218 August Haussleiter, *An der mittleren Ostfront* (Nuremberg, 1942), cited in Rolf Günter Renner, 'Grundzüge und Voraussetzungen deutscher literarischer Russlandbilder während des Dritten Reichs', in Volkmann (ed.), *Russlandbild*, 416.

219 Hitler, *Monologe*, 91 (17 Oct. 1941).

220 Bergér, *Friedrich der Grosse*, 54; Koser, *Geschichte*, vol. 3, 345, 351; Ritter, *Frederick the Great*, 180, 192.

221 Kaplick, *Warthebruch*, 23–5.

222 L[udwik] P[owidaj], 'Polacy i Indianie', I, *Dzennik Literacki* 53, 9 Dec. 1864. I am very grateful to Patrice Dabrowski for bringing this to my attention and for kindly translating these passages. The historian Johann Friedrich Reitemeier, celebrating 'German cultivation of the wilderness' in the eastern Wendish lands, compared this to what Europeans had done in North America: Wolfgang Wippermann, 'Das Slawenbild der Deutschen', 70.

223 A good nineteenth-century example is Ernst Wichert's *Heinrich von Plauen*; the analogies are even more obvious in Hans Venatier's *Vogt Bartold*. Detailed analysis of other works in Wolfgang Wippermann, '"Gen Ostland wollen wir reiten": Ordensstaat und Ostsiedlung in der historischen Belletristik Deutschlands', in Wolfgang Fritze (ed.), *Germania Slavica* (Berlin, 1981), vol. 2, 187–255.

224 L[udwik] P[owidaj], 'Polacy i Indianie', II, *Dzennik Literacki* 56, 30 Dec. 1864.

225 Julius Mann, *Die Ansiedler in Amerika* (Stuttgart, 1845), cited Kriegleder, 'The American Indian', 490.

226 Harry Liebersohn, *European Travelers and North American Indians* (Cambridge, 1998), 1–9, 115–63.

227 Kriegleder, 'The American Indian in German Novels', 497–8.

228 See Adolf Halfeld, *Amerika und der Amerikanismus: Kritische Betrachtungen eines Deutschen und Europäers* (Jena, 1927); Berg, *Deutschland und Amerika*; Philipp Gassert, *Amerika im Dritten Reich* (Stuttgart, 1997); Herbert A. Strauss, 'Stereotyp und Wirklichkeiten im Amerikabild', in Willi Paul Adams and Knud Krakau (eds.), *Deutschland und Amerika* (Berlin, 1985), 19–38.

229 Ziegfeld, *1000 Jahre deutsche Kolonisation und Siedlung*, 39–41; Forstreuter, *Der endlose Zug*, 105–11.

230 The words *Stamm* or *Stämme* were increasingly common locutions among historians like Hermann Aubin, because this was a way of minimizing the true 'nationhood' of east European peoples.

231 *Diensttagebuch*, 522–3 (1 Aug. 1942).

232 Hitler, *Monologe*, 91 (17 Aug. 1941).

233 Hitler, *Monologe*, 334, 377 (8 Aug., 30 Aug. 1942).

234 Karel C. Berkhoff, *Harvest of Despair: Life and Death in the Ukraine under Nazi Rule* (Cambridge, Mass., 2004), 253–304. Ulrich Herbert, *Hitler's Foreign Workers: Enforced Foreign Labor in Germany under the Third Reich* (New York, 1997) on the dependence of the 'Altreich' on this involuntary workforce.

235 Jachomowski, *Umsiedlung*, 194–7 (quotation, 197); fundamental on the

Zamość campaign and its effects, Wasser, *Himmlers Raumplanung*, 133–229.

236 Aly and Heim, *Vordenker*, 189.

237 Breckoff, 'Zwischenspiel an der Warthe', 149; Lumans, *Himmler's Auxiliaries*, 197.

238 See 'Wehrbauer im deutschen Osten', *Wir sind Daheim: Mitteilungsblatt der deutschen Umsiedler im Reich*, 20 Feb. 1944.

239 Koehl, *RFKDV*, 151, 169–72.

240 Bürgener, *Pripet-Polessie*, 129.

241 Bernhard Chiari, 'Die Büchse der Pandora: Ein Dorf in Weissrussland 1939 bis 1944', in Müller and Volkmann (eds.), *Wehrmacht: Mythos und Realität*, 879–900; Bernhard Chiari, *Alltag hinter der Front: Besatzung, Kollaboration und Widerstand in Weissrussland 1941–1944* (Düsseldorf, 1998); Bräutigam, *Ostgebiete*, 92. Berkhoff, *Harvest of Despair*, has material on attempted forced-labour exactions from Polessia.

242 Gerald Reitlinger, *The House Built on Sand: The Conflicts of German Policy in Russia 1939–1945* (London, 1960), 239, 246; Koehl, *RFKDV*, 171–2.

243 Klinkhammer, 'Partisanenkrieg', 819–36, esp. 829–33.

244 Bergius, 'Die Pripetsümpfe als Entwässerungsproblem', 667.

245 *Vorentwuf (Raumordnungsskizze) zur Aufhebung eines Raumordnungsplanes für das Ostland v. 17.11.1942. Bearbeiter: Provinzialverwaltungsrat Dr. Gottfried Müller*, in Rössler and Schleiermacher (eds.), *'Generalplan Ost'*, 189–97; Koos Bosma, 'Verbindungem zwischen Ost- und Westkolonisation', ibid. 198–213; Burleigh, *Germany Turns Eastwards*, 238–9.

246 Chiari, 'Büchse der Pandora', 900. See the soldiers' letters in Ortwin Buchbender and Reinhold Sterz (eds.), *Das andere Gesicht des Krieges: Deutsche Feldpostbriefe 1939–1945* (Munich, 1982).

247 Berkhoff, *Harvest of Despair*, 276–8; Shmuel Spector, 'Jewish Resistance in Small Towns of Eastern Poland', in Norman Davies and Antony Polonsky (eds.), *Jews in Eastern Poland and in the USSR, 1939–1946* (London, 1991), 138–44.

248 Primo Levi, *If Not Now, When?* (Harmondsworth, 1986).

249 Primo Levi, *If This is a Man* and *The Truce* (Harmondsworth, 1979), 309–51.

250 Levi, *If Not Now, When?*, 67–8.

Chapter Six: Landscape and Environment in the Post-war Germanys

1 Künkel, *Auf den kargen Hügeln der Neumark*, 19–20.

2 On Gennin and its mill, Berghaus, *Landbuch der Mark Brandenburg*, vol. 3, 96, 235, 374–8.

3 See 'Der Autor: Ein Nachruf', *Auf den kargen Hügeln der Neumark*, 10–12.

Among his non-fiction books were *Das grosse Jahr* (1922), *Schicksal und Willensfreiheit* (1923), *Der furchtlose Mensch* (1930), *Das Gesetz deines Lebens* (1932) and *Die Lebensalter* (1938). The novels included *Anna Leun* (1932), *Schicksal und Liebe des Niklas von Cues* (1936), *Die arge Ursula* (1942), *Laszlo, die Geschichte eines Königsknaben* (1943) and *Die Labyrinth der Welt* (1951).

4 The title of Künkel's final chapter: *Auf den kargen Hügeln der Neumark*, 117–46.

5 Ibid., 126, 133.

6 Ibid., 44.

7 Heinrich Bauer's almost contemporary work on Brandenburg also mourned a 'lost paradise' superior to the 'mass civilization' of the present: Bauer, *Die Mark Brandenburg*, 47.

8 Künkel, *Auf den kargen Hügeln der Neumark*, 37–8.

9 See above, 13, 178.

10 Herbert Kraus, 'Einführung und Geleit', *Auf den kargen Hügeln der Neumark*, 8.

11 Eva Hahn and Hans Henning Hahn, 'Flucht und Vertreibung', in Etienne François and Hagen Schulze (eds.), *Deutsche Erinnerungsorte*, vol. 1 (Munich, 2001), 335–51; Norman Naimark, *Fires of Hatred: Ethnic Cleansing in Twentieth-Century Europe* (Cambridge, Mass., 2001), 108–38.

12 Hahn and Hahn, 'Flucht und Vertreibung', 335–51.

13 For a mystical-sentimental version of how the Marienburg fortress and the surrounding land 'belonged to each other', see Paul Fechter, *Zwischen Haff und Weichsel* (Gütersloh, 1954), 290–1.

14 Paul Fechter, *Deutscher Osten: Bilder aus West- und Ostpreussen* (Gütersloh, 1955), 29–30.

15 Karlheinz Gehrmann, 'Vom Geist des deutschen Ostens', in Lutz Mackensen (ed.), *Deutsche Heimat ohne Deutsche: Ein ostdeutsches Heimatbuch* (Braunschweig, 1951), 137.

16 Fechter, *Deutscher Osten*, 20; Gehrmann, 'Vom Geist', 130–7.

17 Lutz Mackensen, 'Einführung', in Mackensen (ed.), *Deutsche Heimat ohne Deutsche*, 8; Hanns von Krannhals, 'Die Geschichte Ostdeutschlands', ibid., 47, 55–61; Fechter, *Deutscher Osten*, 20; Kaplick, *Warthebruch* (sub-titled 'A German Landscape in the East'), 1; Fritz Gause, 'The Contribution of Eastern Germany to the History of German and European Thought and Culture', in *Eastern Germany: A Handbook*, edited by the Göttingen Research Committee, vol. 2: *History* (Würzburg, 1963), 429.

18 Agnes Miegel, 'Meine Salzburger Ahnen', *Ostland* (Jena, 1940), 13. See also Inge Meidinger-Geise, *Agnes Miegel und Ostpreussen* (Würzburg, 1955), 17.

19 See the ballad 'The Ferry', *Gedichte und Spiele* (Jena, 1920); 'Abschied vom

Kinderland', *Aus der Heimat: Gesammelte Werke*, vol. 5 (Düsseldorf, 1954), 129; 'Heimat und Vorfahren', 354. See also Anni Piorreck, *Agnes Miegel: Ihr Leben und ihre Dichtung* (Düsseldorf and Cologne, 1967), 118–19 and Meidinger-Geise, *Agnes Miegel und Ostpreussen*, 36.

20 'Gruß der Türme', *Unter hellem Himmel: Gesammelte Werke*, vol. 3, 118, 123.

21 Piorreck, *Agnes Miegel*, 183–92.

22 Agnes Miegel, 'Kriegergräber', *Ostland* (Jena, 1940), 37. See also Ernst Loewy, *Literatur unterm Hakenkreuz* (Frankfurt/Main, 1966), 236–7; and (from an apologetic position), Piorreck, *Agnes Miegel*, 207–8.

23 Piorreck, *Agnes Miegel*, 258–62 (on 'Mother Prussia'); 'Zum Gedächtnis', *Du aber bleibst in mir: Flüchtlingsgedichte* (1949), 14–15; 'Es war ein Land' [1952], *Es war ein Land: Gedichte und Geschichten aus Ostpreußen* (Cologne, 1983), 206–8.

24 Agnes Miegel, 'Es war ein Land'.

25 Wolfgang Paul, 'Flüchtlinge', *Land unserer Liebe: Ostdeutsche Gedichte* (Düsseldorf, 1953), 17; Gehrmann, 'Vom Geist', 129. See also Hans Venatier, 'Vergessen?', in *Land unserer Liebe*, 28–9.

26 Herbert von Hoerner, 'Erinnerung', in *Land unserer Liebe*, 35; Joachim Reifenrath, 'Verlassenes Dorf', ibid., 7.

27 Fechter, *Deutscher Osten*, 7; Miegel, 'Truso': *Es war ein Land*, 60–7.

28 An internet search under 'Agnes Miegel' reveals the efforts now being made in cities all across Germany, especially by the Greens, to rename the schools once again because of Agnes Miegel's record in the Third Reich.

29 For one of many examples, see Hanns von Krannhals, 'Die Geschichte Ostdeutschlands', 63–4, where the purportedly continuing 'Asiatic' threat ('Asia ante portas') is worked into a comprehensive German victimology.

30 Hahn and Hahn, 'Flucht und Vertreibung', 338, 346–51; Günter Grass, *Über das Selbstverständliche: Politische Schriften* (Munich, 1969), 32–41 (quotation, 33).

31 Heinz Csallner, *Zwischen Weichsel und Warthe: 300 Bilder von Städten und Dörfern aus dem damaligen Warthegau und Provinz Posen vor 1945* (Friedberg, 1989), 4–5, 176.

32 Ibid., 110, 141.

33 *Von der Konfrontation zur Kooperation: 50 Jahre Landsmannschaft Weichsel-Warthe* (Wiesbaden, 1999); *50 Jahre nach der Flucht und Vertreibung: Erinnerung – Wandel – Ausblick. 19. Bundestreffen, Landsmannschaft Weichsel-Warthe, 10./11. Juni 1995* (Wiesbaden, 1995).

34 James Charles Roy, *The Vanished Kingdom* (Boulder, 1999), 28.

35 Helmut Enss, *Marienau: Ein Werderdorf zwischen Weichsel und Nogat* (Lübeck, 1998).

36 Fechter, *Zwischen Haff und Weichsel*, 294–5.

37 Ibid., 345–9.

38 Enss, *Marienau*, 60–1, 66–71, 122–36, 150–6, 262–5.

39 Ibid., 336.

40 Ibid., 715.

41 Ibid., 694.

42 Dönhoff, 'Vorwort', *Namen, die keiner mehr nennt*. See also Dönhoff, *Kindheit in Ostpreussen* (Berlin, 1988), 221.

43 Dönhoff, *Namen, die keiner mehr nennt*, 25.

44 See Ingrid Lorenzen, *An der Weichsel zu Haus* (Berlin, 1999), 97. Also ibid., 44, 110.

45 This was the subject of Günter Grass's novella, *Im Krebsgang* (Göttingen, 2002).

46 Grundig, *Chronik*, vol. 2, 161–74.

47 Brilliantly described in the reportage of Swedish writer Stig Dagerman, *German Autumn* (London, 1988), 5–17. See also Zuckmayer, *A Part of Myself*, 391; Hermann Glaser, *Deutsche Kultur 1945–2000* (Munich, 2000), 76.

48 Leo Harting in *A Small Town in Germany*.

49 Max Frisch, *Tagebuch, 1946–9*, cited in Schneider (ed.), *Deutsche Landschaften*, 625.

50 Otto Kraus, the conservative Bavarian nature conservationist, quoted in Schua and Schua, *Wasser: Lebenswelt und Unwelt*, 167.

51 Applegate, *A Nation of Provincials*, 228–36; Lekan, *Imagining the Nation in Nature*, 254.

52 Jan Palmowski, 'Building an East German Nation: The Construction of a Socialist *Heimat*, 1945–1961', *CEH*, 37 (2004), 365–99.

53 Hinrichs and Reinders, 'Bevölkerungsgeschichte', in Eckhardt and Schmidt (eds.), *Geschichte des Landes Oldenburg*, 700–2.

54 Wegener, 'Die Besiedlung', 166–8; Jäger, *Einführung*, 228; Makowski and Buderath, *Die Natur*, 221.

55 Meyer, 'Zur Geschichte des Moorgutes Sedelsberg', 156, 161; Walter Gipp, 'Geschichte der Moor- und Torfnutzung in Bayern', *Telma* 16 (1986), 310–16; Behre, 'Entstehung und Entwicklung', 32–3.

56 Glaser, *Deutsche Kultur*, 256; Hermand, *Grüne Utopien*, 128.

57 Hans-Peter Harres, 'Zum Einfluss anthropogener Strukturen auf die Gewässersituation', in Böhm and Deneke (eds.), *Wasser*, 92–103; Dominick, *Environmental Movement*, 140.

58 Cioc, *The Rhine*, 146–71; Kinzelbach, *Tierwelt des Rheins*, 31; Tittizer and Krebs, *Ökosystemforschung*, 72–163; Schwoerbel, 'Technik und Wasser', 400–3.

59 Sandra Chaney, 'Water for Wine and Scenery, Coal and European Unity: Canalization of the Mosel River, 1950–1964', in Susan B. Anderson and Bruce

H. Tabb (eds.), *Water, Culture and Politics in Germany and the American West* (New York, 2001), 227–52. Chaney's careful analysis shows that neither the best hopes of supporters nor the worst fears of opponents materialized.

60 Garbrecht, *Wasser*, 213.

61 Hydro provided just three per cent of the Federal Republic's energy needs in 1983: ibid., 220.

62 Bavaria's Otto Kraus, for example: see Dominick, *Environmental Movement*, 161.

63 On the numbers, see Giesecke, Glasebach and Müller, 'Standardization', 81. Also Meurer, *Wasserbau*, 320–1; Feige and Becks, 'Wasser für das Ruhrgebiet', 33–55.

64 Deneke, 'Grundwasserabsenkungen im Hessischen Ried oder die Technisierung der äusseren Natur', in Böhm and Deneke (eds.), *Wasser*, 197–201; Kluge and Schramm, *Wassernöte*, 206–10. The problem was hardly unique to Germany: Carbognin, 'Land Subsidence: A World-wide Environmental Hazard', 20–32.

65 *Die Welt*, 6 Nov. 1970: Dominick, *Environmental Movement*, 140. On the Alliance, ibid., 140–4.

66 Ibid., 128; Chaney, 'Water', 235–44.

67 On Metternich's *Die Wüste droht* (1947), and Hornsmann's *Als hätten wir das Wasser*, published by the Alliance for the Protection of German Waters in the 1950s, see Dominick, *Environmental Movement*, 142, 148–9.

68 Brüggemeier, *Tschernobyl*, 202.

69 Hermand, *Grüne Utopien*, 118–19; Dominick, *Environmental Movement*, 148–58; Brüggemeier, *Tschernobyl*, 202–5; Lekan, *Imagining the Nation in Nature*, 255.

70 Albrecht Lorenz and Ludwig Trepl, 'Das Avocado-Syndrom. Grüne Schale, brauner Kern: Faschistische Strukturen unter dem Deckmantel der Ökologie', *PÖ* 11 (1993–4), 17–24.

71 Alwin Seifert, 'Die Schiffbarmachung der Mosel', *NuL* 34 (1959), 54–5; Chaney, 'Water', 238, 240; Zeller, 'Alwin Seifert', 306–7; Jens Ivo Engels, '"Hohe Zeit" und "dicker Strich": Vergangenheitsbewältigung und -bewahrung im westdeutschen Naturschutz nach dem Zweiten Weltkrieg', in Radkau and Uekötter (eds.), *Naturschutz*, 363–404.

72 On mini-dustbowls on the dried out former Danubian moors in Bavaria, see Zirnstein, *Ökologie*, 204.

73 Dominick, *Environmental Movement*, 137.

74 Arne Andersen, 'Heimatschutz', in Brüggemeier and Rommelspacher (eds.), *Besiegte Natur*, 156–7; Lekan, *Imagining the Nation in Nature*, 253–4.

75 *Der Spiegel*, 18 Nov. 1959, discussed in Dominick, *Environmental Movement*, 187–9.

76 Dominick, *Environmental Movement*, 138.

77 Brüggemeier, *Tschernobyl*, 208–9, drawing on the account in Hans-Peter Vierhaus, *Umweltbewusstsein von oben* (Berlin, 1994).

78 Edda Müller, *Die Innenwelt der Umweltpolitik: Sozial-liberale Umwelt-politik* (Opladen, 1986); Franz-Josef Brüggemeier and Thomas Rommelspacher, *Blauer Himmel über der Ruhr* (Essen, 1992).

79 Hermand, *Grüne Utopien*, 131–5; Dominick, *Environmental Movement*, 146–7; Brüggemeier, *Tschernobyl*, 212–16; Sandra Chaney, 'For Nation and Prosperity, Health and a Green Environment: Protecting Nature in West Germany, 1945–70', in Christof Mauch (ed.), *Nature in German History* (New York and Oxford, 2004), 109–12.

80 McNeill, *Something New under the Sun*, 335.

81 Hermand, *Grüne Utopien*, 163, 181–5.

82 For differentiated accounts of these successes (and their limits) see Brügge-meier, *Tschernobyl*, 216–42; Cioc, *The Rhine*, 177–85; Lelek and Buhse, *Fische des Rheins*, 2, 34–5, McNeill, *Something New under the Sun*, 352–3.

83 The wind-powered generator at Karlsruhe-Maxau produces 130,000 Kilo-watt-hours of electricity a year.

84 See Chapter 4, 222.

85 See Ministerium für Umwelt, Baden-Württemberg, *Hochwasserschutz und Ökologie: Ein 'integriertes Rheinprogramm' schützt vor Hochwasser und erhält naturnahe Flussauen* (Stuttgart, 1988); Internationale Kommis-sion zum Schutze des Rheins gegen Verunreinigung, *Ökologisches Gesamtkonzept für den Rhein: 'Lachs 2000'* (Koblenz, 1991), esp. 10–14, 19–22.

86 Tittizer and Krebs, *Ökosystemforschung*, 39–40. On 'bio-prospecting', see Edward O. Wilson, *The Future of Life* (New York, 2002), 125–8.

87 See Ragnar Kinzelbach, 'Wasser: Biologie und Umweltqualität', in Böhm and Deneke (eds.), *Wasser*, 57–9, and the articles in the same collection by Robert Mürb and Josef Mock.

88 See the debates, for example, in Hailer, *Natur und Landschaft am Ober-rhein*. Wolfgang Meinert notes, however, that the temperature differences between the main river and its side-arms at different seasons (side-arms were colder in winter, warmer from April onwards) proved attractive to fish populations: Meinert, 'Untersuchungen über Fischbestandsver-schiebungen zwischen Rhein bzw. Altrhein und blind endenden Seiten-gewässern in der Vorderpflaz', in Kinzelbach (ed.), *Tierwelt des Rheins*, 131–49.

89 Cioc, *The Rhine*, 185–201.

90 Margaret Thatcher, 14 May 1982 to the Scottish Conservative Party Confer-ence, *Chambers Biographical Dictionary* (1997); McNeill, *Something New under the Sun*, 352 (on Ronald Reagan).

91 Lothar Späth, *Wende in die Zukunft: Die Bundesrepublik auf dem Weg in*

die Informationsgesellschaft (Reinbek, 1985), 149–56.

92 The Soviet author Abadashev, cited in McNeill, *Something New under the Sun*, 333.

93 Andreas Dix, 'Nach dem Ende der 'Tausend Jahre': Landschaftsplanung in der Sowjetischen Besatzungszone und frühen DDR', in Radkau and Uekötter (eds.), *Naturschutz*, 351–2, 357–8.

94 Christian Weissbach, *Wie der Mensch das Wasser bändigt und beherrscht: Der Talsperrenbau im Ostharz* (Leipzig and Jena, 1958), 23.

95 Ibid., 11–12, 22, 31.

96 Ibid., 31, 35. On the Saxon dams, see also Such, 'Entwicklung', 70.

97 Mary Fulbrook, *Anatomy of a Dictatorship: Inside the GDR 1949–1989* (Oxford, 1995), 36, 80; Ian Jeffries and Manfred Melzer, 'The New Economic System of Planning and Management 1963–70 and Recentralisation in the 1970s', in Jeffries and Melzer (eds.), *The East German Economy* (London and New York, 1987), 26–40; Charles Maier, *Dissolution* (Princeton, 1997), 87–92.

98 Dieter Staritz, *Geschichte der DDR 1949–1985* (Frankfurt/Main, 1985), 157–62. See also Dieter Hoffmann and Kristie Macrakis (eds.), *Naturwissenschaft und Technik in der DDR* (Berlin, 1997).

99 Walter Ulbricht, *Whither Germany?* (Dresden, 1966), 404, 417, 425, on the 'scientific-technical revolution'; Glade, *Zwischen Rebenhängen und Haff*, 49 (on the 'Cosmonaut District'); Jonathan R. Zatlin, 'The Vehicle of Desire: The Trabant, the Wartburg and the End of the GDR', *GH* 15 (1997), 358–80.

100 Glade, *Zwischen Rebenhängen und Haff: Reiseskizzen aus dem Odergebiet* (Leipzig, 1976), 5–18, 85–94 (quotation, 92). See also Michalsky, 'Zur Geschichte des Oderbruchs' for similar expressions of confidence, and above, Chapter 1.

101 On the 'wonderland of technology' see above, Chapter 4.

102 Glade, *Zwischen Rebenhängen und Haff*, 85–6, 90–2, 95, 103, 104. On visitors to the construction site of the Rappbode Dam 'overcome' by its sheer size, Weissbach, *Wie der Mensch das Wasser bändigt und beherrscht*, 26.

103 Joan DeBardeleben, '"The Future Has Already Begun": Environmental Damage and Protection in the GDR', in Marilyn Rueschemeyer and Christiane Lemke (eds.), *The Quality of Life in the German Democratic Republic* (Armonk, NY, 1989), 153–5.

104 Merrill E. Jones, 'Origins of the East German Environmental Movement', *GSR*, 256. The lower the pH number, the higher the acidity. Battery acid has a pH of 1.0, vinegar 2.4. See McNeill, *Something New under the Sun*, 101.

105 Volker Gransow, 'Colleague Frankenstein and the Pale Light of Progress:

Life Conditions, Life Activities, and Technological Impacts on the GDR Way of Life', in Rueschmeyer and Lemke (eds.), *Quality of Life*, 199; Burghard Ciesla and Patrice G. Poutrus, 'Food Supply in a Planned Economy', in Konrad A. Jarausch (ed.), *Dictatorship as Experience: Towards a Socio-Cultural History of the GDR* (New York, 1999), 152–7.

106 Brüggemeier, *Tschernobyl*, 269.

107 This is a key argument in Maier, *Dissolution*.

108 Jones, 'Environmental Movement', 236. On the GDR chemical industry, see Raymond G. Stokes, 'Chemie und chemische Industrie im Sozialismus', in Hoffmann and Macrakis (eds.), *Naturwissenschaft und Technik in der DDR*, 283–96.

109 DeBardeleben, '"The Future Has Already Begun"', 152.

110 Dietrich Uhlmann, 'Ökologische Probleme der Trinkwasserversorgung aus Talsperren', *Abhandlungen der Sächsischen Akademie der Wiss. zu Leipzig*, Bd. 55, Heft 4 (1983), 3; Brüggemeier, *Tschernobyl*, 265. But note that after 1980 ways were found to come up with industrial processes that used less water, cutting total industrial usage by some ten per cent.

111 Dix, 'Landschaftsplanung', 335–6, 343–53.

112 DeBardeleben, '"The Future Has Already Begun"', 157; Elizabeth Boa and Rachel Palfreyman, *Heimat – A German Dream: Regional Loyalties and National Identity in German Culture 1890–1990* (Oxford, 2000), 131–2; Palmowski, 'Building an East German Nation'.

113 Hermand, *Grüne Utopien*, 144–6; Rudolf Bahro, *The Alternative in Eastern Europe* (London, 1978; German original published 1977 as *Die Alternative*), 267, 407. See also ibid., 428–30.

114 Ernst Neef et al., 'Analyse und Prognose von Nebenwirkungen gesellschaftlicher Aktivitäten im Naturraum', *Abhandlungen der Sächsischen Akademie der Wiss. zu Leipzig*, Bd. 54, Heft 1 (1979), 5–70, esp. 10–11; Karl Mannsfeld et al., 'Landschaftsanalyse und Ableitung von Naturraumpotentialen', ibid., Bd. 55, Heft 3 (1983), 55, 95–6.

115 Dietrich Uhlmann, 'Künstliche Ökosysteme', ibid., Bd. 54, Heft 3 (1980), 5.

116 Ibid.

117 See also Uhlmann, 'Ökologische Probleme der Trinkwasserversorgung aus Talsperren'.

118 Uhlmann, 'Künstliche Ökosysteme', 15.

119 Ibid., 31–2.

120 Neef et al., 'Analyse', 6.

121 Ekkehard Höxtermann, 'Biologen in der DDR', in Hoffmann and Macrakis (eds.), *Naturwissenschaft und Technik in der DDR*, 255–6.

122 Gerhard Timm, 'Die offizialle Ökologiedebatte in der DDR', in Redaktion Deutschland Archiv, *Umweltprobleme in der DDR* (Cologne, 1985).

123 DeBardeleben, '"The Future Has Already Begun"', 156.

124 Jones, 'Environmental Movement', 240–1.

125 Jones, 'Environmental Movement', 243; DeBardeleben, '"The Future Has Already Begun"', 158–9.

126 Jones, 'Environmental Movement', 241–58; Fulbrook, *Anatomy of a Dictatorship*, 225–36; Gransow, 'Pale Light of Progress', 196, 201–5.

Epilogue: Where It All Began

1 Günter Grass, *Too Far Afield* (San Diego, New York and London, 2000), first published in 1995 by Steidl Verlag, Göttingen, as *Ein weites Feld*. The English title retains the geographical sense of the original, which is important, although it is unable to carry the metaphorical meaning of 'a large problem'.

2 Ibid., 416–17.

3 Ibid., 419.

4 Joachim Richau and Wolfgang Kil, *Land ohne Übergang: Deutschlands neue Grenze* (Berlin, 1992), 58.

5 On the Seelow memorial, Glade, *Zwischen Rebenhängen und Haff*, 11–14; Nippert, *Oderbruch*, 50–60; and on the recovered bodies, 'Immer noch vermisst', a German TV broadcast on the ZDF channel (11 November 2003): http://www. zdf.de/ZDFde/inhalt/5/o,1872, 2080581,00.html

6 Richau and Kil, *Land ohne Übergang*, 27.

7 Christa Wolf, *A Model Childhood* (New York, 1980), 50, the rather misleadingly translated title of *Kindheitsmuster* (Berlin and Weimar, 1976).

8 Karl Schlögel, 'Strom zwischen den Welten. Stille der Natur nach den Katastrophen der Geschichte: Die Oder, eine Enzyklopädie Mitteleuropas', *FAZ*, 13 Nov. 1999 ('Bilder und Zeiten').

9 Glade, *Zwischen Rebenhängen und Haff*, 98–102.

10 *Das Oderbruch: Bilder einer Region* (n.p., 1992), 5.

11 Nippert, *Oderbruch*, 9, 216.

12 Cited in Makowski and Buderath, *Die Natur*, 181. Immermann was writing in 1836.

13 Glade, *Zwischen Rebenhängen und Haff*, 94.

14 Nippert, *Oderbruch*, 216–17.

15 Two examples are the photographer and writer of *Land ohne Übergang*. Wolfgang Kil lived in the 'Prenzelberg' and occasionally in Letschin/Oderbruch; Joachim Richau combined his time between Berlin-Woltersdorf and the Oderbruch.

16 Demographic and employment details from the LEADER Aktionsgruppe Oderbruch, available at: http://www.gruenliga.de/projekt/nre

17 Region-by-region details of changes in agricultural production in Brandenburg during the 1990s at: http://www.zalf.de/lsad/drimipro/elanus/html_

projekt/pkt31/pkt.htm

18 Nippert, *Oderbruch*, 217–19.

19 LEADER Aktionsgruppe Oderbruch: http://www.gruenliga.de/projekt/nre

20 The following account draws on: an official Land Brandenburg source, '"Jahrhundertflut" an der Oder': http://www.mlur.brandenburg.de; Bernhard Hummel, 'Nach uns die Sintflut', *Jungle World* 32, 5 Aug. 1998; Peter Jochen Winters, 'The Flood', *Deutschland: Magazine on Politics, Culture, Business and Science*, Oct. 1997, 14–17.

21 See Chapter 1.

22 Winters, 'The Flood', 16.

23 On the 'forces of nature': Winters, 'The Flood', 17.

24 An official Land Brandenburg breakdown of the costs, totalling 317 million euros, can be found in 'Hochwasserschäden', at the same site as '"Jahrhundertflut" an der Oder 1997'.

25 '"Jahrhundertflut" an der Oder 1997'.

26 Winters, 'The Flood', 17.

27 Hummel, 'Nach uns die Sintflut'.

28 Ibid.

29 'Deichreparatur am Oderbruch offenbart Grauen des Krieges': http://www.wissenschaft.de/wissen/news/drucken/156089.html

30 See 'Ökologischer Hochwasserschutz', from BUND-Berlin: http://www.bund-berlin.de

31 '"Jahrhundertflut" an der Oder 1997'.

32 See Isolde Roch (ed.), *Flusslandschaften an Elbe und Rhein: Aspekte der Landschaftsanlayse, des Hochwasserschutzes und der Landschaftsgestaltung* (Berlin, 2003), esp. the articles by Christian Korndörfer and Jochen Schanze; Bernhard Müller, 'Krise der Raumplanung: Chancen für neue Steuerungsansätze?', in Müller et al. (eds.), *Siedlungspolitik auf neuen Wegen: Steuerungsinstrumente für eine ressourcenschonende Flächennutzung* (Berlin, 1999), 65–80. See also the website established by environmental and climate historians Guido Poliwoda and Christian Pfister: http://www.pages.unibe.ch/shighlight/archive03/poliwoda.html

33 'Hochwasserschutz und Naturschutz', Deutsche Bundesstiftung Umwelt: http://www.umweltstiftung.de/pro/hochwasser.html

34 Land Brandenburg, 'Alte Oder': http://www.mlur.brandenburg.de; LEADER Aktionsgruppe Oderbruch.

35 'Wasserhaushaltsuntersuchungen im Oderbruch': http://www.wasy.de/deutsch/consulting/grund/oderbruch/index.html. WASY was responsible for the hydrological parts of the project, which it undertook in partnership with another consultancy firm, the Büro für ländliche Entwicklung Agro-Öko-Consult GmbH.

36 'Leben lernen im Oderbruch': http://www.unternehmen-region. de/_media/

InnoRegio_Dokumentation_2000_S08–31.pdf

37 Http://www.bundjugend-berlin.de/presse/pm2002–11.html; and http://www.oekofuehrerschein.de

38 'Alte Oder'.

39 Ibid.

40 See Chapter 1.

41 Wilson, *The Future of Life*, 114–18 (quotation, 118).

42 See Thomas Deichmann, 'Trittin greift nach der Grünen Gentechnik', *Die Welt*, 9 Oct. 2002, and a longer online version at: http://www.welt.de/daten/2002/10/09/1009de361129.htx

43 Gerald Mackenthun, 'Gen-Mais im Oderbruch', Barnimer Aktionsbündnis gegen Gentechnik: http://www.dosto.de/gengruppe/region/oderbruch/monsanto_moz.html. See also Birgit Peuker and Katja Vaupel, upated by Esther Rewitz, 'Gefährliche Gentechnik', BUND Brandenburg: http://www.bundnessel.de/47_gen.html

44 Wilson, *The Future of Life*, 118.

45 'Alte Oder'; http://www.zalf.de/lsad/drimipro/elanus/html_projekt/pkt31/pkt3.html

46 Hummel, 'Nach uns die Sintflut'.

47 Around 75 million out of 135 million Marks.

48 Winters, 'The Flood', 17.

49 Hummel, 'Nach uns die Sintflut'.

50 See Chapter 5.

51 Hummel, 'Nach uns die Sintflut'.

52 Extensive details on the organization can be found at: http://www.bund-berlin.de/index

53 See Chapter 6.

54 See Chapter 4.

55 Georg Gothein, 'Hochwasserverhütung und Förderung der Flussschiffahrt durch Thalsperren', *Die Nation* 16 (1898–9), 536–9 (quotation, 537).

56 Hummel, 'Nach uns die Sintflut'.

BIBLIOGRAPHY

This book uses many different source materials: archival holdings, books, articles and technical expositions, literary works (for adults and children), maps, paintings, photographs, and (in the epilogue) electronic publications. The bibliography lists all manuscript, printed and electronic sources used and cited in the notes. The archives and libraries that provided visual or cartographical materials are identified in the section acknowledging their permission to use these in the book. The full names of the newspapers and journals that provided sources can be found in the list of abbreviations preceding the notes. I have followed the usual practice of distinguishing between printed sources and secondary works (listed here as 'Other Books and Articles'). It is a useful convention, although the line of division – always blurred – is unusually difficult to draw in a work that ranges from the eighteenth century to the present. It is especially hard to know where to place the writings of modern zoologists, botanists and ecologists. So, for example, readers will find Ragnar Kinzelbach's superb works on the Rhine under 'Other Books and Articles', but they could with equal justification have been listed as a printed source.

Archival Holdings

Generallandesarchiv Karlsruhe [GLA]
Materials on Rhine 'corrections' and on flooding, in 237/16806, 24088–91, 24112–13, 24156, 24177, 30617, 30623–4, 30793, 30802, 30823, 30826, 35060–2, 44817, 44858

Materials on Johann Tulla in the Nachlass Sprenger

Printed Sources and Document Collections

Abercron, W., 'Talsperren in der Landschaft: Nach Beobachtungen aus der Vogelschau', *VuW* 6, June 1938, 33–9

Abshoff, Emil, 'Talsperren im Wesergebiet', *ZfBi* 13 (1906), 202–6

Adam, Georg, 'Wasserwirtschaft und Wasserrecht früher und jetzt', *ZGW* 1, 1 July 1906, 2–6

Algermissen, J. L., 'Talsperren: Weisse Kohle', *Soziale Revue* 6 (1906), 137–64

Allgemeine Anordnung Nr. 20/VI/42 über die Gestaltung der Landschaft in den eingegliederten Ostgebieten, in Rössler and Schleiermacher (eds.), '*Generalplan Ost*', 136–47

Anderson, Emily (ed.), *The Letters of Beethoven*, vol. 2 (New York, 1985)

André, F[ritz], *Bemerkungen über die Rectification des Oberrheins und die Schilderung der furchtbaren Folgen, welche dieses Unternehmen für die Bewohner des Mittel- und Niederrheins nach sich ziehen wird* (Hanau, 1828)

'Anleitung für Bau und Betrieb von Sammelbecken', *ZbWW*, 20 July 1907, 321–4

Aubin, Hermann, 'Die historische Entwicklung der ostdeutschen Agrarverfassung und ihre Beziehungen zum Nationalitätsproblem der Gegenwart', in Volz (ed.), *Der ostdeutsche Volksboden*

Aus Wriezen's Vergangenheit (Wriezen, 1864)

B. [C. Bachmann?], 'Die Talsperre bei Mauer am Bober', *ZdB* 32, 16 Nov. 1914

Bachmann, C., 'Die Talsperren in Deutschland', *WuG* 17, 15 Aug. 1927, 1133–56

Bachmann, C., 'Wert des Hochwasserschutzes und der Wasserkraft des Hochwasserschutzraumes der Talsperren', *DeW* (1938), 65–9

Badermann, 'Die Frage der Ausnutzung der staatlichen Wasserkräfte in Bayern', *Kommunalfinanzen* (1911), 154–5

Bahro, Rudolf, *The Alternative in Eastern Europe* (London, 1978)

Bamberger, Ludwig, *Erinnerungen* (Berlin, 1899)

Bär, Max, *Die deutsche Flotte 1848–1852* (Leipzig, 1898)

Barth, Fr., 'Talsperren', *BIG* (1908), 261–72, 279–83, 287–8

Baumert, Georg, 'Der Mittellandkanal und die konservative Partei in Preussen: Von einem Konservativen', *Die Grenzboten* 58 (1899), 57–71

Bechstein, O., 'Vom Ruhrtalsperrenverein', *Prometheus* 28, 7 Oct. 1916, 135–9

Becker, 'Beiträge zur Pflanzenwelt der Talsperren des Bergischen Landes und ihrer Umgebung', *BeH* 4, Aug. 1930, 323–6

Beheim-Schwarzbach, Max, *Hohenzollernsche Colonisationen* (Leipzig, 1874)

Bendt, Franz, 'Zum fünfzigjährigen Jubiläum des "Vereins deutscher Ingenieure"', *Die Gartenlaube* (1906), 527–8

Benjamin, Walter, 'The Work of Art in the Age of Mechanical Reproduction', in *Iluminations*, transl. Harry Zohn (London, 1973), 219–53

Berdrow, W., 'Staudämme und Thalsperren', *Die Umschau* (1898), 255–9

Bergér, Heinrich, *Friedrich der Grosse als Kolonisator* (Giessen, 1896)

Berghaus, Heinrich Carl, *Landbuch der Mark Brandenburg*, 3 vols. (Brandenburg, 1854–56)

Bergius, Richard, 'Die Pripetsümpfe als Entwässerungsproblem', *ZfGeo* 18 (1941), 667–8

Bernoulli, Johann [Jean], *Reisen durch Brandenburg, Pommern, Preussen, Curland, Russland und Pohlen in den Jahren 1777 und 1778*, 6 vols. (Leipzig, 1779–80)

Biesantz, Dr., 'Das Recht zur Nutzung der Wasserkraft rheinischer Flüsse', *RAZS* 7 (1911), 48–66

Biese, Alfred, *The Development of the Feeling for Nature in the Middle Ages and Modern Times* (London, 1905)

Borchardt, Carl, *Die Remscheider Stauweiheranlage sowie Beschreibung von 450 Stauweiheranlagen* (Munich and Leipzig, 1897)

Borchardt, Carl, *Denkschrift zur Einweihung der Neye-Talsperre bei Wipperfürth* (Remscheid, 1909)

Borkenhagen, Hermann, *Das Oderbruch in Vergangenheit und Gegenwart* (Neu-Barnim, 1905)

The Bormann Letters, ed. Hugh Trevor-Roper (London, 1945)

Boyd, Louise, 'The Marshes of Pinsk', *GR* 16 (1936), 376–95

Brecht, Bertolt, *Die Gedichte von Bertolt Brecht in einem Band* (Frankfurt/Main, 1981)

Breitkreutz, Ernst, *Das Oderbruch im Wandel der Zeit* (Remscheid, 1911)

Brusch, G., 'Betonfertigteile im Landbau des Ostens', in Hans-Joachim Schacht (ed.), *Bauhandbuch für den Aufbau im Osten* (Berlin, 1943), 188–98

Bubendey, H. F., 'Die Mittel und Ziele des deutschen Wasserbaues am Beginn des 20. Jahrhunderts', *ZVDI* 43 (1899), 499–501

Buchbender, Ortwin and Reinhold Sterz (eds.), *Das andere Gesicht des Krieges: Deutsche Feldpostbriefe 1939–1945* (Munich, 1982)

Buck, J., 'Landeskultur und Natur', *DLKZ* 2 (1937), 48–54

Bürgener, Martin, *Pripet-Polessie: Das Bild einer polnischen Ostraum-Landschaft. Petermanns Geographische Mitteilungen, Ergänzungsheft 237* (Gotha, 1939)

Bürgener, Martin, 'Geographische Grundlagen der politischen Neuordnung in den Weichsellandschaften', *RuR* 4 (1940), 344–53

Candèze, Ernst, *Die Talsperre: Tragisch abenteuerliche Geschichte eines Insektenvölkchens*, transl. from the French (Leipzig, 1901)

Carus, V.A., *Führer durch das Gebiet der Riesentalsperre zwischen Gemünd und Heimbach-Eifel mit nächster Umgebung* (Trier, 1904)

Cassinone, Heinrich and Heinrich Spiess, *Johann Gottfried Tulla, der Begründer der Wasser- und Strassenbauverwaltung in Baden: Sein Leben und Wirken* (Karlsruhe, 1929)

Christaller, Walter, 'Grundgedanken zum Siedlungs- und Verwaltungsaufgaben im Osten', *NB* 32 (1940), 305–12

Christiani, Walter, *Das Oderbruch: Historische Skizze* (Freienwalde, 1901)

Clapp, Edwin J., *The Navigable Rhine* (Boston, 1911)

Claus, Heinrich, 'Die Wasserkraft in statischer und sozialer Beziehung', *Wasser- und Wegebau* (1905), 413–16

Clausewitz, Carl von, *On War*, ed. Michael Howard and Peter Paret (Princeton, 1976)

Clauß, Ludwig Ferdinand, *Rasse und Seele* (Munich, 1926)

Csallner, Heinz, *Zwischen Weichsel und Warthe: 300 Bilder von Städten und Dörfern aus dem damaligen Warthegau und Provinz Posen vor 1945* (Friedberg, 1989)

Czehak, Viktor, 'Über den Bau der Friedrichswalder Talsperre', *ZöIAV* 49, 6 Dec. 1907, 853–9

Dagerman, Stig, *German Autumn* (London, 1988)

Deichmann, Thomas, 'Trittin greift nach der Grünen Gentechnik', *Die Welt*, 9 Oct. 2002

Descartes, René, *Discourse on Method and Related Writings*, transl. Desmond M. Clarke (Harmondsworth, 1999)

Detto, Albert, 'Die Besiedlung des Oderbruches durch Friedrich den Grossen', *FBPG* 16 (1903), 163–205

Deutscher Volksrat: Zeitschrift für deutsches Volkstum und deutsche Kultur im Osten (Danzig), 1/19, 13 Aug. 1919

'Die Ablehnung des Mittellandkanals: Von einem Ostelbier', *Die Grenzboten* 58 (1899), 486–92

'Die biologische Bedeutung der Talsperren', *TuW* 11, April 1918, 144

'Die deutsche Kriegsflotte', *Die Gegenwart*, vol. 1 (Leipzig, 1848), 439–72

Die Ennepetalsperre und die mit ihr verbundenen Anlagen des Kreises Schwelm (Schwelm, 1905)

Die Marktgemeinde Frain und die Frainer Talsperre: Eine Stellungnahme zu den verschiedenen Mängeln des Talsperrenbaues (Frain, 1935)

Die Melioration der der Ueberschwemmung ausgesetzten Theile des Nieder- und Mittel-Oderbruchs (Berlin, 1847)

Die Polnische Schmach: Was würde der Verlust der Ostprovinzen für das deutsche Volk bedeuten? Ein Mahnwort an alle Deutschen, hsg. vom Reichsverband Ostschutz (Berlin, 1919)

'Die Thalsperren im Sengbach-, Ennepe- und Urft-Thal', *Prometheus* 744 (1904), 249–53

'Die Wasser- und Wetterkatastrophen dieses Hochsommers', *Die Gartenlaube* (1897), 571–2

'Die Wasserkräfte des Riesengebirges', *Die Gartenlaube* (1897), 239–40

Döblin, Alfred, *Reise in Polen* [1926] (Olten and Freiburg, 1968)

Dominik, Hans, *Im Wunderland der Technik: Meisterstücke und neue Errungenschaften, die unsere Jugend kennen sollte* (Berlin, 1922)

Dominik, Hans, 'Riesenschleusen im Mittellandkanal', *Die Gartenlaube* (1927), 10

Dönhoff, Marion Gräfin, *Namen, die keiner mehr nennt* (Düsseldorf and Cologne, 1962)

Dönhoff, Marion Gräfin, *Kindheit in Ostpreussen* (Berlin, 1988)

Doubek, Franz A., 'Die Böden des Ostraumes in ihrer landbaulichen Bedeutung', *NB* 34 (1942), 145–50

Ehlers, 'Bruch der Austintalsperre und Grundsätze für die Erbauung von Talsperren', *Zdb*, 8 May 1912, 238–40

Ehnert, Regierungsbaurat, 'Gestaltungsaufgaben im Talsperrenbau', *Der Bauingenieur* 10 (1929), 651–6

Eichel, Eugen, 'Ausnutzung der Wasserkräfte', *EKB* 8 (1910), 24 Jan. 1910, 62–4

Eigen, P., 'Die Insektenfauna der bergischen Talsperren', *BeH* 4, August 1930, 327–31

'Eine Dammbruchkatastrophe in Amerika', *Die Gartenlaube* (1911), 1028

'Einiges über Talsperren, insbesondere über die Edertalsperre', *ZfBi* (1904), 270–1

Ellenberg, Heinz, 'Deutsche Bauernhaus-Landschaften als Ausdruck von Natur, Wirtschaft und Volkstum', *GZ* 47 (1941), 72–87

Engels, Friedrich, 'Siegfrieds Heimat' [1840], in Schneider (ed.), *Deutsche Landschaften*, 335–9

Engels, Friedrich, 'Landschaften' [1840], in Schneider (ed.), *Deutsche Landschaften*, 476–83

Enss, Helmut, *Marienau: Ein Werderdorf zwischen Weichsel und Nogat* (Lübeck, 1998)

Enzberg, Eugen von, *Heroen der Nordpolarforschung: Der reiferen deutschen Jugend und einem gebildeten Leserkreise nach den Quellen dargestellt* (Leipzig, 1905)

Ernst, Adolf, *Kultur und Technik* (Berlin, 1888)

Ernst, L., 'Die Riesentalsperre im Urftal', *Die Umschau* (1904), 666–9

Etwas von der Teich-Arbeit, vom nützlichen Gebrauch des Torff-Moores, von Verbesserung der Wege aus bewährter Erfahrung mitgetheilet von Johann Wilhelm Hönert (Bremen, 1772)

Eynern, Ernst von, *Zwanzig Jahre Kanalkämpfe* (Berlin, 1901)

Fechter, Paul, *Zwischen Haff und Weichsel* (Gütersloh, 1954)

Fechter, Paul, *Deutscher Osten: Bilder aus West- und Ostpreussen* (Gütersloh, 1955)

Feeg, O., 'Wasserversorgung', *JbN* 16 (1901), 334–6

Fessler, Peter, 'Bayerns staatliche Wasserkraftprojekte', *EPR* 27, 26 Jan. 1910, 31–4

Festschrift: 75 Jahre Marinewerft Wilhelmshaven (Oldenburg, 1931)

Festschrift zur Weihe der Möhnetalsperre: Ein Rückblick auf die Geschichte des Ruhrtalsperrenvereins und den Talsperrenbau im Ruhrgebiet (Essen, 1913)

Fischer, Karl, 'Die Niederschlags- und Abflussbedingungen für den Talsperrenbau in Deutschland', *ZGEB* (1912), 641–55

Fischer-Reinau, 'Die wirtschaftliche Ausnützung der Wasserkräfte', *BIG* (1908), 71–7, 92–7, 102–6, 111–12

Fontane, Theodor, *Wanderungen durch die Mark Brandenburg* [*WMB*], Hanser Verlag edition, 3 vols. (Munich, 1992)

Fontane, Theodor, *Before the Storm* [1878], ed. R. J. Hollingdale (Oxford, 1985)

Forstreuter, Adalbert, *Der endlose Zug: Die deutsche Kolonisation in ihrem geschichtlichen Ablauf* (Munich, 1939)

Fraas, Karl, *Klima und Pflanzenwelt in der Zeit: Ein Beitrag zur Geschichte* (Landshut, 1847)

Frank, Herbert, 'Das natürliche Fundament', in *Neue Dorflandschaften*, 9–23

Frank, Herbert, 'Dörfliche Planung im Osten', *Neue Dorflandschaften*, 44–5

Freud, Sigmund, 'Thoughts for the Times on War and Death', *The Penguin Freud Library*, vol. 12 (Harmondsworth, 1991), 57–89

Freudenberger, Hermann-Heinrich, 'Probleme der agrarischen Neuordnung Europas', *FD* 5 (1943), 166–7

Freytag, E., 'Der Ausbau unserer Wasserwirtschaft und die Bewertung der Wasserkräfte', *TuW* (1908), 398–401

Freytag, Gustav, *Soll und Haben* (Berlin, 1855)

Freytag, Kurt, *Raum deutscher Zukunft: Grenzland im Osten* (Dresden, 1933)

Froese, Udo, *Das Kolonisationswerk Friedrich des Grossen* (Heidelberg, 1938)

Fuchs, R., *Dr. ing. Max Honsell* (Karlsruhe, 1912)

50 Jahre nach der Flucht und Vertreibung: Erinnerung – Wandel – Ausblick. 19. Bundestreffen, Landsmannschaft Weichsel–Warthe, 10./11. Juni 1995 (Wiesbaden, 1995)

Gause, Fritz, 'The Contribution of Eastern Germany to the History of German and European Thought and Culture', in *Eastern Germany: A Handbook*, ed. Göttingen Research Committee, vol. 2: *History* (Würzburg, 1963), 429–47

Gehrmann, Karlheinz, 'Vom Geist des deutschen Ostens', in Mackensen (ed.), *Deutsche Heimat ohne Deutsche*

Garvens, Eugenie von, 'Land dem Meere abgerungen', *Die Gartenlaube* (1935), 397–8

Gerstäcker, Friedrich, *Die Flusspiraten des Mississippi* (Jena, 1848)

Gerstäcker, Friedrich, *Nach Amerika!* (Jena, 1855)

'Geschichte des Vertrages vom 20.7.1853 über die Anlegung eines Kriegshafens an der Jade: Aus den Aufzeichnungen des verstorbenen Geheimen Rats Erdmann', *OJ* 9 (1900), 35–9

Gilly, David, *Grundriss zu den Vorlesungen über des Praktische bei verschiedenen Gegenständen der Wasserbaukunst* (Berlin, 1795)

Gilly, David, *Fortsetzung der Darstellung des Land- und Wasserbaus in Pommern, Preussen und einem Teil der Neu- und Kurmark* (Berlin, 1797)

Gilly, David and Johann Albert Eytelwein (eds.), *Praktische Anweisung zur Wasserbaukunst* (Berlin, 1805)

Glade, Heinz, *Zwischen Rebenhängen und Haff: Reiseskizzen aus dem Odergebiet* (Leipzig, 1976)

Glass, Robert, 'Die Versiedlung der Moore und anderer Ödländereien', *HHO* 2 (1913), 335–55

Goethe, Johann Wolfgang von, *The Sorrows of Young Werther* (New York, 1990)

Goethe, Johann Wolfgang von, *Faust*, Part II [1831], Penguin edition (Harmondsworth, 1959)

Gothein, Eberhard, *Geschichtliche Entwicklung der Rheinschiffahrt im 19. Jahrhundert* (Leipzig, 1903)

Gothein, Georg, 'Die Kanalvorlage und der Osten', *Die Nation* 16 (1898–9), 368–71

Gothein, Georg, 'Hochwasserverhütung und Förderung der Flussschiffahrt durch Thalsperren', *Die Nation* 16 (1898–9), 536–9

Gräf, Heinrich, 'Über die Verwertung von Talsperren für die Wasserversorgung vom Standpunkte der öffentlichen Gesundheitspflege', *ZHI* 62 (1909), 461–90

Grass, Günter, *Über das Selbstverständliche: Politische Schriften* (Munich, 1969)

Grass, Günter, *Ein weites Feld* (Göttingen, 1995), transl. as *Too Far Afield* (San Diego, New York and London, 2000)

Grass, Günter, *Im Krebsgang* (Göttingen, 2002)

Grassberger, R., 'Erfahrungen über Talsperrenwasser in Österreich', *Bericht über den XIV. Internationalen Kongress für Hygiene und Demographie, Berlin 1907*, vol. 3 (Berlin, 1908), 230–40

Grautoff, Ferdinand, 'Ein Kanal, der sich selber bauen sollte', *Die Gartenlaube* (1925), No. 26, 520–1

Grebe, Wilhelm, 'Zur Gestaltung neuer Höfe und Dörfer im deutschen Osten', *NB* 32 (1940), 57–66

Greifelt, Ulrich, 'Die Festigung deutschen Volkstums im Osten', in Hans-Joachim Schacht (ed.), *Bauhandbuch für den Aufbau im Osten* (Berlin, 1943), 9–13

Gundt, Rudolf, 'Das Schicksal des oberen Saaletals', *Die Gartenlaube* (1926), no. 11, 214–15

Günther, Hanns, *Pioniere der Technik: Acht Lebensbilder grosser Männer der Tat* (Zurich, 1920)

Günther, Hans, *Rassenkunde des deutschen Volkes* (Munich, 1922)

Günther, Werner, 'Der Ausbau der oberen Saale durch Talsperren', dissertation, Jena 1930

Gutting, Willi, *Die Aalfischer: Roman vom Oberrhein* (Bayreuth, 1943)

Gutting, Willi, *Glückliches Ufer* (Bayreuth, 1943)

Halbfaß, W[ilhelm], 'Die Projekte von Wasserkraftanlagen am Walchensee und Kochelsee in Oberbayern', *Globus* 88 (1905), 33–4

Halfeld, Adolf, *Amerika und der Amerikanismus* (Jena, 1927)

Hamm, F., *Naturkundliche Chronik Nordwestdeutschlands* (Hanover, 1976)

Hampe, Karl, *Der Zug nach dem Osten: Die kolonisatorische Grosstat des deutschen Volkes im Mittelalter* (Leipzig and Berlin, 1935; first edn. 1921)

Heidegger, Martin, *The Question Concerning Technology and Other Essays* [1954] (New York, 1977)

Helmholtz, Hermann von, *Science and Culture: Popular and Philosophical Essays*, ed. David Cahan (Chicago, 1995)

Hennig, Richard, 'Deutschlands Wasserkräfte und ihre technische Auswertung', *Die Turbine* (1909), 208–11, 230–4

Hennig, Richard, 'Aufgaben der Wasserwirtschaft in Südwestafrika', *Die Turbine* (1909), 331–3

Hennig, Richard, 'Die grossen Wasserfälle der Erde in ihrer Beziehung zur Industrie und zum Naturschutz', *ÜLM* 53 (1910–11), 872–3

Hennig, Richard, *Buch berühmter Ingenieure: Grosse Männer der Technik, ihr Lebensgang und ihr Lebenswerk. Für die reifere Jugend und für Erwachsene geschildert* (Leipzig, 1911)

Hennig, Richard, 'Otto Intze, der Talsperren-Erbauer (1843–1904)', in Hennig, *Buch berühmter Ingenieure*, 104–21

Herzog, S., 'Ausnutzung der Wasserkräfte für den elektrischen Vollbahnbetrieb', *UTW* (1909), 19–20, 23–4

Hesse-Wartegg, Ernst von, 'Der Niagara in Fesseln', *Die Gartenlaube* (1905), 34–8

Hill, Lucy A., *Rhine Roamings* (Boston, 1880)

Hinrichs, August, 'Land und Leute in Oldenburg', in *August Hinrichs über Oldenburg*, ed. Gerhard Preuß (Oldenburg, 1986)

Hinrichs, August, 'Zwischen Marsch, Moor und Geest', in *August Hinrichs über Oldenburg*, ed. Gerhard Preuß (Oldenburg, 1986)

Hitler, Adolf, *Mein Kampf* (Munich, 1943 edn.)

Hoerner, Herbert von, 'Erinnerung', *Land unserer Liebe: Ostdeutsche Gedichte* (Düsseldorf, 1953), 35

Honsell, Max, *Die Korrektion des Oberrheins von der Schweizer Grenze unterhalb Basel bis zur Grossh. Hessischen Grenze unterhalb Mannheim* (Karlsruhe, 1885)

Hugenberg, Alfred, *Innere Colonisation im Nordwesten Deutschlands* (Strasbourg, 1891)

Hugo, Victor, *The Rhine* (New York, 1845)

Hummel, Bernhard, 'Nach uns die Sintflut', *Jungle World* 32, 5 Aug. 1998

Hurd, Archibald and Henry Castle, *German Sea-Power* (London, 1913)

Internationale Kommission zum Schutze des Rheins gegen Verunreinigung,

Ökologisches Gesamtkonzept für den Rhein: 'Lachs 2000' (Koblenz, 1991)

Intze, Otto, *Zweck und Bau sogenannter Thalsperren* (Aachen, 1875)

Intze, Otto, *Thalsperren im Gebiet der Wupper: Vortrag des Prof. Intze ... am 18. Oktober 1889* (Barmen, 1889)

Intze, Otto, *Bericht über die Wasserverhältnisse der Gebirgsflüsse Schlesiens und deren Verbesserung zur Ausnutzung der Wasserkräfte und zur Verminderung der Hochfluthschäden* (Berlin, 1898)

Intze, Otto, *Talsperrenanlagen in Rheinland und Westfalen, Schlesien und Böhmen. Weltausstellung St. Louis 1904: Sammelausstellung des Königlich Preussischen Ministeriums der Öffentlichen Arbeiten. Wasserbau* (Berlin, 1904)

Intze, Otto, 'Die geschichtliche Entwicklung, die Zwecke und der Bau der Talsperren' [lecture of 3 Feb. 1904], *ZVDI* 50, 5 May 1906, 673–87

Jacquinot, 'Über Talsperrenbauten', *ZdB*, 29 Sep. 1906, 503–5

Jaeckel, Otto, *Gefahren der Entwässerung unseres Landes* (Greifswald, 1922)

Kaminski, A.J., *Nationalsozialistische Besatzungspolitik in Polen und der Tschechoslovakei 1939–1945: Dokumente* (Bremen, 1975)

Kann, Friedrich, 'Die Neuordnung des deutschen Dorfes', in *Neue Dorflandschaften*, 97–102

Kaplick, Otto, *Das Warthebruch: Eine deutsche Kulturlandschaft im Osten* (Würzburg, 1956)

Kapp, Ernst, *Vergleichende allgemeine Erdkunde* (Braunschweig, 1868)

Kapp, Ernst, *Grundlinien einer Philosophie der Technik* (Braunschweig, 1877)

Karmarsch, Karl, *Geschichte der Technologie seit der Mitte des 18. Jahrhunderts* (Munich, 1872)

Kelen, Nikolaus, *Talsperren* (Berlin and Leipzig, 1931)

Keller, Hermann, 'Natürliche und künstliche Wasserstrassen', *Die Woche* (1904), vol. 2, no. 20, 873–5

Keyser, Erich, *Westpreussen und das deutsche Volk* (Danzig, 1919)

Keyser, Erich, 'Die deutsche Bevölkerung des Ordenslandes Preussen', in Volz (ed.), *Der ostdeutsche Volksboden*

Kirschner, O., 'Zerstörung und Schutz von Talsperren und Dämmen', *SB* 67, 24 May 1949, 277–81, 300–3

Kissling, Johannes Baptist, *Geschichte des Kulturkampfes im Deutschen Reiche*, 3 vols. (Freiburg, 1911–16)

Klössel, M. Hans, 'Die Errichtung von Talsperren in Sachsen', *PVbl* (1904), 120–1

Kobbe, Ursula, *Der Kampf mit dem Stausee* (Berlin, 1943)

Kobell, Franz von, *Wildanger* [1854] (Munich, 1936)

Köbl, J., 'Die Wirkungen der Talsperren auf das Hochwasser', *ANW* 38 (1904), 507–10

Koch, L., 'Im Zeichen des Wassermangels', *Die Turbine* (1909), 491–4

Koch, P., *50 Jahre Wilhelmshaven: Ein Rückblick auf die Werdezeit* [1919] (Berlin, n.d.)

Koehn, Theodor, 'Der Ausbau der Wasserkräfte in Deutschland', *ZfdgT* (1908), 462–5, 476–80, 491–6

Koehn, Theodor, 'Über einige grosse europäische Wasserkraftanlagen und ihre wirtschaftliche Bedeutung', *Die Turbine* (1909), 110–19, 153–6, 168–76, 190–6

Kohl, H. (ed.), *Briefe Ottos von Bismarck an Schwester und Schwager* (Leipzig, 1915)

Kollbach, Karl, 'Die Urft-Talsperre', *ÜLM* 92 (1913), 694–5

Korn, A., 'Die "Weisse Kohle"', *TM* 9 (1909), 744–6

Kossinna, Gustav, *Die Herkunft der Germanen* (Würzburg, 1911)

Kötzschke, Rudolf, 'Über den Ursprung und die geschichtliche Bedeutung der ostdeutschen Siedlung', in Volz (ed.), *Der Ostdeutsche Volksboden*, 7–26

Krannhals, Hanns von, 'Die Geschichte Ostdeutschlands', in Mackensen (eds.), *Deutsche Heimat ohne Deutsche*, 38–64

Kretz, 'Zur Frage der Ausnutzung des Wassers des Oberrheins', *ZfBi* 13 (1906), 361–8

Kreuter, Franz, 'Die wissenschaftlichen Bestrebungen auf dem Gebiet des Wasserbaues und ihre Erfolge', *Beiträge zur Allgemeinen Zeitung* 1 (1908), 1–20

Kreutz, W., 'Methoden der Klimasteuerung: Praktische Wege in Deutschland und der Ukraine', *FD* 15 (1943), 256–81

Kreuzkam, Dr, 'Zur Verwertung der Wasserkräfte', *VW* (1908), 919–22, 950–2

Krohn, Louise von, *Vierzig Jahre in einem deutschen Kriegshafen Heppens-Wilhelmshaven: Erinnerungen* (Rostock, 1911)

Kruedener, Arthur Freiherr von, 'Landschaft und Menschen des osteuropäischen Gesamtraumes', *ZfGeo* 19 (1942), 366–74

Krüger, W., 'Die Baugeschichte der Hafenanlagen', *JbHG* 4 (1922), 97–105

Kullrich, 'Der Wettbewerb für die architektonische Ausbildung der Möhnetalsperre', *ZbB* 28, 1 Feb. 1908, 61–5

Künkel, Hans, *Auf den kargen Hügeln der Neumark: Zur Geschichte eines Schäfer- und Bauerngeschlechts im Warthebruch* (Würzburg, 1962)

Küppers, Wilhelm, 'Die grösste Talsperre Europas bei Gemünd (Eifel)', *Die Turbine* 2 (1905), 61–4, 96–8

Kurs, Victor, 'Die künstlichen Wasserstrassen im Deutschen Reiche', *GZ* (1898), 611–12

Lampe, Felix, *Grosse Geographen* (Leipzig and Berlin, 1915)

'Landwirtschaft und Talsperren', *Volkswohl* 19 (1905), 88–9

Lauterborn, Robert, 'Beiträge zur Fauna und Flora des Oberrheins und seiner Umgebung', *Pollichia* 19 (1903), 42–130

Leclerc, Georges-Louis, Comte de Buffon, *Histoire Naturelle*, 44 vols. (Paris, 1749–1804), vol. 12

Letters of Euler on Different Subjects in Physics and Philosophy Addressed to a German Princess, transl. from the French by Henry Hunter, 2 vols. (London, 1802)

Levi, Primo, *If This is a Man; The Truce* (Harmondsworth, 1979)

Levi, Primo, *If Not Now, When?* (Harmondsworth, 1986)

Levi, Primo, *Moments of Reprieve: A Memoir of Auschwitz* (New York, 1987)

Lieckfeldt, 'Die Lebensdauer der Talsperren', *ZdB*, 28 Mar. 1906, 167–8

Lindner, Werner, *Ingenieurwerk und Naturschutz* (Berlin, 1926)

Link, E[rnst], 'Die Zerstörung der Austintalsperre in Pennsylvanien (Nordamerika) II', *ZdB*, 20 Jan. 1912, 36–9

Link, E[rnst], 'Talsperren des Ruhrgebiets', *ZDWW*, June 1922, 99–102

Link, Ernst, 'Ruhrtalsperrenverein, Möhne- und Sorpetalsperre', *MLWBL* (1927), 1–11

Link, Ernst, 'Die Sorpetalsperre und die untere Versetalsperre im Ruhrgebiet als Beispiele hoher Erdstaudämme in neuzeitlicher Bauweise', *DeW*, 1 Mar. 1932, 41–5, 71–2

Link, E[rnst], 'Die Bedeutung der Talsperrenbauten für die Wasserwirtschaft des Ruhrgebiets', *Zement* 25 (1936), 67–71

Loacker, Albert, 'Die Ausnutzung der Wasserkräfte', *Die Turbine* 6 (1910), 230–8

Lorenzen, Ingrid, *An der Weichsel zu Haus* (Berlin, 1999)

M., 'Landschaftsgestaltung im Osten', *NB* 36 (1944), 201–11

Machiavelli, Niccolo, *The Prince*, ed. Harvey C. Mansfield (Chicago, 1985)

Machui, Artur von, 'Die Landgestaltung als Element der Volkspolitik', *DA* 42 (1942), 287–305

Mackensen, Lutz (ed.), *Deutsche Heimat ohne Deutsche: Ein ostdeutsches Heimatbuch* (Braunschweig, 1951)

Mäding, Erhard, 'Kulturlandschaft und Verwaltung', *Reichsverwaltungsblatt* (1939), 432–5

Mäding, Erhard, *Landschaftspflege: Die Gestaltung der Landschaft als Hoheitsrecht und Hoheitspflicht* (Berlin, 1942)

Mäding, Erhard, 'Die Gestaltung der Landschaft als Hoheitsrecht und Hoheitspflicht', *NB* 35 (1943), 22–4

Mäding, Erhard, *Regeln für die Gestaltung der Landschaft: Einführung in die Allgemeine Anordnung Nr. 20/VI/42 des Reichsführers SS, Reichskommissars für die Festigung deutschen Volkstums* (Berlin, 1943)

Maire, Siegfried, 'Beiträge zur Besiedlungsgeschichte des Oderbruchs', *AdB* (1911), 21–160

Marsh, George Perkins, *Man and Nature*, ed. David Lowenthal (Cambridge, Mass., 1965)

Mathy, Karl, 'Eisenbahnen und Canäle, Dampfboote und Dampfwagentransport', in C. Rotteck and C. Welcker (eds.), *Staats-Lexikon*, vol. 4 (Altona, 1846), 228–89

Mattern, Ernst, *Der Thalsperrenbau und die deutsche Wasserwirtschaft* (Berlin, 1902)

Mattern, Ernst, 'Ein französisches Urteil über deutsche Bauweise von Staudämmen und Sperrmauern', *ZdB*, 24 Jun. 1905, 319–20

Mattern, Ernst, 'Die Zerstörung der Austintalsperre in Pennsylvanien (Nordamerika) I', *ZdB*, 13 Jan. 1912, 25–7

Mattern, Ernst, *Die Ausnutzung der Wasserkräfte* (Leipzig, 1921)

Mattern, Ernst, 'Stand der Entwicklung des Talsperrenwesens in Deutschland', *WuG* 19, 1 May 1929, 858–66

Meinhold, Helmut, 'Das Generalgouvernement als Transitland: Ein Beitrag zur Kenntnis der Standortslage des Generalgouvernements', *Die Burg* 2 (1941), Heft 4, 24–44

Meisner, A., 'Die Flussregulierungsaktion und die Talsperrenfrage', *RTW*, 6. Nov. 1909, 405–8

Merian, Matthäus, *Topographia Electorat Brandenburgici et Ducatus Pomeraniae, das ist, Beschreibung der Vornembsten und bekantisten Stätte und Plätze in dem hochlöblichsten Churfürstenthum und March Brandenburg*, facsimile of 1652 edn. (Kassel and Basel, 1965)

Meyer, Aug[ust], 'Die Bedeutung der Talsperren für die Wasserversorgung in Deutschland', *WuG* 13, 1 Dec. 1932, 121–5

Meyer, Konrad, 'Planung und Ostaufbau', *RuR* 5 (1941), 392–7

Meyer, Konrad, 'Der Osten als Aufgabe und Verpflichtung des Germanentums', *NB* 34 (1942), 205–8

Meyer, Konrad, 'Zur Einführung', *Neue Dorflandschaften*, 7

Micksch, Karl, 'Energie und Wärme ohne Kohle', *Die Gartenlaube* 68 (1920), 81–3

Middelhoff, Hans, *Die volkswirtschaftliche Bedeutung der Aggertalsperrenanlagen* (Gummersbach, 1929)

Miegel, Agnes, 'Die Fähre', *Gedichte und Spiele* (Jena, 1920)

Miegel, Agnes, 'Abschied vom Kinderland', *Aus der Heimat: Gesammelte Werke*, vol. 5 (Düsseldorf and Cologne, 1954), 126–31

Miegel, Agnes, 'Gruss der Türme', *Unter hellem Himmel* (1936), reprinted in *Aus der Heimat*, 118–25

Miegel, Agnes, 'Kriegergräber', *Ostland* (Jena, 1940)

Miegel, Agnes, 'Meine Salzburger Ahnen', *Ostland* (Jena, 1940), reprinted in *Es war ein Land: Gedichte und Geschichten aus Ostpreussen* (Cologne, 1983)

Miegel, Agnes, 'Zum Gedächtnis', *Du aber bleibst in mir: Flüchtlingsgedichte* (1949)

Miegel, Agnes, *Die Meinen: Erinnerungen* (Düsseldorf and Cologne, 1951)

Miegel, Agnes, 'Es war ein Land' [1952], *Es war ein Land: Gedichte und Geschichten aus Ostpreussen* (Cologne, 1983)

Miegel, Agnes, 'Truso' [1958], *Es war ein Land: Gedichte und Geschichten aus Ostpreussen* (Cologne, 1983)

Miller, Oskar von, 'Die Ausnutzung der deutschen Wasserkräfte', *ZfA*, August 1908, 401–5

Ministerium für Umwelt, Baden-Württemberg, *Hochwasserschutz und Ökologie: Ein 'integriertes Rheinprogrammm' schützt vor Hochwasser und erhält naturnahe Flussauen* (Stuttgart, 1988)

Mitteilungen der deutschen Volksräte Polens und Westpreussens, 14 Mar. 1919

Monologe im Führer-Hauptquartier 1941–1944: Die Aufzeichnungen Heinrich Heims, ed. Werner Jochmann (Hamburg, 1980)

Morgen, Herbert, 'Ehemals russisch-polnische Kreise des Reichsgaues Wartheland: Aus einem Reisebericht', *NB* 32 (1940), 320–6

Morgen, Herbert, 'Forstwirtschaft und Forstpolitik im neuen Osten', *NB* 33 (1941), 103–7

Mügge, W., 'Über die Gestaltung von Talsperren und Talsperrenlandschaften', *DW* 37 (1942), 404–18

Mühlenbein, C., 'Fische und Vögel der bergischen Talsperren', *BeH* 4, August 1930, 326–7

Mühlens, Dr P., 'Bericht über die Malariaepidemie des Jahres 1907 in Bant, Heppens, Neuende und Wilhelmshaven sowie in der weiteren Umgegend', *KJb* 19 (1907), 39–78

Müller, Dr, 'Aus der Kolonisationszeit des Netzebruchs', *SVGN* 39 (1921), 1–13

Müller, Wilhelm, 'Wasserkraft-Anlagen in Kalifornien', *Die Turbine* (1908), 32–5

Nankivell, Joice M. and Sydney Loch, *The River of a Hundred Ways* (London, 1924)

Naumann, Arno, 'Talsperren und Naturschutz', *BzN* 14 (1930), 77–85

Neue Dorflandschaften: Gedanken und Pläne zum ländlichen Aufbau in den neuen Ostgebieten und im Altreich. Herausgegeben vom Stabshauptamt des Reichskommissars für die Festigung deutschen Volkstums, Planungsamt sowie vom Planungsbeauftragten für die Siedlung und ländliche Neuordnung (Berlin, 1943)

Neuhaus, Erich, *Die Fridericianische Colonisation im Netze- und Warthebruch* (Landsberg, 1905)

Niemann, Harry (ed.), *Ludwig Starklof 1789–1850: Erinnerungen, Theater, Erlebnisse, Reisen* (Oldenburg, 1986)

Nietzsche, Friedrich, *On the Genealogy of Morals* (1887)

Noeldeschen, Friedrich Wilhelm, *Oekonomische und staatswissenschaftliche Briefe über das Niederoderbruch und den Abbau oder die Verteilung der Königlichen Ämter und Vorwerke im hohen Oderbruch* (Berlin, 1800)

Nußbaum, H. Chr., 'Zur Frage der Wirtschaftlichkeit der Anlage von Stau-Seen', *ZfBi* (1906), 463

Nußbaum, H. Chr., 'Die Wassergewinnung durch Talsperren', *ZGW* (1907), 67–70

Oberländer, Richard, *Berühmte Reisende: Geographen und Länderentdecker im 19. Jahrhundert* (Leipzig, 1892)

Oberländer, Theodor, *Die agrarische Überbevölkerung Polens* (Berlin, 1935)

Ott, Josef and Erwin Marquardt, *Die Wasserversorgung der kgl. Stadt Brüx in Böhmen mit bes. Berücks. der in den Jahren 1911 bis 1914 erbauten Talsperre* (Vienna, 1918)

Otto, Frank [pseud. for Otto Spamer], *'Hilf Dir Selbst!' Lebensbilder durch Selbsthülfe und Thatkraft emporgekommener Männer: Gelehrte und Forscher, Erfinder, Techniker, Werkleute. Der Jugend und dem Volke in Verbindung mit Gleichgesinnten zur Aneiferung vorgeführt* (Leipzig, 1881)

Paul, Gustav, *Grundzüge der Rassen- und Raumgeschichte des deutschen Volkes* (Munich, 1935)

Paul, Wolfgang, 'Flüchtlinge', *Land unserer Liebe: Ostdeutsche Gedichte* (Düsseldorf, 1953), 17

Pauli, Jean, 'Talsperrenromantik', *BeH* 4, August 1930, 331–2

Paxmann, 'Bruch der Talsperre bei Black River Falls in Wisconsin', *ZdB*, 25 May 1912, 274–5

Pflug, Hans, *Deutsche Flüsse – Deutsche Lebensadern* (Berlin, 1939)

Poschinger, Heinrich von (ed.), *Unter Friedrich Wilhelm IV: Denkwürdigkeiten des Ministerpräsidenten Otto Freiherr von Manteuffel, Zweiter Band: 1851–1854* (Berlin, 1901)

P[owidaj], L[udwik], 'Polacy i Indianie', I, *Dzennik Literacki* 53, 9 Dec. 1864

P[owidaj], L[udwik], 'Polacy i Indianie', II, *Dzennik Literacki*, 56, 30 Dec. 1864

Präg, Werner and Wolfgang Jacobmeyer (eds.), *Das Diensttagebuch des deutschen Generalgouverneurs in Polen 1939–1945* (Stuttgart, 1975)

'Prinzip Archimedes', *Der Spiegel*, 14/1986, 77–9

Quin, Michael J., *Steam Voyages on the Seine, the Moselle & the Rhine*, 2 vols. (London, 1843)

Raabe, Wilhelm, *Pfisters Mühle* (1884)

Raabe, Wilhelm, *Stopfkuchen*, transl. Barker Fairley as 'Tubby Schaumann': Wilhelm Raabe, *Novels*, ed. Volkmar Sander (New York, 1983), 155–311

Rappaport, Philipp A., 'Talsperren im Landschaftsbilde und die architektonische Behandlung von Talsperren', *WuG* 5, 1 Nov. 1914, 15–18

Rauter-Wilberg, Paula, 'Die Kücheneinrichtung', in *Neue Dorflandschaften*, 133–6

Rehmann, Dr., 'Kleine Beiträge zur Charakteristik Brenkenhoffs', *SVGN* 22 (1908), 101–31

Reifenrath, Joachim, 'Verlassenes Dorf', *Land unserer Liebe: Ostdeutsche Gedichte* (Düsseldorf, 1953), 7

Richau, Joachim and Wolfgang Kil, *Land ohne Übergang: Deutschlands neue Grenze* (Berlin, 1992)

Riehl, Wilhelm Heinrich, *The Natural History of the German People*, transl. David Diephouse (Lewiston, NY, 1990)

Ritter, Carl, 'The External Features of the Earth in Their Influence on the Course of History' [1850], *Geographical Studies by the Late Professor Carl Ritter of Berlin*, transl. William Leonard Gage (Cincinnati and New York, 1861), 311–56

Roloff, Regierungsrat, 'Der Talsperrenbau in Deutschland und Preussen', *ZfB* 59 (1910), 555–72

Rössler, Mechtild and Sabine Schleiermacher (eds.), *Der 'Generalplan Ost'* (Berlin, 1993)

Rudorff, Ernst, 'Ueber das Verhältniss des modernen Lebens zur Natur', *PJbb* 45 (1880), 261–76

Russwurm, 'Talsperren und Landschaftsbild', *Der Harz* 34 (1927), 50

Schauroth, Udo von, 'Raumordnungsskizzen und Ländliche Planung', *NB* 33 (1941), 123–8

Schepers, Hansjulius, 'Pripet-Polesien: Land und Leute', *ZfGeo* 19 (1942), 278–87

Schick, Ernst, *Ausführliche Beschreibung merkwürdiger Bauwerke, Denkmale, Brücken, Anlagen, Wasserbauten, Kunstwerke, Maschinen, Instrumente, Erfindungen und Unternehmungen der neueren und neuesten Zeit, zur belehrenden Unterhaltung für die reifere Jugend bearbeitet* (Leipzig, 1838)

Schlögel, Karl, 'Strom zwischen den Welten. Stille der Natur nach den Katastrophen der Geschichte: Die Oder, eine Enzyklopädie Mitteleuropas', *FAZ*, 13 Nov. 1999 ('Bilder und Zeiten')

Schlüter, Otto, *Wald, Sumpf und Siedelungsland in Altpreussen vor der Ordenszeit* (Halle, 1921)

Schmidt, Albert, 'Die Erhöhung der Talsperrenmauer in Lennep', *ZfB* (1907), 227–32

Schoenichen, Walter, *Zauber der Wildnis in deutscher Heimat* (Neudamm, 1935)

Schönhoff, Hermann, 'Die Möhnetalsperre bei Soest', *Die Gartenlaube* (1913), 684–6

Schöningh, E., *Das Bourtanger Moor: Seine Besiedlung und wirtschaftliche Erschliessung* (Berlin, 1914)

Schröder, Arno, *Mit der Partei vorwärts! Zehn Jahre Gau Westfalen-Nord* (Detmold, 1940)

Schultze-Naumburg, Paul, 'Ästhetische und allgemeine kulturelle Grundsätze bei der Anlage von Talsperren', *Der Harz* 13 (1906), 353–60

Schultze-Naumburg, Paul, 'Kraftanlagen und Talsperren', *Der Kunstwart* 19 (1906), 130

Schütte, Heinrich, *Sinkendes Land an der Nordsee?* (Oehringen, 1939)

Schwanhäuser, Catharine, *Aus der Chronik Wilhelmshavens* [1926] (Wilhelmshaven, 1974)

Schwarz, Paul, 'Brenkenhoffs Berichte über seine Tätigkeit in der Neumark', *SVGN* 20 (1907), 37–101

Schwenkel, Hans, 'Landschaftspflege und Landwirtschaft: Gefahren der zerstörten Landschaft, Aufgaben der Zukunft', *FD* 15 (1943), 118–37

Schwenkel, Hans, 'Landschaftspflege und Landwirtschaft', *NB* 35 (1943), 7–18

Seifert, Alwin, 'Die Versteppung Deutschlands', in *Die Versteppung Deutschlands? Kulturwasserbau und Heimatschutz* (Berlin and Leipzig, n.d. [1938]), 4–10

Seifert, Alwin, 'Die Zukunft der ostdeutschen Landschaft', *BSW* 20 (1940), 312–16

Seifert, Alwin, *Im Zeitalter des Lebendigen* (Dresden, 1941)

Seifert, Alwin, 'Die Schiffbarmachung der Mosel', *NuL* 34 (1959), 54–5

Sello, Georg, *Der Jadebusen* (Varel, 1903)

Seraphim, Peter-Heinz (ed.), *Polen und seine Wirtschaft* (Königsberg, 1937)

Seraphim, Peter-Heinz, *Das Judentum im osteuropäischen Raum* (Essen, 1938)

Sering, Max, *Die innere Kolonisation im östlichen Deutschland* (Leipzig, 1893)

Soergel, Kurt, 'Die Bedeutung der Talsperren in Deutschland für die Landwirtschaft', dissertation, Leipzig 1929

Soldan, W. and C[arl] Heßler, *Die Waldecker Talsperre im Eddertal* (Marburg and Bad Wildungen, 1911)

Späth, Lothar, *Wende in die Zukunft: Die Bundesrepublik auf dem Weg in die Informationsgesellschaft* (Reinbek, 1985)

Splittgerber, A., 'Die Entwicklung der Talsperren und ihre Bedeutung', *WuG* 8, 1 July 1918, 205–12, 253–61

Stadelmann, Rudolph, *Preussens Könige in ihrer Thätigkeit für die Landescultur*, 3 vols. (Leipzig, 1878–85)

Staden, Berndt von, 'Erinnerungen an die Umsiedlung', *JbbD* 41 (1994), 62–75

Staritz, Ekkehart, *Die West-Ostbewegung in der deutschen Geschichte* (Breslau, 1935)

Starklof, L[udwig], *Moor-Kanäle und Moor-Kolonien zwischen Hunte und Ems: Vier Briefe* (Oldenburg, 1847)

Steele, Andrew, *The Natural and Agricultural History of Peat-Moss or Turf-Bog* (Edinburgh, 1826)

Steinert, Martin, 'Die geographische Bedeutung der Talsperren', dissertation, Jena 1910

Storm, Theodor, *Der Schimmelreiter* (Berlin, 1888)

Stöve, L., *Die Moorwirtschaft im Freistaate Oldenburg, unter besonderer Berücksichtigung der inneren Kolonisation* (Würzburg, 1921)

Stromberg, Josef, 'Die volkswirtschaftliche Bedeutung der deutschen Talsperren', dissertation, Cologne 1932

Stumpfe, E., *Die Besiedelung der deutschen Moore mit besonderer Berücksichtigung der Hochmoor- und Fehnkolonisation* (Leipzig and Berlin, 1903)

Sympher, Leo, 'Der Talsperrenbau in Deutschland', *ZdB* 27 (1907), 159–61, 167–71, 175–8

'Talsperrenbauten in Böhmen', *Die Talsperre* (1911), 125–6

Teschner, Clara, 'Landschaftsgestaltung in den Ostgebieten', *Odal* 11 (1942), 567–70

'Thalsperren am Harz', *GI*, 31 May 1902, 167–8

Thielsch, K., 'Baukosten von Wasserkraftanlagen', *ZfgdT*, 20 Aug. 1908, 357–62

Thienemann, A[ugust], 'Hydrobiologische und fischereiliche Untersuchungen an den westfälischen Talsperren', *LJbb* 41 (1911), 535–716

Thiesing, Professor, 'Chemische und physikalische Untersuchungen an Talsperren, insbesondere der Eschbachtalsperre bei Remscheid', *Mitteilungen aus der Königlichen Prüfungsanstalt für Wasserversorgung und Abwässerbeseitigung zu Berlin* 15 (1911), 42–3, 140–1

Thomas, Louis, *Das Buch wunderbarer Erfindungen* (Leipzig, 1860)

Tietze, Walter, 'Die Oderschiffahrt: Studien zu ihrer Geschichte und zu ihrer wirtschaftlichen Bedeutung', dissertation, Breslau 1906.

Timm, Gerhard, 'Die offizielle Ökologiedebatte in der DDR', in Redaktion Deutschland Archiv, *Umweltprobleme in der DDR* (Cologne, 1985)

Treitschke, Heinrich von, *Origins of Prussianism (The Teutonic Knights)* [1862], transl. Eden and Cedar Paul (New York, 1969)

Treitschke, Heinrich von, *Deutsche Geschichte im 19. Jahrhundert, Erster Teil* [1879] (Königstein/Ts, 1981)

Tulla, J[ohann] G[ottfried], *Die Grundsätze, nach welchen die Rheinbauarbeiten künftig zu führen seyn möchten: Denkschrift vom 1.3.1812* (Karlsruhe, 1812)

Tulla, J[ohann] G[ottfried], *Denkschrift: Die Rectification des Rheines* (Karlsruhe, 1822)

Tulla, J[ohann] G[ottfried], *Über die Rectification des Rheines, von seinem Austritt aus der Schweiz bis zu seinem Eintritt in das Großherzogtum Hessen* (Karlsruhe, 1825)

Turner, Frederick Jackson, 'The Significance of the Frontier in American History' [1893], in *The Frontier in American History* (Tucson, 1986), 1–38

'Über die Bedeutung und die Wertung der Wasserkräfte in Verbindung mit elektrischer Kraftübertragung', *ZGW* (1907), Nr. 1, 4–8

'Ueber Talsperren', *ZfG* 4 (1902), 252–4

Ulbricht, Walter, *Whither Germany?* (Dresden, 1966)

Umlauf, J., 'Der Stand der Raumordnungsplanung für die eingegliederten Ostgebiete', *NB* 34 (1942), 281–93

Valentin, Veit (ed.), *Bismarcks Reichsgründung im Urteil englischer Diplomaten* (Amsterdam, 1937)

Vasmer, Max, 'Die Urheimat der Slawen', in Volz (ed.), *Der Ostdeutsche Volksboden*, 118–43

Venatier, Hans, *Vogt Bartold: Der grosse Zug nach dem Osten* (Leipzig, 1944)

Venatier, Hans, 'Vergessen?', *Land unserer Liebe: Ostdeutsche Gedichte* (Düsseldorf, 1953), 28–9

Vogel, Friedrich, 'Die wirtschaftliche Bedeutung deutscher Gebirgswasserkräfte', *ZfS* 8 (1905), 607–14

Vogt, Martin (ed.), *Herbst 1941 im 'Führerhauptquartier'* (Koblenz, 2002)

Völker, H., *Die Edder-Talsperre* (Bettershausen bei Marburg, 1913)

Volz, Wilhelm (ed.), *Der ostdeutsche Volksboden: Aufsätze zu den Fragen des Ostens. Erweiterte Ausgabe* (Breslau, 1926)

Von der Konfrontation zur Kooperation: 50 Jahre Landsmannschaft Weichsel-Warthe (Wiesbaden, 1999)

Weber, J., 'Die Wupper-Talsperren', *BeH* 4, August 1930, 313–23

Weber, Marianne, *Max Weber: A Biography*, transl. and ed. Harry Zohn (New York, 1975)

Weber, Max, 'Capitalism and Society in Rural Germany', in Hans Gerth and C. Wright Mills (eds.), *From Max Weber: Essays in Sociology* (London, 1952), 363–85

'Wehrbauer im deutschen Osten', *Wir sind Daheim: Mitteilungsblatt der deutschen Umsiedler im Reich*, 20 Feb. 1944

Wehrmann, *Die Eindeichung des Oderbruches* (Berlin, 1861)

Weissbach, Christian, *Wie der Mensch das Wasser bändigt und beherrscht: Der Talsperrenbau im Ostharz* (Leipzig and Jena, 1958)

Wermuth, Adolf, *Ein Beamtenleben: Erinnerungen* (Berlin, 1922)

Werth, Heinrich, 'Die Gestaltung der deutschen Landschaft als Aufgabe der Volksgemeinschaft', *NB* 34 (1942), 109–11

Wichert, Ernst, *Heinrich von Plauen: Historischer Roman*, 2 vols. (Dresden, 1929, 22nd edn.)

Wickert, Friedrich, *Der Rhein und sein Verkehr* (Stuttgart, 1903)

Winters, Jochen, 'The Flood', *Deutschland: Magazine on Politics, Culture, Business and Science*, Oct. 1997, 14–17

Wickop, Walter, 'Grundsätze und Wege der Dorfplanung', in *Neue Dorflandschaften*, 46–57

Wiepking-Jürgensmann, Heinrich Friedrich, 'Friedrich der Grosse und wir', *DG* 33 (1920), 69–78

Wiepking-Jürgensmann, Heinrich Friedrich, 'Der deutsche Osten: Eine vordringliche Aufgabe für unsere Studierenden', *DG* 52 (1939), 193

Wiepking-Jürgensmann, Heinrich Friedrich, 'Das Grün im Dorf und in der Feldmark', *BSW* 20 (1940), 442–5

Wiepking-Jürgensmann, Heinrich Friedrich, 'Aufgaben und Ziele deutscher Landschaftspolitik', *DG* 53 (1940), 81–96

Wiepking-Jürgensmann, Heinrich Friedrich, 'Gegen den Steppengeist', *DSK*, 16 Oct. 1942, 4

Wiepking-Jürgensmann, Heinrich Friedrich, 'Dorfbau und Landschaftsgestaltung', in *Neue Dorflandschaften*, 24–43

Wingendorf, Rolf, *Polen: Volk zwischen Ost und West* (Berlin, 1939)

Woldt, Richard, *Im Reiche der Technik: Geschichte für Arbeiterkinder* (Dresden, 1910)

Wolf, Christa, *Kindheitsmuster* (Berlin and Weimar, 1976), transl. as *A Model Childhood* (New York, 1980)

Wolf, Kurt, 'Über die Wasserversorgung mit besonderer Berücksichtigung der Talsperren', *MCWäL* (1906), 633–4

Wolff, C.A., *Wriezen und seine Geschichte im Wort, im Bild und im Gedichte* (Wriezen, 1912)

Wulff, C., *Die Talsperren-Genossenschaften im Ruhr- und Wuppergebiet* (Jena, 1908)

Zantke, S., 'Die Heimkehr der Wolhyniendeutschen', *NSM* 11 (1940), 169–71

Zeymer, Werner, 'Erste Ergebnisse des Ostaufbaus', *NB* 32 (1940), 415

Ziegfeld, A. Hillen, *1000 Jahre deutsche Kolonisation und Siedlung: Rückblick und Vorschau zu neuem Aufbruch* (Berlin, n.d. [1942])

Ziegler, P., 'Ueber die Notwendigkeit der Einbeziehung von Thalsperren in die Wasserwirtschaft', *ZfG* 4 (1901), 49–58

Ziegler, P., *Der Talsperrenbau* (Berlin, 1911)

Zigler, Emil, 'Unsere Wasserkräfte und ihre Verwendung', *ZbWW* 6, 20 Jan. 1911, 33–5, 51–3

Zinssmeister, Jakob, 'Industrie, Verkehr, Natur und moderne Wasserwirtschaft', *WK*, January 1909, 12–15

Zinssemeister, Jakob, 'Die Beziehungen zwischen Talsperren und Wasserabflusss', *WK* 2, 25 Feb. 1909, 45–7

Zinssmeister, Jakob, 'Wertbestimmung von Wasserkräften und von Wasserkraftanlagen', *WK* 2, 5 Jan. 1909, 1–3

Zuckmayer, Carl, *A Part of Myself* (New York, 1984)

'Zum Kanal-Sturm in Preussen', *HPBl* (1899), 453–62

Websites and Other Internet Sources

BUND-Berlin, 'Ökologische Hochwasserschutz': http://www.bund-berlin.de

'Deichreparatur am Oderbruch offenbart Grauen des Krieges': http://www.wissenschaft.de/wissen/news/drucken/156089.html

Deutsche Bundesstiftung Umwelt, 'Hochwasserschutz und Naturschutz': http://www.umweltstiftung.de/pro/hochwasser.html

http://www.bundjugend-berlin.de/presse/pm2002-11.html

http://www.oekofuehrerschein.de

http://www.pages.unibe.ch/highlights/archive03/poliwoda.html

http://www.zalf.de/lsad/drimipro/elanus/html_projekt/pkt31/pkt.htm

'Immer noch vermisst', ZDF-TV broadcast, 11. Nov. 2003: http://www.zdf/.
    de/ZDFde/inhalt/5/0,1872
'"Jahrhundertflut" an der Oder': http://www.mlur.brandenburg.de
Land Brandenburg, 'Alte Oder', http://www..mlur.brandenburg.de
LEADER Aktionsgruppe Oderbruch: http://www.gruenliga.de/projekt/nre
'Leben lernen im Oderbruch': http://www.unternehmen.region.de/_media/
    InnoRegio_Dokumentation_2000_S08-31.pdf
Mackentum, Gerald, 'Gen-Mais im Oderbruch', Barnimer Aktionsbündnis gegen
    Gentechnik: http://www.dosto.de/gengruppe/region/oderbruch/monsanto_
    moz.html
Peuker, Birgit and Katja Vaupel (updated by Esther Rewitz), 'Gefährliche
    Gentechnik', BUND Brandenburg: http://www.bundnessel.de/47_gen.html
'Wasserhaushaltsuntersuchungen im Oderbruch': http://www.wasy.de/deutsch/
    consulting/grund/oderbruch/index.html

Other Books and Articles

Ackermann, Josef, *Heinrich Himmler als Ideologe* (Göttingen, 1970)
Adorno, Theodor and Max Horkheimer, *The Dialectic of Enlightenment* (New
    York, 1972)
Albiez, Gustav, 'Die Goldwäscherei am Rhein', in Kurt Klein (ed.), *Land um
    Rhein und Schwarzwald* (Kehl, 1978), 268–71
Alexander, David, *Natural Disasters* (New York, 1993)
Altenbockum, Jasper von, *Wilhelm Heinrich Riehl 1823–1897* (Cologne, 1994)
Aly, Götz, Peter Chroust and Christian Pross, *Cleansing the Fatherland: Nazi
    Medicine and Racial Hygiene* (Baltimore, 1994)
Aly, Götz, *'Final Solution': Nazi Population Policy and the Murder of the Euro-
    pean Jews* (London, 1999)
Aly, Götz, '"Jewish Resettlement": Reflections on the Political Prehistory of the
    Holocaust', in Herbert (ed.), *National Socialist Extermination Policies*, 53–82
Aly, Götz and Susanne Heim, *Vordenker der Vernichtung* (Hamburg, 1991)
Andermann, Kurt (ed.), *Baden: Land – Staat – Volk 1806–1871* (Karlsruhe,
    1980)
Andersen, Arne, 'Heimatschutz', in Brüggemeier and Rommelspacher (eds.),
    Besiegte Natur, 143–57
Applegate, Celia, *A Nation of Provincials: The German Idea of Heimat* (Berkeley,
    1990)
Augé, Marc, *Non-Places: Introduction to an Anthropology of Supermodernity*
    (London and New York, 1995)
Bakker, H.S., *Norderney* (Bremen, 1956)
Bartov, Omer, *The Eastern Front, 1941–1945: German Troops and the Barbari-
    sation of Warfare* (London, 1985)

Bassin, Mark, 'Friedrich Ratzel's Travels in the United States: A Study in the Genesis of his Anthropogeography', *HGN* 4 (1984), 11–22

Bassin, Mark, 'Race contra Space: The Conflict between German *Geopolitik* and National Socialism', *PGO* 6 (1987), 115–34

Bassin, Mark, 'Imperialism and the Nation State in Friedrich Ratzel's Political Geography', *PHG* 11 (1987), 473–95

Bauer, Arnold, *Rudolf Virchow: Der politische Arzt* (Berlin, 1982)

Bauer, Heinrich, *Die Mark Brandenburg* (Berlin, 1954)

Bauer, Yehuda, *Rethinking the Holocaust* (New Haven and London, 2001)

Bayerl, Günter, Norman Fuchsloch and Torsten Meyer (eds.), *Umweltgeschichte: Methoden, Themen, Potentiale* (Münster, 1996)

Bechtluft, H.H., 'Das nasse Geschichtsbuch', in W. Franke and G. Hugenberg (eds.), *Moor im Emsland* (Sögel, 1979), 40–59

Beck, Rainer, *Unterfinning: Ländliche Welt vor Anbruch der Moderne* (Munich, 1993)

Behre, Karl-Ernst, *Meeresspiegelbewegungen und Siedlungsgeschichte in den Nordseemarschen* (Oldenburg, 1987)

Behre, Karl-Ernst and Hajo van Langen (eds.), *Ostfriesland: Geschichte und Gestalt einer Kulturlandschaft* (Aurich, 1995)

Behre, Karl-Ernst, 'Die Entstehung und Entwicklung der Natur- und Kulturlandschaft der ostfriesischen Halbinsel', in Behre and van Lengen (eds.), *Ostfriesland*, 5–37

Berg, Peter, *Deutschland und Amerika 1918–1929: Über das deutsche Amerikabild der zwanziger Jahre* (Lübeck and Hamburg, 1963)

Berkhoff, Karel C., *Harvest of Despair: Life and Death in the Ukraine under Nazi Rule* (Cambridge, Mass., 2004)

Berman, Marshall, *All That Is Solid Melts into Air: The Experience of Modernity* (Harmondsworth, 1988)

Bernhardt, Christoph, 'Zeitgenössische Kontroversen über die Umweltfolgen der Oberrheinkorrektion im 19. Jahrhundert', *ZGO* 146 (1998), 293–320

Bernhardt, Christoph, 'The Correction of the Upper Rhine in the Nineteenth Century: Modernizing Society and State by Large-Scale Water Engineering', in Susan C. Anderson and Bruce H. Tabb (eds.), *Water, Culture, and Politics in Germany and the American West* (New York, 2001), 183–202

Biedermann, Hans, *Dictionary of Symbolism* (New York, 1994)

Bierganz, Manfred, 'Wirtschaft und Verkehr', in *Die Eifel 1888–1988* (Düren, 1989), 573–614

Bing, Ludwig (ed.), *Vom Edertal zum Edersee: Eine Landschaft ändert ihr Gesicht* (Korbach and Bad Wildungen, 1973)

Bird, Elizabeth Ann R., 'The Social Construction of Nature: Theoretical Approaches to the Study of Environmental Problems', *ER* 11 (1987), 255–64

Birn, Ruth Bettina, *Die Höheren SS- und Polizeiführer: Himmlers Vertreter im Reich und in den besetzten Gebieten* (Düsseldorf, 1986)

Blackbourn, David, *The Fontana History of Germany 1780–1918: The Long Nineteenth Century* (London, 1997)

Blackbourn, David, '"Taking the Waters": Meeting Places of the Fashionable World', in Martin Geyer and Johannes Paulmann (eds.), *The Mechanics of Internationalism* (Oxford, 2001), 435–57

Blaschke, Karl, 'Environmental History: Some Questions for a New Subdiscipline of History', in Peter Brindlecombe and Christian Pfister (eds.), *The Silent Countdown: Essays in European Environmental History* (Berlin, 1990), 68–72

Bloch, Marc, *The Historian's Craft* (Manchester, 1954)

Bluhm, Hans-Georg, 'Landschaftsbild im Wandel', in *Saison am Strand*, 30–1

Blum, Rainer, *Seismische Überwachung der Schlegeis-Talsperre und die Ursachen induzierter Seismizität* (Karlsruhe, 1975)

Blumenberg, Adolf, *Heimat am Jadebusen: Von Menschen, Deichen und versunkenem Land* (Nordenham-Blexen, 1997)

Boa, Elizabeth and Rachel Palfreyman, *Heimat – A German Dream: Regional Loyalties and National Identity in German Culture 1890–1990* (Oxford, 2000)

Böhm, Reiner and Michael Deneke (eds.), *Wasser: Eine Einführung in die Umweltwissenschaften* (Darmstadt, 1992)

Boldt, Hans (ed.), *Der Rhein: Mythos und Realität eines europäischen Stromes* (Cologne, 1988)

Bosma, Koos, 'Verbindungen zwischen Ost- und Westkolonisation', in Rössler and Schleiermacher (eds.), *'Generalplan Ost'*, 198–214

Bramwell, Anna, *Blood and Soil: Richard Walter Darré and Hitler's 'Green Party'* (Abbotsbrook, 1985)

Brandt, Klaus, 'Vor- und Frühgeschichte der Marschengebiete', in Eckhardt and Schmidt (eds.), *Geschichte des Landes Oldenburg*, 15–35

Braudel, Fernand, *Capitalism and Material Life 1400–1800* (London, 1974)

Braudel, Fernand, *On History* (Chicago, 1980)

Braudel, Fernand, *Civilization and Capitalism*, vol. 1 (London, 1981)

Braumann, Fred and Helmut Müller, 'Der Naturpark Drömling in Sachsen-Anhalt', *NuN* 152 (1994), 9–17

Bräutigam, Otto, *Überblick über die besetzten Ostgebiete während des 2. Weltkrieges* (Tübingen, 1954)

Breckoff, Olrik, 'Zwischenspiel an der Warthe – und was daraus wurde', *JbbD* 41 (1994), 142–9

Bredekamp, Horst, *The Lure of Antiquity and the Cult of the Machine* (Princeton, 1995)

Brogiato, Heinz Peter and Werner Grasediek, 'Geschichte der Eifel und des Eifelvereins von 1888 bis 1988', in *Die Eifel 1888–1988* (Düren, 1989), 141–542

Broszat, Martin, *Nationalsozialistische Polenpolitik 1939–1945* (Stuttgart, 1961)

Browning, Christopher R., *The Final Solution and the German Foreign Office* (New York, 1978)

Browning, Christopher R., *The Path to Genocide* (Cambridge, 1992)

Browning, Christopher R., *Nazi Policy, Jewish Workers, German Killers* (Cambridge, 2000)

Brüggemeier, Franz-Josef, *Tschernobyl, 26. April 1986: Die ökologische Herausforderung* (Munich, 1998)

Brüggemeier, Franz-Josef and Thomas Rommelspacher (eds.), *Besiegte Natur: Geschichte der Umwelt im 19. und 20. Jahrhundert* (Munich, 1987)

Brüggemeier, Franz-Josef and Thomas Rommelspacher, *Blauer Himmel über der Ruhr* (Essen, 1992)

Brüggemeier, Franz-Josef and Thomas Rommelspacher, 'Umwelt', in Wolfgang Köllmann, Hermann Korte, Dietmar Petzina and Wolfhard Weber (eds.), *Das Ruhrgebiet im Industriezeitalter*, vol. 2 (Düsseldorf, 1990), 518–26

Burleigh, Michael, *Germany Turns Eastwards: A Study of Ostforschung in the Third Reich* (Cambridge, 1988)

Burrin, Philippe, *Hitler and the Jews* (London, 1994)

Buttimer, Anne, *Geography and the Human Spirit* (Baltimore, 1993)

Carbognin, L., 'Land Subsidence: A World-wide Environmental Hazard', in Goudie (ed.), *The Human Impact Reader*, 20–32

Carlton, J.T., and J.B. Geller, 'Ecological Roulette: The Global Transport of Non-indigenous Organisms', *Science* 261 (1993), 78–83

Chaney, Sandra, 'Water for Wine and Scenery, Coal and European Unity: Canalization of the Mosel River, 1950–1964', in Susan B. Anderson and Bruce H. Tabb (eds.), *Water, Culture and Politics in Germany and the American West* (New York, 2001), 227–52

Chaney, Sandra, 'For Nation and Prosperity, Health and a Green Environment: Protecting Nature in West Germany, 1945–70', in Christof Mauch (ed.), *Nature in German History* (New York and Oxford, 2004), 93–118

Chiari, Bernhard, *Alltag hinter der Front: Besatzung, Kollaboration und Widerstand in Weissrussland 1941–1944* (Düsseldorf, 1998)

Chiari, Bernhard, 'Die Büchse der Pandora: Ein Dorf in Weissrussland 1939 bis 1944', in Müller and Volkmann (eds.), *Wehrmacht: Mythos und Realität*, 879–900

Chickering, Roger, *'We Men Who Feel Most German': A Cultural Study of the Pan-German League* (London, 1984)

Chickering, Roger, *Karl Lamprecht: A German Academic Life* (Atlantic Highlands, 1993)

Christian, David, *Maps of Time: An Introduction to Big History* (Berkeley, 2004)

Ciesla, Burghard and Patrice G. Poutrus, 'Food Supply in a Planned Economy', in Konrad A. Jarausch (ed.), *Dictatorship as Experience: Towards a*

Socio-Cultural History of the GDR (New York, 1999), 143–62

Cioc, Mark, 'Die Rauchplage am Rhein vor dem Ersten Weltkrieg', *BzR* 51 (1999), 48–53

Cioc, Mark, *The Rhine: An Eco-Biography 1815–2000* (Seattle, 2002)

Coldewey, Dettmar, 'Bevor die Preussen kamen', in Grunewald (ed.), *Wilhelmshaven*, 163–75

Coleman, W., 'Science and Symbol in the Turner Frontier Hypothesis', *AHR* 72 (1955), 22–49

Cronon, William C., *Nature's Metropolis: Chicago and the Great West* (New York, 1992)

Cronon, William C., 'The Uses of Environmental History', *EHR* 17 (1993), 1–22

Crosby, Alfred, *Ecological Imperialism: The Biological Expansion of Europe, 900–1900* (Cambridge, 1986)

Danckert, Werner, *Unehrliche Leute: Die verfemten Berufe* (Berne, 1963)

Darby, H.C., *The Draining of the Fens* (Cambridge, 1940)

Darby, H.C., 'The Relations of Geography and History', in Griffith Taylor (ed.), *Geography in the Twentieth Century* (London, 1957), 640–52

Das Oderbruch im Wandel der Zeiten 1747–1997 (Wriezen, 1997)

Das Oderbruch: Bilder einer Region (n.p., 1992)

Daum, Andreas, *Wissenschaftspopularisierung im 19. Jahrhundert* (Munich, 1998)

Davies, Norman and Roger Moorhouse, *Microcosm: Portrait of a Central European City* (London, 2002)

DeBardeleben, Joan, '"The Future Has Already Begun": Environmental Damage and Protection in the GDR', in Rueschemeyer and Lemke (eds.), *Quality of Life in the German Democratic Republic*, 144–64

Deeters, Walter, 'Kleinstaat und Provinz', in Behre and van Langen (eds.), *Ostfriesland*, 135–85

Demeritt, 'Ecology, Objectivity and Critique in Writings on Nature and Human Societies', *JHG* 20 (1994), 22–37

Deneke, Dietrich, 'Eingriffe der Menschen in die Landschaft: Historische Entwicklung – Folgen – erhaltene Relikte', in Ernst Schubert and Bernd Herrmann (eds.), *Von der Angst vor der Ausbeutung: Umweltgeschichte zwischen Mittelalter und Neuzeit* (Frankfurt/Main, 1994), 59–71

Deschner, Günther, 'Reinhard Heydrich', in Smelser and Zitelman (eds.), *Nazi Elite*, 85–97

Dieckmann, Christoph, 'The War and the Killing of the Lithuanian Jews', in Herbert (ed.), *National Socialist Extermination Policies*, 240–75

Diehl, Wolfgang, 'Poesie und Dichtung der Rheinebene', in Geiger, Preuß and Rothenberger (eds.), *Der Rhein und die Pfälzische Rheinebene*, 378–93

Dienel, Hans-Liudger, 'Homo Faber: Der technische Zugang zur Natur', in Werner Nachtigall and Charlotte Schönbeck (eds.), *Technik und Natur* (Düsseldorf, 1994), 13–84

Dietz, Bettina, 'Exotische Naturalien als Statussymbol', in Hans-Peter Bayerdörfer and Eckhardt Hellmuth (eds.), *Exotica: Inszenierung und Konsum des Fremden 1750–1900* (Münster, 2003)

Diner, Dan, '"Grundbuch des Planeten": Zur Geopolitik Karl Haushofers', *VfZ* 32 (1984), 1–28

Dipper, Christof, *Deutsche Geschichte 1648–1789* (Frankfurt/Main, 1991)

Dix, Andreas, 'Nach dem Ende der "Tausend Jahre": Landschaftsplanung in der Sowjetischen Besatzungszone und frühen DDR', in Radkau and Uekötter (eds.), *Naturschutz und Nationalsozialismus*, 331–62

Doering-Manteuffel, Sabine, *Die Eifel: Geschichte einer Landschaft* (Frankfurt/Main, 1995)

Dollfus, Jean, *L'Homme et le Rhin: Géographie Humaine* (Paris, 1960)

Dominick, Raymond H., *The Environmental Movement in Germany: Prophets and Pioneers, 1871–1971* (Bloomington, IN, 1992)

Duby, Georges, *History Continues* (Chicago, 1994)

Dunin-Wasowicz, T., 'Natural Environment and Human Settlement over the Central European Lowland in the 13th Century', in Brindlecombe and Pfister (eds.), *The Silent Countdown*, 90–105

Eckhardt, Albrecht and Heinrich Schmidt (eds.), *Geschichte des Landes Oldenburg* (Oldenburg, 1987)

Eckstein, Karl, 'Etwas von der Tierwelt des Oderbruches', in Mengel (ed.), *Das Oderbruch*, vol. 2, 143–74

Eichberg, Henning, 'Stimmung über die Heide: Vom romantischen Blick zur Kolonisierung des Raumes', in Großklaus and Oldemeyer (eds.), *Natur als Gegenwelt*, 197–233

Eichberg, Henning, 'Ordnen, Messen, Disziplinieren', in Johannes Kunisch (ed.), *Staatsverfassung und Heeresverfassung in der europäischen Geschichte der frühen Neuzeit* (Berlin, 1986), 347–75

125 Jahre deutsche Polarforschung: Alfred-Wegener-Institut für Polar- und Meeresforschung (Bremerhaven, 1993)

Engels, Jens Ivo, '"Hohe Zeit" und "dicker Strich": Vergangenheitsbewältigung und -bewahrung im westdeutschen Naturschutz nach dem Zweiten Weltkrieg', in Radkau and Uekötter (eds.), *Naturschutz und Nationalsozialismnus*, 363–404

Fagan, Brian, *The Little Ice Age* (New York, 2000)

Fahrmeier, Andreas, Oliver Faron and Patrick Weil (eds.), *Migration Control in the North Atlantic World* (New York and Oxford, 2003)

Fauter, Harald, 'Malaria am Oberrhein in Vergangenheit und Gegenwart', dissertation, Tübingen 1956

Fehn, Klaus, '"Lebensgemeinschaft von Volk und Raum": Zur nationalsozialistischen Raum- und Landschaftsplanung in den eroberten Ostgebieten', in Radkau and Uekötter (eds.), *Naturschutz und Nationalsozialismus*, 207–24

Feige, Wolfgang and Friedrich Becks, *Wasser für das Ruhrgebiet: Das Sauerland als Wasserspeicher* (Münster, 1981)

Fels, Edwin, *Der wirtschaftliche Mensch als Gestalter der Erde* (Stuttgart, 1954)

Fischer, Ludwig, 'Die Urlandschaft', in Radkau and Uekötter (eds.), *Naturschutz und Nationalsozialismus*, 183–205

Fischer, Norbert, 'Der neue Blick auf die Landschaft', *AfS* 36 (1996), 434–42

Flemming, Hans Walter, *Wüste, Deiche und Turbinen* (Göttingen, 1957)

Fluck, Hans-Rüdiger, 'Die Fischerei im Hanauerland', *BH* 50 (1970), 466–89

Föhl, Axel and Manfred Hamm, *Die Industriegeschichte des Wassers* (Düsseldorf, 1985)

Förster, Jürgen, 'Wehrmacht, Krieg und Holocaust', in Müller and Volkmann (eds.), *Wehrmacht: Mythos und Realität*, 948–63

Franke, Peter (ed.), *Dams in Germany* (Düsseldorf, 2001)

Freudenberger, H.H., 'Die Landwirtschaft des Oderbruches', in Mengel (ed.), *Das Odernbruch*, vol. 2, 176–275

Fries, Jürgen, 'Anpassung von Talsperren an die allgemein anerkannten Regeln der Technik', *GWF* 139 (1998): *Special Talsperren*, 59–64

Fritzsche, Peter, *A Nation of Flyers* (Cambridge, Mass., 1992)

Froriep, Henrik, 'Rechtsprobleme der Oberrheinkorrektion im Grossherzogtum Baden', dissertation, Mainz 1953

Frühauf, Helmut, *Das Verlagshaus Baedeker in Koblenz 1827–1872* (Koblenz, 1992)

Fulbrook, Mary, *Anatomy of a Dictatorship: Inside the GDR 1949–1989* (Oxford, 1995)

Funk, Albrecht, *Polizei und Rechsstaat* (Frankfurt/Main, 1986)

Gaddis, John Lewis, *The Landscape of History: How Historians Map the Past* (Oxford, 2002)

Gamm, Hans-Jochen, *Der braune Kult: Das Dritte Reich und seine Ersatzreligion* (Hamburg, 1962)

Garbrecht, Günther, *Wasser: Vorrat, Bedarf und Nutzung in Geschichte und Gegenwart* (Reinbek, 1985)

Garbrecht, Günther (ed.), *Historische Talsperren* (Stuttgart, 1987)

Garbrecht, Günther, 'Der Sadd-el-Kafara, die älteste Talsperre der Welt', in Garbrecht (ed.), *Historische Talsperren*, 97–109

Garbrecht, Günther, 'Hydrotechnik und Natur: Gedanken eines Ingenieurs', in *100 Jahre Deutsche Verbände der Wasserwirtschaft 1891–1991: Wasserwirtschaft im Wandel der Zeit* (Bonn, 1991), 14–41

Gassert, Philipp, *Amerika im Dritten Reich* (Stuttgart, 1997)

Geiger, Michael, Günter Preuß and Karl-Heinz Rothenberger (eds.), *Der Rhein und die pfälzische Rheinebene* (Landau, 1991)

Geiger, Michael, 'Die pfälzische Rheinebene: Eine natur- und kulturräumliche Skizze', in Geiger, Preuß and Rothenberger (eds.), *Der Rhein und die pfälzische Rheinebene*, 17–45

Geiss, Immanuel, *Der polnische Grenzstreifen 1914–1918* (Lübeck and Hamburg, 1960)

Geppert, A., *Die Stadt am Kanal: Papenburgs Geschichte* (Ankum, 1955)

Gerhard, Gesine, 'Richard Walther Darré – Naturschützer oder "Rassenzüchter"?', in Radkau and Uekötter (eds.), *Naturschutz und Nationalsozialismus*, 257–71

Gerlach, Christian, *Krieg, Ernährung, Völkermord* (Hamburg, 1998)

Gerlach, Christian, 'German Economic Interests, Occupation Policy and the Murder of the Jews in Belorussia, 1941/43', in Herbert (ed.), *National Socialist Extermination Policies*, 210–39

Giedion, Siegfried, *Mechanization Takes Command* (New York, 1948)

Giesecke, Jürgen, Hans-Jürgen Glasebach and Uwe Müller, 'German Standardization in Dam Construction', in Franke (ed.), *Dams in Germany*, 78ff.

Gießler, Helmuth, 'Wilhelmshaven und die Marine', in Grunewald (ed.), *Wilhelmshaven*, 229–49

Gilbert, Martin, *The Holocaust* (New York, 1985)

Gilhaus, Ulrike, *'Schmerzenskinder der Industrie': Umweltverschmutzung, Umweltpolitik und sozialer Protest in Westfalen 1848–1914* (Paderborn, 1995)

Gipp, Walter, 'Geschichte der Moor- und Torfnutzung in Bayern', *Telma* 16 (1986), 305–17

Glacken, Clarence, *Traces on the Rhodian Shore: Nature and Culture in Western Thought from Ancient Times to the End of the Eighteenth Century* (Berkeley, 1967)

Glaser, Hermann, *Deutsche Kultur 1945–2000* (Munich, 2000)

Goldsmith, Edward and Nicholas Hildyard, *The Social and Environmental Effects of Large Dams* (San Francisco, 1984)

Goudie, Andrew (ed.), *The Human Impact Reader* (Oxford, 1997)

Goudsblom, Johann, *Fire and Civilization* (London, 1992)

Gransow, Volker, 'Colleague Frankenstein and the Pale Light of Progress: Life Conditions, Life Activities, and the Technological Impacts on the GDR Way of Life', in Rueschemeyer and Lemke (eds.), *Quality of Life in the German Democratic Republic*, 194–209

Groh, Dieter and Ruth Groh, *Weltbild und Naturaneignung* (Frankfurt/Main, 1991)

Gröning, Gert and Joachim Wolschke-Bulmahn, 'Naturschutz und Ökologie im Nationalsozialismus', *AS* 10 (1983), 1–17

Gröning, Gert and Joachim Wolschke-Bulmahn, *Die Liebe zur Landschaft*, part III: *Der Drang nach Osten: Zur Entwicklung im Nationalsozialismus und während des Zweiten Weltkrieges in den 'eingegliederten Ostgebieten'* (Munich, 1987)

Gröning, Gert and Joachim Wolschke-Bulmahn, 'Politics, Planning and the

Protection of Nature: Political Abuse of Early Ecological Ideas in Germany, 1933–45', *PIP* 2 (1987), 127–48

Große, Norbert et al., 'Der Einfluß des Fischbestandes auf die Zooplanktonbesiedlung und die Wassergüte', *GWF* 139 (1998): *Special Talsperren*, 30–5

Großklaus, Götz and Ernst Oldemeyer (eds.), *Natur als Gegenwelt: Beiträge zur Geschichte der Natur* (Karlsruhe, 1983)

Grove, Richard, *Green Imperialism: Scientists, Ecological Crises and the History of Environmental Concern, 1600–1860* (Cambridge, 1994)

Grundig, Edgar, *Chronik der Stadt Wilhelmshaven*, 2 vols. (Wilhelmshaven, 1957)

Grunewald, Arthur (ed.), *Wilhelmshaven: Tidekurven einer Seestadt* (Wilhelmshaven, 1969)

Gudermann, Rita, *Morastwelt und Paradies: Ökonomie und Ökologie in der Landschaft am Beispiel der Meliorationen in Westfalen und Brandenburg, 1830–1880* (Paderborn, 2000)

Gut, Johannes, 'Die badisch-französische sowie die badisch-bayerische Staatsgrenze und die Rheinkorrektion', *ZGO* 142 (1994), 215–32

Haarnagel, Werner, *Probleme der Küstenforschung im südlichen Nordseegebiet* (Hildesheim, 1950)

Hagen, William, *Germans, Poles and Jews: The Nationality Conflict in the Prussian East, 1772–1914* (Chicago, 1980)

Hahn, Eva and Hans Henning Hahn, 'Flucht und Vertreibung', in Etienne François and Hagen Schulze (eds.), *Deutsche Erinnerungsorte*, vol. 1 (Munich, 2001), 335–51

Hailer, Norbert (ed.), *Natur und Landschaft am Oberrhein: Versuch einer Bilanz* (Speyer, 1982)

Hansemann, Jörg, 'Die historische Entwicklung des Torfabbaues im Toten Moor bei Neustadt am Rübenberge', *Telma* 14 (1984), 127–43

Hard, Mikael, 'German Regulation: The Integration of Modern Technology into National Culture', in Mikael Hard and Andrew Jamison (eds.), *The Intellectual Appropriation of Technology: Discourses on Modernity, 1900–1939* (Cambridge, Mass., 1998), 33–67

Harres, Hans-Peter, 'Zum Einfluß anthropogener Strukturen auf die Gewässersituation', in Böhm and Deneke (eds.), *Wasser*, 91–118

Harvey, Elizabeth, '"Die deutsche Frau im Osten": "Rasse", Geschlecht und öffentlicher Raum im besetzten Polen 1940–1944', *AfS* 38 (1998), 191–214

Harvey, Elizabeth, *Women and the Nazi East* (New Haven and London, 2003)

Heckmann, Erich, 'Überliefertes Brauchtum in einer jungen Stadt', in Grunewald (ed.), *Wilhelmshaven*, 391–409

Hehn, Jürgen von, *Die Umsiedlung der baltischen Deutschen: Das letzte Kapitel baltischdeutscher Geschichte* (Marburg, 1982)

Heim, Susanne (ed.), *Autarkie und Ostexpansion: Pflanzenzucht und Agrarforschung im Nationalsozialismus* (Göttingen, 2002)

Heise, Bernhard, 'From Tangible Sign to Deliberate Delineation: The Evolution of the Political Boundary in the Eighteenth and Early Nineteenth Centuries', in Wolfgang Schmale and Reinhard Stauber (eds.), *Menschen und Grenzen in der frühen Neuzeit* (Berlin, 1998), 171–86

Hempel, Ludwig, 'Zur Entwicklung der Kulturlandschaft in Bruchländereien', *BdL* 11 (1952), 71–80

Henderson, W.O., *Studies in the Economic Policy of Frederick the Great* (London, 1963)

Herbert, Ulrich, *Hitler's Foreign Workers: Enforced Foreign Labor in Germany under the Third Reich* (New York, 1997)

Herbert, Ulrich (ed.), *National Socialist Extermination Policies* (New York and Oxford, 2000)

Hermand, Jost, *Grüne Utopien in Deutschland* (Frankfurt/Main, 1991)

Herrmann, Bernd with Martina Kaup, *'Nun blüht es von End' zu End' all überall': Die Eindeichung des Nieder-Oderbruches 1747–1753* (Münster, 1997)

Hinrichs, Ernst, 'Grundzüge der neuzeitlichen Bevölkerungsgeschichte des Landes Oldenburg', *Vorträge der Oldenburgischen Landschaft* 13 (1985), 5–41.

Hofen, Nikolaus, 'Sagen und Mythen aus der Vorderpflaz', in Geiger, Preuß and Rothenberger (eds.), *Der Rhein und die pfälzische Rheinebene*, 394–410

Hoffmann, Dieter and Kristie Macrakis (eds.), *Naturwissenschaft und Technik in der DDR* (Berlin, 1997)

Horn, Hannelore, *Der Kampf um den Bau des Mittellandkanals* (Cologne and Opladen, 1964)

Höxtermann, Ekkehard, 'Biologen in der DDR', in Hoffmann and Macrakis (eds.), *Naturwissenschaft und Technik in der DDR*, 233–59

Hughes, Thomas P., *Networks of Power: Electrification in Western Society, 1880–1930* (Baltimore, 1983)

Hummerich, Gunther and Wolfgang Lüdde, *Dorfschiffer* (Norden, 1992)

Jachomowski, Dirk, *Die Umsiedlung der Bessarabien-, Bukowina- und Dobrudschadeutschen* (Munich, 1984)

Jackson, Donald C., 'Engineering in the Progressive Era: A New Look at Frederick Haynes Newell and the US Reclamation Service', *TC* 34 (1993), 539–74

Jacobeit, Wolfgang, *Schafhaltung und Schäfer in Zentraleuropa* (East Berlin, 1961)

Jäger, Helmut, *Einführung in die Umweltgeschichte* (Darmstadt, 1994)

Jakubowski-Tiessen, Manfred, *Sturmflut 1717: Die Bewältigung einer Naturkatastrophe in der frühen Neuzeit* (Munich, 1992)

Jakupi, Antje, Peter M. Steinsiek and Bernd Herrmann, 'Early Maps as Stepping Stones for the Reconstruction of Historic Ecological Conditions and Biota', *Naturwissenschaften* 90 (2003), 360–5

Jansen, Christian and Arno Weckbecker, *Der volksdeutsche 'Selbstschutz' in Polen 1939/40* (Munich, 1992)

Jeffries, Ian and Manfred Melzer, 'The New Economic System of Planning and Management 1963–70 and Recentralisation in the 1970s', in Jeffries and Melzer (eds.), *The East German Economy* (London and New York, 1987), 20–40

Johnson, H.C., *Frederick the Great and His Officials* (London, 1975)

Jones, E.L., *The European Miracle: Environments, Economies and Geopolitics in the History of Europe and Asia* (Cambridge, 1981)

Jones, Merrill E., 'Origins of the East German Environmental Movement', *GSR* 16 (1993), 235–64

Kaiser, Gerhard, 'Vision und Kritik der Moderne in Goethes *Faust II*', *Merkur* 48/7 (July 1994), 594–604

Kasson, John, *Civilizing the Machine* (New York, 1977)

Kaup, Martina, 'Die Urbarmachung des Oderbruchs: Umwelthistorische Annäherung an ein bekanntes Thema', in Bayerl, Fuchsloch and Meyer (eds.), *Umweltgeschichte*, 111–31

Kellenbenz, Hermann, *Deutsche Wirtschaftsgeschichte*, 2 vols. (Munich, 1977–81)

Keller, Walter, *Der Karlsgraben: 1200 Jahre, 793–1993* (Treuchtlingen, 1993)

Kershaw, Ian, *Hitler, 1936–45: Nemesis* (London, 2000)

Kiesewetter, Hubert, *Industrialisierung und Landwirtschaft: Sachsens Stellung zum Industrialisierungsprozess Deutschlands im 19. Jahrhundert* (Cologne, 1988)

Kindleberger, Charles, *Economic Growth in France and Britain* (London, 1964)

Kinzelbach, Ragnar, 'Veränderungen der Fauna im Oberrhein', in Hailer (ed.), *Natur und Landschaft am Oberrhein*, 66–84

Kinzelbach, Ragnar (ed.), *Die Tierwelt des Rheins einst and jetzt* (Mainz, 1985)

Kinzelbach, Ragnar, 'Zur Entstehung der Zoozönose des Rheins', in Kinzelbach (ed.), *Tierwelt des Rheins*, 5–49

Kinzelbach, Ragnar, 'Wasser: Biologie und Umweltqualität', in Böhm and Deneke (eds.), *Wasser*, 39–71

Klenke, Dietmar, 'Autobahnen und Naturschutz in Deutschland', in Matthias Freese and Michael Prinz (eds.), *Politische Zäsuren und gesellschaftlicher Wandel im 20. Jahrhundert* (Paderborn, 1996), 465–98

Klessmann, Christoph, 'Hans Frank: Party Jurist and Governor-General in Poland', in Smelser and Zitelman (eds.), *Nazi Elite*, 39–47

Klinkhammer, Lutz, 'Der Partisanenkrieg der Wehrmacht 1941–1944', in Müller and Volkmann (eds.), *Wehrmacht: Mythos und Realität*, 815–36

Klueting, Edeltraud, 'Die gesetzliche Regelung der nationalsozialistischen Reichsregierung für den Tierschutz, den Naturschutz und den Umweltschutz', in Radkau and Uekötter (eds.), *Naturschutz und Nationalsozialismus*, 77–105

Kluge, Thomas and Engelbert Schramm, *Wassernöte: Umwelt- und Sozialge-schichte des Trinkwassers* (Aachen, 1986)

Knobelsdorff-Brenkenhoff, Benno von, *Eine Provinz im Frieden erobert: Bren-ckenhoff als Leiter der friderizianischen Retablissements in Pommern 1762–1780* (Cologne and Berlin, 1984)

Kocka, Jürgen, 'Ideological Regression and Methodological Innovation: Histo-riography and the Social Sciences in the 1930s and 1940s', *HM* 2 (1990), 130–7

Koehl, Robert L., *RKFDV: German Resettlement and Population Policy 1939–1945* (Cambridge, Mass., 1957)

Köllmann, Wolfgang (ed.), *Quellen zur Bevölkerungs-, Sozial- und Wirtschaftsstatistik Deutschlands 1815–1875*, vol. 2 (Boppard, 1989)

Koser, Reinhold, *Geschichte Friedrich des Grossen*, 3 vols. (Darmstadt, 1974)

Kossler, Gerd-Peter, *Natur und Landschaft im Rhein-Main-Gebiet* (Frank-furt/Main, 1996)

Koßmann, Horst, 'Fische und Fischerei', in Geiger, Preuß and Rothenberger (eds.), *Der Rhein und die pfälzische Rheinebene*, 204–11

Kramer, Johann, *Kein Deich – Kein Land – Kein Leben* (Leer, 1989)

Krause, Reinhard A., *Die Gründungsphase deutscher Polarforschung 1865–1875* (Bremerhaven, 1992)

Krenzlin, Anneliese, *Dorf, Feld und Wirtschaft im Gebiet der grossen Täler und Platten östlich der Elbe: Eine siedlungsgeographische Untersuchung* (Remagen, 1952)

Kriegleder, Wynfrid, 'The American Indian in German Novels up to the 1850s', *GLL* 53 (2000), 487–98

Krüger, Bruno, *Die Kietzsiedlungen im nördlichen Mitteleuropa* (Berlin, 1962)

Kuhn, Götz, *Die Fischerei am Oberrhein* (Stuttgart, 1976)

Kunisch, Johannes, *Absolutismus: Europäische Geschichte vom Westfälischen Frieden bis zur Krise des Ancien Regime* (Göttingen, 1986)

Kunz, Andreas, 'Binnenschiffahrt', in Ulrich Wengenroth (ed.), *Technik und Wirtschaft* (Düsseldorf, 1993), 382–98

Kunz, Andreas, 'Seeschiffahrt', in Ulrich Wengenroth (ed.), *Technik und Wirtschaft*, (Düsseldorf, 1993) 356–81

Kunz, Egon, 'Flussbauliche Maßnahmen am Oberrhein von Tulla bis heute mit ihren Auswirkungen', in Hailer (ed.), *Natur und Landschaft am Oberrhein*, 34–50

Küster, Hansjörg, *Geschichte der Landschaft in Mitteleuropa* (Munich, 1995)

Küther, Carsten, *Räuber und Gauner in Deutschland* (Göttingen, 1976)

Ladurie, Emmanuel Le Roy, 'Writing the History of the Climate', in Ladurie, *The Territory of the Historian* (Chicago, 1979), 287–91

Lampe, Klaus, 'Wirtschaft und Verkehr im Landkreis Oldenburg von 1800 bis 1945', in Eckhardt and Schmidt (eds.), *Geschichte des Landes Oldenburg*, 709–62

Lärmer, Karl and Peter Beyer (eds.), *Produktivkräfte in Deutschland, 1800 bis 1870* (Berlin, 1990)

Lee, Lloyd E., 'Baden between Revolutions: State-Building and Citizenship, 1800–1848', *CEH* 24 (1991), 248–67

Lehmann, Hartmut and James Van Horn Melton (eds.), *Paths of Continuity: Central European Historiography from the 1930s to the 1950s* (Cambridge, 1994)

Leiss, William, *The Domination of Nature* (New York, 1972)

Lekan, Thomas, *Imagining the Nation in Nature: Landscape Preservation and German Identity, 1885–1945* (Cambridge, Mass., 2004)

Lekan, Thomas, 'Organische Raumordnung: Landschaftspflege und die Durchführung des Reichsnaturschutzgesetzes im Rheinland-Westfalen', in Radkau and Uekötter (eds.), *Naturschutz und Nationalsozialismus*, 145–65

Lelek, Anton and Günter Buhse, *Fische des Rheins – früher und heute* (Berlin and Heidelberg, 1992)

Leopold, Luna B., *A View of the River* (Cambridge, Mass., 1994)

Lepper, Carl, *Die Goldwäscherei am Rhein* (Heppenheim, 1980)

Liebersohn, Harry, *European Travelers and North American Indians* (Cambridge, 1998)

Limerick, Patricia Nelson, *The Legacy of Conquest: The Unbroken Past of the American West* (New York, 1988)

Lindenfeld, David F., *The Practical Imagination: The German Sciences of State in the Nineteenth Century* (Chicago, 1997)

Linse, Ulrich, *Ökopax und Anarchie: Eine Geschichte der ökologischen Bewegung in Deutschland* (Munich, 1986)

Liulevicius, Vejas G., *Warland on the Eastern Front: Culture, National Identity and German Occupation in World War I* (Cambridge, 2000)

Löbert, Traude, *Die Oberrheinkorrektion in Baden: Zur Umweltgeschichte des 19. Jahrhunderts* (Karlsruhe, 1997)

Lochert, Martin, 'Zur Geschichte des Talsperrenbaus im Bergischen Land vor 1914', *NBJ* 2 (1985–6), 110–14

Loewy, Ernst, *Literatur unterm Hakenkreuz* (Frankfurt/Main, 1966)

Lopez, Barry Holstun, *Of Wolves and Men* (New York, 1978)

Lorenz, Albrecht and Ludwig Trepl, 'Das Avocado-Syndrom. Grüne Schale, brauner Kern: Faschistische Strukturen unter dem Deckmantel der Ökologie', *PÖ* 11 (1993–4), 17–24

Lumans, Valdis O., *Himmler's Auxiliaries: The Volksdeutsche Mittelstelle and the German National Minorities of Europe, 1933–1945* (Chapel Hill, 1993)

MacDonogh, Giles, *Prussia: The Perversion of an Idea* (London, 1994)

Maier, Charles S., *Dissolution: The Crisis of Communism and the End of East Germany* (Princeton, 1997)

Maier, Helmut, 'Kippenlandschaft, "Wassertaumel" und Kahlschlag: Anspruch und Wirklichkeit nationalsozialistischer Energiepolitik', in Bayerl, Fuchsloch and Meyer (eds.), *Umweltgeschichte*, 247–66

Makowski, Henry and Bernhard Buderath, *Die Natur dem Menschen untertan: Ökologie im Spiegel der Landschaftsmalerei* (Munich, 1983)

Mannsfeld, Karl et al., 'Landschaftsanalyse und Ableitung von Naturraumpotentialen', *Abhandlungen der Sächsischen Akademie der Wiss. zu Leipzig*, Bd. 55, Heft 3 (1983), 5–109

Marx, Leo, *The Machine in the Garden* (New York, 1965)

Masters, Roger D., *Fortune Is a River* (New York, 1999)

Mayer, Arno J., *Why Did the Heavens Not Darken? The 'Final Solution' in History* (New York, 1990)

McCormick, Michael, *Origins of the European Economy* (Cambridge, 2001)

McNeill, John, *Something New under the Sun: An Environmental History of the Twentieth Century* (London and New York, 2000)

McNeill, William H., *Plagues and Peoples* (New York, 1976)

Meade, R.B., 'Reservoirs and Earthquakes', in Goudie (ed.), *The Human Impact Reader*, 33–46

Meidinger–Geise, Inge, *Agnes Miegel und Ostpreussen* (Würzburg, 1955)

Meinert, Wolfgang, 'Untersuchungen über Fischbestandsverschiebungen zwischen Rhein bzw. Altrhein und blind endenden Seitengewässern in der Vorderpfalz', in Kinzelbach (ed.), *Tierwelt des Rheins*, 131–49

Mellor, Roy E.H., *The Rhine: A Study in the Geography of Water Transport* (Aberdeen, 1983)

Mengel, Peter Fritz (ed.), *Das Oderbruch*, 2 vols. (Eberswalde, 1930–4)

Mengel, Peter Fritz, 'Die Deichverwaltung des Oderbruches', in Mengel (ed.), *Das Oderbruch*, vol. 2, 299–389

Merquior, J.G., *The Veil and the Mask* (London, 1979)

Meurer, Rolf, *Wasserbau und Wasserwirtschaft in Deutschland* (Berlin, 2000)

Meyer, Ernst, *Rudolf Virchow* (Wiesbaden, 1956)

Meyrowitz, Joshua, *No Sense of Place: The Impact of Electronic Media on Social Behaviour* (Oxford, 1989)

Michalsky, Werner, *Zur Geschichte des Oderbruchs: Die Entwässerung* (Seelow, 1983)

Milmeister, Jean, *Chronik der Stadt Vianden 1926–1950* (Vianden, 1976)

Mitcham, Carl, *Thinking through Technology* (Chicago, 1994)

Mock, Josef, 'Auswirkungen des Hochwasserschutzes', in Böhm and Deneke (eds.), *Wasser*, 176–96

Mosse, George L., *The Crisis of German Ideology: Intellectual Origins of the Third Reich* (London, 1966)

Mrass, Walter, 'Zu einigen Organisations- und Zielmodellen für Naturschutz und Landschaftspflege zwischen 1935 und 1945', *NuL* 56 (1981), 270–3

Müller, Bernhard et al. (eds.), *Siedlungspolitik auf neuen Wege: Steuerungsinstrumente für eine ressourcenschonende Flächennutzung* (Berlin, 1999)

Müller, Edda, *Die Innenwelt der Umweltpolitik: Sozial-liberale Umweltpolitik* (Opladen, 1986)

Müller, Rolf-Dieter, 'Industrielle Interessenpolitik im Rahmen des "Generalplan-Ost"' *MGM* 42 (1981), 101–51

Müller, Rolf-Dieter, *Hitlers Ostkrieg und die deutsche Siedlungspolitik* (Frankfurt/Main, 1991)

Müller-Weil, Ulrike, *Absolutismus und Aussenpolitik in Preussen* (Stuttgart, 1992)

Müller, Rolf-Dieter and Hans-Erich Volkmann (eds.), *Wehrmacht: Mythos und Realität* (Munich, 1999)

Mürb, Robert, 'Landwirtschaftliche Aspekte beim Ausbau von Fliessgewässern', in Böhm and Deneke (eds.), *Wasser*, 119–36

Murken, Theodor, 'Vom Dorf zur Grossstadt', in Grunewald (ed.), *Wilhelmshaven*, 176–97

Murken, Theodor, 'Wilhelmshavener Kaleidoscop', in Grunewald (ed.), *Wilhelmshaven*, 371–90

Musall, Heinz, *Die Entwicklung der Kulturlandschaft der Rheinniederung zwischen Karlsruhe und Speyer vom Ende des 16. bis zum Ende des 19. Jahrhunderts* (Heidelberg, 1969)

Musall, Heinz, Günter Preuß and Karl-Heinz Rothenberger, 'Der Rhein und seine Aue', in Geiger, Preuß and Rothenberger (eds.), *Der Rhein und die pfälzische Rheinebene*, 46–73

Naimark, Norman, *Fires of Hatred: Ethnic Cleansing in Twentieth-Century Europe* (Cambridge, Mass., 2001)

Neef, Ernst et al., 'Analyse und Prognose von Nebenwirkungen gesellschaftlicher Aktivitäten im Naturraum', *Abhandlungen der Sächsischen Akademie der Wissenschaften zu Leipzig*, Bd. 54, Heft 1 (1979), 5–70

Nipperdey, Thomas, *Deutsche Geschichte 1800–1866* (Munich, 1983)

Nippert, Erwin, *Das Oderbruch* (Berlin, 1995)

Norden, Wilhelm, *Eine Bevölkerung in der Krise: Historisch-demographische Untersuchungen zur Biographie einer norddeutschen Küstenregion – Butjadingen 1600–1850* (Hildesheim, 1984)

Nye, David E., *American Technological Sublime* (Cambridge, Mass., 1994)

Oberkrome, Willi, *Volksgeschichte: Methodische Innovation und völkische Ideologisierung in der deutschen Geschichtswissenschaft 1918–1945* (Göttingen, 1993)

Olbrisch, Hans-Dieter, 'Otto Intze', *NDB*, vol. 10 (Berlin, 1974), 176–7

Oldemeyer, Ernst, 'Entwurf einer Typologie des menschlichen Verhältnisses zur Natur', in Großklaus and Oldemeyer (eds.), *Natur als Gegenwelt*, 15–42

Olmer, Beate, *Wasser, Historisch: Zu Bedeutung und Belastung des Umweltmediums im Ruhrgebiet 1870–1930* (Frankfurt/Main, 1998)

Outwater, Alice, *Water: A Natural History* (New York, 1996)

Overbeck, Hermann, *Kulturlandschaftsforschung und Landeskunde* (Heidelberg, 1963)

Palmowski, Jan, 'Building an East German Nation: The Construction of a Socialist *Heimat*, 1945–1961', *CEH* 37 (2004), 365–99

Patel, Kiran Klaus, *'Soldaten der Arbeit': Arbeitsdienste in Deutschland und den USA 1933–1945* (Göttingen, 2003)

Patel, Kiran Klaus, 'Neuerfindung des Westens – Aufbruch nach Osten: Naturschutz und Landschaftsgestaltung in den Vereinigten Staaten von Amerika und in Deutschland, 1900–1945', *AfS* 43 (2003), 191–223

Paul, Roland, 'Alte Berufe am Rhein', in Geiger, Preuß and Rothenberger (eds.), *Der Rhein und die pfälzische Rheinebene*, 272–80

Pearce, Fred, *The Dammed* (London, 1992)

Peters, Jan, Hartmut Harnisch and Lieselott Enders, *Märkische Bauerntagebücher des 18. und 19. Jahrhunderts* (Weimar, 1989)

Philippi, Georg, 'Änderung der Flora und Vegetation am Oberrhein', in Hailer (ed.), *Natur und Landschaft am Oberrhein*, 87–103

Pielou, E.C., *Fresh Water* (Chicago, 1998)

Pimm, Stuart L., *The Balance of Nature: Ecological Issues in the Conservation of Species and Communities* (Chicago, 1991)

Piorreck, Anni, *Agnes Miegel: Ihr Leben und ihre Dichtung* (Düsseldorf and Cologne, 1967)

Pohl, Dieter, 'The Murder of Jews in the General Government', in Herbert (ed.), *National Socialist Extermination Policies*, 83–103

Pois, Robert A., *National Socialism and the Religion of Nature* (London, 1986)

Prahl, Augustus J., 'Gerstäcker und die Probleme seiner Zeit', dissertation, Johns Hopkins, 1933

Prehn, B. and S. Griesa, 'Zur Besiedlung des Oderbruches von der Bronze- bis zur Slawenzeit', in H. Brachmann and H.-J. Vogt (eds.), *Mensch und Umwelt* (Berlin, 1992), 27–32

Preuß, Günter, 'Naturschutz', in Geiger, Preuß and Rothenberger (eds.), *Der Rhein und die pfälzische Rheinebene*, 233–43

Pyne, Stephen, *Vestal Fire: An Environmental History Told through Fire, of Europe and Europe's Encounter with the World* (Seattle, 1997)

Radkau, Joachim, 'Was ist Umweltgeschichte?', in Werner Abelshauser (ed.), *Umweltgeschichte: Umweltverträgliches Wirtschaften in historischer Perspektive – Acht Beiträge* (Göttingen, 1994), 11–28

Radkau, Joachim and Frank Uekötter (eds.), *Naturschutz und Nationalsozialismus* (Frankfurt/Main, 2003)

Raeff, Marc, 'Some Observations on the Work of Hermann Aubin', in Hartmut Lehmann and James Van Horn Melton (eds.), *Paths of Continuity* (Cambridge, 1994), 239–49

Ramsden, John, *The Dambusters* (London, 2003)

Real, Leslie A. and James H. Brown (eds.), *Foundations of Ecology: Classic Papers with Commentaries* (Chicago, 1991)

Reboly, Alice, *Friderizianische Kolonisation im Herzogtum Magdeburg* (Burg, 1940)

Rechenbach, H. (ed.), *Moordorf: Ein Beitrag zur Siedlungsgeschichte und zur sozialen Frage* (Berlin, 1940)

Reichhardt, Hans J., 'Von Treckschuten und Gondeln zu Dampfschiffen', in *Zwischen Oberspree und Unterhavel: Von Sport und Freizeit auf Berlins Gewässern – Eine Ausstellung des Landesarchivs Berlin* (Berlin, 1985), 19–42

Reinhardt, Waldemar, 'Witterung und Klima im Raum Wilhelmshaven', in Grunewald (ed.), *Wilhelmshaven*, 32–40

Reinhardt, Waldemar, 'Die Besiedlung der Landschaft an der Jade', in Grunewald (ed.), *Wilhelmshaven*, 133–52

Reinhardt, Waldemar, 'Die Stadt Wilhelmshaven in preussischer Zeit', in Eckhardt and Schmidt (eds.), *Geschichte des Landes Oldenburg*, 637–59

Reitlinger, Gerald, *The House Built on Sand: The Conflicts of German Policy in Russia 1939–1945* (London, 1960)

Renner, Rolf Günter, 'Grundzüge und Voraussetzungen deutscher literarischer Russlandbilder während des Dritten Reichs', in Volkmann (ed.), *Russlandbilder*, 387–419

Reuss, Martin, 'The Art of Scientific Precision: River Research in the United States Army Corps of Engineers to 1945', *TC* 40 (1999), 249–301

Riechers, Burkhardt, 'Nature Protection during National Socialism', *HSR* 21, 40–7

Rieger, Bernhard, '"Modern Wonders": Technological Innovation and Public Ambivalence in Britain and Germany between the 1890s and 1933', *HWJ* 55 (2003), 154–78

Ritter, Gerhard, *Frederick the Great*, transl. Peter Paret (Berkeley, 1968)

Roch, Isolde (ed.), *Flusslandschaften an Elbe und Rhein: Aspekte der Landschaftsanalyse, des Hochwasserschutzes und der Landschaftsgestaltung* (Berlin, 2003)

Rödel, Raimund, *Die Auswirkungen des historischen Talsperrenbaus auf die Zuflussverhältnisse der Ostsee* (Greifswald, 2001)

Rollins, William H., *A Greener Vision of Home: Cultural Politics and Environmental Reform in the German Heimatschutz Movement, 1904–1918* (Ann Arbor, 1997)

Rollins, William H., 'Whose Landscape? Technology, Fascism and Environmentalism on the National Socialist Autobahn', *AAAG* 85 (1995), 494–520

Rommelspacher, Thomas, 'Das natürliche Recht auf Wasserverschmutzung', in Franz-Josef Brüggemeier and Thomas Rommelspacher (eds.), *Besiegte Natur*, 42–63

Roseman, Mark, *The Wannsee Conference and the Final Solution* (New York, 2003)

Rouvé, Gerhard, 'Die Geschichte der Talsperren in Mitteleuropa', in Garbrecht (ed.), *Historische Talsperren*, 297–325

Roy, James Charles, *The Vanished Kingdom* (Boulder, 1999)

Rubner, Heinrich, *Deutsche Forstgeschichte 1933–1945: Forstwirtschaft, Jagd und Umwelt im NS-Staat* (St Katharinen, 1985)

Rueschemeyer, Marilyn and Christiane Lemke (eds.), *The Quality of Life in the German Democratic Republic* (Armonk, NY, 1989)

Rüthning, Gustav, *Oldenburgische Geschichte*, vol. 2 (Bremen, 1911)

Safrian, Hans, *Die Eichmann-Männer* (Vienna and Zurich, 1993)

Sahlins, Peter, 'Natural Frontiers Revisited: France's Boundaries since the Seventeenth Century', *AHR* 95 (1990), 1423–51

Saison am Strand: Badeleben an Nord- und Ostsee – 200 Jahre, catalogue, Altonaer Museum in Hamburg/Norddeutsches Landesmuseum (Herford, 1986)

Salewski, Michael and Ilona Stölken-Fitschen (eds.), *Moderne Zeiten: Technik und Zeitgeschichte im 19. und 20. Jahrhundert* (Stuttgart, 1994)

Sammons, Jeffrey L., *Wilhelm Raabe: The Fiction of the Alternative Community* (Princeton, 1987)

Sandgruber, Roman, *Strom der Zeit: Das Jahrhundert der Elektrizität* (Linz, 1992)

Sandkühler, Thomas, *'Endlösung' in Galizien: Der Judenmord in Ostpolen und die Rettungsinitiativen von Berthold Beitz* (Bonn, 1996)

Sandkühler, Thomas, 'Anti-Jewish Policy and the Murder of the Jews in the District of Galicia, 1941/42', in Herbert (ed.), *National Socialist Extermination Policies*, 104–27

Sax, Boria, *Animals in the Third Reich: Pets, Scapegoats, and the Holocaust* (New York, 2000)

Schaffer, Simon, 'Enlightened Automata', in William Clark, Jan Golinski and Simon Schaffer (eds.), *The Sciences in Enlightened Europe* (Chicago, 1999), 126–65

Schama, Simon, *Landscape and Memory* (New York, 1995)

Schatz, Oskar, 'Otto Intze: Zur 125. Wiederkehr des Geburtsjahres des Begründers des neuzeitlichen deutschen Talsperrenbaus', *GWF* 109, Sep. 1968, 1037–9

Schivelbusch, Wolfgang, *The Railway Journey* (New York, 1979)

Schmettow, Matthias G. von, *Schmettau und Schmettow: Geschichte eines Geschlechts aus Schlesien* (Büderich, 1961)

Schmidt, Heinrich, 'Grafschaft Oldenburg und oldenburgisches Friesland im Mittelalter und Reformationszeit', in Eckhardt and Schmidt (eds.), *Geschichte des Landes Oldenburg*, 97–171

Schmidt, Martin, 'Die Oberharzer Bergbauteiche', in Garbrecht (ed.), *Historische Talsperren*, 327–85

Schmidt, Martin, 'Before the Intze Dams: Dams and Dam Construction Techniques in the German States prior to 1890', in Franke (ed.), *Dams in Germany*, 10–35

Schmidt, Rudolf, *Wriezen*, 2 vols. (Bad Freienwalde, 1931–2)

Schmidt, Rudolf, 'Volkskundliches aus dem Oderbruch', in Peter Fritz Mengel (ed.), *Das Oderbruch*, vol. 2, 105–42

Schmiedt, Helmut, *Karl May* (Frankfurt/Main, 1985)

Schmitt, H., 'Germany without Prussia: A Closer Look at the Confederation of the Rhine', *GSR* 6 (1983), 9–39

Schneider, Helmut J. (ed.), *Deutsche Landschaften* (Frankfurt/Main, 1981)

Schönwälder, Karen, *Historiker und Politik: Geschichtswissenschaft im Nationalsozialismus* (Frankfurt/Main, 1992)

Schoolmann, H., *Pioniere der Wildnis: Geschichte der Kolonie Moordorf* (n.p., 1973)

Schott, Dieter, 'Remodeling "Father Rhine": The Case of Mannheim 1825–1914', in Anderson and Tabb (eds.), *Water, Culture, and Politics*, 203–35

Schöttler, Peter, 'Das "Annales-Paradigma" und die deutsche Historiographie (1929–1939)', in Lothar Jordan and Bernd Korländer (eds.), *Nationale Grenzen und internationaler Austausch: Studien zum Kultur- und Wissenschaftstransfer in Europa* (Tübingen, 1995), 200–20

Schremmer, Eckart, *Die Wirtschaft Bayerns: Vom hohen Mittelalter bis zum Beginn der Industrialisierung* (Munich, 1970)

Schua, Leopold and Roma Schua, *Wasser – Lebenselement und Umwelt: Die Geschichte des Gewässerschutzes in ihrem Entwicklungsgang dargestellt und dokumentiert* (Freiburg and Munich, 1981)

Schulte-Mäter, Fritz, *Beiträge über die geographischen Auswirkungen der Korrektion des Oberrheins* (Leipzig, 1938)

Schultz, Hans-Dietrich, *Die deutschsprachige Geographie von 1800 bis 1970* (Berlin, 1980)

Schwalb, Mechthild, *Die Entwicklung der bäuerlichen Kulturlandschaft in Ostfriesland und Westoldenburg* (Bonn, 1953)

Schwarz, Wolfgang, 'Ur- und Frühgeschichte', in Behre and van Lengen (eds.), *Ostfriesland*, 39–73

Schwarzmann, Herbert, 'War die Tulla'sche Oberrheinkorrektion eine Fehlleistung im Hinblick auf ihre Auswirkungen?', *DW* 54 (1964), 279–87

Schwoerbel, Jürgen, 'Technik und Wasser', in Werner Nachtigall and Charlotte Schönbeck (eds.), *Technik und Natur* (Düsseldorf, 1994), 370–410

Scott, James C., *Seeing Like a State: How Certain Schemes to Improve the Human Condition Have Failed* (New Haven, 1998)

Seckendorf, Martin, 'Die "Raumordnungsskizze" für das Reichskommissariat

Ostland vom November 1942: Regionale Konkretisierung der Ostraumplanung', in Rössler and Schleiermacher (eds), 'Generalplan Ost', 175–87

Seidler, Franz W., 'Fritz Todt', in Smelser and Zitelmann (eds.), Nazi Elite, 245–56

Shackleton, Margaret Reid, Europe: A Regional Geography (London, 1958)

Sieferle, Rolf Peter, Fortschrittsfeinde? Opposition gegen Technik und Industrie von der Romantik bis zur Gegenwart (Munich, 1984)

Smelser, Ronald and Rainer Zitelman (eds.), The Nazi Elite (New York, 1983)

Smets, Josef, 'De l'eau et des hommes dans le Rhin inférieur du siècle des Lumières à la pré-industrialisation', Francia 21 (1994), 95–127

Smit, Jan G., Neubildung deutschen Bauerntums: Innere Kolonisation im Dritten Reich – Fallstudien in Schleswig-Holstein (Kassel, 1983)

Smith, Helmut Walser, German Nationalism and Religious Conflict (Princeton, 1995)

Smith, Norman, Man and Water: A History of Hydro-Technology (London, 1976)

Smith, Norman, A History of Dams (London, 1971)

Smith, Woodruff D., 'Friedrich Ratzel and the Origins of Lebensraum', GSR 3 (1980), 51–68

Smout, T.C., 'Problems for Global Environmental Historians', EH 8 (2002), 107–16

Solomon, Maynard, 'Franz Schubert and the Peacocks of Benvenuto Cellini', 19th-Century Music 12 (1989), 193–206

Spector, Shmuel, 'Jewish Resistance in Small Towns of Eastern Poland', in Norman Davies and Antony Polonsky (eds.), Jews in Eastern Europe and in the USSR, 1939–1946 (London, 1991), 138–44

Spehr, Christoph, Die Jagd nach Natur (Frankfurt/Main, 1994)

Spelde, Günther, Geschichte der Lotsen-Brüderschaften an der Aussenweser und an der Jade (Bremen, n.d. [1985])

Squatritti, Paolo, 'Digging Ditches in Early Medieval Europe', PP 176 (2002), 11–65

Staritz, Dieter, Geschichte der DDR 1949–1985 (Frankfurt/Main, 1985)

Staudenmaier, John M., Technology's Storytellers (Cambridge, Mass., 1985)

Steinweis, Alan E., 'Eastern Europe and the Notion of the "Frontier" in Germany to 1945', YES 13 (1999), 56–69

Sternberger, Dolf, Panorama of the Nineteenth Century (Oxford, 1977)

Stokes, Raymond G., 'Chemie und chemische Industrie im Sozialismus', in Hoffmann and Macrakis (eds.), Naturwissenschaft und Technik in der DDR, 283–96

Stossun, Harry, Die Umsiedlungen der Deutschen aus Litauen während des Zweiten Weltkrieges (Marburg, 1993)

Strauss, Herbert A., 'Stereotyp und Wirklichkeiten im Amerikabild', in Willi Paul Adams and Knud Krakau (eds.), Deutschland und Amerika (Berlin, 1985), 19–38

Streim, Alfred, 'Zur Eröffnung des allgemeinen Judenvernichtungsbefehls gegenüber den Einsatzgruppen', in Eberhard Jäckel and Jürgen Rohwer (eds.), *Der Mord an den Juden im Zweiten Weltkrieg* (Stuttgart, 1985), 107–19

Streit, Christian, *Keine Kameraden* (Stuttgart, 1978)

Stukenberg, Wilhelm, *Aus der Kulturentwicklung des Landes Oldenburg* (Oldenburg, 1989)

Such, Wolfram, 'Die Entwicklung der Trinkwasserversorgung aus Talsperren in Deutschland', *GWF* 1939: *Special Talsperren* (1998), 65–72

Tebbenhoff, H., *Grossefehn: Seine Geschichte* (Ostgrossefehn, 1963)

Thom, Achim, 'Aspekte und Wandlungen des Russlandbildes deutscher Ärzte im Dritten Reich', in Volkmann (ed.), *Russlandbild im Dritten Reich*, 421–62

Thomas, Franklin, *The Environmental Basis of Society* (New York, 1925)

Thomas, Keith, *Man and the Natural World* (London, 1983)

Tillessen, Karl, 'Gezeiten, Sturmfluten, Deiche und Fahrwasser', in Grunewald (ed.), *Wilhelmshaven*, 41–64

Tittizer, Thomas and Falk Krebs (eds.), *Ökosystemforschung: Der Rhein und seine Auen – Eine Bilanz* (Berlin and Heidelberg, 1996)

Treue, Wilhelm, *Wirtschafts- und Technikgeschichte Deutschlands* (Berlin and New York, 1984)

Tribe, Keith, 'Cameralism and the Science of Government', *JMH* 56 (1984), 163–84

Trömel, Hans-Peter, *Deichverbände im Oderbruch* (Bad Freienwalde, 1988)

Tuan, Yi-Fu, *Passing Strange and Wonderful: Aesthetics, Nature and Culture* (Washington, DC, 1993)

Tümmers, Horst, *Der Rhein: Ein europäischer Fluss und seine Geschichte* (Munich, 1994)

Turner, Henry A., *German Big Business and the Rise of Hitler* (New York, 1985)

Uhlmann, Dietrich, 'Ökologische Probleme der Trinkwasserversorgung aus Talsperren', *Abhandlungen der Sächsischen Akademie der Wiss. zu Leipzig*, Bd. 55, Heft 4 (1983), 3–21

Uhlmann, Dietrich, 'Künstliche Ökosysteme', *Abhandlungen der Sächsischen Akademie der Wiss. zu Leipzig*, Bd. 54, Heft 3 (1980), 5–34

Uphoff, Rolf, *'Hier lasst uns einen Hafen bau'n!' Entstehungsgeschichte der Stadt Wilhelmshaven 1848–1890* (Oldenburg, 1995)

Veit-Brause, Irmeline, *Die deutsch-französische Krise von 1840* (Cologne, 1967)

Vitek, William and Wes Jackson, *Rooted in the Land: Essays on Community and Place* (New Haven, 1996)

Volkmann, Hans-Erich, 'Zur Ansiedlung der Deutsch–Balten im "Reichsgau" Wartheland', *ZfO* 30 (1981), 527–58

Volkmann, Hans-Erich (ed.), *Das Russlandbild im Dritten Reich* (Cologne, Weimar and Vienna, 1994)

Wagret, Paul, *Polderlands* (London, 1968)

Walker, Mack, *The Salzburg Transaction: Expulsion and Redemption in Eighteenth-Century Germany* (Ithaca, 1992)

Wasser, Bruno, *Himmlers Raumplanung im Osten: Der Generalplan Ost in Polen 1940–1944* (Basel, 1993)

Wassermann, Ekkehard, 'Siedlungsgeschichte der Moore', in Behre and van Lengen (eds.), *Ostfriesland*, 93–111

Wegener, Angela, 'Die Besiedlung der nordwestdeutschen Hochmoore', *Telma* 15 (1985), 151–72

Weigend, Guido Gustav, 'Water Supply of Central and Southern Germany', dissertation, Chicago 1946

Weiser, Christiane Karin, 'Die Talsperren in den Einzugsgebieten der Wupper und der Ruhr als funktionierendes Element in der Kulturlandschaft in ihrer Entwicklung bis 1945', dissertation, Bonn 1991

Weißbecker, Manfred, '"Wenn hier Deutsche wohnten . . ." Beharrung und Veränderung im Russlandbild Hitlers und der NSDAP', in Volkmann (ed.), *Russlandbild im Dritten Reich*, 9–54

Welsch, Wolfgang, 'Postmoderne: Pluralität zwischen Konsens and Dissens', *AfK* 73 (1991), 193–214

Wengenroth, Ulrich, 'Motoren für den Kleinbetrieb: Soziale Utopien, technische Entwicklung und Absatzstrategien bei der Motorisierung des Kleingewerbes im Kaiserreich', in Wengenroth (ed.), *Prekäre Selbständigkeit* (Stuttgart, 1989), 177–205

Wentz, G., 'Geschichte des Oderbruches', in Mengel (ed.), *Das Oderbruch*, vol. 1, 85–238

Wertheimer, Jack, *Unwelcome Strangers: East European Jews in Imperial Germany* (New York, 1987)

West, Hugh, 'Göttingen and Weimar: The Organization of Knowledge and Social Theory in Eighteenth-Century Germany', *CEH* 11 (1978), 150–61

Wettengel, Michael, 'Staat und Naturschutz 1906–1945: Zur Geschichte der Staatlichen Stelle für Naturdenkmalpflege in Preussen und der Reichsstelle für Naturschutz', *HZ* 257 (1993), 366–99

White, Richard, *The Organic Machine: The Remaking of the Columbia River* (New York, 1995)

White, Richard, 'The Natures of Nature Writing', *Raritan*, Fall 2002, 145–61

Wiese, Axel, *Die Hafenbauarbeiter an der Jade, 1853–1871* (Oldenburg, 1998)

Wilcove, D.S., C.H. McLellan and A.P. Dobson, 'Habitat Fragmentation in the Temperate Zone', in Andrew Goudie (ed.), *The Human Impact Reader* (Oxford, 1997), 342–55

Wilhelm, Hans-Heinrich, *Rassenpolitik und Kriegsführung* (Passau, 1991)

Williams, Michael, 'The Relations of Environmental History and Historical Geography', *JHG* 20 (1994), 3–21

Wilson, Edward O., *The Future of Life* (New York, 2002)

Wippermann, Wolfgang, *Der 'Deutsche Drang nach Osten': Ideologie und Wirklichkeit eines politischen Schlagwortes* (Darmstadt, 1981)

Wippermann, Wolfgang, '"Gen Ostland wollen wir reiten": Ordensstaat und Ostsiedlung in der historischen Belletristik Deutschlands', in Wolfgang Fritze (ed.), *Germania Slavica* (Berlin, 1981), 187–255

Wittmann, Heinrich, 'Tulla, Honsell, Rehbock: Lebensbilder dreier Wasserbauingenieure am Oberrhein', *BA* 4 (1949), 5–52

Wittmann, Heinrich, *Flussbau und Siedlung* (Ankara, 1960)

Wöbse, Anna-Katharina, 'Lina Hähnle und der Reichsbund für Vogelschutz', in Radkau and Uekötter (eds.), *Naturschutz und Nationalsozialismus*, 309–28

Woebcken, Carl, *Deiche und Sturmfluten an der deutschen Nordseeküste* (Bremen and Wilhelmshaven, 1924)

Woebcken, Carl, *Die Entstehung des Jadebusen* (Aurich, 1945)

Woebcken, Carl, *Jeverland* (Jever, 1961)

Wolffsohn, Seew, *Wirtschaftliche und soziale Entwicklungen in Brandenburg, Preussen, Schlesien und Oberschlesien in den Jahren 1640–1853* (Frankfurt/Main, Berlin and New York, 1985)

Worster, Donald, *The Wealth of Nature* (New York, 1993)

Wüstenbecher, Katja, 'Hamburg and the Transit of East European Emigrants', in Fahrmeier, Faron and Weil (eds.), *Migration Control in the North Atlantic World*, 223–36

Zang, Gerd (ed.), *Provinzialisierung einer Region* (Frankfurt/Main, 1978)

Zeller, Thomas, *Strasse, Bahn, Panorama: Verkehrswege und Landschaftsveränderungen in Deutschland von 1930 bis 1990* (Frankfurt/Main, 2002)

Zeller, Thomas, 'Ganz Deutschland sein Garten: Alwin Seifert und die Landschaft des Nationalsozialismus', in Radkau and Uekötter (eds.), *Naturschutz und Nationalsozialismus*, 273–307

Zenz, Emil, *Geschichte der Stadt Trier im 19. Jahrhundert*, vol. 2 (Trier, 1980)

Zier, Hans Georg, 'Johann Gottfried Tulla: Ein Lebensbild', *BH* 50 (1970), 379–449

Ziegler, Joachim W. (ed.), *Die Sintflut im Ruhrtal: Eine Bilddokumentation zur Möhne-Katastrophe* (Meinerzhagen, 1983)

Zweckbronner, Gerhard, '"Je besser der Techniker, desto einseitiger sein Blick?" Probleme der technischen Fortschritts- und Bildungsfragen in der Ingenieurzeitung im Deutschen Kaiserreich', in Ulrich Troitzsch and Gabriele Wohlauf (eds.), *Technikgeschichte* (Frankfurt/Main, 1980), 328–56

INDEX